VISIBLE
DIFFERENCES

VISIBLE
DIFFERENCES

Why Race Will Matter
to Americans in the
Twenty-First Century

DOMINIC PULERA

CONTINUUM
New York • London

2002

The Continuum International Publishing Group Inc
370 Lexington Avenue, New York, NY 10017

The Continuum International Publishing Group Ltd
The Tower Building, 11 York Road, London SE1 7NX

Printed in the United States of America

Library of Congress Cataloging-in-Publication Data

Pulera, Dominic J.
    Visible differences : why race will matter to Americans in the
21st century / by Dominic J. Pulera.
        p.   cm.
    Includes bibliographical references and index.
    ISBN 0-8264-1407-9
    1. United States – Race relations. 2. United States – Race
relations – Forecasting. 3. Ethnology – United States. 4. Pluralism
(Social sciences) – United States. 5. Minorities – United
States – Interviews. 6. United States – Census, 22nd, 2000 – Evaluation.
Title.
E184.A1 P85 2002
305.8'00973 – dc21

                                                                2002000377

Grateful acknowledgment is made for permission to quote from:

"Half Breed" by Al Capps and Mary Dean. Copyright © Blue Monday Music. All rights reserved. Used by permission.

Voice and Equality: Civic Voluntarism in American Politics by Sidney Verba, Kay Lehman Schlozman, and Henry E. Brady, Cambridge Mass.: Harvard University Press, Copyright © 1995 by the President and Fellows of Harvard College.

To my mother and father,
who taught me, through their words and deeds,
to respect and appreciate the innate value
of each human being

Contents

Seeing Is Believing

"You don't have elevators like these in Puerto Rico, do you?" a middle-aged man of Northern European descent asked me as we shared an elevator in an upscale Washington hotel 12 years ago. Upon seeing my dark brown eyes and hair, this fellow, who appeared to be slightly ine-briated, had quickly ascertained that I was visibly different from him — and thus a Puerto Rican who hailed from a backward part of the world. He was friendly enough, but his mocking tone and paternalistic attitude clearly indicated that he did not think much of Puerto Ricans. I said nothing to him because I had never encountered ethnic or racial bigotry on a firsthand basis before.

At the time I was only 16 years old, and I had grown up in a rural southeastern Wisconsin community where most people were white. Per-haps ten percent of my high school class was Latino, but there were few black or Asian students. Being white, upper middle class, and somewhat sheltered, I had never personally felt the stinging rebuke of prejudice in my life. So I was wholly unprepared to deal with a bigot, even though I viscerally recoiled from the despicable sentiments that underlay his offhand remarks. My interlocutor's companions quickly sensed my dis-comfort, and one of them hastened to assure me that the man meant no harm by his comments. I shrugged my shoulders in response to her semi-apology for his churlish behavior; soon we went our separate ways, never to meet again.

As the product of an ethnically exogamous marriage — my mother's family comes from different parts of Germany, while my father's an-cestors originate in the Southern Italian region of Calabria — I am difficult to pigeonhole into any one category. My Romance-language surname and "ethnic" forename (I am named after an Italian saint) further confuse people. People often mispronounce my surname or, in-terestingly, pronounce my first name the French way, as in Dominique. Americans periodically ask me about my putative Argentine or Greek or Italian or Mexican or Spanish antecedents. During a visit to an African-

1

American congregation in 1994, the minister even wanted to know if I was black.

My sister, Maria, who lives in suburban Los Angeles, encounters the firsthand effects of presumptive kinship every day. Latinos, Europeans, Middle Easterners, and even South Asians often speak to her in their native tongue. Due to her complexion, the predominance of Latinos in metro Los Angeles, and the mellifluous series of vowels that make up her name, she is probably mistaken for Hispanic most frequently. Every American has his or her own informal schema of sameness and difference; unlike my friend from the hotel elevator, however, most of us do not make invidious distinctions between and among groups of people.

The peopling of North America probably began 30,000 to 40,000 years ago. America's indigenous people trace their ancestry to migrants from northeastern Asia. Over the years, a number of bands and clans decided to set out in pursuit of the proverbial greener pastures elsewhere. In all likelihood, they came in waves, and walked over a land bridge through the Bering Strait to what is now Alaska. However, as Michael D. Lemonick writes, "[T]he details of the migration, including how many waves there were, when they happened and the routes by which wanderers subsequently moved east and south over the millennia, are still largely mysterious."[1] Regardless of how they arrived, by 1500 somewhere between one million and ten million First Americans lived on the land that makes up the present-day United States. These individuals were part of innumerable smaller groups, all of which had their own distinct customs, languages, and living arrangements.[2]

Their world was altered forever by the arrival of European explorers. The Genoan navigator Cristoforo Colombo — whom the Spaniards call Cristóbal Colón and we refer to as Christopher Columbus — is commonly credited as the European "discoverer" of America. (The term discovery is a loaded one, because it denigrates the ethnic indigenous groups who were already here. Contemporary historians prefer the terms contact and encounter.) When Columbus sailed west from Europe in 1492, he hoped to find the fabled riches of India and the Far East. Instead, he landed at one of the islands in the Bahamas on October 12, 1492. Columbus also visited present-day Cuba and Haiti on his first trip to the New World. He christened the Caribbean islands the Indies and the indigenous people there Indians, based on his mistaken perception that he had visited India. Columbus's peregrinations launched a frenzied farrago of exploration in the New World. His Spanish patrons then competed for spoils with the Dutch, English, French, and Portuguese. Thus the conquest, creation, development, and settlement of the United States were spearheaded by the Europeans and their American cousins.

Race came to the fore as the new nation grew larger and expanded its geographic boundaries, while the American population became more ethnically heterogeneous and nonwhites experienced differential treatment and racial discrimination much of the time. Mass immigration from Asia, Europe, and Latin America, as well as the conquering and purchase of Mexican, American Indian, and Native Alaskan lands, brought new peoples into the American nation. Millions of West Africans were forced against their will to come to the United States as slaves; America's "peculiar institution" and the ensuing era of segregation in the South were transgressions of such magnitude that their reverberations continue to be felt today. Race constitutes a stubbornly resistant malady in the United States because of "the color line" — a visible (and invisible) barrier that separates whites from nonwhites. It is animated by a historical legacy of racism, prejudice, and discrimination, in addition to contemporary dynamics that are usually at least tangentially related to past events.[3]

Over the years, theorists have developed various types of explanatory models, with perhaps the most persuasive one being offered by the Swedish sociologist Gunnar Myrdal. In his landmark 1944 book, *An American Dilemma: The Negro Problem and Modern Democracy,* Myrdal defined the race issue as an ineluctable clash of ideals and ambitions — between noble theories (the American Creed of brotherly love and equal opportunities for all) and ignoble practices (ethnic prejudice and limited opportunities for people of color).[4] Myrdal focused his attention on white oppression and black subjugation, but his conception of the American Dilemma can be applied more broadly to almost any situation in American life where an ethnic or racial group suffers because prejudiced members of the majority group discriminate against its members.

The American Dilemma is the exact opposite of the American Dream, which has served as a unifying national ideology, in varying guises, since the nineteenth century. Jennifer Hochschild, for one, characterizes the American Dream as "the promise that all Americans have a reasonable chance to achieve success as they define it — material or otherwise — through their own efforts, and to attain virtue and fulfillment through success."[5] For immigrants, realizing America's promise means having the freedoms and economic opportunities they never had in their homelands. For native-born Americans, it means that each succeeding generation can improve their standard of living.[6] Sometimes the American Dilemma and American Dream intersect, as in the cases of whites who came to the United States from England and made their fortunes with the aid of black slave labor, or in situations where people of color feel that racism and discrimination prevent them from realizing their American Dreams.

In any event, visible differences often affect how we Americans relate to one another. As Carl Degler notes, "to categorize people on the basis of how they look undoubtedly aids in understanding the world — and perhaps controlling it a little. For without such quick and constant categorizing of impressions, the world appears to the beholder as little more than a mass of unrelated, disparate things, animals, persons, and ideas."[7] Before the advent of television and the global media, visible differences were far less salient; humans in many parts of the world rarely saw others who looked perceptibly different in a racial sense, or knew that some nations and peoples were much richer than others.[8] Indeed, we categorize people based upon intersectional factors such as age, race, gender, accent, ethnicity, religion, social class, national origin, sexual orientation, and physical appearance.

Visible differences come in two varieties. Mutable — or largely mutable — factors include accents, attire, beauty, carriage, demeanor, and weight. Immutable — or largely immutable — factors include gender, height, facial features, hair texture, sexual orientation, and skin color. The most significant visible differences are skin color and physical characteristics, which often become inextricably intertwined with cultural, ethnic, linguistic, religious, and socioeconomic factors.

Although "observable physical differences easily translate themselves into intellectual and moral distinctions," to quote Carl Degler again, they become invidious ones only if they affect human behavior.[9] Dichotomous thinking (us versus them, the same and the Other) can lead to atrocities and long-lasting enmities. In comparative terms, at least, intergroup relations in the United States — the world's most racially and ethnically heterogeneous society — are remarkably amicable. America's cultural, intellectual, and political elites continue to be disproportionately white, although blacks, Hispanics, Asian Americans, Native Americans, and Pacific Islanders have made considerable progress in the last 30 years. Likewise, mainstream American culture generally reflects the sensibilities of those Americans who are white, centrist, secular, heterosexual, middle-class, and able-bodied. The mainstream culture largely ignores minorities, ideological extremists, religious folk, homosexuals, the poor, and persons with disabilities. As a result, many Americans, including members of the aforementioned groups, feel like outsiders in the land of their birth.

Visible differences certainly play a role in racial identity development. One's racial identity is merely part of the broader identity s/he forges by middle age; it generally has occupational, religious, and socioeconomic components, too. Beverly Daniel Tatum rightly asserts, "The concept of identity is a complex one, shaped by individual characteristics, family dynamics, historical factors, and social and political contexts."[10] In early childhood, youngsters begin to develop a sense of racial awareness based on the verbal and visual cues provided by their caregivers, peers, and the media. The youngest Americans first encounter race around age three or four, and they achieve a sense of race constancy, or unchanging racial group membership, about three years later. Then the sequential development of racial identity accelerates in adolescence and continues well into adulthood. The process of racial identity development is more difficult for minorities than for members of the racial majority, because they are less likely to see themselves reflected in the media, societal institutions, and so forth.[11]

For minorities, race generally trumps other factors in most contexts, while white people in the primarily white sections of the United States can still go through life without ever really thinking about race. In general, when we evaluate a person's actions and beliefs, it is difficult to isolate with certainty which aspects of her identity are most important. Take, for instance, the case of white women and affirmative action. Which dimensions of the typical white woman's identity might be preeminent when she formulates an opinion about the issue? Her age? Her race? Her gender? Her marital status? Her religious beliefs? Her social class? Her sexual orientation? Her American identity? Or, perhaps, some other circumstances unique to her status as a white American woman?[12] In evaluating such situations, the contrast between perception and reality can be quite important, especially when it comes to race, which is a subject that lends itself to misconceptions, stereotypes, and the like.[13]

For the last three decades, we have lived in what Michael Lind aptly describes as "Multicultural America." Lind divides American history into three periods: "Anglo-America (1789–1861), Euro-America (1875–1957) and Multicultural America (1972–present)."[14] The first 74 years of the American nation were characterized by the dominance of people of Northern European origin. In the second period, which stretched for 82 years, most Americans traced their heritage to Europe, and racial minorities were either ignored or mistreated by the nation's white majority.

Since the early 1970s, the United States has become a genuinely multi-racial nation. Decision-makers and the media now pay attention to the rights, feelings, and opinions of Latinos and Asians as well as blacks and Native Americans.[15] Racial liberals generally defend multiculturalism, the ideology of the new order, on the grounds that diversity initiatives are necessary to ensure that every group of Americans receives fair treatment. Racial conservatives typically oppose such initiatives because they contend that multicultural efforts — affirmative action and inclusive curricula chief among them — Balkanize America and privilege one group over another. Virtually everyone in the mainstream of American life celebrates diversity, at least in the abstract; race is a topic that lends itself to bromides, platitudes, and homilies.

The American cultural, business, political, and intellectual elites almost unanimously embrace the diversity imperative, which I define as the idea that the nation's decision-makers must continually strive to represent people in roughly proportional terms relative to their share of the population. The diversity imperative is more of an idea or a benchmark than a hard-and-fast plan of action; yet the notion influences people in politics, business, advertising, the media, and other realms of American life.[16] Affirmative action is the coercive enforcement mechanism that undergirds the diversity imperative, while America's changing demographics and the politics of inclusion are important normative forces that sustain it as well.

Promoters of the diversity imperative seek to heighten the visibility of traditionally marginalized groups, and they also posthumously recognize the unheralded heroes of yesteryear. The multiculturalists sincerely believe that every group of Americans needs, craves, and deserves recognition. Besides, they know that inclusive appeals can be very profitable for businesses and politicians. Yet the diversity imperative rarely focuses on the specific subgroups that comprise whites or blacks or Hispanics or Asians or American Indians. A Chippewa, therefore, is expected to be satisfied by having a Crow represent him as a Native American on a television program. With so many people jostling for attention and recognition, small ethnic groups like the Hmong are largely doomed to invisibility in the American mainstream.

Likewise, certain types of diversity seem to be valued more than others — race is usually more significant than socioeconomic status, while gender takes precedence over sexual orientation. Indeed, we usually regard it as a sign of progress when a woman or minority succeeds a white male in the workplace, or otherwise penetrates what has previously been an all-white-male circle. Women and minorities often receive considerable media attention when they break through the glass ceiling. The fanfare surrounding such firsts, milestones, pioneers, and trail blazers typically focuses on the historic nature and symbolic resonance of the accession, appointment, election, or achievement.

It is possible to classify American race relations in terms of paradigms (monoracial, biracial, multiracial) that relate to the issues at hand and the population composition of a given area. The monoracial paradigm, whereby whites were the primary focus of attention in American life, characterized race relations from 1789 to 1954. It is now only operational in the parts of America where whites comprise the overwhelming majority of the population. Still, the only time many white Americans think about race is when they perfunctorily answer the race/ethnicity question on a job application or the census form. But they never really stop to consider their own racial identity, although they might discuss ethnicity and religion with their friends and family. Whiteness was not treated as an explicit phenomenon until recently, even though the United States has been a white-majority country throughout its history.[17] Within a few decades, however, most white Americans will no longer be able to ignore racial issues. The luxury of race unconsciousness or, more accurately, race obliviousness, will be the province of those Americans who live in the most remote parts of our country.

Race became a national issue during the twentieth century in large part due to the migration of blacks from the South to other regions of the country. In what became known as "the Great Migration," millions of blacks left Dixie for more hospitable surroundings elsewhere during the 60-year period from 1910 to 1970. In 1910, 89% of American blacks lived in the 16-state South and the District of Columbia. Only 77% of them remained there by 1940, and their numbers dropped to 53% in 1970. The "pull" factors — jobs and greater prosperity in Western, Northern, and Midwestern cities — persuaded many African Americans to leave the South. And the "push" factors of unremitting racial hostility and the introduction of the mechanized cotton picker in the mid-1940s, which reduced the need for as many sharecroppers, drove them out of Dixie.[18]

The arrival of large numbers of blacks in Western, Midwestern, and Northeastern urban areas made race a truly national issue.[19] The South became less black in percentage terms — Mississippi, for instance, was a black-majority state before the Great Migration — even as racial issues assumed greater importance there in the waning days of Jim Crow. At the same time, race riots occurred in cities such as Chicago and Los Angeles.

Once virtually all-white cities (Milwaukee and Detroit come to mind) soon had sizable black populations. These demographics helped make George Wallace a national political figure during the 1960s and 1970s.[20]

After the whites-only paradigm thankfully lapsed into obsolescence at the national level in the 1950s, it was replaced by the black-and-white variant of the biracial paradigm. Today this paradigm, which characterized America's history from 1954 to 1990, is itself obsolescent at the national level. The census in 1990 was the first in the nation's history where the sum total of nonblack minorities outpaced the aggregate number of African Americans.[21] Nonetheless, the black-and-white paradigm retains its outsized importance in the minds of middle-aged and elderly Americans — not just as one variant of American race relations, but as *the* all-encompassing norm. To be sure, it continues to be an accurate frame of reference in much of America, from Detroit to Mississippi to the District of Columbia.

But Americans are starting to look beyond the black-and-white perspective for two reasons. For one, it neglects fast-growing groups (Hispanics, Asian Americans, American Indians, and mixed-race persons) that comprise at least 18% of the American population. These emerging and newly empowered groups resent the traditional focus on black-and-white issues since it usually ignores them and their interests. Moreover, racial issues require far more complicated solutions than during the 1960s and 1970s, when the black-and-white perspective was ascendant and the one-dimensional social-policy debates revolved around the efficacy of traditional social-welfare programs. The advent of a multiracial society has led to new topics of discussion — bilingual education, illegal immigration, and so forth — that were practically nonexistent 30 years ago.

The collective face of America, then, is changing. This development is part of what some observers call "the browning of America," as the complexion of the country slowly, subtly becomes darker. Racial events and issues affect the lives of Americans unevenly: America's multicultural splendor reaches only some of us, depending on factors like our social class and where we live. Yet we Americans "vote" about race every time we date; select our friends; listen to music; watch movies and television; touch the radio dial; choose places to live and vacation; select schools for our children; patronize bars, nightclubs, and restaurants; and worship in churches, mosques, synagogues, and temples. This book is about those choices, and it proceeds on the premise that race is the most significant cleavage in American life. *I contend that the observable differences in physical appearance separating the races are the single most important factor shaping intergroup relations, in conjunction with the social, cultural, economic, and political ramifications that accompany this visual divide. These dynamics animate the unceasing struggles for power, recognition, and resources that occur between, among, and within American racial groups.*

The United States is presently undergoing a fundamental demographic shift unlike any other in its history. America is shifting from a predominantly white country to one where people of color are increasingly numerous and consequently becoming more visible. As a result, race affects the lives of more Americans than ever before. *Visible Differences* is the first ostensibly objective work to cover, in a comprehensive fashion, America's ongoing demographic transition. In doing so, this book analyzes the challenges of managing diversity and avoiding diversity dilemmas without offering prescriptions or lapsing into vitriolic polemics.

I confess to an optimistic bent, although it is tempered by realpolitik. Thus I celebrate the generally positive nature of race relations in America, particularly in the last three decades. Ethnic disparities and inequities exist in the United States, of course, but no other large multiethnic nation or empire in the history of the world compares to America in its ability to integrate and assimilate so many different peoples. The United States has always been "a house divided," and race relations in the land of milk and honey have always been characterized by conflict and compromise. The $64,000 question, of course, is whether there will be more conflicts than compromises in the future, and what forms and shapes they will take.

In my attempt to answer this question, I consciously sought out a wide range of experiences to inform my analysis. The vignettes and overall coverage, I hope, reflect the diversity of U.S. communities and the American people. I perused countless books and monographs about race and ethnicity, including memoirs, polemics, academic treatments, works of fiction, and specific case studies, in addition to innumerable journal, periodical, and newspaper articles. Furthermore, I discussed race and ethnicity with Americans from every racial group, including a sizable number of foreign-born people.

I also made fact-finding forays throughout the United States to burnish my analysis. I visited Puerto Rico, Washington, D.C., and all 50 U.S. states, in addition to nine Canadian provinces and five Mexican states. My field research took me to Appalachia, South Florida, Indian Country, New York City, Southern California, the border regions, the Mississippi Delta, dozens of ethnic enclaves, all of the nation's largest cities, and so many other places.[22] I attended the Alaska State Fair in Palmer over the Labor Day weekend. I crossed the border from Nuevo Laredo to Laredo in the Saturday-afternoon crush. I blended in with the masses of Italian Americans at the Staten Island Mall on a Friday evening. I overheard elderly men conversing in Lakota at the Lakota Thrifty Mart in Eagle Butte on a Thursday afternoon. After seven years of these experiences, I gained a tremendous amount of appreciation for the amazing ethnic and topographical diversity that typifies our nation.

As a white person, it was especially interesting for me to go to the parts of America where whites are a distinct minority. In the course of my travels across America during the last seven years, I have visited many parts of our country where white people are not a major part of the demographic makeup. In particular, I focused on restaurants and supermarkets, places that are easily accessible and open to all, where one can observe a cross-section of the community in action. I spent time in black-majority places such as Detroit, Michigan, and Gary, Indiana (where I was once the only white patron at the public library). One Saturday afternoon, my father and I visited a bustling supermarket in the black section of Charleston, South Carolina, where the pharmacist was the only other white person in the store. My family and I have had similar experiences in Monterey Park, California, and so many other places.

It is valuable for whites, especially analysts of race and ethnicity, to experience, even in a superficial sense, what it is like to be a minority. Most people of color, after all, experience feelings of minority status at some point or another, if only when they look at broadcast television or watch one of Hollywood's many offerings (there still are mainstream movies such as *Breakdown,* the 1997 Kurt Russell vehicle in which every character is white). The typical white person rarely experiences true minority status, because s/he can always move to an area where Caucasians are the majority group. In any event, the power structure in America continues to be overwhelmingly white, so the average white American, especially if s/he is Christian, heterosexual, and able-bodied, is unlikely to feel any significant estrangement from it.

All too often, analysts lump together members of the American racial groups — especially whites — without considering the ethnic and religious diversity of each entity. So I made a particular effort to explore the diversity of every subgroup. For instance, I went to parts of America where most whites are descended from immigrants who came here between 1890 and 1924, and then to others where nearly all the residents trace their ancestry to England, Scotland, Ireland, and Wales — and to people who arrived in the United States before 1800. I also visited such places as Japan, Italy, Spain, Russia, Sweden, Austria, Hong Kong, Argentina, and the Dominican Republic to gain firsthand impressions of the lands and peoples that have shaped the backgrounds of many Americans. These travels enabled me to hone my ability to pick out the national look of a person, and also in many cases to determine the origin of a person's surname.

As America becomes more Latin, I am frequently mistaken for Hispanic and spoken to in the language of Lorca and Cervantes, especially along the U.S.-Mexico border and in big cities with lots of Latinos. The increasingly blurry racial boundary between whites and Hispanics may eventually reconfigure whiteness, and even race, as a U.S. construct. This development heralds the widening scope and growing significance of the multiracial model of race relations, which will someday be universally accepted by Americans as the only way to make sense of our diversity.

Throughout *Visible Differences,* I show how, why, when, and where race matters to Americans and, as importantly, who is most affected by it. I try, whenever possible, to provide the historical context to supplement my analysis of contemporary dynamics and predictions about the future. In Part One, *The Multiracial Nation,* I highlight the effects of minority empowerment and greater numbers of nonwhites on the American experience, and set the stage for our entire discussion. In Part Two, *America's Enduring Dilemmas,* I focus on the socioeconomic disparities that separate various groups of Americans, along with how these disparities affect the diversity imperative and result in cultural conflicts that influence race relations. I also deal with cultural geography, or why Americans live where they do, and how it matters; in this regard, it is de rigeur, if somewhat inaccurate, to state that Americans inhabit parallel worlds and separate universes, with little or no social contact across racial and class lines. In Part Three, *Whites Still Matter Most,* I analyze how race intersects with politics and policy, which may be the most significant venue for mediating racial group interactions or, as Harold Lasswell described it, determining "who gets what, when, how."[23] I focus on politics rather than policy, because that is where the greatest mass participation occurs. Then, in the Epilogue, I look at whether the differences separating Americans are in fact reconcilable — a subject of considerable importance to our inquiry and the future of the United States.

PART ONE

The Multiracial Nation

~ chapter one ~

Classifying by Race

At around 3:00 p.m. on September 11, 2001, four cars blaring loud music drove slowly through the neighborhood where my sister lives in Glendale, California. Passengers in the cars threw "what looked like eggs and rocks" at the apartment houses in the neighborhood, which is home to many Armenians from Iran. The nativists were presumably angry about the terrorist attacks earlier that day on the World Trade Towers in New York and the Pentagon in Washington. Considering the news reports, they had surmised that Arabs/Muslims/Middle Easterners were responsible for the attacks and, as result, decided to scapegoat some Armenians. An hour or so later, the police came to investigate the disturbances, but the angry nativists did not return again. Still, the streets that night were much quieter than usual, as the Armenians stayed in their apartments rather than run the risk of encountering some vengeful American vigilantes.[1]

To some Americans, the Armenian immigrants were suspects, whom they mistakenly believed to be similar in appearance and language and religion to the terrorists who perpetrated a horrific attack on the American people. Many Armenians, of course, were sensitive about this point, and sought to distinguish themselves from Arabs and Muslims. During the evening parade on Ventura Boulevard in the San Fernando Valley on September 14, the National Day of Remembrance, my sister sighted six or seven carloads of Armenians, predominantly young women, waving tiny American flags and chanting, "Armenians are not Muslims."[2] This saga reflects the position Armenians occupy in the popular imagination — between Europeans and Middle Easterners.

It was not entirely surprising that these events unfolded in and around Glendale. During the last 15 years, ethnic Armenians from Iran, Lebanon, and the former Soviet Republic of Armenia have spun a self-sustaining web of grocers, doctors, lawyers, pharmacists, beauticians, and restaurateurs in this middle-class city located 15 minutes north of downtown Los Angeles.[3] Cyrillic letters adorn dozens of storefronts, and Armenian is heard around town as often as Spanish. Elderly Armenians stroll the streets of their new home, just as if they lived in Gyumri or Yerevan. Entire apartment buildings house foreign-born Armenians. Armenian religious and political leaders visit the city. Armenian Orthodox churches dot the landscape. And fresh groups of Armenian immigrants arrive each year.

Armenian Americans are increasingly visible in Glendale, as evidenced by everything from the Armenian-language materials at the Glendale Public Library to the composition of the student body at Glendale Community College. Two of the five City Council members are Armenians. In 2001, the first Armenian was elected to the Glendale Unified School District Board. Glendale's Armenian community numbers 55,000 to 65,000 people out of 195,000.[4] The Armenian-speaking newcomers, who typically have olive skin, black hair, dark brown eyes, and surnames that end with the suffixes "ian" and "yan," qualify as Caucasians. The Armenians soon grasp the realities of living in a multiracial society, especially when they shop at the Glendale Galleria, where every one of the city's multitudinous ethnic groups seems to be represented on Saturday afternoons. People of Armenian ancestry constitute the single largest white subgroup in Glendale — they account for roughly half of the Caucasians there. Thus residents of Glendale often think that any white person with dark hair and brown eyes is Armenian.

The Armenian immigrants to Glendale soon learn about race — a concept foreign to them — and their status as white people. Glendale is a typically multiethnic California city: Whites constitute 54.2% of the population, while Latinos account for 19.7%, Asians 16.0%, multiracials 8.5%, and blacks 1.1%. These figures are somewhat misleading, because many of the people who selected the multiracial option are, in all likelihood, Armenians who checked white and Other and wrote in Armenian.[5] It is unlikely that the Armenian immigrants who populate Glendale ever thought of themselves as white before they came to the United States. In their southwestern Asian homeland, the population is predominantly Armenian, so there is no need for racial classification. When they differentiate themselves from their rivals, they do so in ethnic terms — Turks, Iranians, Azerbaijanis, and the like.

In the United States, however, Armenian Americans find themselves required to check "White, non-Hispanic" on all kinds of forms, in part because early in the twentieth century federal courts twice decided that Armenians were "white persons," based on their culture, skin color, and the conventional anthropological wisdom at the time.[6] These decisions reflected the general consensus that Armenians should be quietly subsumed into the racial majority group. Since the Armenian immigrants continue to be concentrated in Glendale, and they observe many of their traditional customs, the non-Armenian segment of the population usually looks at them as Armenian first, and white second.

Today young Armenian Americans quickly become sensitive to the nuances of race — they attend the Glendale public schools, where Asian and Hispanic students abound — while their elders typically do not interact much with non-Armenians. In recent years there have been reports of tensions between young Armenians and Mexicans at Herbert Hoover High School, for instance.[7] But overall, Glendale's Armenians encounter little xenophobia or overt prejudice, although Koreans, Mexicans, Euro-Americans, and others sometimes disparage them for their supposed clannishness and reluctance to assimilate. The Armenians of Glendale, after all, seem very comfortable in their home away from home, where it is possible for people to speak nothing but Armenian while they work, shop, socialize, and worship.

But the American-born children of the Armenian immigrants and the youthful members of the Soviet-era diaspora are culturally indistinguishable from other white Californians. These bilingual youths listen to the same music, watch the same movies, and eat the same foods (outside of the home) as their non-Armenian peers. Indeed, the young Armenians in Glendale are already following in the path of other white immigrant groups before them, as they go to college, intermarry, leave the ethnic enclave, and succeed in the mainstream. Meanwhile, Glendale clearly benefits from its Armenian-immigrant population — and, indeed, all its newcomers — who enrich the culture, economy, and politics of this vibrant, multiethnic community.

RACE, POWER, AND PRIVILEGE

In the moments before she died a horrible, senseless death, Amy Biehl knew what it was like to be visibly different. She had the calamitous misfortune of being white, in the wrong place and at the wrong time, during that volatile period toward the end of the apartheid era of racial separation, and of white-minority rule, in South Africa. Fired up after a meeting of a radical political organization, a mob of angry young blacks glimpsed her in Guguletu Township, near Cape Town, South Africa, on August 25, 1993. In a nanosecond they labeled her by the crudest and commonest test of racial classification: eyeballing another person. And they only noticed her white skin, not her fervent anti-apartheid beliefs, her frequent visits to their area, or her friendships with residents of Guguletu. The men surrounded her car, as she was driving three black friends home, and kicked, stoned, and stabbed the 26-year-old blond Fulbright scholar from California. Biehl died in a police van only minutes after she had made it to a gas station for help. In short, she fell victim to a form of retribution from individuals who preached "one settler, one bullet," and saw her merely as another white oppressor, like the English and Afrikaners they despised.[8]

Eventually, four of the assailants were convicted of her murder and sentenced to 18-year prison terms. In 1997 they admitted to the murder and apologized to the Biehl family, who forgave them, in an effort to get amnesty from South Africa's Truth and Reconciliation Commission, which was convened to hear testimony about the crimes of the apartheid era. A year later, the Truth Commission granted the convicted murderers amnesty for the killing of Amy Biehl, on the grounds that the crime was committed for political reasons, namely their angry disenchantment resulting from racial oppression.[9]

Since Amy Biehl's death, her parents, Linda and Peter Biehl, have tried to honor their daughter's memory by carrying out what they think would have been her vision for post-apartheid South Africa, a vision she never lived to realize because of racial hatred. The Southern California couple set up the Amy Biehl Foundation, which has approximately $2.5 million in assets, to achieve these goals. The Biehls quit their jobs and relocated to South Africa so they could work full-time on efforts to aid the people of Guguletu Township and nearby communities. They rely on donations and a volunteer staff to achieve their goals. So far they have started a print shop, a construction firm, and several bakeries, ventures that employ dozens of black South Africans. In addition, they fund museums, scholarships, adult literacy projects, and programs for latchkey children in Guguletu. Moreover, the Amy Biehl Foundation, with the Biehls at the helm, is responsible for the construction of schools, housing, and golf courses for the people of Guguletu. Even more remarkably, they have became almost like a second set of parents to each of the four young black men who murdered their daughter; the Biehls go to movies, restaurants, and amusement parks with them.[10]

This story of race and reconciliation stems from the magnanimity of the Biehls; they could have very easily retreated from the place where their daughter was murdered. They chose not to take this route and, incredibly, have made a remarkable difference in hundreds of South African lives. To be sure, their race, affluence, and clout as Americans give them standing in a society where much of the economic power still is in the hands of whites. Thus the Amy Biehl saga continues to illustrate, in a transnational sense, the intersection of race, power, and American privilege.

Presently, two competing perspectives seek to explain why there are visibly different races of humankind: the "Out of Africa" and Multiregional evolution theories. This dispute occurs over how, when, and where modern humans originated and developed racial differences. The crux of the "Out of Africa" theory is that *Homo sapiens*, or modern humans, arose in a single place, Africa, approximately 100,000 years ago. They supposedly supplanted the existing humanlike precursors there due to their superior cognitive abilities. Then some of these modern humans left Africa about 80,000 years ago in response to population pressures, and spread throughout the globe. Proponents of this theory attribute visible, racial differences to geography, and the necessary acclimation that gradually occurred as various groups of human beings established settlements in different parts of the world.[11]

On the other hand, Milford Wolpoff and Rachel Caspari, the husband-and-wife team of unabashed Multiregionalists, write:

> The Multiregional evolution hypothesis argues modernity was approached over a long time period as successful new features and behaviors appeared in different places and spread across the human range as people migrated or exchanged genes. There was no singular event of modernization, no Rubicon to be crossed by widespread populations. Instead, their continued contacts through migrations and mate exchanges created a network of genetic interchanges that linked even the most far-flung peoples.[12]

The truth is hard to ascertain in such matters, but the Out-of-Africa theory, with its touchy-feely view of human commonalities, seems to be the preferred perspective in the scientific world.

Regardless of precisely how it happened, humans eventually evolved different physiognomies, skin colors, and other such features, in response to different climatic and environmental conditions. Over the millennia, then, they developed different ethnic groups with separate languages, religions, and so forth, which resulted in what we know today as visible differences. Because of limited mobility, most areas were racially, ethnically, and linguistically homogeneous. Race, in other words, did not exist for the average person. To be sure, the Roman and Greek elites, along with those in the Middle East and elsewhere, who had exposure to the outside world because of trade and military conquests, developed some rudimentary sense of difference. Due to the nonexistence of media and public education, these ideas did not take hold at the mass level, however.

This started to change in the fifteenth century, when European explorers began to journey throughout the world in search of precious metals, unsaved souls, and territorial gains. Race as a Western construct dates back to these journeys. The European explorers encountered visibly different groups of people during their travels to Asia, Africa, and the Americas. They meticulously documented their impressions of the lands they explored, and the peoples they encountered. Consequently, the intellectual elites of Western Europe became much more knowledgeable about the world's ethnic heterogeneity. Over the years European scholars synthesized the explorers' first-person accounts with existing scientific works. They categorized the foreign lands and peoples, and speculated endlessly about why their homelands often seemed to be more advanced than the European colonies.[13]

Not surprisingly, European scientists and philosophers developed chauvinistic theories of European superiority, which justified the many exploratory ventures and colonization efforts by Western nations in the New World. The eighteenth-century scientists Carolus Linnaeus and Johann Friedrich Blumenbach were influential in developing classification schemas that relied on racial and geographical criteria to sort humanity into mutually exclusive races. But it was nineteenth-century European intellectuals who accelerated the marking of invidious distinctions between and among the races.[14]

As a result, there was an upsurge in polygenism, the racist (and now-discredited) theory that the various racial groups of humankind evolved separately of each other in different areas — without any kind of common lineage whatsoever, according to its most extreme forms. The generals, monarchs, and merchants of the Occident used this type of pseudoscientific reasoning to explain the global dominance of their nations in the nineteenth century, as well as to excuse, or at least rationalize, the ravages of colonialism and imperialism during that period.[15] The notion of racial privilege developed as Western society began to benefit more and more from the development of the modern industrial economy, while many of the other nations of the world languished in poverty.

Although the human races traditionally have been classified by academicians based on inherited physical characteristics such as physique, eye shape, hair type, and skin color, such distinctions frustrate those scientists who question the utility of race as a basis for classifying human beings.[16] For instance, if one used the presence or absence of anti-malarial genes as a basis for a taxonomy, he would group Swedes with Xhosas, a black ethnic group native to South Africa, while Greeks and Italians and most other sub-Saharan Africans would be kept separate from their fellow whites and blacks, respectively.[17] On the basis of skin color, such a classification method would seem silly, of course. This may be true, but Americans and others continue to make distinctions based primarily on visible differences, not anti-malarial genes or any other non-visual criteria.

Race is a socially constructed phenomenon. Its meaning, like so many concepts and labels, must be contextualized within a legal, social, cultural, political, and historical framework.[18] Usually, the more racially homogeneous a society, the more restrictive its definition of membership in the majority group. The political elites in each society create the ordering schemas that structure the identification of the citizenry. They regulate the composition of their nations through immigration laws, citizenship and naturalization regulations, and the general atmosphere of cultural acceptance and employment opportunities available to those who differ from the majority. Humans continue to give race considerable meaning, due to the intersection of race, power, and privilege.

The world's largest economy, the one with the highest Gross Domestic Product (GDP), is the United States, followed by China, Japan, Germany, and India. In 1999 Americans had the second-highest GDP per capita of any country in the world, apart from the tiny Western European nation of Luxembourg. The United States has 4.6% of the world's people and accounts for 22.7% of the GWP (Gross World Product).[19] Latter-day Malthusians fret over the explosive population growth in the non-Western parts of the world, which are falling even farther behind the West in economic terms.[20] Underfed, undereducated poor people are potential constituents for anti-American rabble-rousers. Destabilizing economic conditions and political polarization around the globe may foment resentment of the United States, which poor foreigners see as a largely white fantasyland.

White Americans are, in the aggregate, the most prosperous group of people on Earth. Not only do they live in the richest country in the world, but their incomes and wealth, when measured in group terms, outpace the U.S. national average. Social scientists, naturally, have attempted to explain the disparities among peoples and nations. No one has developed a universally accepted explanation. At one time it was considered acceptable to speculate about whether such differences had racial and genetic underpinnings, although such views have little place in mainstream thought today. Some scholars focus on external factors, from climate to colonialism to geography, in their theorizing about human and national variations; such hypotheses offend few people. Other academics contend that culture, not ethnicity or external factors, is the principal reason that many Asian, African, and Latin American nations remain mired in poverty.[21]

The United States remains the wealthiest, most powerful, and most influential nation in the world. No other nation possesses its human capital, physical resources, military might, and attractiveness to immigrants. To the chagrin of homegrown protectionists who resent what they see as American cultural imperialism, U.S. brands and products, like *Baywatch*, Levi's, Mickey Mouse, Coca-Cola, and McDonald's, dominate the worlds of ideas, commerce, entertainment, and popular culture.[22] Throughout U.S. history Americans have squabbled over what role we should play in global affairs. After the dawn of what Henry Luce called "the American Century" in the 1940s, it became unavoidable that the United States would play an expansive role in global affairs. During the Cold War the United States and the Soviet Union grappled with each other for dominance in various political theaters around the globe.

In the post–Cold War era scholars and policymakers increasingly agree that the umbrella notion of national security should encompass quality-of-life issues for people around the globe. The nations with youthful, predominantly poor populations have the power to make policy decisions about the environment, family planning, and migration issues that threaten our security over the long term. At this point, the differences separating the world's rich nations and its poorest ones are so substantial that to raise them to level of a "Second World" country like South Korea would require far more money than the industrialized countries have to spend. Moreover, the United States spends billions of dollars each year on economic and military aid, in the form of loans and grants, to help poorer peoples around the world.[23] But this aid does little to combat the most pressing, and seemingly intractable, global problems: malnourishment, starvation, and inadequate health care.

Residents, especially native-born citizens, of the United States enjoy certain privileges as their birthright. Unlike people in so many nations around the world, we never have to worry about the possibility that our country will be plagued by anarchy and political instability. Inflation, the bane of so many countries in the developing world, is not a big issue in America. While we rightfully become concerned about inflation rates in the low double digits, we never really have to worry about losing all of our savings due to rampant inflation to the tune of 100% or 200% in a year. The fact that we speak English, the second language of most educated people around the globe, as our native tongue is a vital component of American privilege. Our currency, the greenback, is the most coveted, stable, and convertible currency instrument in the world. Although the purchasing power of the U.S. dollar depends on the exchange rate at a given time, it is the unofficial world currency, accepted by people who neither speak English nor have ever visited the United States. All these factors testify to the dominance of American values and culture, as well as the strength and ingenuity of the American people and institutions.

Americans usually do not stop to consider their advantages until they travel abroad, especially in developing countries, where the linguistic and monetary benefits of American citizenship aid American travelers immeasurably. Middle-class American tourists often go to foreign countries, primarily those in the Third World, where the cost of living is low relative to U.S. standards. If they venture outside of the resort areas, they will probably observe conditions — unpaved roads, no electricity, few telephones, few households with running water — that the typical American would see as unbelievably retrograde. They benefit from American privilege whenever they travel to areas, principally in developing countries, where they can indulge their First World habits at Third World prices. However, ordinary Americans frequently find themselves regarded as rich foreigners in developing countries, like Vietnam, where the GDP per capita in 1999 was an estimated $1,850.[24] It is only in such circumstances that the typical American, who represents a society whose sheer global might and dizzying array of consumer choices are the source of envy and admiration around the globe, realizes the full extent of his or her advantages. Not surprisingly, some foreigners complain about the "Ugly American," a mythical prototype of a loudmouthed, ill-mannered boor from the States who flaunts his money and consequently incites jealousy of American prosperity, strength, and power.[25]

Of course, race, power, and privilege are not evenly distributed in the United States. This issue has long been a sticking point in America's image worldwide, particularly when it intersects with race and ethnicity. White supremacy once limited the opportunities for people of color to develop completely their human capital and full potential in the workplace, the schools, and elsewhere. During the Cold War the Soviet Union tried to score political points at America's expense over its unfair treatment of

African Americans.[26] As a result of the cultural and demographic changes of the last 35 years, the United States is now presenting a face to the world that better represents our demographics. Blacks in South Africa saw *The Cosby Show* during the 1980s and thought that African Americans had it made. When Mexicans in Jalisco and Guanajuato hear about their friends and family members who work in Dallas and Los Angeles or at one of the small-town beef-, pork-, or poultry-processing plants and make $8 or $9 an hour, they see the United States as a land of opportunity, not a place that discriminates against Mexicans.

Indeed, the United States actually has a tremendous amount of socio-economic mobility, at least compared to the other wealthy, industrialized nations of the world. The prospect of intergenerational progression in the socioeconomic sphere entices millions of people to come to America. The Indian family that runs a Dunkin Donuts in suburban Chicago may appear to be poor on the surface because many family members work long hours in the business and the profits overall are not great at first. But they are building equity, and their kids probably will not be working at Dunkin Donuts. After all, the United States, more than any other country in the world, allows people from diverse backgrounds to develop fully their human capital. Yet, at the same time, millions of native-born Americans languish in poverty or near-poverty. The economic situation in the United States, however, is such that most of us feel we have a stake in the system.

THE ETHNO-RACIAL PENTAGON

Bhagat Singh Thind tried to become white, but the Supreme Court would not let him. A Hindu from Punjab, India, he came to the United States as a 21-year-old immigrant in 1913. Thind soon decided to become a citizen of his adopted land. Because Asians were excluded from American citizenship at the time, he claimed to be white on the basis that contemporary anthropologists grouped Asian Indians with "Caucasians." The federal government disagreed with a district court's acceptance of Thind's argument about naturalization, and his case ended up before the Supreme Court.[27] The majority opinion, authored by Justice George Sutherland, offered a very blunt description of racial differences and dismissed Thind's argument that as a Caucasian, by virtue of his "Aryan" ancestry, he was a white person who qualified for naturalization.

In his opinion, Justice Sutherland stated quite clearly that he did not see Asian Indians as white people. According to Sutherland's opinion,

"...[T]he term 'race' is one which, for the practical purposes of the statute, must be applied to a group of living persons *now* possessing in common the requisite characteristics, not to groups of persons who are supposed to be or really are descended from some remote, common ancestor, but who, whether they both resemble him to a greater or less extent, have, at any rate, ceased altogether to resemble another."[28] Using this rationale, the Court reversed Thind's naturalization in 1923. Underlying the Court's decision was the idea that an Asian Indian, being nonwhite, was somehow unworthy of citizenship in what was then a predominantly white country.

Between 1909 and 1942 there were 12 court cases — of which only *Thind* made it to the Supreme Court — about the racial classification of Asian Indians. Generally the courts held that Asian Indians were nonwhite, and employed such rationales as common knowledge, congressional intent, legal precedent, and scientific evidence to do so.[29] The typical resident of the world's second most populous nation is a biological amalgam of 3,500 years of mixing among the light-skinned Aryan conquerors of northern India, the darker-skinned Dravidians of the South, various isolated groups of indigenous peoples, and others. Thus race, at least as we understand it, has no meaning to Indians, who focus instead on religious affiliations, linguistic identifiers, geographical origins, even caste status.[30]

In the 1960s and 1970s, when a resurgence in ethnic pride and the existence of affirmative-action benefits incentivized Americans to assume nonwhite identities, it is no wonder that the Indian-American elites successfully sought to be considered racial minorities, in order to qualify for federal contracting set-asides.[31] Still, it is profoundly ironic that a high-caste Hindu, who might lose opportunities at home due to India's affirmative-action rules that benefit lower-caste people, can come to the United States and automatically receive preferential treatment as a member of a racial minority group. Bhagat Singh Thind, if he were alive, would undoubtedly marvel at how things have changed for Indian Americans in the last 80 years.

Since the first U.S. Census in 1790, the decennial enumeration of Americans has always included questions about race, although the categories and their components have changed over the years.[32] From 1790 to 1950 racial judgments were made by an enumerator from the Census Bureau. The 1960 census was an intermediate step between the old and new systems: Direct interviews, self-classification, and enumerators' observations all factored into data collection. Since 1970 these judgments have been based, for the most part, on self-identification — that is, what we say we are.[33]

During the 1960s and 1970s the federal government's civil-rights infrastructure needed uniform and comparable racial and ethnic statistics. So the bureaucrats designed a uniquely American racial identification schema, which was delineated in a document known as Statistical Policy Directive No. 15 and adopted in 1977.[34] Directive 15 designated four de jure races (white, black, Asian and Pacific Islander, and American Indian) and two ethnic categories (Hispanic and non-Hispanic). The schema underwent some minor alterations 20 years after its promulgation. In 1997 the federal government broadened the number of acceptable terms to describe the people in some of the categories, and it decided to make "Pacific Islander" a fifth racial choice, apart from Asian Americans.[35]

The following categories were the ones designated by the Office of Management and Budget, in the revised version of Statistical Policy Directive No. 15:

- White: "A person having origins in any of the original peoples of Europe, the Middle East, or North Africa."

- Black or African American: "A person having origins in any of the black racial groups of Africa."

- Hispanic or Latino: "A person of Mexican, Puerto Rican, Cuban, South or Central American, or other Spanish culture or origin, regardless of race."

- Asian: "A person having origins in any of the original peoples of the Far East, Southeast Asia, or the Indian subcontinent including, for example, Cambodia, China, India, Japan, Korea, Malaysia, Pakistan, the Philippine Islands, Thailand, and Vietnam."

- American Indian or Alaskan Native: "A person having origins in any of the original peoples of North and South America (including Central America), and who maintains tribal affiliation or community attachment."

- Native Hawaiian or Other Pacific Islander: "A person having origins in any of the original peoples of Hawaii, Guam, Samoa, or other Pacific Islands."[36]

Because Hispanics are often considered to be a separate racial group, the five major categories constitute what David Hollinger describes as the "ethno-racial pentagon." The five ethno-racial groups that make up the pentagon are roughly equivalent to "races": whites, blacks, Hispanics, Asian Americans, and American Indians. These dovetail with the attendant colloquial categories — white, black, brown, yellow, and red.[37] The recent addition of "Pacific Islander" to the U.S. government's racial choices does not create an ethno-racial hexagon. The 398,000 Pacific Islanders — Hawaiians, Samoans, Guamanians, Tongans, Fijians, and others — are not yet a sufficiently large enough group to make their presence felt nationally.

The U.S. classification schema has created some interesting issues and dilemmas. It took shape in the censuses of 1980 and 1990, but really became more complicated in the Census of 2000, which found 281,421,906 people in the 50 U.S. states and the District of Columbia. Without including Hispanic origin as a question, the America of 2000 was 75.1% white, 12.3% black, 5.5% Some Other Race, 3.6% Asian, 2.4% multiracial, 0.9% American Indian, and 0.1% Pacific Islander. When the Hispanic-origin question is included in the census, in 2000, the United States was 69.1% white, 12.5% Hispanic, 12.1% black, 3.6% Asian, 1.6% multiracial, 0.7% American Indian, 0.2% Some Other Race, and 0.1% Pacific Islander.[38] There are 194.5 million non-Hispanic white Americans, but nearly one-half of Hispanics identify as white, and a fair number of the multiracials probably qualify as white in a visual, if not cultural, sense. The 2000 census found that Latinos have nearly reached numerical parity with African Americans. There are 35.3 million Latinos and nearly 34 million non-Hispanic blacks. However, African Americans account for 12.6% of the U.S. population if you include the 1.4 million people who classify themselves as black and an additional race.[39]

With every passing year, the United States becomes proportionately less white, because of the components of population growth — fertility, life expectancy, and net immigration.[40] Natural increase (births and deaths) fuels the growth of the nonwhite population. White and Asian-American females have lower birth rates than black, Hispanic, and American Indian females, for a variety of reasons, such as their relative affluence and greater amount of exposure to higher education. Whites, moreover, are disproportionately elderly at this point — they have higher life expectancy rates and high nonwhite birth rates skew the average age of minority populations — so mortality is another factor that limits population growth for whites. The large-scale immigration from Asia, Africa, and Latin America since the late 1960s also contributes to the growth of America's minority population. People of color have accounted for more than 75% of the legal immigrants to the United States in the last two decades.

Each part of the ethno-racial pentagon agglutinates dozens of different groups that are separated by culture, ethnicity, language, religion, and even long-standing antagonisms left over from their native lands.[41] Pan-ethnic marriages — which are increasingly common, particularly among whites — solidify the categories.

WHITES. White Americans continue to be a predominantly European group. Fifty-eight million Americans trace some or all of their ancestry to Germany, while nearly 39 million claim to be of Irish extraction. Approximately 33 million of us boast English ancestors, while 14.7 million Americans just as proudly celebrate their biological links to Italy. Twelve and one-half million Americans embrace France as an ancestral homeland — slightly more than 2 million of them do so by virtue of their French-Canadian ancestry. Over 9 million people of Polish extraction live in the United States, and more than 6 million of us celebrate our Dutch heritage. Five million six hundred thousand Americans describe themselves as Scotch-Irish, while 5.4 million people claim Scottish blood. Other notable white ancestry groups include the Swedes (4.7 million), Norwegians (3.9 million), Russians (3 million), and Welsh (2 million).[42] In addition, there are 2 to 4 million white Americans of non-European extraction: The Lebanese, Armenians, Iranians (especially Persians), and Syrians claim the most coethnics.[43] As the years go by, each white ancestry group — at least those with few immigrants — becomes ever larger, due to ethnic intermarriage, while the number of full-blooded group members declines.

BLACKS. Most native-born African Americans trace their roots back to the nations of West Africa, although African blacks and Caribbean blacks continue to immigrate to the United States in substantial numbers. There are 1,155,490 West Indian Americans, including 435,024 people of Jamaican extraction and 289,521 Haitian Americans. Of the 500,000-plus sub-Saharan African Americans, people of Nigerian descent are the largest group.[44] Although African Americans and their immigrant brethren usually get along fairly well, there are occasional competitive tensions and complaints about the alleged haughtiness of the newcomers, who frequently see fewer race-related obstacles than their native-born counterparts.[45] Youthful Somali refugees and African Americans have squared off in such locales as Boston, San Diego, and Minneapolis; although both groups are black, the Somalis are Muslims and differ culturally and linguistically from native-born blacks.[46] These differences do not stop black immigrants from intermarrying with African Americans, and thus creating a panethnic black identity — especially among black immigrant youths who find African-American teen culture seductive.

HISPANICS. The U.S. Hispanic population is heavily Mexican; no other Latino group comes close to the numbers and influence of Mexican Americans. Of the 35,305,818 Latinos, 20,640,711 (58.5%) are of Mexican descent; another 3,406,178 (9.5%) identify as Puerto Rican; and 1,241,685 (3.5%) claim Cuba as the trunk of their family tree. The Hispanic population also includes sizable numbers of Dominicans (764,945), Salvadorans (655,165), Colombians (470,684), Guatemalans (372,487), Ecuadorians (260,559), Peruvians (233,926), Hondurans (217,569), and Nicaraguans (177,684). Central Americans account for 1,686,937 Hispanics, or 4.8% of the total Latino population. There are 1,353,562 South Americans in the U.S.; nearly four percent of U.S. Hispanics trace their heritage to this region. The remaining 6.1 million Latinos encompass a wide range of backgrounds, including Spaniards (100,135), people who identify as Spanish (686,004), and those who classify themselves using a panethnic referent (450,769 wrote in Latino, 1,733,274 checked off "other Hispanic" without getting more specific, and 2,454,529 wrote in Hispanic).[47] The prevailing practice nationwide is to classify Latinos as a de facto race — and putatively disadvantaged racial minority — even though the Census Bureau always reminds us, "Persons of Hispanic origin may be of any race." Latinos, in the popular shorthand, are regarded as a mutually exclusive racial group. Thus white usually means non-Hispanic white, black means non-Hispanic black, and so forth.

ASIANS. This group, which once consisted primarily of native-born Chinese and Japanese Americans, has become extremely heterogeneous due to recent immigration patterns. The United States is home to 2.43 million Chinese Americans, 1.85 million Filipinos, 1.68 million Asian Indians, 1.12 million Vietnamese, 1.08 million Koreans, and 796,700 Japanese Americans, among others. These Americans increasingly coalesce across ethnic lines at the universities and in Corporate America, where student organizations and diversity initiatives encourage pan-Asian identification. Newcomers in particular find the "Asian" category confusing: They think of themselves in terms of their individual nationalities, and find it difficult to forget latent ethnic antagonisms from the Old World.[48] The notion of a panethnic Asian identifier is attacked by some Americans of South Asian descent, who contend that they have little in common with the Chinese, Koreans, Japanese, Vietnamese, and others from East Asia and Southeast Asia.[49] However, as Lynette Clemetson points out,

"Roughly one in six Asian-Americans is married to an Asian of a different ethnic background."[50] Thus the pan-Asian identity continues to develop, in ways that would bewilder the typical resident of an Asian country.

AMERICAN INDIANS. Before the first whites came to the New World, Native Americans referred to themselves by their tribal identifiers and often fought acrimonious wars with their enemies. They only began to develop a panethnic identity, or what Stephen Cornell calls "supratribal consciousness," in response to discrimination by white society and the whites' definition of Indians as a singular racial entity.[51] Still, the vast majority of Native Americans identify with one Indian tribe, even if they are part white or their heritage includes ancestors from two or more tribes. Fully 13.6% (281,069) of American Indians are Cherokee, while 13.0% (269,202) identify as Navajo, and 5.2% (108,272) are Sioux. Another 5.1% (105,907) characterize themselves as Chippewa, compared to 4.2% (87,349) who are Choctaw. The Pueblo, Apache, and Lumbee each claim at least 50,000 coethnics. In addition, this category includes tens of thousands of Eskimos and Aleutians. Although many Native Americans continue to be wary of Indians outside their tribe, pan-Indian organizing efforts are stronger than ever, as tribes cooperate with each other in order to combat environmental problems and preserve Native American gains in gaming and other venues.[52]

Panethnic unity and ethno-racial group consciousness and cohesiveness are impeded by ethnic, linguistic, religious, and socioeconomic differences. Yet it is common for businesspeople, media analysts, and social scientists to discuss the races solely in big-picture terms. These decision-makers and opinion leaders speak in vague generalities: white America, the black community, the Asian-American experience; and they note how Hispanics feel, or women think, about a given issue. The assumption implicit in these rhetorical formulations — however misleading and untrue it may be in some cases — is that people with similar ethnic backgrounds think the same and have had comparable experiences. Sometimes there is a disconnect between elite and mass conceptions of racial group interests, and the elite spokespeople distort popular opinion on a given issue by representing their feelings as those of their constituents.[53] Those who deviate from the perceived group interests of the race, like Supreme Court Justice Clarence Thomas, are pilloried as race traitors and abused with in-group racial epithets. In general, recent immigrants to the United States are reluctant to identify with the panethnic groups. A Nigerian immigrant I interviewed thought of herself as Ibo, her ethnic group back home. Moreover, a Peruvian American told me she dislikes it when people lump her in with the Mexicans. The ethnic advocates who represent panethnic organizations typically ignore these ethnic-specific responses, which undercut their efforts to present a united front to the public.

The Reverend Jesse Jackson serves as the black community's roving ambassador-at-large. Jackson, a two-time candidate for the Democratic presidential nomination in 1984 and 1988, materializes whenever and wherever there is a newsworthy issue or crisis that affects African Americans. His tremendous popularity among blacks makes the 60-year-old president and founder of the Rainbow/PUSH Coalition a powerful figure in the Democratic Party and gives him considerable leverage in his efforts to open up America's premier capitalistic enclaves — Wall Street and Silicon Valley — to blacks and other minorities. However, the recent revelations of his extramarital affair and child born out of wedlock and questionable practices regarding the funding of organizations under his control may have diminished his effectiveness.[54]

The Reverend Al Sharpton, a middle-aged African-American New Yorker, increasingly rivals Jesse Jackson as the self-appointed national spokesman for discontented blacks. Sharpton leads protests against police brutality in New York and elsewhere. He makes frequent appearances around the country in situations where there have been racially charged incidents involving African Americans. Sharpton is considerably more militant than Jackson. In recent years, Sharpton has become a national political player, and he continues to be a formidable political power-broker in New York. He intends to seek the Democratic presidential nomination in 2004.[55] Sharpton's presidential candidacy will undoubtedly raise his public profile, even as African Americans increasingly note that no single person can speak for black people in America.[56]

SOCIAL CONSTRUCTIONS OF RACE

When Cher released the album *Half Breed* in 1973, she certainly was attuned to the currents of her times. The third track on the album, "Half Breed," was a song about a woman who was half Cherokee and half white. With the sound of war drums in the background, Cher belts out a ballad about the unpleasantness that can plague a person who is biracial and never completely accepted by either group. The refrain of "Half Breed" emphasizes this point: "Half-breed, that's all I ever heard / Half-breed, how I learned to hate the word / Half-breed, she's no good they

warned / Both sides were against me since the day I was born."[57] The
subject of the song endures mocking at school, and she and her family
have a peripatetic lifestyle because of their inability to fit in anywhere.

The cover art on the album depicts Cher, whose black hair, dark
brown eyes, and ambiguous skin tone give her a polyethnic look, in Native American garb. In fact, the viewer/listener could plausibly assume
that Cher is Native American.[58] Cher, however, gets her exotic looks
from her Armenian-American father, rather than her mother (who reportedly is Irish, French, English, German, and Cherokee).[59] Cher may
have empathized with mixed bloods, who often confront issues of identity and belonging, due to her own experiences as a youth, when she felt
like a bit of an outsider, due to her olive skin and black hair.[60]

Cher's album, *Half Breed,* typified and contributed to Native American chic, a trend that was very popular among whites in 1973. Marlon
Brando made history the same year when he refused to accept his Oscar
for Best Actor in *The Godfather* because of his anger over the mistreatment of American Indians. Native Americans in South Dakota made
history of a different kind during their 71-day occupation of Wounded
Knee in 1973. Indeed, American Indian issues had come to the forefront of the American consciousness in the aftermath of the civil rights
movement. For the first time ever, American Indian ancestry became an
unqualified benefit in America.

As a result, a number of whites such as Cher rediscovered their "Indian" ancestry or, in a few cases, fabricated one out of thin air. Black
culture, to be sure, had also become quite popular with whites in the
early 1970s, but none of the white people who listened to soul music or
flocked to blaxploitation films claimed to be part black. And no prominent white artist would have dared to title her album *Mulatto.* Cher was
able to flirt with an Indian identity without giving up her whiteness. In
essence, she could be white and Indian at the same time. This is a considerably more optimistic situation than the one she depicts in "Half Breed."
After all, whites openly discuss — and brag about — their real or imag-
ined American Indian ancestry. As in Cher's case, an infinitesimal amount
(one-quarter or less) of Indian blood lends Caucasians a glamorous air
of exoticism, without calling into question their whiteness.

Until recently, the cultural and legal norms of the nation validated
what became known as the "one-drop rule," meaning that even minuscule amounts of nonwhite blood disqualified ostensibly white people
from being part of the Caucasian race, instead making them the race of
their nonwhite ancestor. This socially and legally constructed notion of

race originated for blacks as a manifestation of whites' obsession with maintaining racial purity, while its usage for American Indians stemmed from their high rates of racially exogamous marriages, and a desire to maintain tribal membership rolls despite increasingly fractionalized blood-quantum threshold levels. These issues date back to the first English contact and encounters with blacks and Indians during the Age of Discovery. The English viewed both blacks and Indians as inferior, primitive groups. But they enslaved blacks and subjugated them, while Indians were subjected to lesser forms of demeaning treatment, even though there were specific instances of great cruelty and inhumanity.[61]

The European explorers seem to have regarded Amerindians better than black Africans for a variety of reasons. For one, they simultaneously encountered chimpanzees, who looked humanlike, and black Africans, whose civilizations they saw as "backward"; as a result, the whites equated black Africans with members of the animal kingdom. Their negative perceptions of the color black — which stemmed from long-standing European fears of the night, and of darkness — also biased them against black Africans. Perhaps most importantly, the Englishmen found the natural environment of North America infinitely preferable to that of Africa, due to its more temperate climate, less densely populated areas, and proportionally smaller number of diseases that threatened the Europeans' immune systems.[62]

In later years the white/black/red dynamics were affected primarily by numbers — namely, the threat of each minority group to the racial majority. By 1900 the descendants of African slaves constituted 11.6% of the U.S. population.[63] This percentage was much higher in the Deep South states of Louisiana, Mississippi, Alabama, Georgia, and South Carolina, where numerous counties had African-American majorities. There was a great deal of paranoia in the South during the era of slavery, because the fear of a slave rebellion, in which whites were murdered by vengeful slaves, was omnipresent. (This only happened on a few occasions, such as when Nat Turner and his compatriots went on a killing spree in 1831, but it always worried the slaveholders nonetheless.) Later, in the era of segregation, whites were uncomfortably aware that the oppression of African Americans created, unsurprisingly, anger and resentment that might erupt at any time.

As the United States expanded to its current size, American Indians were never more than one percent of the population, while African Americans were the dominant minority group. Due in part to their relatively small numbers, and the conditions under which most Americans came into contact with them — news of battles rather than slavery — Indians were regarded differently than blacks by the white majority. (This is not to say that there were not acts of terrible violence committed by whites against specific Indian tribes. The Trail of Tears during the 1830s, the Sand Creek massacre of 1864, and the Wounded Knee massacre of 1890 come to mind.) Meanwhile, the stereotypes about Indian poverty and dependency had not yet taken hold in a systematic fashion.

After vanquishing them in battle and stealing most of their land, whites mythologized Indians as "noble savages" because the First Americans never represented much of a numerical threat to them, and seemed to be exotic relics of America's rough-and-ready Western past. Great Indian warriors such as Tecumseh and Sitting Bull inspired white respect, if not admiration, for their courage, tenacity, and dogged determination to protect their way of life. Wild West shows and pulp novels about cowboys and Indians were popular, not only in America but in Europe as well.[64] American Indians were also used by white mythologists in the creation of a national narrative; Thanksgiving is perhaps the best example of this phenomenon.[65]

Indians, then, are the only people of color to have graced the nation's mass-circulation currencies. The Indian Head cent, which circulated from 1859 to 1909, features a mythical depiction of Liberty sporting a feathered headdress. And the Buffalo five-cent piece, which circulated from 1913 to 1938, portrays the wizened visage of a Native American man in a traditional headdress, and has a bison — that unmistakable staple of life for Plains Indians — on the obverse of the coin.[66] Moreover, the countenance of Sacajawea, a Shoshone teenager who served as a guide and interpreter for the Lewis and Clark expedition in 1804 and 1805, adorns the gold dollar coin that began circulating in 2000. Had Native Americans been ten percent of the population, and close to a majority in certain states, where they threatened the existing power structure, these instances of symbolic inclusion might never have happened.

Native Americans continued to be an important part of the national mythology in the postwar era. The Western, a dominant film and television genre in the 1950s and 1960s, turned out to be even more enduring than the pulp novels and Wild West shows. Whites and Indians squared off endlessly in these quintessentially American cinematic parables, and the Caucasians were portrayed, almost unanimously, as the heroes and good guys. Native American characters, who often were played by white men, usually had one of three roles to play: villains, faithful and subservient henchmen, or faceless extras added to create an "authentic" picture. In particular, the Lone Ranger and his loyal Indian sidekick, Tonto, entertained Americans with their heroics.[67] Baby Boomer schoolchildren spent millions of hours playing cowboys and Indians, although kids rarely wanted to be the Native Americans, who were the preordained losers in the game.

Throughout the twentieth century Indians, either real or mythical, proved to be potent commercial icons and brand names. They promoted the sales of disparate products, ranging from apples to cigars to motorcycles. In recent years Indians have served as commercial icons as well. Chrysler's Jeep Cherokee line was but one example of their potential naming power. The Apache helicopter is another example. Moreover, thousands of school, community, and professional sports teams adopted Indian mascots and team names, like the Atlanta Braves, Chicago Blackhawks, Cleveland Indians, Washington Redskins, and Kansas City Chiefs. And in the 1960s white environmentalists began celebrating Indians as the archetypal conservationists, whose wise stewardship of natural resources sets an example for non-Indians to emulate.[68] As a result of this valorization, many Americans, particularly those who live in areas with few Indians, probably have positive views of indigenous people.

Notwithstanding their disdain for Africans, the European male colonists had no compunction about forming sexual unions with African females. Black-white marriages were very rare, and subject to legal proscriptions and intense social stigmatization, but this did little to slow the slaveowners, their male relatives, and the overseers who sexually abused the African women. The resulting light-skinned, biracial children of these illicit, frequently extramarital relationships were raised as slaves, or defined as something less than their white offspring, to keep the peace at home and not disrupt the double standard of the times. That is how the "one-drop rule" came about, with fine distinctions made among mulattoes (part-black in general), quadroons (one-quarter black), and octoroons (one-eighth black).[69]

Whites formed sexual unions with Indians, too. These couplings usually involved white men and Indian women, especially in the areas where white females were in short supply. Although fewer social sanctions existed against such relationships, and thousands of actual marriages occurred between white men and Indian women, whites still preferred racially endogamous marriages. However, mixed bloods, as persons of part-Indian and part-white ancestry became known, could assimilate much better into white society than full-blooded Indians. In addition, blacks formed unions with American Indians, especially in the Southeast, but whites frowned upon such couplings.[70] Before the 1970s, according to the U.S. Bureau of the Census, "Persons of mixed white and other parentage were usually classified with the other race. A person of mixed parentage other than white was usually classified by the race of his father, except that mixtures of Negro and Indian were classified as Negro unless the Indian stock was clearly predominant or unless the individual was accepted in the community in which he resided as an Indian."[71]

African Americans coalesced as a cohesive racial group in the years between 1850 and 1920. During this period many American states had statutes that quantified the amount of black blood required to be considered a Negro — with the attendant indignities of second-class citizenship in a segregationist era.[72] In an 1896 case, *Plessy v. Ferguson,* the Supreme Court lent its imprimatur to the "one-drop rule." The Justices upheld Louisiana's segregation of train cars and, by extension, its racial classification of the defendant, Homer Plessy, who was one-eighth Negro and visually white.[73] Some octoroons, quadroons, and mulattoes even left the black race permanently: They took advantage of their light skin color and Caucasian facial features and passed as white. From 1880 to 1925 hundreds of thousands of mulattoes became whites. In doing so, they departed the South to make new homes for themselves and their families in the West, Midwest, or Northeast. Mulattoes who passed for white and permanently crossed the color line gave up their families, friends, and other accouterments of their former lives. Perhaps more common, and certainly less traumatic, was part-time passing, for such purposes as having comfortable accommodations, regular options for entertainment, and especially to obtain more lucrative employment. Interestingly, many mulattoes refused to pass as white, and they remained black because of their deeply ingrained sense of racial loyalty.[74]

By the 1920s, as white America firmed up its acceptance of the "one-drop rule," increasing amounts of "internal miscegenation" between mulattoes and unmixed blacks created "new people," who were brown in color, and whose genotype included African, European, and, frequently, American Indian ancestry. The Census Bureau's classification schema reflected these new realities in the black community. From 1850 to 1920 the nation's enumerators measured varying amounts of black blood. After 1920, however, they gave up trying to quantify it, and henceforth black meant everyone with some African blood who was visibly different from whites.[75]

These factors led to intraracial color discrimination among African Americans. Almost all the leading teachers, preachers, doctors, professors, shopkeepers, and businesspeople of the African-American community were light-skinned, or actually biracial, until the civil rights movement of the 1950s and 1960s. African Americans used a wide variety of colloquial terms to characterize the kaleidoscopic array of colors within black America. An exceptionally insulting term, "high yellow," referred to those mulattoes who mimicked the racial exclusion of white society and sought to distinguish themselves from other blacks through social rituals and other exclusionary mechanisms. One such ritual was the blue-vein test, whereby only persons whose veins were visible through their skin could be members of specific social clubs. Another was the brown paper bag test, whereby only those individuals with skin lighter than the color of brown paper bags could join certain church congregations.[76]

Since the days of black nationalist Marcus Garvey in the 1910s and 1920s, some African Americans have equated darker skin with being really "black," forcing some of their light-skinned brothers and sisters to prove their racial bona fides. Blackness became an ideological stance during the late 1960s, when cries of "Black Power" alternated with "Black Is Beautiful," just as skin lighteners and hair straightening went out of fashion. In the competition to be "blacker than thou," African Americans grew their hair naturally and sported large Afros. Nonetheless, black marital partners frequently have different skin tones; thus it is not uncommon for an African-American family to be multihued. After centuries of internal miscegenation, interracial colorism — both by lighter blacks against darker African Americans, and by darker blacks against their lighter counterparts — still occurs.[77]

A similar dynamic has informed the acceptance of American Indians by whites. Mixed bloods — like the white/Cherokee humorist Will Rogers, who dressed, acted, and lived like other white men — were usually warmly accepted by Caucasians.[78] Their full-blooded brethren, however, faced discrimination from mixed bloods and the dominant society. Today traditional Indians and their Indianness are the subject of respect and admiration from whites and Native Americans alike. This trend really took off during the 1960s when the counterculture embraced Native American ideas and practices. Today New Age devotees seek out Indian curios, symbols, and rituals in their search for enlightenment.[79] This renewed interest in shamans, powwows, tribal lore, and sweat lodges also corresponds with the continuing resilience of Native American chic: the popularity of traditional Indian rugs, dolls, jewelry, blankets, pottery, beadwork, and clothing. White appropriators and interpreters of Indian culture, like Kevin Costner and his Oscar-winning film, *Dances with Wolves,* have spurred this veritable efflorescence of Indian iconography as well.

Today there are 2,068,883 non-Hispanic American Indians, 407,073 Hispanic Indians, and 1,643,345 non-Hispanic multiracials with an American Indian identifier.[80] Of course not all of those who identify as American Indian in a racial sense are enrolled members of federally recognized tribes. Moreover, there are millions of Americans, particularly blacks and whites, who have Native American ancestry but do not identify with the group racially. It is not uncommon for persons who are one-sixteenth or even one-thirty-second or one-sixty-fourth American Indian to claim to be one for racial purposes. Each census shows increasing numbers of Americans asserting American Indian identities; meanwhile, the number of "real" Indians declines. There are more Native Americans than could be expected from natural increase, because some Americans, especially people who formerly identified as white, are declaring themselves American Indians for a variety of reasons, including the popularity of Indianness, a desire to partake of casino riches, and the possibility of affirmative-action benefits.[81]

There are three types of Indians. Full bloods trace their ancestry solely to one tribe. Then there are purely Indian persons whose heritage comes from two or more tribes. And some biracial and multiracial Americans self-identify as Indian, despite their white, black, or Asian blood. The answer to the question — Who is an Indian? — is dependent on a particular tribe's membership policies regarding the granting, denial, revocation, and qualification of Indianness. The tribal imprimatur is necessary if one wants to receive tribal benefits, occupy tribal land, and participate in tribal programs.[82]

In an era when only an estimated 34% of Indians are full bloods, tribes divide into two camps in terms of how rigidly they define Indianness. The first camp is quite liberal. It consists of tribes that have abolished any requirement of a specific blood-quantum level, or have reduced the fractionalized amounts of Indian blood needed to be considered a tribal member. The second camp is much stricter. Its members require half-Indian ancestry for tribal membership. Smaller tribes find it difficult to be this selective — it is nearly impossible for their members to find marital partners. Prospective brides and grooms are biologically related to many of the eligible candidates, or they find the available choices unsatisfactory.[83] But there are few immigrants to replenish the American Indian population. The 407,073 Hispanics who choose American Indian to identify themselves racially are culturally Latino, not Native American. Only a small number of Canadian Indians, the persons who are closest ethnically to most Native Americans, immigrate to the United States. Consequently, it is becoming less common to see full-blooded Indians, many of whom have lustrous black hair, copper-colored skin, and prominent cheekbones.

Racial exogamy is the preliminary step toward eliminating the ethno-racial categories. Notwithstanding persistent stigmas about interracial relationships, which stem from religious injunctions, racial prejudices, and calls for group solidarity, there are fewer social sanctions and more possible partners of every different combination than ever before in the United States. Racial exogamy is most common among the younger generations. Affluence and exposure to higher education also seem to increase the probability of racial exogamy for native-born Americans. (Foreign-born residents and naturalized citizens, not surprisingly, have low rates of racial exogamy.) Interracial marriages usually involve a white and a minority, not two nonwhites of different races. As of 1998, 3.0% of whites were engaged in racial exogamy, compared to 5.0% of blacks, 15.0% of Asians, and 16.7% of Hispanics. American Indian rates of racial exogamy exceed 70%. Of the intergroup married couples, 52% of them are white/Hispanic duos, 19% are white/Asian partnerships, 12% are white/American Indian unions, and 9% are white/black pairs.[84] Rates of intermarriage are only the most permanent indicator of racial couplings: They do not measure dating or cohabitation by race. Young Americans are very likely to have befriended or dated someone of another race at one time or another, particularly if they live in an ethnically and racially heterogeneous area and associate with people of different races who come from the same socioeconomic background.[85]

Due to the growing number of interracial marriages and relationships, there is now a tangible community of mixed-race Americans. They have their own magazines, support groups, advocacy organizations, and political causes (namely, recognition for multiracial people). Many of these mixed-race Americans complain about the zero-sum nature of racial pigeonholing, which leaves little room for people to have multiple racial identities.[86] The 2000 census counted mixed-race Americans for the first time. The non-Hispanic multiracials total 4.6 million, or 1.6% of the U.S. population, almost all of whom are biracial.[87] Interestingly, some of the people who selected "two or more races" on the census form are not, in all likelihood, multiracial. The available evidence suggests that some white and black immigrants checked the category in order to give their ethnic group more visibility.[88] In any event, Hawaii has the largest percentage of non-Hispanic multiracials: They constitute 18.1% of the Aloha State, compared to 4.9% in Alaska and 4.1% in Oklahoma. West Virginia and South Carolina have the smallest percentages of non-Hispanic multiracials in the country; only 0.8% of the residents in each state selected this term to define themselves.

Parents differ on how they acculturate their children to mixed-race identities. Some parents of multiracial children aggressively promote multiracialism. Others adopt a laissez-faire, let-the-kids-decide attitude about the matter. Champion golfer Tiger Woods, a self-described "Cablinasian," personifies the quintessential American multiracial: He is one-eighth white, one-eighth Native American, one-quarter black, one-quarter Chinese, and one-quarter Thai.[89] Multiracial people like Woods are increasingly common in advertising campaigns that seek to represent America. Due to the growing significance of multiracial Americans, particularly in the nation's largest cities, it has become hip in America's youth culture to include multiracials in media portrayals of contemporary youngsters.[90] In any event, multiracials are certainly the most diverse "racial" group America has ever seen.

Regardless, the "one drop rule" remains relevant today. A majority-white person can self-identify as a black or American Indian and, in some cases, Asian or Hispanic — and be considered a de jure racial minority in the United States — based on his or her fractionalized amounts of non-white blood. Many African Americans and American Indians have some European ancestry, as a result of centuries of racially exogamous couplings. Approximately 75% to 90% of black Americans are part white, and possibly one in four has Indian blood too.[91] Most blacks recognize their mixed heritage but identify solely as African American, to reflect how they see themselves as well as to promote racial solidarity.[92]

In practice, as one writer noted more than two decades ago, "a person's own declaration of his ethnic identity is simply accepted unless it obviously conflicts with reality. . . . "[93] Some whites (and Native Americans) are dismayed when they see blond, blue-eyed "Indians" receiving preferential treatment. This practice extends, in some circumstances, to Hispanics as well. In one instance, a young man of English/German origins with a modest academic record and unimpressive test scores was admitted to a selective university based on the fact that he had a Mexican great-grandfather.[94] At one point during a college discussion about racial identity, one of my classmates, a young Eurasian woman, said she identified as white, but added laughingly that she checked "Asian American" on the financial-aid forms. As a rule, there are many incentives for mixed-race people to emphasize the nonwhite aspect of their identity, in order to qualify for affirmative-action programs.

During the last ten or 15 years, racial classifications have come under increasing fire in the United States for a number of reasons. The most important reason, of course, is the growing number of children from multiracial backgrounds. Another significant reason is the sizable population of immigrants from places such as Arabia, the Caribbean, and Latin America; these people encompass a wide range of skin tones, facial features, and hair textures. Yet another reason is that the environment in Multicultural America is receptive to claims made by previously unrecognized groups, ranging from transgenders to multiracials to persons with disabilities. Although few people seriously discuss eliminating racial categories altogether, there has been grumbling about the inadequacy of the ethno-racial pentagon ever since its creation in 1977. In particular, many multiracial activists feel that the existing racial categories are insufficiently detailed enough to account for the nation's diversity.

Because of such concerns, in 1993 the Office of Management and Budget began what turned out to be a four-year review process to assess the validity of the racial and ethnic standards. This review sparked a heated debate that was the subject of two sets of congressional hearings, detailed stories in newspapers and periodicals, spirited discussions in Internet chat rooms, and a Multiracial Solidarity March in Washington. The most contentious issue was whether the Census Bureau should create a multiracial box, in addition to the five existing categories, for the decennial enumeration in 2000. Ethnic advocates worried that such a category might lead many of their constituents to embrace an amorphous, ill-defined multiracial status. Naturally, the ethnic advocates want to maximize their numbers, which affect everything from legislative redistricting to the allocation of federal dollars to monitoring for various types of discrimination. Rather than include a separate multiracial category, however, the federal government decided to allow census respondents to check multiple racial categories.[95]

With the development of the new categories, it is only a matter of time before every business or institution that collects racial and ethnic data has to adjust to the new, more complicated system in order to be in compliance with federal regulations. By 2003, the old model — white, black, Hispanic, Asian, American Indian — has to be expanded to take into account Pacific Islanders and multiracial people. These changes, along with the plethora of ethnic/racial combinations in the last census, almost certainly will complicate the collection, evaluation, and presentation of racial and ethnic data.[96] The old standards, while easier to tabulate, no longer accurately measured the increasing richness of America's multiethnic splendor.

Furthermore, it appears that the non-Hispanic multiracials are going to be classified as minorities. The Office of Management and Budget, under the Clinton administration, decided that, for administrative and reporting purposes, a biracial person who is part white will be classified by his nonwhite racial identifier.[97] This is a very interesting development because many of the non-Hispanic multiracials appear white in a visual sense, and are white in a cultural sense as well. Due to the heterogeneity of the groups that make up the multiracial community, we have not seen the development of a distinct multiracial identity with a specific ethnic basis, as in the Métis of Canada or the Afro-Chinese of Jamaica.

The nation's growing population of people from North Africa and the Middle East contributes to the increasing complexity of ethnic and racial classification in America. Most people in North Africa and the Middle East have the pigmentation and physiognomic characteristics that we commonly associate with white people. In the United States, they usually identify as white, and often intermarry with European Americans; their descendants are garden-variety white Americans. To be sure, this highly diverse population group includes some people who are not white by American standards and who, for that matter, do not view themselves as white people. Some scholars, activists, and policymakers argue that, despite their high income levels and impressive rates of educational achievement, many non-European white Americans, especially Arabs, are stigmatized and marginalized on the basis of ethnicity, religion, and national origin.[98]

Indeed, Arab Americans and non-Arab Middle Eastern Americans, such as Iranians, are often considered a quasi-minority group in America. Media analyses frequently refer to whites *and* Arabs or whites *and* Iranians as mutually exclusive groups, when in fact most Arab Americans and Iranian Americans are white people. Conversely, this white/Other dichotomy rarely surfaces in the coverage of Armenian Americans, who are a long-established white ethnic group, or small Middle Eastern subgroups such as Turks or Chaldeans. These issues remain largely a regional phenomenon, limited to the parts of America where North Africans and Middle Easterners make up a substantial percentage of the population.

In this era of multiculturalism and identity politics, there is a growing movement within the Arab-American and Middle Eastern communities to distinguish themselves from European Americans. Some members of these groups want their own box on the census, distinct from European Americans, either as a subset of the white category, or as a separate category altogether. Arab-American ethnic advocates argue that a census box will improve the collection of data about Americans of North African and Middle Eastern descent, an issue that takes on added importance because of the activists' concerns about census undercounts.[99] (The ancestry question is presently the only source of census data on Americans of North African and Middle Eastern origin.)

The possibility of an Arab-American or Middle Eastern census category surfaced during the Office of Management and Budget's review of the racial and ethnic categories in the mid-1990s. The OMB eventually rejected the idea, in part because Arab Americans and non-Arab Middle Eastern Americans only account for one to two percent of the U.S. population — and they are concentrated in a few places, such as the Detroit area and Greater Los Angeles.[100] Still, the OMB indicated "that further research should be done to determine the best way to improve data on this population group."[101] This matter, along with the issue of whether people from North Africa and the Middle East should become a protected class akin to Hispanics, will undoubtedly continue to be part of the discourse on ethnic and racial classification.

~ **chapter two** ~

White Like Who?

"Look, look. I see a big yellow car. See the yellow car go," said Jane to her little sister Sally. Upon seeing an airplane, older brother Dick added, "Look up, Sally. You can see something. It is red and yellow. It can go up, up, up. It can go away."[1] With words like these, and the simple, illustrated stories that accompanied them, a brother-and-sister duo named Dick and Jane taught reading to 85 million first graders (most American adults today) from 1930 to 1970. As the protagonists of the three paperback primers used in most elementary schools during that period, these fictional, Northern European-looking characters socialized impressionable young children with their duties and responsibilities as Americans. The nostrums contained within the pages of the bland stories emphasized learning entire words, and were reinforced by the pictures.[2]

Dick and Jane had no surnames or distinguishing regional characteristics — a shrewd bit of ecumenism that made them broadly acceptable to white children around the country. These syrupy accounts, which highlighted the banalities of childhood, implicitly celebrated white hegemony and traditional family values through their portrayals of social class, gender roles, and family relationships.[3] With their Anglo-American names and middle-class suburban lifestyle, Dick and Jane personified the homogenizing influences of the assimilationist national ethos in the years preceding Multicultural America. The Dick-and-Jane stories provided those outside the mainstream — minorities, white ethnics, the poor — with a model of the majority culture's acceptable value system, and prepared them for participation in civil society.[4]

However, the demographics of Multicultural America sounded the death knell for Dick, Jane, and Sally. Educators embraced phonics to teach students reading, while feminists challenged the traditional gender roles described in the stories, and civil rights activists denounced the racially exclusionary nature of the primers. The stories about Dick, Jane, and Sally were most popular during the conformist 1950s. Although the last edition, published in 1965, included more disobedience and "enlightened" gender roles, along with black characters, Dick and Jane were clearly obsolete by this time. Nonetheless, the Dick-and-Jane primers were sold for five more years, and were used in some classrooms during the 1970s.[5] Dick and Jane live on in the present through the commercialized artifacts of nostalgia: calendars, stationery, wrapping paper, and the like.

The history of Dick and Jane illustrates how ethnic and racial minorities were largely excluded from America's textbooks during the middle part of the twentieth century. The filmmakers, advertising gurus, textbook creators, and television producers of yesteryear may not have consciously excluded people from the spotlight, although the effect was the same when they created products in their own image. Today's textbooks, at least, resemble Benetton ads in their portrayals of diversity, so that even public schoolchildren in the whitest corners of America see nonwhite faces when they do their lessons. The ever-present disputes over curricula reflect the larger debates about how a multiracial nation like the United States should go about making all of its residents and citizens feel included, without sacrificing a sense of national unity and purpose.[6]

THE COLOR OF A NATION

During the evening of December 8, 1998, the fifty-seventh anniversary of Pearl Harbor Day in Japan, a coterie of Japanese nationalists took up residence in a massive, raised platform in the Shinjuku district of Tokyo. They adorned the speaker's box with a simple white banner with black lettering that read "December 8" and "57 years." Amid the glitter and neon of Japan's premier nightlife area, speaker after speaker vented his or her feelings of anger toward the United States. One particularly arresting orator, a middle-aged Japanese woman with tears streaming down her face, delivered an impassioned harangue that invoked the U.S. nuclear bombing of Hiroshima and Nagasaki in 1945, and assailed the American military presence in Okinawa.

This fervent nationalist's anti-American imprecations seemed anachronistic, more than five decades after Japan and the United States fought what amounted to a race war in the Pacific, and several years after the denouement of a long-running trade conflict and war of words between the two nations, which lasted from the late 1970s to the early 1990s. She and her counterparts attracted few listeners, and my family and I encountered no anti-American incidents during our uniformly pleasant stay in the land of the Rising Sun.

As a rule, Japan and the United States enjoy amicable relations. There is considerable cross-pollination between the two nations in terms of consumer products and popular culture. Americans readily recognize Japanese brands such as Sony, Suzuki, Honda, Toyota, and Toshiba. American consumers embrace Japanese pop culture, from karaoke to Hello Kitty merchandise to Pokémon trading cards and paraphernalia. In Japan, meanwhile, some businesspeople have begun using American management practices to revitalize their ailing companies. And American fashions, musicians, and movies reach receptive audiences in Japan. Even the film *Pearl Harbor* was a surprise hit there. Not surprisingly, the Japanese version of *Pearl Harbor* downplayed the wartime hostilities and focused more on the romance between the two protagonists.[7]

To be sure, Westerners whose coloration and physiognomy identify them as non-Japanese *gaijin* can never be truly "Japanese" — even if they speak the language and marry a native of the homogeneous island nation. Some Japanese scholars contend that the Japanese, while suspicious of all foreigners, prefer Westerners over other Asians for two reasons. For one, they disdain non-Japanese Asians, like the nation's Korean minority, as inferior. And while the Japanese can, of course, easily spot foreigners from the West in their midst, they sometimes find it difficult to ferret out the non-Japanese Asians among them.[8] Conversely, Japanese Americans periodically argue that their Eastern characteristics mark *them* as perpetual outsiders in the United States, due to the American tendency to see whites and blacks as those who look "American."[9] These phenomena reflect the demographics of each country.

The accouterments of nationhood usually include an independent government, sovereign borders, a national flag, a national currency, a common language, a dominant religion, and often, a majority ethnic group. Unlike most nations in the world, the United States is a country where people are bound not by a singular ethnic or racial identity but rather by a set of common values, experiences, and principles.[10] There is no state religion in America, although a majority of Americans are Protestants. Nor is there an official language, although most Americans speak English — and fluency in American English is essential to success in America.

The United States once had an ethnic majority: British Americans. One hundred years ago a solid majority of Americans (nearly three out of five) traced their roots to Great Britain. While America remained a predominantly European-origin nation until the 1990s, British Americans were but a plurality of the nation by 1920, although 75% of Americans at that time hailed from northwestern Europe.[11] Even today, many Americans who trace their ancestry to the British Isles do not look at themselves as "having" ethnicity. Although people of Welsh and, especially, Scottish ancestry often organize cultural activities around their ethnic identities, there is no English-American identity per se. The cultural and linguistic dominance of the American Anglo-Saxons is reinforced by the fact that many African Americans have English surnames, which makes the Anglo-Saxon identity seem even more quintessentially American.

Unlike in the past, American citizenship no longer has racial significance. At one time, the United States had patently discriminatory citizenship regulations. Native-born white persons have been U.S. citizens since the Constitution took effect in 1789. Blacks, who were considered to be "three-fifths" of humans by the drafters of the Constitution, became citizens in 1868. The remaining non-citizen American Indians were granted U.S. citizenship in 1924. And Asians were finally allowed to become naturalized Americans beginning in 1952. Since 1868 the United States has had birthright citizenship. If a child is born on U.S. soil, regardless of the legal status of his parents, he is an American citizen.[12] Moreover, legal residents of five years or longer are eligible to apply for naturalization.

Although U.S. citizenship remains a valuable prerogative — it confers upon its holders the basic rights of participation in the American polity — foreign-born Americans are displaying an unusual reluctance to become naturalized citizens. Doing so closes the door, in many cases, on ever returning permanently to one's original country. This may explain why naturalization rates are so low for Mexicans and Central Americans. Aside from bureaucratic barriers like the difficulty and expense of naturalization, a long-term reluctance to commit oneself to the United States may be the single most significant reason that only 37.3% of foreign-born Americans have obtained U.S. citizenship.[13] Unlike most other affluent nations in the West, the United States made it fairly easy (until recently) for newcomers to enter the country and later become citizens.

Over the years the definition of whiteness and criteria for membership in the dominant U.S. racial group have gotten much broader as well. Irish, Jewish, Slavic, Greek, and Italian immigrants once faced ethnic discrimination from native-born European Americans of Anglo-Saxon, Teutonic, and Scandinavian stock. These so-called Nordic peoples were initially skeptical about the dark-skinned Caucasians in their midst. Except for some Anglo-Saxon Southerners, who at first considered their Greek-, Italian-, and Arab-immigrant neighbors to be racial Others,

Americans generally accepted the Southern and Eastern Europeans as whites. However, the newcomers initially ranked lower on the status scale than old-stock Americans, those who traced their antecedents to Northern and Western Europe.[14]

Since the immigrants were closer than African Americans to the racial majority group at the time, they faced much less resistance from those folks regarding intermarriage, employment opportunities, and so forth, once they embraced assimilation and shed the most conspicuous aspects of their foreignness.[15] These intraethnic differences seldom surface anymore, unless a white person has a conspicuously "ethnic" appearance. The ethnic origins of white Americans differ greatly by region. A Swedish American from Minnesota might look a little unusual to residents of Providence, Rhode Island, for instance, where most whites are Irish, Italian, Portuguese, or French-Canadian. But the Minnesotan would almost certainly benefit, at least in some situations, from being a white person in Providence, regardless of his ethnicity.

At any rate, with the widespread intermarriage between and among white subgroups, the persistent ethnic differences of the past are rapidly fading into history. Eighty, 90, and 100 years ago Irish Americans and Italian Americans were suspicious of each other, and often battled in the political arena. In many urban neighborhoods in the Northeast, the Irish went to one Catholic church while the Italians went to another. By the 1950s an exogamous marriage of an Irish American to an Italian American was so common, outside of the most insular ethnic enclaves, that it merited little eyebrow-raising by relatives. Today many middle-aged Northeasterners are half Irish and half Italian. The Midwestern analogue to the Irish/Italian duo is the Swedish/Norwegian couple. Swedish Americans and Norwegian Americans are culturally similar and they share the Lutheran religion. After assimilation wiped out the linguistic and nationalistic differences that separated the two groups, there were a large number of Scandinavian intermarriages in the Upper Midwest.

As Caucasian immigration remains relatively small (in percentage terms), white Americans continue to intermarry among themselves, resulting in individuals with ever more variegated ethnic identities. Although surnames still give us clues into the proportionality of a person's ethnic heritage, widespread intermarriage among whites from different ethnic subgroups has made it common for younger whites to have surnames that do not reflect their ethnic roots. A person of Dutch, English, Swedish, Italian, and Scottish ancestry may bear an English surname, simply because her father got it from his father, and so forth. Consequently, millions of white Americans have no discernible look that can be traced to a single European, Middle Eastern, or North African country.

The United States remains a predominantly Christian — and Protestant — nation. In 1999 the Gallup Organization estimated that 59% of American adults were Protestants, with significant doctrinal and stylistic differences separating mainline and evangelical sects.[16] An ethnic component intersects with geography and socioeconomic status to determine religious affiliation. The Episcopalian Church typically has been regarded as a bastion of affluent old-stock Americans, while Lutherans tend to be of German and Scandinavian origins. And Baptists are a religious group with a strong presence in the South, both among whites and blacks, who usually worship in separate congregations. The vast majority of African Americans belong to Protestant churches, which serve as the nerve centers of black communities.[17] White Anglo-Saxon Protestants (WASPs) — the ethno-religious group made up of old-stock Americans, primarily of English origins — were once the dominant group in the United States. WASPs account for an ever-smaller percentage of the U.S. population. Other ethno-religious groups, such as Irish Catholics and American Jews, have become indispensable segments of the Power Elite.[18]

The non-Protestant population of America encompasses a sizable amount of diversity, including a fair number of people whose beliefs are not part of the Judeo-Christian framework. Twenty-eight percent of American adults identify as Roman Catholic: This group is predominantly white and Latino.[19] Six million Jews live in the United States, the largest number of any country in the world, including Israel.[20] Eight percent of American adults are atheists, agnostics, or persons who decline to designate a religious group. And six percent of American adults worship deities outside the traditional Judeo-Christian framework.[21] There is a growing population of Muslim Americans, who include Europeans, South Asians, Middle Easterners, and native-born African Americans.[22] Ramadan has become an important part of the American holiday season, along with Hanukkah, Kwanzaa, and Christmas. Meanwhile, Buddhists, Hindus, and others are gaining adherents, largely through immigration rather than conversion.[23] In general, the millions of marriages across denominational lines — e.g., a Methodist who marries a Catholic — are eroding the ethno-religious boundaries that once mattered so much to Americans.

Significant numbers of white Americans selectively celebrate elements of their ancestral backgrounds. This phenomenon, which the sociologist

Herbert Gans describes as "symbolic ethnicity," encompasses activities, like eating kielbasas and dancing polkas, that do not antagonize Americans outside the ethnic group, and which have only a superficial connection to the Old World.[24] In this vein, whites celebrate Oktoberfest and *Syttende Mai* and Greek Independence Day. The sociologist Richard Alba has found that a majority of native-born white Americans are of mixed European ancestries, and their closest connection with the Old World is to the ethnic cuisine. Since the 1970s there has been an upsurge of kitschy boosterism and light-hearted ethnic chauvinism. Pins, decals, T-shirts, bumper stickers, and kitchen magnets announce "Kiss Me, I'm Polish," or proclaim that "Italians Are Better Lovers."[25]

Irish Americans are a particularly large and prominent American ethnic group. There are more full-blooded Irish people in the United States than in Ireland.[26] Therefore, it is perhaps not surprising that Celtic cultural artifacts — the tunes of U2, Irish cinematic flicks, memoirs by Frank McCourt (*Angela's Ashes, 'Tis*), the mock-imitation Irish pubs that appear throughout America — are oh-so-cool in the United States.[27] Irish import shops dot America; these knickknack stores specialize in products from the Old Country, in addition to distinctly American items like travel guidebooks. Ireland, a nation of 3,841,000, is arguably more important than India, with its 1,030,000,000 people, to the average American — Irish Americans outnumber Asian Indian Americans by better than 23-to-1. These sociocultural dynamics, where ethnic affinity and national priorities cleave together, have far-reaching consequences in almost every facet of American life.

Countless American communities still have ethnic celebrations annually. These festivities recognize their ethnic roots, where locals and tourists eat ethnic foods, watch dance performances, listen to traditional music, and otherwise reinforce their affiliations with the Old World. Some of these ethnic festivals are little more than church affairs, while others, such as the extravaganzas each summer in Milwaukee (Asian Moon Festival, Polish Fest, Festa Italiana, German Fest, African World Festival, Irish Fest, Mexican Fiesta, Indian Summer Festival, and Arabian Fest) attract tens of thousands of visitors. Festivals that cater to ethnic groups with large numbers of immigrants usually draw few tourists. In Dearborn, Michigan, the annual Dearborn Arab International Festival attracts Arab Americans from throughout the Detroit metropolitan area, but relatively few non-Arab tourists join the festivities. Conversely, tourists definitely outnumber Dutch Americans at the Tulip Time festivals each May in Pella, Iowa, and Holland, Michigan.[28] Tulips, along with windmills and wooden shoes, remain potent symbols of Dutch-American identity, even though Americans of Dutch descent are now virtually indistinguishable from other whites of Northern European ancestry.

Festivals and parades often are a vital part of ethnic merrymaking. Most large cities celebrate Saint Patrick's Day and Columbus Day with colorful pageantry and boisterous processions. Indeed, the holiday honoring Ireland's patron saint outpaces all others. Each Saint Patrick's Day, Americans honor Gaelic folk by trotting out the shamrocks, posting pictures of leprechauns, wearing articles of green clothing, and eating corned beef and cabbage. Cinco de Mayo (May 5) and Mexican Independence Day (September 16) are the two premier Mexican-American holidays. As the Mexican-American population has grown, these holidays have become high-profile events in the United States.

Liberal multiculturalists are heartened by celebrations of non-Western and non-European cultures. They contend that the United States is governed by de facto "white" or "white male" norms and standards, including the notions of fact, merit, neutrality, objectivity, and quality, which, in their minds, are Eurocentric constructs that exclude women, minorities, homosexuals, and others who are not white heterosexual men.[29] In recent years the study of whiteness, and a burgeoning literature about it, has helped to demystify the idiosyncrasies of Caucasians. Some colleges and universities now offer courses in whiteness studies. Writers, academics, and students examine whiteness as an overarching phenomenon: They interrogate the legal, cultural, political, economic, and biological significance of race, racial categories, and racial privilege. They also focus on various aspects of the white experience, such as country music, professional wrestling, and stock car racing, that have been heretofore unexplored through a racial lens. The antiracist activists of the whiteness-studies movement embrace multiculturalism. They hope their efforts to disseminate information about the nation's majority race will promote greater understanding of "white privilege," and thus eradicate racism and promote diversity.[30]

Critics of the U.S. status quo assert that it makes whites automatic insiders in America. There is a certain comfortable myopia — an ignorance of and lack of interest in those different from oneself and one's peer networks — that accompanies such a status. If you asked many white Americans who personifies the "All-American" look to them, their mental picture would be of a person with some variation of Northern and Western European characteristics, possibly with blond hair and blue eyes. Blondness continues to be a mythical ideal for many American women, and not just white females either; Latinas and black women often sport blond dye jobs too.[31] The United States, of course, is simply too heterogeneous to be characterized by a single national look. Nor do all whites feel as if they are insiders in American society. Some whites, to be sure, think of themselves as disadvantaged due to their disabilities, ethnic heritage, sexual orientation, or socioeconomic status.

In outsider narratives, Americans of Asian descent discuss the initial movement they realize they are regarded as "foreign" by many Americans despite, in many cases, their family's multigenerational history in the United States. They may be asked, "Where are you from?" or someone might compliment their proficiency in spoken English.[32] A young Hong Konger, a naturalized American, once lamented to me, "I am a citizen. But look at me, I'm Chinese." With an air of resignation, he implicitly conceded that he was never going to be fully accepted by his fellow Americans due to his physiognomy. And I once knew a Taiwanese immigrant who characterized whites as "Americans," blacks as "the coloreds," and his coethnics as "Chinese," in a frank and unvarnished acknowledgment of how he saw the U.S. racial hierarchy. America's changing demographics have not materially altered these kinds of perceptions yet, because the types of media images presented to us — and to the world — still portray Americans as a largely white group.

It must perplex white immigrants when they find about their status as members of the omnipotent racial majority. Shortly after coming to America many of them personally encounter blacks, Latinos, and Asians for the first time in their lives. This diversity probably bewilders people accustomed to the racial homogeneity of Kiev or Amman or Sarajevo. Most white immigrants do fairly well in this country. The extent to which their success is attributable to skin color rather than work ethic remains a matter of conjecture. Nonetheless, the typical European, North African, or Middle Easterner continues to be closer to the racial mainstream in the United States than the average migrant from Asia, Latin America, the Caribbean, or sub-Saharan Africa. At this point, no definitive quantitative evidence exists to prove that a white immigrant receives intangible benefits from his whiteness — at the expense of his similarly situated nonwhite counterpart. However, it is relatively easy to find anecdotal evidence to support this theory in almost any community with a sizable immigrant population.

Immigration is a vital part of globalism, as the importance of individual nation-states and geopolitical boundaries decreases steadily. In this era of easy mobility, most national borders are porous and permeable, and can be traversed with virtual impunity by data, persons, and products. Some issues — global warming, organized crime, nuclear terrorism, environmental degradation, copyright protections — require cooperation between and among nations. The lingua franca of the world is English, in its myriad varieties, a development that Europeans and others who resent the United States view with alarm.[33] Residents of the global village, a figurative entity that reflects the increasing closeness of various cultures, herald the imminent demise of nation-states. Accordingly, these "global citizens" or "citizens of the world" eschew what they see as narrow-minded, flag-waving nationalism in favor of broad-minded, cosmopolitan globalism.[34]

One aspect of globalism that clearly affects American workers is the global labor market; they compete with low-wage laborers in China, Guatemala, Indonesia, and elsewhere. During the past two decades, the United States has run up huge trade deficits with many of its trading partners, including Japan, China, and Mexico, as we bought more of their imports than they purchased of our exports. Americans believe that globalization is good for U.S. companies, American consumers, and the U.S. economy, but we are closely divided about whether its positive aspects outweigh the negative ones with regard to the environment and the creation of U.S. jobs.[35] White Americans, at least, seem to feel a greater connection to Europe than to any other part of the world; these feelings of kinship affect American trade policies and influence U.S. diplomatic efforts.[36]

BECOMING AMERICAN

" ... [W]hy should the Palatine Boors be suffered to swarm into our Settlements," fulminated Benjamin Franklin in a 1751 diatribe against German immigrants to his native state, "and by herding together establish their Language and Manners to the Exclusion of ours? Why should Pennsylvania, founded by the English, become a Colony of Aliens, who will shortly be so numerous as to Germanize us instead of our Anglifying them, and will never adopt our Language or Customs, any more than they can acquire our Complexion."[37] Franklin's intemperate remarks reflected the views of other New World Englishmen, who as a group disliked the German immigrants who came to Pennsylvania during the 1720s, 1730s, and 1740s.[38]

Similar expressions of dislike for German newcomers cropped up later in American history. Native-born white Protestants despised German Catholics and their opposition to temperance. During World War I, German Americans faced mass hysteria over their supposedly divided loyalties. People stopped eating German foods. Place names were changed. The speaking of the German language was discouraged.[39] These instances of xenophobia became less common as the Germans assimilated into American society. Ben Franklin would probably be dismayed to learn that people of German descent now outnumber his beloved English folks in America. Nearly one in four Americans claims German ancestry, but no separate German culture exists on these shores.

As we can see from the trajectory of my German-American family, the fears that German immigrants and their progeny would never assimilate were unfounded. My mother is of German-Catholic descent. Neither one of my maternal grandparents spoke English as their first language. They communicated with each other in different, but mutually intelligible, dialects of German. All of my great-uncles and great-aunts married non-Germans, and the spellings and pronunciations of their names were anglicized to be more "American." In Wisconsin, the most German-American of all the states, no one in the younger generation of my mother's family speaks German fluently. None of them regularly visits Germany. My mother proudly embraces her German heritage, including the traditional nickname my grandmother bestowed upon her, and corresponds periodically with relatives in Europe, but she does not eat sauerkraut, drink Budweiser, celebrate Oktoberfest, or domesticate dachshunds.

After all, most German Americans do not make a big deal out of their ethnic heritage, judging by their limited support of efforts to preserve the German culture and language in the United States. Peter Beinart accurately describes German Americans as "America's invisible ethnic group."[40] More than 30% of white Americans have German ancestry, and few people even stop to consider the extent of the German-American presence in our nation. Take Freddy Krueger, who terrorized the teenagers of Elm Street in so many films during the 1980s. Even though few German Americans would want to claim him, Krueger was part of the flock — and, at the same time, a quintessentially *American* cinematic villain. Indeed, the integration of Germans into American society is a testament to the stubborn power of the assimilation process.

Social cohesion continues to be a topic of great significance in our era, just as it was 250 years ago. The national motto, *e pluribus unum*, which means "out of many, one," adorns American coins. The Pledge of Allegiance, which is recited every weekday morning by many schoolchildren, refers to "one nation, indivisible." We characterize ourselves as the American people and describe our country as the United States; these singular references imply an unshakable unity. Although certain beliefs, norms, and ideals bind most Americans — capitalism, freedom, individualism, democracy, self-reliance, the American Dream — we disagree passionately about the specifics of how to order our society.[41]

There are competing metaphors (the melting pot, the salad bowl) to explain the nation's assimilation process and efforts to manage diversity. The melting-pot theory, though discredited and constantly under attack, remains the operative guideline for assimilation. This explanation of ethnic group relations posits that people from different lands and cultures are thrown together in the United States (the pot) and the subsequent amalgamation and assimilation (the melting) create a new people.[42] As Arthur M. Schlesinger Jr. writes: "Historically and culturally this republic has an Anglo-Saxon base; but from the start the base has been modified, enriched, and reconstituted by transfusions from other continents and civilizations. The movement from exclusion to inclusion causes a constant revision in the texture of our culture. The ethnic transfusions affect all aspects of American life...."[43] Take place names, which are an important indicator of a nation's cultural heritage. Spanish place names pop up in the Southwest; British place names appear, aptly enough, in New England. And at least 20 names of the U.S. states originate from Indian words.[44] In some cases, though, the foreign attachments are lost, like the anglicized pronunciations of Amarillo or New Orleans.

An analogous process occurs in the culinary realm, as ethnic cuisines, albeit homogenized versions of them, have become quite popular with the American palate. Even Americans who have little exposure to our nation's multicultural splendor regularly eat Cajun and Chinese, drink margaritas and tequila, and consume faux-Mexican food at Chi-Chi's or Taco Bell. In more cosmopolitan venues, we might eat Thai, feast upon shish kebab, or snack on lox and bagels. Gourmands mix culinary traditions, creating "fusion" cuisines like Tex-Mex and French-Vietnamese food, with the same zest and frequency that Dennis Rodman changes his attire and hair color.

This culinary eclecticism may confuse and even disconcert some of those Americans who consider hot dogs and apple pie to be the metaphorical dietary staples of the United States. But the meat-and-potatoes traditionalists are being surpassed by the nonwhite immigrants, culinary hipsters, and health-conscious yuppies who patronize specialized markets and shop in the ethnic-foods aisles of mainstream supermarkets.[45] In the market for condiments, salsa (a catchall term for picante sauce, pico de gallo, and other spicy, eye-watering seasonings) outsold ketchup for most of the 1990s. The two condiments are in a neck-and-neck battle for consumers' taste buds, although the red-colored accompaniment to hamburgers, French fries, and hot dogs is reportedly on top again.[46] Despite all the cultural cross-pollination, certain culinary phenomena (fry bread, pig's feet) remain solely the province of a particular racial group. This demonstrates the persistence of ethno-cultural differences in America, in the face of powerful homogenizing forces.

Diverse culinary tastes are the hallmark of a heterogeneous, multiethnic society. Such societies rarely last for centuries, in the absence of widespread amalgamation, because persistent differences make it difficult to sustain a viable political entity. Contemporary multiethnic dystopias, such as Nigeria and Indonesia, are constantly in danger of dissolution. Other multiethnic nations, like Canada and Belgium, have little overt strife. Self-styled American nationalists have always been skeptical of multiculturalism, which they feel creates "hyphenated Americans," who are presumed to have dual loyalties, to their country of origin and to the United States. Nonetheless, it is customary for native-born Americans to use ancestral identifiers — Irish, Italian, Swedish, Hungarian, Romanian, Lebanese — as a convenient descriptive shorthand to describe themselves and other people in the United States. For instance, a monolingual, native-born Finnish American may characterize himself (and be characterized by others) as a Finn.

These references persist, even though the assimilation process and the inexorable passage of time have erased most of the characteristics that would identify the typical native-born American as a foreigner. Americans often use dual flags, the U.S. banner and one from an Old World country, to symbolize their hyphenated identities. Some Americans, though, do not identify with any other country besides the United States. If pressed, they will delineate their European roots and might relate some fuzzy tales of crowded ships and pioneer experiences, but they feel no real connection to the Old World.

It is difficult to define what, exactly, makes one an American. By March 2002, there were more than 286.5 million of us, according to the Census Bureau's estimates, and every one of us has our own take on what it means to be an American. As Americans, we certainly value our freedoms, particularly the right to free speech, the right to bear arms, and the right to practice our religion freely. As Americans, the citizens

of the world's foremost consumer society, we certainly are able to fulfill our material expectations in ways that would be incomprehensible
to people in so many other countries. As Americans, we are reasonably
assured that there will be social, economic, and political stability. In a
recent poll conducted by Maritz Marketing Research for *American Demographics,* 83% of Americans identified themselves as unequivocally
American. The percentages differed by ethnicity: 90% (European Americans), 64% (Middle Eastern Americans), 61% (Latinos), 54% (African
Americans), and 33% (Asian Americans).[47]

Indeed, 12.4 million of us identified as Americans in response to the
census question about ancestry during the last decennial count. These
American Americans are concentrated in the U.S. South, where many
whites are 200 and 300 years removed from the British Isles.[48] After
all, their progenitors came to the United States in the seventeenth and
eighteenth centuries, and only their Anglo-Saxon surnames and physiognomies betray their ethnic heritage. Some people, no doubt, continue to
believe that native-born Americans of English, Welsh, Scottish, Scotch-
Irish, or Irish-Protestant descent are the "truest" Americans, due to their
prominence in early American history and the continuing influence of
Anglo-American ideals and culture. Such distinctions clash with the unwritten rules and ethos of Multicultural America, where a person who
arrived in the United States two years ago from Damascus can plausibly claim to be as "American" as someone whose ancestors sailed to
Plymouth on the *Mayflower* in 1620.

Black persons in the United States inhabit two, never quite mutually
exclusive spheres, as blacks and as Americans, wrote W. E. B. Du Bois
nearly a century ago.[49] Afrocentrism is a homegrown response to this
eternal dilemma of African-American identity. Afrocentrists focus more
on their connections to Africa than they do on their relationship with
other nonblack Americans. They teach black children Swahili; wear
kente cloth, the 1990s version of the dashiki; and celebrate Kwanzaa, a
seven-day, end-of-the-year commemoration of African values, from December 26 to January 1.[50] During the 1960s and 1970s thousands of
African Americans took African names in place of their American ones.
This practice did not catch on with most blacks, however, but it remains
an acceptable and celebrated form of black pride. African Americans have
often seen sub-Saharan Africa as a racial paradise (the promised land,
their Old World), based largely upon the perception of shared similarities, particularly in terms of skin color, facial features, and hair texture.
In the past native-born blacks have left the United States for substantial

periods of time, even departing forever, because they despaired of ever experiencing equality here.

But African Americans who visit and live in sub-Saharan Africa do not always find the region culturally congenial — and not just for linguistic reasons. Africans, their putative kinfolk, often see African Americans not as fellow Africans, but as Americans, who are affluent participants in the world's economic, military, and political behemoth. African Americans who relocate to Ghana are sometimes dismayed to discover that they encounter official corruption, natives who see them as foreigners, and people who try to extract as many dollars from them as possible.[51] Likewise, native-born Irish Americans often discover how American they are when they go to Ireland. U.S.-born Mexican Americans frequently have similar experiences in Mexico. Furthermore, since most black Americans trace their ancestry to West Africa, it is not surprising that people in East Africa and Southern Africa do not treat them as long-lost cousins. If a Russian American went to Germany or Bulgaria, for instance, he would not be treated by the natives as if he were a kindred spirit, just because he is white. The same is true in Africa, except the natives are black.

To be sure, African Americans who visit the land of their ancestors are delighted by their feelings, once and for all, of being part of the racial majority. But many of them have found, upon self-reflection, that they are purely American, after visiting the Motherland. The political corruption, heartbreaking poverty, interethnic genocide, and lack of First World material comforts reinforce this message.[52] Pan-Africanism, at least in its most recent incarnation, revolves mainly around trade issues. Between 1991 and 1999 five African-African American Summits were held in different parts of Africa. Delegates from both continents met to promote American investment in sub-Saharan Africa, along with greater trade between the United States and Africa.[53] These events reflect the growing identification with Africa among black Americans, especially the elites, who have become a familiar sight in Accra, Dakar, Cape Town, and elsewhere.

Cultural role-playing occurs when Americans cross racial boundaries in willful defiance of their informal, racially circumscribed social roles. The ignoble, and interrelated, traditions of blackface and minstrelsy date back well over 150 years.[54] Similarly, white Americans have long appropriated American Indian cultural forms for their own uses.[55] Some whites identify with African-Americans' "outsider" status in American society, and seek to act and speak in an authentically "black" manner.[56] For example, there are white racial boundary-crossers who imitate the exaggerated walk, sullen slouch, urban patois, and expressionless eyes and faces of black gang members. They are denigrated as *wannabes* and *wiggers* by blacks and whites alike.[57] The black analogue to the blond kid with dreadlocks is an urban tough who sports stock-car gear. Unlike these young men, many Americans embrace assimilation by dyeing their hair, changing their names, eliminating their accent, undergoing cosmetic surgery, using colored contact lenses, and altering their ethnic clothing and hairstyles. Such efforts to change one's appearance, perhaps to look more European, are a particularly touchy subject among African Americans.[58]

Besides different-looking people, language may be the most important indicator of ethnic and racial change. Most native-born Americans have little linguistic dexterity. The Census Bureau reports that in 1990, the most recent year for which data are available, 86.2% of Americans "5 years old and over" spoke only English. Native speakers of immigrant tongues such as Russian, Mandarin Chinese, and, of course, Spanish are increasing in number, while the speakers of such languages as Greek, German, and Italian are declining in number. More Americans speak Tagalog than Polish, and more of us are fluent in Korean and Vietnamese than Greek.[59] Spanish is the de facto second language of the United States. ATMs, billing instructions, reservations numbers, directions for product usage, and even signs warning restaurant patrons about wet floors are offered in English and Spanish. Thousands of U.S. businesses post signs that read "Se habla español," meaning that at least one employee or staff member speaks Spanish. And Spanish is the most commonly studied foreign language in American public high schools.[60]

Spanish, of course, is not the only language used in linguistic outreach programs. These attempts to be inclusive embrace all kinds of foreign languages, depending on the location of the marketing campaign. Mainstream businesses seek to reach ethnic consumers in their native tongues. Their advertising campaigns and customer service efforts might use Hmong in Saint Paul, Minnesota; Armenian in Glendale, California; Creole in Brooklyn and South Florida; Portuguese in Fall River and New Bedford, Massachusetts; Polish on the Northwest Side of Chicago; and so forth. These forms of linguistic accommodation are, fittingly, a venerable tradition in what has always been "a nation of immigrants."

The use of the English language is an important indicator of assimilation. First initiated in 1968, bilingual education has become an important part of the public-school system. In theory, bilingual-education programs are meant to bring immigrant children into the English-speaking mainstream as quickly as possible. By teaching immigrant youths in their native language, proponents of bilingual education hoped that limited-English-proficient students would learn more and eventually gain a better understanding of English. Unlike immigrants and their progeny in the period before Multicultural America, when students went to school knowing no English and learned it there to survive, bilingual education may amount to a "crutch" for students, one that hampers their ability to learn English *or* their native language well.[61] Spanish-speaking students are the primary consumers of bilingual education, but big-city school district administrators routinely note that there might be 40 or 65 or 110 languages spoken in their educational systems. Many of these students take English as a Second Language (ESL) in lieu of bilingual education.

Important forces, from the mockery of their English-speaking friends to the requirements of the American workplace, virtually dictate that most immigrant youths will learn English rapidly. Indeed, many immigrant kids switch as effortlessly from accentless English to their native tongue as a bodybuilder moves from the bench press to leg extensions. Their children in turn are going to grow up as monolingual English speakers, especially if both parents come from different ethnic backgrounds. Thus, after three generations, Americans typically are no longer proficient in their ancestral language(s).

Likewise, most Americans try to accommodate this country's Anglo-Saxon origins in the naming process. In the past, most immigrants tried to become fully "American" as quickly as possible. Many European immigrants and their children anglicized the pronunciations and spellings of their names, so as to speed their acceptance by the native-born majority.[62] Even today the most common surnames in America — Smith, Johnson, Williams, Jones, and Brown (in that order) — all come from England.[63] African Americans tend to have Anglo-Saxon surnames, but since the 1960s, millions of black parents have given their children forenames with distinctive spellings and pronunciations.[64] Four Spanish surnames, by the way, are among the 30 most common American surnames: Garcia, Martinez, Rodriguez, and Hernandez.[65] And if one takes a look at the White Pages in many major U.S. metropolitan areas, s/he will see that quintessentially American appellations like Wilson and Bennett are giving way to such surnames as Romero and Nguyen.

By selecting identifiably ethnic names for their children, immigrants to the United States signal pride in their native heritage. Still, immigrants frequently adopt anglicized nicknames, forenames, or even new surnames. An assimilation-minded Asian-American couple might name their son

Kevin, while a Hispanic duo could christen their daughter Brittany.[66] As a result, there is an ever-increasing number of uniquely American names, such as Kevin Chen and Brittany Torres, that reflect the diverse ethnic influences that shape our nation today.

Whither assimilation? The racial differences between most contemporary immigrants and the rest of the American population are larger than at any other time in U.S. history. Moreover, affirmative action and similar programs may encourage racial separatism. And unlike in the past, there has been no significant break in the tide of immigrants. Since about 1970 the percentage of foreign-born residents of the United States (those with non-citizen parents) has been slowly increasing every year. Our foreign-born population, a group that included 9.5% of all Americans in 1999, is 43.0% Hispanic (the vast majority of them from Mexico), 25.3% white, 24.5% Asian, 7.0% black, and 0.2% American Indian.[67]

Sometimes the values these immigrants bring with them clash with the sensibilities of native-born Americans, and vice versa. They periodically have problems adjusting to a culture that seems far more open — and, in some cases, decadent — than what they are used to back home. Westerners may regard their traditionally medical practices as barbaric or woefully inadequate. Children from some traditional cultures may be taught to avoid making eye contact with teachers and other authority figures; that kind of behavior is seen as shifty by many Americans. Mexican, Central American, and Haitian immigrants come from places with widespread police corruption. Their understandable wariness of the police can lead to misunderstandings with American cops. Frequently, their children pick up these attitudes, perhaps in a modified form, and then pass them on to their children. Thus Old World approaches and sensibilities sometimes affect the behavior of multiple generations of native-born Americans.

Immigrants' attitudes toward assimilation depend, naturally, on their ages and the quality and types of their interactions with Americans and American institutions. Many Americans today believe that the United States is racked by disunity and dissension, in part because of immigrants who refuse to assimilate. But is this really true? For one, people of color expect more from America, and are freer to make more blunt criticisms of the United States, than people in, say, the 1920s or 1950s. And a respectable case can be made that vigorous criticism of the status quo is patriotic, since it might jolt people out of their somnolence and lead to changes that will ultimately strengthen the country. However, most racial conservatives and many not-so-conservative folks have watched with growing skepticism as the diversity imperative and excesses of multiculturalism have led to what they see as resurgent racial separatism.[68]

INDIAN COUNTRY

First-time visitors to Tahlequah, Oklahoma, might be initially puzzled when they look at the street signs that mark main thoroughfares such as Choctaw Street, Grand Avenue, Downing Street, and Muskogee Avenue. As they drive around this white-majority town of 14,458 in northeastern Oklahoma, where 26.3% of the residents identify as American Indian, they may notice that each of these street names is listed in English, of course — and then followed by a word or two in Cherokee, a language that looks vaguely Nepali to the untrained eye.[69] Moreover, Cherokee script adorns the front window of the local Bank of America, and it appears above the entrance to the U.S. Post Office. Even though most Cherokee do not read or speak their ancestral language, these examples of symbolic bilingualism celebrate Tahlequah's Cherokee heritage and culture. (The city is the capital of the Cherokee Nation — and the tribe's offices are located a few miles south of town in the W. W. Keeler Tribal Complex.)

The people of Tahlequah honor Native Americans in many ways. They venerate Sequoyah, the man who invented the Cherokee syllabary. His name graces several businesses, a public park, an elementary school, and an institute at Northeastern State University (NSU). NSU, appropriately enough, offers courses in the Cherokee language, houses the Center for Tribal Studies, grants bachelor's degrees in Native American studies, has a Native American Student Association (NASA), and holds a yearly Symposium on the American Indian. One out of four NSU students has Indian ancestry, and 70% of the Native Americans on campus identify as members of the Cherokee Nation. The university offers a congenial environment for Indian students, replete with a supportive faculty, a large Native American student body, funding for Indian activities and organizations, and a plethora of cultural opportunities on and off campus.[70]

Indeed, Native American artifacts, institutions, place names, and, most importantly, people are an integral part of Tahlequah. The town's longtime commitment to embracing its diversity goes beyond symbolism, however, and is reflected in the ranks of Tahlequah's educators and businesspeople. The high rates of racial intermarriage and sizable number of mixed bloods indicate the generally harmonious nature of ethnic relations there. Race is simply not a binary phenomenon in Tahlequah: Many whites are part Indian, and many Native Americans are part white. At Tahlequah Senior High School, Principal Gary McClure notes that 25% of his tenth, eleventh, and twelfth graders are identifiably Native American, while another 23% have some degree of Indian blood. According to McClure, who graduated from TSHS in 1970 and returned to his alma mater as a teacher in 1975, there is "such a mix that nobody pays any attention to it," and the Native American influence is "so accepted, so part of growing up" that whites like himself embrace it without hesitation.[71]

Most Cherokee now live lifestyles that are virtually identical to those of their white peers, so many of the causal factors that lead to racism elsewhere do not exist in Cherokee County. In Tahlequah, there is little of the wariness — and hostility — that sometimes characterizes white/Indian relations in the Great Plains and Mountain West. Still, some Native American residents of Cherokee County say they experience covert prejudice, or at least feel a little uncomfortable when they go to Tahlequah's predominantly white venues. In the main, though, race relations in Tahlequah are clearly among the best of any place in or around Indian Country.

Indian Country is a loosely knit federation of semi-sovereign territorial homelands, whose origins date back to the 370 treaties between the United States and various Indian nations that were concluded from 1778 to 1871. These government-to-government treaties traded peace and land for U.S. federal services, like free schooling and health care in perpetuity.[72] In a landmark Supreme Court decision, *Cherokee Nation v. Georgia* (1831), Chief Justice John Marshall famously characterized American Indian tribes as "domestic dependent nations" and analogized the Indian-U.S. relationship to "that of a ward to his guardian."[73] The next year, in a second case, *Worcester v. Georgia,* Marshall expanded on his previous intellectualizations and stated, "A weak state, in order to provide for its safety, may place itself under the protection of one more powerful, without stripping itself of the right of government, and ceasing to be a state."[74]

At the same time, the U.S. government created Indian reservations to isolate Native Americans, in places where they would be forgotten and no longer pose a problem to white society. The reservations were frequently situated outside of a given tribe's territory or included only a fraction of their old stomping grounds. To add insult to injury, much of what they received was eventually stolen from them by land-hungry white settlers.

Although Indians may have had a more fluid and communal notion of landownership than whites, with territorial notions of where they could hunt, fish, and live, the sordid fact remains that European Americans displaced them from their traditional living grounds. If insidious methods of cheating them — offers of muskets, "fire water," and horses in exchange for land, scouting duties, and military assistance — failed, whites forcibly displaced them or even brutalized and murdered them.[75]

At the same time they coveted their land, whites sought to assimilate the Indians into American society and make them into pseudo-Caucasians. Doing so entailed ridding them of any vestiges of their old ways, and required speaking English, becoming Christians, taking Christian names, wearing white attire, sporting white haircuts, and living like European Americans. At government-sponsored boarding schools, Indian youths were instructed by white, English-speaking teachers about Christian pieties. Any attempts the Indians made to speak their native tongues were swiftly punished. Whites believed that, eventually, the Indians would intermarry with Caucasians and disappear completely. The logical end result of this kind of thinking was the 1950s-era federal government policy of "termination," which sought to end certain Indian tribes entirely and integrate their members into the general population.[76]

Federal Indian policy became more Indian-friendly in subsequent years. Indeed, a rabid dislike for the historical treatment of Native Americans and the federal agencies whose edicts affected reservation Indians was one of the few ideological constants among the assorted radicals who made up the Indian Civil Rights Movement during the late 1960s and early 1970s. The American Indian Movement (AIM), whose members admired the Black Panthers and promoted Panther-like militant rhetoric and community programs, won lots of Indian support for their efforts to take on the White Man. On rural reservations, cries of "Red Power" echoed the black radicals' chants of "Black Power" in urban America. Despite some high-profile actions, like the seizure of Alcatraz Island near San Francisco from 1969 to 1971, the most practical offshoot of this era of activism was an emphasis on pan-Indian solidarity — and a renewed interest in the dusty treaties and antiquated legal precedents of the past.[77] Long dormant tribal groups organized to win federal recognition. Existing communities stepped up their efforts to assert their treaty rights and achieve greater self-determination. Such efforts dated back to the Indian Reorganization Act of 1934.[78]

Today Indian entities come in various types: bands, groups, pueblos, villages, and, most commonly, tribes. There are 562 federally recognized

Indian entities in the United States.[79] It is extremely difficult for prospective Indian nations to gain federal recognition, either through an act of Congress or the U.S. Department of the Interior's arduous recognition process.[80] The federal government provides a major source of income — the only substantial source, in some cases — for impoverished Indians on many rural reservations.

Various federal agencies, like the Indian Health Service (IHS) and, most notably, the Bureau of Indian Affairs (BIA), have a mandate to improve the lives of Indians, particularly those who live on reservations. With a $2.2 billion-a-year budget, the IHS has limited resources and a spotty track record. It fights a constantly uphill struggle to maintain the health of one of America's most vulnerable ethno-racial groups, whose members suffer disproportionately from ailments like diabetes, liver disease, and tuberculosis.[81] Critics of U.S. Indian policies reserve special venom for the Bureau of Indian Affairs. This division of the Department of the Interior serves as a paternalistic overseer over many tribal affairs, and has a reputation for corruption, inefficiency, and insufficient responsiveness to its service population.[82] To top things off, the present fiscal climate is unreceptive to dramatic new infusions of federal government spending on American Indians.

Many Native Americans live on reservations or trust lands — the literal and metaphorical heart of Indian Country. Federally recognized reservations are communities specifically set aside by the U.S. Government for Indians. Trust lands are property-tax-exempt parcels of land held in trust for the Indians by the U.S. Secretary of Interior. Just because land is on a reservation does not mean it is trust land; conversely, some trust lands are outside reservation boundaries. Overall, the United States is home to more than 300 federal Indian reservations. Thirty-three states have at least one federal Indian reservation within their boundaries. These reservations differ dramatically in terms of their acreage, remoteness, ethnic composition, and topographical characteristics.[83]

The non-reservation Indians fall into three groups. The first group consists of those who are fully assimilated into white society; these individuals often have professional jobs and live in the suburbs. The second group lives in the Indian neighborhoods of major cities such as Denver, Seattle, Phoenix, Minneapolis, and Los Angeles. And the third group resides near reservations, in the border towns such as Farmington, New Mexico, and Mobridge, South Dakota. As a rule, the greatest residential concentrations of American Indians exist on and around the reservations.

Most Indian reservations display unmistakable signs of sovereignty. Usually a portent of some kind (often a standard-issue green highway sign) indicates that one has entered an Indian "nation" or "reservation" — or, in Canada, a reserve. There may be some signage in the tribe's traditional language. The tribal logo is usually emblazoned on the local water tower and the driver's side of tribal police cars. To be sure, there are limits to tribal nationhood. Indians use American money, most of them speak English as their first language, and non-Indians have equal access to reservation roads. But there may be separate tribal laws, courts, schools, libraries, hospitals, constitutions, governments, radio stations, junior colleges, fire departments, and police forces. Regardless of their location, Native Americans increasingly recognize Denver as the locus of Indian Country, a position that the Mile High City has earned due to its fortuitous location, a day's drive or a two-hour plane ride from many of the nation's biggest reservations, and the fact that no large tribes, who might overshadow pan-Indian activities, hold sway in north-central Colorado.[84] Indian Country even has its own newspaper of record — named, aptly enough, *Indian Country Today.*

Many reservation dwellers inhabit isolated redoubts of Third World poverty that are surrounded by indifferent or hostile whites. Crime, suicide, diabetes, alcoholism, and domestic abuse bedevil Indian Country. On the nation's poorest Indian reservations it is not uncommon for six, seven, or eight Indians to live in two-room hovels, without adequate insulation, indoor plumbing, or transportation to jobs off the reservation. Except for climatic and topographical differences, the typical reservation looks similar, whether it is in Alabama or California or Wisconsin. Mobile homes and cookie-cutter residences — HUD (after the U.S. Housing and Urban Development Department) homes, in the local parlance — dot the landscape, along with copious amounts of scrap metal, children's toys, and old vehicles.

A disproportionate number of American Indian households lack electricity, telephones, indoor plumbing, and other amenities that most Americans consider to be indispensable staples of life in the twenty-first century. All too many Indian children and adults do not get enough to eat, or consume fatty foods that eventually ruin their health. To exacerbate matters, reservation-dwelling Native Americans are often victims of violent crimes. Moreover, tribal police departments are frequently understaffed and have outdated equipment, which makes it difficult for them to patrol the vast expanses of land under their jurisdiction.[85] Despite the aforementioned shortcomings of reservation life, being encircled on the "rez" by one's friends, family, and coethnics can be heartening, with bonds of community that seldom exist elsewhere. Yet this closeness brings with it the minor irritations of small-town life everywhere: boredom, infighting, periodic attacks of claustrophobia, and a paucity of jobs and economic opportunities.

For all the manifestations of Indian sovereignty, the most profitable and lucrative one — a veritable cash cow that generates hundreds of millions in profits each year — is Indian gaming. It dates back to the 1970s, but first assumed great significance only after the passage of the Indian Gaming Regulatory Act (IGRA) in 1988, which jump-started the tribal gaming boom by authorizing states to negotiate compacts with tribes. Two hundred one of the 562 federally recognized tribes operate gaming facilities. There are 321 tribal gaming operations in 29 states. Indian gaming took in $10.6 billion in revenue in 2000, the most recent year for which data are available. Indian casinos are either on reservations or on off-reservation trust lands. It is very difficult to get land taken into trust by the U.S. Secretary of the Interior, because then the trust lands become exempt from local property taxes and it is almost impossible to reverse the process.[86]

Profits from their gaming operations have enabled tribes to start new businesses; expand existing ones; celebrate their heritage; build new homes, schools, and health-care facilities; and even to buy back land stolen from them during the nineteenth century. The most amazing success stories — the Shakopee Mdewakanton Sioux's Mystic Lake Casino in suburban Minneapolis, and the Mashantucket Pequots' Foxwoods Resort Casino near Ledyard, Connecticut — are of small tribes situated in close proximity to heavily populated metropolitan areas. Such spectacular and highly unusual examples have created the misleading stereotype that most Indians are now millionaire casino operators. Many tribes operate casinos, but only a few of these gaming establishments are mammoth, and highly lucrative, one-stop vacation destinations, replete with shops, hotels, restaurants, big-name entertainers, and, of course, the ubiquitous slot machines and blackjack tables. Gaming is a panacea for those tribes fortunate enough to have successful operations that provide tribal members with jobs as dealers, gaming managers, security officers, maintenance personnel, and food-service workers. Overall, 250,000 American jobs (75% of which are held by non-Indians) are attributable to Indian gaming.[87]

Indian gaming continues to be controversial, inside and outside Indian Country. Stories of the fabulous profits generated by "the new buffalo" have engendered white resentment and influenced the various negotiations over extending state-tribal gaming pacts. Indian gaming operations also face opposition from religious groups, who oppose lotteries and gambling of *any* kind, on the grounds that casinos entice people to spend money they can ill-afford to lose. And not every tribe wants gambling — for spiritual and practical reasons. (In some cases, the gaming profits have occasioned bloody intratribal battles over how to allocate the new riches.) Expansion of Indian gaming is still occurring, particularly in California, where the tribes are making major progress toward achieving their goal of becoming a down-home alternative to Las Vegas.[88] Not surprisingly, Indians nationwide also are diversifying into other businesses, in the event that the casino boom dissipates during the next decade.[89]

Anti-gaming efforts are only one element of a concerted white backlash against Indian sovereignty, with a concomitant Indian counterreaction. Tribes fight with states and localities and even the federal government over a wide variety of issues, including hunting and fishing rights; the disposal of toxic waste; repatriation of artifacts and human remains; liquor sales by non-Indian vendors near "dry" reservations; attempts by states to tax gasoline and cigarette sales to non-Indians by reservation businesses; and the exercise of traditional religious expression, whether it is the use of peyote in their religious ceremonies or their desire to worship on ancestral lands in national parks.[90]

Many whites oppose any dispensations or "special rights" for minorities, including those that benefit American Indians. In recent years Native Americans have encountered resentment from non-Indians due to their muscular exercise of treaty rights. White opponents of Indian sovereignty give little credence to the treaties and historical trajectories that undergird the Indian nations' government-to-government relationships with the United States. They especially dislike the attempts of various Indian tribes to reclaim their ancient lands, or at least gain compensation for their disinheritance.[91]

Nationally, Indians have launched counteractions on two fronts, sometimes simultaneously, to protect their hard-won sovereignty and economic gains. First, they are using the "carrot" of the jobs they create for non-Indians and off-reservation businesses, like the local vendors who provide services and supplies to Indian-owned casinos. Second, they are using the "stick" of their newfound clout to dispense campaign contributions to friendly politicians, while they retain high-powered lobbyists to influence state legislators and members of Congress.[92] These efforts have been largely successful; most national political figures are sympathetic, or at least indifferent, to the Indians' position in favor of sovereignty.

To be sure, the Indians see unpleasant historical parallels to the existing efforts to curtail Native American sovereignty. It seems to them that whenever they have something valuable, such as mineral deposits of coal, oil, uranium, and natural gas, unctuous Caucasians attempt to swindle them out of it or mean-spirited whites try to take it from them.[93] The military men and political leaders of yesteryear who literally paved the way for many of today's interstate highways, shopping malls, and suburban housing developments by virtue of their treaty negotiations with the Indians never envisioned that Native Americans would someday use these treaties to their advantage. While everyone can empathize with a convenience-store owner who cannot compete with the tribal store down the street that arbitrarily undercuts her prices, they also have to acknowledge that the Indians' exemption from state cigarette and gasoline taxes is a right guaranteed to them by treaties and case law.

Therein lies a key difference between American Indians and African Americans. The latter group lacks nation-to-nation treaties that spell out the terms of their relationship to the United States. So their situation is more tenuous in a legal (but not necessarily ethical) sense, as liberal blacks propose redistributive remedies to compensate African Americans for the effects of their past oppression. Moreover, relatively few Americans feel threatened by Indian sovereignty, since Native Americans make up less than one percent of the U.S. population. The controversies over Indian sovereignty tend to occur in rural, sparsely populated parts of the country, where Indian reservations abut white communities. Therefore, these issues rarely surface, to a significant extent, in national politics.

What does the future hold for American Indians and Indian Country? From the view of those who want to preserve traditional Native American customs, the assimilation process that white reformers dreamed about a century ago has worked all too well. Most Indians have European names, marry non-Indians, speak only English, and maintain tenuous, if any, ties to their cultural traditions. Fewer younger Native Americans have traditional surnames like Dull Knife, Blue Bird, Many Horses, Little Thunder, or Crow Dog. Even fewer Indians speak their traditional languages, despite the valiant attempts by tribal elders and ethno-linguists to preserve them. Young people are able to absorb their native tongue only in places like the Navajo Indian Reservation, where many adults still speak the traditional language. Smaller tribes, particularly those that are not isolated geographically, find it difficult to maintain their linguistic heritage.[94]

In the meantime, Indians continue to marry non-Indians in large numbers, a development that is steadily reducing the population of full-blooded Native Americans. For tribal members who live on reservations, this increases the numbers of Americans eligible to become part of Indian Country — that is, for tribes with liberal membership requirements. Considering the present identification schema, this means that more Americans will be citizens of Indian Country in the future. Wealthy and powerful Native American tribes will resist any efforts to infringe upon their special dispensations, even as the tribal representatives will appear white or, less frequently, black, and their claims to Indianness are based on ever-decreasing blood-quantum levels.[95] Yet it does not seem very likely that the rights and benefits of Indian sovereignty will be extended to America's two other indigenous ethnic groups, Native Alaskans and Native Hawaiians.

The issues facing Multicultural America increasingly affect the world's other white-majority countries too. Few wealthy nations in the West remain ethnically homogeneous. Only such places as Japan or Norway, with harsh weather, geographical isolation, limited employment opportunities for outsiders, and stringent restrictions on immigration, do not receive lots of immigrants. Since the 1950s, Western Europe has been besieged by immigrants from Eastern Europe, North Africa, the Middle East, sub-Saharan Africa, the Indian subcontinent, and elsewhere. Many newcomers arrived as noncitizen "guest workers" to ease labor shortages in the 1950s and 1960s, or as political refugees who fled the Nineties-era upheavals in places like Somalia and Yugoslavia. Many of the world's predominantly white nations, including Ireland, now receive immigrants and confront questions of race and national identity.[96]

This development is the subject of vitriolic debate in the West. Within Western Europe, every nation except for Spain, Italy, Iceland, Norway, Finland, and Denmark is ethnically and racially heterogeneous. Many Western Europeans unilaterally oppose any immigration. According to the European nativists, immigrants are responsible for the rising crime rates in Western Europe.[97] Two other predominantly European nations — Canada and Australia — have begun to deal with issues related to migration as well. Canada's liberal immigration policies have altered the demographic composition of its largest cities, particularly Toronto and Vancouver.[98] The same is happening in Australia, where immigrants, predominantly from Asia, are bringing racial diversity to what has been and continues to be an overwhelmingly white country.[99] As a result, most people in the affluent Western nations have some degree of familiarity with the demographic changes associated with immigration.

The nations of Western Europe, along with Japan, are slowly beginning to accept greater numbers of immigrants, largely because they do not have enough people to sustain their national economies during the coming decades. Economic reasons are spurring the affluent countries to encourage immigration: In Spain, Italy, Japan, Greece, and Germany, persons aged 65 and older now outnumber youths in the 0–14 category. Several other nations — France and the United Kingdom among them — are rapidly approaching this demographic milestone as well.[100] It is becoming increasingly more difficult for these nations to finance their generous retirement programs, due to the earlier retirement ages of beneficiaries, longer life expectancy rates for pensioners, and limited number of taxpaying workers. Barring increased immigration or a significant uptick in fertility rates, Spain, Italy, and Germany will decrease in population during the next 50 years.[101]

The affluent Western nations differ dramatically in their willingness to accept immigrants from non-Western nations. Neither Spain nor Italy, however, seems inclined to accommodate an influx of immigrants. To be sure, some Spaniards and Italians support moves to increase the flow of immigrants and move away from a monoethnic model of nationality, but this is a minority view at present. *Deutschland* is becoming more immigrant-friendly out of necessity; in 2000 Germany liberalized its regulations governing naturalization and citizenship.[102] Someday Japan may follow suit, as it slowly begins to accept foreigners as permanent residents and workers, even though the Japanese remain highly reluctant to grant them citizenship and voting rights.[103] In all likelihood, almost every Western nation will be forced to admit more immigrants, who will take care of their elderly and help finance their pension systems. These developments will eventually lead people in the West to accept, if not embrace, multiculturalism.

∾ chapter three ∾

Latino America

Spanish is not a foreign language in Hialeah, Florida, the heavily Cuban city northwest of Miami. According to the various estimates, 80% to 90% of Hialeahans speak *español*. Spanish is heard as often as English around town, and Hialeahans shift with ease between the two languages. Most native-born Hispanic Hialeahans can speak Spanish, even if they cannot read or write it very well. To be sure, Spanish surnames are rarely, if ever, mispronounced or anglicized in Hialeah. And Spanish-language radio and the local Telemundo affiliate are popular with the locals. In fact, Telemundo, the Spanish-language television giant, has its headquarters in Hialeah, on West 8th Avenue.[1] Moreover, "[t]he Spanish collection," at the main branch of the public library, "includes more than 8,000 books, videos, compact disks, and magazines for adults and children."[2]

Even though Spanish-language signage and cultural phenomena predominate in much of the city, many Hialeahans are fluent in English and Spanish. Native-born Cuban Americans do not choose so much as combine the Cuban and American aspects of their heritage. Due to the steady influence of Latin cultural traditions at home and around them, the assimilation process proceeds differently for Cuban Americans than for smaller ethnic groups elsewhere. Rates of ethnic endogamy remain high. There is a large pool of Cuban Americans from which to choose one's partner. Yet the young people of Hialeah are thoroughly American in their attitudes and expectations. Indeed, Hialeah is a center of Latino America, which is a transnational entity of Latinos and Latin Americans, often embodied in a single person, who is bilingual, bicultural, and even, occasionally, binational.[3]

People of Cuban ancestry dominate Hialeah, making it the tenth-largest Cuban city in the world. This Miami suburb of 226,419 has surpassed Miami proper to be the center of Cuban America. Cuban Americans account for 140,651, or 62.1%, of Hialeah's residents. Overall, the city is 90.3% Hispanic and 8.1% Anglo. (By contrast, only 34.1%

of Miami's 362,470 residents are Cuban.) There are 2.3 million people in Miami-Dade County; the county's population is 28.9% Cuban and 57.3% Hispanic.[4] Most of the Cuban exiles of Hialeah and South Florida are white, in contrast to Cuba, where blacks and mulattoes account for 63% of the population. Some people contend that white Cuban Americans discriminate against nonwhite Cuban Americans, especially those who are visibly African.[5]

Hialeah is home to third-generation Cuban Americans and people who arrived in the United States last week. It is home to people who left Cuba as adults and others who were born in America and have little firsthand knowledge of their ancestral homeland. These factors affect the mindsets of Hialeahans and how they view democracy and capitalism.[6] Although Hialeah is home to many Latin American immigrants, this working-class, industrial city has few of the international banks and businesses of Miami. And it draws few of the American, European, and Latin American tourists, students, and businesspeople who come to South Florida seeking excitement, enlightenment, and entrepreneurial riches.

Hialeah gradually became a bastion of Cuban-American influence in the years after the Cuban Communists led by Fidel Castro overthrew Cuba's capitalist dictatorship in 1959. After the Communists began to rule Cuba, there was a mass exodus of white professionals and landowners from Cuba to South Florida. These migrants, and their coethnics who followed them, crossed the Straits of Florida by plane or boat and settled in Miami, Hialeah, Kendall, Coral Gables, and other cities in South Florida. The Cuban Adjustment Act of 1966 mandated that Cuban exiles were to be granted automatic political asylum in the United States. This policy was modified in 1995 to grant asylum to Cuban nationals only if they reach U.S. shores.[7]

These exiles recreated the rhythms and ambiance of Cuba in Miami, particularly in the ethnic enclave known as Little Havana. Calle Ocho is its center, just as Mulberry Street was once the focal point of New York's Little Italy. Many Cuban Americans have prospered over the years. They helped transform Miami from a quiet Southern city to the fast-paced global metropolis of today — the capital of Latin America, as some people refer to it.[8] Americans of Cuban ancestry rarely return to Cuba, though, due to the long-standing U.S. embargo that dates back to 1962. It restricts most travel by Americans to that island nation and generally prohibits commercial intercourse between the United States and Cuba. Therefore, many of the native-born Cuban Americans in Hialeah have never visited the land of their parents and grandparents.

The typical native-born American would find the Latin influence in Hialeah to be quite different from what s/he was used to back home. S/he would probably be surprised by the prevalence of the Spanish language — and the Cuban and Latin cultural influences there. S/he might be surprised to learn about the diversity of Latino Americans. Yes, the blond lady in line at the Hialeah Wal-Mart is Cuban, and so is the black gentleman strolling around the Westland Mall. S/he also might be puzzled by the importance of Fidel Castro to the lives and politics of many people in Hialeah, nearly all of whom either left Cuba — or are descended from people who left — because they despised Fidel Castro and Cuba's Communist government. Even today, anti-Castro politics is a mainstay of Cuban Miami.[9]

The average Hialeahan can relate stories of how Castro's government dispossessed his or her family, which spurred them to leave Cuba for the United States. This is why most Cuban Americans in Hialeah and elsewhere took the side of Elián González's Miami relatives in the custody dispute over the young Cuban boy in 1999 and 2000. Most Americans, however, supported the Immigration and Naturalization Service's return of the boy to his Cuban father.[10] Such ideological differences, along with the Latin flavor of Hialeah, make it seem more exotic than, say, Mesa or Toledo. Yet, upon further reflection, one concludes that the city is clearly and unambiguously American — Latino American, perhaps, but American nonetheless.

LA RAZA

Sammy Sosa is a bona fide Dominican hero. Dominicans respect, admire, and revere the home-run slugger for his athletic prowess, hard-earned wealth, generous philanthropy, and the relentlessly positive image he projects to the media in the United States, Latin America, and around the world. His picture hangs in Dominican homes, shops, and offices. A highway near Santo Domingo bears his name. And a taxi driver giving some foreigners a tour of the Dominican capital points with pride to Sosa's palatial residence there. Every Dominican, it seems, knows that Sosa was once a shoeshine boy in San Pedro de Macorís.[11] As Sosa puts it, "Our financial situation was so critical I simply didn't have the time to do much else besides work and earn money. When I did play baseball, I played on the street, using balled-up rags for baseballs and sticks for bats."[12]

Many of the poor Dominican boys who hope to emulate Sosa's example share his black skin, dark brown eyes, and Dominican features. Sosa has a very Dominican visage: A sizable number of Dominicans are similar in appearance to the home-run slugger. After all, persons of mixed heritage, like Sosa, constitute the vast majority — 73% to be exact — of Dominicans, while whites make up 16% of the population and unmixed blacks account for 11%.[13] If Sosa were to trace his genealogy, the Chicago Cub would undoubtedly find African slaves, Spanish overlords, and perhaps a Taíno or two (they were the native people who eventually disappeared into genetic oblivion) among his forebears.

Wealth and power continue to be the province of the Dominican Republic's white minority, and the most successful *dominicanos* (excluding the professional baseball stars) share the coloration and facial features of Oscar de la Renta, not Sammy Sosa. Most young biracial and black Dominicans enjoy few opportunities for upward mobility, due to the pervasive poverty that characterizes so much of the island. Spanish-speaking Dominicans, regardless of their skin color, rarely confront any kind of explicit colorism or racism in the Dominican Republic. But relatively few dark-skinned people reach the highest pinnacles of Dominican society. Sosa magnanimously skirts the issue of race, but Dominicans typically frown upon blackness and are reluctant to identify as African, traits they associate with neighboring Haiti, their despised adversary.[14]

Sammy Sosa, like many successful black and biracial Latin Americans, married a woman who is phenotypically white. However, most Dominicans would not view Sonia and Sammy Sosa as an interracial couple. They would see Mrs. Sosa as a white Dominican and Sammy Sosa as representative of the nation's mixed-race majority. It is common in Latin America for an affluent dark-skinned man to marry a woman with a light complexion. By virtue of his economic success and the race of his marital partner, a man who might be viewed as black in the United States is often considered to be white or near-white in much of Latin America. In any event, race is irrelevant to those Latin Americans who believe in the inclusive notion of *la raza* — the idea that the Spanish-speaking inhabitants of the Western Hemisphere are a single people united by history, culture, and language.

Beginning with Columbus's trips to the New World in the 1490s, Spain sought colonies and treasures in the Western Hemisphere. In the sixteenth century Spanish explorers vanquished and colonized mighty Amerindian groups such as the Aztecs, Incas, and Mayas, who were ill-prepared for the horses, firepower, and infectious diseases the white men brought with them. Without much success, the Spaniards attempted to enslave the Indians to work in their mines and fields. To implement their imperial objectives, they enslaved Africans and brought them to several colonies in large numbers: Cuba, Ecuador, Venezuela, Puerto Rico, and the Dominican Republic.[15] Spain also introduced the Roman Catholic religion and Spanish language to the Amerindians of its Latin American colonies.

At the same time, the Iberian conquerors established an elaborate system of racial privilege that favored Spaniards and non-Spanish European immigrants over Amerindians, African slaves, *mestizos* (mixed-race persons of Spanish and Indian blood), and *zambos* (mixed-race persons of African and Indian blood). From the middle of the sixteenth century until the beginning of the nineteenth century, Spain expanded its colonial power, through the immigration of Spaniards to its colonies, along with the looting of native lands for precious metals and the cultivation of cash crops such as tobacco and sugar cane. Dissatisfaction with this faraway Iberian overlord, coupled with the growing weakness of Spain's global position, led to the Latin American wars of independence in the early nineteenth century, which threw off the yoke of Spanish oppression but did little to alter the existing hierarchies of racial privilege. In essence, Latin Americans traded one group of whites (the Spaniards) for another (homegrown oligarchs, many of whom were of Spanish descent).

Contemporary Latin America is largely the product of Spanish sexual and military conquests — and the resulting vestiges of the colonization process. Spain indelibly marked its colonies in the New World with Spanish place names and gave the disparate peoples there a common identity, complete with Spanish surnames, the Spanish language, and Roman Catholicism. These characteristics shaped the cultures of all the Spanish-speaking Latin American countries. Today Spain continues to have a quasi-familial relationship with the residents of Spanish America. It is an important participant in the annual Ibero-American Summits, and political exiles and wealthy students from the Americas often choose to spend time in España. Spanish corporations (Mapfre, Endesa, Banco Bilbao, Banco Santander, Telefónica) dominate Latin American commerce; these companies derive much of their profits and revenues from their Latin American operations.[16] The two-way traffic in cultural products — books, music, movies — between Spain and Latin America also maintains the ties between the erstwhile colonizer and its former colonies.

Spanish men, from the very beginning, had little compunction about forming sexual unions with the indigenous women of the New World.[17] Many *conquistadores* and Spanish colonists formed sexual unions with the native women. This process of *mestizaje* (miscegenation) created the *mestizo*. The children of these sexual unions — there were few marriages of Spaniards to Indians — resided in an unhappy limbo. They were not fully Spanish or Indian, and the Spaniards discriminated against them in favor of full-blooded Iberians, although they outranked people who were purely Indian. The mestizos in turn formed unions with the Indians, thus introducing Spanish blood into the indigenous population. Consequently, the percentage of full-blooded Indians declined slowly while the mestizo population grew steadily larger.

Today the Latin American notion of race is based on cultural characteristics (values, norms, attire, language, lifestyle, social standing), not just appearance. Latin Americans have friendly and not-so-friendly nicknames and descriptive colloquialisms that refer to gradations of color. A redhead, for instance, wins the appellation *la pelirroja*, while a woman with a blond mane might be called *la rubia*, and a raven-haired lady will be described with the adjective *morena*.[18] Although the "national look" differs by country, there is a single Latin American look, at least according to stereotype. This look was created by centuries of ethnic mixing among Spaniards, Amerindians, and Africans, and it was refined by further mixing with the European, Middle Eastern, and Chinese and Japanese immigrants who have come to Latin America in the last century. It usually entails having dark brown eyes, brown or black hair, and some shade of olive or brown skin color.

Latin Americans who deviate from this perceived racial norm are not always accepted by the other natives. One Chinese Mexican told my sister that she was called an "ugly duckling" in school by her brown-skinned Mexican classmates. Another time she surprised some would-be marauders who brazenly spoke to each other about robbing her in her presence. (They assumed that, with her Chinese appearance, she was a foreign tourist who did not understand Spanish and was thus an easy target.) Considering the Northern and Western European origins of many Americans, it is not surprising that Latin Americans frequently presume that gringos and gringas are blond and blue-eyed.[19] Conversely, Caucasians with brown eyes and black hair may be mistaken for natives in Spanish-speaking countries; they might be addressed in Spanish by *latinoamericanos*.

Besides Spain, the United States has played the largest role of any foreign country in the development of Latin America. Much of what is now the United States, including three of our four most populous states, was under Spanish dominion until the nineteenth century. The United States purchased Florida from Spain in 1819, increasing the size of America by 58,666 square miles. The acquisition of Texas in 1845 added 388,687 square miles to the United States. And the U.S. victory in the Mexican War dramatically shrank the size of Mexico, giving the United States 529,189 square miles of land as part of the Treaty of Guadalupe Hidalgo, which ended the war in 1848. Moreover, the Gadsden Purchase of 1853 added 29,670 square miles to the U.S. land mass. Forty-five years later, Spain ceded the island of Puerto Rico to the United States. In total, the Spanish once controlled one million square miles of the present-day United States.

During the nineteenth century, some Americans believed it was the United States' Manifest Destiny to extend throughout the Americas. This vision did not come to fruition, although the United States exercised considerable economic, political, and military influence over Central American countries and the Spanish-speaking parts of the Caribbean: Cuba, Puerto Rico, and the Dominican Republic. From 1902 to 1934 the Platt Amendment to the Cuban Constitution allowed the United States to intervene any time it saw fit in Cuban affairs. Puerto Rico became an American possession in 1898, as part of Spain's concession to the United States after losing the Spanish-American War. Twice, in 1916 and 1965, U.S. troops intervened in the Dominican Republic. Throughout the Americas U.S.-owned fruit and mining companies busily exploited the land; the term banana republic came out of this era. During the Cold War, U.S. military strategists worried that the Communists might gain a foothold in Latin America and sweep all the way up to Mexico and our southern border. There were persistent rumors of involvement by the Central Intelligence Agency (CIA) in the affairs of Chile, El Salvador, Nicaragua, and other places where Marxists gained power or appeared to be popular.[20] Today the old left-right battles of the Cold War are fading memories, and the U.S. gospel of open markets and cultural fusion is sweeping the Americas (with the conspicuous exception of Cuba).

Spanish-speaking Latin America consists of 18 countries, in addition to the American commonwealth of Puerto Rico. An agglomeration of 337 million people, it starts in the north in Mexico, then snakes south to encompass Guatemala, El Salvador, Honduras, Nicaragua, Costa Rica, and Panama. In the Caribbean, it includes Puerto Rico and the Spanish-speaking islands of Cuba and the Dominican Republic. Then there are the Spanish-speaking parts of South America: Argentina, Bolivia, Chile, Colombia, Ecuador, Paraguay, Peru, Uruguay, and Venezuela. More than 400 years after the Spanish conquest of the Americas, the Spanish language and cultural traditions dominate every one of the former Spanish colonies in this part of the world.

The nations of Latin America fit into multiple racial categories. Bolivia is the only one that is still majority-Indian. Peru has an Amerindian plurality, and more than four out of ten Guatemalans identify as full-blooded *indígenas*. Two countries, Argentina and Uruguay, are predominantly white, while two others, Chile and Costa Rica, boast sizable white and mestizo populations. Cuba and the Dominican Republic have black-and-mulatto majorities. Ten Spanish-speaking Latin American nations are mestizo-majority: Mexico, Colombia, Paraguay, Guatemala, Honduras, Nicaragua, Ecuador, Panama, Venezuela, and El Salvador. Of all the Latin American nations, Ecuador, Colombia, Nicaragua, and Venezuela are the most ethnically and racially heterogeneous — their populations include significant numbers of whites, blacks, mestizos, and Amerindians.[21] Socioeconomic divisions that usually parallel ethnic divisions continue to bedevil every racially diverse Latin American society. The out-groups vary by country, but in general whites and light-skinned mestizos and mulattos rank highest on the social scale.

Central America is largely mestizo, and the six percent of Hispanic Americans who trace their heritage to this part of Latin America represent a variety of different physical types. Most people in Guatemala, El Salvador, Honduras, Nicaragua, Costa Rica, and Panama speak Spanish, practice the Catholic religion, and have few ties to African or indigenous traditions and cultures. The cultural assimilation process is most advanced in El Salvador and Honduras and least far along in Guatemala. Ninety-four percent of Salvadorans are mestizo, and only five percent identify as Amerindian.[22] Ninety percent of the Honduran population is mestizo, while seven percent are Amerindian, two percent see themselves as black, and one percent identify as white.[23] Few whites live in Guatemala, a country where 56% of the residents are *ladinos* (a group that includes mestizos and Amerindians who live as mestizos) and 44% are Amerindians, mainly Maya. Four out of ten Guatemalans speak an Amerindian language, and some do not speak Spanish. But even in Guatemala, the Spanish culture is making inroads into the traditional Indian bastions of the country.[24]

Each Central American country has what might be termed a national look, or a couple of national looks, which the locals recognize as the norm for their nation. The different Indian ethnic groups in each country contributed mightily to these varied looks, as did the white immigrants to Central America. The blacks of Nicaragua and Panama — and, to a

far lesser extent, Honduras and Costa Rica — shaped how people look
in those countries as well. Since few people migrate to Central America,
most people there will eventually be mestizo; sizable black populations
may continue to exist in Nicaragua and Panama. When racially endogamous unions occur in Central America, they are often a function of social
class or geographical isolation. The white elites of Nicaragua, Costa Rica,
and Panama tend to choose marital partners from their social circles. And
Indians in isolated communities, particularly in Guatemala and Panama,
often marry someone from their ethnic group. As a rule, however, race
means little to most Central Americans, and will mean even less to them
in the future.

Racial divisions still affect the lives of Cubans, however. Spaniards
dominated Cuba almost immediately upon first contact in the 1490s.
Its pre-Columbian indigenous residents (the Arawak) perished or inter-
mingled with Spaniards and the numerous black slaves who worked on
the sugar cane plantations. The manumission of slaves in Cuba occurred
in 1886. Afro-Cubans, who lived in segregated enclaves and faced subtle
discrimination despite legal statutes that proscribed bigotry against them,
were largely locked out of the requisite training and education to ascend
to the most powerful positions in Cuban society. The Communist revolutionary Fidel Castro, who rose to power in 1959 and has led Cuba since
then, saw antiblack racism as an enervating flaw of bourgeois society and
rapacious capitalism.[25]

Castro's seizure of power led to a mass exodus of white Cubans over
the next two decades that made Cuba a blacker country.[26] Mulattoes account for 51% of Cuba's population, while whites make up 37%, blacks
11%, and the Chinese 1%.[27] Conversely, more than eight out of ten
Cuban Americans identify as white. In Cuba and metropolitan Miami,
one sees people who resemble Nordic Spaniards, with their fair skin and
sandy brown hair; others, who look like Mediterranean Spaniards, have
olive skin and black hair. Still others are mulatto or black — although
Afro-Cubans are far more common in Cuba than in the United States.
Thus Daisy Fuentes, Andy Garcia, Jon Secada, and Orlando "El Duque"
Hernandez represent four different physical types that typify the diversity
of the Cuban population.

Although Afro-Cubans are doing better than they were in the days
before the Revolution, white Cubans continue to wield most economic
and political power. Black Cubans complain about racial profiling by the
police and their inability to obtain the plum jobs in the tourist economy.
The Castro regime prefers to focus on socioeconomic factors instead of

race. Its unwillingness to examine seriously racial inequities in Communist Cuba makes it very unlikely that race-specific remedies will be used as a means of combating racism and discrimination on the island.[28]

The same kind of myopia with regard to racism and discrimination exists in Puerto Rican society. The original inhabitants of Puerto Rico, the Taíno Indians, have not been a distinct group for at least 400 years. Still, many Puerto Ricans have some Taíno blood. They often refer to themselves using the adjective *boricua,* a term that symbolizes the indigenous heritage of the islanders.[29] African slaves and their descendants have played an important role in the island's economy over the years. Slavery was abolished in Puerto Rico in 1873. Today islanders come in all colors, races, and ethnic backgrounds. Many Puerto Ricans have at least a smidgen of African blood.[30] Yet the stigma of slavery makes Puerto Ricans unwilling to identify as black — a reluctance that exists throughout Latin America. In the 2000 census, which asked the race question in Puerto Rico for the first time in 50 years, 80.5% of Puerto Ricans identified as white, 8.0% said they were black, 6.8% selected Some Other Race, 4.2% checked mixed race, 0.4% chose American Indian, and 0.2% were Asian. (The island is 98.8% Hispanic.)[31]

Whiteness is clearly preferred by Puerto Ricans, and the closer one looks to the racial ideal, the better his life chances there. A disproportionate number of the island's social, political, and economic leaders look as if they just arrived by plane from Spain. Their skin tones, hair texture, and physiognomic characteristics bear no traces of the 400 years of mixing that have shaped the Puerto Rican population and its culture. Indeed, black Puerto Ricans and dark-skinned mulattoes complain about indignities and subtle discrimination, such as a muttered comment or a missed job promotion.[32] The racial mores on the U.S. mainland often confuse mixed-race people from the Caribbean, especially Puerto Ricans, who find to their surprise that many Americans see them as black.[33] Nonetheless, Ricky Martin, Jennifer Lopez, Benicio del Toro, Marc Anthony, and Rosie Perez all look Puerto Rican, even though they do not share the same skin color or physiognomic characteristics.

Racial discrimination is not uncommon in Mexico, the world's most populous Spanish-speaking country. In 1519 the Spanish conqueror Hernán Cortés arrived in the New World with a small contingent of *conquistadores;* by 1521 Mexico, which was known in colonial times as New Spain, was a Spanish colony. Many of the Spaniards in New Spain had multiple liaisons with Indian women. Over the years, the ranks of the Indians were decimated by European diseases and by their backbreaking drudgery in service of Spanish colonialism. The mestizo population soared, while the indigenous population dropped markedly. Even so, there was a complicated racial hierarchy, with *peninsulares* (Spaniards born in Spain) at the top. They were followed by *criollos* (Spaniards born in Mexico) and Euromestizos (mestizos with a European orientation).[34]

Eventually the percentages of full-blooded Indians and Caucasians (usually of Spanish descent) decreased steadily. Thousands of African slaves, Arab and Chinese immigrants, and European newcomers also contributed to this distinctly Mexican mixture. Once Mexico achieved its independence from Spain in 1821, less European blood came into the national gene pool. Mexico's mixed-race plurality became a majority around 1910. The last time the Mexican government asked the race question in the national census was in 1921, so the precise demographics of Mexico remain a mystery. Pockets of unmixed Europeans still exist, such as the German Mennonites of Chihuahua and the Mexicans of Spanish descent in Mexico City and elsewhere, but the vast majority of Mexicans are mestizos of some type or another.[35]

The mestizo population in Mexico encompasses a wide range of physiognomic characteristics and differences in skin coloration. Some Mexicans have moderately light skin and Indian facial features, while others have relatively dark skin and European looks. As a rule, mestizos whose looks bear few traces of *mestizaje* rank higher on the social scale than those Mexicans who resemble their Aztec forebears. Many members of the nation's elite look as if they are full-blooded Spaniards, and many more appear to be primarily Spanish, with only a hint of Indian ancestry. Mexico's advertisements, television programs, and consumer products usually feature people who resemble Germans or Spaniards. Chinese Mexicans, Afro-Mexicans, the darkest mestizos, and full-blooded Indians are most likely to feel excluded in Mexican society. These Mexicans regularly experience discrimination in social circumstances.[36]

Indians, of course, are far and away the largest of Mexico's minorities. There are approximately 10 million Mexican Indians, who live mainly in the southeastern Mexican states of Oaxaca and Chiapas, along with the states of Quintana Roo and Yucatán. Many of these indigenous Mexicans resist assimilation, and they resent being at the bottom of Mexican society on almost every socioeconomic indicator (poverty, illiteracy, malnutrition, infant mortality, and so forth). The burgeoning Indian-rights movement, which sponsored a march to Mexico City in 2001, has not yet succeeded in improving the conditions of the Mexican Indians.[37] Indians, in other words, serve as the nation's racial Other, even as the government promotes the idea that Mexico is an ethnically homogeneous mestizo nation.

LATINO AMERICANS

In the fall of 1996 the annual Homecoming celebration was canceled at Garden City High School in Garden City, Kansas, because the school's administrators feared that fights would disrupt the festivities. A number of Mexican nationals attending GCHS had made it be known that they did not intend to stand for the Pledge of Allegiance during the Homecoming assembly. In response, some young Anglo guys decided they were going to compel the Latinos — by force, if necessary — to say the Pledge.[38] Some Anglos in town, after all, remain skeptical of the Mexican, Central American, and Southeast Asian immigrants who have come to work in the Garden City area's beef-processing plants since the early 1980s.[39] Members of Garden's Mexican-American community, whose roots in southwestern Kansas date back nearly a century, do not mix much with the Hispanic newcomers either.[40]

Garden's public schools, of course, reflect the changing face of this heterogeneous community of 28,415 people (the city is 49.8% white, 43.9% Hispanic, 3.5% Asian, and 1.2% black). Today, 49.5% of the 1,900-plus students at Garden City High School are Anglo. Another 40% identify as Hispanic; three-quarters of the Latinos trace their ancestry to Mexico, while substantial numbers come from Guatemala and El Salvador as well. Another 8% are Asian American, primarily from Southeast Asia, and the rest identify as black or Native American.[41]

GCHS stands out among secondary schools in the Midwest, due to its minority-friendly environment and the sheer diversity of its student body. Appropriately enough, all the major directional signs in the hallways at GCHS appear in three languages: English, Spanish, and Laotian. Spanish-language posters warn GCHS students not to violate the school's dress code because some Latinas favor low-cut blouses that offend Middle American sensibilities. And the Behavior Curriculum is posted in every classroom throughout the school district in English, Spanish, Laotian, and Mandarin. GCHS students, moreover, learn about such holidays as the Tet Celebration and Mexican Independence Day in their social studies classes. Educators also receive extra compensation if they learn to speak another language, and the school actively recruits minority teachers.[42]

Principal Kevin Burr, a native of Dodge City, another heavily Hispanic meatpacking town, came to GCHS in 1997. Burr immediately set out to improve the school's ethnic climate, and he was so successful at it that his colleagues named him Kansas Principal of the Year in 2000. The centerpiece of his reconciliation effort is an organization called "We Are GCHS," which promotes school spirit and fosters ethnic harmony through activities that encourage the students to work together and fraternize with each other. Although ethnic divisions between native-born Anglo students and foreign-born Latinos continue to exist, teenagers in Garden City no longer worry that ethnic discord will spoil any part of their high school experience. The majority of the GCHS students — Anglos, Latinos, and Laotians alike — now accept multiculturalism unquestioningly.[43] After four years at GCHS, they are well prepared to be citizens, workers, and neighbors in Multicultural America.

Since the beginning of Anglo-Saxon settlement in the Southwest, ethnic differences have affected the relationship between Anglos and Latinos. Take New Mexico, for example. The initial Anglo-Saxon pioneers were culturally, linguistically, and ethnically distinct from the Hispanos, whose ancestors colonized New Mexico in the seventeenth and eighteenth centuries. Another factor that certainly affected the Anglo-Saxon reaction to the Hispano is that many, if not most, of New Mexico's Spanish-speakers are racially mixed persons. To New Mexicans, the term Hispano includes people who are of Indian and Spanish ancestry as well as full-blooded Spaniards (the word literally means "Spaniard" or "Spanish American"). The early Anglo-Saxon settlers felt little kinship with the Hispanos, and the two groups repeatedly clashed over symbolic and substantive issues in their dealings with each other.[44]

Throughout much of America, whites regularly treated mixed-race Latinos as if they were a separate race. Sometimes Mexican Americans attended segregated schools. They were frequently barred from prestigious neighborhoods. Moreover, they endured racist comments by Anglos about "dumb Mexicans" and, in some communities, confronted restaurants with signs that read "No Mexicans Served," or another variation of this racially dismissive refrain. And they were excluded, at times, from business and community affairs. In 1954 the U.S. Supreme Court took up a number of these issues in a case involving Jackson County, Texas, where Anglos classified Mexican Americans as whites but treated them differentially.[45] Indeed, Mexican Americans once faced widespread discrimination in Texas, California, and elsewhere, although the racism they encountered paled in comparison to the rigid system of racial privilege that governed the American South at the time.[46]

Over the years, the decennial census instructions varied in terms of how to classify people of Latin American ancestry. In the 1930 census, "it was decided that all persons born in Mexico, or having parents born in Mexico, who were not definitely white, Negro, Indian, Chinese, or Japanese, would be returned as Mexicans."[47] But in the 1960 census, enumerators received instructions that Mexicans, Puerto Ricans, and other Latin Americans were to "be classified as 'White' unless they were definitely Negro, Indian, or some other race."[48] Gradually policymakers came to see these Americans, who once had been identified by their national origins or as Spanish-speaking people, as members of a de jure minority group.[49] The protected-class status of Hispanics today is partially due to historic discrimination, particularly against Mexicans in the Southwest, and it is also attributable to contemporary disparities.

Interestingly, the Hispanic category also includes Americans of Spanish descent — that is, white people of European ancestry. Spain, after all, colonized the Latin American countries that send lots of immigrants to the United States. As a result, most Latin Americans speak Spanish and have varying amounts of Spanish blood. By defining the Hispanic group to include Spaniards, the government bureaucrats eliminated the need to get into messy permutations about the after-effects of Spanish colonialism in the Americas. Since then, Spanish Americans have been subsumed into the Hispanic "racial" category, and little information exists about them as a specific group.

During the last 20 years, Hispanics have been transmogrified in the popular imagination from a pseudo-white group to a racial minority. Mexicans and Puerto Ricans, the nation's largest Spanish-speaking groups, were classified as minorities in the late 1960s and early 1970s. To codify this status, the federal government created the Hispanic category. The elites of the Spanish-speaking community quickly embraced the new identity, and a variety of panethnic advocacy groups, advertising agencies, political organizations, and media companies sprang up to serve the Latino population. In 2000, 47.9% of U.S. Latinos checked white in response to the census question about race, 42.2% chose Other, 6.3% picked two or more races, 2.0% selected black, 1.2% checked American Indian, and 0.5% said they were Asian or Pacific Islander (the totals do not add to 100 because of rounding).[50]

The Latino subgroups differ in terms of how their members self-identify themselves by race. Cuban Americans as a group identify mainly as white — 83.8% of them classify themselves this way. More than 64% of Colombian Americans come down in the white camp. Mexican Americans and Puerto Ricans, though, are divided almost evenly between white and Other. Fewer than 30% of Dominican Americans identify as white; another 30% see themselves as black, with 40% choosing Other. Salvadoran Americans favor Other over white by a margin of 59.1% to 38.53%. Guatemalans choose Other, too, but they do so by only 11.5 percentage points. And a plurality of Panamanian Americans (35.5%) identifies as black.[51] Race as a topic within the Latino community does not receive a great deal of attention from the general public, but it certainly continues to matter to Hispanics.

To be sure, there are color-based hierarchies within the U.S. Latino population. White Latinos typically are at the top of the Latin social scale, although they sometimes face subtle discrimination from other Hispanics, who may not consider them to be "Latino." Black Hispanics, who numbered 710,353 in the last census, face the worst possible situation of all. Most Americans see them as being solely black, as do many of their fellow Hispanics. Yet they are about as "black" in the African-American sense as Somali refugees or first-generation Nigerian immigrants. But if they emphasize their Spanish heritage and culture, native-born African Americans accuse them of trying to duck their blackness (this has been known to happen, especially in the past).[52]

The bigger issue, though, involves the masses of multiracial mestizos, who come to the United States suffering from racial disadvantages in their native lands. These inequitable disparities, then, may be exacerbated by U.S. conditions. But there is a high probability that U.S. affirmative-action programs that assist mixed-race Hispanics are correcting for at least some inequities that never occurred on U.S. soil, and which are largely or wholly unrelated to American dynamics. Nonwhite Mexicans, Puerto Ricans, Nicaraguans, and others are likely to migrate to the United States in greater numbers than white Latin Americans, due to the paucity of economic opportunities for them at home. The white oligarchs who run many Latin American countries have little incentive to come to the United States, save a drastic shift in power that endangers their privileges, like the one that occurred in Cuba 43 years ago. Regardless, the typical U.S. Hispanic is more similar in appearance to Caucasians than he is to blacks, the nation's traditional racial Other. Americans may refer to whites *and* Hispanics as two separate racial entities, but the dichotomy lacks the searing intensity and historical resonance of the black-white juxtaposition.

The fact that many Latinos are white in a visual sense complicates the notion that the entire Hispanic community should be part of a protected class that is intended, primarily, to help people of color. To be sure, the Latino category is so ecumenical in part because it can be very difficult to determine who is — or is not — white in Latin America. Many Latin Americans appear white in a visual sense, even though they are part Indian and/or part African. A white Puerto Rican, for instance, may have a sibling who appears to be a person of color. Therefore, it is nearly impossible, in many cases, to characterize Latin Americans in a racial sense.

The issue of race and protected-class status is sometimes a difficult one to assess when one considers matters related to race, recognition, and resources for U.S. Hispanics. Many Latinos have brown skin and facial features that blend Indian and Spanish characteristics. Yet, in a cultural sense, native-born Hispanics are often very similar to native-born Anglos. Many of them check white — white Hispanic — on the census form, particularly in such places as South Texas and northern New Mexico. In these parts of the country, however, they view themselves as Hispanic, Latino, Hispano, or some other identity different from that of the Anglos, even though both groups are "white." And there are some Latinos who emphatically consider themselves to be people of color, even though they would be considered white by most, if not all, Americans.

In any event, it is easy for white Latin Americans to embrace the present racial classification schema in the United States. Few immigrants, after all, would quibble with affirmative-action programs that help them achieve economic success in America.[53] However, it remains uncertain whether white Latin Americans face any more discrimination than any other white people. Spaniards and white Latin Americans may not speak English when they come to America, but neither do most Poles, Russians, and Ukrainians, and no sees them as minorities and allows them to benefit from affirmative action. White Latin Americans may experience some cultural dislocation when they arrive in the United States, but so do Bosnians, Iranians, and the Lebanese, and they are not part of a protected class either. To be sure, white Hispanics often defend their protected-class status by arguing that there are cultural similarities that unite all people of Latin American origin, and by making the case that all people with Spanish surnames face discrimination in the United States on the basis of their culture and ethnic heritage.

Indeed, the Hispanic identity can serve as a broad unifying notion for Latinos, even though some of them, due to their visual appearance, can choose to embrace it selectively if they wish to do so. White Hispanics who lack foreign accents and other foreignisms simultaneously benefit from being de facto whites and de jure nonwhites. However, except for Cubans, relatively few Spanish-speaking whites of unmixed European, Middle Eastern, or North African ancestry immigrate to the United States.[54] Still, it is one of the quirks of our present ethnic classification system that a white person from Spain or Spanish-speaking Latin America automatically becomes a Hispanic and a "person of color" when s/he immigrates to the United States. In any event, Americans from all ethnic groups frequently refer to Mexicans, Puerto Ricans, and other Latinos as "the Spanish" or "Spanish people." These imprecise synonyms refer to their heritage and language more so than their ethnicity or nationality.[55]

The Hispanic/Latino category is not especially cohesive or monolithic. U.S. Hispanics are divided by dialect, social class, race, ethnicity, national origin, and even religion — and unified by the Spanish language, their Spanish surnames, and their Latin American culture.[56] National origin is the most significant difference, of course. There are national holidays, traditions, and musical preferences that separate the various Latin American groups. Hispanics may make invidious distinctions between and among the numerous Latino subgroups. These distinctions reflect their suspicions, antipathies, and national rivalries. Latin Americans even speak Spanish differently. Although the ordinary Chilean could communicate in mutually intelligible Spanish with the typical Salvadoran, there are different pronunciations and slang words in each patois, which might hinder their conversational flow. In sum, race, nationality, and socioeconomic status are perhaps the most important factors that divide Latinos.

These divisions make it somewhat difficult to organize Latino Americans except on the broadest basis and at the elite levels. Due to the differing migration streams and geographical concentrations, most Hispanics have little interaction with or exposure to Latinos from other ethnic groups, except in large cities and at the elite levels. (Three out of four Latinos live in Texas, Illinois, Florida, California, and New York.) It takes a while for people to develop a panethnic identity, and to see themselves as having a common political agenda with people who come from cultures and countries different from their own. Most Hispanics use their national identifiers as self-reference points, but well-educated, native-born Latinos will use the panethnic identifiers, too, along with ethnic-specific ones.[57]

Panethnic Latino organizations such as the League of United Latin American Citizens (LULAC) typically draw their members from the ranks of acculturated, native-born Hispanics, whose ties to their ancestral homelands are usually more tenuous than those of recent immigrants. The typical Cuban or Mexican or Colombian immigrant probably would not be able to tell you anything about the National Council of La Raza (NCLR), the nation's leading Latino advocacy group. But his middle-class, college-educated coethnic likely would know something about it, and may even be a member.

The existing studies indicate that Latino panethnic unity is fragile indeed. For instance, the Latino National Political Survey (LNPS), which polled Mexican Americans, Cuban Americans, and Puerto Ricans, found that more members of each group surveyed considered themselves to be closer to Anglos than they were to other Hispanics outside their specific ethnic group.[58] Another study found that Latinos felt they shared more in common with other Latino subgroups than with Anglos and African Americans, but 52% of all Hispanics polled agreed that "Latinos in the United States share few political interests and goals."[59]

The biggest pan-Hispanic unifier is the Spanish-language media, which provide Latino Americans with visibility and an alternate point of view, both of which are absent in mainstream media content and programming. Spanish is a handy referent for most Hispanics, except for the few who only speak their Amerindian languages. Latinos have many Spanish-language media options. The United States has 34 Spanish-language daily newspapers, 265 Spanish-language weeklies, 352 Spanish-language magazines, and 594 Spanish-language radio stations.[60] Moreover, there are two major television networks (Univision and Telemundo) and hundreds of commercial Web sites that cater to Latinos.

Mainstream media outlets increasingly appeal to Spanish-speaking consumers by offering them Spanish-language versions of their traditional products (Yahoo en español, CNN en español, Time-Warner's *People en Español,* the Miami Herald's *El Nuevo Herald*). These Spanish-language products vary in terms of whether they contain completely different content, or whether they are just Spanish-language translations of the English-language media product.[61] In any event, these forms of media enable Latin American immigrants to maintain their ties to the Spanish-speaking culture, even though they live in a society where English, not Spanish, is the predominant language.

Of all the Spanish-language media, none are more important in creating a sense of community than Spanish-language television. The Univision Network is the United States' fifth largest television network. Univision and its less successful competitor, Telemundo, offer their viewers a cultural and linguistic alternative to the Anglo fare of mainstream television networks — and promote feelings of kinship among Spanish speakers throughout the world. Spanish-language television viewers watch broadcasts of Latin American news, movies, and variety shows, and tune in to the popular *telenovelas* (melodramatic soap operas).[62] The format has stars such as Cristina Saralegui, the Cuban-American host of "El Show de Cristina," a popular talk show on Univision, who is rivaled by Laura Bozzo, a Peruvian whose show "Laura en America" runs on Telemundo.[63] Another leading figure is Univision news anchor Jorge Ramos, a Mexican national who draws large audiences in major American cities with his nightly newscast, "Noticiero Univision."[64] The Spanish-language networks offer such fare as "Sábado Gigante" (Univision) and "Padre Alberto" (Telemundo) that resonate with Spanish-speaking audiences.

Spanish-language television has encountered increasing criticism from Latino Americans. Some U.S. Hispanics dislike Spanish-language television's foreign storylines and the racial homogeneity of its on-air personalities (virtually all the actors, hosts, and news anchors on Univision and Telemundo could pass for Spaniards or Argentines).[65] Many Hispanics, of course, never watch Spanish-language television. When native-born Latinos, especially those who are monolingual English speakers, want programming that reflects their interests and sensibilities, they turn to mainstream media outlets.

Spanish-language media outlets come in two types: monoethnic and panethnic. The nation's two leading Spanish-language radio networks — Radio Unica Communications and Heftel Broadcasting Corporation — take somewhat divergent approaches. Radio Unica tries to create panethnic, Latino programming that works nationally, while its competitor does niche marketing and specifically focuses on local markets.[66] Monoethnic publications and radio stations appeal to the sensibilities of a specific ethnic group in a specific area. Take Miami's Cuban-American radio stations, whose Caribbean rhythms and interminable discussions of Castro and foreign policy would be a turnoff to the typical Mexican. In Chicago, there are popular radio stations that focus on Mexican regional music, not panethnic Latino pop, and cater only to Mexicans, who make up 70.3% of the city's huge Hispanic population.[67] Chicago's Cubans, Puerto Ricans, and Central and South Americans probably do not listen to those stations very much.

The Spanish-language media usually focus on panethnic issues of interest to the broadest possible spectrum of Spanish-speaking Americans. The television programs go one step further, and downplay national differences as much as possible. Spanish-language periodicals integrate the members of the Latino subgroups as best they can, and highlight panethnic Latino celebrities for whom ethnicity and nationality are less important than their Spanish-language cultural identity. Jennifer Lopez is presently the best example of this phenomenon. The Spanish-language media's coverage of J. Lo rarely focuses more than a little bit on her Puerto Rican heritage, but rather cursorily categorizes her as Hispanic.

Language continues to be an important issue for Latinos. Spanish-speaking immigrants — or, at least their children — learn English out of necessity: It is a prerequisite for many well-paying jobs. The linguist Richard Teschner estimates that 25% of Hispanics are monolingual English speakers, another quarter of them are monolingual Spanish speakers, and 50% of them are conversant in both languages. By the third generation, native-born Latinos rarely speak Spanish fluently. However, the steady stream of Spanish-speaking newcomers keeps the language alive in the Hispanic community.[68]

Spanglish, a hybrid tongue of Spanish and English, is the dialect of Latino America. According to Lizette Alvarez, "Spanglish has few rules and many variations, but at its most vivid and exuberant, it is an effortless dance between English and Spanish, with the two languages clutched so closely together that at times they actually converge. Phrases and sentences veer back and forth almost unconsciously, as the speaker's intuition grabs the best expressions...."[69] Spanglish is most common in the areas with large numbers of assimilating Latinos: Miami (where it is called Cubonics), Los Angeles, the South Bronx, and U.S. border towns in Texas (where people refer to it as Tex-Mex). Some Hispanics contend that this deviation from standard English (and Spanish) confuses its speakers and limits their ability to speak English *or* Spanish properly. Mexican linguists fear the invasion of English, particularly along the U.S. border with Mexico, will corrupt the purity of the Spanish language as it is spoken there.[70] Due to this linguistic heterogeneity, the most prescient marketers realize that different marketing strategies are needed to reach each generational cohort of Latinos, particularly the youths who grew up in a Spanish-dominant home environment but feel more comfortable speaking English.[71]

BETWIXT AND BETWEEN TWO WORLDS

On a sunny Saturday afternoon in February 1999, my family and I stopped for a snack at a Wendy's restaurant in Mayagüez, a coastal city of 98,434 in western Puerto Rico. In terms of its decor, setup, and menu items, this particularly Wendy's resembled any other Wendy's franchise in the United States. Even the menu was in English. But all the patrons disregarded the English-language menu boards and placed their orders in Spanish: They referred to Wendy's flagship product as *una hamburguesa*, not a hamburger as it said on the menu.

During the 15 minutes we spent at this particular Wendy's restaurant, we never heard a single word of English spoken. The language on the menu board was irrelevant to the patrons in the half-filled dining room, who chatted quietly and enjoyed their meals of hamburgers, French fries, and soft drinks. Except for the Puerto Rican faces and the sounds of Caribbean Spanish, this fast-food restaurant in Mayagüez could have been a Wendy's in Modesto or Milwaukee. The English-language menu board was simply one of the cultural dichotomies common on the island, such as the English-language U.S. postage stamps that everyone in Puerto Rico uses on their letters and packages.

However, the English-language menu seemed incongruous in an island commonwealth where only one-quarter of the residents speak English fluently. Most Puerto Ricans also differ dramatically in appearance from "Wendy," the perpetually young white girl with red hair who is simultaneously an American icon and an instantly recognizable symbol of one of the nation's leading purveyors of hamburgers and French fries. This quintessential American chain, with its well-known, grandfatherly founder, Dave Thomas, has planted its flag in the far reaches of the American nation, along with such competitors as McDonald's, Pizza Hut, and Kentucky Fried Chicken. Puerto Ricans, of course, enjoy fast food as much as any other Americans.

To this day, I am not quite sure why the menu at this particular Wendy's franchise was in English, when the other American fast-food restaurants on the island generally advertise their wares in Spanish. I never asked the staff of the Wendy's in Mayagüez about the English-language menu. At the time of my visit to this particular Wendy's restaurant, I had not yet gone to enough fast-food franchises on the island to realize that such a menu was somewhat unusual. In any event, the cultural and linguistic compromise at the Wendy's in Mayagüez exemplifies Puerto Rico's dual cultural influences, those of the United States and Latin America. The island commonwealth is betwixt and between two worlds.

Many Puerto Ricans would say there is no cultural schizophrenia in their homeland. Puerto Rico, after all, is heavily weighted toward Latin

America and the Spanish-speaking global culture. After all, four centuries of Spanish rule, from 1493 to 1898, left their imprint on the island, which was named "rich port" by the Spaniards. After losing the Spanish-American War, Spain yielded Puerto Rico to the United States as a result of the Treaty of Paris, which the two nations signed in December 1898.[72] This island, with a land mass of 3,339 square miles, borders the Atlantic Ocean on the north and the Caribbean Sea on the south. It is the most populous of the outlying areas of the United States, which include Guam, American Samoa, the U.S. Virgin Islands, and the Commonwealth of the Northern Mariana Islands. Like Puerto Ricans, Guamanians, Samoans, Virgin Islanders, and Northern Mariana Islanders are American citizens, use U.S. dollars, and have the right of free travel to the U.S. mainland.[73]

Since the voters of Puerto Rico approved commonwealth status in a plebiscite in 1952, the contradictions of that status have been manifold — and a never-ending source of discussion and contentiousness on the island. Commonwealth status is known in Puerto Rico as *Estado Libre Asociado* (ELA), which translates to Free Associated State. Although *puertorriqueños* are subject to American foreign policy and can be drafted for military service, they cannot vote for President or elect voting members of the U.S. Congress. Puerto Ricans have their own laws and system of government, although the island is governed by the Constitution and U.S. federal laws. The federal minimum-wage law applies in Puerto Rico, just like on the mainland, but Puerto Ricans pay no federal income taxes on income earned in Puerto Rico. Puerto Ricans are American citizens and carry U.S. passports, but the islanders are not counted by the U.S. Census Bureau as part of the resident American population. These factors embolden supporters of statehood for Puerto Rico to push for full integration with the rest of the United States.

To be sure, a number of cultural differences distinguish Puerto Rican islanders from their fellow Americans. They use U.S. dollars as their currency, but sometimes refer to them as *pesos* or *dólares*. Road distances are measured in kilometers, while the speed-limit signs are posted in miles per hour. As in Mexico and other Latin American countries, gasoline is measured and sold in liters. Unlike other American public school students, Puerto Rican youngsters are taught primarily in Spanish. As Ronald Fernandez, Serafín Méndez Méndez, and Gail Cueto point out, "English as a second language continues to be a required subject throughout the [Puerto Rican public school] system's primary and secondary schools, as well as in institutions of higher education."[74] When it comes to the national anthem, *"La Borinqueña"* takes precedence over "The Star-Spangled Banner" in Puerto Rico. At every toll booth, the U.S. flag flies side by side with the Puerto Rican banner, which has a white star inside a navy-blue triangle, set against alternating red and white stripes. Furthermore, islanders pay a lot more attention to the World Cup than to the Super Bowl. Puerto Rico remains a popular vacation destination for Americans, who account for many of the 4.2 million annual visitors who fuel its $2.1 billion-a-year tourism industry.[75]

Indeed, Puerto Rico is an American border region — one that, as Ellis Cose puts it, "lies at the intersection of the United States and Latin America."[76] Puerto Ricans, after all, have been American citizens since 1917.[77] However, Puerto Rico is part of the Caribbean and Latin America: San Juan, the island's most populous city, is much closer to Caracas than it is to Chicago. Still, familiar American businesses — Sears, K-Mart, Wal-Mart, Walgreen's, and others — loom large in the island's retail world. American food, tobacco, and liquor products are also popular on the island.[78] But in Puerto Rico and elsewhere in Latin America, being Puerto Rican has a meaning and significance beyond that of a normal U.S. state identity, such as that of an Alabamian or an Oregonian. Puerto Ricans seem to consider their homeland to be a semi-sovereign nation in many respects.[79]

In any event, Puerto Ricans, both islanders and mainland residents, complain that many of their fellow Americans do not see them as U.S. citizens. As David Jackson and Paul de la Garza note, "For Puerto Ricans, it is a peculiar part of the American experience to be treated as a foreigner in your own land. To be told with scorn to go back to your own country, when you're already there."[80] The vernacular used by mainland Americans and Puerto Rican islanders reflects this dichotomy, with references to the two groups of people as Americans and Puerto Ricans, and descriptions of the United States and Puerto Rico as mutually exclusive entities. The most accurate reference, although rarely used, is to juxtapose Puerto Rico with "the mainland" or "the States."

Puerto Ricans, as a group, are poorer and less educated than the U.S. national average. Of the major Hispanic subgroups, Puerto Ricans (resident on the mainland) have the highest percentage of persons and families below the poverty line, the lowest percentage of family incomes above $50,000 a year, the lowest percentage of married-couple family types, and the highest percentage of Hispanic households headed by single mothers. Among Hispanics, they also have the highest unemployment rate and the largest percentage of people not in the labor force. Only on high school graduation and college completion rates do Puerto Ricans outrank the Hispanic average.[81]

Resident Puerto Ricans are, in the main, much more prosperous than non-resident ones. In 1989, for instance, the mean per capita household income in Puerto Rico was $4,099. At the same time it was $14,052 in the U.S., and $8,370 for Puerto Ricans living in the States.[82] Not surprisingly, federal transfer payments play an important role in the Puerto Rican economy.[83] Of course Puerto Rico is a major consumer of goods from the States.[84] Moreover, Puerto Rico has the economic and political stability typical of the United States. No one in Puerto Rico ever has to worry about rampant inflation or the prospect of a political revolution, in contrast to some of their fellow Latin Americans. Puerto Ricans enjoy a higher standard of living than that enjoyed by people in all the Latin American countries except for Chile and Argentina (before the recent economic problems in the latter country).

Migration from Puerto Rico to the U.S. mainland has been a defining feature of postwar Puerto Rican life. The migration boom picked up in the immediate aftermath of World War II, when mainland employers recruited Puerto Ricans to fill vacant jobs in the thriving U.S. economy. Hundreds of thousands of Puerto Ricans took advantage of economical airfares and left behind the overpopulated island. The 1950s were the peak decade for net emigration from Puerto Rico to the U.S. mainland, when 470,000 Puerto Ricans came to the States. Since the 1950s, at least 100,000 island residents have made the journey each decade to the mainland, with migration pressures at their lightest during the 1970s. The Puerto Rican migrants settled in urban barrios, particularly in New York, Chicago, and Philadelphia. As the promise of well-paying manufacturing jobs proved to be elusive, many migrants became part of the urban underclass. This is most evident in New York City, where 40% of Puerto Ricans live in poverty (the percentages for Puerto Ricans elsewhere in the country are lower).[85]

Due to the fact that Puerto Ricans are American citizens and can move freely between the island and the mainland, there is a considerable amount of what demographers describe as "circular migration." Some Puerto Ricans live on the island for a few years, then go to the mainland for a while, and eventually return to Puerto Rico. Each year thousands of Puerto Ricans leave *la isla* for the mainland, if only to get an education and English-speaking experience in the business world, while thousands of other Puerto Ricans depart from the States to live in Puerto Rico.[86] Many migrants relish the cultural and linguistic homogeneity of Puerto

Rico. But they might not be judged by their peers as fully Puerto Rican, especially if they grew up in the States. The extent to which a Puerto Rican becomes "Americanized" during his or her time on the mainland depends on the frequency (and duration) of the person's trips to the island, closeness to relatives there, ability to speak Spanish, economic ties to businesses there, and so forth.

Approximately 7,200,000 Puerto Ricans live in the United States. According to the most recent census, 3,406,178 of them live on the mainland, while the majority of Puerto Ricans (3,808,610) reside on the island. Nearly 61% of mainland Puerto Ricans live in the Northeast, while 22.3% reside in the South, 9.6% call the Midwest home, and 7.2% live in the West. Nearly half of all mainland Puerto Ricans live in just three states: New York (1,050,293), Florida (482,027), and New Jersey (366,788). Puerto Ricans also have a substantial presence in Pennsylvania (228,557), Massachusetts (199,207), Connecticut (194,443), Illinois (157,851), and California (140,570).

Certain parts of urban America are heavily influenced by Puerto Ricans. More than 20% of mainland Puerto Ricans (789,172) reside in New York City.[87] Yet the Puerto Rican influence in New York City is waning and declining in absolute numbers, as Puerto Ricans return to Puerto Rico or move elsewhere in the States.[88] Today Puerto Ricans constitute only 36.5% of the Big Apple's Latino population, which includes 406,806 Dominicans, 186,872 Mexicans, and 777,704 other Hispanics, many of whom are from South America. One hundred thirteen thousand Puerto Ricans live in Chicago, the site of the second largest mainland Puerto Rican community. Philadelphia, with its 91,527 Puerto Ricans, is home to the nation's third largest aggregation of mainland Puerto Ricans. The other cities rounding out the top ten are Newark (39,650), Hartford (39,586), Springfield, Massachusetts (35,251), Bridgeport (32,177), Jersey City (29,777), Boston (27,442), and Paterson (24,013). Nearly one-third, or 32.6%, of Hartford's 121,578 residents are Puerto Ricans; this makes it the mainland's most heavily Puerto Rican city.[89]

Interestingly, there are significant factors related to political socialization that affect Puerto Ricans on the mainland differently than if they remained on the island. To participate fully in the American polity, Puerto Ricans have to establish residency in one of the 50 states. The resident Puerto Ricans therefore enjoy more of the fruits of American citizenship than their island counterparts. However, there is a remarkable difference between the dismal Puerto Rican voter turnout rates on the mainland

and the sky-high rates of electoral participation on the island, where politics is a cacophonous circus of rallies, colorful banners, and triumphal marches through the streets. Unlike other Hispanic immigrants to the U.S. mainland, Puerto Ricans can vote in American elections immediately. Most of them rarely exercise this privilege in the States, where they feel their participation matters less than it does in Puerto Rico.[90] Nor is the political situation the result of selective migration: The Puerto Rican voter turnout rates are high enough — and the migration rates substantial enough — that this is not an adequate explanation.

Perhaps the most dramatic difference between the island and the mainland occurs with regard to racial identification. Puerto Ricans on the mainland identify as white less frequently than their counterparts on the island. According to the 2000 census, eight out of ten Puerto Ricans said they were white. On the mainland, however, the percentages are very different. In 1990, the most recent year for which data are available, only 46.4% of Puerto Ricans classified themselves as white, 45.9% chose Other, 6.5% picked black, 1.0% selected Asian and Pacific Islander, and 0.3% identified as Native American in a racial sense.[91] Selective migration does not explain this disparity. Based on my fieldwork in mainland Puerto Rican communities, and my visit to the island, it seems to me that the racial composition of each group is similar.

Clearly, there are very different conceptions of race on the island versus on the mainland. Puerto Rico, to be sure, is influenced by Latin American conceptions of race, whereby people who would not be considered white by North Americans identify — and are accepted — as such by Puerto Ricans. Moreover, in Puerto Rico it is difficult to raise the racial issue because the Spanish-language culture serves as the tie that binds Puerto Ricans together. Spanish-speaking Puerto Ricans, especially the mixed-race and black islanders, may be more reluctant to see themselves as white on the mainland because they do not share a linguistic and cultural bond with the Caucasians there. In addition, the multiculturalism of the States leads many mainland Puerto Ricans to see themselves as people of color.

Meanwhile, the status question — statehood, commonwealth, or independence — suffuses Puerto Rican politics. There have been referenda on the question of Puerto Rico's status in 1967, 1993, and 1998.[92] The two major sides are statehood and the stay-the-course situation of commonwealth status, with independence and other options measuring negligible support. The incessant debate over the status question involves substantive and symbolic issues. Substantive issues include voting seats in the U.S. Congress; a voice in selecting the nation's President; the imposition of federal income taxes; and the overall benefits of commonwealth status. Symbolic facets of the island-wide discussion include the virtues of being the fifty-first star on the U.S. flag; the future of Puerto Rico's semi-national contestant in the Miss Universe Pageant; and the viability of having a separate team at the Olympic Games.[93]

The admixture of substance and symbolism comes together in the language issue. The possibility of English-language requirements on an island full of Spanish-speaking people concerns the monolingual natives. The Spanish language is the most visible proxy issue related to Puerto Rican identity, and efforts to promote English-language instruction in the public schools are seen by many islanders as attempts to destroy their cultural heritage. The linguistic issue goes to the core of the Puerto Rican identity. Almost all Puerto Ricans, including the English speakers, feel most comfortable speaking Spanish.[94]

Besides, the 2000 election results dealt a blow to proponents of statehood for Puerto Rico. The pro-commonwealth Popular Democratic Party capitalized on some scandals in the Pedro Rosselló administration and narrowly ousted the New Progressive Party from the statehouse. Popular Democratic Party nominee San Juan Mayor Sila M. Calderón won 48.8% of the vote, while the New Progressive Party's Carlos Pesquera took 46.0%, and the Puerto Rican Independence Party's Rubén Berríos Martínez won 5.2%. Moreover, the Popular Democratic Party won Puerto Rico's non-voting U.S. House seat, and it gained control of the Puerto Rican House and Senate too. Calderón and her partisans seek even greater autonomy in the commonwealth arrangement.[95] At her inauguration as governor, Calderón signaled her pro-commonwealth tilt: "We value our U.S. citizenship. We are loyal to the democratic principles that link us together, but first — before anything else, we are Puerto Ricans. We live, think, pray and love in Spanish and we are not willing to ever hand over the language that our heart speaks with."[96]

Puerto Ricans continue to be deeply ambivalent about statehood, and they are not ready to relinquish the Spanish language in exchange for the political legitimacy conferred by statehood. In Puerto Rico it seems very unlikely that public sentiment will swing dramatically in favor of statehood anytime soon. Nor do most islanders want to embrace completely English-language learning and other significant forms of cultural fusion with the mainland. Until this occurs, Puerto Rico will almost certainly never become a state. Never before has a state gained admission to the

Union when so many of its residents differed culturally, linguistically, and racially from the preponderance of Americans.

The U.S. relationship with Mexico will continue to be our nation's most important diplomatic priority in Latin America. A number of factors — geographical proximity, the volume of trade, the number of Mexican Americans — undergird this relationship. To promote the naturalization of Mexican Americans and to strengthen Mexico's influence on the United States, our southern neighbor now allows Mexican-origin persons who live abroad to maintain dual nationality but not dual Mexican citizenship. Mexican-American dual nationals are able to transcend anti-foreigner restrictions on investments and property purchases in Mexico, but they still cannot vote in Mexican elections.[97]

Mexican Americans maintain ties to the old country in other ways as well. They patronize hole-in-the-wall *taquerías*. They frequent mom-and-pop *tiendas* and giant *supermercados* that stock Mexican foods, music, movies, magazines, greeting cards, and consumer products. They travel by car, bus, train, and air between the U.S. and Mexico. They send billions of dollars in remittances — $9.6 billion in 2001 — to relatives at home in Mexico via banks, post offices, and currency exchanges.[98] And they make millions of telephone calls to the motherland, often using the inexpensive phone cards available at groceries, pharmacies, and gas stations throughout the United States. Moreover, many Americans of Mexican descent retain vestiges of Mexican culture: They venerate the Virgin of Guadalupe, watch Spanish-language television, and celebrate Cinco de Mayo and Mexican Independence Day.[99] In doing so, these Mexican Americans actively promote closer cultural, economic, and political ties between Mexico and the United States.

Meanwhile, it appears that the hard-line U.S. policy toward Cuba, with its focus on isolating Castro and his Communist regime, will remain unchanged until the aging revolutionary dies or is incapacitated. American businesspeople worry that the U.S. trade embargo against Cuba is keeping them out of that nation's developing marketplace. Since Castro allowed Cubans to have dollars in 1993, the major cleavage in Cuban society has been between those who have dollars and those who do not. The stores, restaurants, and nightclubs catering to the dollar economy have much better merchandise and services. Canadian and Western European tourists spend hundreds of millions of dollars in Cuba annually, and Cuban Americans send $1 billion each year in remittances to their

Cuban relatives.[100] One hundred seventy-six thousand Americans visited Cuba in 2000, including 22,000 tourists who flouted the U.S. government's strict limitations on travel to Cuba, which prohibit Americans, except those receiving special governmental permission, from spending money there.[101]

The United States is already preparing for the post-Castro era. There almost certainly will be a massive outflow of refugees from Cuba to our shores.[102] Moreover, the embargo is unlikely to last long once the Castro era ends in Cuba. As soon as the travel restrictions are lifted, Americans are very likely to travel to Cuba in large numbers. For Cuban Americans, especially those who were born in Cuba, the passing of Castro will mark the end of an era. The presence of Castro has defined two generations of Cuban-American politics and culture, and it will be interesting to see how the older exiles feel about Cuba without Castro. What role Cuban Americans will play in a post-Castro Cuba remains uncertain at this point.

Back in the United States, the continued presence of new immigrants fuels the retention of Latino cultural traditions, and it prevents a panethnic Hispanic category from gelling. Ethnic and national differences remain resilient: Latinos often hang embroidered ornaments with the national flag from their country of origin (these are usually made out of yarn) from the rearview mirrors in their vehicles. The average foreign-born Latino probably never relinquishes his national identity in favor of the panethnic one. Since the continuing inflow of Latin American immigrants shows no sign of abating, these issues will continue to shape ethnic identification in the Latino community.

Among the college-educated Latino elites, and those who are part of the traditional civil rights community and the diversity infrastructure in Corporate America, the Hispanic/Latino identity is a given. For younger Hispanics, especially those who have been exposed to the notion of *la raza* at the university, and who marry a Latino from a different ethnic group, the panethnic notion of Hispanics as a separate "racial" group will take off. But the Latino National Political Survey found that Puerto Rican and native-born Mexican-American and Cuban-American respondents were more likely to marry an Anglo than a Hispanic outside their ethnic group.[103] Meanwhile, the traditional assimilation process is working its magic on many native-born Hispanics, who embrace selective elements of their Latino heritage but also enjoy activities and cultural products with no ties to the Spanish-language culture.

Rock en Español, meanwhile, is increasingly popular with Americans of all ethnic backgrounds. This development is attributable to a combination of factors: the Latino demographic boom, constant airplay on Spanish-language radio stations, and a willingness by established Latin American stars to record songs and albums in English. Ricky Martin remains the Latin crossover success story of the decade; he released his first English-language album in 1999 and it went multiplatinum. Two of his contemporaries, Marc Anthony and Enrique Iglesias, also came out with their first English-language albums the same year.[104] The Colombian artist Shakira, who released an English-language album in 2001, is the latest Latin superstar to try for crossover success in the United States.[105] While some Latin stars have recorded albums in English, a number of prominent American artists, namely Rick Treviño and Christina Aguilera, have recorded albums in Spanish.

Similarly, Latinos are playing an increasingly important role in other aspects of American popular culture, such as movies and television. American-born, English-dominant Latinos have a growing number of role models in the entertainment industry, including Jimmy Smits, Esai Morales, Benjamin Bratt, John Leguizamo, and Jennifer Lopez. These actors regularly play Anglo characters, and no one questions their ability to do so. Few Americans seem to think of these actors as "minorities" per se. When Benjamin Bratt, who is half Peruvian, dated Julia Roberts for a time, the mainstream press did not focus on his ethnicity. Indeed, the gradual evolution of Latino entertainment from the margins of American society to the mainstream mirrors the history of other large immigrant groups, like the Irish and the Italians, who once were outsiders but now shape and define generic Americana.[106]

PART TWO

America's Enduring Dilemmas

～ chapter four ～

Unequal Life Chances?

Few white kids growing up in Saint Paul, Minnesota, ever stop to think that the way they learn to speak at home, in the schoolyard, and in the workplace distinguishes them from Americans who live outside the Midwest.[1] Native English speakers in Saint Paul speak accentless American English; there is no Southern drawl, no Brooklyn accent, in their speech patterns. They learn at an early age about the various types of American speech through the portrayals of Southerners, New Yorkers, and others in television programs and motion pictures. Young white residents of Saint Paul probably do not think about how they speak English, unless they come into contact with someone who speaks a different type of regional English. After all, virtually everyone around them sounds the same. The general culture reinforces the feeling that their version of American English is the preferred one, unless, of course, they speak like a character out of *Fargo*.[2]

The advent of radio and television promoted the development of a homogeneous form of American English — an accentless dialect that is based on Midwestern speech patterns. Despite this linguistic homogenization, dialects such as Southern Regional English remain stubbornly resilient.[3] As long as a resident of Saint Paul stays in the Upper Midwest where his accent is regarded as normal, he will never experience the feeling of being different — or face any kind of accent discrimination — just because of how he speaks English. But if he leaves Saint Paul for Macon or Paterson to go to college or find employment, he may encounter regional prejudice on the basis of his speech patterns.[4]

The homogeneous accent of Saint Paul's white residents developed during the twentieth century, as the European immigrants and their American-born children assimilated into the English-speaking culture. As a result, most whites in Saint Paul speak English as their first language. Few white people born there after 1964 can even remember a grandparent who spoke with a foreign accent. There have been relatively

105

few white immigrants to Saint Paul in recent years, a demographic fact that contributes to the city's linguistic homogeneity.

Within the white population, of course, there are differences in terms of how well people speak English. These linguistic differences often correlate to socioeconomic status. Generally, educated people speak proper English, without the solecisms and nonstandard colloquialisms that often typify the speech of the uneducated. Regardless of how well they speak English, however, white residents of Saint Paul usually have no regional accent — unless, of course, one considers the accentless speech of the Midwest to be a regional accent.

In Saint Paul, as elsewhere, audible differences often go hand in hand with visible differences. Like its neighbor, Minneapolis, Saint Paul has become increasingly heterogeneous in recent years. According to the most recent census, whites make up 64.0% of the city, while Asians comprise 12.3%, African Americans account for 11.4%, Latinos constitute 7.9%, multiracials make up 3.1%, and Native Americans are 1.0%. Saint Paul is home to the nation's largest Hmong community; eight and one-half percent of Saint Paul's 287,151 residents are Hmong. Many of the city's 24,389 Hmong attend the Saint Paul Public Schools.[5] Saint Paul also is home to a sizable Latino population. Indeed, more than four out of ten students in the Saint Paul public schools grow up speaking a language other than English.[6]

Proficiency in English is important to get a good job in Saint Paul, Minneapolis, or almost anywhere else in America, which is why those immigrants who achieve some degree of fluency in English, especially those who speak the language without a perceptible accent, do best economically.[7] Furthermore, black vernacular English is alive and well in Saint Paul, where there is a significant population of poor and working-class people who speak nonstandard English.[8] To be sure, many of Saint Paul's African Americans speak standard English, meaning that their grammar, syntax, and tonal inflections are indistinguishable from those of other middle-class Americans. The linguistic diversity that now typifies the city, due to immigration and domestic-migration patterns, indicates that Saint Paul is no longer the white-bread bastion of Northern Europeans that it once was.

When we open our mouths, after all, we tell people many things about ourselves, such as our social class, our level of education, our regional antecedents, and whether we learned American English from a native speaker. To some extent, these audible cues affect our life chances.[9] Accent discrimination, at least as it relates to national origin, is clearly illegal, but it remains unclear at this point whether accent discrimination based on regional origin is actionable bias.[10] This is not to say that an employer can openly discriminate against native-born Americans because s/he does not like how they speak American English. If the owner of a telemarketing firm in Saint Paul advertised that s/he only sought employees who spoke like native-born residents of the Twin Cities, s/he might receive some unfavorable publicity.

However, for ordinary jobs throughout most of America, particularly ones that involve frequent oral communication, any kind of regional or foreign accent is likely to be a hindrance, as is ungrammatical language. Therefore, some Southerners and Northeasterners try to reduce or eliminate their accents, by going to speech coaches and specialists, so they sound more like other Americans and do not incur any accent penalties that might limit their advancement.[11] In sum, the typical native-born resident of Saint Paul probably has a slight advantage over a similarly situated native-born resident of the South or Northeast because he learns to speak accentless American English as his birthright.

INTERSECTIONAL IDENTITIES

Oprah Winfrey is presently only one or two years away from becoming the first black female billionaire in U.S. history. Born poor in central Mississippi in January 1954, she survived a rough-and-tumble childhood and found great success in television at an early age. Winfrey is now one of the 400 wealthiest Americans. Her net worth stands at $900 million, according to *Forbes* magazine.[12] Winfrey's cash cow is the eponymous, syndicated *The Oprah Winfrey Show,* which has aired since 1986. Female viewers of daytime television respond to Winfrey's maternal empathy and relate to her yo-yo dieting and persistent weight problem.

The 48-year-old dynamo has even become a verb *and* a noun: Her first name is synonymous with a form of weepy, confessional release that some critics disparage as unseemly and exploitative. Despite some tough competitors, including Jerry Springer in recent years, Winfrey has continued to stay on top, due to her sensitivity to the needs of women, her core audience. By 2000, she had become such an institution in daytime television that major-party presidential candidates Al Gore and George W. Bush appeared on her show to court voters. Never before has a daytime talk show host wielded so much influence in American life.

Winfrey's reach, moreover, extends far beyond television. She writes best-selling books about diet and exercise; promotes books, mainly works of fiction, through Oprah's Book Club; acts in acclaimed movies such as *Beloved* and *The Color Purple;* stars in *O: The Oprah Magazine,* a monthly periodical that features her on the cover; dabbles in cable television and the Internet, through Oxygen Media; and gives millions to charity. As a celebrity, her appeal to women transcends race and socioeconomic class. Oprah's personal life and professional success continue to be fodder for the black media and mainstream press alike.

Her life story, in short, provides compelling evidence that the American Dream touches black lives as well as white ones. Oprah Winfrey has become a symbol of sorts. White conservatives often cite her story as a sign that any African American can make it out of poverty.[13] Yet it is unrealistic to point to the second-richest person in black America and imply that racism and discrimination do not affect the life chances of African Americans. Indeed, the contrast between Oprah's gilded lifestyle and that of the ghetto poor provides a dramatic example of the tremendous socioeconomic diversity that characterizes American racial groups.

Most African Americans are direct descendants of slaves, and the black experience continues to be affected by the vestiges of slavery, which linger on in various guises.[14] Today the forms of legal oppression that once circumscribed African Americans' life chances are largely nonexistent, but it took a century of civil rights activism and societal change to get to this point. The *Plessy* decision by the Supreme Court in 1896 created the doctrine of "separate but equal," which led to de jure segregation of blacks from whites in the South, until the Court's ruling in the *Brown* decision of 1954.[15] During this 58-year period and beyond, the program of second-class citizenship for blacks was known as "Jim Crow," which meant that black children in the South went to segregated schools with inferior schoolbooks, lower-paid teachers, and crumbling building facilities. Buses, passenger trains, drinking fountains, swimming pools, public libraries, public restrooms, park benches, and state universities were segregated, too. Private businesses, including hotels, restaurants, and movie theaters, also maintained strict racial segregation.[16]

The civil rights movement of the 1950s and 1960s ended de jure segregation and led to the drive for a level playing field. However, it was clear from the beginning of the civil rights movement that the end of segregation was only the first step toward achieving full equality for African Americans in every sector of American society. While non-Southern white Americans generally supported the efforts to eradicate segregation, they were far less supportive of the affirmative-action policies and social-welfare programs that benefited many African Americans during the 1960s, 1970s, 1980s, and 1990s.

The vexing question, of course, is how to define equality and "equal opportunity," and then how to go about achieving it. Whereas civil rights activists once advocated colorblindness in public policy and private actions, they now embrace programs, like affirmative action and mandatory busing, that take into account the respective numbers of blacks and whites in each context.[17] By many conventional indicators, including college enrollment, cultural icons, home ownership, out-of-wedlock births, math and reading proficiency, and the employment of young black men, it has never been a better time to be an African American. In particular, the percentage of poor blacks is at its lowest ever — at least since the federal government started measuring race and poverty.[18]

Yet African Americans worry about the possibility that their new-found prosperity could disappear in the event of a protracted economic recession or the curtailment of affirmative action. And affluent blacks are uncomfortably aware that all too many of their less fortunate co-ethnics continue to wallow in poverty.[19] Although few African Americans are multimillionaires like Oprah Winfrey, there is a well-established and thriving black middle class, in addition to an equally well-established and thriving black upper class.[20] Prince George's County, Maryland, has become the premier black suburban county in America. Many blacks outearn the whites in the county — and not by a little bit. This dynamic has unsettled some of the longtime white residents of Prince George's County, as the area's affluent blacks make their voices heard in civic and political affairs.[21]

Racism, alas, has not disappeared. In fact, it remains the preeminent "ism," along with the likes of sexism, classism, lookism, heterosexism, and so forth. I define racism, simply, as the willful ordering of human beings into hierarchies, based on one's arbitrary dislikes of members of entire racial groups. Old-fashioned forms of racism, like murders or shouted racial epithets, are much rarer than in the past. Now more nuanced and ambiguous situations have come to pass. That said, there are many types of racism: cultural racism, symbolic racism, environmental racism, even unconscious racism.[22] According to the existing definitions of institutional racism, white Americans do not have to take any specific actions to be considered racists, if the institutional structures of the United States delimit the opportunities available to people of color.[23] It is distinctly unfashionable (and morally reprehensible) for someone to be a racist. Credible allegations of racist behavior can irreparably damage one's personal reputation and professional career.

The extent to which racism still serves as a hindrance to nonwhites' hopes, or merely functions as a convenient rationalization for them to excuse their failures, is a subject of hot controversy.[24] In fact, this issue is at the heart of what Leonard Steinhorn and Barbara Diggs-Brown refer to as "the perception gap."[25] Whites often feel that blacks and other minorities see racism everywhere, when there are non-racial explanations for many issues. Since we cannot always figure out where someone is coming from, we know that race is not a factor for certain only in those situations where both parties are from the same race. Moreover, promiscuous charges of racism have devalued the currency of the term and inured Americans to the seriousness of the allegation and offense.[26] Discrimination is the logical after-effect of racism, or any of the other "isms." It involves putting prejudice, or the theory behind the "ism," into practice, into action. Occasionally Americans engage in zero-sum reductionism about which groups have experienced the most racism and discrimination throughout our nation's history — blacks or Hispanics or Asians or Native Americans.

An important debate about discrimination involves standardized tests, which many educators deem to be culturally biased because blacks and Hispanics tend to have poorer scores on them than whites and Asian Americans. Now many states have standardized tests in core subjects like math, science, and English; these exams, which are increasingly common as a prerequisite to graduate from high school or move on to the next grade, may hurt poor minority students, who fail them more often than their white peers. This method to ensure that students have basic competency in their core subjects is the target of lawsuits, protests, and investigations.[27]

Although the Educational Testing Service's Scholastic Assessment Test (SAT), which is a key determinant of admission to most elite colleges and universities, provides some means of comparison among the various secondary schools, it is an imperfect measuring tool of preparation for college, and a faulty indicator of professional success. Poor kids often attend substandard public schools, where they are unable to take the requisite high-school courses to prepare them for such exams. This does not mean that they cannot master such material. It means that they do not have the opportunity to test their mettle. And some youths from affluent school districts simply are not good test-takers. Score gaps on the SAT persist between and among the races: The mean scores of whites and Asians are similar, and they outscore blacks by 200 points, and outpace Hispanics by about 130 points, on average. These kinds of disparities have led some colleges or universities to downplay the SAT as a determinant when they decide whom to admit as students.[28]

Discrimination, like racism, is sometimes difficult to measure. The most commonly used definition is a form of proportional representation, which is known in legal circles as "disparate impact," meaning that any kind of numerical disparity is prima facie evidence of discrimination.[29] The presumption is, that if we do not get equal results, something went awry. Dinesh D'Souza, the conservative thinker, argues in favor of a highly controversial notion: "rational discrimination." To paraphrase his complex argument, if persons are members of ethnic groups with higher-than-average rates of criminal activity, or other such malefactions, it may be rational for people to discriminate against them *on that basis*.[30] This logic informs the controversial practice of profiling, by which cabdrivers, shopkeepers, law-enforcement personnel, and others make cursory and often stereotypical judgments about people based on their color, behavior, mannerisms, and trappings (or lack thereof) of material success.

People of color complain about the corporate version of "rational discrimination," which is referred to as redlining, whereby businesses refuse to provide services to residents of inner-city neighborhoods, based on the seemingly unprofitable nature of such ventures.[31] Pressure from the federal government, along with the prospect of reaching untapped markets, led businesspeople to make tentative moves into the inner city during the 1990s. Much to their surprise, they found that the inner-city market could be quite profitable. Now urban dwellers in low-income neighborhoods have greater access to banks, retailers, grocery stores, insurance companies, and movie theaters.[32]

Regardless, expressions of "rational discrimination" and groupthink persist. African Americans complain about the indignities they sometimes face when they drive expensive cars, shop in upscale venues, and hail taxis. DWB, "driving while black," is the three-word phrase African Americans use to describe the tendency, common in some jurisdictions, of law-enforcement officers to stop blacks for no apparent reason except their suspicions that the drivers might be criminals. SWB, "shopping while black," is an equally pernicious form of racial harassment — from the perspective of African Americans. Sometimes store personnel follow black shoppers unnecessarily, ostensibly on the grounds that the African-American consumers are prospective thieves; clerks or security guards also may falsely accuse them of shoplifting. HATWB, "hailing a taxi while black," refers to the difficulties African Americans have in getting cabs to stop for them, because some cabdrivers fear black passengers will rob them. The cab issue cuts across all socioeconomic lines in the African-American community: Danny Glover, Cornel West, and others are among the famous and widely publicized victims of HATWB. African Americans compare these types of rejection, harassment, and unwarranted attention, in addition to other expressions of what experts classify as "retail racism," to modern-day lynchings.[33] At the same time, businesses, federal agencies, and other institutions hasten to assure people of color that they will be treated fairly.

Our environment shapes our aspirations and level of attainment. Consequently, it can be difficult for Americans who live in poor areas to achieve social mobility — in essence, to avoid replaying their parents' lives.[34] The intergenerational transmission of social standing animates the American class structure — upper class, upper middle class, middle class, working class, poor. It is difficult to define these categories by dollar amounts because the cost of living differs around the country, and expenses vary from person to person based on the number of one's dependents.

The most commonly cited indicator of material prosperity — money income — allows us to see ethnic divisions in relief. Whites and Asian Americans are less likely than blacks, Hispanics, and American Indians to be below the federal government's officially defined poverty line, or to have children or elderly group members in poverty.[35] The panethnic group categories mask intragroup differences. Cuban Americans, for instance, outpace Mexicans and Puerto Ricans on just about every socioeconomic indicator.[36] As a rule, many immigrants come to the United States with few, if any, assets, but they are upwardly mobile and do not remain poor forever. Group-based analyses can be problematic for ethnic groups that include large numbers of recent immigrants who may lack the education and skills to rise rapidly up the socioeconomic ladder. The data for these new arrivals can obscure the progress being made by their native-born coethnics.

Although whites generally do well based on such indicators as annual income and educational attainment, there are many exceptions to the rule within this ethno-racial group. The specious notion of "white privilege" is that all whites (and especially all white males) are unilaterally privileged vis-à-vis people of color. Proponents of this rule posit that "white privilege" transcends mere economics. They believe it empowers white Americans by giving them confidence and self-assurance that race will never be a barrier to their hopes, dreams, and aspirations. According to this line of reasoning, white, able-bodied, heterosexual men — who comprise about 30% of the adult population but continue to wield most of the power in American society — are the ultimate exemplars and possessors of racial privilege.

The legal theorist Cheryl Harris equates white skin with property, based on what she sees as the advantages of membership in the dominant group.[37] The best test of how whites feel about their race, and whether it confers unearned benefits upon them, is to ask them whether they would switch to another race, and how much money they would require to do so.[38] Most white Americans never think about this issue — and, if asked, many would jest about the possible rewards of affirmative action or make some self-conscious assertions of ethnic pride. A tacit acknowledgment of what liberals describe as "white privilege," in addition to the power differential between whites and minorities, may explain why most Americans tolerate and even countenance explicitly racial organizations from minorities but not from whites, e.g., a black student group but not a White Student Union.

Since the mid-1960s, Americans of Asian descent have been regarded by white society as a "model minority," because their socioeconomic standing was much higher than that of other nonwhites, and they assimilated into the mainstream without challenging the central tenets of the American ethos. The model minority stereotype holds that Asian-American students do well in school, especially in math and computers, because of their solid work ethic and ingrained cultural characteristics. According to the model minority stereotype, Asians prosper in American society because they unequivocally eschew identifying as a racial minority group with specific grievances.[39]

To be sure, Asian Americans have higher median household incomes than whites, but Caucasians outpace them in terms of their per-capita incomes, and have a lower percentage of group members below the poverty level. And Asian-American professionals are affected negatively by stereotypes of passivity and "foreignness." At times, Asian immigrants face difficulties in the workplace due to their accents or language problems. The model minority image denies that some Asian Americans do poorly and may require assistance from the government or private institutions.[40] Like any stereotype, this one neglects to take into account those Asian Americans who support affirmative action and actively identify with people of color and the Multicultural Left.

Regardless, many whites and nonwhites alike are left out of the global economy in the Information Age. Its leading lights are what Robert B. Reich calls "symbolic analysts," and Richard J. Herrnstein and Charles Murray classify as members of the "cognitive elite." Symbolic analysts typically have impressive educational credentials. They manipulate logic and use ideas to make their livings — in other words, the old dichotomy of working with one's head rather than one's hands. Now many of the jobs that require physical labor also entail technological training.[41]

Social analysts focus on the issue of universal access to personal computers and the up-to-date software required to use them, at home *and* at school, or in other public places, like libraries. In what has been labeled the "digital divide," whites are more likely to have computers at home than blacks and Hispanics, and to use them there. Again, in public schools, the one place where inequities may be remedied, minority students (and white youths in rural areas) often lack the sophisticated hardware and software found at suburban schools with predominantly white enrollments. Because basic computer literacy is necessary for many jobs (especially the well-paying positions), this racial gap in technological access, awareness, and knowledge concerns policymakers.[42]

OPPORTUNITIES TO SUCCEED

Coy Samons knows that education pays. Even though neither of his parents had a college degree, they recognized his potential when he was very young and encouraged him to go to college. His teachers did likewise. As a result of this encouragement and his own hard work, Samons became the first person in his family to earn a four-year degree. A native of Floyd County, Kentucky, Samons received a bachelor's degree from Alice Lloyd College, earned a master's from Morehead State University, and had additional graduate training in secondary-school principalship. In 1995, at age 30, Samons was selected to be the assistant principal of Betsy Layne High School in Betsy Layne, Kentucky. The following year this tall, mustachioed man with brown hair, a light complexion, and a commanding manner became the principal of Betsy Layne, his alma mater. He served in this position for two years before taking the top job at the high school in Prestonsburg, Kentucky.[43]

After 14 years as an educator and administrator, Samons was chosen in February 2001 to be director of the East Kentucky Regional GEAR-UP (Gaining Early Awareness and Readiness for Undergraduate Programs) Project, a program of the U.S. Department of Education.[44] Samons works for Morehead State University — officials at MSU's Institute for Regional Analysis and Public Policy applied for the $4.7 million, five-year federal grant that funds this particular GEAR-UP partnership.[45] The GEAR-UP partnership with Morehead State University covers Floyd, Johnson, Martin, and Pike counties in eastern Kentucky; whites account for 97.8% of the 147,200 area residents.[46] The rural isolation, the limited number of well-paying jobs, and the intergenerational transmission of poverty limit the life chances of many people there.

Samons and his colleagues are using the GEAR-UP grant money to encourage young people to attend college and break the cycle of poverty and dependency that affects so many families in Appalachia. To achieve this goal, Samons is aided by Kevin Hall, the assistant director of the East Kentucky Regional GEAR-UP Project, who himself is a first-generation college graduate with an advanced degree. Samons and Hall work in tandem with the teachers and administrators from 23 of the middle schools in the four-county area. They also benefit from the assistance of their partners in the local business world and the educational establishment. Every year Samons and Hall speak to the seventh graders at the local middle schools about the impact of post-secondary education on one's earning abilities — and then they outline the financial aid available to promising students. Moreover, they conduct separate workshops for the parents.[47]

Students who participate in GEAR-UP benefit from a variety of enrichment activities: internships, academic summer camps, after-school programs, tutoring programs in math and science, and field trips to local businesses such as factories and medical centers. Eight thousand youths in eastern Kentucky will have participated in the East Kentucky Regional GEAR-UP Project's activities by 2005. Student apathy is perhaps the biggest obstacle that Samons, Hall, and their fellow educators face — specifically, the enervating notion that it is simply impossible for youths from disadvantaged backgrounds to get an education and significantly improve their socioeconomic status. Nonetheless, the educators hope to increase the number of students in eastern Kentucky who go on to college or vocational school by ten to 20 percent.[48]

The federal GEAR-UP program is a practical application of the social contract, the idea that we-are-all-in-this-together and, accordingly, should maintain certain standards of decency and welfare to preserve the fabric of community. In the seventeenth, eighteenth, and nineteenth centuries, the United States basically operated according to the principles of Social Darwinism, and the ethos of "survival of the fittest" reigned supreme.[49] Reforms during the Progressive Era, New Deal, and Civil Rights Era established a stingier American version of the cradle-to-grave social-welfare systems of Scandinavia. During the New Deal, from 1933 to 1937, the federal government constructed an expansive social safety net for the disadvantaged. The twin pillars of the New Deal were the creation of Social Security and welfare — primarily, Aid to Families with Dependent Children (AFDC). And in 1938, for the first time, there was a federal minimum wage. In subsequent years, a bipartisan political consensus protected the welfare state, and even expanded it.[50]

Then, in the 1960s, President Lyndon B. Johnson's Great Society initiatives increased social spending dramatically and created scores of new programs, including Head Start, Medicare, and Medicaid. The benefits of these programs have become known as "entitlements" — that is, Americans feel they are *entitled* to them. At the same time, the civil rights movement culminated in the passage of the Civil Rights Act of 1964, the Voting Rights Act of 1965, the Fair Housing Act of 1968, and a host of other legislative initiatives in the 1970s, such as the Equal Credit Opportunity Act.[51]

Perhaps not coincidentally, ethnic and racial discord is less of a distraction in the most expansive social-welfare states in the world, those in Canada, Scandinavia, and Western Europe. The price that people in the aforementioned nations pay for general benefits — more vacation time, universal health care, paid family leave — is higher taxes and greater bureaucratic regulation. It is debatable whether this would be a desirable model for America. But Americans clearly are not ready to pay that price at this time. Our counterparts in Canada, Scandinavia, and Western Europe also may have to make do with a less muscular conception of the social contract, as their governments find it will be impossible to fund such generous benefits in the future.

On another front, the expansion of rights for previously neglected minorities in the United States during the 1960s and 1970s resulted in the formation of protected classes.[52] Every American, of course, is protected by the laws of the United States and the Fourteenth Amendment's requirement that everyone should be guaranteed "the equal protection of the laws." In a conflict between individual rights and group rights, however, some Americans — namely people of color — receive special protections in the form of affirmative action because they are perceived to face pervasive discrimination. A corollary of protected-class status is known as identity politics: Blacks, women, homosexuals, persons with disabilities, and others cite their identities as "victims" or powerless people to make claims for power, recognition, and resources.

Affirmative action is the bedrock of protected-class status; it compensates women and minorities in the present for the opportunities denied to women and minorities in the past. This shift from seeking "equal chances" to a tacit acceptance of the elusive goal of "equal results" has engendered controversy and led to increasing skepticism about the goals and significance of the civil rights movement.[53] The issue of responsibility for past misdeeds results in the pangs of "white guilt" some Caucasians experience over the injustices of yesteryear. But when if ever should compensatory mechanisms be phased out? Do whites have to pay for the sins of their fathers (and, in many cases, grandfathers, great-grandfathers, and other more distant progenitors) in perpetuity, even if the payers are not the actual people who committed the crimes?

These types of issues always surface in any serious discussion of affirmative action, though seldom in an intellectually creative fashion. Jewish Americans are a numerical minority, one that faced subtle discrimination in the past, but the government does not view them as a legal minority or protected class, at least in the sense that they suffer deprivation because of their Jewishness. Likewise, some Arab Americans assert that they feel unwelcome in the United States due to the stereotypes of terrorism and fanaticism that some Americans associate with Middle Easterners and the Muslim religion. Moreover, there are a number of white ethnic groups that could make plausible claims that their socioeconomic and demographic indicators trail the national average, the typical means of measuring discrimination for ethno-racial minority groups.

White liberals play an important role in the policy debates over these issues. To be sure, they face an intriguing predicament. They embrace — in theory — the need for diversity and other tenets of the multicultural gospel, but they do so without having personally experienced racism and deprivation. White liberals, of course, add diversity to the multiculturalists' rainbow coalition. America is a white-majority country, and any movement for social justice, especially one that purports to be transracial in its reach and objectives, has to have white members to be taken seriously by the mainstream media and Middle America. Still, white liberals often run into hostility on all fronts. Their rhetoric and actions may be resented by more-conservative whites, who view them as liberal do-gooders. Minorities, moreover, may be skeptical of what they see as white liberals' hypocrisy and paternalism.[54]

Multicultural conservatives are not especially popular with many of their coethnics either. Soon after the rise of the Multicultural Left in the 1960s and 1970s, there was a concomitant rise of a Multicultural Right during the 1980s. It consisted of blacks, Hispanics, and Asian Americans who disagreed with the prevailing left-liberal models of white oppression and minority subjugation. While minority conservatives disagree on many issues, they concur that race no longer prevents people of color from fully realizing their American Dreams. They have not made a great deal of progress in changing the minds of their coethnics, particularly in the African-American and Latino communities, where right-wing minorities are often viewed as the dupes of the white establishment. As with white liberals, however, multicultural conservatives have symbolic significance, particularly when they back colorblind initiatives that typically win the most support in white America.[55] After more than three decades of protected classes and burgeoning minority population growth, these issues are more salient than ever.

Race and social class continue to intersect in debates over social policy.[56] Political pragmatists who support expansive social-welfare programs, like the sociologist William Julius Wilson, propose universal (meaning transracial) solutions to social problems. Such programs benefit *all* disadvantaged Americans, and are most defensible in the political arena, where race-specific policies remain unpopular.[57] In the early 1980s the national mood turned solidly against generous social-welfare programs, at least those that working Americans viewed as undeserved handouts to people who had not earned them. Entitlements such as Medicare, Social Security, veteran's benefits, unemployment compensation, and the mortgage interest deduction never waned in popularity among white Americans during this period. Welfare, on the other hand, came to be seen by millions of Americans as the government program that most symbolized the excesses of big-government liberalism. This topic inevitably became a racial proxy issue because African Americans were disproportionately represented among long-term welfare recipients; the stereotypical and misleading portrait of a welfare mother was a single black woman with four or five children.[58]

Congress enacted a massive welfare-reform statute in 1996, thus ending welfare's 20-year reign as the domestic policy issue that consistently vexed whites. The states are now responsible for determining who gets welfare and how much, so long as there is a five-year lifetime limit on aid.[59] This development was a triumph for the advocates of devolution and states' rights, who argue that their approach is more efficient. According to this line of reasoning, devolution makes government programs more responsive to their intended beneficiaries. These debates usually have a racial subtext, because the federal government traditionally intervenes (at least it has during the last 48 years) to protect minorities from abuses by state and local governments.

The tax code, like almost every other part of American life, has racial dimensions, only because it intersects with socioeconomic indicators. Whites, on average, tend to have more money than non-Asian minorities, so they are overrepresented in percentage terms in the higher tax brackets, while non-Asian minorities are concentrated in the lower tax brackets. This ineluctable reality colors every aspect of tax reform and fiscal policy. As a rule, most federal revenues come from individual income taxes, social insurance and retirement receipts, corporate income taxes, and excise taxes (in that order).[60] The Earned Income Tax Credit for low-income families benefits a higher percentage of minorities than whites, whereas the capital-gains tax rate, which is levied on the sales of stocks, yachts, and such, affects Caucasians more so than people of color. The same is true of the estate tax, due to the fact that most rich people are white. This issue is not as cut-and-dried as it used to be, due to the growing presence of the black upper class, which now includes a number of centimillionaires in its ranks.[61] In 2000 Viacom's purchase of Black Entertainment Television (BET) made Robert Johnson, BET's founder, the first black billionaire in American history.[62] As more people of color achieve great success in America, it will become increasingly difficult to analyze the nation's tax structure in racial and ethnic terms.

The government's appropriation of our tax dollars, including the allocation of federal funds among the respective states, is another fiscal matter with racial connotations. The biggest items in the federal budget are Social Security; national defense; income security; net interest on the debt; Medicare; health; education, training, employment, and social services; veterans benefits and services; and transportation.[63] Medicaid, for instance, disproportionately benefits minorities.[64] And people of color comprise the majority of food-stamp recipients; whites constitute 40.1% of this group, while blacks account for 36.3%, Hispanics 18.3%, Asians 3.0%, and American Indians 1.6%.[65] In any event, significant tax cuts or major new social programs appear unlikely at this point.

Indeed, there are limits to what the federal government — or any state or local government, for that matter — can do to correct social inequities. For example, 38.7 million Americans, or 14.0% of the U.S. population, had no health insurance coverage in 2000. This group includes disproportionate numbers of blacks, Hispanics, and Asian Americans.[66] The poor have Medicaid, and affluent Americans are covered by private carriers, so it is the working poor, lower-middle-class, and some middle-class Americans who have to skimp on this crucial human necessity and coveted fringe benefit, which ranks with food and shelter in importance. The present fiscal and political climate in the United States is such that we will not have universal health care for some time, if at all. Most American voters have insurance coverage, so the issue is of little importance to them; and they are unwilling to pay higher taxes to fund universal care. This fiscal frugality affects nearly every social-welfare issue.

In the private sector, there are numerous efforts that fill social needs — in place of government spending. Some are run by churches, while others are nonsectarian. Some are funded by wealthy conservatives, while others receive grants from foundations and local, state, or federal governments. As a rule, white Americans donate slightly more of their household income (in percentage terms) than blacks and Hispanics to charity.[67] This modest differential may reflect the fact that African-American and Latino households tend to have less disposable income, on average, than their white counterparts, so they do not make as many formal donations to charitable causes. When it comes to volunteering one's time, the evidence is mixed. In 1997, 43% of American adults answered affirmatively in response to a question about whether they had participated in charity work "at least once in the prior 12 months." Only 31% of Hispanic adults reported they had done charity work, while 34% of American Indians, 41% of Asians, 44% of African Americans, and 45% of whites said they had done so.[68] (Another survey also put white rates of volunteerism higher than those of blacks and Hispanics.)[69]

Despite all the options one has in America to maximize his or her potential, millions of Americans of all races never take advantage of the opportunities available to them. Some Americans are limited by their angry paranoia, self-destructive behavior, or diminished aspirations and expectations. Such feelings of nihilism can translate into (but not excuse) dysfunctional behavior, and lead to a reluctance to participate in the white-dominated political and economic system.[70] Substance abuse is another side-effect of poverty and powerlessness. The seductive lure of alcohol tempts many American Indians on rural reservations into an enervating and self-destructive descent into despair, with domestic abuse and premature death often a result. The danger is that hopelessness becomes a self-fulfilling prophecy, or the proverbial vicious circle: Some poor Americans may not fully exert themselves in school or in the workplace, because they feel the system is stacked against them. Of course, when they do not succeed, their failures confirm their own suspicions as well as reinforce outsiders' negative stereotypes about them.

These feelings of alienation and estrangement affect the belief systems of some Americans. It is not uncommon for people of color, particularly blacks, to embrace conspiracy theories that ostensibly explain how white racists prevent minorities from getting ahead in America.[71] Another manifestation of this distrustful impulse is jury nullification, which basically means that predominantly black juries set African-American defendants free, not out of a conviction of their innocence, but, rather, a desire to send a "message" to white people.[72] The phenomenon of black rage is interesting in this regard. This, basically, is the notion that some blacks get so angry over America's mistreatment of African Americans in the past — and, to them, at least, in the present — that they go around in a state of continual anger.[73] Black rage has surfaced as a legal defense in a number of criminal trials of African-American defendants.[74] Not surprisingly, this viewpoint is not embraced by everyone.

Some minority students distrust white society, so they denigrate their academically successful peers for "acting white" by getting good grades and attending school regularly. There are other reasons besides peer pressure to explain academic underperformance by people of color, like teachers who expect less from them and parents who have no time to badger recalcitrant youths about their schoolwork.[75] Anecdotal evidence, primarily from top-notch Shaker Heights High School in Shaker Heights, Ohio, an integrated, upper-middle-class community in suburban Cleveland, shows that these self-defeating pathways to loserdom persist even in enclaves of prosperous blacks.[76] White youths, to be sure, often denigrate their high-achieving classmates. Caucasians frequently let their intellectually precocious coethnics know they will not be popular with their peers if they appear too smart. However, the social pressures not to succeed appear to be strongest in certain predominantly black and Latino inner-city schools.

For blacks, these kinds of taunts and self-defeating conundrums nevertheless continue into adulthood. The psychologist Claude M. Steele, working in tandem with a number of his colleagues, has found that black college students may be disconcerted by the stereotypes they think nonblack students hold about their credentials and qualifications. This "stereotype threat" can affect their academic performance negatively, if and when it becomes a self-fulfilling prophecy.[77] After college, some successful African Americans from low-income families feel "survivor's guilt" about their achievements, which make them part of the white professional world, but result in their being considered "sellouts" (to white people) by envious coethnics.[78]

Many African Americans continue to believe that racism and discrimination are significant barriers to their advancement in the United States.[79] Hendrik Hertzberg writes, "I have yet to meet a well-informed, unbigoted black American who would not firmly endorse the following statement: If you're black, you have to be twice as good to travel the same socioeconomic distance as a white person in this country — twice as talented, twice as ambitious, twice as determined."[80] Black professionals also complain that white people expect less of them than their Caucasian counterparts. Stephen Carter describes this phenomenon as "the best black syndrome," whereby whites are astonished by an African American's competence, talent, and, of course, "articulate" speaking style.[81] To prosper in the mainstream world, many African Americans practice what David K. Shipler refers to as "black biculturalism," meaning that they successfully circumnavigate around the shoals of racial difference, altering their music, attire, body language, and style of speaking depending on whether the context is primarily black or predominantly white.[82]

It is difficult, of course, to determine how the emerging class of the black megarich — and its nascent social and political clout — will affect the future of American society. At the very least, the successes of these highly creative, resourceful, indefatigable individuals (and their middle-class and upper-middle-class coethnics) demonstrate that America is now a society where everyone has a reasonable chance to make it. Except for some African despots, the richest black people in the world are Americans. These developments contribute to social stability and indicate that the United States is no longer squandering a valuable part of its human capital, as it did during the Jim Crow era.

GROWING PAINS

During the 1990s Arizona's school-funding formula exacerbated ethnic and generational divisions in the Dysart Unified School District in northwest suburban Phoenix.[83] Under Arizona law, the state provides the same amount of money for every Arizona student. Therefore, Dysart, like any other school district in Arizona, has to pass an override election whenever it wants to raise more money to enhance its programs. Back in the mid-1990s, Dysart was a poor, heavily Hispanic district with a reputation for fiscal mismanagement, low test scores, and political feuding. The district's financially precarious situation resulted in overcrowded classes, low teacher salaries, and limited extracurricular activities.[84]

In the mid-1990s and late 1990s, the Anglo retirees who comprised a major part of the Dysart electorate consistently refused to support bonds or overrides to raise their property taxes to benefit the district's schools. Retirees from the Sun City West expansion area gained control of the school board in November 1997. At the same time there was a burgeoning movement to deannex four retirement communities from the school district.[85] During this tumultuous period, in mid-1998, Dr. Margo Olivares-Seck became superintendent of the Dysart Unified School District. Olivares-Seck quickly implemented a top-down management model — among other reforms, she initiated a leadership shakeup at every school in the district — that rankled some parents and community activists. Furthermore, the district, under Olivares-Seck's stewardship, restored its reputation for fiscal responsibility.[86]

These efforts did not go unnoticed in the retirement communities, where the residents applauded Olivares-Seck's approach to budgetary matters as well as her attempts to involve them in the district's affairs.[87] Not coincidentally, in May 2000 the Dysart electorate voted by a two-to-one margin to approve a budget override that would allow an eight percent property tax increase. With the extra funds, the district reduced class size, increased teacher pay, recruited more teachers, and offered more extracurricular activities.[88]

No single factor completely explains the astonishing turnaround, but Olivares-Seck's leadership, the educators' focus on accountability and results, the pro-student tilt of the local political elite, and the changing makeup of the district's electorate (lots of young families and Baby Boomer retirees) all shape the new political landscape. And as Dysart's student population swells due to in-migration, the percentage of Anglo youths keeps increasing each year.[89] The acrimony of 1997 and 1998 is history now. A majority of the school board now supports the district, and no one mentions deannexation anymore. Some retirees still grumble about the schools and vote accordingly, but they are outnumbered by voters who do not reflexively oppose increased funding for Dysart. If the educators, the school board, the local political leadership, and the parents and retirees continue to work together, the Dysart Unified School District will never again be riven by significant ethnic and generational conflicts.[90]

Indeed, the United States is a generationally stratified society. Age correlates with race: The older the generational cohort, the whiter its members. Conversely, the younger the cohort, the higher its percentage of nonwhite faces. According to the Census Bureau, America's under-18 population is 64.6% white, 15.8% Hispanic, 14.5% black, 4.1% Asian and Pacific Islander, and 1.0% American Indian. Our 65-and-older population is 83.9% white, 8.1% black, 5.3% Hispanic, 2.2% Asian and Pacific Islander, and 0.4% American Indian (the totals do not add to 100 because of rounding). The varying median ages of the ethno-racial groups — whites (38.1), Asians (32.0), blacks (30.3), American Indians (28.2), and Latinos (26.5) — also give us an idea of how age and race intersect for the people in each ethno-racial category.[91] The age gap is fueled by the fact that immigrants and people of color tend to have larger families than whites. In addition, many immigrants are younger, on average, than native-born Americans. Differing life expectancy rates also contribute to the generational stratification of American society.

Elderly Americans accounted for 12.4% of the American population in 2000; this percentage is projected to increase to 13.2% by 2010, 18.5% in 2025, and 20.3% in 2050.[92] Members of America's fabled Baby Boom generation, who were born between 1946 and 1964, will begin contributing to the growth of the elderly population in nine years. The Baby Boomers continue to be a major generational force. Boomers dominate politics, entertainment, Corporate America, and almost every other important sector of U.S. society. The first Boomers, who were born in the early years of postwar prosperity, will become senior citizens in 2011. This cohort includes nine million African Americans, whose views about social issues and the aging process differ, to some extent, from those of their white counterparts.[93] Many of these individuals, who learned to read with Dick and Jane, will live to see the day when a majority of America's schoolchildren are people of color.

In recent years, policymakers have increasingly concluded that the root causes of many social problems can be traced back to the experiences a young person has in early childhood. Some parents, even those with the best intentions, do not have the time, the financial resources, and/or the educational training to provide the requisite enrichment opportunities for their young children. Consequently, there has been an increase in government spending on initiatives that promote early childhood learning.[94] These efforts supplement the offerings of Head Start, a program created in 1965 as part of the Great Society. The Head Start program attempts to prepare low-income children, those in the three-to-five age group, for school. In 1998 Head Start received federal funding of more than $4.3 billion and served 822,000 children, the majority of whom were four-year-olds. The service population of Head Start in 1998 was 36% black, 32% white, 26% Hispanic, 3% American Indian, and 3% Asian American.[95]

Publicly funded pre-kindergarten programs are taking off nationwide, in an effort to ensure that American students develop into happy, productive, well-adjusted adults. The nation's most expansive pre-kindergarten program for four-year-olds is in Georgia, where proceeds from the state lottery go to help young people.[96] Policymakers increasingly feel that this type of pre-emptive spending is worthwhile, to avoid the costs of prisons, teen pregnancies, juvenile delinquency, and poor educational results decades later.[97] In other words, children will have a better shot at developing their potential, and the taxpayers will have a lighter load to bear.

The United States offers every one of its residents a basic public education. Public schools provide children with education from kindergarten through twelfth grade, with the only cost being minimal fees each year. After high school, American students have a wide array of options, from inexpensive community and technical colleges to some of the world's best institutions of higher learning. Education is an important leveler for Americans because it gives them unparalleled opportunities for social mobility. Although every American child is legally able to obtain a free K-12 public education, the student expenditures per capita vary dramatically from school district to school district. Most funding for education still comes from local property taxes. Wealthier communities, not surprisingly, have better-funded schools than poorer ones. Students in districts with low student expenditures per capita confront overcrowded classes, limited course offerings, diminished extracurricular activities, and smaller, dingier facilities.[98]

Efforts to achieve any kind of equalization of public-school funding among districts through such measures as revenue sharing inspire contentious debates about fairness, and sometimes degenerate into class warfare.[99] Due to the correlation between race and income, public schools with lower student expenditures per capita usually are in predominantly black, Hispanic, or American Indian areas.[100] In any event, most public schools utilize "tracking," or ability grouping, in structuring their curricula. Tracking remains a controversial method of sorting students. Poor children of all races and non-Asian minority youths are overrepresented in basic classes, instead of regular or advanced ones, where they may be deprived of the intellectual stimuli found in mixed classrooms.[101] These factors indicate that social class continues to play a significant role in determining our life chances.

The divide between public and private schools suffuses the American educational system, and it takes on racial overtones as well. Whites comprise 77.4% of all students enrolled in public schools, from nursery school through college, but they constitute 83.9% of the students in private schools.[102] Public schools have a disproportionate number of minority students because many white parents send their children to private and parochial schools, on the grounds that such schools provide students with a safer environment, more personalized attention, and less peer pressure to engage in antisocial behavior.

There are numerous educational options for parents who wish to explore alternatives to public education. Charter schools, which enrolled 0.8% of public school students in 1998–99 (252,009 students in 27 states), have proven to be another alternative to the traditional public school education. Most charter schools do not differ markedly in their racial makeup from the local public schools.[103] At least one million American youths go to school at home; the homeschooling movement encompasses a tremendous amount of religious and ideological diversity.[104] Vouchers, meanwhile, enable tens of thousands of American children to use public money or funding from wealthy donors to attend private and parochial schools. (Public money is, or has been, used for this purpose in Florida, Cleveland, and Milwaukee.)[105] School choice allows students to choose the public school they want to attend, instead of being guided by geography or judicial edicts that mandate busing for racial balance. Due to the number of students who fail to prosper in traditional educational environments, parents and educators will almost certainly continue to seek alternatives to public education in the coming years.

These debates involve so much passion because there is a clear link between educational attainment and income, although this depends on the quality of the school, the student's course of study there, and, of course, his or her grades. With few exceptions, the more education one has, the better his or her earning capabilities. People with professional degrees, not surprisingly, earn the most, followed by those with doctorates, master's degrees, bachelor's degrees, associate degree holders, people who attended some college without getting a degree, high school graduates, people who attended high school but did not graduate, and, finally, those who have less than a ninth-grade education. By way of example, the median income of a person with a bachelor's degree was $62,188 in 1998, compared to $34,373 for a high school graduate, and a mere $16,154 for someone who did not complete ninth grade.[106]

Males as a group — and white males in particular — have traditionally gained the most financial benefits as a result of their educational credentials.[107] Furthermore, families where the householder has a college degree have a mean net worth more than twice that of those with some college, three times that of those with only a high school diploma, and a whopping seven times that of those who have no high school diploma.[108] High school graduation rates are roughly equal for younger blacks and whites, but parity is long off in terms of their rates of college completion. Slightly more than one-quarter of Americans 25 and older have completed four years of college: Whites have higher college completion rates than blacks and Hispanics, but theirs are far lower than those of Asian Americans.[109] Such figures help explain the income and wealth gaps that cleave along ethnic lines.

To help fund their universities, many states try to attract retirees, in part because their disposable incomes create more jobs and sustain economic prosperity. But seniors also have other salutary attributes and qualities, like their quietness, lack of crime, propensity toward volunteerism, and absence of school-age children. And they contribute little to traffic congestion or to air pollution, due to their limited driving habits. There are disadvantages as well, especially if poorer retirees spend down their resources and have to rely on state funding for health-related problems. This happens in Florida, where 17.6% of the residents are 65 and older, and a racially diverse population of youngsters is filling the state's public schools.[110]

In a number of states, seniors form communities based on the common threads of age, class, and interests. Retirees to Florida might live in a huge condominium development with others who come from the Northeast. Retirees to Arizona might live in a suburban-style ranch home in one of the giant planned communities in metropolitan Phoenix. The elderly in these areas are not hostile to children — they love their grandchildren dearly, but they usually interact little with them, or other children, for that matter. Since the elderly subsist on fixed incomes, they can be skeptical about initiatives that cost them more in taxes. Elderly whites vote in greater numbers than members of other racial groups. They frequently support age-specific measures at the expense of new schools, parks, and other improvements that primarily benefit younger persons — and are needed to preserve social order and develop human capital. The racialization of age-related issues provides the basis for yet another fault line in American society.[111]

Demographic pressures are most acute in states and localities with higher-than-average numbers of elderly whites *and* youthful nonwhites. Nowhere is this more evident than in the popular retirement spots, such as Florida, California, and Arizona.[112] And on the national scene, Medicare and Social Security have racial significance — for a number of reasons. People of color make up an increasingly significant percentage of those who are supporting such programs, just as their numbers of beneficiaries go up, too. Since blacks, Hispanics, and American Indians make less money, on average, than your typical whites and Asian Americans, they have fewer assets, smaller pensions, and receive fewer benefits from Social Security. Since whites, particularly white females, live longer than members of other racial groups, they get more of a payoff from income security programs like Social Security than their minority counterparts.[113] These factors also explain why whites, on average, have more retirement income in the form of savings and pensions than people of color, with the possible exception of native-born Asian Americans.[114]

As these dynamics receive wider attention, and minorities continue to make up an ever-greater percentage of the taxpaying public, younger people of color might start asking the age-old political question — *What's in it for us?* — that usually leads to the birth of social movements and the enactment of dramatic political reforms. Thus we may be headed for heightened age-race conflicts in areas with large numbers of elderly whites and youthful nonwhites, at least where finite resources exist for use in the public sector.[115]

In any event, demographers project that the aging of America has the potential to affect dramatically the future economic and political course of the nation. Some potential side-effects of the generational shift may benefit all of us. Crime rates may drop, particularly in states with large percentages of elderly people and correspondingly small percentages of youths. America, at least among the elderly, could become a matriarchy, since women have longer life-expectancy rates (seven years, on average) than men. Moreover, the opportunities for entrepreneurs in economic sectors that appeal to the elderly — luxury cars, funeral parlors, health care, condominium development, pharmaceutical sales — will almost certainly increase.[116] Barring more babies or more immigrants, the aforementioned developments are inexorable ones. And it is entirely possible that life expectancy rates will soar — and exacerbate the impending age-related imbroglio even more.

Thirty years from now, seniors will account for nearly one in five Americans, up from one in eight today. Within 40 years the elderly may constitute one-third of the American electorate, nearly twice their proportion in the 1990s. These demographic shifts raise the specter of white elders agitating for enhanced program benefits, while nonwhite taxpayers resist or even oppose these advocacy efforts, because they face higher taxes to finance the nation's income security programs, even as the eligibility requirements governing *their* eventual collection of benefits become more restrictive.[117] These tensions will become especially pronounced in 2015 and beyond, as the United States approaches the point when the elderly will outnumber youths under 15, a milestone that has already been reached in several European nations.

There is hope on the horizon, however, and much of it centers around the efforts of policymakers to create alternatives to the increasingly expensive costs of higher education. Indeed, the cost of a college or university education at most institutions of higher learning continues to outpace the rate of inflation — a development that threatens to exclude many prospective students.[118] Educators will try to accommodate the rising number of college students, in an era of limited funding for public education, as the Baby Boomers' reproductive riches head for the nation's campuses over the next 15 years.

There are some fiscally responsible models that point to how we can aid students in their efforts to get a college education. After completing a K-12 education in Georgia, for instance, students are able to take advantage of a program financed by the lottery — the HOPE (Helping Outstanding Pupils Educationally) Scholarships. The program allows each Georgian to earn a college degree (for free) at any of the state's institutions of higher education, provided s/he makes a B average in high school and maintains that level of scholastic standing throughout college. More than 500,000 Georgians have benefited from the HOPE Scholarships, which are open to all who qualify — regardless of their race, gender, or social class.[119] Other states are trying this approach: The Bright Futures program in Florida imitates Georgia's HOPE Scholarships.[120] More recently, West Virginia started offering its students PROMISE (Providing Real Opportunities for Maximizing In-state Student Excellence) scholarships.[121] The spirit of such reforms is trendy now, as people in the public and private sectors work together to create greater educational opportunities for the poor and middle class.

A number of demographic distinctions — chief among them race and cohort — are going to play havoc with the predictions that can be made about the impact of aging on America's future. First of all, by the time the Baby Boomers begin to retire in 2011, the elderly population will be more ethnically diverse than it is today. Even though the elderly population will always be far whiter than the youngest generations of Americans, people of color should constitute a critical mass among seniors by the end of this decade. The extent to which they become involved in the advocacy organizations remains to be seen. While there are a number of issues that bind our elders together, it is possible that the minority aged may pursue a slightly different agenda, one with less stridency, which might head off some of the potential age-related ethnic conflicts that could develop.[122]

Against this backdrop, another factor will come into play: the increasing significance of one's generational cohort among the elderly in determining one's positions on age-related issues. Demographers traditionally have made distinctions among the elderly population, such as between the "young old" (ages 65 to 69) and the "old old" (ages 85 and older).[123] These points of demarcation will matter even more as the Baby Boomers begin to reach retirement. They were socialized differently than the Greatest Generation and the children of the Depression Era, so there is no telling how they might vote on age- and race-related equity issues. It is entirely possible that they will be more inclined to support the construction of new schools, parks, playgrounds, and other capital improvements that primarily benefit young people.

Scientific advances continue to provide us with greater foreknowledge to predict our genetic futures — and to protect ourselves from ill health and the infirmities of old age. At the same time, there are growing fears that the use of genetic profiling and ever-more sophisticated genetic tests might result in the misuse of this information, and in genetic discrimination or genetic redlining. This artificial prescience can be emotionally unsettling and financially damaging for those who are at risk for, or diagnosed as having, an inherited disease.[124]

Not surprisingly, biotechnology companies, drug manufacturers, and health and life insurance companies covet this information. Insurers charge high-risk clients more for coverage, or even exclude them entirely from the pool of healthy Americans.[125] In the coming years, with the development of expensive new drugs and procedures that will prolong — and improve the quality of — our lives, health insurance companies will almost certainly clash with the public over what should, and should not, be covered by their policies.

Money, of course, plays a very important role in our health care system. Throughout our nation's history, race and class have affected the quality of care available to people, and this is not likely to change in the future.[126] Still, there have been some advances in a number of different fields. For example, minority advocates have made significant progress in expanding the reach of medical test studies, so that more is known about how to treat women and minorities for their ailments.[127] Yet the nation's socioeconomic divide will take on added significance in future policy discussions regarding race and health care. In the coming decades, one's financial situation may dictate whether s/he has access to the cornucopia of medical advances that will be available to Americans, so that one can live longer and with fewer health problems.

The end result of these biotechnological advances might be Nietzschean superpeople, who possess no discernible mental or physical imperfections. Wealthy Americans are already able to purchase body parts, like corneas or livers, from people in poor countries.[128] In the future, affluent parents might use embryo screening and prenatal genetic testing to select the attributes — height, weight, gender, intelligence, skin tone — they want in their children.[129] New hierarchies, based on who has access to these biomedical benefits, could develop.[130] These hierarchies might stratify our society even further.

Consequently, the development of a comprehensive system of laws, ethics, and morality governing biomedical issues will become increasingly important to Americans, during what numerous observers are already predicting will be "the biotech century."[131] The most pressing issue of the new era is how to distribute scarce resources in health-care management. These decisions involve extraordinarily thorny questions about our intrinsic worth — and considerations of how we have lived our lives. In other words, should a dissolute 35-year-old substance abuser receive priority billing for a spare liver, ahead of a clean-living, 57-year-old grandmother? Should multimillionaires be given preference over custodians, if access to a particular type of medical technology is solely an issue of money?

Americans are an egalitarian people, and therefore we find these kinds of questions to be profoundly troubling. Race is largely absent from these discussions, but if there proves to be a socioeconomic basis for access to critical services, and the costs are such that some are excluded on the basis of their financial situation, the existing divide in terms of race and wealth and income could affect these dynamics. Medical ethicists, policymakers, and scientists face the difficult task of coming up with equitable, as well as politically feasible, solutions to these intractable dilemmas.

During this century, we, as a society, will ask — and answer — such questions with increasing frequency. Accordingly, we may see some kind of universal health coverage during the next century. Or, in an atmosphere of tight budgets, spiraling health-care costs, and disgruntled, overburdened youthful taxpayers, Americans might not be discouraged from choosing euthanasia or assisted suicide, if they have spent all their funds and cannot care for themselves. Such issues rarely, if ever, assume racial dimensions in contemporary public-policy debates and discussions.

However, this is set to change, due to the rapidly aging population — and the continuing socioeconomic disparities between, among, and within races. It is impossible to determine how, exactly, this will play out, but the Boomers as a group will probably be more sensitive to the ethnic dimensions of these issues for a couple of reasons. For one, there are more minorities in the Baby Boom generation than in the present group of elderly. Moreover, the Boomers have different sensibilities about race than many of their elders. They are the first generation of Americans for whom race, at least at the national level, has been a topic of concern throughout their lives (the oldest Boomers were only eight when the Supreme Court outlawed segregated schools in *Brown v. Board of Education*). To be sure, the growing clout of minority voters will also make policymakers take notice of any age-related ethnic disparities that may arise in the future.

chapter five

The Geography of Race

South Philadelphia is one of the most fabled ethnic enclaves in the United States, and the Italian Market continues to be the social center and premier tourist attraction of that neighborhood. Seventy-eight years after the mass immigration from Italy subsided, Philadelphia's resident Italians still support this bustling, multiblock shopping area of several dozen indoor stores and outdoor stalls along 9th Street between Christian Street and Washington Avenue. This must-see stop for students of Italian Americana dates back to the late nineteenth century, when poor, underemployed immigrants from Sicily, Campania, Calabria, Basilicata, and elsewhere in Italy began leaving the land of Dante and da Vinci for jobs in America.

What began as an immigrant ghetto has evolved, metamorphosed, and gentrified into the present-day cornucopia of sights, sounds, and smells. Travel writers and tourists often rhapsodize about the Italian Market's colorful quaintness and its quasi-foreign feel, but this shopping district, though not an outdoor ethnic museum yet, is slowly becoming more American than Italian. Most shoppers and vendors, including the Italian Americans, communicate in English. At one time Italian immigrants and their offspring predominated among the throngs of people who crowd the sidewalks, but the shoppers today range from affluent professionals to elderly men and women whose clothing and mannerisms would allow them to pass for natives in Bari, Messina, or Catanzaro.

Ironically the tremendous economic success of Italian Americans as a group threatens to diminish the Italian character of Il Mercato Italiano. Dozens of stores have gone out of business in the past two decades because there were no family members willing to work in the shop or stall after the proprietor died or retired. The descendants of the bakers, butchers, and restaurateurs now heal sick people, interpret the intricacies of legal matters, and manage corporate enterprises with budgets that exceed the entire yearly revenues of all the shops in the Italian Market. Many vendors, especially those who sell fruits and vegetables or cheap clothing and knickknacks, are Asian; moreover, some African Americans work in the Italian shops.

Meanwhile, the growing Asian population in South Philadelphia promises to revitalize — and perhaps change the nature of — the Italian Market. The area is now home to an expanding population of Chinese, Cambodian, and Vietnamese immigrants. A few blocks away from Fante's, Claudio's, and DiBruno's, a mainly Asian strip mall caters to the neighborhood's latest crop of newcomers. In fact, it is only a matter of time before the Italian Market gives way to an Italian-Asian fusion shopping area — at least that is what appeared to be happening when I visited South Philadelphia in August 2000 and July 2001. Some Italian shops will undoubtedly remain there for many years, even if Asians eventually predominate in the neighborhood. The Italian character of South Philadelphia is too deep and too rooted to disappear anytime soon.

Americans of Italian descent continue to affect the cultural, economic, and political affairs of the City of Brotherly Love, which was once governed by a fellow with the unmistakably Italian-American name of Frank Rizzo. All around Philadelphia and its suburbs, one sees the familiar signs of Mediterranean heritage — black hair, dark brown eyes, olive skin. South Philadelphia, in particular, remains one of the most Italian parts of America. Almost every block seems to have a stand selling *gelato*. Murals of legendary Italian-American recording artists such as Mario Lanza and Frank Sinatra adorn buildings. And there are dozens of Italian-surnamed lawyers, doctors, dentists, realtors, optometrists, and travel agents.

But the assimilation process has proceeded remarkably well. Few native-born Philadelphians under age 50 speak Italian. Moreover, most Italian Americans in the Philadelphia area marry outside their ethnic group, although there are enough full-blooded Italians to ensure that endogamous marriages sometimes occur by happenstance. The typical South Philly teenager or twentysomething with an Italian surname such as Ricci, Gallo, Ferrara, Lombardi, or Giordano does not play bocce, attend Italian-language services at the local Catholic church, or purchase the Italian magazines and newspapers available at local specialty shops.

Although young Italian-American Philadelphians identify with their Italian roots, their ties to Italy are usually tenuous at best. If you ask them about their ethnic heritage, they will proudly reply "Italian," even though people in Italy would see them as American. They probably have never visited Italy, or have gone there only once or twice. They do not maintain close contact with relatives in the old country. And if they earn a college degree, it is highly probable that they will never live in what ethnics often fondly refer to as the old neighborhood. Elderly Italian Americans may fly the red-white-and-green banner of Italy and attend meetings at the Sons of Italy lodge or Italian-American Club, but their offspring largely disdain such shows of ethnic pride and are reluctant participants in fraternal organizations.

Italian Americans in South Philadelphia, as elsewhere, increasingly identify as white first and Italian second. When the Italians first came to Philadelphia, they identified solely as Italians. For the first-generation immigrants, being Italian was simultaneously an ethnic identity and a national identity. Their race was taken for granted: Everyone, even the darkest Mediterranean Italians, was considered white by Philadelphians. As the American-born children and grandchildren of the immigrants entered the mainstream, however, they often married whites from other ethnic groups. These intermarriages, along with the inexorable passage of time, erased interethnic boundaries. And in recent years, the Italian Americans have lived in close proximity to a large African-American population, a demographic fact that has promoted dichotomous black/white thinking. In this respect, the geography of race in South Philadelphia resembles that of most urban areas in the Midwest and Northeast.

RACE AND PLACE

From 1962 to 2000, three flags — the Stars and the Stripes, the navy-blue South Carolina banner, and the Confederate battle flag — flew atop the Statehouse dome in Columbia, South Carolina.[1] But only one of these banners brought thousands of marchers and protesters to Columbia, inspired impassioned discussions between and among neighbors, sparked a boycott by the NAACP that has cost the Palmetto State millions in tourist dollars, and generated debate that dominated the political discourse in South Carolina for much of the 1990s. It was the third flag on the pole, known colloquially as the Stars and Bars, with its blue stripes and white stars against a red background, that aroused virulent controversy.

The Confederate battle flag was hoisted to its rarefied perch in 1962 by white legislators, who were infuriated by integration and the advances of the civil rights movement. Today the white South Carolinians who endorse the Confederate totems defend them on the grounds of regional pride and heritage preservation. Black South Carolinians, like African Americans around the country, view the flag as an affront to their dignity and a contemporary symbol of hate. After months of heated discussion in 1999 and 2000, South Carolina's legislators concluded that the flag was giving their state a bad reputation, so they voted to lower it. The flag came down on July 1, 2000, and it was relegated to the Confederate Soldier's Memorial in front of the Capitol. This compromise did not satisfy the NAACP, which was angered that the Confederate battle flag still received official sanction on state property in South Carolina. Conversely, flag supporters throughout the South bitterly denounced the decision as a betrayal.[2]

The fight over Confederate symbols has heated up in recent years. For the most part, opponents of the flag have succeeded in community after community in their efforts to banish Confederate iconography from such places as public schools and government buildings. The antiflag movement triumphed in neighboring Georgia in January 2001. Between 1956 and 2001 the state flag there incorporated a St. Andrew's cross that took up two-thirds of the banner. The Peach State's new flag features the Great Seal of Georgia and includes a banner of the five flags from the state's history.[3] Likewise, in Mississippi, where the state banner has incorporated the Confederate battle flag since 1894, the state electorate voted to keep the present banner by a 65%-35% margin in a referendum in April 2001. The flag-is-bad-for-business argument did not sway Mississippians. White residents of the Magnolia State strongly support the flag, while their black counterparts oppose it, but do not assign much importance to the issue.[4]

Throughout America, but especially in the Deep South, the Stars and Bars is emblazoned on caps, decals, T-shirts, tattoos, belt buckles, jacket patches, truck grilles, bumper stickers, and license plates. Although Confederate iconography, from statuary to the song "Dixie" to team names and mascots, is now politically incorrect, millions of white Southerners refuse to abandon the symbols they cherish so deeply.[5] These symbols seem to be especially popular with young white men, who delight in expressing their Southern pride in this way. They do not particularly care if white outsiders and their African-American neighbors regard the Confederate battle flag as a symbol that is synonymous with racial intolerance to many people of color — and Caucasians, for that matter. All the hubbub over these Confederate symbols undoubtedly strengthens their resolve to defend them.

These debates, of course, involve considerations of race and place. Our sense of place, or where we are from, is about who we are — and who we are not.[6] Indeed, the character of a place is fundamentally shaped by its original settlers. The demographics and social dynamics remain largely unchanged for decades, even centuries, in areas with few immigrants and little domestic in-migration. Regional differences remain astonishingly persistent. The tremendous ethnic heterogeneity of America is perhaps the most salient indicator of our nation's regional differences, followed by the regional accents that still typify American English. A simple way to experience the ethnic and cultural diversity of America is to drive coast to coast on an interstate highway, such as Interstate 90, which links Boston to Seattle, and get off at an exit every 100 miles or so.

Nonetheless, there are powerful homogenizing forces at work, chief among them national television and the interstate highway system. The first standardized speech patterns and the second contributed to the growth of the cookie-cutter franchises (Holiday Inn, Motel 6, Burger King, Wal-Mart, The Home Depot) that dot America.[7] The lodging, entertainment, and shopping options in Syracuse are not markedly different from those in Sioux Falls. Regardless of the ethnic character of an area, civic boosters around the United States celebrate their communities based on factors such as climate, industry, natural wonders, sports teams, art museums, theatrical groups, colleges and universities, and famous sons and daughters. The cultural and economic geography of many American towns, cities, and metropolitan areas is structured by race and socioeconomic class. When Americans discuss residential living patterns, we rarely mention race because place names and geographical descriptions (e.g., downtown, the South Side) have commonly understood meanings.

For whites, blacks, and every other racial group, homeownership is the cornerstone of the American Dream. Real estate is an important component of the typical American's financial portfolio. Neighborhoods with high rates of homeownership are usually stable. The residents assiduously maintain their properties and are vigilant about crime and anything else that threatens their safety and the upward spiral of their property values. More than two-thirds (67.4%) of Americans owned their homes in 2000. The white rate of homeownership was 73.8%, while the minority homeownership rates were considerably lower, but rising each year (47.2% for blacks, 46.3% for Hispanics, 52.8% for Asians and Pacific Islanders, and 56.2% for American Indians).[8]

Sometimes American communities embrace secession as a means of attracting attention, or in order to get out of being part of an urban entity because of high taxes and unfair resource allocation. For years the San Fernando Valley of Los Angeles, which is home to approximately 40% of Angelenos, has been the hotbed of a secession movement.[9] At one time, Staten Islanders favored secession, but many of their grievances were addressed by New York's political leadership, so the issue seems to have disappeared from the public discourse. Secession movements rarely succeed, but they do focus attention on the grievances of those people whose dissatisfaction prompted the activism in the first place.

The United States continues to be a de facto segregated nation. It is a cliché, albeit an accurate one, that the most segregated hour of the week is 11:00 a.m. Sunday morning in church.[10] The cultural sphere is surely almost as segregated as the religious one, when it comes to our tastes in music, movies, books, cyberspace, television, and other forms of entertainment. Few American adults have genuinely integrated groups of friends, apart from work. And there are not many public spaces and facilities, such as buses, parks, schools, and libraries, that everyone uses on a regular basis.[11] Moreover, the paucity of public bus, train, and subway routes between cities and suburbs restricts the movement of low-income people and preserves the socioeconomic homogeneity of the suburbs.[12] In the most extreme cases, de facto segregation is enforced by glares, epithets, and attacks, including cross burnings. As a rule, Americans endorse integration in theory but a variety of factors, ranging from cultural comfort levels to residential living patterns, prevent us from becoming a genuinely integrated society at every level.

The most segregated parts of America tend to be cities in the urban Midwest and South, those in which the population profile still remains starkly black and white. Hispanics appear to be hyper-segregated in a number of American cities; many Latin American immigrants live in ethnic enclaves while they become acclimated to American life.[13] Naturally, affluent minorities and ethnic and racial groups with few members in a given area, who pose no threat to the dominant group, generally reside in integrated neighborhoods. African Americans, of all the minority groups, live in the greatest segregation. The high rates of black residential isolation reflect, to some extent, past injustices, such as the restrictive covenants that prevented them from buying certain homes, and the redlining that made it difficult for them to obtain home loans. Liberals argue that blacks face more racial animosity than any other nonwhite group; some Americans simply refuse to live near them.[14] To be sure, ethnically heterogeneous communities with stable population dynamics and property values, like Oak Park, Illinois, do exist.

Still, America's public schools are resegregating, especially for poor urban black and Latino students, despite a quarter-century of mandatory busing to achieve desegregation. Because public schools draw upon the local population, this development reflects the paucity of native-born whites in urban America. Busing, the controversial remedy for segregation in urban and some suburban schools, continues to be unpopular with many whites and an increasingly large number of blacks, who see it as ineffective, disruptive, and unnecessary.[15] In sum, these issues demonstrate how we vote with our feet when we make choices about our social interactions and residential living patterns.

To make sense of these social and political divisions, the Census Bureau divides the United States into four regions: the Northeast, the South, the Midwest, and the West. Moreover, there are numerous sub-regional categories, which have distinct identities, such as Appalachia, the Deep South, Mountain West, New England, and the Pacific Northwest. The Census Bureau's schema defines the regions as follows:

- Northeast: Connecticut, Maine, Massachusetts, New Hampshire, New Jersey, New York, Pennsylvania, Rhode Island, and Vermont.

- South: Alabama, Arkansas, Delaware, Florida, Georgia, Kentucky, Louisiana, Maryland, Mississippi, North Carolina, Oklahoma, South Carolina, Tennessee, Texas, Virginia, West Virginia, and the District of Columbia.[16]

- Midwest: Illinois, Indiana, Iowa, Kansas, Michigan, Minnesota, Missouri, Nebraska, North Dakota, Ohio, South Dakota, and Wisconsin.

- West: Alaska, Arizona, California, Colorado, Hawaii, Idaho, Montana, Nevada, New Mexico, Oregon, Utah, Washington, and Wyoming.

In any event, the burgeoning Sun Belt continues to be the economic and political powerhouse of the United States. The states of the South and West are especially attractive to native-born domestic migrants and immigrants alike; low taxes, well-paying jobs, a temperate climate, and quality-of-life issues lure people to the Sun Belt.[17]

America's domestic and international migrants select their destinations for many reasons, including climate, peer networks, cost of living, employment opportunities, the proximity of kinfolk and coethnics, and, for many Mexican and Caribbean immigrants, the nearness to their native land. Whites, as a group, are spread out fairly evenly among the regions. But many white subgroups continue to be concentrated in just a few places. Jews are most prominent in New York, California, and Florida. Americans of Czech heritage — a bare majority of them, anyway — remain fond of the Midwest, particularly the industrial cities. Similarly, Norwegian Americans favor the Midwest, while slightly more than one-half of Italian Americans reside in the Northeast, especially in Connecticut, Pennsylvania, Massachusetts, New York, New Jersey, and Rhode Island. Hispanics are particularly well represented in the West, largely due to the huge Latino population in California and the sizable contingents of Spanish-surnamed people in Nevada, Arizona, and New Mexico. However, Puerto Ricans mainly migrate to the Northeast and Florida, while Cubans prefer Florida and New Jersey. The typical Asian American is a Westerner, primarily because of the proximity of Asian-majority Hawaii and California (where over one-third of Asian Americans dwell) to the Pacific Rim.[18] Many members of long-standing white ethnic groups, such as Welsh Americans, are so well assimilated that they feel comfortable living and working in almost any part of America.

For recent immigrants, ethnic enclaves serve as protective cocoons of family, friends, and peer networks. The newest Americans enjoy living among their coethnics, who help them negotiate the cumbersome ins-and-outs of American life, which can be daunting for people who lack financial resources and the ability to speak English. Ethnic enclaves recreate the Old World in miniature, with bakeries, groceries, travel agencies, video stores, currency exchanges, and other commercial establishments that allow the immigrants to conduct their business in a culturally and linguistically congenial atmosphere. To survive and flourish, an ethnic enclave needs a steady stream of newcomers to keep the immigrant traditions alive. This is why the Chinatowns of America are flourishing, while no city has a Little Italy that rivals its counterpart of 50 years ago.

Recent immigrants have formed or revitalized ethnic enclaves throughout the United States. Little Saigon, the thriving enclave of Vietnamese in Westminster, California, is largely the creation of the refugees from South Vietnam who fled to the United States after America withdrew from Southeast Asia in 1975. Dark-skinned black Haitians — some who fled the brutal and corrupt autocracy that governed their homeland from 1957 to 1986, others who have abandoned the anarchic chaos of Haiti since then — people the Little Haitis of Miami, Delray Beach, and Flatbush. Chicago's long-established Polish-American community once again became a Mecca, in the 1990s, for immigrants from Poland, who congregate in neighborhoods on the city's Northwest Side.[19] Moving beyond the enclave is usually seen as a sign of progress by immigrants and their second-generation children, who interpret a suburban home in a vanilla community as proof that they have finally made it. Thus ethnic enclaves often fade away as their residents become overwhelmingly assimilated and middle class. Typically, the most exotic and vibrant ethnic enclaves have been found in the nation's largest cities, although there are now many ethnic enclaves in suburban America.[20]

The Northeast, more so than any other region, encompasses tremendous ethnic and racial heterogeneity. As elsewhere, the bastions of diversity are the large cities, such as Boston, Philadelphia, and New York. Each of these cities encompasses a large white population, with sizable numbers of Jews, Irish Americans, and Italian Americans, along with good-sized African-American and Latino communities. Puerto Ricans are still the dominant Hispanic subgroup in the region. Every large Northeastern city has a significant Puerto Rican community. Most cities in the region also have rapidly growing Asian populations. The New York metropolitan area is stunning in its heterogeneity. Every imaginable ethnic group in the world is represented there, including small communities of Turks, Afghans, Eritreans, and others. And, of course, there are huge contingents of Jews, Koreans, Chinese, Puerto Ricans, South Americans, Irish Americans, Italian Americans, African Americans, and black immigrants. Metro New York, with its 21.2 million people, looms large in the region, but the Northeast also includes Pennsylvania, a heterogeneous state with large swaths of rural America.

In New England, there are still bastions of old-stock Yankees, whose Anglo-Saxon Protestant forebears once made up the vast majority of Americans. This is especially true in Maine, Vermont, and New Hampshire, the three whitest states in America. Nonetheless, the traditional Yankee (remember Fred Tuttle, the Vermont farmer who had his 15 minutes of fame in 1996) is very much a minority in New England. English surnames are still common in the region, but many of those who have them are part Irish or part French Canadian, or even part Italian or part Portuguese. These four white ethnic groups make up an important part of the white population in Rhode Island, the nation's most heavily Catholic state, even though their distinctive ethnic cultures have largely vanished during the last 90 years. At one time, the Jews and white ethnic Catholics of the Northeast resented their lack of representation in the halls of power; it remains to be seen whether the black, Latino, and Asian residents of the region will achieve similar successes.

Even in the Midwest, long stereotyped by coastal sophisticates as the white-bread heartland, there is a sizable amount of diversity — and not just in the big cities. The large urban areas of the Midwest (Chicago, Detroit, Indianapolis, Milwaukee, Saint Louis, and others) are showcases of the region's ethnic and racial diversity. Conversely, many rural parts of the heartland are overwhelmingly white. Some of the whitest parts of America — northern Michigan, southern Indiana, southern Illinois, southern Missouri, southern Ohio, and much of the Great Plains, except for Indian reservations and meatpacking towns — lie in the Midwest. In ethnic terms, the Midwestern cities and suburbs include sizable numbers of Americans of Southern and Eastern European descent, while Germans, Scandinavians, and people of Anglo-Celtic origin predominate in the rural areas. To be sure, the rural white heartland has embraced a number of immigrants, particularly Mexicans and refugees from places like Bosnia. It is increasingly rare for Midwestern communities to be virtually all-white, except in such places as Upper Michigan and rural North Dakota, which lose many of their young people to out-migration because of the limited economic opportunities available to them in those areas.

Meanwhile, the West, particularly California, is home to some of the nation's best-known polyethnic communities.[21] Nearly 51% of all Westerners live in California. Most population centers in the Golden State do not reflect the ethnic dynamics that one sees elsewhere in the West, at least outside of places like Seattle, Phoenix, and Denver. For one thing, there are relatively few Asian Americans in the Mountain West. But California has cities such as Daly City (31.6% Filipino) and Monterey Park (41.2% Chinese). After all, the Bay Area and Greater Los Angeles are outranked only by the tri-state New York metropolitan area in terms of having the most ethnic, racial, religious, and socioeconomic diversity in America. Asians and Latinos constitute an ever-increasing share of the population in the Pacific Northwest, just as they do in California. Seattle and, to a lesser extent, Portland have polyethnic mixes that reflect the Pacific Northwest's demographic composition. And Alaska and Hawaii, of course, present very different versions of the West. Alaska includes people from all five parts of the ethno-racial pentagon, but the primary groups in the state are whites and Native Alaskans. Hawaii is the only state in the nation where Asians and Pacific Islanders constitute a clear majority — that is, if you count the multiracials who identify as part Asian or part Pacific Islander.[22]

The Mountain West is probably what most Americans think of when the words "West" and "Western" enter their minds. To be sure, the biggest cities in the region (Phoenix, Denver, Tucson, Las Vegas, and so on) are ethnically diverse. Fast-growing states such as Nevada, Arizona, and Colorado have large Hispanic populations. And American Indians account for a sizable part of the population in the rural expanses of the West. But there still are plenty of virtually all-white communities in the rural Mountain West.

As in the South, an old/new dichotomy is unfolding in the Mountain West, but this one has little to do with race and a lot to do with social class and competing visions of development. The debate over the future of the American West stems from the cultural conflicts between the old-timers — ranchers, loggers, miners, and others who work in extractive industries — and the newcomers, who include computer programmers, health-care professionals, and telecommuting symbolic analysts within their ranks. Traditional Westerners speak of the "War on the West," a phrase that indicates their dislike for the land-use policies of the federal regulatory agencies, including the Forest Service and the Bureau of Land Management, that oversee the vast expanses of public land in the rural West. The most acrimonious conflicts occur in Nevada, where the federal government owns 83.1% of the land, the highest percentage of any state in the nation.[23]

Meanwhile, the racial dynamics of certain parts of the South are undergoing substantial changes. Non-Southern whites began moving to the South in large numbers after World War II, for the same reasons that brought others to the Sun Belt. This influx of Yankee migrants nationalized certain parts of the South, such as the Atlanta, Charlotte, and Dallas-Fort Worth metropolitan areas, where many residents do not have Southern accents.[24] Moreover, there has been a reverse migration of African Americans back to the South, a trend that began during the 1970s. The "push" factors include the continuing presence of racial animosity in the North and the paucity of well-paying manufacturing jobs in urban areas. The "pull," meanwhile, is a dramatically improved Southern racial climate, in addition to continuing family ties and the lure of a safe, inexpensive rural or suburban environment. Today, 54.4% of African Americans live in the 16-state South and the District of Columbia.[25] Race relations, for the most part, have never been better in the South, although many Southerners socialize mainly with people from their own racial group — as do most Americans.

At the same time, an influx of Hispanics and Asians into Southern states such as Georgia, Maryland, Virginia, and North Carolina is beginning to disrupt the biracial status quo that has defined the South for over two centuries. These migrants settle in large metropolitan areas, including Greater Atlanta, Dallas-Fort Worth, and the polyglot communities of Fairfax County, Virginia, and Montgomery County, Maryland. They also go to small towns near and around poultry-processing plants in Georgia, Alabama, Arkansas, Oklahoma, and the Carolinas. As a result, the traditional black-and-white perspective on race relations in the

South, though still the dominant theme, is slowly evolving to encompass other ethno-racial groups, particularly Latinos.[26]

AT HOME IN AMERICA

The Census of 2000 counted no blacks, Hispanics, American Indians, or Pacific Islanders in Shullsburg, Wisconsin. This quaint, picturesque city in the rolling hills of rural southwestern Wisconsin is one of the whitest places in America.[27] According to the census, 1,240 of the 1,246 residents of Shullsburg are Caucasian — the town is 99.5% white. Shullsburg's minority population in 2000 included two Asian youths and four multiracial persons, only one of whom was an adult. Shullsburg remains homogeneous because there are no jobs or educational institutions to attract immigrants or domestic migrants to this sparsely populated corner of the Badger State. So the residents of the area are mainly descended from the German, Irish, English, and Swiss settlers who came to Shullsburg during the nineteenth century (the city was founded in 1827).[28]

This perfectly unremarkable community 28 miles east of Dubuque, Iowa, is characterized by a constant population — it grew by only ten people during the 1990s. All the communities in this part of southwestern Wisconsin have similar demographics. Shullsburg is the second-largest city in Lafayette County, Wisconsin, which itself is 98.7% white. This area is ethnically and, to a large extent, socioeconomically homogeneous. Most people in Shullsburg are neither rich nor poor. This homogeneity, when coupled with the low population density and the communal spirit that owes much to the agricultural influence in the area, gives Shullsburg and environs a tranquillity that residents of large cities would find idyllic and, perhaps, stifling.

Race and ethnicity are simply not issues in Shullsburg. There are few immigrants there, and most of the residents are thoroughly assimilated Euro-Americans. Diversity happens elsewhere: It is something the residents read about in magazines or see documentaries about on television. Most people in Shullsburg do not interact with ethnic or racial minorities on a regular basis. When Shullsburgers go to the grocery store in nearby Darlington or Platteville, they usually see only white faces. When they go to the Lafayette County Fair, a popular gathering spot every year, they see very few, if any, minorities. When they go to Shullsburg's Cheesefest, a hometown celebration every October, the faces of the revelers look as if they would if one were attending a festival in Bavaria, Cornwall, or County Kerry.

This is not to say that the residents of Shullsburg are hostile to minorities. A black family or a Latino couple would probably enjoy living in this close-knit heartland community. But the demographics of Shullsburg and the neighboring towns reveal the tremendous differences that characterize the racial geography of population divisions, such as cities, suburbs, and rural areas. Parts of Wisconsin are quite diverse. Milwaukee, for instance, is 45.4% white, 36.9% black, 12.0% Latino, and 2.9% Asian. But this demographic reality has little significance in Shullsburg, or in many other parts of rural Wisconsin. Yet fewer and fewer American communities resemble Shullsburg in a demographic sense.

The United States is now a predominantly urban and suburban nation. Slightly more than eight out of ten Americans (80.3% of us) live in metropolitan areas. Most Americans are accustomed to the advantages of being close to large cities — great shopping, world-class restaurants, renowned art museums, and the like — but do not necessarily want to contend with the disadvantages of urban living, such as crime, poor schools, and air pollution. When African Americans moved en masse to the large cities of the Midwest and Northeast, whites frequently decamped to the suburbs to avoid the perceived costs of the black influx. Lily-white suburbs still exist, even though African Americans, Latinos, and Asians are now an important part of contemporary suburbia, and immigrants increasingly skip the big cities and go right to the suburbs.[29]

Urban America, as a rule, encompasses tremendous ethnic, racial, and socioeconomic diversity in a compressed amount of space. Many of America's biggest cities — Chicago, Dallas, Houston, Los Angeles, and New York — fall into the polyethnic category. Phoenix is the largest city with a white majority. Atlanta, Baltimore, Detroit, Memphis, Newark, New Orleans, and the District of Columbia, among others, boast black majorities. Santa Ana, El Paso, and San Antonio, meanwhile, are the most populous Hispanic-majority cities. During the 1990s, the cities with large influxes of immigrants, such as Chicago, Houston, and New York, grew in size, while the cities with few immigrants (e.g., Detroit, Cleveland, and Milwaukee) lost population.[30] As a rule, city dwellers have a great deal of familiarity with racial, ethnic, and socioeconomic diversity, if only in a superficial sense; still, the typical urbanite experiences this heterogeneity only in passing. Some stunning examples of residential segregation exist in the suburbs and urban areas of the Midwest and South. Many whites remain wary of predominantly black urban areas, which tend to be poorer and have higher crime rates than the suburbs. African Americans, conversely, may avoid the virtually all-white suburbs because they feel unwelcome there.

The most dramatic example of residential segregation in the Midwest can be found in Detroit, Michigan, and its environs. More than eight out of ten residents of the Motor City are black, but there are predominantly white suburbs such as Livonia and Sterling Heights within 30 minutes of downtown Detroit. More surprisingly, some suburbs that border Detroit, such as Dearborn to the west and Warren to the north, have few blacks. In fact, the residential segregation in metropolitan Detroit is so pervasive that when one drives around the area, s/he can always tell when s/he has entered the city: Black people suddenly become visible everywhere. Many white suburbanites rarely visit Detroit, unless they drive through it on Interstate 75 or Interstate 94 en route to somewhere else.

Greater New Orleans has a similar, if slightly less dramatic, set of demographics. The city itself is two-thirds black, with many of the same problems as Detroit. Many whites have fled to suburbs such as Metairie, which abuts New Orleans, and across the Pontchartrain Causeway to places like Mandeville and Covington.[31] The residents of Metairie worry about the big-city problems that sometimes spill over into their community from New Orleans. By contrast, their compatriots across the causeway feel the 24-mile-long bridge insulates them from the crime, taxes, and poverty of New Orleans. Many people in Mandeville and Covington only go to New Orleans to work or to take advantage of a cultural opportunity such as a show or a sporting event. As in Detroit, there is no sense of regional integration between the white-majority suburbs and the black-majority city. Due to the socioeconomic gaps that undergird these metropolitan divisions, it seems unlikely that any significant amount of metropolitan integration will occur in these parts of America anytime soon.

Such divisions are largely nonexistent in rural America, which continues to be a moderately heterogeneous part of the country. To be sure, there are many rural communities, particularly in the Midwest and Mountain West, where nearly all of the residents are white. Ethnic endogamy occurs regularly in such places. For instance, it might be possible to find a youngster in eastern Montana or western Wisconsin who is three-quarters English, even though his ancestors left the East Coast well over a century ago. In such places, there has been little in-migration — and not a little out-migration — since the original white settlers established their presence there. Until recently, the rural parts of the West, Midwest, and Northeast were predominantly white, except for those counties near Indian reservations. But many Southern and Midwestern communities with beef-, pork-, and poultry-processing plants are now home to sizable populations of Latinos. These areas were once black-and-white or virtually all-white.

People of color are well represented in parts of rural America. Indeed, the rural Deep South is home to most of the nation's predominantly black counties. African Americans predominate in the Mississippi Delta. Blacks outnumber whites in the Black Belt of Alabama (this part of central Alabama received its name because of the richness of its soil, not its demographics). And most rural Southern communities, apart from those in central Appalachia, tend to be racially mixed, with a fair number of African Americans. However, there are few blacks to be found in the sparsely populated rural counties of the Great Plains, Upper Midwest, and Mountain West. Hispanics are prevalent in parts of rural America — namely in the Southwest and the border region. And Native Americans have a major presence throughout much of rural America, particularly in the Midwest and Mountain West. Rural America may be more homogeneous and unchanging in its ethnic and racial patterns than its urban and suburban counterparts, but it too is affected by the diversity that now characterizes so many places in Multicultural America.

States, like urban, suburban, and rural areas, differ dramatically in terms of their ethnic and racial composition. One state, Hawaii, has a white minority. Two states, California and New Mexico, have white pluralities. Although members of each ethno-racial group live in every state, 14 states are at least 85% white: Maine (96.5% white), Vermont (96.2% white), New Hampshire (95.1% white), West Virginia (94.6% white), Iowa (92.6% white), North Dakota (91.7% white), Montana (89.5% white), Kentucky (89.3% white), Minnesota (88.2% white), Idaho and South Dakota (88.0% white), Nebraska and Wisconsin (87.3% white), and Indiana (85.8% white). Ohio is the whitest big state in the nation — 84.0% of the people in the Buckeye State are Caucasian. Indeed, there are 33 white-majority states with populations less than 85% white. Some white-majority states, like Arkansas, have one major racial minority group. Others are ethnic medleys, such as Washington State, which has numerically significant black, Hispanic, Asian, and American Indian populations. Of course some predominantly white states contain multiracial cities, and there certainly are monoracial areas within the multiracial states.

The ethnic origins of white people often vary by state. People of German, Irish, and English ancestry are present in large numbers in almost every state. Irish Americans and Italian Americans are especially common in the Northeast, particularly in the big states: New York, Pennsylvania, and New Jersey. Americans of German and Scandinavian descent predominate in Iowa, Minnesota, Wisconsin, and the Dakotas. The 1990 census (this is the most recent year for which data are available) found that 53.7% of Wisconsinites had German ancestry. Several other Midwestern states were not far behind Wisconsin in terms of being German-American bastions: South Dakota (51.0% German), North Dakota (50.9% German), Nebraska (50.3% German), Iowa (50.2% German), and Minnesota (46.1% German). Moreover, Americans of French, or French Canadian, descent continue to be especially prominent in Louisiana and the Northeastern states of Maine, Vermont, New Hampshire, and Rhode Island. People who identify as Scotch-Irish abound in such states as Kentucky, Tennessee, and West Virginia. As a rule, whites who trace most, if not all, of their heritage to the British Isles are most common in the South.

Even today relatively few Americans of Southern and Eastern European ancestry live in the rural parts of the South and Midwest. If someone with Greek, Syrian, Italian, Spanish, Armenian, or Lebanese forebears moves into a close-knit Southern or Midwestern community, the newcomer might be questioned (politely, of course) by some of the locals about his or her ethnic heritage. When my sister, her Lebanese-American friend, and I stopped at a fast-food restaurant in northeastern Tennessee in July 1999, a gentleman of Scotch-Irish origin approached my sister and asked her, point-blank, "What are you?" To her credit, she replied, "An American. What are you?" However, the ethnic and racial isolation of such places has diminished sharply in the last 50 years. It is no longer conceivable, as it was in the days before World War II, that white Americans in parts of the Midwest, Northeast, and Mountain West might go for months or possibly years without ever personally encountering people of color.

No U.S. states presently have black majorities, although African Americans account for roughly three-fifths of the residents of the District of Columbia. Thirteen states have black populations of at least 14.8%. Mississippi is the blackest state in the Union, followed by Louisiana, South Carolina, Georgia, Maryland, Alabama, North Carolina, Virginia, Delaware, Tennessee, Arkansas, Illinois, and New York. Conversely, nine states have black populations of less than one percent. Montana has the smallest percentage of African Americans of any state, and Vermont, Maine, Idaho, New Hampshire, South Dakota, North Dakota, Wyoming, and Utah are the other states that very few blacks call home. Almost every African American is part of some context where s/he is a minority.

Blacks can enjoy a sense of majority status by living in a black-majority city or neighborhood, where there are African-American role models for their children and multitudinous black-friendly cultural activities and economic opportunities. It is a positive, affirming experience for blacks to live in such places as Atlanta, Chicago, or the District of Columbia, where ample opportunities exist for intraracial dating, networking, and socializing. African Americans who live and work on the West Side of Chicago, for instance, may not interact with whites on a regular basis. Their coworkers, their children's playmates, and their co-religionists are all native-born blacks, many of whom probably trace their roots to the Mississippi Delta. On a Saturday afternoon it is possible to drive for 12 or 15 blocks on Chicago's West Side and see only African Americans — no whites, no Mexicans, no Chinese, no Asian Indians.

These days blacks will confront little overt prejudice from whites, no matter where they live. Yet they may feel unwelcome in some "white" venues, especially if they are the recipients of stares or second glances that telegraph the thought, "What are *you* doing here?" Many black denizens of primarily white areas are third- and fourth-generation residents — due to a ranch, the railroad, a military base, or some other economic entice-ment that attracted their progenitors. Others are retirees who cherish an easygoing atmosphere, a low crime rate, and the general absence of big-city problems. Still others are white-collar transplants who take jobs in academia or business that require them to relocate to places with few African Americans.

Racial isolation can be a problem for them. Their children may be the only blacks at school. They may have to drive long distances to wor-ship at a church with a predominantly African-American congregation. And they may miss the black-oriented restaurants, nightclubs, and cul-tural events readily available in most large American cities. Furthermore, African Americans who believe in racial endogamy may have a tough time finding a spouse locally. Due to diversity programs and the evolu-tion of racial attitudes, blacks are very likely to receive a warm welcome from their coworkers in Boise and Burlington and Green Bay. Still, the intangible effects of minority status — always being the only black family at the local Denny's, the thankless task of answering white peers' earnest questions about racial issues — can drive African Americans to conclude that they "need a little color" in their lives.[32]

California is unquestionably ground zero for multiracial living in the United States. The Golden State, which is home to nearly 34 million Americans, holds a mythical place in the national imagination. California wins such accolades because of its sheer size; its trendsetting social movements; its palm trees and crowded but beautiful beaches; its Hollywood glamour and extraordinarily expensive real estate; its temperate weather (the lack of snow in Southern California has long been a key selling point for Midwesterners); and, perhaps most importantly, the perception that boundless opportunities exist there for anyone who is willing to work hard and take some risks. Beginning with the Gold Rush in 1848, hundreds of thousands of whites from all social classes came over the desert from the East, South, and Midwest to seek their fortunes in California. They were joined by African Americans from the South, who fled racially stultifying lives in Dixie for Oakland, Los Angeles, San Francisco, and elsewhere.[33]

The migrants still come today (approximately one-quarter of new immigrants to the U.S. settle in California), but now they arrive by foot, van, or bus from Mexico, Guatemala, and El Salvador, and by jumbo jet from Taipei, Tehran, Moscow, Seoul, and Yerevan. The domestic migration of native-born Americans to California has slowed because of crime, air pollution, cultural diversity, economic problems, housing costs, racial tensions, and traffic congestion.[34] After a devastating recession in the early 1990s, California bustled again with economic activity during the mid- and late 1990s, particularly in Hollywood and the technological sector.[35] Now the state is once again in the middle of an economic downturn, although it seems to be weathering it better than most of the other Western states.[36]

California, which was a predominantly white state in the 1950s and 1960s, lost its white majority during the 1990s.[37] The most recent census found that the state was 46.7% white, 32.4% Hispanic, 10.8% Asian, 6.4% black, and 2.7% multiracial. Only a few parts of California remain untouched by racial diversity, mostly in the sparsely populated northern reaches near the Oregon border. To be sure, there are still white-majority outposts in Palm Springs, metropolitan San Diego, the San Fernando Valley neighborhoods of Los Angeles, and elsewhere. Southern California is also home to the largest collection of non-European whites, particularly Armenians and Iranians, anywhere in the country. New York City may be more diverse, but Southern California beats out the Big Apple to claim the title of the nation's premier multicultural showcase, based on the high-profile growing pains that have accompanied its ethnic heterogeneity.

The Golden State, which is home to approximately 40% of America's undocumented immigrants, is a racially and economically stratified place. During the recession of the early 1990s, resurgent nativism — the undocumented Mexican immigrant was the principal scapegoat — plagued the state. These overt manifestations of ethnic hostility had largely disappeared by the late 1990s, as the economy began to boom again. Furthermore, many people who disliked the state's explicit multiracialism exited California for the Pacific Northwest and Mountain West during the 1990s.[38] William Booth aptly notes: "Whether the state and its cities shatter into small, balkanized ethnic slices — or mingle as a whole — is one of the most pressing challenges to face California in the new century."[39]

Texas offers a model of multicultural integration that differs from California's. Both states are ethnically and racially heterogeneous and have roughly similar percentages of Hispanics. According to the 2000 census, whites account for 52.4% of Texans, Hispanics 32.0%, blacks 11.3%, Asians 2.7%, and multiracials 1.1%. The cultural geography of the Lone Star State is quite diverse. East Texas is primarily black and white. West Texas, apart from the border counties, is mainly Anglo with some blacks and Latinos. The border region continues to be the province of Mexican Americans and Mexican immigrants, with some Anglos thrown in for good measure. San Antonio, of course, is heavily Latino. Moreover, Dallas and Houston have joined Chicago and New York on the short list of the nation's genuinely triethnic cities. Latinos narrowly outnumber Anglos in Dallas 35.6% to 34.6%, while blacks constitute 25.6% of the population. Hispanics, by contrast, outdistance Anglos and blacks in Houston, where 37.4% of the residents identify as Latino, 30.8% see themselves as Anglo, and 25.0% are black. Overall, Texas has had a stronger Hispanic influence for much longer than California, and the state's informal assimilation model seems to be more traditional and less focused on identity politics than the one in the Golden State.[40]

Unlike the Mexican Americans of Texas, California Latinos do not feel a comfortable sense of unchallenged majority status in an entire swath of their state. Even metropolitan Los Angeles is far from being unilaterally Hispanic, although Los Angeles itself has a Latino plurality. Forty-six and one-half percent of Angelenos (but 70% of the public school students) are Hispanic; 29.7% identify as Anglo; 10.9% characterize themselves as black; and 9.9% are Asian. In metropolitan Los Angeles, four cities of at least 100,000 inhabitants have Latino majorities: Pomona (64.5% Latino), El Monte (72.4% Latino), Santa Ana (76.1% Latino), and East Los Angeles (96.8% Latino). Conversely, every major Texas city along the Rio Grande is overwhelmingly Hispanic, from Brownsville (91.3% Hispanic) to McAllen (80.3% Hispanic) to Laredo (94.1% Hispanic) to El Paso (76.6% Hispanic). Neither Dallas nor Houston is a racial Shangri-la, but Texas's two largest polyethnic cities do not compete with Los Angeles in the ethnic-conflict department.

In the main, Texas remains far more peaceful than California, particularly when it comes to relations between Anglos and Latinos. Analysts attribute this relative tranquillity to the following factors: the Texas model of managing diversity; rates of American citizenship (80% of Hispanic Texans are citizens, compared to approximately half of California Latinos); the spread-out geography of the U.S.-Mexico border in Texas, as opposed to the Tijuana-San Diego pressure point; and Texas's public welfare system, which is less generous to undocumented immigrants than California's.[41]

THE BORDER REGIONS

"We share the same land, air and water. We are two cities committed to a harmonious and friendly relationship on behalf of our communities." This message, in English and Spanish, adorns a bronze plaque that is posted near the official boundary between Matamoros, Tamaulipas, and Brownsville, Texas, the southernmost part of the Lone Star State. Near this expression of cross-border amity and goodwill is a much larger, unsubtle reminder that two sovereign nations abut each other: a red-white-and-blue-striped water tower. The water tower is very close to the boundary line, and it is clearly visible in Matamoros.

The water tower was one of the symbols of American sovereignty that my father and I observed when we walked across the International Bridge that links Brownsville to Matamoros on a pleasant Sunday afternoon in February 1998. U.S. Border Patrol cruisers sat in the gully beneath the bridge. Their occupants vigilantly watched the no man's land between the two sovereign nations for undocumented immigrants and drug smugglers. The Brownsville-Matamoros sector, after all, is a key entry point for illegal border crossers from Mexico, Central America, and elsewhere.[42] Moreover, couriers with millions of dollars in cash sometimes cross the International Bridge, en route to the drug bosses in Matamoros, who frequently shed blood to protect and expand their ill-gotten enterprises.[43]

These issues are facts of life in the Brownsville-Matamoros area. Together, these two communities number more than one-half million — 139,722 Americans live in Brownsville and 416,428 Mexicans reside in Matamoros.[44]

The symbiotic relationship between the ethnically similar communities of Matamoros and Brownsville is evolving into a partnership, as the poorer Mexican city valiantly tries to catch up to its richer American counterpart. Hundreds, perhaps thousands, of locals walk or drive across the toll bridge each day, to shop, work, or visit friends and family. For the most part, the people of Brownsville do not view Mexico as a foreign country. "So strong is this feeling of a common bond," observes one writer, "that many of the residents on both sides of the Rio Grande think of the two cities as one."[45]

Brownsville is the kind of place where the devaluation of the Mexican peso in 1994 — and the increased border safeguards after the terrorist attacks of September 11 — affected the health of merchants, because fewer Mexican shoppers frequented Brownsville's businesses and, in the latter case, fewer Americans went to Matamoros.[46] During the Mexican presidential election of 2000, there was considerable interest in Brownsville as to who might win, and whether there would be instability in the border region as a result.[47] Environmental conditions also play a role in this cross-border interdependence. Toxins from factories in Matamoros cross through the air above the International Bridge and in the water below it, and may cause Brownsville's much higher-than-average rates of birth defects like anencephaly and spina bifida.[48] Indeed, the closeness of Brownsville and Matamoros highlights the increasing irrelevance of national boundaries in the U.S.-Mexico border region.

Up north, the political boundary separating the United States from its northern neighbor, Canada, is known, variously, as "the border" to Americans, "the line" to English Canadians, and *la frontière* to French Canadians. Numerous treaties and heated words over territorial acquisitions by America shaped the line, before and after Canadian nationhood in 1867. This 5,524.5-mile border between Canada and the United States begins in the west with Alaska and the Yukon, stops by British Columbia, then starts up again with Washington, and continues eastward past Idaho to Montana, North Dakota, Minnesota, Michigan, New York, Vermont, New Hampshire, and ends in Maine.[49] In the days before bridges, expressways, ferries, and motorized boats, the line used to be a formidable barrier because of the Great Lakes and the Saint Lawrence River. Since the vast majority of Canadians live in the southern part of their nation, usually within two hours driving distance of the line, almost every Canadian is familiar with the border region.[50]

In the sister cities, such as the two Niagara Falls and the Sault Ste. Maries (which locals refer to as Soo, without regard to the national boundary), family ties and business relationships stretch across the line. American shopkeepers in border towns often accept Canadian currency and give their customers change back in U.S. dollars. The periodic fluctuations in the currency exchange rates result in specials at diners and gas stations that favor whatever currency is stronger at the time. American businesses catering to tourists from the Great White North often fly Canadian flags alongside U.S. banners, sometimes as far as 300 miles from the boundary line. These expressions of binational friendship are mainly directed to English-speaking Canadians.[51] For Canadian Anglophones, their proximity to the culturally and linguistically similar American behemoth heightens the necessity of defining what, exactly, makes them different from Americans. So most of the drama and conflict in the U.S.-Canadian border region comes as a result of interactions between Americans and English-speaking Canadians.[52]

America's border with its southern neighbor, Mexico, took shape through conquest and purchase. This 1,951.36-mile border, nearly two-thirds of which tracks the Rio Grande, begins in the west by California and extends eastward past Arizona and New Mexico to Texas.[53] Twenty-four million people live in the U.S.-Mexico border region.[54] In such areas, the cross-border traffic and corresponding economic initiatives foster a sense of regional identity. The depth of this regional identity depends on the demographics and population density of each community. Much of San Diego feels far removed from Mexico, even though the city's southern boundary abuts Baja California, while San Antonio is 150 miles northwest of Nuevo Laredo and it has an identifiable Mexican influence.

In the sister cities, like *Ambos Nogales* or *Los Dos Laredos*, border dwellers may work in one city and live in another; families, particularly Mexican ones, literally enjoy the best of both worlds. Thus it is perfectly natural for a panhandler in McAllen, Texas, to ask a guy if he speaks English, or for a Laredo disk jockey to query a lovesick Latino about whether the Casanova who stole his girlfriend is Mexican or American. The formal boundary line is irrelevant to pollutants as well. Mexico and the United States spar constantly over air and water pollution, largely because of Mexico's ineffective environmental standards.[55] Both nations also duel over the region's scarce supply of water, which is crucial for farmers and city dwellers alike.[56] The unofficial motto of the border region might as well be *sin fronteras*, which translates to "without borders" in English.

The notion of a border transcends geopolitical lines and encompasses the cultural dichotomies that Mexican immigrants deal with on a daily basis. The border region extends to the swap meet in Vernon, California, just east of Los Angeles, where Mexicans and Central Americans have their own bustling version of the Italian Market in South Philadelphia. The border region extends to Elgin, Illinois, in west suburban Chicago, where Mexicans eat at *taquerías*, purchase meat at *carnicerías*, buy bakery goods at *panaderías*, wash their laundry at *lavanderías*, purchase furniture at *mueblerías*, pay bills and wire money to Mexico at currency exchanges, and shop at *supermercados* where, in the case of one giant store, every product, it seems, comes directly from Mexico.

One of the most intriguing instances of the porous nature of the border is the increasing interest of Mexican politicians in Mexican Americans and particularly the Mexican immigrants who live in the United States. As America's Mexican-origin population has grown to more than 20 million, the Mexican government has been more careful to include the interests of Mexicans north of the border in their policy calculations. Several million Mexicans who live in the United States are eligible to vote in Mexico, and many Mexican Americans influence the voting decisions of people there as well. Not surprisingly, Mexican presidential candidates routinely campaign in large U.S. cities, such as Chicago and Los Angeles.[57] To be sure, there are countless Mexicans who live in the United States, but who do not have any interest in staying in America over the long term. They simply want to earn enough money to live comfortably in Mexico upon their return. These "temporary" immigrants, many of whom are undocumented, eke out an existence while they live their daily lives in what amounts to a psychological border region.

At this point, more Americans are closer — racially, culturally, and economically — to Canadians than to Mexicans. The per capita annual incomes, one important measurement, are similar for Americans and Canadians: In 1999 Americans weighed in at a healthy $33,900, while Canadians were not too far behind with $23,300. Mexicans brought up the rear with a mere $8,500.[58] This disparity, not surprisingly, is evident in many of the U.S. communities that border Mexico. The standard of living in U.S. border towns is far superior to that of their Mexican counterparts, even though some U.S. border communities are among the poorest places in America. These disparities color border-town life and create intractable problems over such issues as illegal drugs and undocumented immigration. Whenever one traverses the Mexican-American border region, s/he is constantly reminded of the clash between North and South, developed and developing countries, and the First and Third Worlds.[59] But in the English-speaking parts of Canada, one can momentarily forget that s/he is in a foreign country.

Canada, of course, is not *exactly* the same as the United States. There are colorful notes instead of greenbacks. Gas is sold in liters rather than gallons. Road signs indicate distances in kilometers instead of miles. The maple-leaf flag flies rather than the Stars and Stripes. And Canadian patois, with its British-style spellings (but not necessarily pronunciations) and expressions, such as "in hospital" or "at university," differs slightly from American English. Another minor difference is the Canadian government's policy of official bilingualism (English and French), which affects everything from the inscriptions on highway signs to the packaging of Canadian consumer products. Our neighbors to the north also have fewer minorities, stronger unions, lower crime rates, less religious fervor, and a more expansive welfare state. As a group, Canadians are divided about the benefits of living so close to America, and they split over whether they think Americans exercise too much influence over their culture and economy. Americans, for the most part, view Canada as an ally, a friend, and a culturally congenial place to visit. For us, Canada is undoubtedly the least foreign country in the world.[60]

The North American Free Trade Agreement (NAFTA) is gradually lowering barriers to trade among the three nations of North America.[61] (Canada is our largest trading partner, followed by Mexico and Japan.) NAFTA stimulated the growth of the burgeoning *maquiladora* (assembly plant) movement. An estimated one million workers in Mexican border towns assemble clothing, microwaves, televisions, toys, VCRs, and auto parts for American, Canadian, Japanese, South Korean, and other international companies. This arrangement appeals to foreign businesses because of Mexico's low wage scales, weak labor laws, lax environmental regulations, and proximity to the United States for processing, distribution, and sales.[62]

Overall, NAFTA has dramatically strengthened the U.S.-Mexican trade relationship — and the U.S.-Canadian trade relationship as well. Three hundred sixteen thousand U.S. workers have lost or threatened jobs as a result of NAFTA. Many of these individuals were displaced manufacturing workers who suffered at least some decrease in their wages. But NAFTA has benefited American companies and, by extension, American workers by creating more jobs due to the fact that U.S. suppliers provide 82% of the components used by the *maquiladoras.*[63] Now American employers and manufacturers turn almost reflexively to Mexican companies, particularly those in the industrialized northern states, to solve their labor needs competently, expeditiously, and inexpensively.[64]

Migration patterns have played a major role in shaping the composition of the border areas, particularly in the Southwest. Whenever social or economic turmoil takes place in Mexico or, more recently, northern Central America, there usually is a corresponding increase in illegal migration from those countries to the United States. The migrants clean homes, tend lawns, work construction, care for children, bus and wait tables, wash and park cars, pick grapes, lettuce, and strawberries, along with myriad other low-skill jobs. The Border Patrol, known to undocumented immigrants as *la migra,* is achieving a higher profile (thanks to a larger budget and more humanpower), as America fortifies its southern border. Due to the dramatic socioeconomic disparities between the United States and Mexico, migration pressures are most substantial in California, Arizona, New Mexico, and Texas. Many border towns serve as way stations for the northbound migrants. Border-town residents, many of whom are Mexican Americans, observe these migrants with a mixture of disdain, skepticism, and sympathy.

The U.S.-Mexico border region has much more of a militarized, adversarial air than its Canadian counterpart. There are Border Patrol checkpoints along the highways near the U.S.-Mexico border, where Border Patrol officers check passing cars for undocumented immigrants. It also is a common sight in the U.S.-Mexico border region to see Border Patrol officers in their white SUVs diligently scouring the fields, deserts, and ravines for illegal immigrants. When efforts to tighten up the border succeed in one area — like Operation Gatekeeper in San Diego — the illegal migration shifts elsewhere to places like Douglas, Arizona, without decreasing in aggregate numbers overall.[65]

Until the events of September 11, 2001, led to a sharp crackdown along the U.S.-Mexico and U.S.-Canada borders, these migration flows showed no signs of abating. The migration flows decreased temporarily in the months after the post-9/11 crackdown in the U.S.-Mexico and U.S.-Canada border regions, but undocumented immigration began to rise again in 2002.[66] Indeed, there is no end in sight to the migration flows so long as Mexico and the nations of Central America remain far poorer than the United States. Before 9/11, the number of DEA, Customs, and Border Patrol officers along the Mexican border dwarfed the presence those agencies had along the Canadian border. After 9/11, however,

Congress approved a sharp increase in personnel for the U.S.-Canada border region, which terrorists may use to gain entry into the United States.[67]

Considering the ethnic, cultural, national, and socioeconomic differences that separate Mexico and the United States, it is not surprising that the two nations have had a tumultuous relationship since Mexico became an independent country in 1821. The tensions have periodically been resolved through military means, such as the Mexican War of 1846 to 1848 and the undeclared conflict that sent U.S. troops into Mexico in search of the bandit Pancho Villa in 1916 and 1917. Over the years Mexico's intellectual classes were fashionably anti-American, and the nation's political leadership often embraced this viewpoint as well. Moreover, Mexico's poverty, Spanish language, mestizo identity, and overwhelming Catholicism made it seem like an alien Other to Americans. But that was then.

Today cultural and economic factors are bringing the two nations together. Seven percent of Americans now claim Mexican ancestry, and the Spanish language became firmly entrenched as the U.S.'s second tongue in the 1980s and 1990s. Countless American tourists visit Mexico (the top destination for Americans who go abroad), either on day trips to border towns or as part of package tours to Cancun, Cozumel, Acapulco, Puerto Vallarta, Los Cabos, or any of Mexico's other resort communities. Mexico, moreover, is clearly embracing free-market capitalism, and it is beginning to emulate the good-government model of the United States. In the end, NAFTA will eventually create a giant free-trade block in North America, a development that will unite Americans and Mexicans more so than almost any other factor.

Nonetheless, Americans in the border region have a number of concerns about Mexico. For one, the steady stream of migrants discombobulates some communities; rural ranchers find themselves almost helpless to stem the flow of migrants across their land. Americans remain rightfully concerned about the increasing power of Mexican drug traffickers, who recently supplanted the Colombians as the main suppliers of illegal narcotics (particularly cocaine, marijuana, and methamphetamines) to American drug users.[68] Many border-staters also fear the impending introduction of Mexican trucks onto U.S. highways, in accordance with the provisions of NAFTA, due to the differing truck safety standards of the two nations. To be sure, Mexican trucks will have to meet rigorous safety standards before they can be driven on U.S. highways.[69]

Mexico, for its part, is not ignoring the border either. To drive this message home, in the late 1990s the Mexicans erected massive Mexican tricolor flags in prominent locations near the U.S. border (Tijuana, Ciudad Juárez, Piedras Negras, and Nuevo Laredo, among others).[70] Many border-dwellers maintain their skepticism about the people, culture, and institutions on the other side, even though they may visit it on a regular basis to shop, work, or play. Mexico's political and economic system is starting to resemble the U.S. version of representative democracy and free-market capitalism, so the people of Mexico's industrial North, at least, may begin to grow closer to Americans and the United States.

Canada, like Mexico, is not immune to cross-border tensions with the United States. Since the two nations are among the richest in the developed world, the points of conflict bear little resemblance to those separating Mexico and America. For years English-speaking Canadians have worried about U.S. cultural imperialism. Many Canadians enjoy American books, music, films, magazines, and television — supposedly at the expense of Canadian writers, artists, actors, editors, and broadcasters. Ottawa, therefore, requires Canadian radio and television broadcasters to meet certain threshold levels with regard to their use of Canadian content. These regulations focus primarily on the nationality of the product creators and, for films and television dramas, the site of production. Canadians hope that this cultural protectionism will nurture local creative types and safeguard their delicate sense of national identity.[71] In addition, many Canadians tend to be skeptical about foreign companies that seeks to purchase Canadian businesses.

The huge volume of trade between Canada and the United States — over $300 billion in commerce crosses the line each year — occasionally results in other contentious disputes, such as those in recent years over steel, wheat, salmon, lumber, tomatoes, and livestock.[72] Furthermore, Canadians sometimes complain that the strictness of U.S. border-crossing procedures forces them to spend an unnecessarily long amount of time waiting in line to gain entry into the United States.[73] Despite these occasional disagreements, Canada remains one of America's closest allies, and our cross-border squabbles are roughly analogous to fights between siblings.

The population of the United States continues to assume a more multiracial character with each passing year, and it keeps shifting South and West. Texas is likely to become the nation's third white-plurality state in 2004.[74] Within a decade New Mexico will in all likelihood become the nation's first Hispanic-plurality state. (As of 2000, New Mexico was 44.7% Anglo, 42.1% Hispanic, 8.9% Native American, 1.7% black, 1.4% multiracial, and 1.0% Asian.) California will probably reach this demographic milestone in the middle of the 2010s.

Likewise, Arizona, which has the fourth-highest percentage of Hispanics of any state in the nation — the other border states outrank it — is becoming more Latino each year. Hispanics make up 25.3% of Arizona's population today, while this percentage will probably top 30% in 2010. High Latino birth rates and the continuing influxes of immigrants from Latin America continue to reshape the political, cultural, and economic dynamics of Arizona, as well as in Texas, Florida, and California.

Overall, ten U.S. House seats shifted from the Northeast and Midwest to the South and West after the Census of 2000. Four states (Texas, Florida, Arizona, and Georgia) gained two seats, while California, Colorado, Nevada, and North Carolina gained one each. Meanwhile, New York and Pennsylvania lost two seats apiece, and eight states — Connecticut, Illinois, Indiana, Michigan, Wisconsin, Ohio, Oklahoma, and Mississippi — each lost one. The new census figures also affect the allocation of federal funds among the states, as well as the distribution of funds within states.[75]

This decennial powershift will continue in the foreseeable future. In 2020 the Census Bureau projects that more than three-fifths of Americans will live in the South and West. By then, Florida will probably have passed New York to become America's third most populous state. Thus, 28% of Americans (up from 25% today) will reside in just three states: California, Texas, and Florida.[76] These highly heterogeneous anchors of the Sun Belt are increasingly the center of Multicultural America.

On the international front, we will not see substantial North American integration at the mass level for some time. Indeed, it is difficult for Chinese-American New Yorkers, French-Canadian Nova Scotians, and Amerindian Mexicans from Chiapas to see much, if anything, in common with each other. At the present time, it is unlikely that the respective citizens of Canada, Mexico, and the United States would allow any kind of supranational political entity to take precedence over their separate Canadian, Mexican, and American identities. Nor is there a North American currency in our future. Americans certainly are not going to give up their familiar greenbacks for a bland, multinational currency that might include images of Nezahualcoyotl and Queen Elizabeth II. And the prospect of dollarization — the replacement of the peso and loonie with greenbacks — causes Mexican and Canadian nationalists fits of apoplexy.[77]

True North American integration will have to wait until everyone speaks a common language. American English is the most likely candidate for such a linguistic common denominator. Americans, of course, speak English as their native tongue. Most Canadians are native English speakers as well. In Mexico, however, English-language fluency is most prevalent among the cultural, political, and economic elites. Growing numbers of Mexicans can speak some English because they have spent time north of the border, or they have friends and relatives who have done so. In any event, it is increasingly common in the United States to see consumer products with labeling or instructions in English, French, and Spanish, the three principal languages of North America.

North American integration is still a work in progress. At this point few companies qualify as genuinely North American businesses, in that the Mexican, Canadian, and U.S. markets each contribute significant amounts of revenue to their bottom lines. However, a number of businesses, particularly in the banking, trucking, and railroad sectors, are making progress in this regard. The North American Industry Classification System (NAICS), which "was developed jointly by the U.S., Canada, and Mexico to provide new comparability in statistics about business activity across North America," is one such indicator of North American integration.[78] And in academia, scholars in a variety of disciplines are trying to promote North American integration. The North American Integration and Development Center at UCLA is a leader in this field.[79]

The most authentic example of North American integration may occur in the Lower Rio Grande Valley of Texas. The cross-border traffic inspired by NAFTA brings thousands of Mexicans to the Lower Rio Grande Valley, a place where thousands of Americans and Canadians spend their winters. These Winter Texans mix easily with the largely Mexican-American population of South Texas, and they often travel to Mexico during their sojourns in the Lone Star State. During the next two decades, the relentless forces of globalization will undoubtedly create even more examples of North American integration.[80]

~ chapter six ~

The Perils of Exclusion

Mattel has been quite enlightened in its product development, at least for a mainstream toy company. It first introduced Barbie, its Nordic-looking flagship doll, in 1959. Female Baby Boomers quickly embraced the blond, blue-eyed figurine. In deference to the rapidly expanding purchasing power of minority consumers, Mattel released Christie, a black friend for Barbie, in 1968, followed by Julia (1969), Brad (1970), and Curtis (1975). Mattel introduced Black Barbie, its first full-fledged African-American equivalent to the blond and brunette flagship dolls, in 1980. Despite the introduction of multihued dolls and toys, minorities in the toymaking field — those who create, market, and distribute multicultural alternatives to the mainstream fare at Wal-Mart and Toys "R" Us — still complain about the relative absence of colorful faces and culturally accurate toys in the parade of childhood playthings.[1]

Mattel, meanwhile, continues to fine-tune its product lineup, to be ever-more inclusive and responsive to market conditions. Barbie, after all, is a $1.5 billion-a-year business for Mattel, and its revenues will only increase if the company meets the demands of the marketplace.[2] Mattel's multicultural products include Mexican Barbie, Native American Barbie, and Puerto Rican Barbie, in addition to less curvaceous models and a wheelchair-bound doll. In 1991 Mattel introduced a Shani line (the name means "marvelous" in Swahili) of three black Barbies — Asha, Shani, and Nichelle — with different skin tones, to reflect the diversity of the African-American community.[3] These forays into the multicultural marketplace have not been without some controversy. The introduction of Puerto Rican Barbie, for instance, resulted in spirited discussions both in Puerto Rico and on the U.S. mainland over whether the doll was an appropriate representation of Puerto Ricans.[4] Mattel's competitors also confront similar issues in their marketing campaigns and product-development efforts.

Indeed, all the major toy manufacturers now seek to accommodate ethnic consumers with more diverse and culturally sensitive choices for their children. Mattel has been particularly aggressive in reaching out to the Latino market. The company now offers consumers a *Quinceañera* Barbie (the term refers to the coming-of-age celebration that occurs when Latin American females turn 15) in an effort to reach out to young Latinas. And in March 2002 Mattel introduced an omniracial Barbie named Kayla; this doll has olive skin and brown hair. Dolls such as Kayla are the wave of the future in the toy world. With the increasing number of Latino, Middle Eastern, multiracial, and multiethnic Americans with Mediterranean European roots, dolls such as Kayla appeal to dozens of ethnic groups—and thus, in theory, have tremendous commercial potential.

Nonetheless, Mattel and its competitors have come under fire from Asian Americans, who contend that there are far too few Asian-American dolls. Mattel and Hasbro, its chief competitor, often make dolls in three varieties: white, black, and Latino. This was the case with the "Barbie for President 2000" doll. Asian-American leaders roundly criticized Mattel for failing to create an Asian-American version of the election-year toy. There are two main reasons for the paucity of Asian-American dolls. First, Asian Americans constitute less than four percent of the U.S. population. Secondly, toymakers believe that they do not have to produce many Asian dolls because Asian-American girls prefer to play with white dolls. Typically, the Asian dolls available to American consumers portray Asians as foreigners, e.g., a doll wearing a kimono. These types of dolls reinforce the pernicious stereotype that Asian Americans never completely integrate into American society.[5]

Dolls and toys matter in racial terms, because almost every child spends a significant amount of his or her time playing with them. White children tend to select dolls that look as they do. Caucasians have an overabundance of candidates to choose from at mainstream retailers. Minority children are not so fortunate. Before the 1960s it was common for black girls to play with white dolls, largely because they had few other choices, or because they associated whiteness with positive qualities. The psychologists Kenneth and Mamie Clark conducted doll tests with young African-American children during the 1940s. They discovered that the black youths often preferred white dolls. Segregation, the Clarks concluded, led black children to have low self-esteem. The Clarks' research influenced the Supreme Court's decision in *Brown v. Board of Education,* and helped to convince the Court that segregated schools harmed African-American children.[6] Indeed, black psychologists fear that a paucity of racially compatible playthings causes African-American children irreparable harm in terms of their developing a positive racial identity and a healthy sense of self-esteem.[7]

Today minority parents seek dolls, playthings, and action figures that reflect and affirm their children's ethnic heritage and thus enhance their sense of self-worth. After all, people feel affirmed when they see others who share their ethnic characteristics in the spotlight. Young children, of course, do not express their feelings this way, but they might wonder, "Why aren't there more dolls that look the way I do?" This question is an especially difficult one for parents who come from small ethnic minority groups, such as Samoan Americans and Pakistani Americans.[8] In the past, it was hard for Mediterranean Caucasians to find ethnically compatible dolls for their children, but the increasing heterogeneity of the American population has led toymakers to create omniracial dolls whose features resemble those of many Latinos, multiracials, Middle Easterners, and Mediterranean Europeans.

Toymakers, to be sure, diversify their product offerings in response to market conditions. Since the United States is a white-majority country, white dolls predominate at the toy store and in the toy aisles of major retailers. With few exceptions, toymakers try to create omniracial dolls, so they can reach the largest possible number of consumers. Therefore, the figurines reflect only the general characteristics of specific ethnic groups. In other words, an olive-skinned youngster of Greek, Lebanese, or Spanish descent has to be satisfied with a brunette doll, even if the plastic figurine does not resemble her exactly. And males of all ethnic groups, particularly minority youths, have far fewer dolls to choose from than their female counterparts.[9]

The aforementioned phenomena, which could be interpreted as hopeful signs of cultural cross-pollination, are an antidote to the perils of exclusion. Although the practice has fallen into disrepute, it is still possible to see young black girls with blond Barbies. While no comprehensive data exist on this topic, of course, white girls also are known to play with African-American dolls. No one launches boycotts or instigates riots in the street because s/he cannot find ethnically compatible toys, figurines, and playthings for her or his children. But the issue matters because research demonstrates that a child's self-esteem may be affected by whether s/he has access to ethnically compatible toys, figurines, and playthings.

TOWARD INCLUSION

In the eight decades since Betty Crocker was first introduced to the American public in 1921, the General Mills corporate symbol has become one of the most familiar, respected, and enduring brands in the packaged-foods business. Betty Crocker was created 81 years ago by the Washburn Crosby Company (which would eventually develop into General Mills), in response to the queries about baking the company received as a result of an advertising campaign to sell Gold Medal flour. The company selected the forename Betty because it sounded friendly and chose the surname Crocker out of respect for William G. Crocker, who had retired a short time before as a director of Washburn Crosby. In response to the growing popularity of Betty Crocker, her corporate creators decided to develop a visual image of her in 1936. The first Betty Crocker was matronly and middle class, and her appearance reflected the Northern European majority in America at that time.[10]

Over the years the General Mills corporate symbol came to personify domesticity and the joys of the culinary experience. Between 1955 and 1986 she underwent six makeovers of her attire and hairstyle — but not her Northern European appearance — to remain in step with consumers.[11] In 1995 General Mills decided to create a new, multicultural Betty. To update their corporate symbol, the Fortune 500 company chose 75 American women from diverse ethnic, racial, and geographical backgrounds and used a computer to create a composite picture of their faces. Then General Mills commissioned a watercolor artist to paint Betty's new face; he used the composite picture as his model.[12]

General Mills unveiled the eighth incarnation of Betty Crocker in March 1996, and she immediately replaced her dowdy predecessor on all the Betty Crocker products. "The new Betty," Joseph A. Kirby points out, "is a radical departure from the blue-eyed, motherly looking Crocker of old. She appears to be younger and darker, and features a broad smile, a stylish hairdo, contemporary clothing and accessories, and facial accents that could be interpreted as Caucasian, Hispanic, Asian or Native American."[13] General Mills also had an inclusive anniversary slogan that accompanied the new Betty: "There's a little bit of Betty in all of us."[14] However, this makeover was largely symbolic. Usually Betty Crocker products bear her trademark red spoon with the words Betty Crocker in white print and a small picture of the master cook herself. As a rule, the red spoon is more prominent than Betty Crocker's visage on the products that bear her name.

Nonetheless, Betty is big business: The Betty Crocker brand now includes dozens of products, numerous cookbooks, a weekly newspaper column on cooking, the monthly *Betty Crocker Recipe Magazine*, and a Web site.[15] Betty Crocker's makeover, to be sure, dovetails with General Mills' expansion into ethnic markets with products that target minority consumers. Betty, in short, is still the trusted icon of yesteryear; she just looks like the typical American of the future.

Inclusion is the name of the game in Multicultural America, and affirmative action remains the most common method of promoting diversity. Affirmative action encompasses public and private programs that range from outreach to outright preferences for members of the protected classes in hiring, promotions, admissions, and contracting. Discrimination is the most politically popular rationale for affirmative-action efforts; after all, most reasonable Americans agree that it is only fair to try to help women and minorities make up for their past disadvantages. But vexing questions exist about how, exactly, to measure discrimination. Should socioeconomic status be the principal criterion? Should discrimination be measured by the composition of the local labor pool, or by the makeup of one's clientele or customer base? In addition, multiculturalists cite the diversity rationale as a main reason to support affirmative action.

Affirmative action usually benefits white females and racial minorities. Whites, as a group, rarely receive affirmative-action protections, except on the basis of economic need, even though true diversity goes beyond race and gender to encompass such factors as ethnicity, ideology, social class, and sexual orientation. Still, it is difficult to extend this type of reasoning to every sector of American society. If there are a finite number of highly visible positions in a particular context, such as the spots on a national television newscast, one cannot very easily balance the anchors to represent every racial, ethnic, religious, or socioeconomic group in America. Nonetheless, diversity initiatives, especially in the academy, the government, and Corporate America, increasingly emphasize a wide range of factors in addition to race and gender. In any event, the multiculturalists contend that far too little progress has been made in terms of advancing the employment and educational prospects of women and minorities.

Politicians, corporate honchos, and policymakers seek to demonstrate their responsiveness — to voters, to consumers, and to service populations. The federal government remains vigilant for any numerical imbalances that may exist, particularly in the public sector. For example, officials of the National Park Service are concerned that insufficient numbers of minority Americans visit and enjoy the splendor of U.S. national parks.[16] Since the federal government has a responsibility to take into account the needs of its entire service population on this issue, it is logical that the National Park Service would want to increase the number of black, Hispanic, Asian, and American Indian visitors to its sites.

However, in the private sector, companies often prosper based on their appeal to a narrow slice of the demographic pie, so executives usually target their advertising to a specific generational cohort, socioeconomic group, or ethno-racial category. Take NASCAR racing — it is a sport dominated by white men, with a predominantly white fan base. No one seriously thinks that African Americans or even Latinos are going to flock to stock car races anytime soon, so we rarely hear talk about recruiting black drivers or Hispanic pit bosses. If NASCAR was a public entity, supported by tax dollars, it would be a completely different story.

Many businesspeople implement the diversity imperative more so because it benefits the bottom line than because they consider it to be "the right thing to do" in a normative sense, divorced from economic considerations. Executives at mainstream corporations are mindful that people of color spend more than one trillion dollars on goods and services each year. According to the projections for 2001 from the Selig Center for Economic Growth at the University of Georgia, whites have buying power of more than $6.22 trillion, the African-American market is estimated to be $572.1 billion annually, while Hispanics have buying power of over $452.4 billion on a yearly basis, Asian Americans purchase goods and services to the tune of $253.8 billion annually, and the American Indian market is $34.8 billion a year. In addition, minority buying power is increasing significantly faster than white buying power.[17] Corporations attempt to reach all sorts of consumers, from assimilated American Jews to foreign-born Chinese Americans, with carefully targeted advertising campaigns that invoke, celebrate, and highlight the ethnicity of the target population.[18]

Popular culture is probably the most racially inclusive venue of American life. White consumers avidly follow the exploits of their favorite black actors, athletes, entertainers, and recording artists: Bill Cosby, Lauryn Hill, Kobe Bryant, Shaquille O'Neal, Martin Lawrence, Eddie Murphy, Chris Rock, Will Smith, Wesley Snipes, Chris Tucker, and Denzel Washington. But television is segregated by viewing habits, and by the characters, story lines, and settings of sitcoms. Prime time network television continues to be dominated by white characters and story lines. Advertisers covet affluent young white viewers, and the decisionmakers, most of whom are white themselves, reason that the best way to attract them in a fragmented universe of entertainment options is to offer programming starring people and story lines that mirror the target demographic.[19] Blacks, along with Hispanics, Asian Americans, and Native Americans, often complain that mainstream movies and television shows exclude them entirely; marginalize them as buddies, servants, and sidekicks; or portray them in stereotypical or demeaning roles. Yet a diverse cast of faces often gives a movie, advertisement, music video, or television show credibility with young consumers.

In recent years the fashion world has flirted with gangsta rap and hip-hop, which became the universal constants of youthful angst and adolescent rebellion in the late 1990s. Hip-hop's oversized influence on the American youth culture ranges from the vernacular (dis, def, phat) to clothing (jerseys, down jackets, and exceedingly baggy jeans) to lifestyle (casual evocations of racial harmony). Caucasians purchase 71% of rap music, according to estimates. Young white fans of hip-hop and gangsta rap are often cultural voyeurs, chillin' to the tunes of Tupac, Snoop, and Jay-Z, in communities where there are no drive-bys or gang wars. They enjoy rap's paeans to hard-core materialism and the pursuit of pleasure, and its superficial focus on the verities of life in the 'hood. Softer forms of rap, as embodied by the feel-good rhymes of Will Smith, came to the fore in the late 1990s.[20]

The fashion world is another example of cross-cultural pollination. Ralph Lauren's signature Polo collection, as well as the threads of Lauren-clone Tommy Hilfiger, became hip with inner-city blacks and Hispanics during the late 1990s. In return, these clothiers of white preppies began to include African-American models in their Nordic ensembles. And they offered consumers more streetwise designs, of the type favored by fashionable urbanites and their imitators. Likewise, many white kids purchased items of clothing by FUBU and other urban designers. Still, it is difficult to determine the extent to which race relations are affected by the ecumenism and superficial inclusiveness of America's youth culture.[21]

For the last three decades, multiculturalists have largely succeeded in pointing out the importance of previously ignored or undervalued cultural contributions by women and minorities and others, like homosexuals, the poor, and certain ethnic groups. From the beginning of the American nation until the late 1960s, it was virtually unquestioned that the lens of U.S. history should focus on a small group of white men — some American, some European — who were commonly acknowledged to have played a dominant role in shaping American culture and that of the Western world. But the academics who came of age during the 1960s gradually have reshaped disciplinary perspectives to encompass curricula and teaching styles that reflect the rhythms of life in a heterogeneous, multiracial nation.

In Multicultural America, public school students receive considerable exposure, at least in the curriculum, to the heterogeneity of America's past, present, and future. Students around the country celebrate Black History Month every February, with readings, discussions, and posters about African-American heroes and cultural events. Students also celebrate Women's History Month in March and Hispanic Heritage Month from September 15 to October 15. Left-wing academics now characterize the canon of Great Books as a white male construct. So literature majors are just as likely to read Toni Morrison as they are William Shakespeare, while Chaucer often takes a back seat to Sandra Cisneros. Meanwhile, courses about Western civilization have fallen out of fashion, in favor of ethnic studies courses. Critics worry that the inclusion of diverse narratives "dumbs down" the curriculum, in the interest of boosting self-esteem for members of historically underrepresented groups. The multicultural impulse affects the nation's icons as well. We recognize the achievements of women and minorities more so than ever before, while traditional American heroes — such men as George Washington, Thomas Jefferson, and Abraham Lincoln — receive less attention than in the past.[22]

Martin Luther King Jr. is one of the leading heroes in the American pantheon. The civil-rights icon will forever have an important place in American history due to his pivotal role in the drive to obtain equal rights for African Americans. He wins historical plaudits, too, for his vision of integration and racial harmony, as embodied by his "I Have a Dream" speech at the Lincoln Memorial in August 1963. We beatify King for his visionary leadership and noble espousal of nonviolence during the civil rights movement. King is honored with a federal holiday, which was first celebrated in 1986. Each state pays tribute to King with a holiday as well. And virtually every city with a sizable black population has a roadway named after the Nobel Peace Prize-winning integrationist. The annual King holiday serves as a time to remember the slain leader's teachings and significance, often with plays, speeches, and other activities that attempt to evoke and recapture the spirit of his extraordinary life.[23]

In the Mexican-American community, Cesar Chavez is far and away the leading icon: He is the Chicano Martin Luther King.[24] The United Farm Workers leader led peaceful, nonviolent protests and boycotts to better the working conditions of migrant workers from the 1960s until his death in 1993. He had his greatest impact in California, where parks, schools, libraries, and roadways are named after him in such places as Oxnard, San Jose, Union City, Bakersfield, San Francisco, and East Los Angeles. California honors Chavez with a state holiday. In addition, California public school students learn about Chavez as part of the curriculum.[25] Each year Chavez's status as the premier Mexican-American hero becomes increasingly unassailable. Today most communities with a substantial Mexican-American presence recognize Chavez in some form or another.

At the same time, bureaucrats, businesspeople, and diversity professionals coordinate efforts to promote the diversity imperative and the tenets of multiculturalism, through diversity workshops and sensitivity training in schools, businesses, and government offices. In their advertisements and recruiting materials, companies signal their receptiveness to female and minority employees with the following phrases and acronyms: Equal Opportunity Employer (EOE); Women and minorities are encouraged to apply; and M/F/D/V (Minority/Female/Disabled/Veteran). Corporations, public bureaucracies, and educational institutions often have goals and timetables for increasing the employment of women and minorities, in addition to special programs to groom females and people of color for leadership positions. In addition, diversity issues factor into bonuses, promotions, and performance reviews for managers and executives in the public and private sectors alike.[26]

White males, to be sure, continue to wield much of the power in Corporate America and, to a lesser extent, in the public sector and educational institutions. Some female and minority professionals continue to complain that subtle but pervasive discrimination — a "glass ceiling" that blocks their advancement to the most powerful decision-making positions — exists in Corporate America and elsewhere.[27] White males still dominate the upper echelons of Fortune 500 companies, but there is more diversity in Corporate America than ever before.[28] Some of America's most venerable corporations are run by women, including Avon (Andrea Jung), Hewlett-Packard (Carly Fiorina), and Xerox (Anne Mulcahy). And minorities head the following corporate behemoths: Kellogg (Carlos Gutierrez), Fannie Mae (Franklin Raines), American Express (Kenneth Chenault), AOL Time Warner (Richard Parsons), and Merrill Lynch (Stanley O'Neal, the president and chief operating officer, is scheduled to become CEO in 2004).

Most large companies eagerly share with the world their undying commitment to diversity, inclusion, and the like. Companies seek to advance — and profit — from diversity in the workplace and the marketplace for a variety of reasons: to attract minority workers in a tight labor market; to encourage nonwhite consumers to use their services; to preempt a civil rights organization's willingness to initiate a boycott, with attendant negative publicity, against the company; and to establish a good track record in the event of employee lawsuits or government investigations of alleged bias in pay, promotions, and responsibilities. Meanwhile, racial optimists point to the burgeoning number of minority-owned businesses to support their contention that racial discrimination no longer exists in the business world.[29]

It is an unfortunate fact of a capitalist, free-market economy that competition leads to winners and losers. Almost from the point that affirmative action was created in the 1960s, complaints of unfairness and reverse discrimination have abounded. After three decades of sustained affirmative-action programs, with myriad effects in large corporations and public employment, opposition to affirmative action has become prevalent among whites. Most Americans embrace the notion of equal opportunity, but we disagree about what it means and how we should go about achieving it. The American public remains very skeptical about preferential treatment, although Americans are more supportive of benign, less rigid forms of affirmative action.[30]

There is usually a racial dimension to the affirmative-action issue. Blacks and Hispanics tend to support such programs, which is not surprising considering that many members of these groups see affirmative action as a bulwark against discrimination and a means to advance themselves socioeconomically. There are notable exceptions to the rule, however. Millions of white men enthusiastically and vociferously support affirmative action. Furthermore, much of the opposition to such programs is coordinated by conservative blacks and Hispanics, who feel that affirmative action stigmatizes them and makes their coethnics dependent on government. They also contend that such programs are unfair to non-beneficiaries. White men, particularly police officers, firefighters, union workers, and public employees in racially heterogeneous areas, are most affected by affirmative-action dictates. A sizable number of white men feel that such programs favor women and minorities at their expense.[31] Affirmative action itself remains popular in Washington and Corporate America, but the Reagan-Bush appointees to the federal judiciary have invalidated many affirmative-action rules, programs, and initiatives, primarily in terms of public contracting, higher education, and voting rights.

Supporters of affirmative action usually try to get white women to focus on their shared interests with minorities in this regard. They usually forget to take into account that affirmative-action programs frequently focus far more on race than gender. For one, minorities often see white women as white first and women second. They contend that white women benefit from racial privilege, perhaps not as much as their white male compatriots, but more so than a similarly situated person of color. Moreover, white women do not always see themselves as having much in common with minorities. They are white, after all, and most white adults do not interact a great deal with people of color in social settings. White females usually have lots of white male relatives. Thus, they may hear their white brothers, sons, uncles, cousins, nephews, husbands, and fathers grumble about reverse discrimination. In addition, any financial rewards they enjoy due to affirmative action usually benefit white males in their families, considering the present rates of intermarriage. And white females are often slotted as privileged whites by affirmative-action officers, as evidenced by some of the most celebrated litigants (Sharon Taxman, Cheryl Hopwood, Yvette Farmer, Jennifer Gratz, Julia McLaughlin, and Barbara Grutter) in reverse-discrimination cases.

Asian Americans are ambivalent about affirmative action, too. They might be disadvantaged by diversity requirements in higher education, but they benefit from the efforts to promote inclusion in public contracting and corporate positions. As a group, they seem to support minority preferences, although there is considerable debate on this issue in Asian America.[32] These issues indicate that many Asian Americans, especially those who are native-born, assimilated, middle-income members of the group, are not racial minorities in a traditional sense. Asian Americans with the aforementioned characteristics usually are warmly accepted by their fellow Americans. This is not always the case for foreign-born, less-affluent Asian Americans, those individuals who rarely stray from their ethnic enclaves.

Affirmative action in higher education continues to make headlines, due to a number of important court cases in the last six years that have invalidated affirmative-action programs for students of color. Proponents of affirmative action in higher education contend that affirmative action helps develop America's human capital — and that it enables motivated and qualified minority students to benefit from existing educational opportunities. Moreover, the multiculturalists argue that white students profit from their exposure to ethnic heterogeneity; such experiences prepare them for the workplace, where they will have to appeal to diverse groups of consumers and work with and manage heterogeneous groups of people.[33] Colleges and universities take many factors besides grades, test scores, and extracurricular activities into account when they select students.

Texas, Florida, and California eliminated affirmative action in higher education in response to legal decisions and political considerations. To preserve diversity in higher education, the three states have enacted laws that guarantee any in-state student admission to a state college or university if s/he meets the class-rank requirement: the top four percent in California, the top ten percent in Texas (where the student can also choose the school s/he wants to attend), and the top 20 percent in Florida. Despite the courts' skepticism about affirmative action, college and university administrators are reluctant to stop using it as a means to diversify their student populations. Educators and policymakers throughout America have become increasingly creative in their efforts to embrace ethnic diversity in higher education without using traditional affirmative-action programs to do so. As a result, there has not been a major decrease in minority enrollment at the state universities in Texas, Florida, and California, although the ratios at some of the most prestigious schools in California have shifted a bit.[34]

ONE NATION, INDIVISIBLE

Storm Lake, Iowa, is probably the only small town in the rural white heartland where a local CPA advertises his services to potential clients in English, Spanish, and Laotian around tax filing time. Trilingualism has become a way of life in Storm Lake, a multiethnic community of 10,076 in the northwestern part of the Hawkeye State, whose civic boosters call it "The City Beautiful." This linguistic inclusiveness is a relatively recent development; old-timers remember when German, Swedish, and Norwegian were the principal foreign languages spoken in these parts. Indeed, Storm Lake was racially homogeneous as recently as 1970, when the town's population consisted largely of Germans, Scandinavians, and other people of Northern European descent. Storm Lake's transformation into a multiracial community dates back to the mid-1970s, when Laotian refugees began coming to the town as part of the U.S. government's resettlement policy.[35]

Then, in 1982, IBP, one of the world's leading meatpacking companies, opened shop in Storm Lake. To fill the factory's low-wage positions, IBP's managers encouraged the Laotians to recruit their coethnics to work in the pork-processing plant. These successful recruiting efforts greatly expanded the Laotian population of Storm Lake. In the early 1990s, legal and illegal immigrants from Mexico and Central America began migrating to Storm Lake to work at IBP too.[36] Today 2,121 Latinos and 790

Asians make their home in Storm Lake: The city is 69.8% white, 21.1% Latino, and 7.7% Asian. The sounds of Lao and Spanish fill the air in Storm Lake. Some people from both ethnic groups wear their traditional garb around town. The checkout lines at Hy-Vee and Wal-Mart bear witness to the town's multiethnic character. And white students constitute a distinct minority in at least one of the public schools.

These changes do not sit well with everyone in town. The anti-immigrant crowd in Storm Lake claims the newcomers bring crime with them and provide unnecessary competition for native-born Iowans in the marketplace. They also allege that the immigrants require costly services, such as emergency care at local hospitals and expenditures on English as a Second Language in the public schools. But the Euro-American nativists are particularly troubled by a nagging sense that Storm Lake is not what it used to be, and these old-stock Iowans will tell you how it was better before *they* came. By contrast, the defenders of the newest Storm Lakers argue that the vast majority of Laotians and Hispanics are hardworking, upstanding citizens, whose presence enriches — and revitalizes — the community. The Storm Lake Diversity Task Force, a project initiated by the pro-immigrant civic leadership, promotes intercultural events, such as monthly potluck dinners, that celebrate diversity, encourage interaction, and bridge the city's racial divide.

Although social and economic segregation exists in Storm Lake, most Storm Lakers are now tepid supporters of diversity, or at least have grudgingly accepted the new face of their community. While Storm Lake still attracts attention from the national press due to its racial tensions, it is increasingly being recognized as a model of interracial amity. The City Beautiful will undoubtedly continue to be a microcosm of demographic change in rural America, but the news stories about the town in 2010 and 2020 will probably characterize it as yet another American success story, where people from heterogeneous backgrounds come together, learn to live side by side, and eventually create bonds of family and community that transcend race and ethnicity.

Anti-immigrant sentiments, to paraphrase H. Rap Brown's aphorism about violence, are as American as cherry pie. The particulars differ, but the fundamentals are always the same: competition for jobs and wages and fears of cultural dislocation, particularly due to ethnic, linguistic, and religious differences. There was a brief outpouring of anti-immigrant sentiment in the early 1990s, which stemmed from native-born Americans' fears about the costs of immigration. According to the stereotypes, immigrants either did not pull their own weight (the erroneous notion that the newcomers were burdensome charges who took advantage of generous social services) or they were obsequious worker bees (the equally insidious notion that the newcomers toiled for long hours and low wages and consequently made homegrown American workers look bad in comparison). An amorphous sense of cultural dislocation — the opinion that the largely Latino and Asian immigrants were simply too alien and too foreign to suit Anglo sensibilities — also influenced the national mood about immigration.[37] These issues play out in multiple ways, from laws that declare English the official language (25 states have such statutes) to municipal ordinances that restrict the number of people who can live in a given residence.

White backlash against immigration and the related issue of multiculturalism still exists, albeit in an attenuated form. But the new nativism largely faded after the U.S. economy surged and unemployment rates dipped so low that many Americans were no longer afraid that immigrants would take their jobs. Meanwhile, economists heatedly debate whether immigration is a net plus or minus for the U.S. economy, and the pro-immigration crowd appears to have the upper hand in the current discussions. Many immigrants have little formal education, so they work at menial jobs — and their presence in the labor market sometimes has the effect of depressing wages for blue-collar work.[38] During the boom years of the mid- and late 1990s, Americans became more immigrant-friendly. It seemed, after all, as if there were plenty of jobs for everyone. Until the terrorist attacks on September 11, 2001, Americans strongly favored the generous immigration allowances that brought hundreds of thousands of newcomers to the United States each year during the 1990s. However, it is possible that the national mood about immigration may change, due to concerns about foreign terrorists and the scarcity of well-paying jobs in an economic recession.

America's largest racial groups — whites and blacks — are continually integrating immigrants into their intraracial coalitions. European immigrants tend to be easily accepted, if not embraced, by native-born whites. Euro-Americans generally feel magnanimous toward the new arrivals. They fondly recollect the stories and examples of their own immigrant ancestors, and presume that the Europeans will quickly pull their own weight and become "good Americans." Arab immigrants, along with Turks, Iranians, and Armenians, are also accepted without much hostility on the part of native-born white Americans, although they might be initially put off by the newcomers' religious beliefs, foreign-sounding names, and unfamiliar facial features. At least three million foreign-born whites have arrived in the United States since the 1960s, and their American-born children are virtually indistinguishable from other Caucasians here.

Two factors — rapid upward mobility and tremendous ethnic heterogeneity — enable white immigrants to assimilate quickly and assume the generic white identity. The third- and fourth-generation descendants of the Southern and Eastern European immigrants who came to the United States during the period from 1890 to 1924 are now wholly American, meaning that few of them feel any tangible connection to any country besides the United States. These European Americans are very likely to be of mixed ethnic origins and, in any event, those who still trace their heritage to one country have few of the distinguishing characteristics that would mark them as foreign. In the 1950s and 1960s, social scientists sometimes asked respondents to rank the various ethnic subgroups in the white population, and to assess the veracity of stereotypical conceptions about the different groups. Today such a survey would be difficult to conduct, with results of limited utility, because the ethnic and religious distinctions between and among native-born whites simply do not have the same salience that they did even a quarter century ago.

Just as whites are becoming accustomed to large-scale immigration from the Middle East and Eastern Europe, intraracial relations are becoming more complicated for African Americans, too, because of the increasing number of black African, Caribbean, and Latin American immigrants in their midst. At one time, the term black was instantly synonymous with English-speaking, native-born Americans of African descent: This one-dimensional conception of race is changing due to the presence of over one million foreign-born blacks in the United States. Miami's Little Haiti, one of the nation's premier black-immigrant communities, looks and feels quite different from the African-American neighborhoods of Overtown and Liberty City, which exist in close proximity to this colorful ethnic enclave of Creole-speaking refugees from Hispaniola.[39] Although the two groups do not interact much and sometimes clash over cultural matters, African Americans are, in the main, sympathetic to the plight of Haitian refugees. Jamaicans also have a large presence in South Florida, but as English-speakers, they integrate more easily than Haitians into the African-American community.[40]

Black immigrants have the highest profile in New York, especially in the Flatbush neighborhood of Brooklyn, which is home to thousands of West Indians who coexist peaceably with their African-American neighbors. African-American New Yorkers share a racial, though not an ethnic bond, with the city's large Jamaican and Haitian communities.[41] In the late 1990s African Americans embraced two black immigrants — a Haitian (Abner Louima) and a Guinean (Amadou Diallo) — who were well-known victims of police brutality in New York City. Overall, the young black immigrants and their native-born progeny are quickly subsumed into the respective ranks of white and black, as the ethnic, cultural, linguistic, and religious bases for intraracial differences fade, dissipate, and eventually disappear.

Since the 1960s racial strife has taken precedence over intraracial — read white-versus-white — cultural conflicts as the principal source of disharmony in the United States. At one time, numerous cultural conflicts (evolution, temperance, the teaching of German in public schools) had ethnic overtones or ethno-religious connotations.[42] Class conflicts were frequently fought among ethnically similar groups of whites, such as when cash-strapped Midwestern farmers fulminated against avaricious Eastern bankers a century ago. Today we rarely hear the rhetoric of class resentment in mainstream discourse — in what has become a fundamentally middle class nation. Americans tend to be far less oriented toward redistributing the wealth than their counterparts in other capitalist democracies. The prominence of other divisions, chiefly racial ones, may prevent social class from having the same kind of significance in America that it has in, say, Great Britain.[43] But many parts of the United States, those that are almost exclusively white, do not really confront race-related issues. In the others, the tenor and nature of interracial contact and relations depend on the population groups in the area — and the various factors that affect their relationships.

Most Americans have little interest in fighting over race, ethnicity, and religion, at least compared to the people who live in Bosnia, Kosovo, Kashmir, Johannesburg, Northern Ireland, and other datelines for ethnic strife. Yet some places, such as Chicago and New York City, have particular histories of racial tensions. Moreover, ethnic and racial conflicts now occur in Fargo, Minneapolis, and other formerly homogeneous cities, as racial heterogeneity begins to affect much of the United States. Images of race come from the mainstream media for many white Americans, who do not interact with minorities on a regular, sustained basis. These media portrayals often caricature race and generally focus on a few hot-button issues, such as the O. J. Simpson saga during the mid-1990s.[44]

Racial attitudes are structured by one's upbringing, socioeconomic status, educational background, and contact with members of other racial and ethnic groups. In today's atmosphere, where there is no small amount of white guilt over past transgressions and present inequities, most Americans hasten to prove that they are tolerant, unprejudiced, and open-minded with regard to racial matters. The contact hypothesis, a longtime tenet of social science, posits that sustained interracial contact in a neutral, noncompetitive environment disproves stereotypes and promotes racial comity.[45] Highly competitive situations, primarily with poor or working-class protagonists, who joust over scarce resources in the schools or the workplace, are the spawning grounds for racial friction.

No one knows for sure the precise breakdown of Americans' feelings about race. Respondents in opinion polls, especially white people, are affected by who does the asking, how the questions are asked, and to whom they are asked. Thus polls are merely a snapshot of the views of a particular group of people at a particular period in time. Moreover, we Americans consistently overestimate the number of minorities in the United States, a misconception that may affect our feelings about the claims made by people of color for power, recognition, and resources.[46] Whites and minorities differ on various issues, particularly regarding the degree to which discrimination continues to be an impediment for people of color. Due to the reticence of some survey respondents to give their true — and politically incorrect — views about racial issues to pollsters, it is nearly impossible to say how many Americans are prejudiced. But almost every measure of survey data in the last 50 years demonstrates that there has been an evolution of American racial attitudes on key indicators, from racial intermarriage to residential integration.[47]

Organized racist activity remains relatively rare in the United States. The Southern Poverty Law Center, an organization that monitors extremist activity, counted 676 active U.S. hate groups in 2001.[48] Most hate groups can claim only a handful of members and sympathizers. American racists continue to be a notoriously fractious and disunited bunch, who are divided by doctrinal differences and personal rivalries. We are intimately familiar with lowbrow haters from the television coverage of sparsely attended and heavily publicized Klan rallies. Lowbrow haters are the barely literate poor whites who delight in twisting their faces into anger using intemperate, epithet-laden language for the omnipresent television cameras at such events. Highbrow haters, by contrast, wear suits and ties, speak in measured tones, and cloak their despicable arguments in specious intellectualism. White supremacists such as Don Black and Matt Hale, both of whom have thriving Web sites, regularly appear on television. They try to seem reasonable and persuade Americans to endorse viewpoints that win few supporters these days.

The American public is utterly unreceptive to the racists' bilious message of hate. Communities usually refuse to permit Klan members to rally or neo-Nazis to march, and only do so under court order. When these instances of racial theater occur, the protesters often outnumber the racists — and not by a little bit, either. Likewise, hate crimes are widely publicized but relatively atypical examples of racial animosity.[49] Whites, of course, do not have a monopoly on hatred in the United States. Critics often single out Louis Farrakhan, the head of the Nation of Islam, the country's largest black-nationalist group, who has made numerous anti-Semitic and anti-white utterances over the years, and whose organization includes many members who endorse such views.[50] At the same time the activists and leaders of the traditional civil rights community struggle to win public backing for their left-of-center objectives.

Many Americans consider our racial problems to be largely solved, and have little patience for grievances that lack the moral immediacy of the social issues that spurred the civil rights movement four decades ago. This lack of interest in issues of racial justice greatly frustrates ethnic advocates because even their putative constituents often have little interest in the agendas that they develop and the issue positions they propound. Therefore, civil rights leaders consistently look for issues that will allow them to recapture the moral high ground that they so clearly occupied in 1955, 1960, and 1965. The spate of black church burnings in 1995–1996 seemed at first to be a clear-cut example of evil that resembled the civil-rights-era atrocities of the 1950s and 1960s. But it soon became evident that many of the fires had been set by disgruntled teenagers and twentysomethings — white and black alike — who were motivated more by youthful rebellion and anti-religious feelings than racial animosity. By raising such issues as church burnings and police brutality, the minority elites seek to restore the moral dimension of their struggle for equal rights.[51] Indeed, there are few parts of America where large numbers of people overtly express their disdain for another group of Americans based on race, ethnicity, or national origin.

While African-American, Hispanic, and Asian-American academics and ethnic advocates may see themselves as having a common agenda, the individuals they purport to lead and speak for rarely share this rosy view of rainbow unity. African Americans still fight with whites for their piece of the economic pie, and increasingly they feel they are being pushed aside in favor of the rapidly growing immigrant populations of Hispanics and Asians. In some respects, many blacks are skeptical about the new immigration; a predominantly English-speaking group, they share with some whites feelings of antipathy toward foreign-language signage and other instances of cultural change. In addition, they fear competition from other groups for the special dispensations they feel are warranted them — and that other minorities obtain without a history of slavery and segregation. Moreover, inner-city blacks are often wary of the immigrant entrepreneurs, particularly Koreans, who brave high crime rates and open ethnic hostility to operate gas stations, liquor stores, and convenience marts in blighted neighborhoods.[52]

Indeed, the survey data show that minorities are as skeptical about each other as they are about whites. People of color remain deeply divided on the issue of whether they get a fair shake in white society, but they continue to be somewhat suspicious about others outside their ethno-racial group. The central issue of minority group relations, then, is whether individual nonwhite groups would rather ally with whites to achieve their goals instead of forming trans-minority group coalitions. So far, at least, the evidence suggests that people of color are just as likely to ally with Caucasians as with other minorities.[53]

In the nation's warm-weather ethnic cauldrons, blacks and Hispanics compete for resources and fight pitched battles with each other, over such issues as city jobs and control of the public schools. The cultural clashes seem to occur most frequently between Latino immigrants and native-born African Americans. These tensions are perhaps most pronounced in Miami. Indeed, African Americans resent the dominance of Cuban Americans in Miami and its environs. A powershift — from Anglos to white Cubans — occurred in Miami during the 1960s and 1970s. Many blacks, who faced widespread discrimination in South Florida before the civil rights era, remain poor, bitter, and largely disenfranchised. It is difficult for African Americans in South Florida to watch the white Cuban refugees prosper while many blacks languish in poverty. Cuban Americans, of course, are very proud of their stellar track record in the United States. The white Latinos contend that Miami's blacks lag behind the region's other ethnic and racial groups because they do not take advantage of all the opportunities available to them in South Florida.[54]

African Americans remain far more powerful in Los Angeles than their counterparts in Miami, but the city's Mexicans and Central Americans are rapidly gaining on them. Los Angeles will soon be a Hispanic-majority city, and poor and working-class blacks increasingly feel out of place there. Onetime bastions of black Los Angeles, such as the cities of Compton and Inglewood, are now becoming heavily Latino. South Central Los Angeles was once mostly black, but it probably had a Latino majority by the mid-1990s. Watts, the site of the 1965 riots that focused attention on the grievances of black Angelenos, is now three-fifths Latino. African Americans are leaving Los Angeles for the surrounding suburbs and elsewhere, driven away by crime, gangs, bad schools, high housing prices—and the rising clout and numbers of the city's Hispanic population.[55]

WORDS AS WEAPONS

In November 1996, *Emerge* magazine published a scathing cover story about Supreme Court Justice Clarence Thomas. The unflattering cover art depicted the bespectacled jurist as a lawn jockey with a full-toothed smile. Moreover, the accompanying headline characterized the nation's leading black conservative as "Uncle Thomas," and stated that he was a "Lawn Jockey for The Far Right."[56] The article inside the magazine featured an illustration of Justice Thomas shining Justice Antonin Scalia's shoes. This illustration was a snide pictorial reference to the perception that Thomas took his cues from Scalia, due to their philosophical commonalities and frequent concurrences on the bench.

Indeed, Justice Thomas is commonly labeled—smeared might be the proper word, depending on your ideological predilections—as an "Uncle Tom" by some of his fellow blacks, who resent the Georgia native's right-wing stances and dislike the results of his jurisprudence. A member of the Supreme Court since 1991, Thomas is very unpopular with the elite segments of the African-American community, like the editorial staff of the now-defunct *Emerge,* because of his conservative positions on such issues as voting rights, affirmative action, and school busing to achieve racial integration. He clearly is disdainful of the standard liberal orthodoxies, and will not be dissuaded or diverted from his potentially groundbreaking efforts to reshape the body of American law by a few sneers or unpleasant remarks.

The epithet-cum-sobriquet that has bedeviled Thomas since he became a national figure entered the lexicon during the 1850s: Uncle Tom was the title character in Harriet Beecher Stowe's best-selling antebellum novel about slavery.[57] According to *Random House Webster's College Dictionary,* which flags the entry with its standard disclaimer about "disparaging and offensive" words and phrases, an Uncle Tom is "a black person who is regarded as being abjectly servile or deferential to whites."[58] Nonblacks rarely use the term, which is essentially off-limits to them.

During the twentieth century, African Americans co-opted the term and gave it widespread currency, transforming a literary reference into a contemptuous, in-group slur for black men. Subsequent derivations of the phrase — the verb tenses "tommed" and "tommin' " — refer to the act of being an Uncle Tom. The term is so biting that Mexican Americans speak disdainfully of *tío tacos* and Native Americans periodically disparage their ideologically wayward coethnics as *Uncle Tomahawks*. Thomas, meanwhile, has been a member of the Court for over a decade now. He has begun to carve out his own judicial identity, separate from Scalia, although both men continue to be the Court's most conservative members.[59] The saga of Clarence Thomas and Uncle Tom highlights the importance of words as weapons in our multiracial society.

Racial slurs and vile epithets continue to be part of American racial dialogues, if only at the interpersonal level. It is no accident that slurs and profanities are among the first words that immigrants learn. Offensive slang words often stem from uncertain origins, or originate from inept translations or adaptations of foreign words. Slurs come in pan-ethnic and ethnic-specific varieties. Derogatory references like *gook* and *slant eyes* are applied indiscriminately to Asian Americans with epicanthic folds, while *Chink* and *Jap*, for instance, are ethnic-specific slurs that refer to Chinese and Japanese people, respectively. Contemporary racists call Hispanics *spics*, while *wetback* is a racial insult for undocumented immigrants — ostensibly because they swim or wade through the Rio Grande to get to the United States.

Then there are in-group terms that minorities use to disparage their co-ethnics whom they perceive to be pro-white sycophants. Often they do so by using culinary analogies that mean a person is white inside, regardless of her external coloration: *Oreos* (blacks), *coconuts* (Hispanics), *bananas* (Asians), and *apples* (American Indians). African Americans make plantation analogies, particularly in the political context, and ridicule those blacks who are allegedly too close to the white power structure — the master in today's lingo — with barbed witticisms about the master-slave relationship. Mexicans sometimes refer to assimilated Mexican Americans as *pochos;* the term, according to Earl Shorris, refers to a Mexican American "who has traded his language and culture for the illusory blandishments of life in the United States."[60] Despite the offensive nature of these terms, they continue to be part of our vernacular.

Verbal weaponry implicates ethnic iconography as well. Many Native Americans find Indian athletic iconography demeaning and racist, and say they experience mental anguish when they hear fans chant,

"Go Braves," or see them waving Redskins pennants. The prominent professional teams with Indian-related names — the Atlanta Braves, the Chicago Blackhawks, the Cleveland Indians, the Kansas City Chiefs, the Washington Redskins — have thus far refused to change their names or get rid of the pseudo-Indian chants and icons that their fans love so much. An estimated 2,500 high school and college teams still have Indian team names, logos, and mascots, while at least 600 institutions have dropped these pejoratives, usually after an extended period of reflection and acrimonious debate.[61] Chief Illiniwek, the mascot of the University of Illinois, is especially controversial.[62] White fans, in particular, often view their Indian team names and mascots as almost sacrosanct, and they fight passionately to retain them.

In addition, Indians protest the usage of the word *squaw*, which is a derogatory reference to females of their race, in place names around the United States. Five states — Maine, Oregon, Montana, Oklahoma, and Minnesota — ban the use of place names that include the S-word. Still, at least 900 U.S. place names include it, such as Michigan's Squaw Island, California's Squaw Valley, Arizona's Squaw Peak Recreation Area, and Missouri's Squaw Creek National Wildlife Reserve.[63] It is only a matter of time before many of these places will be renamed. With few exceptions, there has not been much acrimony in the debates over whether to excise the word *squaw* from place names.

Most Americans refuse to discuss race in mixed company. They shy away from the volatile topic because they do not want to offend their fellow discussants, just as they avoid discussions of politics and religion. When Americans do voice their complaints and feelings about racial issues, they usually frame their discussions in terms of class, crime, and the like. There is a de facto realm of the legitimate in popular and elite discourse. Certain topics are essentially off-limits; if a person brings them up, he risks being ostracized by the mainstream.[64] However, Americans often circumvent the strictures of political correctness through the use of code words and proxy issues. The most open and honest dialogues about race may occur on the Internet, where people say what they really think in the mistaken belief they are anonymous.[65]

Away from the think tanks, academic conferences, blue-ribbon panels, and television talk shows, ordinary Americans discuss racial issues, often disregarding multicultural sensitivities, in taverns, bowling alleys, and lunch rooms; and at job sites, family reunions, and around the dinner table. Professional provocateurs such as the late Khallid Abdul Muhammad and former Ku Klux Klan leader David Duke thrive on inflammatory rhetoric, which attracts a niche audience, even though it permanently estranges them from the mainstream. Comedians are the one group of Americans who are allowed to push the envelope, to some extent, on racial issues — when they offend, they succeed. In recent years, Chris Rock has established himself as the nation's preeminent comedic commentator on racial issues. His clever takes on the ironies, hypocrisies, and double-talk that attend race in America resonate with many Americans, particularly his fellow African Americans.[66] Americans, to be sure, relish straight talk on racial issues, so long as the comedian, politico, or speaker does not seem racist or mean-spirited in his or her remarks.

The differences between racist expressions and merely impolitic words are sometimes blurry, and may depend on the context. Americans sometimes half-jokingly engage in racially charged repartee. This ethnic banter occurs without incident only among old friends who are quite comfortable with each other, but it is largely off-limits in the workplace or the schoolyard. There is a limited level of acceptance for Americans to use offensive terms among themselves, to be affectionate or mildly insulting, e.g., a couple of Irishmen calling each other *micks*. But if an outsider uses the forbidden terms, or indulges in ethnic humor — usually ribald jokes that highlight stereotypes and frequently are overtly bigoted and racist — he might be on the receiving end of glares, foul words, a beating, or even death.

The general consensus regarding racist speech (hateful tirades that denigrate human beings based on their ethnicity, religion, or race) breaks down, to some extent, when it comes to discussions of controversial social policies. Some leftists view any criticisms of affirmative action, bilingual education, and other multicultural initiatives as racist speech, even if the critics of these programs make reasonable arguments in mainstream language. During the 1980s many leading universities adopted speech codes that were designed to restrict "hate speech" and prevent minorities from being harassed while on campus. Civil libertarians protested, often successfully, that these efforts ran aground of First Amendment protections for free speech.[67] The speech codes reflected the earnest attempts of university administrators to make students from traditionally underrepresented groups feel welcome on campus.

The discussions of "acceptable" speech involve considerations of talk radio, literary works, and more. When it comes to "acceptable speech," talk radio is 180 degrees in the opposite direction from the left-wing campuses. Although mainstream conservative hosts (Rush Limbaugh comes to mind) rankle liberals, it is the so-called shock jocks (Bob Grant certainly qualifies as a member of this group) who regularly rant against feminists, civil rights activists, and other multiculturalists. The more outrageous their assertions, it seems, the higher their ratings.[68] Civil libertarians may scoff at talk radio, but they are wary of efforts to censor or restrict the books stocked at stores, taught in schools, and shelved at libraries. The repetitious use of the N-word in Mark Twain's *Adventures of Huckleberry Finn* makes it offensive to black schoolchildren — and has even led to its removal from some classroom reading lists.[69] Harper Lee's *To Kill a Mockingbird,* published in 1960, recently met a similar fate in at least one school district, even though it won the Pulitzer Prize in 1961 and was made into an Academy Award-winning movie starring Gregory Peck in 1962. These conflicts over the spoken word and the written word will increase in significance as minorities become increasingly numerous and wield more political and economic clout.

Politicians, businesspeople, and other public figures and institutions are particularly careful to avoid any kind of connection whatsoever to intolerance — and intolerant remarks. No one wants to be tarred with the brush of racism. Politicians will lose votes. Corporations will lose customers. Non-profit organizations will lose funding. Damage control, as a result, usually occurs quickly in such a situation. Typically, if a person makes a rhetorical faux pas, he has to apologize effusively and immediately, or he will be unceremoniously demoted or terminated from his position. Athletes often lose lucrative commercial endorsements after they make rhetorical blunders. But O'Shea Jackson, better known as the hard-core rapper Ice Cube, has suffered few losses in his budding movie career, despite his antiwhite and anti-Korean diatribes in the early 1990s. Americans apparently viewed Ice Cube's raps as vacuous posturing and a form of entertainment.

Public figures, especially celebrities and corporate chieftains, usually strive to avoid controversy, so as to avoid tarnishing their image — or, in the case of businesspeople, that of their corporation. Vigilant employers fear lawsuits by disgruntled employees who might sue them over a racially hostile work atmosphere, so they prohibit any kind of prejudicial behavior: racist e-mails, insensitive remarks, and offensive actions.[70] Most Americans, after all, agree that racial diversity is something positive, even though we do not always agree about how to facilitate inclusion in specific venues and contexts.

Crude, earthy language still remains part of our vernacular, however, as evidenced by the plethora of in-group and out-group epithets for white people. For starters, there are ethnic-specific terms. A prejudiced white person might speak of his fellow Caucasians as Irish *micks,* German *krauts*, Polish *polacks*, Italian *wops* and *dagos*, and Jewish *kikes* and *Hymies*. In addition, he may use the word *jew* as a verb in the context of buying and selling, in a reference to that perennial bugaboo of anti-Semites: envy of Jewish economic success. Gentiles periodically denigrate affluent Jewish women as *JAPs* (*Jewish-American Princesses*). Jews, to be sure, have their own derisive Yiddish words for gentiles: *shiksa* for non-Jewish females and *shegetz* for non-Jewish males. European Americans might denigrate Arabs as *ragheads, towel heads,* or *camel jockeys*. And there still are Americans who might find crude ethnic jokes about blondes or Polish Americans humorous; both types of ethnic humor rely on punch lines that disparage members of these groups as unintelligent. Educated Americans generally frown upon any kind of ethnic stereotyping, even when the scapegoats are members of the racial majority group, who presumably benefit from "white privilege."

Then there are the general terms for whites as a group. African Americans and other people of color might disparage white people by calling them *Okies, crackers, honkies, rednecks, white trash,* or, in the case of white men, *white boys*. Whites and minorities alike frequently use the terms *white trash* and its analogue, *trailer trash,* a derogatory term for whites who live in mobile home communities, to describe the poorer members of the Caucasian race. White people often use such terms as *cracker, hillbilly,* and *white trash* among themselves, as a way of denoting class distinctions. Of these terms, *white trash* is probably the most vicious — this contemptible slur takes into account race and socioeconomic status as it analogizes garbage and human beings.[71] *Cracker* is not a positive term by any means, but it lacks the brute force of *white trash*. No one wants to be called a *hillbilly* either, but the usage of this term would not precipitate a bout of fisticuffs (the surest barometer of the viciousness of a slur) as quickly as if someone started throwing around the epithet *white trash*.

While the term *redneck* is still pejorative in some contexts — and may be synonymous with the adjectives ignorant and racist depending on its usage — it increasingly is adopted by whites, particularly in the South, as a badge of honor. Country musicians rhapsodize about *rednecks,* but, tellingly, they never celebrate *crackers, hillbillies,* and *white trash*. The comedian Jeff Foxworthy has created a cottage industry as a result of his wildly popular comedy routines about *rednecks* and the *redneck* way of life, with restaurants, greeting cards, desktop calendars, multiple best-selling books, a failed television sitcom, two multiplatinum comedy albums, and marquee appearances around the country.[72] There are books and Web sites that celebrate *rednecks,* as well as cultural events such as the annual Redneck Games in East Dublin, Georgia. Many of the people who embrace the term *redneck* as a self-identifier are neither poor nor intolerant of ethnic, racial, and religious diversity. To the self-described *rednecks,* the R-word represents a cultural identity that reflects one's pride in a down-home way of life.[73]

The most controversial slur of all is one applied to African Americans — the word *nigger.* All the other hateful epithets used by racists to disparage African Americans — *coons, spooks, darkies, jungle bunnies, spearchuckers,* and the like — pale in comparison to the N-word.[74] Andrew Hacker writes, "This word has the force to pierce, to wound, to penetrate, as no other has."[75] Most older African Americans remember how often they were called the N-word as children, or were reduced, metaphorically, to being merely a *nigger.* The N-word is so vicious that it has gained currency for other ethnic groups: Bigots refer to Arabs as *sand niggers,* and they dismiss Great Plains Indians as *prairie niggers.* Disenfranchised people of all races use the term *nigger* as a self-referential shorthand to express their feelings of oppression and marginalization. Usually the media refer to this vile epithet using a delicate shorthand — the N-word, the 'N' word, or n———.[76]

The N-word, of course, is controversial in black America, even though some African Americans use it in their daily lives. Depending on the context, the N-word might be a term of affection — or of derision — when it is used by an African American who is speaking about or to another African American. Indeed, the N-word is a favorite of black rappers and a staple of the comedic routines of many African-American humorists. And the phrase "bad nigger" is a badge of honor for some black men. It means that an African-American man lives his life as he sees fit, without regard to the social conventions of white society. Nonetheless, many African Americans believe that the N-word is so hateful that it should not be used by blacks in any context. This is one of the reasons why a group of African Americans launched an ultimately unsuccessful campaign in the late 1990s to remove the N-word from *Merriam-Webster's Collegiate Dictionary.* Spike Lee and others worry that the prevalence of the term in U.S. popular culture desensitizes Americans to its meaning.[77] In any event, everyone, even hard-core racists, realizes that the N-word is off-limits to nonblacks; some whites, therefore, delight in using it to offend people.

The N-word is a staple of white-supremacist Web sites on the Internet, which allow haters to reach the entire world for a pittance. Cash-strapped

white supremacists and other bigots had few opportunities to disseminate their messages and spew their venomous rhetoric before the advent
of the World Wide Web. The typical Web site for haters offers a prosaic
message of bile and bigotry, along with opportunities to purchase racist
publications and other accouterments of the white-supremacist lifestyle.
Anti-hate watch groups — the Southern Poverty Law Center and the Simon Wiesenthal Center chief among them — are vigilant in tracking the
on-line efforts of far-right hatemongers, who delight in crude attacks on
gays, Jews, blacks, and nonwhites in general. These forums (newsgroups,
chat rooms, Web sites, and electronic bulletin boards) embolden haters
by creating a sense of community for them. Although most Internet service providers (ISPs) allow racist Web sites, parents can choose to install
anti-hate software filters on their computers to prevent their youngsters
from accessing hate sites. Even many racial liberals reason that majority
opinion is against the haters anyway, and that however despicable or re-
volting we find them, it is best to ignore their poisonous messages rather
than try to censor them.[78]

The diversity imperative is going to matter more to Americans in coming
years, and in places where it has never mattered before, due to the influx
of nonwhite immigrants and growing numbers of minority babies. There
are still venues in American society where the nation's diversity is not even
close to being represented in proportional terms — Congress, Wall Street,
NASCAR racing. By 2010 or 2015 most Americans will regard all-white-
male lineups as peculiar, or even as prima facie evidence of discriminatory
employment practices. Racial milestones, like the first black employee at a
fast-food restaurant or the first Chinese-American family on a city block,
occur regularly and with little fanfare. Norman Y. Mineta became the
first Asian American to join the Cabinet in 2000, for instance, and the
mainstream media barely took notice. And the selection of Angela Perez
Baraquio as Miss America 2001 — she was the first woman of Asian
ancestry to wear the crown — received little attention either.

Now that Latinos account for one in eight Americans, we celebrate
the "firsts" and other demographic milestones that involve people with
Spanish surnames on a regular basis. Sometime during the next decade
the United States will probably get its first Hispanic Supreme Court Justice. President Bush is very likely to fill a vacancy on the nine-member
Court with a Latino jurist.[79] We can also expect Hispanics to press aggressively for greater representation in the workforce, particularly for public

jobs. Latinos have already clashed with African Americans in areas such as Houston and Los Angeles where blacks hold public-sector positions in percentages that exceed their share of the population.[80] These debates will occur with increasing frequency in the future.

Once more females and people of color hold positions of power, it will become increasingly difficult for members of these groups to blame their troubles solely on racism or sexism and discrimination. But unskilled immigrants keep coming to the United States, thus providing the ethnic advocates with fresh bodies to sustain their group-based claims of exclusion. At any rate, we Americans have already made considerable progress in eliminating the exclusionary practices that once sharply delimited the opportunities open to women, minorities, persons with disabilities, and others. The most telling sign that we are making progress on the ethnic-equity and gender-equity fronts comes whenever a minority or woman receives a major appointment or promotion and the occurrence is common enough that it is no longer newsworthy — at least in terms of race or gender.

Moreover, in some circumstances, whites will be recruited to satisfy diversity requirements. On occasion white students may even receive minority scholarships, as do some of the Caucasians who attend Historically Black Colleges and Universities (HBCUs). Whites are unused to being seen in this light, and many minorities are skeptical of the isolated instances of affirmative-action programs that benefit white people due to their race. But the proportionalistic logic dictates representation by numbers, and in those cases where whites are underrepresented, the correctives may involve forms of affirmative action.

Global market forces increasingly affect the diversity imperative in the United States. Foreign consumers exercise influence in this regard through their purchases and consumption habits. When a Thai teenager buys a Britney Spears CD instead of one by Lil' Kim, she augments the white star's fan base — and increases the probability that music promoters will choose up-and-coming singers with the same sound and pigmentation in the future. Approximately one-half of the revenues for such U.S. media as books and movies come from the global marketplace. This fact increasingly shapes the content (settings, story lines, and cast makeup) of American films.[81] In this environment, it becomes more difficult for black producers and directors to get Hollywood's white decision-makers to fund big-budget films with "black" themes. Studio executives are often reluctant to back such projects, which they perceive to have limited appeal outside the African-American community. Even though there is significant evidence that black-themed films can be quite profitable, the actors in such movies often receive salaries that are not always commensurate with their box-office appeal, at least vis-à-vis similarly situated white actors.[82]

During the next decade Hollywood will probably start making more movies starring ethnic Chinese actors, as China embraces capitalism and its people become part of the worldwide market for entertainment products. While the Chinese have shown a willingness to embrace Western films starring people of European ancestry, they certainly would not be averse to seeing Western cultural imports that include ethnic Chinese as protagonists. Jackie Chan, a Hong Konger, has become the first star from China to make the successful transition from Hong Kong's cinema to mainstream Hollywood films. His English may not be perfect, but he is following in the footsteps of Europeans like Arnold Schwarzenegger and Jean-Claude Van Damme, who parlayed their muscular physiques into lucrative careers as action stars. The growing power of foreign consumers to dictate the content of American cultural products subtly erodes U.S. national sovereignty, and is a little-discussed consequence of globalization.

Foreign businesspeople make decisions regarding diversity issues, too, such as how they market to Americans and where they site their operations in the United States. The German auto manufacturers BMW and Mercedes-Benz have assembly plants in the Deep South (BMW in South Carolina, Mercedes-Benz in Alabama); they are required by federal law to hire African Americans, in order to be in compliance with affirmative-action rules. Such dictates apply to businesses nationwide, of course, but the demographic pressures that exist in Alabama and South Carolina are largely absent in states such as Iowa, Idaho, and Maine, where whites far outnumber people of color.

English, Dutch, French, German, Italian, and Japanese fashion mavens regularly make hiring and advertising decisions that determine the direction of American style. Magazine editors and fashion designers are cautious about featuring females other than lithe, Nordic-looking women, for fear of adversely affecting the sales of magazines, clothing, and cosmetics. So the top models are just as likely to hail from Canada, Corsica, Russia, Germany, Great Britain, southern Brazil, or the Czech Republic, as they are to come from the ample battalions of American females.[83]

PART THREE

Whites Still Matter Most

~ chapter seven ~

Accommodating Diversity

"We are one," Mayor-elect Larry Delgado told the cheering crowd of supporters on March 3, 1998, that gathered in a ballroom at the Radisson Hotel in Santa Fe to celebrate his landslide victory in the day's balloting. "We always have to remember that. We're all one."[1] Delgado, fittingly, addressed Santa Fe's ethnic divide in his Tuesday night victory speech — it had been a major theme of his inclusive mayoral campaign. The brouhaha over diversity dated back to the late 1970s, when Santa Fe's temperate climate, excellent amenities, Southwestern cachet, and reputation for fine art began to receive international attention. More than two decades ago foreign visitors and Anglo jet-setters began to descend in large numbers upon this city of 62,203 in northern New Mexico.[2]

The influx of affluent Anglo migrants from such places as California and New York in the 1980s and 1990s drove up the property values and cost of living in and around Santa Fe, which used to be a Hispanic-majority city with low prices and ethnic harmony. Consequently, many of the Hispanic locals felt little kinship with the new residents, who patronized exclusive retailers, restaurants, art galleries, and cultural venues such as the Georgia O'Keeffe Museum and the renowned Santa Fe Opera. The character of New Mexico's capital city, which had been founded by the Spaniards in 1609, gradually shifted to encompass a wide range of cultural and ideological diversity. Santa Fe had been traditionally Catholic, Hispanic, and culturally conservative. Many of the new migrants were secular in outlook, Anglo, and culturally liberal.[3] As a result, there were periodic clashes between the two groups on local issues.

Not surprisingly, the frosty ethnic climate affected the city's politics. Some old-stock Hispanos rallied behind Debbie Jaramillo, a city councilor who decried the cultural and demographic changes remaking Santa Fe. She was elected Santa Fe's mayor in 1994. Jaramillo proved to be a forceful, if spottily successful, opponent of development during her four years in City Hall. A series of tactical missteps and ethical blunders compromised her effectiveness, though, and she only garnered 11% of the vote in her 1998 race for reelection. Santa Fe became more polarized in the mid-1990s, in part because Jaramillo made little effort to reach out to the city's growing Anglo population.

By contrast, her successor, Larry Delgado, embraces Santa Fe's diversity. He worked to create the city's Department of Intercultural Affairs, a move that symbolically affirmed the importance of inclusion. "Everyone who lives in this city," he regularly tells his fellow Santa Feans, "should be recognized and appreciated in this city."[4] Delgado's words take on special significance in Santa Fe, due to the delicate ethnic balance there. Hispanics now constitute 47.8% of the population, and Anglos account for 47.1%. Anglos presently make up a majority of the electorate in Santa Fe. They will probably outnumber Latinos within a few years, unless the present migration patterns change.

Larry Delgado is the consummate conciliator: His heritage and temperament enable him to bring Santa Feans together. A tall, affable man in his mid-sixties with fair skin and aquamarine eyes, Delgado is the descendant of Spaniards who came to New Mexico in the early 1700s. He speaks impeccable Castilian Spanish and proudly embraces his cultural heritage. Delgado, moreover, is a lifelong Santa Fean; his father served as the city's postmaster, and both parents were well-regarded members of the community. He himself spent three decades as a highway designer with the New Mexico Highway Department. After retiring in 1986, Delgado taught school for several years before entering public life in 1990. That year he ran for and won a northside seat on the Santa Fe City Council. Delgado earned a reputation as a thoughtful, pragmatic lawmaker during his eight years as a councilor.[5]

In 1998 this son of Santa Fe ran for mayor of his hometown. Delgado's pleasant demeanor, tireless campaigning, slow-growth platform, record of volunteerism and civic involvement, and extensive network of donors and campaign workers propelled him to victory over the front-runner, former Mayor Sam Pick. The Spanish American won over many voters because he occupied the middle ground on the issue of growth; the pro-growth camp favored Pick, while the no-growth partisans backed Jaramillo. Delgado also promised to "treat everyone equally," and told voters he would have "an administration that includes everyone," regardless of whether a person had been a Santa Fean for "20 generations or 20 months." In the end, he won 44% of the vote in the nonpartisan mayoral race, while Pick took 32%, and Jaramillo barely broke into the double digits.[6]

As mayor, Delgado has been very attentive to the symbolic and substantive aspects of politics in multiethnic Santa Fe. He is a visible figure in the city, attending numerous weddings, speaking to schoolchildren, issuing hundreds of proclamations recognizing ordinary citizens, and discussing issues with his constituents in chance encounters at the grocery store. Santa Fe's chief executive spends much of his time on growth-related issues, as he tries to improve city-county relations, attract well-paying jobs to the city, develop affordable housing for working- and middle-class Santa Feans, and preserve what he terms the "specialness" of his hometown.[7] His efforts met with the approval of the Santa Fe electorate. Mayor Delgado won a comfortable reelection victory over his three challengers in March 2002.[8]

Meanwhile, the city's ethnic climate continues to improve. Now only the most obstinate nativists refuse to acknowledge that the newcomers love Santa Fe as much as they do. In addition, the strong economy of the 1990s benefited most Santa Feans, including the Hispanos who felt displaced by the Anglo migrants to northern New Mexico. Anglos exercise an increasingly significant amount of influence in the city's affairs, a development that does not sit well with everyone in Santa Fe's Hispanic community. The city council now has six Anglo members and only two Latinos.[9] There is "still a lot of work to be done" with regard to intergroup relations, as Mayor Delgado points out, but it is finally possible to envision the day when ethnic differences will no longer divide the people of Santa Fe.[10] The peaceful integration of the Anglo newcomers in northern New Mexico testifies to the warm spirit and generous outlook of Santa Feans, as embodied by the exemplary career and inclusive leadership of Larry Delgado.

MAJORITY RULE

Throughout the 2001 campaign there was talk in New York that John C. Liu would make history and become the first Asian American elected to the New York City Council. The 34-year-old actuary was the leading contender in the race to represent District 20, which encompasses Flushing, Queens. This neighborhood of 160,000 a few miles southeast of LaGuardia Airport is 37% white, 35% Asian, 22% Hispanic, and 6% black.[11] The Asian community itself is divided by ethnicity and nationality; it includes a sizable Chinese-origin population (mainlanders and Taiwanese alike), along with many Koreans and a number of Asian Indians. Not surprisingly, Liu ran as an assimilationist candidate, whose accentless English and longtime residence in the area (he moved to the United States at age five) belied the fact that he had been born in Taiwan.[12]

As one who had been involved in civic issues for years, Liu focused on the basics — affordable housing, improving the public schools, sprucing up downtown Flushing — in his campaign. Liu faced a Chinese-born opponent (Ethel Chen), a Korean-born adversary (Terence Y. Park), and an Italian-American challenger (Richard Jannaccio) in the Democratic primary. Before the primary, Liu raised a substantial amount of money for his campaign. He also was endorsed by several prominent New York politicians and the Queens County Democratic Organization.[13] On primary day, September 25, 2001, Liu narrowly edged Ethel Chen to win the crucial Democratic nomination in the district. Then, on November 7, 2001, he easily defeated three challengers to become the first person of Asian descent to be elected to the New York City Council.[14]

The results of the race symbolized the ethnic and generational transformation of Flushing. Liu succeeded Julia Harrison, the elderly white Democrat who represented the district for 16 years, from 1986 to 2002, before she was forced out by term limits. Harrison came to power at a time when the white-ethnic nature of Flushing was beginning to fade after more than seven decades. Harrison steadfastly refused to embrace her new constituents on matters big and small, and made no secret of her disdain for what she saw as their reluctance to assimilate. She never encountered any serious electoral problems as a result of her positions, because most of her white constituents probably sympathized with her views on immigration and assimilation.[15] The Asians, moreover, were not a cohesive enough voting bloc to defeat her. Still, Harrison encountered spirited opposition in the Democratic primary in 1997 from John Liu, a year after she was forced to issue a perfunctory apology for the intemperate remarks she made to the *New York Times* regarding the Asian immigrants to Flushing. Liu, then only 30 years old, ran a strong race against Harrison in the Democratic primary, and he earned her enmity as a result.[16]

In January 2002, Liu took his seat on a city council that included a great deal of ethnic diversity, due in large part to the term limits that forced veteran incumbents to retire.[17] He is already being seen by Asians throughout New York City as "their" representative.[18] Based on the electoral dynamics of his district, Liu can be expected to focus on issues that have substantial appeal to middle-class, native-born New Yorkers as well as those who are recent immigrants. Whites will probably continue to account for a majority of the voters in District 20, so Liu will almost certainly look out for their interests while he focuses on satisfying the needs of his core constituency in the Asian-American community.

Politics was fought, for the most part, between and among whites in the years before John Liu's Democratic Party embraced blacks and other people of color as an important part of its coalition during the 1960s. When the European immigrants became naturalized citizens, they reciprocated by supporting the politicians who helped them — and who seemed amenable to their presence in the United States. Nineteenth-century Irish immigrants joined the Democratic Party largely due to the domination of the GOP by native-born Protestants. In turn, Norwegians, Swedes, and Welshmen backed the Republicans a century ago, because they disliked the Irish-Catholic influence in the Democratic Party.[19] In Rhode Island, for instance, Yankee Protestants supported the Republicans, and French-Canadian, Irish, and Italian Catholics backed the Democrats. Politics, in such circumstances, served as a venue for working out broader cultural, social, and economic conflicts.[20]

From about 1932 to the late 1960s, class-conscious politics reigned supreme as ethnic urbanites staunchly supported Democrats because they felt the politics of economic redistributionism offered by that party materially benefited them. But cultural politics have assumed increasing importance since the 1960s. Lunch-bucket Democrats have, on occasion, left their ancestral home to back country-club Republicans on issues like taxes, abortion, crime, and affirmative action.[21] Conversely, affluent white liberals embrace the Democratic Party because its social agenda is generally consonant with their support for environmental protection, backing of abortion rights, and more permissive attitudes, generally, toward moral issues. Meanwhile, social scientists continue to debate the primacy of cultural attitudes versus economic self-interest as factors in determining Americans' political predilections.

Political cleavages exist largely because of the cultural and socioeconomic divisions in American society. Indeed, one's socioeconomic status often affects her or his feelings about the size and scope of government and the necessity of a public-sector safety net. Democrats usually favor a bigger government and a more expansive social-welfare system than Republicans. Whites, Asians, and men of all races are more likely than blacks, Hispanics, American Indians, and women of all races to support Republicans. In addition, race often intersects with religion to influence the political preferences of white Americans. For cultural and economic reasons, white Protestants, such as Dutch Americans and Euro-

American Southerners, tend to be the most Republican ethno-religious group. Mormons vote almost unanimously Republican; eighty-eight percent of Mormon voters backed GOP presidential nominee George W. Bush in 2000.[22] White Catholics, however, are a mixed bag politically — they are no longer hostile to the Republican Party, but they remain receptive to Democratic entreaties.[23] American Jews are second in Democratic Party loyalty only to African Americans; seventy-seven percent of them supported Democrat Al Gore in the 2000 presidential election.[24]

Indeed, each major political party is an unwieldy coalition of disparate groups — a reality that leads to diversity dilemmas that reflect the different core constituencies of the respective parties. Republicans struggle to maintain their fragile coalition of white social and economic conservatives, who clash sometimes over the party's priorities, while reaching out, half-heartedly, to minority voters. Democrats have to reconcile a fractious multiracial coalition, while trying to retain a strong enough base among white voters to stay competitive in national elections. African Americans routinely support Democratic candidates with 80% or more of their votes. Mexican Americans and Puerto Ricans generally cast more than 60% of their ballots for Democrats. Cuban Americans, conversely, usually back the Republican Party, due to their relative affluence and hawkish views on foreign policy. And Asian Americans are closely divided between the two parties.[25] Ethnic groups that monolithically back one political party run the risk of being neglected by the party in power if their members overwhelmingly support the opposition, and there is no real chance they will consider switching their allegiances in future elections.

Although at least one-quarter of American voters characterize themselves as political independents, no national third party has emerged to win their support. This is true for at least three reasons. For starters, the two-party system includes procedural obstacles that make it difficult for third parties to be considered viable political options. Moreover, independents differ so much on the issues that no political party could possibly hope to develop a coherent platform to win their support. Finally, most Americans do not want to "waste" their votes in races where third-party candidates have little chance of winning. Nonetheless, there are innumerable minor parties. The Greens, the Libertarians, and the Constitution Party all ran presidential candidates in 2000. It now appears highly unlikely that the Greens — or any other third party, for that matter — will build a viable political entity that wins wide public support. Sometimes blacks and Hispanics feel themselves caught between the Scylla of sometimes indifferent but modestly responsive Democrats and the Charybdis of frequently uncaring and utterly hostile Republicans. However, most dissatisfied African Americans and Latinos remain reluctant to desert the Democrats, because doing so would marginalize them, given the sorry record third parties have compiled at the state and national levels.

Each of the regions, states, and localities of the United States has a political culture, which is the sum total of that area's political leanings and the policies in effect there.[26] For all practical purposes, whites matter most in every statewide election (except those in Hawaii) and certainly in national elections, due to their income levels, citizenship rates, levels of educational attainment, and feelings of political efficacy. As a general rule, whites lean Republican, particularly those Caucasians who live in the Deep South, Great Plains, and rural parts of the Mountain West. White voters disagree with people of color on many policy issues, but they outvote minorities and consequently see their policy preferences take effect. The Northeast and Pacific Northwest are solidly Democratic, while the South and Mountain West are heavily Republican. And the Midwest is full of bellwether states, such as Ohio and Illinois, that favor politicians from both parties in roughly equal proportions. Rural residents traditionally support the GOP, while urbanites back Democrats, a tribute no doubt to the sizable minority presence in many cities. Suburbanites, who constitute a plurality of the national electorate and the voting-age population of many states as well, are closely divided between the two parties.[27]

The issue agenda of contemporary American politics is composed of domestic and foreign issues, with further subdivisions, especially on domestic matters, into economic and social/cultural categories. Politicians from both parties try to frame election campaigns and policy debates in terms advantageous to their issue agendas, so they can galvanize the maximum amount of support for their candidates, proposals, and positions. There are few single-issue voters, or persons who cast their ballots based on one issue alone, but de facto partisan litmus tests do exist. Democrats typically support abortion rights and the agenda of the Multicultural Left. Republicans usually oppose abortion rights. Moreover, they tend to be skeptical about many multicultural initiatives. In the South and industrial Midwest there are still Democratic officeholders who hold positions at odds with their party on abortion, gun control, and affirmative action. The Republican apostates are concentrated in California, the Northeast, and Pacific Northwest: Their brand of social liberalism and economic conservatism is barely recognizable to Southern Republicans. Both political parties have moved to the center in the last five years because they recognize that most Americans do not favor the ideological extremes.

Political socialization begins at an early age, with the cues one receives from her or his parents, peers, and authority figures. These cues in turn structure one's likelihood of participation, types of participation, and electoral behavior.[28] In writing about political participation, Sidney Verba, Kay Lehman Schlozman, and Henry E. Brady note:

> Americans who wish to take part politically have an array of options: they may express their views directly by communicating with public officials or indirectly by attempting to influence electoral outcomes; they may give time and effort or contribute dollars; they may work alone or in concert with others; they may be active at the national, state, or local level. Since different forms of political activity are differentially effective in conveying information or exerting pressure, it matters how citizens take part.[29]

However, many of us are skeptical about whether our participation really matters when the federal government seems to be influenced primarily by lobbyists, special interests, and the politicians who respond to them. Therefore, many Americans do not regularly participate in the political process.[30]

Whites have the highest rates of political participation, followed by blacks; Hispanics and Asians are at a disadvantage in this regard because of the relatively high percentages of young people and non-citizens within their ranks.[31] Low electoral participation by minority immigrants and their progeny is sometimes attributable to their socialization in political cultures where military dictators or corrupt politicians either restrict or devalue their participation.[32] Whenever possible, the Democrats try to encourage turnout among minority voters, particularly blacks, Puerto Ricans, and Mexican Americans, who can be relied upon to support Democratic candidates. The Republicans' core constituency, on the other hand, includes higher-income voters, especially whites, who are very likely to get to the polls or cast absentee ballots. Therefore, white Republicans tend to be unenthusiastic about reducing barriers to political participation. They fear that doing so might lead to increased voting by minorities, poor whites, and others sympathetic to the Democratic message.

Voter turnout in the United States is quite low for an advanced industrial nation. Voter turnout in the 2000 presidential election was 50.7%

of the electorate. It ranged from the highs of 68% (Minnesota) and 65% (Alaska and Wisconsin) and 64% (Vermont) to the lows of 41% (Arizona, Hawaii, and Nevada), 43% (Texas), and 44% (Georgia).[33] Nonvoting does not necessarily signal disenfranchisement. Millions of Americans of all ethnic backgrounds, a group that includes those whose political views place them solidly outside the mainstream, do not deign to participate in the electoral process. Many nonvoters do not feel excluded from the political system; rather, they do not feel any pressing need to vote or otherwise participate in it. Nonvoting, at bottom, is less a political statement than a personal choice.[34]

These events occur in the context of the white dominance, particularly at the highest levels, of the American political system. Affluent white donors and white-dominated political action committees provide the campaign funds politicos need to ensure their electoral survival. Consequently, lobbyists and influence peddlers, who are overwhelmingly white, have considerable access to and influence over lawmakers.[35] Wealthy candidates, moreover, are at the front of the line in the American political process, in large part due to *Buckley v. Valeo,* a 1976 Supreme Court decision. This legal precedent allows candidates to make unlimited personal expenditures in their electoral efforts; it protects such outlays as free speech.[36] Rich white candidates frequently do well in American politics. Their wealth often enables them to winnow the field of competitors. Many self-financing candidates appear amateurish in comparison to experienced public officials, however, and they frequently have inadequate organizations at the local level.[37]

Still, white male multimillionaires regularly seek and win political office. The laundry list of successful self-financing candidates includes Virginia Governor Mark Warner and New York City Mayor Michael Bloomberg, along with the following members of the U.S. Senate: Jon Corzine, Mark Dayton, John Edwards, Herbert Kohl, Peter Fitzgerald, and Jay Rockefeller. But other wealthy, free-spending white guys, including Al Checchi, Steve Forbes, Guy Millner, and Michael Huffington, have failed to realize their political ambitions. Although substantial personal expenditures do not guarantee victory, these self-financing, modern-day plutocrats benefit from the widespread perception that they cannot be bought or influenced by the special interests.

A countervailing trend, legislative term limits, is opening up opportunities for women and minorities in the political process. Laws limiting the number of terms a legislator can spend in public office exist in 17 states. (The Supreme Court has ruled that such limitations may apply to state and local, but not federal, offices.) Term limits have roiled the political landscape in several states, including Ohio, Michigan, and California, where the rapid turnover in the legislative bodies has allowed minorities and women to bolster their numbers and influence. By forcing veteran white male lawmakers to retire from office, term limits eliminate a significant barrier — the power and perquisites of incumbency, which restrict competition in the electoral sphere — to the advancement of minority and white female candidates and officeholders. As a result, there is greater fluidity in the legislative process, along with less reliance on the seniority system, when it comes to assigning committee positions and other indicators of political power.[38]

In many states with legislative term limits, women and minority legislators have assumed positions of power and influence that they ordinarily would not have had access to in the past. The results have been perhaps most dramatic in the California legislature, where Latino Democrats have been especially prominent since term limits began to take effect in the late 1990s. However, term limits also have the side effect of allowing junior lawmakers and minority legislators to exercise power only for a limited amount of time. Senior lawmakers of color and their white female counterparts have to retire eventually just like their white male colleagues.[39] Furthermore, one might argue that this diversification of the political class means little, unless dramatic changes in policy occur as a result of the different faces in power.

In recent years, people of color have become more involved in the campaign-finance process. Asian Americans raised millions of dollars for the Democrats in 1995 and 1996, a fund-raising milestone that led to allegations of an "Asian connection" between Beijing and Washington. Proponents of this theory argue that Asian nationals and Asian Americans affiliated with Beijing supported the Democratic Party during the 1995–1996 campaign cycle, as part of a conspiracy to affect American policies toward the People's Republic of China.[40] Hundreds of thousands of dollars in improper donations were made to the Democrats — all of which were returned to their donors in the months after the scandal broke in late 1996. All too often, the scandal coverage did not sufficiently distinguish between the illicit donations offered by Asian nationals and the legitimate financial contributions made by Asian Americans.[41] Some American Indian tribes, flush with profits from gaming, have become major players in the political arena, as they fight for greater sovereignty through their generous donations to politicians of both parties.[42] Moreover, the expansion of the black, Hispanic, and

Asian-American corporate and entrepreneurial classes ensures that there will be greater minority participation in the campaign-finance process during the coming years.

A PLACE AT THE TABLE

Washington Senator Maria Cantwell probably owes her Senate victory in 2000 to the Internet boom of the late 1990s. Cantwell, a 43-year-old former congresswoman, was an executive at RealNetworks, a Seattle-area high-tech firm, from 1995 to 2000. She amassed $40 million in stock during her tenure there, which enabled her to launch a self-financed run for the United States Senate in 2000 against Republican Senator Slade Gorton. During the campaign, she outspent Gorton, spending $11.5 million, almost all of it her own, to Gorton's $6.4 million. Cantwell, a native of Indianapolis who served one term in the U.S. House from 1993 to 1995, cast herself as a moderate Democrat. Gorton, however, attempted to characterize her as a tax-and-spend Democrat. Conversely, she raised the issue of whether Gorton was a career politician who was concerned more about the special interests than ordinary Washingtonians.[43]

The race went into overtime, due to the fact that a majority of the voters had cast absentee ballots. In the end, Cantwell won by a narrow margin — 2,229 votes out of 2,461,379. This was the last Senate race of the 2000 campaign to be decided, weeks after the November 7 election, and the Senate was tied 50–50 as a result. As is usually the case in Washington elections, there was a regional divide. Western Washington, the multiethnic, socially liberal part of the state, strongly supported Cantwell. Eastern Washington, the predominantly white, socially conservative part of the state, overwhelmingly backed Gorton.[44] But most voters live in western Washington, not in the east, where the vibe is often more Mountain Western than Pacific Northwestern.

Because of her gender and ideological positions, Senator Cantwell serves as a proxy for most women and ethnic minorities in Washington State. With her election in 2000, Washington became the third state in the 107th Congress (California and Maine are the others) to have an all-woman delegation in the United States Senate. Cantwell undoubtedly represents the views of a majority of Washington women on most issues — they supported her in the campaign. And Cantwell seems well positioned to represent the ethnic minorities of Washington (the Evergreen State is 78.9% white). Due to the political predilections of Washington's women and minorities, and the fact that Cantwell can be counted on to support most aspects of multicultural liberalism, it would seem that Cantwell is a better proxy for their interests than Gorton, who was fairly conservative on many issues. As a result, they occupy one of the seats or places at the metaphorical "table" where important decisions are made and power is allocated to the various groups in American society.

The notion of responsiveness is, at its core, a simple one. First, persons provide money and votes to candidates, either independently, or through interest groups, like the AFL-CIO or the National Rifle Association. They do so because they fully expect to see their issues mentioned in the public discourse and their interests represented in policy deliberations. In return, public officials take symbolic and substantive actions (through their words and deeds) that benefit members of the groups that put them in office. In both political parties, the leaders remain white, middle-aged, non-ideological pragmatists who avoid espousing controversial positions that may stir up the troops but alienate centrists in the process.

Many Christian conservatives, like minority voters, are willing to sacrifice ideological purity to assure the victories of friendly allies who will be able to do more than merely propound ideas, plans, and theories. The Christian Right is divided into pragmatic and purist camps, based on their members' willingness to compromise with secular Republicans. As more Christian conservatives gravitate toward the political mainstream, a sizable minority of them are willing to vote for Democrats on occasion.[45] Likewise, blacks and non-Cuban Hispanics will periodically support friendly Republican candidates, although most of them continue to be skeptical of the GOP in general. This partisan cross-pollination may result in greater responsiveness to voters' concerns, because fewer groups will be taken for granted — or written off — by politicos and officeholders.

Political figures continually attempt to demonstrate their affinity for various groups in the electorate, often through their participation in photo opportunities. During these scripted appearances, politicos affirm their fondness for members of a given group through symbolic words and actions — and hope for votes and financial support in return. In making ethnic and racial appeals, a politician may eat pierogies or inhale some tamales, speak a few words of German or Spanish, and march in a Saint Patrick's Day parade or officiate at a stock car race. Candidates even journey to foreign countries on fact-finding expeditions to curry favor with American voters who trace their roots back there. On Martin Luther King Jr.'s birthday in January, politicians frequent black churches, where they pay their respects to the congregations and address issues with salience to African Americans. Prominent Democrats always make time to address the annual convention of the NAACP, and they also appear at the National Council of La Raza's assemblage each summer. Few white politicians speak to predominantly Caucasian audiences about racial issues; they typically save these discussions, which usually include anecdotes involving people from the target group, for their minority audiences.

Few, if any, public figures target all demographic groups equally. Not surprisingly, they often focus much of their attention on undecided voters and the constituencies that comprise their base. In general, Republican venues include evangelical churches, stock car races, and anything involving country music. The Democrats rarely neglect black churches, feminist meetings, and labor gatherings. It is a form of counterscheduling when a public figure visits a group whose members are cool to his positions, such as a liberal Democrat who braves the inevitable booing and shows up at a stock car race, or a right-wing Republican who marches in New York City's National Puerto Rican Day Parade. In doing so, the intrepid politician demonstrates that s/he embraces cultural and ideological diversity — and is confident enough to venture beyond the confines of her or his partisan turf.

There is perhaps no better way for a politico to appeal to an ethnic community than to speak to its members in their native tongue. Language, of course, serves as the touchstone of a national culture, and it is second only to ethnicity as a key tie that binds people together. Most Americans — regardless of their nativity — realize that English will never be displaced as America's principal language, but that does not stop them from taking pride in their traditional languages. The politico whose linguistic repertoire includes a language besides English often learned it from his immigrant parents, and when he speaks it to his coethnics he reinforces his ancestral connection to them. Speaking a foreign language to members of an ethnic group different from one's own allows an outsider to cross the divides of culture and pigmentation. It is a time-honored tradition for politicians to utter some words in the appropriate language at ethnic events, as in speaking Polish at a meeting to celebrate Pulaski Day in Chicago.[46] Monolingual candidates frequently advertise in the foreign-language media to win votes and raise funds. They also deploy bilingual surrogates to disseminate their messages for them.

Most ethnic voters excuse the rough edges of linguistic-outreach efforts by inclusive politicos — thick accents, unintentional solecisms, the

occasional grammatical peculiarities — and revel in the experience of being courted in their native tongues. To be sure, the language used in
political appeals varies by region: French in Louisiana's Cajun country; Portuguese in southeastern Massachusetts; Navajo in northwestern
New Mexico and northeastern Arizona; Cantonese and Mandarin in San
Francisco (although few non-Chinese politicos attempt to speak it); and
Spanish in Arizona, New Mexico, South Florida, South Texas, northeastern Illinois, Southern California, and New York City. Other languages
are coming to the fore as immigrants begin to flex their political muscles. Miami Mayor Manny Diaz greeted the audience at his November
2001 inauguration in English, Spanish, and Haitian Creole, in deference
to three distinct groups: Anglos and African Americans, Latinos, and
Miami's large Haitian community.[47]

As befits its status as America's second language, Spanish is the most
widely utilized foreign language in the political arena. In 2000 Democrat Al Gore and Republican George W. Bush both spoke rudimentary
Spanish in their efforts to woo Hispanics.[48] In some parts of America,
such as New York City, Anglo mayoral candidates such as Democrat
Ruth Messinger (her party's nominee in 1997) and Republican Michael
Bloomberg (the winner in 2001) have learned some basic Spanish to communicate with Latino voters. Two Texas Democrats — Dan Morales and
Tony Sanchez — even held a Spanish-language televised debate in their
gubernatorial contest in 2002.[49] At least two of the nation's leading Republicans (Texas Governor Rick Perry and New York Governor George
Pataki) have taken Spanish lessons. But, in the end, linguistic dexterity
and conspicuous multilingualism matter only tangentially in American
politics. A candidate, like the monolingual Bill Clinton, who says the
right things and supports the right programs, will win votes without
speaking anything besides American English.

Americans do not necessarily vote for their coethnics, regardless of
ideology, although they might do so out of ethnic pride — which is sometimes hard to distinguish from ethnic chauvinism. With few exceptions,
partisan affiliations trump race, gender, and ethnicity at the ballot box. In
other words, a white Democrat will beat a black Republican hands-down
among African Americans. Similarly, Democratic women will choose a
male Democrat over a female Republican in almost every case. Despite
the gender gap (chasm would be a better description) between male and
female voters, women do not automatically vote for other women as a
matter of course. Female candidates who face multiple white male op-

ponents sometimes mistakenly conclude that gender-specific appeals may lead to easy victories for them.

Notwithstanding their willingness to support ideologically congenial white male proxies, women and minorities are not averse to descriptive representation. Therefore, white male officials or candidates frequently appoint or spotlight white women and racial minorities in an effort to appear attuned to the needs of such persons. Out of electoral necessity, the Democrats are particularly sensitive to race, gender, and ethnicity. The big-city political machines of yesteryear routinely slated Irish, Jewish, and Italian candidates in carefully calibrated numbers, so as not to appear to be favoring one group over another. At present, Democratic and, to a lesser extent, Republican, Party leaders slate females, blacks, and Hispanics in ever-increasing numbers. It has become commonplace for male gubernatorial candidates to select female running mates. At the national level, though, 1984 Democratic presidential nominee Walter F. Mondale has been, to date, the only major-party candidate in American history to choose a woman to be his No. 2. Regardless, the diversity imperative surely will become more important in this rarefied realm.

On another front, the growing perception among people of color that the Republicans are antiblack and anti-immigrant has hurt the GOP nationally, particularly in California. In all likelihood, blacks and immigrants do not care about the minutiae of each subject; more importantly, they feel Republicans are hostile to them — and what they perceive to be their interests. Republicans, to be sure, have long recognized that they need to recruit more people of color to their party. They espouse a "big tent" philosophy, which means (in theory, at least) that the GOP includes and welcomes persons of differing races and views on thorny issues.[50] At their 1996 national convention, the Republicans highlighted a tableau of the GOP's few leading nonwhites. They also included bland speeches by party luminaries that invoked inclusion and characterized the Republicans as the "party of Lincoln."[51] In November of that year Democrats won their customary percentages in the black and Hispanic communities.

In 2000 the Republicans nominated their first presidential candidate whose multicultural bona fides seemed largely in order, and the GOP national convention was conspicuously multiracial. George W. Bush's associates made sure that the convention lineup of speakers and entertainers resembled America. One prominent speaker, retired General Colin L. Powell, pointedly endorsed affirmative action. This emphasis on inclusion was so atypical of the GOP that the Republicans quickly came under fire for being an exclusionary organization that sought to delude the American public into thinking it was a rainbow of colors when in fact most of the delegates at the convention were white.[52]

Indeed, it takes a lot more than a few speeches to reach minorities when GOP politicians seek to curtail multicultural initiatives and social-welfare programs that benefit people of color.[53] In the late 1990s, though, Republicans distanced themselves from such contentious issues as affirmative action, bilingual education, immigration reform, and cutbacks in aid to legal immigrants, so as to avoid further antagonizing minority and immigrant voters.[54] Republican outreach efforts in minority communities often turn out to be successful, especially for moderate candidates who avoid ideological confrontations. Moreover, inclusive Republicans win plaudits from the mainstream media for going the extra mile to reach out to new constituencies. (Due to the nature of the multiethnic coalition that keeps them in power, the Democrats rarely face any questions regarding diversity issues from the ever-vigilant media.) Cynics, both in the Democratic Party and the corps of political journalists, speculate that Republicans make nominal efforts to win support from minorities primarily to appear tolerant to white swing voters.[55]

Foreign policy continues to be quite important, too, as a means of accommodating diversity in the U.S. political system.[56] Extant political antagonisms around the globe, such as those between India and Pakistan, do not necessarily fade on American shores, where proxy fights in our political venues influence the formulation of U.S. foreign policy.[57] Global issues rarely rank as top concerns for most American voters, so those ethnic groups whose members feel intensely passionate about such matters tend to exercise a disproportionate amount of influence in our nation's foreign affairs. As Paul Glastris points out, "Recent immigrant groups, particularly Asians, are learning to play the same fund-raising and lobbying games that more established ethnic groups do."[58]

The end of the Cold War broadened conceptions of American national security to encompass groups and issues that were largely neglected during the bipolar era of U.S.-Soviet relations. These developments allow the ethnic interest groups, working independently or in concert with politicians and organizations in the Old World, to play a greater role in the formulation of U.S. foreign policy.[59] American economic and military aid to foreign countries is a major concern to these ethnic lobbies. This is one of the reasons that Armenia receives lots of U.S. foreign aid relative to its size and what some would describe as its strategic significance.[60] But Americans from a particular ethnic group do not always feel a close connection to their coethnics abroad, as evidenced by the reluctance of many assimilated Mexican Americans to pay much attention to issues related to Mexico, Mexican immigration, or the U.S.-Mexico relationship.[61]

The United States' relationship with Israel is perhaps the most significant issue with ethno-religious connotations in the foreign-policy arena. Israel, to be sure, has been a consistent American ally in the Middle East. Many Christian Americans feel a deep attachment to Israel because of its connection to the Holy Land. And most Jewish Americans, of course, feel very close to the Jewish state. The clout of the American Israel Public Affairs Committee, which is well known for its advocacy on every important issue affecting the U.S.-Israeli relationship, is partially responsible for the $3 billion in aid that the Jewish state receives annually from the United States.[62] Issues such as Palestinian statehood and the location of the U.S. Embassy in Israel (it presently is in Tel Aviv but many Israelis want it moved to Jerusalem, which they view as the true capital of the Jewish homeland) are an essential part of politics in New York. Jews make up a greater percentage of the New York electorate — 18.3%, according to one estimate — than in any other state.[63]

On the national level, every major political candidate is usually pro-Israel, and there is widespread agreement among leaders of all political stripes that Israel should continue to be the source of billions of dollars in American foreign aid. In the past, some political candidates even eschewed contributions from, and connections to, Arab Americans, for fear that they would be seen as anti-Israel. As the United States pursues the war against terrorism, the troubled Israeli-Palestinian relationship continues to make headlines and complicate efforts to promote stability in the Middle East. So issues involving Israel almost certainly will continue to be of great significance in American foreign policy.

Besides Israel, Cuba is another country that figures prominently in U.S. foreign policy, due to the voluble and powerful contingent of Americans who maintain close ties to that Caribbean nation. One of the most important — and controversial — ethnic lobbying groups is the Cuban American National Foundation, whose leaders played a major role in creating the Cuban litmus test for national political candidates. It requires unyielding opposition to Fidel Castro's dictatorship and enthusiastic support for the longtime U.S. embargo against Cuba. In recent years, however, a growing number of leading American politicians have questioned the viability of current U.S. policies toward Cuba.[64]

Republicans' vehement anti-Castro diatribes, coupled with their fervent support of free enterprise, won them the vast majority of Cuban-American votes for decades. Bill Clinton broke the GOP lock on Cuban-

American voters, due to the Republicans' growing "anti-immigrant" reputation, and because he satisfied the Castro litmus test when he signed into law the Helms-Burton Act, which further reinforced the U.S. embargo against Cuba, in 1996.[65] However, the Clinton administration did not make any friends in the Cuban-exile community when it returned Elián González to his biological father and opposed permanent U.S. residency for the Cuban boy.[66] The Bush administration's policy toward Cuba continues in the tradition of other Republican presidents in its support for the embargo and attempts to isolate Castro.[67] Bush's cautious Cuban policy demonstrates that ethnicity and foreign policy can be as combustible a mixture as any that exist in the realm of domestic policy.

THE POLITICS OF SOUTHERN CHANGE

As a young boy growing up in Holmes County, Mississippi, during the 1930s, Robert G. Clark Jr. spent a lot of time with his elderly grandfather, William H. Clark, whom he and the rest of his family affectionately referred to as "Pa." Robert Clark was too young — and his grandfather too old — for field work, so the two would sit and shuck corn to feed the mules. The older man, who had been 11 at Emancipation, told his grandson what it was like to have been a slave, and reflected on the mistreatment of blacks by whites in Mississippi. He said that Jim Crow would never end unless his grandson and other young people worked to change things. The precocious youngster took his grandfather's advice to heart.[68]

For five decades, Robert G. Clark has worked to effect social change in Mississippi, first as an educator and later as a politician. As an educator and coach in central Mississippi from 1952 to 1966, Clark constantly butted heads with the white authorities (he was fired twice), because of his support for integration and attempts to challenge the status quo by educating African Americans. When the Holmes County Board of Education refused to approve a countywide adult education program, Clark decided to enter electoral politics. He ran for state representative as an independent, and the white incumbent, a Democrat named J. P. Love, waged a vitriolic campaign against him.[69] But on November 7, 1967, Clark was elected to the Mississippi House from a rural district in central Mississippi. He defeated Love by a margin of 106 votes out of 6,938, and became the first African-American legislator in Mississippi since the late 1880s.[70] Clark's victory demonstrated the emerging clout of Mississippi's African Americans, just two years after the passage of the Voting Rights Act.

During his 34-year career as a legislator, Robert Clark has earned a reputation for being a moderate lawmaker who favors racial integration, fights for the disadvantaged of all races, and who is willing to compromise if necessary to achieve his goals. A tall, dignified man with ebony skin, dark brown eyes, and close-cropped hair, the 73-year-old Clark has been called "a hell-raiser" and "an Uncle Tom" during his distinguished career.[71] Indeed, many of his white colleagues ostracized him when he first took office in 1968. Clark was a diligent lawmaker, however, and he eventually earned the respect of his fellow legislators.[72] In 1979 he began to chair the House Education Committee. Three years later he spearheaded the passage of his proudest legislative accomplishment — the Education Reform Act of 1982.[73] And in January 1992, Clark's colleagues chose him to be Speaker Pro Tempore. In this capacity, he serves as speaker in the absence of Speaker Tim Ford, and chairs the House Management Committee, which oversees the fiscal affairs of the House.[74]

Clark now has 35 black colleagues in the 122-member Mississippi House, but the African-American legislators are a culturally and ideologically diverse group, so it is difficult for them to reach a consensus on many issues. Nonetheless, the septuagenarian rancher works tirelessly to achieve his main goal: ensuring that African Americans are fully part of the mainstream in Mississippi, especially in terms of the economic opportunities available to them.[75] Recently, Clark played a major role in the unsuccessful campaign to change the Mississippi state flag; he reminded voters that blacks associate the Confederate battle flag with oppression and discrimination, not heritage and valor.[76] Today Speaker Clark is the most enduring figure in Mississippi politics. He gains respect from friend and foe alike for his power, wisdom, reasonableness, and status as a political pioneer.

Politics in the South continues to be influenced by events that stem, at least indirectly, from the Civil War and Reconstruction. Republican leaders freed the slaves, enfranchised black men, and fought for blacks' rights during Reconstruction. A faction within the party, the Radical Republicans, tried as much as possible to humiliate and punish the white South for its disloyalty to the Union. Consequently, the white Southern political elites endorsed what became known as the Compromise of 1877. It resolved a dispute over the outcome of the 1876 presidential election by electing a Republican, Rutherford B. Hayes, to the nation's highest office — in exchange for several concessions, including the removal of the last federal troops from the South.[77]

With the restoration of white supremacy, blacks were disenfranchised through such devices as grandfather clauses, literacy tests, poll taxes, and whites-only primaries.[78] Republicans were cursed as the party of the Union that defeated the Confederacy and then humbled the South during Reconstruction. As a result, white Southerners turned to the Democrats, and their region became known as the "Solid South." From the late 1870s to the early 1960s, Democrats retained effective control of most local, state, and national offices in Dixie.[79]

The political fate of the contemporary South may have been sealed when President Lyndon Johnson signed the Civil Rights Act of 1964 — a development he reportedly forecast at the time.[80] Then the Republican Party became the home of disgruntled white Southerners who disliked integration, affirmative action, and the new black empowerment. In the meantime, millions of Southern blacks entered the electorate in the 1960s after the de jure barriers to suffrage ended; their new voting power transformed the electoral process in the South.[81] Politicians such as Strom Thurmond and George Wallace who had once espoused white supremacism now embraced full African-American participation in Southern politics after decades of fighting black advancement, because they quickly grasped the fundamental reality of the burgeoning black electorate: black voters (and votes) count. In statewide politics, as elsewhere, the traditional white good-ol'-boy Democrats retired, changed or muted their racial attitudes, switched parties, or faced imminent defeat.

Since the early 1970s white Southern Democrats have appealed to blacks and eschewed racial politicking. It is difficult to believe that all these men, especially those from the World War II generation, had sudden epiphanies about the virtues of integration. As pragmatists they realized that accommodation was the order of the day, even as many African Americans grumbled about their continued absence from the halls of power. Today Florida, Alabama, Arkansas, Kentucky, and Louisiana have the most significant numbers of white voters who are willing to vote for national and local Democrats. By contrast, Texas and South Carolina, both of which have sizable minority populations, have trended heavily Republican in the last two decades. The flight of whites to the Republican Party has strengthened the position of black Democrats in intraparty politics: African Americans account for an increasingly significant part of the Democratic Party's base in the South (40% to 50% in Alabama, Georgia, Louisiana, Mississippi, and South Carolina).

Thirty-seven years after the passage of the Voting Rights Act of 1965, which brought African Americans into the political process in the South, "there is now," as Hastings Wyman puts it, "a major black presence in all Southern state governments."[82] This is true even though few overtly racial issues surface in the legislative dialogue. The critical mass of black legislators changes the political calculus so that African-American interests are taken into account in the decision-making process.[83] In 2001, 76 of the 543 state senators in the 13-state South were black. Moreover, 237 of the 1,526 state representatives in the 13-state South were African American. In Mississippi, the blackest state in the Union, more than one-quarter of the state legislators are African Americans. In neighboring Alabama, blacks account for one in four state lawmakers. Louisiana, Georgia, and South Carolina also have large black legislative delegations.[84] Black legislators exercise a significant amount of power in the Southern legislatures, due to their concentration in the Democratic Party — and the fact that this party still controls most legislative bodies in the South. In a number of Southern states, African Americans hold important legislative leadership posts and head prominent legislative committees.[85]

Black legislators now have the power to achieve many of their objectives, especially when it comes to certain types of symbolic initiatives, such as matters related to Confederate iconography. Moreover, they are better positioned than ever before to achieve their goals with regard to pork barrel spending that might benefit their districts. But their power depends, to a large extent, on whether the Democrats control the legislature and the governor's mansion. In any event, many Southern black legislators are not particularly liberal, especially those who come from rural districts, but their priorities on fiscal and social-welfare issues often put them to the left of their white colleagues. This ideological disconnect can make it difficult for them to achieve all their legislative goals.

Now that African Americans compose one-half of the Democratic Party's base in several Southern states, the Democrats face increasing pressure to nominate African-American candidates in statewide races. Perhaps surprisingly, relatively few African Americans have carried the banner for the Democrats statewide in the South. Most African-American candidates are unacceptable on ideological grounds to the vast majority of the white voters, some of whom no doubt would be reluctant to support a black candidate, no matter how conservative. In recent years, though, politically pragmatic Democratic primary voters have chosen white centrist standard-bearers who may not pass every ideological litmus test, but who can triumph in November. It is, of course, easiest for African-American candidates in the South to be elected in black-majority cities and congressional districts. Consequently, the electoral milestones for African-American Southerners usually come in such areas.[86] Democrats also have difficulties melding coalitions of blacks and moderate whites, as native Southern whites leave the Democratic Party and white newcomers bring their Republican voting habits with them.

The stigma attached to being a Southern Republican has receded to the point of being nonexistent in the white South. Conservative whites, particularly the younger ones, embrace the party. However, it is virtually impossible to discern precisely how much of the Southern whites' support for Republicans is attributable to race, rather than to their positions on largely raceless issues such as crime, taxes, military spending, traditional values, and big government.[87] Republicans now govern Arkansas, Florida, Louisiana, Oklahoma, Tennessee, and Texas. The GOP holds 43% of the state legislative seats in the 13-state South.[88] And at the beginning of the 107th Congress in January 2001, Republicans controlled 17 of the 26 U.S. Senate seats and 81 of the 137 U.S. House seats in the 13-state South. Although few white Southerners make distinctions between national and local Democrats anymore, Southern Democrats still win most local offices, especially in rural counties with large black populations. The Democratic primary, however, is no longer the critical election it once was in most of the South. The turnout in Southern Republican primaries routinely exceeds that in Democratic races — at least when there are fiercely contested battles on the GOP side.

Still, Democrats are making a modest comeback in the South. They have managed to create enduring, biracial coalitions in a number of states, including Alabama, Arkansas, Georgia, and the Carolinas. Throughout the South racially charged appeals have declined in frequency. Such attacks do not necessarily spur greater white turnout, and they anger black voters, who often turn out in large numbers to defeat white politicians they consider to be racist. Dozens of politically resourceful Southern Democrats won high office in the 1990s and continue to do so in the twenty-first century (the Democrats took back the Virginia governorship in 2001). With the perquisites of incumbency, most of these Democratic officeholders will undoubtedly enjoy long political careers. These developments bode well for the Democratic Party's future in the South. Georgia Senator Zell Miller, a white Democrat who was governor of Georgia from 1991 to 1999, holds the Rosetta stone of modern Southern politics. Like his ideological compatriot, former four-term

North Carolina Governor James B. Hunt Jr., Miller avoids controversial social issues, like abortion and school prayer, and instead focuses on surefire winners, such as crime, education, and the economy.[89]

Democrats in the Miller-Hunt mold have been winning Southern governorships and U.S. Senate races since 1998. In each election, African Americans played an important, if not decisive, role in the Democratic victory.[90] Democrats now hold four of the five Deep South governorships. From 1998 to 2000 they enjoyed an electoral rebirth south of the Mason-Dixon line for numerous reasons. Close Republican ties to the Religious Right disconcerted secular whites. Economic prosperity and state budget surpluses eliminated, at least temporarily, the possibility of tax increases. The rightward tilt by national Democrats on crime and welfare reform neutralized these issues for party members in the South and elsewhere. And farsighted Democrats co-opted emerging issues, e.g., the perils of suburban sprawl.[91] In sum, the South continues to be fertile ground for Democrats even as the region votes for Republicans time and time again.

Democrats certainly appear to be making a comeback in Florida, the region's second largest state. Like every other big state, Florida is tremendously multiethnic: It is 65.4% Anglo, 16.8% Hispanic, 14.2% African American, 1.6% Asian, and 1.5% multiracial. Northern Florida, for the most part, remains traditionally Southern, with the black-and-white racial dynamics typical of Dixie.[92] Central Florida is more multiethnic, with sizable white, black, and Latino populations. And South Florida is one of the nation's most heterogeneous regions, with America's largest concentration of Cubans and sizable Jewish, West Indian, and African-American communities. Florida's elected officials do not represent the state's diversity in a descriptive sense at this point. Both U.S. Senate seats and all the elected statewide constitutional offices are held by Anglos. At the local, county, and legislative levels, however, the public officials offer the state's various ethnic groups plenty of descriptive representation.

Florida is now the nation's most decisive swing state in presidential elections. The state's numerous Anglo voters lean Republican. In the meantime, the state continues to attract hundreds of thousands of Anglo migrants. Many of them are sympathetic to the GOP, in part because of Florida's lack of a state income tax. Hispanics, the state's largest minority group, often vote Republican. This is largely due to Cuban Americans, who make up 5.2% of the state — and 31% of the Hispanic population there. Florida's other Hispanics have shown a marked tendency to vote Democratic, or at least be more open to the party than the Cubans. African Americans in Florida, of course, are as fervently Democratic as

any of their coethnics in the country. Perhaps surprisingly, considering
the state's demographics, there is racial harmony in Florida politics — at
least at the statewide level. Except for the recent debate over affirmative
action in the state and the dispute over the results of the 2000 presidential election, race rarely surfaces as a topic or point of division in the
legislature or in a statewide campaign.[93]

The racial climate is peaceful in Texas, too, a state where politics is
dominated by Anglo Republicans. Texas shifted rightward in the 1970s
and 1980s, mainly because of the changing predilections of Anglo voters,
who recoiled from the cultural and economic liberalism of the Democratic Party. African Americans make up 12% of the Texas electorate;
they are a Democratic monolith. Latinos constitute 14% of Texas voters — a percentage that increases every year — and they presently identify
with Democrats over Republicans by about a three-to-one margin. Texas
is presently in the middle of a demographic transition that is almost certain to aid the Democratic Party. Unfortunately for the GOP, there is
little room for them to gain any more traction among Anglo voters, who
are now among the most Republican in the nation. Secular conservatives
fear that the Christian Right will frighten away white suburbanites who
lean Republican but do not wish to live in a theocracy. At the same time
Texas Republicans are conducting outreach efforts to persuade Latinos
to join the Lone Star GOP.[94]

People of color play an increasingly important role in Texas politics, as
voters and as candidates. There are several prominent Hispanic Republican elected officials in Texas — namely, Congressman Henry Bonilla
and Tony Garza, who sits on the state's three-member Railroad Commission. (Republican Michael Williams, who is African American, chairs
the Texas Railroad Commission.)[95] Garza is presently the most powerful
Latino politician in Texas. Three of Texas's five most populous cities are
governed by Hispanics: Raymond Caballero of El Paso, Ed Garza of San
Antonio, and Gustavo "Gus" Garcia of Austin (an Anglo-majority city).
Moreover, two of the three major candidates in the Democratic Sen-
ate primary in March 2002 were minorities: The field included former
Dallas Mayor Ron Kirk, an African American, Houston Congressman
Ken Bentsen, an Anglo, and 1996 Democratic Senate nominee Victor
Morales, who is Latino. Likewise, multimillionaire businessman Tony
Sanchez and former Texas Attorney General Dan Morales squared off for
the Democratic gubernatorial nomination in 2002. Sanchez and Morales
were the first significant Latino major-party gubernatorial candidates in
Texas since 1958. Democrats think the rising numbers of Latino voters

will enable them to be competitive at the statewide level again. Republicans hope their minority-outreach efforts will enable them to win enough Hispanic support to dominate Texas politics for years to come. In any event, these developments herald the beginning of a more competitive era in Texas politics.

The latest version of the politics of Southern change is going to revolve around nonblack minorities. Latinos outnumber blacks in Florida and Texas, but nowhere else in the South do Hispanics constitute a significant percentage of the electorate. Non-Southern white migrants also will continue to play a role in this political transformation. Multicultural issues affect the politics of an increasingly large number of Southern communities. White politicians in Dixie regularly run for office in areas where immigrants — and issues related to immigration — are a major part of the local political discourse. In these places, such as Rogers, Arkansas, and Siler City, North Carolina, white politicians often face an electorate that is primarily white and, in many cases, heavily black. These native-born whites and blacks are not always sympathetic to the issues and concerns of the Latino newcomers to their communities.[96]

To be sure, nonblack minorities are beginning to play an active role in the electoral process in places like Georgia and North Carolina. In Georgia, a state where Latinos account for 5.3% of the population, the Republican Party has begun to reach out to Hispanics; state GOP chairman Ralph Reed initiated a Latino outreach initiative in 2001.[97] Moreover, in North Carolina, where Hispanics constitute 4.7% of the population, both political parties have begun talking about how they can bring Latinos into the fold.[98] It will probably be at least 20 years before nonblack minority candidates regularly win statewide office in Georgia, Virginia, and North Carolina. And in many of the other Southern states, such as Louisiana, Mississippi, and Alabama, the population profiles will remain black and white in the foreseeable future.

The parts of the American political system that lead to racial disproportionality are possible flash points for interracial tensions. A current example of this disproportionality is the outsized influence in presidential contests of the first-in-the-nation Iowa caucuses and their analogue a few days later, the New Hampshire primary — both of which occur in predominantly white, low-population states. Every four years, the national media focus a disproportionate amount of attention on the presidential campaigns in Iowa and New Hampshire. Iowa became an important part of the national primary process in 1976, after Jimmy Carter did well in the Democratic caucuses there and established himself as a formidable candidate. New Hampshire's relevance dates back to at least 1952. Presidential candidates often have little chance to do well in the campaign if they do not win — or at least place second — in one of these critical contests.[99]

Due to the influence of Iowa and New Hampshire in determining whether a presidential contender has the necessary momentum to go the distance and win his party's nomination, candidates spend a significant amount of their time campaigning in these states. In recent years, other states have attempted to gain more influence in the presidential selection process, so the primary schedule has become front-loaded, in that the majority of the delegates needed to win a major-party presidential nomination are now selected by the end of March. Iowa and New Hampshire jealously guard their first-in-the-nation status, and schedule their contests earlier than any other state. Our third- and fifth-whitest states, in other words, effectively winnow the presidential field.[100]

The most salient instance of racial disproportionality, however, is the U.S. Senate, the upper body of the national legislature, where states have equal representation. "Senate apportionment," write Frances Lee and Bruce Oppenheimer, "affects four aspects of the institution: representation, election, strategic behavior, and policymaking."[101] Due to the racial demographics of the American states, the constitutional requirement that allocates two Senate seats to each state takes on racial significance. Seven states have two Senate seats and only one at-large House member: Alaska, Delaware, Montana, North Dakota, South Dakota, Vermont, and Wyoming. And beginning in 2003, four states will have equal numbers of U.S. senators and representatives: Idaho, Maine, New Hampshire, and Rhode Island.[102] All of these states — with the exception of Alaska — are whiter than the national average.

There is a growing disparity between the large, multiracial states and the small, monoracial states. A state senator in California represents more constituents than a U.S. Senator from Wyoming, Vermont, Alaska, North Dakota, South Dakota, or Delaware. Approximately 16.3% of Americans elect half the Senate, and 11.2% of Americans choose 40 of the senators — the number needed to support filibusters that hold up or even block legislation. The consequences of this disparity may be heightened in the future. During the twenty-first century, Latinos and Asians will continue to be concentrated in large states, such as California, Texas,

Florida, New York, and Illinois. These population dynamics will almost certainly exacerbate the existing disparities.[103]

Similarly, the Electoral College, which selects the president and vice president, may take on racial significance that it never had in the past.[104] The future of presidential politics will be one of close contests in the Electoral College. In 2004, a presidential candidate could win the presidency in the Electoral College by carrying the 11 most populous states: California (55 electoral votes); Texas (34 electoral votes); New York (31 electoral votes); Florida (27 electoral votes); Illinois (21 electoral votes); Pennsylvania (21 electoral votes); Ohio (20 electoral votes); Michigan (17 electoral votes); New Jersey (15 electoral votes); Georgia (15 electoral votes); and North Carolina (15 electoral votes). The electoral map became more friendly to the Republicans as a result of the reapportionment that followed the Census of 2000. During this decade, Republican Arizona will have ten electoral votes, as many as Democratic Wisconsin; in the last decade Wisconsin had three more electoral votes than Arizona.

It is entirely possible that we may see more instances where a presidential candidate wins the popular vote but loses in the Electoral College. If a Democrat wins by lopsided margins in California, New York, Illinois, New Jersey, and many of the other big states, and the Republican candidate cobbles together a coalition of small states and manages to win large states such as Ohio and Florida by narrow margins, a Democrat could win the popular vote by two or three million but still fail to get 270 electoral votes. This scenario may occur at some point in the next two decades, especially as minorities vote in ever greater numbers in California, New York, Illinois, New Jersey, and elsewhere.

The constitutional compromises of 1787 that created the two houses of the national legislature, along with the Electoral College, might come under fire from liberal multiculturalists and their political allies during the 2010s and beyond. We can expect more people to advocate the abolition of the Electoral College if Democrats continue to win the popular vote (as Al Gore did in 2000) in presidential elections, yet lose the White House because of the Electoral College. Such a change would require a constitutional amendment. The conservative, primarily white, small states — Montana, Wyoming, Idaho, Utah, the Dakotas, Nebraska, Kansas, Oklahoma, New Hampshire, and West Virginia — would almost certainly be joined by other small states, along with the Republican-leaning large states, in opposition to such a proposal.

It is even possible that the process of amending the U.S. Constitution could take on racial significance. To be sure, the last racially significant amendment was made to the Constitution in 1964. Nor are there any racially charged issues that seem likely to motivate the Multicultural Left to push for any constitutional amendments. However, because two-thirds of the House and Senate and three-quarters of the state legislatures must approve any new constitutional amendments, the small- and medium-sized conservative, primarily white states have an effective veto over any dramatic constitutional changes on the racial-policy front. Should a proposed constitutional amendment ever be rejected by the states that are populated mainly by white Americans, the issue could precipitate a racially charged conflict and even result in a constitutional crisis.

chapter eight

Beyond Black and White

When Ben Nighthorse Campbell decided to run for the Colorado House of Representatives in 1982, there initially was some skepticism in the 59th District about this American Indian candidate who sported a ponytail. So a fellow Democrat helped him contact sympathetic locals who then publicly supported his candidacy and, by doing so, signaled that Campbell agreed with the right-of-center mindset prevalent in southwestern Colorado. During the 1982 campaign Campbell met thousands of voters in the district and convinced them that he was a regular guy. His background as a rancher helped him overcome the doubts some voters might have had about his long hair. To his credit, Campbell declined to shorten the length of his hair, in part because his Native American friends would have considered his haircut to be a simple act of political expediency.[1]

Campbell's Indian background actually became an electoral advantage in a district where few of the voters were Native American. The Colorado political cognoscenti took to referring to the race as the "buckskins vs. Brooks Brothers" contest, in reference to Campbell's Indian appearance and the buttoned-down demeanor of his Republican opponent. Campbell ran an energetic campaign, one that took him door to door throughout the district in southwestern Colorado. The first-time candidate triumphed with 57% of the vote. Before his election to the Colorado House, he had never even visited the Colorado State Capitol Building. As would be the case in his subsequent political forays, Campbell's Native American ancestry was the subject of considerable buzz, before and after the election, in Colorado political circles.[2]

Campbell's biography is a story of hardship, tempered by discipline, and distinguished by the protagonist's constant attempts to better himself. The future senior senator from Colorado was born in 1933 in Auburn, California, the son of a father who was mainly Native American and a mother of Portuguese descent. Campbell had it tough as a youngster, due to the fact that his father was an alcoholic and his mother suffered from tuberculosis. He and his sister even lived in an orphanage for a while. Eventually, Campbell dropped out of school and enlisted in the Air Force during the Korean War. He served his country and earned a GED (general equivalency diploma) at the same time. Campbell left the Air Force in 1953. Four years later he graduated from San Jose State University. Campbell later became a devotee of judo and spent four years training in Japan; he competed in the 1964 Olympics in judo and served as the U.S. team captain.[3]

In the mid-1960s Campbell began to embrace his Indian heritage, and to identify as a Native American. When he was growing up in the 1930s and 1940s, he and his family downplayed their Indian roots. But Campbell began to evince an interest in his genealogy by the time he reached his mid-thirties. He researched his roots and eventually became an enrolled member of the Northern Cheyenne tribe in Montana. And he grew his hair long, in the Indian style. During the 1970s Campbell became a noted designer of Indian jewelry — as a jewelry designer, he called himself Ben Nighthorse — and he earned a handsome living at it.[4]

Ben Nighthorse Campbell entered electoral politics in 1982, and within ten years he was a member of the U.S. Senate. During his two terms in the Colorado legislature, Campbell established a reputation as a hardworking, moderate lawmaker. Then, in 1986, he decided to run for the U.S. House from Colorado's Third Congressional District. The moderate Democrat won the election and went to Washington. After three terms in Congress, Campbell successfully ran for the U.S. Senate in 1992.[5] Although the press focused on Campbell's Native American heritage, his biographer, Herman Viola, points out "that he is the first U.S. senator of Portuguese descent."[6]

As a member of the Senate, Campbell has continued his iconoclastic ways. In 1995 he switched to the Republican Party, a move that was not entirely surprising, considering that he had never been friendly with the liberal wing of the Democratic Party. Over the last nine years, Senator Campbell has been known more for his outsized persona than his legislative accomplishments. He is unquestionably the most colorful member of the Senate, due to his ponytail, his refusal to wear neckties, and his collection of motorcycles. Campbell represents the libertarian strain of politics common among Republicans in the Mountain West. He also serves as a national symbol and advocate for Native Americans, a role that he proudly embraces.[7]

Throughout his political career, Campbell does not seem to have been affected negatively by white racism during any of his campaigns. The fact that he is part Native American has never been a hindrance to him for three reasons. First, he is not a liberal, so it is difficult to pin stereo-types on him. Second, he does not seek publicity for his efforts to help Native Americans. Third, because Colorado has a minuscule American Indian population — slightly less than 29,000 — it would be impossible for someone to play ethnic politics with him in this regard, something that might occur in a state with a larger Native American presence.[8] Campbell also appears white in a visual sense, which does not hurt him in his efforts to win support in conservative Anglo areas.

In effect, Campbell benefits from the glamour of his Indian persona, without ever encountering any serious prejudice in the electoral arena. Campbell's political profile certainly appeals to his fellow Coloradans: He won his reelection bid in 1998 by nearly a two-to-one margin. Campbell's switch to the Republican Party was a smart political decision, because Colorado started to trend heavily Republican in the 1990s. To the extent that race matters in Colorado, it is largely an Anglo/Latino dichotomy (Denver is nearly one-third Hispanic), not the black/white duality that still characterizes so much of American life and politics.[9] Even though Campbell identifies as a racial minority, white voters warmly accept him, due to the fact that his cultural values and political stances dovetail with theirs.

INVIDIOUS DISTINCTIONS

When David Duke released his self-published autobiography, *My Awak-ening,* in the winter of 1998–1999, on the eve of his campaign for the U.S. House, the lengthy book left little doubt that he embraced views that were clearly outside the mainstream of even ultraconservative political thought in the United States. The book, which came out as Duke began the campaign, recapitulated his anti-Semitic beliefs and white-supremacist views on racial issues, and left little doubt that the aging radical subscribed to nonviolent racial extremism.[10] Duke ran as an unreconstructed white supremacist during his congressional campaign in 1999. The Republican from suburban New Orleans stressed social and cultural issues in his advertisements and campaign appearances. As a congressional candidate, Duke repeatedly slammed Kwanzaa, denigrated the Malcolm X postage stamp, and criticized the renaming of a New Orleans elementary school that had once honored George Washington.[11]

The onetime neo-Nazi, ex-Klansman, and founder of the National Association for the Advancement of White People found a receptive audience in the predominantly white First Congressional District. After all, many white suburbanites in Greater New Orleans do not care much for the black-dominated central city that attracts so many tourists to Louisiana. When Duke entered the race, Republicans became concerned that he might make the runoff for the seat that had been vacated by Representative Robert Livingston, who had resigned after revelations of marital infidelities. In the May 1999 special election, Republican David Duke polled a strong third with 19% of the vote after a five-month campaign during which he explicitly advocated for the rights of European Americans. Had a conservative Democrat not won 11%, Duke probably would have made the runoff and embarrassed the national Republican Party.[12]

Duke has been giving the Republicans a reputation for bigotry, intolerance, and racism ever since 1989, when he was elected in a special election to the Louisiana House of Representatives from a suburban New Orleans district. In his two high-profile statewide races in Louisiana (a U.S. Senate candidacy in 1990 and a gubernatorial bid in 1991), Duke became the first serious candidate for an important public office in Multicultural America to make a white-rights pitch to the electorate, in tandem with his espousal of traditional conservative positions on issues like taxes, personal morality, and the size of government. Although he won solid majorities of the white vote (60% and 55%, respectively) each time, Duke's electoral prospects dimmed as conventional right-wing politicians began integrating parts of his message into their stump speeches and legislative efforts.[13]

After a few years in the early 1990s as a far-right "mainstream" politician, Duke returned to his roots as a full-time activist who offered gloomy obsequies for white-majority America and wistful invocations of Euro-American virtue and ingenuity. The former Louisiana legislator promotes his anti-Semitic, white-supremacist, minority-bashing message on his Web site, in his writings, and through his speaking engagements around the world.[14] His role in American electoral politics may be over; in November 2000, he left the United States to promote his racist ideas in Europe. Duke may not be returning to the United States anytime soon, due to an ongoing federal investigation of charges that he misused funds donated by followers who supported his white-supremacist activities.[15]

Invidious racial distinctions are far from new phenomena in American public life. From the 1870s to the 1960s the politics of race was almost exclusively black and Southern. There were some exceptions, of course. Chinese and Japanese immigrants served as political scapegoats in California during the late 1800s and early 1900s. In areas with sizable American Indian populations, the First Americans occasionally were convenient foils for unscrupulous white politicians. Ethnic tensions between Anglos and Hispanics sometimes surfaced in the Southwestern political arena, too. From the beginning of the young democracy, issues related to slavery — along with the related matters of sectionalism and states' rights — were debated in Congress, at election time, and around the dinner table.

During the first six decades of the twentieth century, Southern politicians cherished and cultivated antiblack reputations. Since African Americans could not vote in the South and racially liberal whites accounted for only a small percentage of the electorate in Dixie, there was no backlash against such tactics. The white-supremacist politicians differed from one another in their views on economic issues and their stylistic flourishes — namely, how explicitly they attacked blacks, and whether they referred to them as "niggers" and assailed their white opponents as "nigger-lovers."[16] More often than not, race-baiting was a chimerical distraction that took the place of cursory, never mind serious, discussions of substantive issues. Mindful of this Southern bloc of voters, and the racial attitudes of the country at large, national political leaders did little to assist or include African Americans in the polity. Anti-lynching legislation was a hot-button issue in national politics for decades; Southern politicians quashed attempts to discuss the topic. The events that nationalized racial politics did not occur until the 1950s.[17]

With the invigoration of the civil rights movement in the 1950s, a new dimension — opposition to federal efforts to promote integration — infused the politics of race in the South. White Southern politicians soon realized that their electoral survival depended on staunch anti-Communism, support for segregation, and opposition to any civil-rights initiatives. Therefore, segregationist Southern politicians of the 1950s and 1960s, such as Arkansas's Orval Faubus and Mississippi's Ross Barnett, called for "massive resistance" to integration.[18] But the Civil Rights Act of 1964 and the Voting Rights Act of 1965 changed the power dynamic in Arkansas, Mississippi, and elsewhere. Whites were no longer only the aggressors, and blacks the Others, in electoral contests.

As a result of the events and social movements that occurred during the 1960s and the 1970s, numerous social and cultural issues became part of the national discourse — and our politics. Besides the civil rights movement, the antiwar movement, the women's liberation movement, the gay rights movement, the secularization of American society, the legalization of abortion rights in 1973, and even the environmental movement spurred the consideration of new issues and new claims that also opened

up schisms that previously had not existed. Those Americans who re-
sisted the social and cultural changes of the 1960s and 1970s generally
turned to the Republicans, while most tribunes of the new social order
joined the Democrats.[19]

Race, of course, was a subtext of the nation's social and cultural debates as well. Such issues as crime, welfare, and affirmative action played
a role in shaping the nation's issue agenda. Indeed, social class declined
as a motivating force in American politics when white backlash against
integration started breaking up the New Deal coalition in the 1950s. At
the same time, most contemporary issues with racial tinges — taxes, welfare, affirmative action, bilingual education, violent crime — originated
in the 1960s, or began to take on racial significance during that decade.[20]

During the 1960s and 1970s millions of white Americans permanently
left the Democratic Party because they disliked the fact that the national
Democratic leadership aligned itself with the Multicultural Left. In fact,
a Democratic presidential candidate has not garnered a majority of white
votes since 1964. George McGovern, the 1972 Democratic presidential
nominee, was the first major national candidate who fully embraced the
causes and interests of the Multicultural Left. The American people responded by giving him one of the worst drubbings in modern electoral
history; Richard Nixon defeated him by a 61%-37% margin. Indeed, Republican Presidents Richard Nixon, Ronald Reagan, and George Bush —
along with a host of other GOPers at the state and local levels — capitalized on social and cultural issues in the 1960s, 1970s, and 1980s to win
office again and again.[21]

Democrats aided the GOP when they dropped much of their standard
emphasis on economic issues, and espoused controversial positions, such
as support for abortion rights, higher taxes, mandatory busing, affirmative action, enhanced welfare benefits, a dovish national defense, and
the rights of criminal defendants. Therefore, many of the socially conservative Democrats, who favored the party due to their backing of its
initiatives to improve the lives of blue-collar Americans, became disen-
chanted and politically rootless. This was particularly true in the South,
where GOP presidential candidates won smashing victories in election
after election; in 1972, 1984, and 1988, Republicans carried every state
in the old Confederacy. These white Democrats who voted Republican in
presidential contests became known as "Reagan Democrats": They liked
Ronald Reagan's tough-guy patriotism, backed the GOP on issues like
abortion and affirmative action, and had no love lost for poor minorities
or rich whites.[22]

Democrats, not surprisingly, began to search for ways to make an electoral comeback. A group composed mainly of white Democrats formed the Democratic Leadership Council (DLC) in 1985, in an attempt to appeal to Middle America by advocating moderate positions and supporting centrist candidates.[23] During the late 1980s and early 1990s, the end of the Cold War brought wholly different issues to the forefront of public consciousness. Education and the economy replaced national defense and anti-Communism as topics of interest to the American public. As a result, racial issues were not part of the issue agenda in 1992. This dynamic aided Bill Clinton's presidential quest that year.[24]

In contrast to the lingering persistence of racial prejudice in American politics, nativism — at least the type directed at whites, for consumption by other whites — is almost completely absent from contemporary electoral machinations. From the 1850s to the 1960s, intraracial nativism was an intermittent part of American political dialogue, however.[25] Today most U.S. elections, particularly for national offices, are fought solely between and among white candidates, with few or no ethnic or religious differences coming into play. But in states with substantial populations of voters who trace their roots primarily to the British Isles and other parts of Northwestern Europe, Caucasian candidates with Greek, Italian, Jewish, Polish, or Middle Eastern surnames sometimes lose favor with other white voters, who may be suspicious of them and their "foreign" names.

To date, every one of our presidents (and all but one vice-president) has traced his heritage to Northern and Western Europe. Spiro Agnew, the first American of Southern European descent to be vice-president, did not lose any votes because of his Greek ancestry; in fact, his conservative politics won him many fans in the Anglo-Saxon South. Moreover, Massachusetts Governor Michael S. Dukakis, a Greek American who was the Democratic presidential candidate in 1988, encountered no major instances of nativism in the political arena. Still, if New York Governor Mario Cuomo had run for the Democratic presidential nomination in 1988 or 1992, he would have probably encountered some voter skepticism because of his liberalism, New York background, and all the vowels in his forename and surname. Yet such nativism rarely affects electoral deliberations in a significant way.

Race is but one way to win votes by making invidious distinctions between and among groups of people. It is often difficult to decipher the hieroglyphics of ethnic bickering, racial animosity, class resentment, or religious bigotry in electoral politics. By definition, such appeals employ verbal and visual cues that scapegoat someone or an entire group of people. These cues polarize the electorate and pander to voters' fears — and to their prejudices. How this is done varies in terms of the subtlety and content of the appeal. But it usually involves an oppositional dynamic: "We" win, while "they" lose.[26] All but a few candidates and policymakers make ritualistic disavowals of any kind of bigotry, racism, discrimination, prejudice, or intolerance, even if their track records may lead people — at least their ideological opponents — to an opposite conclusion.

Regardless of one's ideological predilections, there are informal standards about who is a mainstream political figure and what constitutes a mainstream political appeal. Jesse Jackson continues to be a pillar of the Multicultural Left, and a leading mainstream figure in the Democratic Party. Al Sharpton, by contrast, has one foot in black-nationalist politics and the other in the political mainstream. Before he left the Republican Party in October 1999, Pat Buchanan was at the far-right end of the mainstream spectrum. Even during the early 1990s, David Duke never came close to being regarded as a mainstream figure; his past involvement in racist organizations and continued espousal of white supremacism made him a political outcast. Nearly four decades after the death of Jim Crow, most Americans consider explicit race-baiting to be an illegitimate and reprehensible tactic. Thus few contemporary politicians in America attempt to win votes by exploiting racial divisions.

Intraracial distinctions also occupy an ignominious place in the annals of ethnic politicking. One such example might be a white candidate who contends that her Caucasian opponent is overly sympathetic to African Americans, or vice-versa in a black-versus-black race. African-American politicians, particularly mayors in black-majority cities, are between the proverbial rock and a hard place. They represent constituents who remember their past exclusion from the white power structure (as recently as the 1960s), and who also fume about contemporary inequities and disparities. Thus some of them embrace a winner-take-all mentality that makes them reluctant to reach out to whites. But they face the vexing challenge of reconciling the pressing needs and heightened expectations of their black core constituencies with the sobering realities and unavoidable compromises necessary to cooperate with the largely white civic and business elites of their cities. Consequently, many African-American mayors eschew overtly racial politics and articulate integrationist messages.[27]

In the District of Columbia, skin color, social class, and other intraracial divisions, along with the traditional black-versus-white dichotomies, animate the city's politics. Washington's current mayor, Anthony Williams, has come under fire for not being "black" enough, a charge that dogs many African-American politicos in the District. His predecessor, Marion Barry, was the consummate race-baiter during his 16 years as Washington's mayor.[28] Barry is attempting a political comeback this year as the candidate of Washington's poor and working-class African Americans in his bid for an at-large seat on the District's City Council, which now has a white majority. The former mayor almost certainly will urge blacks to unite behind him to counterbalance the increasing political power of whites in the city. In addition, he surely will criticize what he sees as the unnecessarily accommodative attitudes of Washington's African-American political leadership. Barry's political appeal may fall flat in multiethnic Washington, a city where blacks now constitute less than 60% of the population.[29]

American politicos embrace one of two approaches — what David T. Canon describes as the "politics of difference" and the "politics of commonality" — when it comes to their campaign tactics and strategies of governance.[30] The "politics of difference" involves demonizing a particular person or group of people, so as to gain an electoral advantage. The "politics of commonality" requires politicos to make rhetorical affirmations of diversity and to celebrate and recognize, at least perfunctorily, *all* the people who make up the polity. When politicians make divisive appeals, they take into account complex electoral calculations — whether they will turn off more voters than they gain by doing so, and whether it will be harder for them to govern after they win using such tactics. The new politics of race still focuses on dividing to conquer, but it is far less overt than its predecessor, which involved naked appeals to racial and ethnic hatreds.

Partisans of each political party periodically seek to divide the electorate so as to gain an advantage in an election campaign or a legislative debate. Race-baiting, which can be defined as any political effort that divides voters by race, is a key component of the Republican "politics of difference." Another way Republicans polarize the electorate is through the use of red-hot social issues, such as gay rights and school prayer, which have little or no racial significance. In response, Democrats criticize Republican "extremism" on abortion, education, gun control, the environment, and other issues. Democrats, moreover, periodically charge that the Republicans intend to eviscerate Medicare and Social Security. They also may stir up minority turnout by excoriating the GOP as a haven of racist hatemongers, or promote class resentment through soak-the-rich rhetoric and advocacy of higher taxes. The explicitness of these types of appeals continues to decline, for the most part, due to the American public's disgust with political in-fighting and excessively ideological tactics and strategies.

The most common variant of interracial politics occurs in areas where African Americans (and other people of color) are a clear minority of the electorate. In such venues, race rarely surfaces in politics. Black candidates, to be sure, are occasionally hurt by their race because whites may hold unflattering preconceptions about African Americans which are then magnified in the political arena. However, white voters often support black candidates. African-American Democrats presently serve as mayors of majority-white cities like Denver and Columbus, and as chief executives of multiethnic cities such as Houston, Jersey City, and San Francisco. And black Democrats regularly win statewide offices in Illinois, a state that is 67.8% white, 14.9% black, 12.3% Latino, and 3.4% Asian.[31] Still, the same liberal positions that black candidates espouse to win favor in the African-American community make it difficult for them to win over white voters in ideologically polarized contests. Racism may play a role, if only a small one, that hurts a black candidate in a tight race. As a result, it can be difficult for African Americans to win elections in statewide contests and legislative and congressional districts where racially polarized voting patterns exist.[32] Only in Asian-majority Hawaii do members of a single nonwhite racial group have enough numerical clout to elect their coethnics to statewide positions, even if the candidates espouse liberal positions on the issues during the campaign.

Minority candidates, particularly blacks and Latinos, face tough questions when they run for office in racially polarized parts of America. Non-Latino voters in a multiethnic city might want to know whether Hispanic candidate X will be known as a *Hispanic mayor* if he is elected, meaning that he lavishes his attention on Hispanics and utilizes his executive prerogatives to benefit them. Or will he be a *mayor who happens to be Hispanic,* whose ethnic background is incidental to his political agenda, governing style, and effectiveness as a leader. Politicos, naturally, are far more likely to be the former type if they have a monolithic ethnic voting majority backing them.

An increasingly common variant of interracial politics occurs when whites are the minority or plurality group, even among registered voters, in a given locality. In such venues, race frequently surfaces in politics — if only because people of color want to make sure that they receive their "fair share" of city services. Many polyethnic cities, including Chicago,

Oakland, New York, and Los Angeles, have white mayors. In some of these cities, Caucasians still account for the majority of the voters. Hispanics are a key swing voter group in Chicago, Dallas, Los Angeles, and New York: It is not uncommon for them to back white candidates who are opposed by most African Americans. However, no one seriously thinks a white person could be elected mayor of racially divided black-majority cities such as Atlanta, Detroit, Memphis, Newark, New Orleans, or the District of Columbia, at least in the current racial and political climate. To be sure, two black-majority cities (Gary and Baltimore) elected white mayors in the 1990s. Moreover, St. Louis, a city that is 51% African American, elected a white mayor in 2001.

White candidates in black-majority jurisdictions sometimes benefit from the perception that, as Caucasians, they will be taken more seriously by white powerbrokers. Their white skin confers upon them automatic outsider status in places where white and African-American voters seek an alternative to the local black political machine. For a variety of reasons — multiethnic coalitions, anemic minority registration and voting rates, the clout of white civic and business elites, and white candidates who simply out-campaign their nonwhite opponents — Caucasians continue to exert political influence in excess of their numbers in many polyethnic places.

THE COALITION-BUILDERS

In 1998 it seemed for a time that Linda Lingle might become Hawaii's first female governor. The Maui Republican made a strong challenge to Democratic governor Benjamin J. Cayetano. In an era of state budget deficits and a lackluster economy, Cayetano, a one-term governor, was vulnerable to a Republican challenger like Lingle, who had compiled an impressive record in her eight years as mayor of Maui. Many voters were skeptical about Cayetano's record. Lingle, therefore, was the front-runner in most polls. But Cayetano mustered a stunning comeback, with a barrage of potent biographical ads and major expenditures during the final two weeks of the campaign. Cayetano eked out a narrow 50.1%-to-48.8% victory, largely on the strength of his appeal to Hawaii's sizable Filipino- and Japanese-American communities.[33]

It is difficult to determine what role, if any, Lingle's ethno-racial background played in her gubernatorial defeat in 1998. To be sure, Hawaii's minority voters strongly backed Governor Cayetano in his reelection bid. And whites, or *haoles* as they are known in Hawaii, overwhelmingly favored Lingle's candidacy. However, Caucasians probably made up only 30% of the Hawaiian electorate in 1998, which means that Lingle must have won a significant amount of support from nonwhite voters to do as well as she did. As a rule, Hawaiians are perhaps the most tolerant group of Americans; ethnic and racial diversity is a fact of life in the Aloha State. Even though the state's various ethnic groups generally get along well with each other, there still are ethnic rivalries and disparities that color their relationships.[34] So it is impossible to discount race as a factor in an election this close.

Linda Lingle faced an uphill battle in her attempt to become Hawaii's second white Republican governor, due to her partisan affiliation, not her race. Social class, more than any other factor, probably cemented Cayetano's victory. Many Hawaiians consider Republicans such as Lingle to be the political proxies of the affluent people in the state. Whites, of course, are well represented in the ranks of prosperous Hawaiians. Inasmuch as Lingle was perceived to be the candidate of affluent white Hawaiians, she lost ground in the minority precincts where Republicans are seen as insensitive to the needs of the less-affluent.

Whites in heavily Democratic Hawaii tend to support the GOP, which limits their ability to elect whites to statewide office.[35] Hawaii has had only one white U.S. Senator in its history.[36] Its first two governors were white but no Caucasian has won the state's top elected job since 1970.[37] Every major statewide official is a minority Democrat — although in Hawaii, they are the majority, in terms of their ethnic background and partisan affiliation. Should Lingle, who now chairs the state Republican Party, succeed in her gubernatorial run in 2002, she will make history as a white Hawaiian and as a Republican. However, it is the second distinction, not the first, that matters to most Hawaiians. Ethnic distinctions still affect the state's politics, but probably matter less than in any other place where whites are a minority of the voters and residents.

Likewise, Western states such as Colorado and Washington are particularly amenable to women and minority candidates and officeholders.[38] Colorado sends Ben Nighthorse Campbell, a Native American Republican, to the U.S. Senate. The state's lieutenant governor, Joe Rogers, is black. Wellington Webb, the mayor of Denver, is African American; blacks constitute only 10.8% of the population in the Mile High City. Elsewhere in the West, there are similar examples of minorities who have triumphed in white-majority jurisdictions. Gary Locke, the governor of Washington since 1997, is the first Chinese-American governor and the first Asian-American chief executive outside of Hawaii. Ron Sims, who is African American, serves as King County Executive, the position that gave Locke the stature to run successfully for governor six years ago.[39] In addition, women make up more than 30% of the state legislators in six Western states: Washington, Nevada, Arizona, Colorado, Oregon, and New Mexico.[40] Arizonans made history of a different type in November 1998, when they elected women to the top five statewide offices, including the governorship.[41] As Jeff Kass points out, these Western politicos "all are benefiting from an unusual mix of history and current events — a less tradition-bound past and a present marked by a huge influx of open-minded residents."[42]

Such factors influence the politics of New Mexico, the nation's most heavily Latino state, where political affiliations largely cleave along ethnic lines. As a rule, Anglos tend to back Republicans, while Hispanics and Native Americans usually support Democrats. The state's well-deserved reputation for peaceful ethnic relations extends to the political arena.[43] Overt ethnic politicking is rare in New Mexico. Even though Anglos constitute a majority of the electorate, the state has a venerable tradition of electing Hispanics to offices at every level of government. New Mexico has had several Latino governors, including Toney Anaya, who served from 1983 to 1987. Dennis Chávez represented the state in the U.S. Senate for 27 years; Joseph M. Montoya later held the same seat for another 12 years.[44] New Mexico also sent two other Hispanics — Republican Manuel Lujan Jr. and Democrat Bill Richardson — to Congress for many years.

Indeed, Latinos presently wield more political power in New Mexico than in any other state. Three of the five New Mexico Supreme Court Justices are Hispanic Democrats. Ben Lujan, a Latino Democrat, serves as state House speaker, and Hispanics hold a variety of other leadership positions in the legislature. Moreover, the roster of New Mexico's statewide officeholders includes four Latino Democrats: Secretary of State Rebecca Vigil-Giron, State Auditor Domingo P. Martinez, State Treasurer Michael A. Montoya, and Attorney General Patricia A. Madrid. Sometimes both of the major-party candidates for a statewide office in New Mexico are Hispanic.

Statewide officeholders in New Mexico, regardless of their ethnic background, systematically reach out to Anglo, Latino, and American Indian voters. Candidates often spend money on Navajo- and Spanish-language advertising campaigns. They usually retain surrogates from each of the state's major ethnic groups. Secretary of State Rebecca Vigil-Giron, the Land of Enchantment's highest ranking Democratic officeholder, exemplifies the inclusive political approach typical of successful politicos in New Mexico. Vigil-Giron, who speaks three languages and traces her ancestry in the New World back to 1695, tailors her office's services to reflect the multicultural realities of New Mexico. The state Constitution requires her to make voting materials available in English and Spanish; election information is also translated into Navajo and several other Native American languages.[45]

Vigil-Giron excels at retail politics, and she makes frequent appearances around the state in order to persuade New Mexicans to involve themselves in the electoral process. The perceptive politico assiduously courts Anglo voters, even though she generally wins her biggest margins in the Hispanic and American Indian precincts of New Mexico.[46] Vigil-Giron and her colleagues practice the politics of inclusion out of necessity. They simply cannot afford to ignore any group of voters in this politically divided state — Democratic presidential candidate Al Gore carried New Mexico by only 366 votes in 2000.

Black Republicans in New Mexico and beyond have considerable experience in the realm of inclusive politicking. They usually find most of their support in the white community, due to black America's virtually unanimous support for the Democrats. Few blacks embrace them because of their Republican tag (the party of Lincoln theme falls flat), and some whites question their GOP bona fides.[47]

Nonetheless, black Republican candidates are no longer unusual or a novelty: They run in majority-black *and* majority-white jurisdictions. In 1990 Gary Franks became the first African-American Republican elected to the U.S. House since the 1930s. He served three terms from a Connecticut congressional district before losing his bid for reelection in 1996.[48] The sole African-American Republican in Congress, Oklahoma Representative J. C. Watts Jr., represents a district with a voting-age population that is seven percent black. He serves as chairperson of the Republican Conference Committee in the U.S. House, the fourth highest-ranking position in the GOP leadership there.[49] Ohio Secretary of State Ken Blackwell, Colorado Lieutenant Governor Joe Rogers, and Texas Railroad Commission Chairman Michael Williams are the best known black Republican elected officials at the state level. At the very least, these officials demonstrate that the stereotypes surrounding African-American political preferences may have to be modified in the future.

Retired General Colin L. Powell, who served as Chairman of the Joint Chiefs of Staff from 1989 to 1993, is the leading star in the black Republican firmament. As Johanna McGeary of *Time* points out, "[Powell's] stellar career, inspiring personal history and reputation for integrity have endowed him with a unique moral stature."[50] While mindful of Powell's social significance, blacks continue to be more skeptical than whites about whether the Jamaican American is genuinely attuned to their interests, or is merely a proxy for white conservatives — many of whom, by the way, see him as a centrist who is insufficiently conservative for their tastes.[51] As one who is unsullied by rough-and-tumble political combat, Powell routinely garners astronomical popularity ratings from his fellow Americans.

Powell consistently refused to enter electoral politics in the 1990s, despite opinion polls that indicated he would have been a formidable presidential candidate and one of the few potential vice-presidential nominees who might have actually affected the election results. He probably avoided running for president or vice president because his emphatic support for gun control, abortion rights, and affirmative action hurt him with the core constituency of the Republican Party. It was better for the African-American Cincinnatus to preserve the illusion that he could win the Oval Office, with attendant political capital, than to test this dicey proposition in the electoral arena. Powell made history once again when he became Secretary of State in George W. Bush's administration, but few African Americans have followed him to the Republican Party.

Alan L. Keyes has run twice for the Republican presidential nomination. No other African-American national candidate has ever won so many white votes and so little support from his fellow blacks. Keyes occupies a special place in Republican Party presidential politics, where he is best known for his erudite orations and boundless self-confidence. Keyes, who is Catholic and a staunch conservative, makes his case on every issue — abortion, gun control, affirmative action, the income tax — solely on intellectual grounds. His distinguished résumé includes a Harvard Ph.D., service in prominent posts in the Reagan State Department and diplomatic corps, and a career in the 1990s as a writer, lecturer, and radio talk-show host. Keyes has used his extraordinary speaking skills and formidable command of political theory to capture the support of conservative purists in the Republican Party. Christian conservatives rally to this didactic and unmistakably cerebral man; some of them regard him as a political prophet due to his diatribes about moral decline in the United States.[52]

Keyes has little choice but to court white voters, because his partisan affiliation and ideological beliefs repel most of his fellow African Americans. He regularly charges that the mainstream news media demonstrate racial bias against him by neglecting to cover his quixotic political campaigns. Keyes contends that the mainstream media largely ignore him because his politics are antithetical to their conceptions of how blacks should view issues.[53] Keyes, ironically, may encounter little hostility in the GOP because there are so few black voters in the Republican primary electorate that white conservatives do not feel threatened by the possibility of an influx of blacks in "their" party. Although Keyes holds hard-right positions on most racial issues — he strenuously opposes affirmative action, for instance — he rarely discusses such matters, preferring instead to focus on values and morality.

Since he entered national politics in 1995, Keyes has won hundreds of thousands of votes. He placed fifth in the GOP presidential sweepstakes in 1996, winning 436,262 Republican primary votes, in addition to nine delegates to his party's national convention.[54] Keyes did even better in 2000; he won 990,014 votes and 21 delegates in his second GOP presidential quest.[55] His participation in the presidential debates always ensured that these usually boring episodes of the campaign sitcom would be eminently watchable, especially when Keyes treated his audiences to lengthy discourses on classical American political theory. After George W. Bush sewed up the Republican presidential nomination in March 2000, Keyes was his only active primary challenger. The small but vocal constituency of true-believing social conservatives fueled Keyes' low-profile campaign in 2000, and he placed a distant third (after Bush and John McCain) in votes and delegates. Still, it is hard to envision Keyes ever winning the presidency. Besides his lack of electoral experience, Keyes is too far right to gain the backing of most Americans. Yet he has already made history. Every primary that Keyes enters, every caucus he contests, every debate he dominates is a minor and little-noted indicator of racial progress, because almost all of Keyes' voters, listeners, and financial supporters are conservative white folks.

Hispanic Republicans face less significant challenges than their African-American partisans — although this depends on their ethnic background and the community they represent. Mexican Americans are loyal to the Democratic Party, although there have been a number of defections over the years, especially in Texas. The most prominent Mexican-American Republican, U.S. Congressman Henry Bonilla, represents a House district that encompasses much of the U.S.-Mexico border region in Texas. Since his election to Congress in 1992, the bilingual Bonilla has served as a point man for the Republican Party in its national minority-recruitment efforts.[56] These outreach initiatives have not been especially successful;

relatively few Mexican Americans outside of Texas regularly support the GOP.

Cuban Americans, however, continue to be heavily Republican, particularly those *cubanoamericanos* who live in South Florida. Miami-area Congresswoman Ileana Ros-Lehtinen became the first Cuban American elected to the House in 1989, when she won the special election to succeed the late Claude Pepper. She was joined in Congress in 1993 by Lincoln Diaz-Balart, who represents another South Florida House district. Both Ros-Lehtinen and Diaz-Balart follow the GOP party line on most economic and foreign policy matters, but they differ with the Republican leadership over such issues as aid to legal immigrants and the need for bilingual education.[57] Florida is the indisputable capital of Hispanic Republicanism. Bob Martinez, a Spanish-American Republican, governed the state from 1987 to 1991. And in Miami-Dade County, Republicans with Spanish surnames hold many political positions. Some Latinos, to be sure, regard Hispanic Republicans as traitors who betray their coethnics by backing a party largely made up of conservative Anglos. Until more non-Cuban Latinos respond to the GOP's overtures, Hispanic Republicans will continue to encounter many skeptics in the Latino community.

Many cities, such as Laredo and Hialeah, are dominated by one Hispanic subgroup so the politicos in those areas do not have to practice coalition politics. In other places, the rule is that Latinos will vote for Latinos against Anglo candidates, provided that the Hispanic politico is ideologically congenial, but will favor their coethnic in an intraethnic battle, e.g., a Cuban versus a Puerto Rican.[58] Miami Mayor Manny Diaz, a Cuban, was elected in 2001 after he defeated Maurice Ferré, a Puerto Rican. Diaz triumphed based on his overwhelming support in the Cuban precincts. He took 70% of the Hispanic vote, while Ferré won 68% of the Anglo vote and 88% among African Americans.[59] Ferré's overwhelming support among Anglos and blacks was probably at least partially attributable to the fact that he was Puerto Rican, not Cuban. Some Anglos and blacks resent the Cuban influence in Miami, and they vote accordingly.

Ethnic differences also affect politics in black America. West Indians and African Americans share common interests on a wide variety of issues, from poverty to police brutality. But there are some key differences that separate the two groups. The Caribbean immigrants often have a different mind-set about racism in America, as well as a transnational focus on events back home and here. Until recently, Jamaican Americans participated more fully in American politics than Haitian Americans because of their English-language facility, their higher levels of American citizenship, and the fact that they were more committed to making their lives in the United States.[60]

As the West Indian communities have begun to flex their political muscles in such places as Miami, Boston, Newark, New York, and elsewhere, African-American politicians have become increasingly responsive to their political concerns.[61] Haitian Americans are becoming involved in electoral politics now that many in their community have decided to stay permanently in the United States. Some Haitian-American politicos represent sizable African-American constituencies and face African Americans in their electoral matchups.[62] Ethnic politicking periodically occurs in such contests.

Fernando Ferrer won a significant amount of support from West Indians, African Americans, and his fellow Hispanics during his campaign to become mayor of New York City in 2001. Ferrer, the Bronx borough president, was the self-styled candidate of "the other New York." His campaign slogan highlighted his theme of "two New Yorks": the New York of affluent whites and the New York of the not-so-affluent Latinos and African Americans. Not surprisingly, Ferrer, who is Puerto Rican, won tremendous support in the Hispanic community. Moreover, Ferrer won the endorsements of a number of black (and Latino) elected officials. What really helped — and, later, hurt — his campaign was the endorsement of the Rev. Al Sharpton, whose backing enabled Ferrer to solidify his support in the African-American community, which supported him by a solid margin on primary day.[63] As a result of his overwhelming backing from Latinos and his majority among African Americans, Ferrer did well in the initial primary, taking first place with 36% of the vote to Mark Green's 31%. Ominously, he won a negligible percentage of the white vote.[64] Still, Ferrer managed to unite the black-brown coalition that multicultural leftists dream about but seldom assemble in cities where the two ethno-racial groups are roughly equal in number.

The acrimonious two-week runoff campaign in New York City divided the Democratic Party so badly that a Republican won the mayoral election. During the runoff, Ferrer campaigned heavily in the city's minority communities. Mark Green, meanwhile, redoubled his efforts to win overwhelming support from white voters, who made up nearly half the New York City electorate in 2001. Some renegade Green backers made telephone calls to white voters suggesting that Sharpton would be a major figure in a Ferrer administration. They also distributed leaflets that included a cartoon that crudely mocked the Sharpton-Ferrer alliance. (The Green campaign disavowed any connection to these activities.) Green himself unleashed a television commercial that challenged Ferrer's credentials, a ploy that infuriated the Ferrer campaign. On election day, Green eked out what appeared to be a narrow victory. He took 83% of the white vote, while Ferrer was supported by 71% of black voters and 84% of Latinos. Almost immediately, the results were called into question because of overcounting and other irregularities. Eventually, the New York City Board of Elections certified Green as the winner by a 51%-49% margin.[65]

But many minority voters were angered by Green's campaign tactics and refused to support him. Meanwhile, Republican Michael Bloomberg capitalized on this discontent in his expensive advertising blitz, which featured the endorsement of popular Mayor Rudolph Giuliani in the last days of the campaign. The billionaire mogul also benefited from his ability to outspend Green and his appeal as a can-do businessman in the aftermath of a crisis. Sharpton did not endorse Green, and some Latinos either backed Bloomberg or refused to vote in the mayoral race. In the end, Bloomberg defeated Green 50%-47% — as Green carried Latinos, whose turnout dipped dramatically from the primary, by only a 49%-47% margin.[66] Bloomberg's unusual electoral odyssey shows that Democrats can never take the minority vote for granted, and that Republicans (especially unorthodox left-of-center Republicans like Bloomberg) can do well among people of color under the right circumstances. At this point, it is uncertain whether Mayor Bloomberg will be able to maintain a high level of support from the Hispanic community of New York City during his four-year term as mayor.

VOTES AND RIGHTS

When William O. Lipinski was growing up in Chicago during the 1940s and 1950s, Irish, Polish, and Italian politicos ran the city. They represented constituents who were one or two or even three generations removed from the immigrant experience, and who were beginning to join the great American middle class in large numbers. These upwardly mobile Americans remained faithful Catholics, and the influence of the Church made them social conservatives (like the Irish-Polish Lipinski). On economic issues the white ethnics supported the New Deal and government policies that, in their eyes, benefited the working man, not the factory owner or corporate executive. As they grew older and more prosperous, many of these Chicagoans moved to the close-in suburbs around the city. They sought more living space and also hoped to put some distance between themselves and the city's poor blacks.[67]

The popular Lipinski has faithfully represented his white ethnic constituents in the political arena, first on the Chicago City Council and then in the U.S. House, to which he was first elected in 1982. He opposes abortion rights and affirmative action, two positions that do not endear him to the left wing of the Democratic Party, but are consistent with the philosophy of the ethnic, urban Democrats of his generation. In the past Lipinski has criticized the national Democratic Party for what he says is its inattention to the issues and interests of his working- and middle-class urban ethnic constituents. Lipinski's middle-of-the-road voting record appeals to the white Chicagoans who predominate in his district, and reelection is never a problem for the 64-year-old lifelong resident of Chicago.[68]

Despite the changing demographics of his Chicago base, Lipinski still represents a constituency that is largely made up of people who are descended from European immigrants. Today three-quarters of Lipinski's constituents reside in south and west suburban Chicago; twenty-five percent of them are Chicagoans, many of whom live in and around Midway Airport and in the city's Bungalow Belt neighborhoods on the Southwest Side. Lipinski's congressional district was approximately 90% white in the early 1990s. At the time he and his colleagues in Chicago's Democratic Party watched their new Hispanic neighbors with interest, due to the Voting Rights Act, which required legislators to maximize the number of majority-minority congressional districts.[69]

After much foot-dragging, Illinois legislators created the state's first Hispanic-majority congressional district in 1991, which united the Windy City's geographically dispersed Puerto Rican and Mexican-American communities. The Voting Rights Act preserved the three existing black-majority districts in metropolitan Chicago. Since the city lost a U.S. House seat overall, two white members of Congress were redistricted into political oblivion in order to make room for the new Hispanic congressional district. Lipinski survived the game of musical chairs when he defeated an Italian-American colleague in 1992. Moreover, he appears prepared to deal with similar dynamics in 2002 (the 2000 census revealed that his district is now nearly one-quarter Hispanic). These dramas related to equity issues in the political arena are a permanent part of the electoral landscape in large multiethnic cities.

Electoral affirmative action is a manifestation of the diversity imperative. It dates back to the Voting Rights Act of 1965, which served as a statutory mandate to eradicate the discrimination that had prevented so many black Southerners from exercising their constitutional right to vote. This enforcement mechanism for remedying African-American electoral exclusion was renewed in 1970, 1975 (when it began to cover Hispanics), and 1982. In the latter year Congress renewed the Voting Rights Act until 2007. Legislators included provisions that were designed to increase the descriptive representation of nonwhites, especially in the next round of congressional redistricting. Racially gerrymandered districts were the principal means of electing minorities to Congress. After all, it is easier for liberal people of color to win in legislative districts tailored to their ethnic and ideological specifications, than for them to contest seats with unfriendly demographic and ideological mixes. Mapmakers frequently drew the district lines to ensure that whites would be a minority in the electorate, thus virtually guaranteeing that a nonwhite would win the seat. Doing so often required that 65% or 70% of the district's residents had to be people of color.[70]

The Voting Rights Act, particularly as it was interpreted by political cartographers in 1991 and 1992, created "communities of interest" that did not necessarily adhere to the standard criteria regarding geographical compactness. These districts were supposed to give minority voters opportunities to elect "representatives of their choice"; the ubiquitous white male lawmakers clearly did not fit the bill. In the course of fleshing out the details, there were occasional squabbles between black and Hispanic legislators and interest groups, but they usually worked together to ensure maximum representation for their coethnics. Republicans were happy to help them, as they sought to squeeze out white Democrats in the U.S. House, by creating as many congressional districts with nonwhite majorities as possible. Some states, like Illinois, faced an imperative to reduce the size of their U.S. House delegations and, at the same time, Voting Rights Act dictates to create more majority-minority seats. Frustrated by their inability to advance faster—and emboldened by the 1982 amendments to the Voting Rights Act that sought to maximize the numbers of nonwhite representatives—ambitious black and Hispanic liberals wholeheartedly embraced a strategy of cooperation with white Republicans in the early 1990s.[71]

In a partnership that wags dubbed an "unholy alliance," black and Hispanic politicians teamed up with white Republicans nationally (and in a number of states). They sought to create more majority-minority, heavily Democratic congressional districts—and consequently more predominantly white, Republican-leaning seats. White Republicans were tired of their minority status in the U.S. House and figured they could open up other seats for their candidates by supporting the creation of House districts crammed full of people of color. To do so, they provided minority Democrats with computer software, legal assistance, and moral support. White Republicans employed this deliberately cynical strategy, despite the principled opposition of conservatives like William Bennett and Linda Chavez, to regain control of the U.S. House, a goal they achieved in November 1994. Black and Hispanic activists were equally calculating. They usually accepted GOP offers of help, notwithstanding speculation that racial gerrymandering might diminish voter turnout in general elections by eliminating the possibility of competitive interparty contests in the heavily minority districts. Republicans privately cheered this development because they hoped it would lower the turnout of likely Democratic voters in statewide elections and presidential contests.[72]

These machinations occurred primarily in 13 states, all of which had lots of minorities, and some of which had to satisfy Voting Rights Act dictates: Alabama, California, Florida, Georgia, Illinois, Louisiana, Maryland, New Jersey, New York, North Carolina, South Carolina, Texas, and Virginia. The U.S. Justice Department watched over the redistricting process, in order to ensure that the plans being drawn up by the state legislators, and sometimes vetoed by governors or rejected by the courts, maximized nonwhites' chances to win congressional seats.[73] Many of the resulting districts, particularly in Illinois, New York, and North Carolina, were exercises in creative cartography, and the media coined unforgettable descriptions that mocked the most misshapen and asymmetrical maps. These serpentine creations provided minority politicos with a means to take a shortcut to Washington, rather than wait for established incumbents to die, retire, make missteps, or become entangled in scandal — the traditional ways to open up seats held by veteran officeholders.

White Democrats faced a Catch-22 when it came to speaking out in opposition to racial gerrymandering. On the one hand, they feared that racial gerrymandering would decimate their ranks. On the other, to appear hostile to such initiatives exposed them to charges of indifference, or even tacit racism, from their most loyal constituents. So they handled the issue of racial gerrymandering as delicately as possible. White Democrats tried to get blacks and Hispanics to accept smaller percentages of minorities in the majority-minority districts. They attempted to make sure that Republicans did not get all the credit for increasing the descriptive representation of blacks and Hispanics in the U.S. House. And they pushed for a more detailed enumeration of the nation's population, in the hopes that it would turn up more minorities. But the incentives for cooperating with Republicans were too great, so many high-ranking minority lawmakers were reluctant to work with white Democrats on redistricting issues.[74] Some black and Hispanic liberals, of course, were genuinely concerned that there would be negative repercussions from the "unholy alliance." They lamented the loss of talented white legislators who were sacrificed on the altar of racial politics, and fretted that fewer legislators overall would have sufficiently large numbers of minority constituents to be obligated to take their views into account.[75]

After the 1992 elections, the "unholy alliance" resulted in a dramatic increase in descriptive representation for people of color. The number of Hispanic-majority seats increased in California, Florida, Illinois, Texas, and New York. Alabama, Florida, North Carolina, and South Carolina gained their first black U.S. Representatives since Reconstruction. Most significantly, Florida went from having zero to three black members of Congress. North Carolinians sent two African Americans to Washington. Georgia's lone black U.S. Representative, John Lewis, was joined by two others, while Maryland, Texas, and Virginia also added African Americans to their congressional delegations. Black and Latino members of Congress had more clout than ever before, at least while the Democrats controlled the U.S. House.

In 1993 and 1994 Congressional Black Caucus Chairman Kweisi Mfume and his fellow black legislators constituted a fairly cohesive voting bloc that, at times, held the balance of power in the lower chamber of Congress. When the Democrats controlled the House, African Americans also benefited from the congressional seniority system because they came from safe districts that allowed them to serve for decades and accumulate the requisite experience to hold powerful committee and subcommittee chairmanships. For a short time, it appeared that the underlying logic of the "unholy alliance" had worked to the advantage of the African-American lawmakers.[76] With the Republican takeover of the U.S. House of Representatives in 1995, however, the Congressional Black Caucus once again became a legislative group with little power or influence in Congress. In any event, black legislators still make up 18% of the House Democratic Caucus. But the question of whether African Americans (or Latinos, for that matter) are receiving significantly more substantive representation in Congress than they did ten years ago is open to debate. In the meantime, most black and Latino members of Congress have fought the GOP's legislative initiatives.

When they won control of the U.S. House in the 1994 elections, white Republicans realized their rewards from participating in the "unholy alliance." This development was due, largely, to their major gains in the South. Nevertheless, scholars differ over how important a role racial gerrymandering played in the GOP takeover of the U.S. House. Some, like Carol M. Swain, contend that it was a major factor, even accountable for the entire margin of Republican victory. Swain and her ideological compatriots focus on the majority-black districts that were created in the South for the 1992 elections. Conversely, some respected experts and lawmakers refuse to attribute any significant Republican gains in the House to racial gerrymandering, perhaps because they do not want to question the broader strategy of electoral affirmative action as a means of promoting greater descriptive representation for people of color.[77] Both sides in this debate are partially right. When the last round of redistricting took place, white Southerners still had not completely embraced the Republican Party, while popular Democratic incumbents held what seemed like lifetime leases on congressional seats. Since then, a combination of Democratic retirements, a favorable issue agenda, and, yes, racial gerrymandering has powered the GOP's congressional gains in Dixie.

Perhaps to the relief of some white Democrats, electoral affirmative action has come under intense fire during the last nine years. Many of the new congressional districts immediately were the subject of litigation. The Supreme Court frequently weighed in on the issue throughout the 1990s, as did the lower courts, and numerous congressional districts were invalidated and redrawn.[78] The Court's general reluctance to endorse racial gerrymandering infuriated African-American elite opinion makers, although electoral affirmative action did not resonate as an issue at the mass level. Several states, including Texas, Georgia, Louisiana, and North Carolina, had to redraw some of their congressional districts to remedy the most egregious instances of racial gerrymandering. The redrawn districts are more compact and have smaller minority constituencies than the previous ones. Moreover, the new electoral geography complicates matters for Republicans in neighboring districts, who now have larger nonwhite constituencies.

These legal maneuverings gave five African-American members of the Class of 1992 redrawn, white-majority congressional districts just in time for the 1996 elections. The power of incumbency enabled them to win over white voters; every member of this political quintet — Florida's Corrine Brown, Georgians Sanford D. Bishop Jr. and Cynthia McKinney, and Texans Sheila Jackson-Lee and Eddie Bernice Johnson — emerged victorious in 1996. In 1998 and 2000 all five of the aforementioned legislators won again, as did North Carolina Democrat Melvin Watt, although African Americans now make up only 44.6% of his district. The national media focused a considerable amount of attention on the electoral successes of U.S. Representatives Brown, Bishop, McKinney, Jackson-Lee, Johnson, and Watt. It remains uncertain at this point the degree to which incumbency, rather than colorblind voting patterns, is responsible for these electoral milestones.[79]

These recent victories by African Americans in congressional districts where whites are the largest voter group undoubtedly contributed to the reluctance of the black and Latino elites to resurrect their once-a-decade "unholy alliance" with white Republicans. Two factors seemed to be working here. First, black incumbents have observed that they can win in white-majority districts (such as those that have resulted from the mid-decade redrawing of lines necessitated by court rulings against racial gerrymandering). As a result, many of them sought districts with smaller percentages of minority voters, so that Democrats would be able to win in other districts. Republicans, predictably, were not thrilled about this idea. The second difference between 1991 and 2001 was that the previous coalition occurred in the context of Democratic congressional hegemony. Many of the nonwhite participants in that unorthodox partnership failed to consider that the Democrats might lose their majority in the U.S. House. In 2001, after six years on the political margins, few black or Hispanic Democrats wanted to do anything that would have extended the Republican lease on the lower chamber of Congress. The courts, moreover, did not seem predisposed to approve redistricting plans that included racial gerrymandering.[80]

The result is that in a number of states, more districts have been created, ones with lower percentages of African Americans than in the past redistricting cycles, that might be won by white — or black — Democrats.[81] For seven years, Georgia's 11-member House delegation has consisted of eight white Republicans and three black Democrats; the new redistricting map is very likely to send several white Democrats to Washington.[82] To be sure, some ethnic advocates sought more descriptive representation for their coethnics regardless of what the consequences would be in terms of the partisan composition of Congress.[83] This type of thinking did not prevail in 2001 and 2002, however, as it did in 1991 and 1992. In sharp contrast to the minority gains of 1992 and the Republican victories of 1994, it seems very unlikely that people of color will dramatically increase their descriptive representation in the 108th

Congress or that Republicans, for that matter, will benefit much from the redrawing of congressional districts nationwide.

The typical white incumbent often finds himself or herself in an untenable position when his or her district gradually shifts to include a more heterogeneous mixture of constituents.[84] It is unusual for a non-incumbent white candidate to win in a district where the majority of the voters are black. African Americans can — and do — vote against perceived interlopers. In such a context, white incumbents sometimes persevere and prevail in election after election, but they face constant pressures to retire and let a person of color represent the district. The exceptions to this unwritten rule of same-race representation usually occur in Hispanic-majority districts with large numbers of noncitizen minorities who cannot vote yet.

Still, there are at least 13 white incumbents who represent House districts where minorities constitute a clear majority of the population, if not the electorate. Six white Democrats represent House districts where a single minority constitutes a majority of the residents, while five white Democrats and two white Republicans represent heterogeneous majority-minority House districts.[85] These incumbents are popular in their districts. They use the perquisites of their office to build rapport with the voters. Eliot Engel represents the most minorities of any white member of Congress; New York's 17th Congressional District is predominantly black and Hispanic. He continually faces primary challenges, although many of his colleagues from majority-minority districts never encounter any ethnic or racial animosity on the home front.[86] Despite the clear willingness of minorities to vote for whites — and whites to vote for people of color — it is still evident that the desire for descriptive representation can be a powerful argument against a white lawmaker in a majority-minority district.

Some black lawmakers face similar electoral threats because Latino voters now make up a majority of the residents, but not necessarily the voters, of their districts. Even today there are African-American legislators who act as if most of their constituents are black, when this is not the case. In any event, three African Americans now represent Latino-majority congressional districts: New York Representative Charlie Rangel and Southern California Representatives Maxine Waters and Juanita Millender-McDonald. A third Los Angeles-area House member, Diane Watson, presently has a Hispanic-plurality constituency. Dallas Democrat Eddie Bernice Johnson represents a multiethnic House district where blacks barely outnumber Latinos, but the electorate is solidly

African American. The same is true of Houston Democrat Sheila Jackson-Lee's congressional district.[87] None of these lawmakers has ever faced a serious Latino challenger.

In the meantime, African-American politicians throughout Southern California hold on, somewhat tenuously, in congressional, legislative, and aldermanic districts where Hispanics are now the numerical majority but comprise a minority of the electorate. Black politicians in the Los Angeles area span the spectrum from those who openly embrace Hispanics to those who defiantly refuse to acknowledge the changing demographics of their constituencies.[88] In 2001 the California legislature spared Maxine Waters, Diane Watson, and Juanita Millender-McDonald from significant primary challenges during the next decade by drawing safe Democratic districts for them in which black voters figure prominently. However, there are no such redistricting panaceas in the cards for the three blacks on Los Angeles' 15-member City Council, all of whom represent districts where Latinos are a major presence.[89]

As Hispanics emerge politically in previously black-dominated communities and neighborhoods throughout the country, we can expect to see a number of acrimonious black-versus-brown electoral battles. Some African-American legislators will undoubtedly adjust well to the new electoral dynamics and provide valuable outreach services to their Latino constituents. Others may try to win reelection with the monolithic support of African Americans, who still outvote Hispanics even in districts where there are two or three times as many Latinos as blacks. In any event, it certainly will be interesting to see how African-American politicos conduct their Hispanic outreach efforts — and how they do so without unsettling their black core constituency.

Racial politics declined in frequency and viciousness during the 1990s. Complex electoral calculations have forced political figures of all races to be warier of scapegoating and clashing with various groups of people. This phenomenon is particularly evident in America's cities, where many blacks now feel that African-American mayors, though symbolically important, are not necessary to improve city services, create well-paying jobs, and so forth. In fact, monochromatic politicking by African Americans in urban areas can be counterproductive: It leads to unnecessary conflicts with white business leaders and poisons relations with the white residents of the surrounding suburbs.[90]

Not so long ago Chicago's politics reeked of racial acrimony. But Mayor Richard M. Daley, who came to power in 1989, has quelled but not extinguished the forces of racial divisiveness through his attention to the black community and coalition-building with Hispanic politicos. In 1999 Daley won more than four out of ten African-American ballots in his successful reelection campaign against Bobby Rush, a former Black Panther who represents Chicago's South Side in Congress.[91] Indeed, Hispanic Chicagoans are becoming a major voting bloc in the Windy City, which is now 26% Latino and heavily Mexican. Despite these signs of progress, the temptation to engage in ethnic politicking in racially polarized areas still exists, especially if large numbers of Others pose a perceived "threat" and do not vote in great numbers.

Take Philadelphia, for example. As recently as 1990, the City of Brotherly Love had a white majority. But the most recent census found that African Americans and Caucasians had reached numerical parity: There are 646,123 black Philadelphians and 644,395 whites in the city. Blacks and whites constitute 85.1% of Philly's 1,517,550 residents; the city is now 8.5% Hispanic and 4.4% Asian. Like so many other large urban centers, Philadelphia remains characterized by residential segregation. West Philadelphia is mainly African American, and Northeast Philadelphia is primarily white. South Philadelphia and central Philadelphia are ethnically diverse. Philadelphia elected its first black mayor, Wilson Goode, in 1983; he served two four-year terms. In 1991, Goode was succeeded by Ed Rendell, a white Democrat who occupied City Hall for eight years. During this period, race seemed to decrease in importance as an issue in Philadelphia politics.

The 1999 mayoral race between John Street, an African-American Democrat, and Sam Katz, a white Republican, never involved racial issues.[92] Yet the election results demonstrated that the city's racial schism continues to affect its politics. Street won a narrow victory, winning virtually unanimous support from African Americans, 94% of whom supported him on Election Day. By contrast, 87% of white voters favored Street's Republican opponent.[93] The 1999 mayoral election results indicate that Philadelphia's politics could easily be polarized by unscrupulous politicos. Someday the city's growing Latino population may hold the balance of political power. If whites and blacks in Philadelphia remain politically polarized, the Hispanic community, should it unite behind a particular mayoral candidate, could choose the mayor in, say, 2003 or 2007. Such a development might permanently change the politics of Philadelphia, a city that still remains largely black and white.

During the twenty-first century, ethnic politicking will become ever more variegated and indecipherable. Rancor and resentment still play a role in determining electoral outcomes, but voters are more likely than ever before to disregard primordial affinities when casting their ballots. In an era when HMO-bashing is more profitable politically than anti-immigrant attacks, explicitly racial appeals will become more sporadic, though no less virulent. Such appeals do not necessarily occur in the most heterogeneous parts of our country. The climate for explicitly racial politicking varies tremendously; it often depends as much on the history and socioeconomic characteristics of an area as on its ethnic and racial demographics.

The increasing heterogeneity of Multicultural America creates new battlegrounds for ethnic politicking, even as this insidious stratagem falls out of favor in its former bastions. For example, we can expect Hispanics and African Americans to square off in cities where those two groups are the dominant ethno-racial entities. A black-versus-brown campaign might feature an African-American mayoral candidate who exhorts his followers to "vote for your own kind," while a Mexican-American politico telegraphs the same message — in Spanish — to his coethnics. Whites or Asian Americans might be compromise candidates in such a context. Similarly, whites or Asians might find themselves the swing voter group that decides the election.

Dallas and Houston seem destined to be pioneers in the realm of multi-ethnic coalition-building during the next few years. Both cities now have Hispanic pluralities but blacks and Anglos constitute most of the voters in each place.[94] African Americans in Dallas and Houston were once focused mainly on working with Anglos to obtain more power, recognition, and resources. During the 1980s and 1990s African Americans watched as Latinos surpassed them in numbers, a development that complicated the blacks' efforts to accumulate political and economic power. Latinos are not uniformly allied with blacks or Anglos in either city. Instead, Hispanic activists work with members of both ethno-racial groups to advance their political goals.

Latinos have already begun to demonstrate their clout in each city's politics. Blacks and Hispanics in Dallas and Houston spar over whom to select to head the local public school systems, both of which are heavily Hispanic.[95] And in Houston last year, Cuban-American Republican Orlando Sanchez forced the incumbent mayor, African-American Democrat Lee Brown, into a runoff election; Brown narrowly won re-election. The Houston race drew national attention because it was the

first head-to-head matchup between a Latino and an African American
for the mayoralty of a large U.S. city. Sanchez, a conservative Republican, formed an unlikely coalition based on ideology and ethnicity. He
won 48% of the vote, and drew strong support from conservative Anglos
and Mexican-American Democrats.[96] Similar contests may occur in the
future, especially since Latinos are likely to account for an ever-increasing
percentage of the population in Dallas and Houston.

⌒ chapter nine ⌒

Conflict and Cooperation

After Raymond Flynn resigned as mayor of Boston in July 1993 to become the United States Ambassador to the Vatican, he set into motion events that would lead to a milestone in Boston's ethnic history. Flynn, an Irish Catholic Democrat, had first been elected mayor in 1983. Like most of his predecessors since 1885, when Hugh O'Brien was elected the first Irish mayor of Boston, Flynn traced his ancestry to the Emerald Isle. It was a given, in a city where the Irish had first begun arriving in substantial numbers during the 1840s, and where they had embraced politics as a means of overcoming the discrimination they faced from the Yankee Brahmins who ran the city.[1]

Over the years, they first won political power in contests with Yankee Protestants. Some Irish politicos cooperated with the Yankee power structure, while others were uncompromising in their opposition to it. But the Irish, encouraged by the Catholic Church, had big families and eventually came to outnumber the Yankees in the city. And Boston's politics came to be dominated by men of Irish descent. Within a generation after Hugh O'Brien made history in Boston, a significant number of his coethnics had already become upwardly mobile. Eventually, many Irish Americans earned college and graduate degrees and moved out of Boston to the suburbs when they became part of the middle class. During this period of Irish-American assimilation and socioeconomic success, the Irish set the agenda in Boston's political world. Flynn was part of this venerable political tradition, which reached its apogee in the 1950s and 1960s.[2]

Ray Flynn's departure ended the Irish domination of the city's politics that had led Irishmen to hold the mayor's office since 1930. Four candidates figured prominently in the campaign to succeed Flynn: Acting Mayor Thomas M. Menino, State Representative James T. Brett, Suffolk County Sheriff Robert Rufo, and City Councilor at Large Rosaria Salerno. Menino placed first, with 27% of the vote, while Brett took 22%

251

and narrowly outpaced Rufo, who had 20%, and Salerno, with 18%, for the right to face Menino in the runoff. Due to the high turnout rates of Irish Americans and their numerical significance in the city, clearly many of them voted for one of the three major Italian-American candidates for mayor over Brett, the son of Irish immigrants.[3]

In the general election campaign, the two candidates debated their respective approaches to crime prevention, budgetary matters, and their plans to improve the city's public schools, but they never engaged in ethnic attacks of any kind. In fact, each man tried to seem like more of a magnanimous multiculturalist than the other. The acting mayor defeated Brett by a 64%-36% margin, as he won support from many Irish Americans, including city workers, who backed him enthusiastically.[4] During his eight years as mayor, Thomas Menino has delivered on his 1993 campaign promise — "We're a changing city but I'll bring the people together" — and it seems that he has a lifetime lease on the job.[5]

Race, rather than ethnicity, is now the dominant social division in Boston culture and politics. During the 1960s and 1970s the city rapidly became more racially diverse than it had been in the past. Racial tensions began to plague Boston in the late 1960s. At the same time the city's black minority emerged as a cohesive political force. Race first began to matter in Boston politics during this period, largely due to the busing issue. As a result of de facto segregation, there were a number of public schools, particularly in South Boston, where the vast majority of the students were white, even though the city's student population was racially heterogeneous. In 1974 a federal judge mandated that busing was necessary to integrate the Boston public schools; many white Bostonians reacted to his edict with tremendous hostility.[6] For 25 years, the busing issue was an integral part of Boston politics, although it mattered less as students of color came to dominate the city's public school system. The busing of students to achieve racial balance in the Boston public schools ended three years ago.[7]

Meanwhile, the ethnic differences that once separated Boston's whites have largely receded into history. The city's two large white Catholic subgroups — the Irish and the Italians — intermarry and cooperate on political issues. The Irish and the Yankees no longer clash over issues in a way that evokes the ethno-religious distinctions of the past. Indeed, the Brahmins barely exist anymore in Boston. There are few Yankees per se left in the city.[8] European Americans in Boston are more likely than ever before to identify as white rather than Irish, Italian, English, or some other ethnic identity, due to the effects of the intergenerational assimilation process and the racial identity politics that has accompanied the city's demographic changes.

These demographic changes, of course, call into question who — and what groups — will dominate Boston politics in the future. The 2000 census found that Boston's population of 589,141 people was 49.5% white, 23.8% black, 14.4% Latino, 7.5% Asian, and 3.1% multiracial. Boston is home to an eclectic assortment of ethnic groups, including Koreans, Indians, Haitians, Cambodians, and Cape Verdeans. The city has one of the nation's largest West Indian communities. More than 27,000 Puerto Ricans call Boston their home.[9] Boston is probably the most heterogeneous city its size, which might come as a surprise to people who remembered the busing battles of the 1970s, which focused the nation's attentions on conflicts between the Irish and their African-American neighbors.

Yet many of the rapidly growing ethnic groups in Boston have not begun to participate in the city's politics in numbers commensurate with their share of the population. As a result, white ethnics, particularly the Irish and Italians, continue to exercise a great deal of influence in Boston politics.[10] Now the city's Haitian community is starting to become involved in the public life of Boston.[11] Marie St. Fleur, who immigrated from Haiti to the United States as a child, was elected to the Massachusetts House of Representatives in 1999. She represents the Roxbury and Dorchester neighborhoods of Boston. In the future, politics in Massachusetts' most populous city will become increasingly complicated, as candidates and elected officials take into account the variegated interests, demands, and issues of the city's multiple ethnic and racial groups.

THE THIRD WAY

Future historians may date the beginning of a revivified national Democratic Party to a precise day — October 3, 1991. That is when then-Arkansas Governor Bill Clinton stood outside the Old State House in Little Rock, Arkansas, and formally announced his candidacy for the 1992 Democratic presidential nomination. In his speech he served notice to Democrats and Republicans alike that he intended to build a multiracial coalition that included substantial numbers of white middle-class voters. "For twelve years," Clinton contended, "Republicans have tried to divide us — race against race — so we get mad at each other and not at them. They want us to look at each other across a racial divide so we don't turn and look to the White House and ask, Why are all of our incomes going down? Why are all of us losing jobs? Why are we losing our future?"[12] Furthermore, he promised the audience that any Republican race-baiting would be met with a firm response from his camp.[13]

These were heartfelt words from a shrewd politician, one who had arisen from modest circumstances in his native Arkansas to graduate from Georgetown University, earn a Rhodes Scholarship to study at Oxford University, and take a law degree from Yale Law School. Clinton was, in many respects, the ideal advocate of integrationist politics. He was equally comfortable at a black church service in Pine Bluff or in a beer joint full of good ol' boys in Hot Springs. Due to his extraordinary interpersonal skills, Clinton managed to balance the sometimes competing concerns of Arkansas's black minority and its white majority. This tall, stocky man with prematurely gray hair and an Anglo-Saxon name developed the ability to appeal to both groups, which was no small feat considering that many of the state's whites had been skeptical, to say the least, about the civil rights movement of the late 1950s and early 1960s.

In a meteoric rise that made him the nation's youngest governor in 1979 (at age 32), this white son of the New South soon displayed a fascination with the politics of race. He pondered how Democrats could build populist coalitions of white working- and middle-class voters with African Americans to defeat country-club Republicans. Except for his defeat for reelection in 1982, Bill Clinton compiled a remarkable record of electoral triumphs in Arkansas as he won reelection time and time again. At the state level, he proved to be an effective leader, noted for his centrist perspective and willingness to be innovative, particularly in the field of education. Arkansas was beginning to shift toward the Republicans at this point, but Clinton's ability to relate to white working-class voters kept him in office.[14]

At the national level, Clinton clearly was frustrated by the Democratic Party's loss of three consecutive presidential elections during the 1980s. As a member of the Democratic Leadership Council, he voiced moderate views on social issues and focused on ways to reconnect with white voters, primarily through his proposals to make government more responsive to the needs of working- and middle-class Americans.[15] As a result, he was seen as a rising star in the Democratic Party, a political maestro who was almost certain to run for the White House someday. After passing on the presidential race in 1988, he decided to run four years later. His campaign was nearly derailed by allegations of philandering, draft evasion, and marijuana use, but Clinton rebounded and handily won the Democratic nomination.

During his 1992 presidential campaign, Bill Clinton consciously sought to rebuild the biracial Democratic Party coalition that had been shattered since the late 1960s.[16] To do so he successfully courted "the forgotten middle class" and celebrated those who "played by the rules," his paean to white working- and middle-class Americans in swing-voter-rich areas like Macomb County, Michigan, the suburban Detroit enclave that was home to lots of Reagan Democrats.[17] At the same time, Clinton won most black votes in the 1992 Democratic primaries for four reasons: his rivals' weaknesses, his aura as a potential winner, his comfort level with African Americans, and his earnest message of racial reconciliation.[18] Calling himself a "New Democrat," in an obvious reference to past electoral debacles, the Arkansan distinguished himself from failed Democratic presidential nominees George McGovern, Walter Mondale, and Michael Dukakis whenever possible.

After vanquishing his Democratic rivals, Clinton saw an opening to inoculate himself against charges of ultraliberalism when the rapper Sister Souljah made what seemed to be a tacit endorsement of black violence against whites in a newspaper interview after the Los Angeles riots in 1992. At a meeting of Jesse L. Jackson's Rainbow Coalition in Washington, D.C., Clinton chastised the assembled members for having Souljah participate in a youth conference earlier in the organization's convention. The Democrats' presidential nominee made front-page news in June 1992, because Jackson, who was at the conference, interpreted Clinton's speech as an attempt to distance the candidate from blacks — and the aging civil rights leader, who continued to personify the excesses of racial liberalism to white urbanites and Southerners.[19]

Clinton's general-election campaign reflected his centrist approach in 1992. In a generational appeal, one that eschewed traditional notions of geographical, ideological, and demographic balancing, Clinton selected Tennessee Senator Albert Gore — a fellow Baby Boomer, political centrist, and Southern Baptist — to run with him. Throughout the summer and fall of 1992, these two fortysomething white guys avoided black audiences, ducked racial issues, and otherwise inoculated themselves against the charges of racial and cultural liberalism that had hurt their Democratic predecessors. Their successful bus tours after the Democratic National Convention took them, for the most part, to predominantly white areas of Middle America, where they burnished their self-described image as "a different kind of Democrat."[20] Clinton also took positions on key issues that helped him establish his New Democratic bona fides with the skeptical white electorate. He advocated a balanced budget, promised a middle-class tax cut, pledged to "end welfare as we know it," and vowed to put 100,000 new police officers on the streets.[21]

Clinton's electoral triumph in 1992 occurred in large part because he ran as a moderate candidate and avoided ideologically polarizing issues in his campaign. He benefited immeasurably from his efforts to protect himself from debilitating Republican attacks on hot-button issues. The political climate in 1992 was unreceptive to such attacks, which would have seemed like diversionary attempts to ignore the "real" issues.[22] In the fall the Democrat also benefited from his general appeal as a political outsider, the sense that he cared about ordinary Americans, and his general focus on growing the economy. These factors helped him assemble a winning multiracial coalition of blacks, Hispanics, Reagan Democrats, and white middle-class suburbanites, in what was the first Democratic presidential victory since 1976.[23]

Throughout the first three years of his administration, Clinton seemed likely to face political problems in 1996 because he failed to live up to his promise of a "New Democratic" administration. Clinton went to Washington as someone who was thoroughly part of the political mainstream in one of America's more conservative states. Within a short period of time, he had forfeited his moderate reputation as a result of the controversial stances he took on some issues. His attempt to allow gays to serve openly in the military backfired with white traditionalists, as did his successful efforts to promote gun control, through the Brady Bill. The Clinton administration's big push to enact a tax increase for upper-income Americans in the budget package of 1993, along with the unsuccessful health-care reform effort of 1994, did not exactly help the Democrats either.[24] Finally, although Clinton had promised voters he would have a Cabinet that resembled America, some Americans saw his appointees as being too close to the Multicultural Left and resented what they considered to be his informal quotas.

Due to these factors, members of Clinton's party suffered a whopping defeat in 1994, as voters sent the president an unequivocal message about his failure to govern as a centrist. Republicans retook the U.S. House and U.S. Senate, and they dramatically reconfigured the political landscape — a development that forced Bill Clinton to the right again. Post-election analysts on the left, not surprisingly, attributed the Republicans' big win to white backlash against the advances made by people of color.[25] To be sure, the Republican victory in 1994 brought racial issues like affirmative action, illegal (and legal) immigration, and welfare reform to the top of the issue agenda of American politics. During the spring and summer of 1995, it seemed likely that the 1996 elections might be the most venomous battles fought over race at the national level in years. The not-guilty verdict in the O. J. Simpson criminal trial in October 1995 further polarized the nation's politics. Multicultural issues like immigration and debates over the primacy of the English language were an important part of the public discourse. Republicans pandered to voters with hard-right rhetoric and conservative policy choices, which included anti-tax diatribes, opposition to affirmative action, tough talk on welfare reform, a muscular approach to crime, and staunch opposition to illegal immigration.[26]

In response to the climate of the times, the president initiated a review of federal affirmative-action programs. After nearly five months of contentious deliberations and political calculations, the review concluded with Clinton's call to "mend" the programs, not "end" them.[27] To keep the White House faithful to multicultural orthodoxy, Jesse Jackson publicly considered both a Democratic primary challenge to Clinton and a third-party run against him. These possibilities led the White House to issue a ringing defense of traditional Democratic efforts to promote equal opportunity.[28] Affirmative action proved to have little staying power as a national political issue; by the end of 1995, the issue agenda of American politics focused primarily on the debates over the federal budget. Race largely disappeared from the political arena, and the tide turned for Clinton and his party.

House Speaker Newt Gingrich and his conservative colleagues in the House Republican Caucus inadvertently allowed Clinton to make a comeback. Budget cuts, deficit spending, and entitlement reforms took central stage in the fall of 1995 and winter of 1995–1996, when partisan disagreements over the federal budget led to two government shutdowns. During this period Gingrich, the leader of the so-called Republican Revolution, made strategic blunders and tactical errors that played right into the Democratic stereotypes of Republicans as members of a cold, uncaring political party of the wealthy. Bolstered by a multimillion-dollar advertising campaign, Clinton successfully seized the political high ground during this period. He skillfully outmaneuvered Gingrich and his fellow Republicans, portraying them as eager to "cut" Medicare and threaten the future of Social Security, along with other entitlement programs and benefits for the middle class.[29]

Gingrich was no match for Clinton in the public relations battle. Clinton demonstrated his formidable political abilities by surging in the opinion polls as a result of his new role as the "protector" of Middle

America from the budget-cutting Republicans. The House Republicans did not do a good job of defending themselves from the Democratic onslaught, and the Democrats' narrative ended up defining them in the eyes of many swing voters, who began to look favorably at the president once again. Clinton's comeback occurred because he remade himself as a centrist — indeed, he began to govern in accordance with the campaign pledges he made in 1992.

During his 1996 reelection campaign, Clinton relied on the counsel of his centrist media consultant, Dick Morris, whom he brought into the White House in 1995 to craft a strategy that Morris described as "triangulation." In doing so, the president aggressively advocated positions that reflected his fiscally responsible brand of social moderation, on issues like tobacco, education standards, family leave, gay marriages, television violence, and college-tuition tax credits.[30] Clinton's most politically motivated (and controversial) decision may have been his signing of the Welfare Reform Act of 1996, which he did to fulfill a 1992 campaign pledge.[31] On the crime issue, meanwhile, Clinton benefited from his get-tough emphasis on the rights of crime victims instead of criminal defendants. The increasing popularity of gun control measures also helped the Democrats in this regard.[32]

In 1996, Clinton encountered little grumbling within the Democratic Party about his rightward tilt, however. Most liberals saw him as the bulwark against the evisceration of their cherished social programs, and viewed voting for Green Party presidential nominee Ralph Nader, the purist alternative, as functionally equivalent to backing the Republican presidential nominee, former Senate Majority Leader Bob Dole.[33] In November 1996 Clinton won an impressive plurality victory over Republican Bob Dole, Reform Party candidate Ross Perot, and the Green Party's Ralph Nader. He profited from the gender gap; earned the support of elderly voters who wanted to protect Medicare and Social Security; and won the backing of most Hispanics (a whopping 72%) and many Asian Americans — largely because of the Republicans' "anti-immigrant" attacks during the 104th Congress.[34] The 1996 election results convincingly demonstrated that many Americans believed Clinton genuinely cared about them and their well-being, although his critics often disparaged the president's empathetic tendencies.

Two years later, Republicans failed to make major gains in the midterm elections, in spite of the uproar over Clinton's extramarital affair with former White House intern Monica Lewinsky and the investigation by Independent Counsel Ken Starr. Democrats, meanwhile, avoided discussing Clinton's peccadilloes whenever possible and instead stressed such issues as education, health care, and Social Security. A substantial turnout by blacks, women, and union members produced virtually unprecedented results for a sitting president's party in midterm elections. In a stunning affirmation of President Clinton's public leadership and his party's record, Democrats lost no governorships or U.S. Senate seats in 1998, and they actually *gained* five U.S. House seats.[35] Newt Gingrich's resignation from the House speakership shortly thereafter made the victory all the sweeter for Democrats.

The 1998 election results reflected the considerable progress Clinton had made in revitalizing the national Democratic Party. His legal troubles notwithstanding, the president boasted sky-high approval ratings that seemed impervious to Republican vilification. Clinton's popularity was largely attributable to his likable persona as well as his stewardship of the U.S. economy during the longest sustained economic boom in American history. Still, it remains to be seen the extent to which Clinton's legacy will be tarnished by his impeachment — on the grounds of his alleged perjury and obstruction of justice during the Lewinsky saga. In February 1999 the president managed to avert the most drastic possible consequence when the United States Senate came far short of summoning up the requisite two-thirds majority to convict him on either charge, and thus remove him from office. The Democrats' trajectory on values issues during the Clinton presidency was inherently contradictory. The person (Clinton) who did so much to neutralize, and even capitalize upon, such issues for them is the same one who later negated many of these gains due to his reckless personal behavior.[36]

African Americans have been, and continue to be, Bill Clinton's most enthusiastic supporters, for a number of reasons. For one, he has a tremendous amount of rapport with them; Clinton enjoys going to black churches, and his exuberant style of politicking plays well with African Americans. And they applauded his support for affirmative action, celebrated his diverse cabinet, judicial, and sub-cabinet appointments, and cheered his rhetorical emphasis on racial harmony and multiethnic inclusion. Most importantly, the sustained period of economic prosperity during his tenure in office benefited many of them substantially, as it did most Americans. To be sure, there were points of conflict, over his periodic hectoring about personal responsibility; his willingness to approve the welfare-reform legislation in 1996, which promised to have a disproportionate impact on poor blacks; and his position in favor of the 1994 anti-crime bill, which many African Americans felt was unduly punitive and would send outsized numbers of black men to jail. However, these were minuscule disagreements compared to his stalwart defense of affirmative action, his aggressive protection of many social-welfare programs, and his advocacy of congenial positions on other matters of importance to most African Americans.[37]

Indeed, polls during Clinton's presidency showed that blacks gave him consistently higher approval ratings than whites. They were also much less likely than whites to support impeaching him or removing him from office because of his disingenuousness over his admittedly inappropriate relationship with Monica Lewinsky. Jesse Jackson completed his rapprochement with Bill Clinton during the height of Zippergate, and he became the most visible figure of Black America's support for the president. Some black Democrats detected a racial subtext to the impeachment efforts. According to their reasoning, Clinton was a proxy for the hopes and aspirations of black Americans. Therefore, they viewed the attacks by white conservative Republicans on their standard-bearer as racist efforts to impede the progress made by African Americans.[38]

Clinton's amalgam of governing and politicking was part of what analysts call the "Third Way." "Clintonism" is an indigenous version of it that has borne spectacular political results. Clintonism is not so much a coherent doctrine or political ideology, except, perhaps, in its amorphousness, its very fluidity, and its lack of coherence. The central tenets of Clintonism include fiscal responsibility and equal opportunities for women and minorities; globalist positions on international affairs, in addition to backing of unfettered free trade; and moderate stances on social issues, balancing a pro-choice position on abortion with support for the V-chip and ratings for television programs.[39] There are Clintonisms, too, those pithy slogans and witticisms that epitomize Third Way thinking, such as Clinton's frequent rhetorical linkages of "opportunity" and "responsibility." Clinton's center-left political approach — how he governed in 1995–1996 as opposed to 1993–1994 — was ideally suited to the political climate of the 1990s.

In retrospect, Bill Clinton's greatest strength as a politician was his ability to build unlikely coalitions of people, even as he sometimes took positions that conflicted with their interests. During his administration, Latino and, to a lesser extent, Asian voters strongly embraced the Democratic Party, a demographic fact that is already leading the Democrats to dominate the politics of California, Illinois, New Jersey, and many other states. Moreover, Clinton certainly stopped the Democrats' hemorrhaging among white voters. In other words, he was successful in creating a mainstream image for the Democrats, especially in contradistinction to the GOP. Not everyone in the Democratic Party loves Clinton and his brand of politics, however. Some liberals believe that he is an opportunist, a pseudo-Republican, who is too willing to embrace social policies, like welfare reform and unreconstructed globalism, that violate traditional Democratic principles. Liberals worry, then, that they have made Faustian bargains with the centrist compromisers in order to regain political power. Yet Democrats know that a left-wing pitch will probably be an electoral loser, so the Clinton paradigm may be the guiding one in the party for a long time to come.[40]

NEW FACES, NEW PACES

On January 2, 2001, President-elect George W. Bush announced that Linda Chavez was his choice to head the Labor Department. Chavez had long been a bête noire of the traditional liberal lobbies, dating back to her stint in the 1980s as the staff director of the U.S. Civil Rights Commission. With her book, *Out of the Barrio,* which criticized government dependency, and her vociferous opposition to affirmative action, Chavez had become a darling of the Right. A onetime liberal Democrat who moved to the right during the 1970s and 1980s, Chavez was the Republican nominee for the U.S. Senate from Maryland in 1986. Most recently, she had served as president of the Center for Equal Opportunity, a policy institution that opposed affirmative action. As a syndicated columnist and regular guest on cable television news shows, Chavez was best known for her controversial right-wing stands on multicultural issues.[41]

By choosing Chavez, Bush signaled to conservatives that he intended to take a tough line on workplace safety, the minimum wage, and affirmative action, all issues on which Chavez could be expected to adopt conventional right-of-center policies. Immediately after her nomination, labor unions geared up to defeat Chavez.[42] Nor were the Hispanic civil rights organizations any more enthusiastic about her nomination. Then it came out on January 7, 2001, that she had harbored an illegal immigrant from Guatemala in her home for two years in the early 1990s; Chavez had neglected to inform the Bush transition team of this fact. Chavez withdrew her nomination two days after the story became public. The Bush transition team had become skittish about her apparent disingenuousness.[43]

The significance of the failed Chavez nomination has to do with what it says about race in America — and George W. Bush's often-articulated desire to embrace and reach out to minorities. At the time of the Chavez nomination, he had only one Hispanic in his Cabinet: Mel Martinez, a Cuban American from Orlando, who had been nominated to head the Department of Housing and Urban Development (HUD). By selecting Chavez, Bush hoped to add a second Hispanic — and another woman — to his Cabinet. It is, of course, difficult to determine what role, if any, Chavez's ethnic background and gender played in her selection. But the native of New Mexico is Spanish on her father's side and thus, in some cases, eligible to be considered a minority.[44] Chavez's appearance would allow her to pass for a native in Spain, but she does not speak Spanish. Still, in Chavez's case, her Spanish surname gives her a modicum of credibility as "the conservative minority woman," a lucrative niche that she seems to have all to herself.

In any event, the Bush team quickly regrouped and on January 11 the President-elect announced that Elaine L. Chao was his choice to be Labor Secretary. Chao, a conservative Republican who came to the United States from Taiwan at age eight, in 1961, inspired little opposition. The Taiwanese American, though conservative, did not antagonize the unions or the Multicultural Left. During her career, which included being head of the Peace Corps and United Way, Chao had been a pragmatic, nonideological leader who had nonetheless never deviated from her conservative principles. In many respects, she was very similar in political outlook to George W. Bush, which may explain why he chose her to join his Cabinet.[45] Incidentally, Chao was the first Cabinet secretary of Chinese descent. Bush's choice of Chavez, and then Chao, demonstrates that he clearly recognizes the axiomatic truth of millennial politics in the United States: that the new faces dictate new paces.

The Bush brothers — both Republicans and the sons of old-school WASPs George and Barbara Bush — are as comfortable as the Democrats on the new playing field of American ethnic politics. President George W. Bush, the eldest son and namesake of the man beaten by Bill Clinton in 1992, and his younger brother, Florida Governor John Ellis "Jeb" Bush, espouse "compassionate conservatism" and offer their own Third Way for the Republicans. These Spanish-speaking paragons of white male privilege embrace traditional conservative positions in favor of balanced budgets, lower taxes, limited government, and the death penalty, but they practice a twenty-first-century politics of inclusion that goes beyond that of most other Republican officials.[46]

George W. Bush, who won the Texas governorship in 1994, earned a well-deserved reputation as a tax-cutting, crime-fighting leader who favored a less expansive social-welfare system. A self-described "uniter" rather than a "divider," Bush governed Texas with a minimum of partisanship and made numerous appointments of blacks and Hispanics to state posts. As governor, Bush stressed "English-plus" instead of English-only, promoted "affirmative access" in place of racial preferences, and refused to oppose bilingual education. From the beginning of his tenure, Governor Bush was careful to distinguish himself from the Mexico-bashing and high-profile theatrics of Pete Wilson, his Anglo Republican colleague in California. His extensive Spanish-language media campaign and frequent visits to Latino-majority areas like El Paso helped him take somewhere between 37% and 49% (exit polls differed) of the Hispanic vote statewide in 1998, as part of his landslide reelection victory.[47]

This political scion's example has pointed the way to other Republican victories, most notably that of his brother, Jeb, who won election as governor of Florida in 1998. Jeb Bush's household is a veritable outpost of Latino America: He and his Mexican-born wife, Columba, have three children; the eldest, George P. Bush, campaigned for his uncle in 2000.[48] After he narrowly lost his hard-right campaign for Florida's top elected post in 1994, W.'s younger brother converted to Catholicism, remade himself politically, sought out African Americans, and even co-founded a charter school in the Liberty City section of Miami. In his second try for the Florida governorship, Bush won a comfortable victory over a moderate Democrat.[49]

Since he became governor of Florida in January 1999, Jeb Bush has made a name for himself as a policy wonk. He immediately began fulfilling his election-year promises, starting with the legislature's agreement to allow state funds to be used for school vouchers.[50] Bush then implemented his controversial One Florida policy, which terminated race-based affirmative action in state university admissions and contracting programs.[51] Both actions demonstrated Jeb Bush's willingness to take significant political risks in order to advance his policy objectives. Bush has proven to be a popular governor, whose right-of-center policies have made him a favorite for reelection in 2002.[52] So it seems probable that the Bush political dynasty will remain alive and well in the Sunbelt for some time to come.

The 1998 elections established George W. Bush as the incontrovertible front-runner in the Republican presidential race, and he quickly decided to enter the race to succeed Bill Clinton. Bush emerged with tremendous stature after winning 68% of the vote in the Lone Star State, in an election year that was not very hospitable to Republicans. With his slight twang and omnipresent cowboy boots, he projects the image of the archetypal West Texan — an unpretentious, down-to-earth guy who nonetheless is brash, sunnily optimistic, and supremely self-confident. Throughout his presidential campaign, the Texas governor conducted photo opportunities with blacks and Hispanics, particularly youths, on an almost daily basis. He also spoke about race and racially tinged issues before mostly white audiences.[53] In 1999 George W. Bush campaigned in general-election mode, as he raised tens of millions of dollars in campaign funds, and flushed most of his Republican primary rivals out of the race before any votes were cast.

John McCain interrupted Bush's lackadaisical romp to the Oval Office when he beat the Republican dynast by a 19-point margin in the New Hampshire presidential primary. Suddenly, McCain, the wisecracking, white-haired outsider with a red-hot message and dramatic biography, became a serious contender, and the Bush campaign mobilized all its formidable resources and humanpower to combat his unexpectedly vigorous challenge. Although McCain appealed to Democrats and Independents, a phenomenon that led to talk of a "McCain Majority," he failed to convince enough registered Republicans to back him. Bush ended McCain's presidential quest, at least in 2000, when he beat him solidly in Virginia and Washington in late February and then trounced him in every big state (Ohio, California, New York) on Super Tuesday. After he secured the GOP nod for the Oval Office, Bush returned to the Herculean task of courting voters in the center of the political spectrum.

Meanwhile, Vice President Albert Gore had briefly succeeded Bill Clinton as the titular head of the newly vibrant multiracial Democratic Party — and as the standard bearer of the Third Way in the United States. During his eight years as vice president, Gore loyally supported Clinton, while he maintained a high-profile role in American politics. In the 1990s the cerebral politico established a well-deserved reputation as a master of liberal interest-group politics, even though he was more conservative than many Democratic Party activists. Gore's assiduous courting of key left-wing constituencies paid off in 2000, when gays, unions, blacks, Hispanics, feminists, and environmentalists backed him in his quest to win the Democratic presidential nomination. Gore dissuaded other prominent Democrats from challenging him, by winning countless endorsements, assembling a top-flight organization, and by raising prodigious amounts of money.[54]

Former New Jersey Senator Bill Bradley was the only Democrat with a national reputation who was brave — or foolhardy — enough to challenge the vice president. Candidate Bradley was openly disdainful of the spirit and substance of Clinton's Third Way proposals. The lanky iconoclast staked out left-leaning stands on gay rights, free trade, police brutality, urban poverty, and universal health care. However, Gore shrugged off his well-funded challenger's feeble attempts to paint him as a closet conservative, and relentlessly attacked Bradley's signature health-care plan. The vice president benefited from his opponent's aloofness and reluctance to counterattack using the traditional slash-and-burn methods of political combat. In the end, Gore managed an amazing shutout, as he defeated Bradley in every primary and caucus.[55] As he prepared for the general-election campaign, Gore sought to take credit for the positive aspects of Clinton's tenure, chiefly the economic expansion, without associating himself too closely with the scandal-plagued occupant of the Oval Office. This proved to be a difficult challenge for him.

The presidential contest between Gore and Bush turned out to be one of the closest in modern American political history. Both men were strong candidates who had united their parties behind them. After eight years of Bill Clinton, many Americans were ready for a change in Washington, even though the country was peaceful and prosperous. Gore ran as an unreconstructed populist who would defend the interests of the average American, while Bush portrayed himself as a "uniter" who would promote bipartisan cooperation in Washington and reduce the extent of the federal government's involvement in our lives. The two men sparred with each other over such issues as tax cuts, missile defense, school vouchers, America's role in world affairs, and the reform of Medicare and Social Security. The opinion polls in the race showed that Gore had the clear advantage in September, while Bush surged into the lead in October after his strong performances in the three televised debates.

By early November 2000, the race was too close to call. Both sides developed impressive voter-mobilization efforts, and the last-minute revelation of Bush's DUI arrest in Maine in 1976 slowed his momentum. In the end, 105,405,100 Americans cast ballots in the presidential contest. Gore won 50,999,897, or 48.38% of those votes, while Bush received 50,456,002, or 47.87% of the total. Green Party candidate Ralph Nader, whose fiery anti-corporate candidacy drew so much attention because Democrats feared he would throw the election to Bush, won 2,882,955 votes (2.74% of the total). And renegade Republican Patrick Buchanan, the Reform Party nominee, did not prove to be a threat to Bush, as he won only 448,895 votes (0.42% of the total).

On the day after the balloting, Gore had 255 electoral votes in his column, and Bush lagged behind at 246. Three states (Florida, Oregon, and New Mexico) were too close to call. However, only Florida had enough electoral votes to give a candidate a majority in the Electoral College. The initial tallies in Florida gave Bush a razor-thin lead of 1,784 votes out of nearly six million cast. So the Bush and Gore teams spent the next five weeks battling over Florida in a standoff that featured legal wrangling, partisan demonstrations, and dueling political and judicial interpretations of electoral law. Gore's camp insisted that undervotes and overvotes be counted manually in four heavily Democratic counties — Volusia, Palm Beach, Broward, and Miami-Dade — in the hope that the Democratic presidential candidate could pick up enough votes to win Florida and the presidency. Bush's team steadfastly opposed the manual recounts and stood by the machine count and the machine recount, both of which named Bush the winner.

On November 26, 2000, the Florida Secretary of State, Republican Katherine Harris, certified Bush as the winner of the state's presidential contest by 537 votes, based on the tally of the machine recount. Gore's legal team kept the battle going in the courts, as they sought to continue the manual recounts. But on December 12, the U.S. Supreme Court extinguished Al Gore's presidential hopes in 2000 when, by a 5–4 vote, it curtailed the vote-counting in Florida on the grounds that the process would be unable to complete in a timely fashion. As a result, Bush won the presidency.[56] On December 13, 2000, Gore conceded the race to Bush in a gracious televised speech, and the nation finally had a president-elect. Bush won the final electoral tally, 271 to 266 (one of Gore's electors from the District of Columbia cast a blank ballot to protest Washington's lack of voting representation in Congress).

The presidential election results in 2000 highlighted the extraordinary racial polarization of the American electorate. According to the Voter News Service exit polls, the national electorate in 2000 was 82% white, 10% black, 4% Hispanic, and 2% Asian. Bush won the white vote by a margin of 54%-42% nationwide, but he still lost the popular vote to Gore by 543,895 votes. White Easterners supported Gore over Bush 52%-44%, while white Westerners backed the Texan 51%-43%, and white Midwesterners supported him 53%-44%. Two-thirds of Southern whites voted for Bush. Forty-seven percent of the voters were white Protestants, and Bush carried them by a margin of 63%-34%. Bush won the white male vote 60%-36%; white men accounted for 39% of the voters.

Bush defeated Gore by the razor-thin margin of 49%-48% among white women, who constituted 43% of the electorate.[57]

Gore clearly was the candidate of minority voters. Ninety percent of African Americans voted for the vice president, and only eight percent supported his Republican opponent. Gore received 85% of the black male vote, and a truly overwhelming 94% of the black female vote. Hispanics voted for Gore by an impressive 67%-31% margin, while Asian Americans supported the vice president by a margin of 54%-41%.[58] These results demonstrated the success of the Democratic Party's continuing identification with the Multicultural Left, even though many minorities do not necessarily agree with all of its positions. Furthermore, a Democrat no longer has to carry the white vote — or even come close to carrying the white vote — to win the presidency anymore.

There also was a significant amount of regional polarization in the election results, as Bush did very well in the South and the Mountain West. The president won every state in the Mountain West except for New Mexico, which was essentially a tie. His highest percentages came in Wyoming (67.7%), Idaho (67.2%), and Utah (66.8%). He also swept the Great Plains, winning Nebraska (62.2%), North Dakota (60.6%), Oklahoma (60.3%), South Dakota (60.3%), and Kansas (58.0%) by big margins. Furthermore, Bush carried every state in the 13-state South, including Al Gore's Tennessee and Bill Clinton's Arkansas. Florida, of course, was a dead heat. Only two of the ten most populous states voted heavily Republican in the 2000 presidential contest: Texas and Georgia. Ohio voted for Bush by 3.5 percentage points. Clearly, the electoral map no longer gives the Republicans a distinct advantage, as it did during the period from 1968 to 1988.

Indeed, Gore easily defeated Bush in California, New York, Illinois, New Jersey, and every Mid-Atlantic and Northeastern state besides New Hampshire. He did best in the District of Columbia (84.8%), Rhode Island (61.0%), New York (60.0%), Massachusetts (59.6%), Maryland (56.5%), New Jersey (56.0%), Connecticut (55.9%), and Hawaii (55.8%). The vice president won many of the battleground states (Wisconsin, Minnesota, Iowa, New Mexico, and Oregon), as well as the decisive swing states of Michigan and Pennsylvania. Several states, including California, Illinois, and New Jersey, have shifted from being marginally Republican to solidly Democratic in presidential races. Each of these states faithfully supported the GOP presidential candidate in every election from 1968 to 1988. But they backed Clinton in 1992 and 1996, and then cemented their allegiance to the Democrats by supporting Gore enthusiastically in 2000. In each state, the growing percentage of minority voters has contributed to its Democratic bent in presidential elections, but only in California have minority voters reshaped the state's political landscape.

George W. Bush became the nation's forty-third president under the most unenviable circumstances since Rutherford B. Hayes acceded to the presidency in 1877. He is only the fourth president — John Quincy Adams, Rutherford B. Hayes, and Benjamin Harrison were the others — to inhabit the White House who did not win the popular vote. Bush struck a conciliatory tone, beginning with his statement of victory on December 13, 2000, when he repeatedly called for unity across racial and partisan lines, and also in his Inaugural Address. He speaks with a moderate voice while he articulates right-of-center positions, and his appointees are an eclectic mix of centrists and ideological conservatives. His cabinet, cabinet-level, and sub-cabinet appointees are certainly the most diverse of any Republican president in history. In fact, the Bush White House has made a determined effort to include women and minorities at every level of the new administration. In doing so, Bush won plaudits from the establishment press, and promoted the nascent GOP outreach efforts in minority communities. His energetic commitment to the diversity imperative even engendered some conservative grumbling about the Bush administration's reverse discrimination against white male appointees.[59]

President Bush faces some compelling challenges in the future — namely, appeasing the Republican right and winning enough support from the American people to triumph over the Democrats. The first challenge may prove to be as difficult as the second. For the time being, the Bush administration maintains excellent relations with the conservative activist community: pro-lifers, tax cutters, the property rights movement, and others. Bush palliates the Republican right by appointing ideologues like Attorney General John Ashcroft and Interior Secretary Gail Norton, and he keeps his lines of communication open to movement conservatives. As a national figure, Bush has adeptly courted — and backed away from — the right wing of his party.[60]

During his presidential campaign, in 1999 and 2000, he emulated Clinton's ideological balancing act. Bush emphasized the need for some government and rhetorically positioned himself as a centrist while he successfully courted his party's dominant ideological group. As a Republican presidential candidate, he dodged tough topics like guns, abortion, and the environment, hedged on such hot-button issues as affirmative action and the Confederate-flag dispute in South Carolina, and avoided getting into specifics that might have diminished his popularity. He was able to move to the center without inciting a mass revolt by conservatives because they, like their liberal counterparts in 1991 and 1992, wanted to win the White House so badly that they were willing to excuse Bush's deviations from conservative orthodoxy (although not on the abortion issue).[61] Movement conservatives would much rather have a center-right Republican than a liberal Democrat in the White House. A true-blue conservative candidate could not be elected president at this time.

President Bush has formidable political skills and all the power and perquisites of the presidency at his disposal, so the Democrats should never underestimate him. He receives good marks for an efficient, well-organized administration, which is staffed by experienced leaders from the academy, Washington, Corporate America, and the states. The Bush administration is certainly right-of-center in an ideological sense, but conservative purists are not likely to be completely satisfied by its positions and programs. Bush, for instance, has displayed a reluctance to oppose affirmative action in all its guises.[62] In any event, Bush's successful leadership of the war on terrorism has earned him extraordinarily high approval ratings, similar to those enjoyed by his father after the completion of the Gulf War in the spring of 1991.

Before the war on terrorism reconfigured the policy agenda, President Bush had made some progress in his efforts to appeal to people of color. Bush has conducted vigorous outreach efforts in the Latino community, which have included a radio address in Spanish, his decision to close the Navy bombing range on the Puerto Rican island of Vieques in 2003, and his consideration of a proposal, since abandoned, to grant amnesty to millions of undocumented Mexican immigrants.[63] Conversely, the president has been less visible in his attempts to win support in the African-American community. Most blacks were skeptical of the Bush administration before the events of 9/11, due to its right-wing bent and the fact that their presidential favorite, Al Gore, lost the election amid allegations of faulty voting machines and electoral intimidation in the African-American precincts of Florida.[64] Regardless, no Republican president has ever done more, at least in a symbolic sense, to reach out to people of color.

MULTIRACIAL DEMOCRACY

The Oakland City Council passed an ordinance — known as the Equal Access policy — in 2001. Councilman Danny Wan, a Taiwanese immigrant, and City Council President Ignacio De La Fuente, who himself is an immigrant from Mexico, sponsored the legislation, which provides linguistic assistance to the Spanish-speaking and Chinese-speaking residents of Oakland. The law dictates that the city must employ bilingual employees — those who speak English and Spanish and those who speak English and Chinese — in the municipal departments where the personnel regularly interact with the public. Moreover, Oakland has to ensure that important documents regarding city services are available in Spanish and Chinese. The ordinance is flexible and takes into account the possibility of demographic change. Any time another non-English-speaking group meets the threshold requirement of 10,000 residents, the city has to accommodate speakers of that language with services similar to those now enjoyed by Spanish-speaking and Chinese-speaking Oaklanders.[65]

The passage of the Equal Access Ordinance indicated that Oakland's political elite recognized and embraced the changing demographics of the city. Despite its multiethnic population, Oakland continues to be best known as the birthplace of the Black Panther Party in 1966.[66] For more than three decades African Americans have been the dominant force in the politics and culture of Oakland, a city of 399,484 that is connected by the Bay Bridge to San Francisco. In 1990, the census found that more than 43% of Oaklanders were black; in recent years blacks have been leaving Oakland and nonblack minorities are taking their place. Oakland's white population is not growing either. Blacks now make up 35.1% of Oakland's population, whites 23.5%, Hispanics 21.9%, and Asians 15.1%. Oakland itself has a thriving Chinatown: The city is 8.0% Chinese. And Oakland's appropriately named International Boulevard is lined with Mexican stores that cater to its growing Mexican population (which accounts for nearly for one in six Oaklanders). This fascinating heterogeneity is a developing story; the Asian and Latin American immigrants continue to settle in Oakland. The city is, after all, a cheaper, less-crowded alternative to San Francisco.

The electorate in Oakland, however, remains mainly black and white. Many of the Latino and Asian immigrants are noncitizens or otherwise do not involve themselves in the political process. Notwithstanding the diverse composition of the city's elected leadership, political debates in Oakland sometimes make it seem as if it were 1970 again, and blacks were fighting to be recognized as an important part of the polity. On one level, African Americans achieved many political successes in Oakland. They elected black mayors, city councilors, state legislators, and members of Congress. On another level, many ordinary black voters found that African-American officials were not always able to live up to the high expectations many in the community had for them. The local black political elite often became entangled in internecine disputes that did little to advance the city's interests, even as the decline of the industrial economy worsened social and economic conditions in black Oakland.[67]

African Americans, to be sure, continue to be an important part of the governing class of this black-plurality city. Oakland's political leadership certainly reflects the city's diversity. The eight-member city council includes two white women, one white man, one Latino man, two black men, and two Asian men. Moreover, one of the two Asian-American councilors, Danny Wan, is openly gay — another first for Oakland. The city clerk is a black woman, the city manager is a black man, and the city auditor and city attorney are both white men.[68] Jerry Brown, a white man who served as governor of California from 1975 to 1983, was elected mayor of Oakland in 1998. He has won strong black support in his bid to revitalize Oakland, an effort that has led him to crack down on crime, take decisive measures to reform the city's public schools, and anger some of his allies in the environmental movement because of his aggressive efforts to promote economic development. Brown's strategy appears to be working: He defeated his African-American challenger, Wilson Riles, to win reelection in March 2002 by a margin of 63.5% to 36.5%.[69] Oakland's politics exemplifies a model of interracial cooperation — one that is increasingly typical of America's multiracial democracy.

Californians may be a famously apolitical bunch, but the Golden State has a diverse electoral geography that mirrors its ethnic heterogeneity and topographical wonders. Campaigns are conducted almost entirely on television, and often turn vitriolic to rouse the apathetic electorate. Caucasians continue to be the dominant voter group, although the Hispanic electoral presence is growing by leaps and bounds. In 2000 the California electorate was 71% white, even though the state's population was slightly less than 47% Caucasian.[70] Indeed, whites continue to exercise an outsized influence in California's politics through the initiative process, which remains an important means of setting policy there, and in turn creating national movements, from rolling back property taxes to eliminating bilingual education.[71]

Republicans are very much in the minority in contemporary California, which now rivals New York as the nation's most Democratic big state. The GOP continues to do well in a number of regions in the state, including the far north, the Anglo precincts of the Central Valley, and the middle-class and affluent parts of Orange, Ventura, Imperial, Riverside,

San Diego, Los Angeles, and San Bernardino counties. Whites account for most of the California Republican electorate, although the party polls well among Asian Americans on occasion. Many white Republicans in California hold moderate views on such social issues as the environment and abortion rights. There are few relatively hard-right Republicans in the state. The dramatic increase in the state's minority population directly correlates to the Republican Party's inability to win significant statewide elections anymore.[72]

The strength of the Democratic Party in California is increasingly attributable to minority voters, although socially liberal whites still account for its largest group of supporters. Democrats predominate in California's black, Latino, Jewish, gay, and urban precincts, including Sacramento, San Jose, Los Angeles, San Francisco, and elsewhere. As elsewhere, African Americans are the staunchest of Democratic constituencies, while the state's heavily Mexican-American Latino electorate is trending almost as solidly Democratic. Asian Americans were once amenable to the GOP message, but during the last six years they have leaned toward the Democrats. Roughly one-third of the California Democratic Party's statewide base is now black, Hispanic, or Asian. This percentage increases every election cycle, and will probably approach 50% by 2010. And in Los Angeles County, the state's single largest source of voters, minorities already account for a majority of the Democrats' support in many elections.[73]

The governor of California is, of course, the most important political figure in the state. Golden State voters backed the white-backlash politics of Ronald Reagan in 1966 and 1970. Then they turned around and supported the multicultural liberalism of Jerry Brown in 1974 and 1978. Brown's successor, George Deukmejian, was more conservative, of course, than Brown on racial matters, but he did little to inflame public opinion on the contentious issues of the day. Republican Pete Wilson's tenure, from 1991 to 1999, during the tumultuous transition from white-majority to white-plurality California, marked the apogee and likely end of white-backlash politics there, if only because it is no longer a politically viable tack anymore.

Now Jerry Brown's onetime Chief of Staff, Gray Davis, is California's governor. He explicitly disavows Wilson's brand of "divisive" politics, with its reliance on wedge issues, and follows his mentor's model of inclusion and pragmatic responsiveness to public opinion. In contrast to his predecessor, who feuded with Mexican politicians over narcotics trafficking, illegal immigration, environmental degradation, and other thorny issues, Davis has emphasized the importance of amicable relations with Mexico.[74] On other issues Davis is a moderate Democrat in the mold of Tony Blair and Bill Clinton, as he endorses tough gun-control measures and tirelessly stresses the importance of improving the state's beleaguered public schools. And he often clashes with liberals in California's Democratic-controlled legislature over the ideological direction of his administration. Davis mouths the party line on hot-button issues of interest to the Multicultural Left but nevertheless defers to the sensibilities of middle-income whites, who still make up an important part of the Golden State electorate. The fallout from California's electrical-utility-rate crisis and its economic problems (along with the state's multibillion-dollar budget deficit) have hurt Davis politically. The governor, a tremendously successful fund-raiser, seems very likely to face a tough reelection race this year.[75]

During the 1990s California was a testing ground for three high-profile referenda that focused national attention on the state's ethnic divisions. In 1994 backers of Proposition 187, the so-called "Save Our State" initiative, sought to prohibit illegal aliens — whom the public viewed as Hispanic, particularly Mexicans — from receiving public schooling, non-emergency health care, and other benefits. The initiative passed by a margin of 59%-41% in November 1994. Whites backed Proposition 187 by a huge margin, while blacks and Asians split on it, and Hispanics opposed it overwhelmingly.[76] Two years later, Californians voted on Proposition 209, the "California Civil Rights Initiative," which banned racial and gender preferences in public contracting, employment, and university admissions. Despite substantial black and Hispanic opposition, white voters lined up to support the initiative, and it was approved by a 54%-46% margin in November 1996.[77] The next initiative to make headlines in California was Proposition 227, the "English for the Children" initiative. It sought to curtail bilingual education programs and offer limited-English-proficient students a year of English immersion before they entered regular classrooms. This initiative appeared on the June 1998 ballot. It won by a 61%-39% margin, but, again, as with Propositions 187 and 209, Latinos solidly opposed it.[78] In any event, the initiative process seems likely to continue to be a forum in which thorny issues will be decided in California.

The state GOP's enthusiastic support for Propositions 187 and 209 tarnished the image of California Republicans in the eyes of many people of color, just as hundreds of thousands of recently naturalized minorities were entering the political process. Pete Wilson tied his 1994 reelection campaign to Proposition 187 and the issue of illegal immigration, with television commercials that raised the specter of ravaging hordes of illegal alien job seekers. This gambit helped him win reelection handily but also made him a veritable poster boy for Republican hostility to Hispanics. Wilson also assumed a pivotal role in scaling back affirmative action in state government, along with the University of California system, and he enthusiastically backed Proposition 209. Meanwhile, thousands of white Republicans fled California during the 1990s; their Latino and Asian replacements were far less supportive of the party of Reagan and Wilson.[79]

In 1997 the California GOP began seriously examining its hemorrhaging support among minority voters. To improve their image with people of color, party leaders emphasized their ideologically congenial positions on cultural issues like abortion, highlighted their traditional message of tax cuts and limited government, and made perfunctory attempts at inclusiveness. In 1998 many California Republicans therefore kept their distance from Pete Wilson and Proposition 227.[80] By this time, it was possible for a Republican candidate to carry the white vote by a solid margin and still lose the election, due to the Democrats' overwhelming margins in the minority communities.

The multicultural backlash that occurred as a result of Pete Wilson's divide-and-conquer strategy became evident when the Republicans lost the California governorship in 1998, for the first time in 16 years. Democrat Gray Davis was on a roll after winning the Democratic nomination against two wealthy opponents, and he never gave up any ground in a centrist campaign that left Republican Dan Lungren with no room to gain traction. Lungren ran a right-wing campaign that was better-suited to the California of 1978 than the California of 1998. His Reaganesque platitudes fell flat with an electorate that no longer responded enthusiastically to conservative Republican appeals. And Dan Lungren tried just about everything short of changing his surname to Garza or Salinas in his futile quest to win Hispanic votes.[81]

Gray Davis happily courted members of California's largest minority group, and their support played a major role in his sizable victory over Lungren. (Davis took 78% of the Latino vote.) Of course Gray Davis's 58%-38% win was by no means solely attributable to black, Hispanic, and Asian discontent with the Republicans. Davis solidly defeated Lungren among the state's numerous white voters; he even won the white male vote.[82] The magnitude of the loss came as a shock to Republicans who, after all, had held the governorship for all but eight years between 1966 and 1998. "We are now stuck as a party that is perceived as anti-immigrant and antiminority, thanks to Pete Wilson," noted Republican consultant Alan Hoffenblum at the time.[83]

Even though Wilson is no longer on the political radar screen, he continues to overshadow the California Republican Party's Latino-outreach efforts.[84] That California Republicans were concerned about their poor showing among Hispanics became evident in 2000, when the state's Democrats successfully sought to honor Cesar E. Chavez with a state holiday and a place in the state's schoolbooks. Golden State Republicans, of course, were never big fans of Chavez, who clashed repeatedly during his lifetime with the agribusiness interests that loyally back the GOP. However, the Republicans refused to oppose a state holiday recognizing Chavez, nor did they block the inclusion of Chavez's story in the state's curricula for public school students. They simply could not afford to offend Mexican-American voters, who would have interpreted their spirited opposition to the efforts to honor Chavez as more evidence of their hostility to Latino interests.[85] In any event, the California GOP will probably not win a sizable share of the Latino vote for at least 20 years, due to the lingering hard feelings from the Wilson era and the tendency of Mexican Americans, along with their far less numerous Central American counterparts, to vote for Democrats based on social and economic issues.

In 2001 and 2002 Republican Richard Riordan attempted unsuccessfully to convince his fellow Republicans that a moderate platform was the only way they would win back the governorship — and regain political ascendancy in the state. Riordan, who had served two terms as mayor of Los Angeles from 1993 to 2001, contended that a centrist candidate like himself with proven appeal to women and Hispanics would be the best GOP gubernatorial nominee in 2002. He basically ignored his conservative primary challengers (businessman Bill Simon Jr. and California Secretary of State Bill Jones) and campaigned against Democrat Gray Davis. Governor Davis responded by pummeling the Riordan campaign with $10 million in negative ads. (The Democrats saw Riordan as the most electorally fearsome Republican in the Republican field.) Moreover, Riordan's ideological profile — he supports abortion rights, backs gay rights, advocates gun control, and refuses to condemn affirmative action or illegal immigration — proved to be more important than his electability to conservative California Republicans. As a result, he lost the GOP gubernatorial primary by an 18-point margin to Bill Simon Jr., the leading conservative candidate, in March 2002.[86]

Divisive ethnic politics are probably not going to resurface again —
to a significant extent, at least — ever again in California politics. The
reason is a simple one: demographics. Minority voters are now too
significant for a white candidate to win a statewide victory based on
white-backlash politics. Similarly, white voters are going to make up the
solid if not overwhelming majority of the state's electorate for at least
the next two decades, so no minority statewide candidate would dare
to make an antiwhite appeal to people of color. Nonwhites, particularly
Hispanics, surely are going to assume more visible and important political posts as their numbers increase. In 1998 Cruz Bustamante, the first
Latino speaker of the California Assembly, became the first Hispanic
elected to a California constitutional office (the lieutenant governorship)
during the twentieth century. The state's 52-member congressional delegation includes six Latinos, four blacks, and two Asian Americans. At the
beginning of 2001, Latinos accounted for seven California senators and
15 assemblymembers, and Hispanics regularly hold leadership positions
in the legislature.[87] Moreover, minority candidates are increasingly common at the statewide level. The visual disconnect between California's
voters and its candidates will continue to diminish rapidly.

During the Los Angeles mayoral campaign in 2001, two Hispanics,
Congressman Xavier Becerra and former Assembly Speaker Antonio
Villaraigosa, hoped to become the first Latino mayor of Los Angeles
in 129 years. Becerra never gained traction as a candidate and finished
fifth, with six percent of the vote, but after a virtually flawless campaign,
Villaraigosa placed first in the April primary balloting, with 30% of the
vote to 25% for another Democrat, James K. Hahn, the city attorney.
Villaraigosa's remarkable showing was attributable to his energetic politicking, as well as his legislative record and three decades as a liberal
activist. Moreover, he received the endorsements and financial backing
of civic leaders and political heavyweights. Throughout the mayoral campaign the native of East Los Angeles called himself "a uniter" and, not
surprisingly, refused to characterize himself in ethnic terms, even as he
benefited from Latino pride in his candidacy. Villaraigosa faced Hahn in
the runoff on June 5, 2001. After a campaign in which Hahn asserted
that Villaraigosa was untrustworthy and soft on crime, the political scion
(Hahn's father, Kenneth, had been a fixture in local politics) beat the
Mexican American by a 53.5%-46.5% margin.[88]

Hahn won because of his solid backing among whites and Asians,
along with his overwhelming four-to-one margin among African Ameri-

cans. Whites, particularly in the San Fernando Valley, paid attention to Hahn's attacks on Villaraigosa's record with regard to crime and related issues. Moreover, Hahn benefited not just from his late father's sterling reputation in the African-American community, but also from black discontent over Latino advances. Villaraigosa, predictably, won a runaway victory among Latinos; however, he failed to win enough support from whites, blacks, and Asians to be genuinely competitive.[89] This election demonstrated convincingly that minorities do not automatically vote for other minorities, and that the politics of interethnic coalitions will continue to be ever-more complex in multiethnic metropolises such as Los Angeles.

At the same time, Rocky Delgadillo was elected City Attorney, the city's second-highest elected post, as a result of a black-brown coalition. The centrist Democrat had a great story: He went from a working-class background in northeast Los Angeles to Harvard as an undergraduate where he was All-American in football. Later, this grandson of Mexican immigrants earned a law degree from Columbia University and joined a corporate law firm in Los Angeles. Delgadillo rose to become the deputy mayor for economic development in the Riordan administration. The first-time candidate's signature issue was reforming the Los Angeles public schools, although the city attorney has limited influence in the educational realm. Delgadillo defeated Los Angeles City Councilman Mike Feuer by a 52%-48% margin due to his support from blacks, Latinos, leading businesspeople and political figures (including Mayor Riordan), and backing from special interests, namely the billboard companies, who disliked Feuer's support for restrictions on billboard advertising in the city. Nearly eight out of ten Hispanics — and 59% of blacks — backed Delgadillo in the nonpartisan race. He lost the Anglo vote by 22 percentage points, and failed to carry the Asian community by six points, but he still won the election.[90]

Despite all the attention focused on the mayoral race, and the failure of Villaraigosa to win much black support, Delgadillo demonstrated convincingly that a Latino candidate can win citywide office on the basis of a multiethnic coalition in which blacks and Hispanics are the largest groups. To be sure, Delgadillo's opponent did not have the same kind of credibility in the black community as did Hahn. Moreover, the city attorney's office lacks the symbolic significance of the mayoralty, so African Americans may not have been as reluctant to support a candidate from an ethnic group that competes with them on so many levels. Still, it is not inconceivable that Delgadillo may someday resurrect his black-brown coalition and win the mayoralty of Los Angeles.

It is far too early to speculate about George W. Bush's future in electoral politics. But President Bush may face a tough reelection campaign, in large part because America is balanced almost evenly between the two parties. The Democrats, moreover, seem unlikely to repeat their mistakes of the past. In other words, their partisans are reconciled to the idea that they need to nominate centrist candidates — those who fit the political profile of Al Gore, John Edwards, Gray Davis, and Joe Lieberman — if they are to win the presidency. However, Al Sharpton seems poised to make a respectable bid for the White House in 2004. It will be difficult for the Democrats to avoid antagonizing Sharpton, who may emerge as the preferred candidate of the Multicultural Left in the presidential primaries. Sharpton's candidacy promises to remind Middle America that the Multicultural Left continues to be an important part of the Democratic Party.

The economy, of course, is another factor that seems likely to influence the election results in 2002 and 2004. President Bush presently faces an economy that has lapsed into recession. A lengthy recession could decimate the Republican Party's chances in 2002 and 2004. President Bush, to be sure, has become extremely popular as a result of his firm handling of the war against terrorism. But his approval ratings (before September 11) were not especially good for a president in his first year, and as his father can attest, voters quickly forget a leader's military and foreign-policy accomplishments, if the economy does poorly for an extended period of time.

At the national level, white voters are going to continue to be the most numerically significant group in the American electorate. They will probably account for 78% to 80% of the voters in 2004. But the past few elections have shown that a Republican can do only so well in white America.[91] So if a Republican hopes to win the presidency or, in an increasing number of states, the governorship or a U.S. Senate seat, s/he is going to have to demonstrate her or his ability to win minority votes. In fact, a candidate's ability to triumph among voters of color is likely to become a major issue in Republican primaries this century.

In the foreseeable future, Florida, Michigan, and Pennsylvania will be the big battleground states in presidential politics, just as they were in 2000. No Republican is going to spend much time in California, New

York, Illinois, or New Jersey. And no Democrat will log many hours in Texas, Ohio, Georgia, or North Carolina. Florida in particular will be the most coveted prize. The state now has ten percent of the electoral votes needed to win the White House. Florida mirrors the ethnic diversity of America about as well as any large state; presidential candidates who hope to win there will have to be genuinely inclusive in their outreach efforts.

In any event, the demographics of Multicultural America bode well for the Democrats. Many people of color continue to view the Republicans as a party of affluent whites who care little about the nation's minority groups. Therefore, they gravitate to the Democratic Party, whose ranks encompass much more ethnic, racial, and religious diversity than those of the GOP. People of color now make up at least 16% of the national electorate. In 2000 Al Gore lost among whites to George W. Bush by 12 points, but he still won the popular vote, due to the fact that he carried nonwhites by a four-to-one margin.

With whites divided in their political loyalties and blacks reluctant to abandon the Democrats, both parties are scrambling to win the loyalty of Hispanics, who remain open to their partisan entreaties, though they lean Democratic. Republicans will not win a majority of any ethno-racial minority group's votes on a regular basis, at least in the near future. The good news for them is that they do not need to do so, *if* they can win by sizable margins among whites. Since Caucasians often support Democrats, the GOP cannot indefinitely afford to lose among people of color and hope to win many elections in the future.

In the absence of some brilliant, as-yet-undetermined panacea that will enable the GOP to reach Vietnamese Americans in Westminster and Garden Grove, Cuban Americans in Hialeah and Union City, and Mexican Americans in Pilsen and El Monte, they will end up as the political equivalent of roadkill. The more perspicacious Republicans know they cannot wait passively for minorities to become more affluent and consequently more amenable to the Republican message; such dithering is a one-way ticket to electoral oblivion. High-income African Americans and Mexican Americans show no permanent signs of leaving their ancestral partisan home. Republicans also hope that the cultural conservatism of minorities, especially Hispanics, will inspire them to pull the GOP lever in the voting booth. Yet these voters will remain loyal to the Democrats unless the party becomes too closely associated with fringe lifestyles and unpopular social causes.

Republicans are trying to avoid a demographic disaster without antagonizing their core constituencies, hence their halting efforts to recruit minority candidates, spotlight their nonwhite officeholders, and communicate their message in softer tones. Only with a minority-friendly presentation and a wholesale restructuring of the GOP agenda to find common issues — crime, taxes, education, health care, school vouchers — that appeal equally to whites and a substantial number of nonwhites will the Republicans be able to make a plausible claim to majority-party status during the next 30 years, particularly in states with substantial multiethnic populations.

∼ epilogue ∽

Reconcilable Differences?

The death of Robert Many Horses on June 30, 1999, came as a shock to many residents of Mobridge, South Dakota. Many Horses, a 22-year-old Native American, was a well-known and well-liked inhabitant of this town of 3,574 in north-central South Dakota. On the evening of June 29, Many Horses, a victim of fetal alcohol syndrome, went drinking with four white teenagers, and he passed out after consuming a prodigious amount of liquor. His blood alcohol level was 0.446 percent. After failing to revive him, one of the white youths decided to play what he thought was an innocuous prank on Many Horses, so he stuffed him face-down into a garbage receptacle. Alas, Robert Many Horses died in the early morning hours of June 30. Many Native Americans in the Mobridge area immediately suspected foul play, due to the circumstances of Many Horses' death. However, the state medical examiner's autopsy showed that Many Horses died because of alcohol poisoning. The federal authorities who investigated the case as a possible hate crime came to a similar conclusion.[1]

Many Native Americans, though, were not satisfied with either judgment. They angrily protested what they saw as white indifference to the murder of a Sioux. One memorable march in Mobridge featured an upside-down American flag. From the Indian perspective, the handling of the Many Horses case reflected their economic marginalization and lack of clout at the ballot box.[2] Native Americans constitute 17.8% of the population in Mobridge, a town that is 79.1% white (Germans predominate, but there are significant numbers of people who have Norwegian, Irish, or English antecedents as well).[3] The death of Many Horses became a rallying cry for the Indian ethnic advocates in the area; they viewed him as a victim of white racism.

Whites, to be sure, wield most economic and political power in Mobridge.[4] The Missouri River separates Mobridge from Indian Country, and a bridge links the "Bridge City" to the Standing Rock Sioux Indian Reservation, whose denizens frequently travel to the town for shopping, entertainment, and health care. Native Americans from the Cheyenne River Sioux Indian Reservation, southwest of Mobridge, often come to the Bridge City as well.[5] Indians in Mobridge and on the reservations tend to be poorer than whites, and this socioeconomic divide, coupled with the alcoholism that bedevils many Native Americans, complicates ethnic relations. But flagrant racism is rare in Mobridge; there are "a lot of good people here who do not put a lot of emphasis on skin color," according to Larry Atkinson, the editor and publisher of the *Mobridge Tribune*.[6] Indeed, it is impossible to generalize about the tenor of race relations in Mobridge, a place where Euro-American kids regularly date and socialize with their Sioux peers, a Native American couple owns a popular restaurant (the Fireside Supper Club) frequented by people of both races, an Indian man represents a white-majority constituency on the City Council, and the white owner of the local Paylessfoods speaks Lakota to his Native American customers.[7]

The tensions engendered by the Many Horses case inspired Atkinson, who is white, and an Indian newspaper editor in North Dakota to create the Hands Across the River Committee in January 2000. It soon evolved into the Mobridge Area Race Relations Council (MARRC). This all-volunteer committee, whose seven-member board includes three whites and four Native Americans, brings in speakers, holds public forums and workshops, investigates citizens' complaints, and clears up misunderstandings that might develop into racial conflicts.[8] The committee's activities, along with the informal efforts of people of both races to promote goodwill on a day-to-day basis, allow us to be optimistic that whites and Native Americans in northern South Dakota will eventually reconcile most, if not all, of the differences that divide them today.

Multiculturalism affects the lives of an increasing number of Americans in the Mobridge area and beyond, because every year the United States becomes a little more ethnically and racially diverse than it was during the previous 12 months. In the Mount Rushmore State, like much of America, this phenomenon is largely attributable to minority birth rates that exceed those of the white population. But immigration and, to a lesser extent, domestic in-migration contribute as much as the birth rates to the ethnic and racial heterogeneity found in such places as Texas, Illinois, California, and New York. More than a decade ago demographers began to consider seriously the possibility that the United States would lose its white majority someday. *Time* did its part with a sensational 1990 story about the end of white-majority America, a demographic milestone the newsmagazine projected would occur sometime during the

2050s. Emblazoned across *Time*'s cover was a watercolor rendering of the American flag, with the title "America's Changing Colors," and the open-ended question: "What will the U.S. be like when whites no longer are the majority?"[9]

The white-minority-America argument consists of a simple syllogism:

a. The United States is becoming proportionally less white each year.

b. This ineluctable development will transform almost every sector of American society. It is, of course, a desirable process because diversity itself is an intrinsic good.

c. Therefore, we should begin preparing for a white-minority America immediately, through affirmative action and other manifestations of multiculturalism, so the transition to the nonwhite-majority America of the future goes smoothly and seamlessly.

Since that cover story in *Time* 12 years ago, "the coming white minority," as Dale Maharidge describes it, has been accepted as an article of faith — largely without debate.[10] At the very least, America may turn into a *white-plurality* country, because whites will not be a minority so much as a plurality of the population. By 2050 the U.S. Census (middle series) projections forecast that America will be 52.8% white, 24.5% Hispanic, 13.6% black, 8.2% Asian, and 0.9% American Indian.[11] Indeed, a more heterogeneous white-majority America, not a white-minority America, seems to be the most likely scenario at this point.[12]

The white-plurality-America scenario presupposes trans-minority group interests — the idea that all racial minorities will form a cohesive majority united in opposition to the white minority in almost every situation. This is a specious argument: People of color frequently ally with whites against each other. Hispanics now rival blacks as the nation's largest minority group, a quantum shift with myriad consequences and ramifications that have yet to be felt. As Americans learn more about race and ethnicity, and events continue to unfold in our largest cities, it is becoming ever-more difficult to predict how well blacks and Latinos will get along with each other. Asian Americans, particularly those who are middle-class suburbanites, tend to align closely with their white neighbors on most issues. Five factors, outlined below, add an element of uncertainty to the process of forecasting America's racial demographics 50 years from now.

POPULATION DISTRIBUTION. The major components of population change (births, deaths, immigration) could be dramatically altered. Minority fertility rates might decline. Or there could be a sudden uptick in white birth rates. Similarly, life expectancy rates might change, abortion could be outlawed or sharply curtailed, and more restrictive immigration policies might be in the offing. There are two wild cards here: Puerto Rican statehood and the breakup of the Canadian nation. Statehood for Puerto Rico would swell the resident population of Hispanics considerably. It would add 3.8 million persons who can claim Hispanic backgrounds to the American population, speeding the day when white-plurality America becomes a reality. Likewise, the breakup of Canada might lead some of the English-speaking prairie provinces, such as Alberta and Saskatchewan, to petition to join the United States.[13] These provinces are predominantly white, and would tip the U.S. racial balance a bit. However, neither scenario is likely to come to pass, at least anytime soon.

IDENTIFICATION SCHEMA. Although the present identification schema defines nonwhiteness broadly, we know that, historically, there has been considerable flux in the classification process. Moreover, mixed-race Americans constitute an ever-larger constituency for more ecumenical categories in future censuses. And the "minority" category, should it exist 30 or 40 years from now, may change in meaning.[14] Whiteness may come to have a more expansive meaning that it has today.[15] How these developments would affect the whole concept of diversity is difficult to imagine.

RACIAL FLIGHT. A massive exodus of whites or another racial group from the United States could happen if conditions seemed inhospitable enough. Few Americans would move unless it appeared that doing so would have multiple advantages, chief among them the ability to maintain or improve their standard of living without suffering a perceptible loss of civil liberties. However, ample English-language employment opportunities and other amenities of American life are now readily available in the prosperous Asian, European, and Latin American countries. It is conceivable, though very unlikely at this point, that millions of white Americans would leave the United States permanently during the twenty-first century. Change in the United States is usually incremental, and our society is stable enough to undertake greater power sharing without unduly discombobulating the racial majority group, at least to the point that lots of them would feel compelled to leave their homeland.

HUMAN CLONING. In the future, the diversity imperative may be undermined by human clones, or a similarly transformative biological or technological development. Depending on how quickly the cloning of humans occurred on a mass scale, some unscrupulous Americans might try to manipulate demographics in favor of one racial group. Although this seems improbable now, scientific developments are moving so rapidly that it would be foolhardy to discount such a possibility. Besides, it will be nearly impossible to regulate human cloning, due to the manifold incentives for cash-starved, developing countries to provide safe havens for rogue traders in biotechnology.[16]

ARTIFICIAL INTELLIGENCE. We face the possibility in the next half-century of dealing with autonomous machines that will be smarter than the most intelligent humans. Thus we confront an important question: Can machines achieve consciousness? If machines are eventually able to have feelings, just like humans, the last major point of separation between smart machines and intelligent humans will be breached.[17] Otis Port of *BusinessWeek* reports that by around 2050, "Neural implants will expand human knowledge and thinking powers — and begin a transition to composite man-machine relationships that will gradually phase out the need for biological bodies."[18] This development could render the whole issue of race academic.

In the interregnum, younger Americans are most likely to be comfortable with the twenty-first century's multiracial environment. Neil Howe and William Strauss describe the generation "born in or after 1982" as "the Millennials."[19] They have had greater exposure to multicultural curricula, in addition to nonwhite playmates and cultural heroes, than most persons aged 50 and older. Despite periodic instances of skinhead violence and widely publicized reports of racial fights in high schools, American youths are increasingly comfortable with mixed groups of teens dating, fraternizing, working together, and attending school with each other. But they lack firsthand familiarity with the traumatic events of the 1960s, which inspired many Baby Boomers' sappy assumptions about racial integration and social justice 30 years ago.[20]

The Millennials are the first generation of American youths to grow up with multiracial sensibilities. As Howe and Strauss point out, "Millennials have never personally seen black-white race issues divide America."[21] Their pop cultural experiences included the likes of Brandy and Chris Rock, Jennifer Lopez and Carlos Santana, Lucy Liu and Jackie Chan. Yet some evidence suggests that these multicultural pioneers may accept benign notions of social segregation. Young adults emphatically agree on the need for equal opportunities for people of all races, but they do not necessarily feel that everyone has to hang out together all the time in integrated social settings.[22]

Every day Americans cast votes in what might be described as the never-ending, national referendum on racial reconciliation. Frequently, we cast affirmative ballots by giving persons of other races the benefit of the doubt on the road, at the mall, and in the workplace. Less frequently, we cast negative ballots by uttering racial epithets, giving dirty looks, rejecting job applications, or not renting properties to qualified buyers. Xenophobes frequently utter the infelicitous phrase, "Go back to (the presumed native country of the person in question)," when they come into contact with immigrants who irritate them. Sometimes nativists instigate their own informal Americanization efforts by crudely exhorting immigrants to speak English, when they hear the unfamiliar sounds of Korean, Spanish, or some other foreign tongue.

All the while, personal, interpersonal, and institutional efforts to reconcile racial differences continue. Throughout the nation, particularly in the South, efforts to achieve racial reconciliation vary in terms of their antecedents, contemporary dynamics, and proposed panaceas. Such efforts all share three central goals: to get beyond past — and, in some cases, present — feelings of rancor, to achieve interracial amity, and to allow more Americans to enjoy the fruits of the American Dream. These events indicate that America's racial tensions continue to plague us.

For at least 30 years, some African Americans have sought indemnification for slavery. Advocates of reparations argue that the United States benefited tremendously from the availability of forced slave labor by people whose ancestors were involuntary immigrants to America. This slave labor played an important role in the development of the economic infrastructure of the United States. At the same time, African Americans received very little, if any, economic compensation for their labors. These disadvantages, which were compounded by a century of legal segregation in the South and the effects of antiblack racism elsewhere in the country, created the conditions that explain why a disproportionate number of African Americans have yet to share in America's material prosperity. Advocates of reparations differ, of course, in terms of how the reimbursement program should be set up, who should qualify for benefits, how the funds should be distributed, and how many funds are necessary to alleviate the stigma and burden of slavery.[23]

The movement to obtain reparations for slavery began to win widespread support in the African-American community during the 1990s, particularly after the U.S. government paid $20,000 to every living survivor of the Japanese-American internment camps during World War II. Since then, there has been a great deal of activity on this front, yet it is very unlikely that white America will ever embrace this cause, especially since many Caucasians consider affirmative action to be a form of reparations.[24] In any event, the idea of reparations keeps blacks on the forefront of the nation's consciousness, even in the absence of a formal government apology for slavery. It is certainly possible that many advocates of reparations view their efforts as a means of getting the nation's policymakers to focus on the needs and claims of African Americans in an era where nonblack minorities, especially Hispanics, are receiving lots of attention, and affirmative action is less popular than it used to be.

Now we turn to Mississippi, where we can assess the state of race relations in the place that, for many Americans, symbolized the worst excesses of white racism against blacks. During the civil rights era, Mississippi made international headlines for the murder of Emmett Till in 1955, the unpleasant reception that greeted James Meredith when he single-handedly integrated the University of Mississippi in 1962, the murder of Medgar Evers in 1963, and the murders of James Chaney, Michael Schwerner, and Andrew Goodman, the three civil rights workers who were trying to register voters in Neshoba County in 1964.[25] African Americans were once lynched with impunity in Mississippi; these extralegal grotesqueries occurred with particular frequency from 1893 to 1927.[26] In a state ruled by white Anglo-Saxon men, and home to some of the vilest white supremacists in the country, many blacks (and whites) lived in degrading poverty. Not surprisingly, the state's whites regarded the incipient civil rights movement, which found fertile ground in Mississippi, with suspicion, hostility, and even murderous hatred. The black-white relationship affected almost every part of Mississippi, due to the fact that most counties had substantial numbers of blacks.[27]

Since the civil rights movement faded into oblivion during the mid-1960s, racial reconciliation has proceeded, slowly and unevenly, in the Magnolia State. Due to such movies as *Mississippi Burning, A Time to Kill,* and *Ghosts of Mississippi,* many Americans see Mississippi, somewhat unfairly, as the quintessential hotbed of racial animosity in this country. To be sure, there are white Mississippians who dislike their black neighbors, and vice-versa. But in recent years, two elderly white killers of Sixties-era civil rights figures have been convicted of murder in Mississippi. In 1994 Byron De La Beckwith went to jail for killing Medgar Evers.[28] Four years later, Samuel H. Bowers was permanently incarcerated for his role in the murder of Vernon Dahmer.[29] And in 2000, Mississippi Attorney General Mike Moore reopened the investigation of the 1964 slayings of Chaney, Schwerner, and Goodman.[30] Furthermore, the administrators of the University of Mississippi, the state's flagship public university, are attempting to make Ole Miss more welcoming to black students and athletes in a variety of ways. The University of Mississippi now discourages, restricts, and, in some cases, prohibits the display of Confederate iconography.[31]

Notwithstanding the black legislators, principals, mayors, executives, lawyers, and professors who constitute an important part of the state's Power Elite, a wage, wealth, and power gap between blacks and whites persists to this day in Mississippi. Although the separate public schools, municipal libraries, water fountains, and swimming pools are receding historical memories, there is still underlying segregation in the social sphere, as evidenced by the predominantly white private academies that persist in parts of Mississippi.[32] There is at least one country club in Mississippi that still does not admit black members. In any event, Mississippi's black population is growing faster than the white population, so it seems likely that African Americans will play an increasingly significant role in the state's affairs.

During the 1950s and 1960s Alabama was second only to Mississippi in its well-justified national reputation for racial rancor. Although the Supreme Court's *Brown* decision in 1954 is normally considered to be the beginning of the civil rights movement, the activism really took off in December 1955 with the Montgomery Bus Boycott, led by a 26-year-old minister named Martin Luther King Jr. George Wallace rose to national prominence in 1963 when he issued his ringing defense of segregation in his inaugural address as governor. Eugene "Bull" Connor, the commissioner of public safety in Birmingham, Alabama, became a national icon of white hatred for blacks when his baton-wielding cops unleashed attack dogs and fire hoses on peaceful civil-rights protesters. White supremacists in Birmingham bombed the Sixteenth Street Baptist Church in 1963, killing four black girls.[33] The Bloody Sunday march across the Edmund Pettus Bridge in Selma in 1965 was perhaps the last major incident of the civil rights movement, before it began to break up amid internal dissension and white indifference.

Alabama's situation has always been different from Mississippi's for a number of reasons. For one, Alabama's black population has always been smaller than Mississippi's. Another difference is that there are significant swaths of northern Alabama where whites, usually of Anglo-Saxon origin, comprise the vast majority of residents. In recent years, there has been a Hispanic influx to some of these areas. Even though the segregationist mores prevailed throughout the state, Appalachian Alabama was largely unaffected by racial tensions, except in the context of statewide issues. So there were large parts of Alabama where race was largely an academic issue, as it continued to be well into the 1990s.

Separation rather than integration continues to be the norm in Alabama. Alabamians of different races live in relative isolation from each other, even in the same town, and they do not intermingle much, except at Wal-Mart and McDonald's. As in Mississippi, many white students attend private schools, which tend to have small black enrollments. Selma, for instance, continues to be a place where blacks and whites do not mingle very often, at least on equal terms, in social settings.[34] Black Alabamians, like their coethnics in Mississippi, have made substantial political and economic gains, but suspicions and recriminations still linger and polarize the races.

But more than at any other time in the history of the Deep South, blacks and whites are making good-faith efforts to get along with each other. There may be periodic conflicts in Wedowee, Lineville, and Greene County, but some whites and blacks are working together to reconcile the state's racial differences in Birmingham, Montgomery, and elsewhere.[35] In 1993 the state removed the Confederate battle flag from the Capitol dome in Montgomery, a gesture of reconciliation that aided its efforts to attract out-of-state businesses to Alabama.[36] And in 2001 a Birmingham jury convicted Thomas E. Blanton Jr. of the murders of the four black girls at the Sixteenth Street Baptist Church.[37] Alabama certainly has made progress in changing the negative image on racial matters that it acquired during the 1950s and 1960s. The state's future stability and prosperity depend on the success of the ongoing attempts to reconcile its racial differences.

It was Bill Clinton who initiated the most prominent effort to promote racial reconciliation in recent years. In June 1997 Clinton announced a national initiative on race and reconciliation, with the slogan "One America in the 21st Century," that he hoped would facilitate a "great and unprecedented conversation about race." Discussions about racial divisions usually occur in the aftermath of some disastrous catalytic event, like the riots of the 1960s that spawned the precursor to Clinton's effort: the National Commission on Civil Disorders — known informally as the Kerner Commission, after its head, Illinois Governor Otto Kerner. But Clinton felt that a placid time was best to examine our past problems and, moreover, to look toward the future, to the coming demographic transformation of America.[38]

To spearhead this effort, Clinton created a seven-member panel (the Advisory Board to the President's Initiative on Race), and he named the distinguished historian John Hope Franklin, an African American, its chair. Throughout its year-long life span, the advisory panel was dogged by controversy over its focus on blacks and whites, its intramural squabbles and organizational difficulties, and its lack of genuinely open discussions about race. To be sure, Franklin and his fellow conciliators held panel discussions and town meetings on a variety of topics in different cities.[39] In 1998 the panel released a report that summarized its findings and delineated its recommendations for policymakers.[40] Even as our leaders attempt to resolve problems that predate Multicultural America, a whole new set of issues, dilemmas, and questions is beginning to demand their attention.

In the meantime, futurists increasingly posit that exogamic marriages and multiethnic babies are the antidote to America's racial problems. This line of reasoning proceeds on the pessimistic — or is it simply realistic? — premise that we cannot transcend racial animosities unless we are so ethnically and racially mixed that the very concept of race becomes functionally irrelevant. If we accept the validity of this theory, race will be significant in our lives for a very long time, judging by the high rates of intraracial marriage among all groups of Americans, with the notable exception of American Indians. Intraracial marriages, with attendant children, usually occur because individuals move in concentric social circles. More than a few Americans, however, do not endorse interracial dating or nuptials, no matter what they tell pollsters.[41]

In their self-congratulatory rush to judgment, trendspotting multiculturalists forget that interracial relationships are not as widespread as people might think, if they live in, say, Southern California, where mixed-race couples are common. Anyone who peruses small-town newspapers for announcements of marriages and engagements in such states as Iowa, Oklahoma, Maine, and Oregon finds that most of the radiant duos featured in those pages are all-white, with more than a few of them from old-stock (Yankee) backgrounds. At the beginning of the twenty-first century, one can travel through entire swaths of the Midwest, Northeast, Mountain West, and Appalachian South and see lots of pink-faced toddlers and youths. These children, whose Northern European ancestors constituted the solid majority of Americans up until at least 1940, are not much more likely than their parents to marry a person of a different race, unless they travel widely, join the military, or move to a multiethnic area.

These dynamics largely reflect the demographic composition of the marriage markets in so many parts of America. White youngsters who attend high school and college in such places as West Virginia, eastern Kentucky, southern Indiana, Upper Michigan, western Nebraska, eastern Oregon, southwestern Wisconsin, and northern New Hampshire will have few minority classmates. So their chances of marrying another white person are almost one hundred percent, especially if they do not leave the aforementioned areas. Indeed, ethnic endogamy remains alive and well in parts of white America. It is possible to visit elementary and secondary schools in northwestern Michigan where many of the students are full-flooded Finns. Each year children of purely German ancestry are born to nonimmigrant parents in Wisconsin; nor is it unusual for a newborn child in Massachusetts to be 100% Irish. Nonetheless, a growing number of Americans have ambiguous racial backgrounds, so it is becoming harder than ever to "place" a person, as America's complexion slowly gets browner. Perhaps someday there will be a new physical type — the American — who has a set of commonly recognizable features and characteristics, similar to the Swedes or the Japanese. In the meantime, racial exogamy is not a pervasive enough phenomenon to be a realistic solution to racial strife.

Domestic migration patterns are another indicator of American racial attitudes. Whole swaths of America harbor unwitting trendsetters in the field of domestic migration patterns: native-born white and, to a far lesser extent, black migrants who have fled heterogeneous metropolitan areas, due to high concentrations of nonwhite immigrants. "Push" factors driving the new regional segregation center around immigration and assorted ephemera related to it, like competition for jobs and feelings of cultural dislocation. "Pull" factors motivating domestic migrants depend on the people and their end destinations, but may include climate, a lower cost of living, a booming job market, and a corporate-friendly environment. Race, to be sure, is not necessarily the paramount concern of the typical domestic migrant, but issues related to racial and ethnic diversity usually influence his or her decision to move to a more homogeneous area of the country.[42]

Domestic migrants often desert cities and suburbs in the racially heterogeneous states and take refuge in the racially homogeneous parts of the Mountain West and Pacific Northwest. They flee the conspicuously multicultural environments of such places as California and New York, and often go to places with negligible populations of recent immigrants. Between 1990 and 2000 the Los Angeles-Riverside-Orange County metropolitan area shed 843,000 whites. Similarly, metropolitan New York lost 680,000 whites. There is evidence, too, that suggests

African Americans have been fleeing urban neighborhoods that are now dominated by Latinos. The tremendous population growth attributable to immigrants and their offspring masks the departures of native-born whites and blacks from the Californias and New Yorks. So even though the census figures for aggregate population appear virtually unchanged for the ten-year period from 1990 to 2000, the racial demographics of many metropolitan areas underwent sweeping changes during those years.[43]

In the end, the consequences of this developing demographic polarization will depend on how durable a phenomenon it proves to be. Perhaps the most significant ramifications affect the young people, the ones who are going to be the cultural, business, and political leaders of tomorrow. Many of them — white and nonwhite — will hail from areas where significant ethnic and racial diversity is the norm. While the days are long gone when a white youth might not see blacks or Asian Americans in person until he went into the Army, or went away to school, clearly some Caucasian youths will have far more exposure to America's multicultural splendor than others. And while it is clear that familiarity with such matters — and the ability to acknowledge, manage, and respect diversity — will be absolutely necessary for almost any job description, at least nationally, it is not so clear that growing up in a multiracial environment gives one special insights in this regard. Most public school teachers, moreover, use curricular materials that familiarize their students with America's heterogeneous demographics.

Increasing racial diversity, much of it fueled by immigration, is changing the faces of countless American communities and inspiring discussions about how to integrate the newcomers without acrimony. Dozens of American towns and cities have diversity committees, whose members discuss the local demographics, formulate plans to promote inclusion and assimilation, and remain vigilant for signs of racial polarization in their communities. Sometimes these committees take shape in the aftermath of a catalytic event that exposes the divisions in a given place. Other times, the committees are organized by people of good faith who wish to prevent schisms and divisions from developing in their communities.

Numerous American towns and cities have been changed immeasurably by immigration during the past few decades and have not had any major problems in integrating the newcomers. Wausau, Wisconsin, a primarily white community in the north-central part of the Badger State, is now home to a sizable Hmong population. A giant pork-processing plant has reshaped the demographics of Guymon, Oklahoma, a white-majority town in the Oklahoma Panhandle where Hispanics now account for 38.4% of the population. White immigrants from Turkey and Arabia prosper in Paterson, New Jersey, a predominantly black and Latino city that contains one of the nation's most comprehensive Middle Eastern shopping districts. To be sure, many parts of America still remain largely untouched by the effects of ethnic and racial heterogeneity. These places are sparsely populated and usually rural.

In any event, America certainly is more united than the skeptics thought, as we saw in the aftermath of the terrorist attacks on the World Trade Center and the Pentagon on September 11, 2001. Almost immediately, there was a widespread outpouring of national support and unity. Americans came together faster than at any other time since World War II, crossing ethnic, racial, religious, and socioeconomic lines to do so.[44] There were nationalistic, pro-American messages everywhere, from billboards to storefronts to automobiles, with such slogans as "United We Stand" and "In God We Trust." Americans of all races watched the patriotic television specials. We used the "United We Stand" postage stamps. The ubiquitous American flags popped up immediately after the attacks, and they waved from black, Hispanic, Asian-American, and American Indian homes and vehicles just as readily as they did from white residences and automobiles.[45]

After all, the terrorists did not make ethnic, racial, religious, and socioeconomic distinctions in their war on America: Every American was a potential target. This realization undoubtedly contributed to the American public's nearly unanimous support for the war against the Taliban and Al Qaeda in Afghanistan. Many Americans contributed money to the relief efforts that aided the families who lost loved ones in the terrorist attacks; as of February 2002, $1.5 billion had been raised for this purpose.[46] It remains to be seen how lasting this new sense of national unity will be, but it definitely is a hopeful sign that Americans are far more united than we had all thought before the terrorist attacks.

Even the treatment of Arab Americans and Muslim Americans in the aftermath of September 11 testified, at least to some extent, to the unity, tolerance, and goodwill of the American people. As is typically the case when the United States becomes involved in a Middle Eastern conflict, there was a sharp uptick in the amount of harassment directed against Arab Americans, Muslim Americans, and individuals who were mistaken for members of these two groups. By February 2002, the Council on American-Islamic Relations had collected in excess of 1,700 instances of bias in the five months since September 2001. These manifestations of the nativist impulse included hate mail, ethnic slurs, public harassment, employment discrimination, and school confrontations.[47] After the September 11 attacks, however, many Americans, from President Bush and his surrogates to millions of ordinary people, consistently made it clear in their words and deeds that Arab Americans and American Muslims were vital members of the American family, not enemies of America.[48]

Therefore, most of us do not lose sleep at night worrying that twenty-first-century America will be a multiethnic dystopia, where one's particularistic loyalties are solely to his or her ethno-racial group. A 1995 *Newsweek* survey found that, in response to the question, "100 years from today, will the United States still exist as one nation?" 61% of whites, 54% of Hispanics, and only 41% of blacks polled answered affirmatively.[49] Their cautious optimism is justified: The American political and economic system enables a diverse society to coexist in harmony most of the time. The economic expansion of the 1990s may have healed some of the ethnic and racial tensions that still bedevil parts of our country, by ameliorating some of the conditions that underlie social maladies and festering resentments.

Looking toward the future, even if whites lose their majority status, they are not going to suffer a corresponding diminution in their economic and political power — that is, if white-plurality states like California and New Mexico, and multiethnic cities such as Chicago and Los Angeles, are any indication. In such situations, power sharing usually takes place; whether it is tokenism or meaningful depends on the circumstances. Indeed, the future stability of the United States may depend on the willingness of socially dominant groups to share power with racial and ethnic minorities. These efforts aimed at integration and reconciliation will affect every one of us in some way during the twenty-first century.

Notes

Prologue: Seeing Is Believing

1. Michael D. Lemonick, "Bones of Contention," *Time* 148 (October 14, 1996): 81. See, too, Charles W. Petit, "Rediscovering America," *U.S. News & World Report* 125 (October 12, 1998): 56–60, 62–64; Karen Wright, "First Americans," *Discover* 20 (February 1999): 52–58, 60–61, 63; Sharon Begley and Andrew Murr, "The First Americans," *Newsweek* 133 (April 26, 1999): 50–57; Marc K. Stengel, "The Diffusionists Have Landed," *Atlantic Monthly* 285 (January 2000): 35–39, 42–44, 46–48; Scott L. Malcomson, "The Color of Bones," *New York Times Magazine* (April 2, 2000): 40–45; Sasha Nemecek, "Who Were the First Americans?" *Scientific American* 283 (September 2000): 80–87; Michael Parfit, "Hunt for the First Americans," *National Geographic* 198 (December 2000): 40–67; Steve Coll, "The Body in Question," *Washington Post Magazine* (June 3, 2001): at W8; Guy Gugliotta, "Earliest Americans Seen as More Diverse," *Washington Post*, July 31, 2001, at A1.

2. Lewis Lord, "How many people were there before Columbus?" *U.S. News & World Report* 123 (August 18–25, 1997): 68–70; Russell Thornton, *American Indian Holocaust and Survival: A Population History Since 1492* (Norman: University of Oklahoma Press, 1987), 15–41; Fergus M. Bordewich, *Killing the White Man's Indian: Reinventing Native Americans at the End of the Twentieth Century* (New York: Doubleday, 1996), 162–203.

3. W. E. B. Du Bois noted that "the problem of the Twentieth Century is the problem of the color-line." W. E. B. Du Bois, *The Souls of Black Folk* (1903; reprint, with an introduction by John Edgar Wideman, New York: Vintage Books/Library of America, 1990), 3; David K. Shipler, *A Country of Strangers: Blacks and Whites in America* (New York: Alfred A. Knopf, 1997), 3–19; Roberto Suro, "The Next Wave; How Immigration Blurs the Race Discussion," *Washington Post*, July 19, 1998, at C1.

4. Gunnar Myrdal, *An American Dilemma: The Negro Problem and Modern Democracy* (1944; reprint, New York: Harper & Row, 1962). For a description of the importance of this book, see David W. Southern, *Gunnar Myrdal and Black-White Relations: The Use and Abuse of* An American Dilemma, *1944–1969* (Baton Rouge: Louisiana State University Press, 1987).

5. Jennifer L. Hochschild, *Facing Up to the American Dream: Race, Class, and the Soul of the Nation* (Princeton, N.J.: Princeton University Press, 1995), xi.

6. Everett Carll Ladd and Karlyn H. Bowman, "The Nation Says No to Class Warfare," *USA Today* 127 (May 1999): 24–26.

7. Carl N. Degler, *Neither Black nor White: Slavery and Race Relations in Brazil and the United States* (New York: Macmillan, 1971), 208.

295

8. Michael Omi and Howard Winant, *Racial Formation in the United States: From the 1960s to the 1990s*, 2d ed. (New York: Routledge, 1994), 61–62; Sharon Begley, "Three Is Not Enough," *Newsweek* 125 (February 13, 1995): 68.

9. Degler, *Neither Black nor White*, 213–214, 288–289.

10. Beverly Daniel Tatum, *"Why Are All the Black Kids Sitting Together in the Cafeteria?" And Other Conversations About Race* (New York: Basic Books, 1997), 18.

11. Tatum, *"Why Are All the Black Kids Sitting Together in the Cafeteria?"* 31–90; Lawrence A. Hirschfeld, *Race in the Making: Cognition, Culture, and the Child's Construction of Human Kinds* (Cambridge, Mass.: Bradford Books/MIT Press, 1998).

12. For reflections on these issues, see Martha R. Mahoney, "Whiteness and Women, in Practice and Theory: A Reply to Catharine MacKinnon," *Yale Journal of Law and Feminism* 5 (Spring 1993): 217–251; Marita Golden and Susan Richards Shreve, eds., *Skin Deep: Black Women and White Women Write About Race* (New York: Anchor Books, 1996).

13. Orlando Patterson, *The Ordeal of Integration: Progress and Resentment in America's "Racial" Crisis* (Washington, D.C.: Civitas/Counterpoint, 1997), 57–60, 148–157.

14. Michael Lind, *The Next American Nation: The New Nationalism and the Fourth American Revolution* (New York: Free Press, 1995). The quotation appears on page 11.

15. Lind, *The Next American Nation*, passim.

16. To the best of my knowledge, my definition of this phrase, in this context, is an original one. To determine how often the words diversity and imperative are paired together, I did a search on Yahoo on March 16, 2002, that combined the keywords "diversity" and "imperative." It came up with 114,000 hits, some of which referred to a "diversity imperative" and others that contained references to diversity and imperative in a single sentence — usually something along the lines of "It is imperative that we have diversity" — rather than using the two-word phrase.

17. Barbara Flagg, " 'Was Blind, but Now I See': White Race Consciousness and the Requirement of Discriminatory Intent," *Michigan Law Review* 91 (March 1993): 953–1017; Ian F. Haney López, *White by Law: The Legal Construction of Race* (New York: New York University Press, 1996), 155–195.

18. Nicholas Lemann, *The Promised Land: The Great Black Migration and How It Changed America* (New York: Alfred A. Knopf, 1991); U.S. Bureau of the Census, *Historical Statistics of the United States, Colonial Times to 1970, Bicentennial Edition, Part 1* (Washington, D.C.: U.S. Bureau of the Census, 1975), 22.

19. Lemann, *The Promised Land*, passim.

20. Dan T. Carter, *The Politics of Rage: George Wallace, the Origins of the New Conservatism, and the Transformation of American Politics* (New York: Simon & Schuster, 1995).

21. Peter Brimelow, *Alien Nation: Common Sense About America's Immigration Disaster* (New York: HarperPerennial, 1996), 64.

22. I visited most of the North American places — and many of the Asian, European, and Latin American datelines — mentioned in this book. In particular, I went to every dateline discussed in the vignettes that open each section and chapter, except for South Africa. Moreover, I refer to some nations in the text, such as Cuba, India, Ireland, Germany, Vietnam, and Australia, that I have yet to visit.

23. Harold D. Lasswell, *Politics — Who Gets What, When, How* (New York: Whittlesey House/McGraw-Hill Book Company, 1936).

Chapter 1: Classifying by Race

1. Maria Pulera, telephone conversations with author, September 11, 2001, September 14, 2001, and September 16, 2001.

2. Pulera, telephone conversations, September 14, 2001 and September 16, 2001.

3. I made 23 trips to Glendale, California, between July 1996 and January 2002, so I am quite familiar with the demographics of this community. For background on the Armenians of Los Angeles County, see Claudia Der-Martirosian, Georges Sabagh, and Mehdi Bozorgmehr, "Subethnicity: Armenians in Los Angeles," in Ivan Light and Parminder Bhachu, eds., *Immigration and Entrepreneurship: Culture, Capital, and Ethnic Networks* (New Brunswick, N.J.: Transaction Publishers, 1993), 243–258.

4. Helen Gao, "Vote Adds Ethnic Diversity to Leadership in Glendale," *Los Angeles Daily News,* April 5, 2001, N3.

5. On the speculation about how some Armenians may have selected the mixed-race option, see Laurent Belsie, "Profile rises for multiracial people," *Christian Science Monitor,* July 17, 2001, 3.

6. Ian Haney López, *White by Law: The Legal Construction of Race* (New York: New York University Press, 1996), 67, 70, 72, 99, 126, 130–131, 156; Matthew Frye Jacobson, *Whiteness of a Different Color: European Immigrants and the Alchemy of Race* (Cambridge, Mass.: Harvard University Press, 1998), 109, 129, 231–232, 240.

7. Massie Ritsch, "Retreats Promote Peace on Campus," *Los Angeles Times,* March 5, 2001, at B1.

8. Bill Keller, "How American 'Sister' Died in a Township," *New York Times,* August 27, 1993, at A1; Robert Reinhold, "Death of an Idealist," *New York Times,* August 27, 1993, A10; Bill Keller, "Rage Has Its Own Rules in South Africa," *New York Times,* August 29, 1993, Sec. 4, p. 6; John Battersby, "Killing of US Student in Racial Attack Shakes South Africa," *Christian Science Monitor,* August 30, 1993, 3; Arlene Getz, "Comrades Come in All Colors," *Newsweek* 122 (September 6, 1993): 32; David Van Biema, "Bright Life, Dark Death," *Time* 142 (September 6, 1993): 45.

9. Suzanne Daley, "South Africans Apologize to Family of American Victim," *New York Times,* July 9, 1997, A9; Patrick Rogers, "Remembering Amy," *People Weekly* 48 (September 8, 1997): 73–74; Paul Harris, "Four Got Amnesty in Amy Biehl Death," *Associated Press News Service,* July 28, 1998.

10. Jon Jeter, "A Daughter's Dream Lives at Scene of Her Death; Amy Biehl's Parents Embrace S. Africa That Took Her," *Washington Post,* February 18, 2001, at A1.

11. For an excellent exposition of the "Out of Africa" theory, see Christopher Stringer and Robin McKie, *African Exodus: The Origins of Modern Humanity* (New York: Henry Holt and Company, 1998).

12. For an equally good discussion of Multiregional evolution, consult Milford Wolpoff and Rachel Caspari, *Race and Human Evolution* (Boulder, Colo.: Westview Press, 1998). The quotation comes from Wolpoff and Caspari, *Race and Human Evolution,* 11.

13. Wolpoff and Caspari, *Race and Human Evolution,* 57–172; Stephan Jay Gould, "The Geometer of Race," *Discover* 15 (November 1994): 64–69; Dinesh D'Souza, *The End of Racism: Principles for a Multiracial Society* (New York: Free Press, 1995), 25–65, 115–161; Ivan Hannaford, *Race: The History of an Idea in the West* (Washington, D.C.: Woodrow Wilson Center Press and Johns Hopkins University Press, 1996); Scott L. Malcomson, *One Drop of Blood: The American Misadventure of Race* (New York: Farrar, Straus and Giroux, 2000), 133–159.

14. Ibid.

15. Ibid.

16. Stringer and McKie, *African Exodus,* 64; Jared Diamond, "Race Without Color," *Discover* 15 (November 1994): 83–89; David L. Wheeler, "A Growing Number of Scientists Reject the Concept of Race," *Chronicle of Higher Education,* February 17, 1995, A9, A15; Natalie Angier, "Do Races Differ? Not Really, Genes Show," *New York Times,* August 22, 2000, at F1.

17. Diamond, "Race Without Color," 86.

18. Haney López, *White by Law,* passim, especially 111–153; Michael Omi and Howard Winant, *Racial Formation in the United States: From the 1960s to the 1990s,* 2d ed. (New York: Routledge, 1994), particularly 53–76; Ruth Frankenberg, *White Women, Race Matters: The Social Construction of Whiteness* (Minneapolis: University of Minnesota Press, 1993).

19. Borgna Brunner, ed., *TIME Almanac 2002* (Boston: Information Please, 2001), 707, 716–717.

20. Matthew Connelly and Paul Kennedy, "Must It Be the Rest Against the West?" *Atlantic Monthly* 274 (December 1994): 61–91; Bruce B. Auster, "It's chaos, and it's here to stay," *U.S. News & World Report* 122 (May 12, 1997): 34; Michael S. Teitelbaum and Jay Winter, *A Question of Numbers: High Migration, Low Fertility, and the Politics of National Identity* (New York: Hill & Wang, 1998); James Gustave Speth, "The Plight of the Poor," *Foreign Affairs* 78 (May/June 1999): 13–17.

21. For divergent views on this issue, see Jared Diamond, *Guns, Germs, and Steel: The Fates of Human Societies* (New York: W. W. Norton & Company, 1997); David S. Landes, *The Wealth and Poverty of Nations: Why Some Are So Rich and Some So Poor* (New York: W. W. Norton & Company, 1998); Thomas Sowell, *Conquests and Cultures: An International History* (New York: Basic Books, 1998); Lawrence E. Harrison and Samuel P. Huntington, eds., *Culture Matters: How Values Shape Human Progress* (New York: Basic Books, 2000).

22. Bernard Wysocki Jr., "The Global Mall: In the Emerging World, Many Youths Splurge, Mainly on U.S. Goods," *Wall Street Journal,* June 26, 1997, at A1; Gloria Goodale, "US Pop Culture Envelops Globe; (Globe not entirely pleased)," *Christian Science Monitor,* August 7, 1998, at B1; Paul Farhi and Megan Rosenfeld, "American Pop Penetrates Worldwide; Nations with New Wealth, Freedom Welcome Bart Simpson, Barbie and Rap," *Washington Post,* October 25, 1998, at A1.

23. U.S. Census Bureau, *Statistical Abstract of the United States: 2000* (120th ed.) (Washington, D.C.: U.S. Government Printing Office, 2000), Tables 1318, 1319, 1320, and 1321; Karen DeYoung, "Generosity Shrinks in an Age of Prosperity," *Washington Post,* November 25, 1999, at A1; Michael Dobbs, "Foreign Aid Shrinks, but Not for All; With Clout in Congress, Armenia's Share Grows," *Washington Post,* January 24, 2001, at A1.

24. Brunner, ed., *TIME Almanac 2002,* 890.

25. David E. Sanger, "Bashing America for Fun and Profit," *New York Times,* October 5, 1997, Sec. 4, at p. 1.

26. Mary L. Dudziak, *Cold War Civil Rights: Race and the Image of American Democracy* (Princeton, N.J.: Princeton University Press, 2000).

27. *United States v. Bhagat Singh Thind,* 261 U.S. 204 (1923); Haney López, *White by Law,* 86–95, 119–120, 148–150, 198.

28. *United States v. Bhagat Singh Thind,* 261 U.S. 204 (1923), 209.

29. Haney López, *White by Law,* 204–208.

30. André Béteille, "Race and Descent as Social Categories in India," in John Hope Franklin, ed., *Color and Race* (Boston: Houghton Mifflin Company, 1968), 166–185; Shashi Tharoor, *India: From Midnight to the Millennium* (New York: Arcade Publishing, 1997), 11–13, 50–138.

31. Yen Le Espiritu, *Asian American Panethnicity: Bridging Institutions and Identities* (Philadelphia: Temple University Press, 1992), 124–126; Joel Millman, *The Other Americans: How Immigrants Renew Our Country, Our Economy, and Our Values* (New York: Viking, 1997), 139–171.

32. Frederick G. Bohme, ed., *200 Years of U.S. Census Taking: Population and Housing Questions, 1790–1990* (Washington, D.C.: U.S. Government Printing Office, 1989). See also Sharon M. Lee, "Racial classifications in the US census: 1890–1990," *Ethnic and Racial Studies* 16 (January 1993): 75–94. For general background on the Census, see Margo J. Anderson and Stephen E. Fienberg, *Who Counts? The Politics of Census-Taking in Contemporary America* (New York: Russell Sage Foundation, 1999); Peter Skerry, *Counting on the Census? Race, Group Identity, and the Evasion of Politics* (Washington, D.C.: Brookings Institution Press, 2000).

33. U.S. Bureau of the Census, *Historical Statistics of the United States, Colonial Times to 1970, Bicentennial Edition, Part 1* (Washington, D.C.: U.S. Government Printing Office, 1975), 3.

34. Jack D. Forbes, "The Hispanic Spin: Party Politics and Governmental Manipulation of Ethnic Identity," *Latin American Perspectives* 19 (Fall 1992): 59–63; Lawrence Wright, "One Drop of Blood," *New Yorker* 70 (July 25, 1994): 50, 52–53. For the original directive, see Appendix, Directive No. 15, "Race and

Ethnic Standards for Federal Statistics and Administrative Reporting," *Federal Register* 60 (August 28, 1995): 44692–44693.

35. Office of Management and Budget, "Revisions to the Standards for the Classification of Federal Data on Race and Ethnicity," *Federal Register* 62 (October 30, 1997): 58782–58790.

36. Ibid., 58789.

37. David A. Hollinger, *Postethnic America: Beyond Multiculturalism* (New York: Basic Books, 1995), 23–50.

38. There were a total of 6,826,228 Americans who selected the multiracial category on the census, 4,602,146 of whom were non-Hispanic and 2,224,082 were Hispanic. Moreover, the "Other" category on the census form mainly serves as a way for Hispanics who do not view themselves as white to identify as such. In the 2000 census, 15,359,073 Americans chose "Some Other Race." When Hispanic is factored into the equation, that number drops to 467,770. In other words, 97% of the people who select "Some Other Race" are Hispanic. The non-Hispanic Others, a group that includes some Cape Verdeans and Arab Americans, have widely divergent reasons for choosing this category. Just because someone checks Other does not mean that that person is recognized as a minority by the general public, however.

39. D'Vera Cohn and Darryl Fears, "Hispanics Draw Even with Blacks in New Census; Latino Population Up 60% Since 1990," *Washington Post,* March 7, 2001, at A1; Frank James, "U.S. Hispanic Population Grows by 58%; Numbers May Boost Group's Political Pull," *Chicago Tribune,* March 8, 2001; Eric Schmitt, "New Census Shows Hispanics Are Even with Blacks in U.S.," *New York Times,* March 8, 2001, at A1; Haya El Nasser, "Census shows greater numbers of Hispanics," *USA Today,* March 8, 2001, 3A; Eduardo Porter, "Number of Hispanics Ballooned in '90s, Set to Pass Total of Blacks," *Wall Street Journal,* March 8, 2001, A24.

40. Jennifer Cheeseman Day, *Population Projections of the United States by Age, Sex, Race and Hispanic Origin: 1995 to 2050,* U.S. Bureau of the Census, Current Population Reports, P25–1130 (Washington, D.C.: U.S. Government Printing Office, 1996), 17–29.

41. David Lopez and Yen Espiritu, "Panethnicity in the United States: a theoretical framework," *Ethnic and Racial Studies* 13 (April 1990): 198–224.

42. These data are from the 1990 census. At this writing, the 2000 figures are not yet available. U.S. Census Bureau, *Statistical Abstract of the United States: 2000,* Table 50.

43. It will be difficult, if not impossible, to come up with a precise estimate of the number of Americans who trace their ancestry to the Middle East or North Africa until the new census data for ancestry are released in mid-2002. In 1990, for instance, 1,766,697 Americans selected a North African or Middle Eastern identity in response to the ancestry question on the census form. (This figure includes Israelis.) Since then, there has been substantial immigration to the United States from North African and Middle Eastern nations. Moreover, ethnic advocates such as Helen Samhan of the Arab American Institute insist that the census undercounts Arab Americans. Samhan says there is an undercount of recent immigrants and that the ancestry question does not elicit responses

from all Americans who are part Arab. According to Samhan, there "are at least three million Arab Americans," an estimate that includes any American with Arab ancestry. The government's estimate would probably be less than half that number. Helen Samhan, telephone conversation with author, September 10, 2001.

44. These data are from the 1990 census. At this writing, the 2000 figures are not yet available.

45. For information about sub-Saharan Africans in America, see Millman, *The Other Americans,* 70–102, 172–209, 285–312; Sanford J. Ungar, *Fresh Blood: The New American Immigrants* (New York: Simon & Schuster, 1995), 37–41, 247–272, 364–365; F. Nii-Amoo Dodoo, "Assimilation Differences among Africans in America," *Social Forces* 76 (December 1997): 527–546. On West Indian Americans, see Suzanne Model, "West Indian Prosperity: Fact or Fiction?" *Social Problems* 42 (November 1995): 535–553; Matthijs Kalmijn, "The Socioeconomic Assimilation of Caribbean American Blacks," *Social Forces* 74 (March 1996): 911–930; Flore Zéphir, *Haitian Immigrants in Black America: A Sociological and Sociolinguistic Portrait* (Westport, Conn.: Bergin & Garvey, 1996); Milton Vickerman, *Crosscurrents: West Indian Immigrants and Race* (New York: Oxford University Press, 1999); Mary C. Waters, *Black Identities: West Indian Immigrant Dreams and American Realities* (New York: Russell Sage Foundation, 1999); Nancy Foner, ed., *Islands in the City: West Indian Migration to New York* (Berkeley: University of California Press, 2001).

46. Kimberly Hayes Taylor, "Somalis in America; Working through a clash of cultures," *Minneapolis Star Tribune,* March 22, 1998, at 1A.

47. For these data, see U.S. Census Bureau, *The Hispanic Population: 2000* (U.S. Census Bureau, May 2001), 3.

The Census Bureau saw an uptick in the number of Hispanic people who identified with a panethnic referent, such as Latino, in the 2000 census. According to the statistician Roberto Ramirez, who works on these issues at the Census Bureau, "There was an increase in the number of people who reported pan terms versus specific terms between Census 1990 and Census 2000." Ramirez and his colleagues have speculated about several hypotheses to explain this occurrence, but only one of them has been scientifically tested. One hypothesis is that the term Latino was new to the Census of 2000, so that people who might have used it before finally had a chance to do so — this theory has been tested by the Census Bureau. See Betsy Martin, "Some Evidence about Questionnaire Design Effects on Reporting of Specific Hispanic Groups in Census 2000 Mail Questionnaires," (Census Bureau, November 7, 2001). Another hypothesis, which has not been tested yet, refers to what might be termed the "generation effect," to describe the Latino consciousness of younger Hispanics, who do not identify with a specific ethnic group, even if they trace all of their ancestry to one particular group.

To be sure, the Census Bureau does tally the numbers of Hispanics with multiple Latino origins. In the argot of the Census Bureau, "panethnic" means people who have reported Latino, Hispanic, and Spanish. Multiple-origin Hispanics, however, are those who report "two or more Hispanic-origin groups," according to Ramirez. When a person selects multiple Hispanic ethnicities, his or her response is coded as multiple-origin Hispanic. This is a mutually exclusive category: The multiple ethnic responses are not allocated among the various Latino subgroups. As of February 2002, the data about the specific number of multiple-origin Hispanics were not yet available. "The Census Bureau," Ramirez points out, "will release the number of people who gave more than one Hispanic origin, but will not release specific combinations." Roberto Ramirez, telephone conversations with author, November 30, 2001, February 11, 2002, and February 13, 2002.

48. Espiritu, *Asian American Panethnicity;* William Wei, *The Asian American Movement* (Philadelphia: Temple University Press, 1993); Norimitsu Onishi, "New Sense of Race Arises Among Asian-Americans," *New York Times,* May 30, 1996, at A1; Nazli Kibria, "The construction of 'Asian American': reflections on intermarriage and ethnic identity among second-generation Chinese and Korean Americans," *Ethnic and Racial Studies* 20 (July 1997): 523–544; Nazli Kibria, "The contested meanings of 'Asian American': racial dilemmas in the contemporary US," *Ethnic and Racial Studies* 21 (September 1998): 939–958; Sharon M. Lee and Marilyn Fernandez, "Trends in Asian American Racial/Ethnic Intermarriage: A Comparison of 1980 and 1990 Census Data," *Sociological Perspectives* 41:2 (1998): 323–342; Nazli Kibria, "College and Notions of 'Asian American': Second-Generation Chinese and Korean Americans Negotiate Race and Identity," *Amerasia Journal* 25 (Spring 1999): 29–51; Helen Zia, *Asian American Dreams: The Emergence of an American People* (New York: Farrar, Straus and Giroux, 2000).

49. Nazli Kibria, "Not Asian, Black or White? Reflections on South Asian American Racial Identity," *Amerasia Journal* 22:2 (1996): 77–86; Lavina Dhingra Shankar and Rajini Srikanth, eds., *A Part, Yet Apart: South Asians in Asian America* (Philadelphia: Temple University Press, 1998).

50. Lynette Clemetson, "Love Without Borders," *Newsweek* 136 (September 18, 2000): 62.

51. Stephen E. Cornell, *The Return of the Native: American Indian Political Resurgence* (New York: Oxford University Press, 1988), 106–127.

52. Daniel Wood, "Indians Hear a High-Tech Drumbeat," *Christian Science Monitor,* February 19, 1998, at p. 1.

53. There is a burgeoning literature about blacks and group interests. See, e.g., Michael C. Dawson, *Behind the Mule: Race and Class in African-American Politics* (Princeton, N.J.: Princeton University Press, 1994), passim; David Harris, "Exploring the Determinants of Adult Black Identity: Context and Process," *Social Forces* 74 (September 1995): 227–241; Randall Kennedy, "My Race Problem — And Ours," *Atlantic Monthly* 279 (May 1997): 55–56, 58–60, 64–66; Mary Herring, Thomas B. Jankowski, and Ronald E. Brown, "Pro-black Doesn't Mean Anti-white: The Structure of African-American Group Identity," *Journal of Politics* 61 (May 1999): 363–386.

54. Eric Slater and Myron Levin, "When Jackson Presses, Funds Tend to Follow," *Los Angeles Times,* March 13, 2001, at A1; Pam Belluck, "Despite Emboldened Critics, Jesse Jackson Isn't Yielding," *New York Times,* March 26, 2001, at A1; William Claiborne, "Jackson's Fundraising Methods Spur Questions," *Washington Post,* March 27, 2001, at A1. For a harshly critical look at

Jackson's career, see Kenneth R. Timmerman, *Shakedown: Exposing the Real Jesse Jackson* (Washington, D.C.: Regnery Publishing, 2002).

55. See, e.g., Eli Kintisch, "Uncivil Affair: The Jackson-Sharpton feud," *New Republic* 223 (December 4, 2000): 19–20, 22; Adam Nagourney, "The Post-Sharpton Sharpton," *New York Times Magazine* (March 18, 2001): 42–47; Mark Hosenball and Evan Thomas, "Jesse and Al's Food Fight," *Newsweek* 137 (April 9, 2001): 41; Scott Sherman, "He Has a Dream; The grand ambition of the Rev. Al Sharpton," *Nation* 272 (April 16, 2001): 11–13, 15–18, 20; Jack E. White, "The Fight for Might," *Time* 157 (May 28, 2001): 46–48; Jack Newfield, "Rev vs. Rev," *New York* 34 (January 7, 2002): 46–49, 70, 106.

56. Ellis Cose, "Rethinking Black Leadership," *Newsweek* 139 (January 28, 2002): 42–43.

57. "Half Breed" was written by Al Capps and Mary Dean.

58. Mary E. Ladd, "The Gunslinger Ballads: Cher and the American West," *Cher Scholar: The Cher Zine/The Gunslinger Ballads.* www.cherscholar.com/cherwest.htm.

59. Lawrence J. Quirk, *Totally Uninhibited: The Life and Wild Times of Cher* (New York: William Morrow and Company, 1991), 275.

60. In her semi-autobiography, *The First Time,* Cher writes about how the intraethnic differences within her own family affected her self-esteem. For instance, Cher describes a childhood trip to Mexico in which she and her fair-skinned mother and sister were interrogated by U.S. border guards who thought that Cher might be a Mexican (her Armenian complexion became darker after she tanned). Cher writes, "That day I learned that white/pale/blond/fair was *better*— or maybe just easier (emphasis Cher's)." Cher also describes how she sometimes felt like an outsider because she was part of a family of blond people: "I was always the dark one. Dark hair, dark eyes, dark skin." Moreover, she admits, "I wanted to be a blonde. I pined to be a blonde. I wanted to trade in my cheekbones for a round face with blue eyes and a little pug nose." Cher as told to Jeff Coplon, *The First Time* (New York: Simon & Schuster, 1998), 19–20, 63. The first quotation appears on page 20. The latter two quotations can be found on page 63.

61. D'Souza, *The End of Racism,* 58–61, 84–87.

62. Ibid.

63. Brunner, ed., *TIME Almanac 2002,* 123.

64. Robert F. Berkhofer Jr., *The White Man's Indian: Images of the American Indian from Columbus to the Present* (New York: Vintage Books, 1979), passim; Brian W. Dippie, *The Vanishing American: White Attitudes and U.S. Indian Policy* (Lawrence: University Press of Kansas, 1982), passim, particularly 81–94.

65. Ann Uhry Abrams, *The Pilgrims and Pocahontas: Rival Myths of American Origin* (Boulder, Colo.: Westview Press, 1999).

66. R. S. Yeoman, *A Guide Book of United States Coins,* 55th ed., 2002, ed. Kenneth Bressett (New York: St. Martin's Press, 2001), 94, 109.

67. Jacqueline K. Greb, "Will the Real Indians Please Stand Up?" in Gary A. Yoggy, ed., *Back in the Saddle: Essays on Western Film and Television Actors* (Jefferson, N.C.: McFarland & Company, 1998), 129–144; Jacquelyn Kilpatrick,

Celluloid Indians: Native Americans and Film (Lincoln: University of Nebraska Press, 1999).

68. Shepard Krech III, *The Ecological Indian: Myth and History* (New York: W. W. Norton & Company, 1999).

69. Joel Williamson, *New People: Miscegenation and Mulattoes in the United States* (New York: Free Press, 1980), 5–59; F. James Davis, *Who Is Black? One Nation's Definition* (University Park: Pennsylvania State University Press, 1991), 31–42; Kathy Russell, Midge Wilson, and Ronald Hall, *The Color Complex: The Politics of Skin Color Among African Americans* (New York: Harcourt Brace Jovanovich, 1992), 9–23; Christine B. Hickman, "The Devil and the One Drop Rule: Racial Categories, African Americans, and the U.S. Census," *Michigan Law Review* 95 (March 1997): 1161–1265.

70. Dippie, *The Vanishing American*, 247–269; William Loren Katz, "History's Missing Chapter: Black Indians," *American Legacy* 3 (Spring 1997): 31–38; Jack D. Forbes, *Africans and Native Americans: The Language of Race and the Evolution of Red-Black Peoples*, 2d ed. (Urbana: University of Illinois Press, 1993), passim.

71. U.S. Bureau of the Census, *Historical Statistics of the United States, Colonial Times to 1970, Bicentennial Edition, Part 1*, 3.

72. Haney López, *White by Law*, 118–119.

73. *Plessy v. Ferguson*, 163 U.S. 537 (1896).

74. Davis, *Who Is Black?* 22, 42–80; Williamson, *New People*, 61–106, 108–109, 111–139.

75. Ibid.

76. See, e.g., Russell, Wilson, and Hall, *The Color Complex*, 24–166; Michael Hughes and Bradley R. Hertel, "The Significance of Color Remains: A Study of Life Chances, Mate Selection, and Ethnic Consciousness Among Black Americans," *Social Forces* 68 (June 1990): 1105–1120; Verna M. Keith and Cedric Herring, "Skin Tone and Stratification in the Black Community," *American Journal of Sociology* 97 (November 1991): 760–778; Lawrence Otis Graham, *Our Kind of People: Inside America's Black Upper Class* (New York: HarperCollins, 1999), 376–393.

77. Ibid.

78. Rogers was nine-thirty-seconds, or about 28 percent, Cherokee. Ben Yagoda, *Will Rogers: A Biography* (New York: Alfred A. Knopf, 1993), especially xii, 3–18.

79. Philip J. Deloria, *Playing Indian* (New Haven, Conn.: Yale University Press, 1998), 154–180.

80. Overall, 4,119,301 Americans selected American Indian in response to the race question in the 2000 census, either as their sole identifier or as one of two or more identifiers. Of these individuals, 59.9% (2,475,956) checked American Indian as their only racial identity. There are 2,068,883 non-Hispanic American Indians and 407,073 Hispanic Indians. Most non-Hispanic multiracials with an American Indian identifier (a population of 1,643,345) belong to one of four groups: non-Hispanic white/American Indian biracials (969,238), non-Hispanic black/American Indian biracials (168,022), non-Hispanic white, black, and American Indian multiracials (94,161), non-Hispanic Asian/American Indian

biracials (43,052). In addition, there are 368,872 others who identify as part-Indian, non-Hispanic multiracials, but who do not fit into any of these four categories.

81. David Harris, "The 1990 Census Count of American Indians: What Do the Numbers Really Mean?" *Social Science Quarterly* 75 (September 1994): 580–593; Karl Eschbach, "The enduring and vanishing American Indian: American Indian population growth and intermarriage in 1990," *Ethnic and Racial Studies* 18 (January 1995): 89–108; Joane Nagel, *American Indian Ethnic Renewal: Red Power and the Resurgence of Identity and Culture* (New York: Oxford University Press, 1996), 83–112; C. Matthew Snipp, "Some observations about racial boundaries and the experiences of American Indians," *Ethnic and Racial Studies* 20 (October 1997): 667–689; Carol Morello, "Native American Roots, Once Hidden, Now Embraced," *Washington Post,* April 7, 2001, at A1; Sara Steindorf, "American Indians on the rise," *Christian Science Monitor,* December 6, 2001, 11, 13.

82. Russell Thornton, *American Indian Holocaust and Survival: A Population History Since 1492* (Norman: University of Oklahoma Press, 1987), 42–239; Rogers Worthington, "Who Belongs to Tribe? Casino Wealth Raises the Stakes," *Chicago Tribune,* May 28, 1994, at Sec. 1, at p. 1; Megan Garvey, "Wealthy Minnesota Tribe Is at Odds Over Quarters; Faction Wins Tribal Vote to Open Membership Rolls," *Washington Post,* April 21, 1995, A3; David Foster, "Intermarriage clouds claims of Indian ancestry," *Milwaukee Journal Sentinel,* January 27, 1997, 13.

83. Ibid.

84. Roger Sanjek, "Intermarriage and the Future of Races in the United States," in Steven Gregory and Roger Sanjek, eds., *Race* (New Brunswick, N.J.: Rutgers University Press, 1994), 103–116; Zhenchao Qian, "Breaking the Racial Barriers: Variations in Interracial Marriage Between 1980 and 1990," *Demography* 34 (May 1997): 263–276; Sean-Shong Hwang, Rogelio Saenz, and Benigno E. Aguirre, "Structural and Assimilationist Explanations of Asian American Intermarriage," *Journal of Marriage and the Family* 59 (August 1997): 758–772; Reynolds Farley, "Racial Issues: Recent Trends in Residential Patterns and Intermarriage," in Neil J. Smelser and Jeffrey C. Alexander, eds., *Diversity and Its Discontents: Cultural Conflict and Common Ground in Contemporary American Society* (Princeton, N.J.: Princeton University Press, 1999), 85–128; Roberto Suro, "Mixed Doubles," *American Demographics* 21 (November 1999): 56–62; Maria P. P. Root, *Love's Revolution: Interracial Marriage* (Philadelphia: Temple University Press, 2001); Darryl Fears and Claudia Deane, "Biracial Couples Report Tolerance; Survey Finds Most Are Accepted by Families," *Washington Post,* July 5, 2001, at A1.

85. On this issue, see Kara Joyner and Grace Kao, "School Racial Composition and Adolescent Racial Homophily," *Social Science Quarterly* 81 (September 2000): 810–825.

86. Michel Marriott, "Multiracial Americans Ready to Claim Their Own Identity," *New York Times,* July 20, 1996, Sec. 1, at p. 1. For personal narratives and some theoretical information, see Maria P. P. Root, ed., *Racially Mixed People in America* (Newbury Park, Calif.: Sage Publications, 1992); Lise Funder-

burg, *Black, White, Other: Biracial Americans Talk About Race and Identity* (New York: William Morrow and Company, 1994); Naomi Zack, ed., *American Mixed Race: The Culture of Microdiversity* (Lanham, Md.: Rowman & Little-field Publishers, 1995); Maria P. P. Root, ed., *The Multiracial Experience: Racial Borders as the New Frontier* (Thousand Oaks, Calif.: Sage Publications, 1996).

87. More than 92% (4,257,110) of the 4,602,146 non-Hispanic multiracials are biracial. The largest subgroups of non-Hispanic biracial Americans are: white/American Indian (969,238), white/Asian (811,240), white/Some Other Race (731,719), white/black (697,077), black/Some Other Race (255,966), Asian/Some Other Race (185,754), black/American Indian (168,022), Asian/Pacific Islander (129,130), and white/Pacific Islander (100,702). Most of the non-Hispanic multiracials who identified as part Some Other Race were probably part Latino. Another 6.7% of the non-Hispanic multiracials (311,029) were triracial, with three racial backgrounds. Only 0.6% (27,155) were part of the Tiger Woods camp, with four racial identities. Amazingly, 6,342 Americans claimed to have five backgrounds, and 510 identified with all six racial identities on the census form — white, black, Asian, American Indian, Pacific Islander, and Some Other Race.

88. Several parts of the country with substantial immigrant populations (Glendale, California, Dearborn, Michigan, and the Haitian-American precincts of Broward and Miami-Dade counties in Florida) registered higher-than-expected counts of mixed-race people in the 2000 census, which suggests that these communities are home to "phantom multiracials." In other words, the Armenians of Glendale, Middle Easterners of Dearborn, and Haitians of Broward and Miami-Dade counties selected two choices — their race, and then they wrote in their ethnic background as a way of drawing attention to their numbers. (Ethnic advocates encouraged this practice, in some cases.) For information about the phantom multiracials, see Laurent Belsie, "Profile rises for multiracial people," *Christian Science Monitor,* July 17, 2001, 3; and on the situation in South Florida, see Andrea Elliott and Jason Grotto, "2000 Census Beyond Black," *Miami Herald,* March 31, 2001, at 1A.

89. Michael A. Fletcher, "Woods Puts Personal Focus on Mixed-Race Identity," *Washington Post,* April 23, 1997, at A1; Earl Woods with Fred Mitchell, *Playing Through: Straight Talk on Hard Work, Big Dreams and Adventures with Tiger* (New York: HarperCollins, 1998), 192–210.

90. Suro, "Mixed Doubles," 62.

91. Davis, *Who Is Black?* 21.

92. Eric Schmitt, "Blacks Split on Disclosing Multiracial Roots," *New York Times,* March 31, 2001, at A1.

93. Robert Reinhold, "Government Expands 'Minority' Definition; Some Groups Protest," *New York Times,* July 30, 1978, Sec. 1, p. 33.

94. Jorge J. E. Gracia, "Affirmative Action for Hispanics? Yes and No," in Jorge J. E. Gracia and Pablo De Greiff, eds., *Hispanics/Latinos in the United States: Ethnicity, Race, and Rights* (New York: Routledge, 2000), 202–203.

95. Suzann Evinger, "How to Record Race," *American Demographics* 18 (May 1996): 36–41; Linda Mathews, "More Than Identity Rides on a New Racial Category," *New York Times,* July 6, 1996, Sec. 1, at p. 1; Clyde Tucker

and Brian Kojetin, "Testing racial and ethnic origin questions in the CPS supplement," *Monthly Labor Review* 119 (September 1996): 3–7; William O'Hare, "Managing Multiple-Race Data," *American Demographics* 20 (April 1998): 42–44; Christy Fisher, "It's All in the Details," *American Demographics* 20 (April 1998): 45–47.

96. Office of Management and Budget, "Provisional Guidance on the Implementation of the 1997 Standards for Federal Data on Race and Ethnicity." (Tabulation Working Group, Interagency Committee for the Review of Standards for Data on Race and Ethnicity, December 15, 2000), 60–72.

97. Ibid.

98. For background on these issues, see Samia El-Badry, "The Arab-American Market," *American Demographics* 16 (January 1994): 22–27, 30; Mehdi Bozorgmehr, Claudia Der-Martirosian, and Georges Sabagh, "Middle Easterners: A New Kind of Immigrant," in Roger Waldinger and Mehdi Bozorgmehr, eds., *Ethnic Los Angeles* (New York: Russell Sage Foundation, 1996), 345–378; Helen Hatab Samhan, "Not Quite White: Race Classification and the Arab-American Experience," in Michael W. Suleiman, ed., *Arabs in America: Building a New Future* (Philadelphia: Temple University Press, 1999), 209–226; Therese Saliba, "Resisting Invisibility: Arab Americans in Academia and Activism," in Michael W. Suleiman, ed., *Arabs in America: Building a New Future* (Philadelphia: Temple University Press, 1999), 304–319; Nadine Naber, "Ambiguous insiders: an investigation of Arab American invisibility," *Ethnic and Racial Studies* 23 (January 2000): 37–61.

99. Gordon Trowbridge, "Arab Americans lose out in census; No ethnic box costs political, economic clout," *Detroit News*, March 26, 2001, at C1.

100. Office of Management and Budget, "Standards for the Classification of Federal Data on Race and Ethnicity," *Federal Register* 60 (August 28, 1995): 44681; Office of Management and Budget, "Recommendations from the Interagency Committee for the Review of the Racial and Ethnic Standards to the Office of Management and Budget Concerning Changes to the Standards for the Classification of Federal Data on Race and Ethnicity," *Federal Register* 62 (July 9, 1997): 36932, 36934, 36936, 36940; Office of Management and Budget, "Revisions to the Standards for the Classification of Federal Data on Race and Ethnicity," *Federal Register* 62 (October 30, 1997): 58785, 58786, 58787.

101. Office of Management and Budget, "Revisions to the Standards for the Classification of Federal Data on Race and Ethnicity," 58787.

Chapter 2: White Like Who?

1. *Fun with Dick and Jane: A Commemorative Collection of Stories* (New York: Collins Publishers, 1996), 12–13.

2. Carole Kismaric and Marvin Heiferman, *Growing Up with Dick and Jane: Learning and Living the American Dream* (New York: Collins Publishers, 1996), passim; Trip Gabriel, " 'Oh, Jane, See How Popular We Are,' " *New York Times*, October 3, 1996, at C1.

3. Ibid.

4. Ibid.

5. Gabriel, " 'Oh, Jane, See How Popular We Are.' "

6. Sandra Stotsky, *Losing Our Language: How Multicultural Classroom Instruction Is Undermining Our Children's Ability to Read, Write, and Reason* (New York: Free Press, 1999).

7. Howard W. French, " 'Pearl Harbor' in Japan: Love or War?" *New York Times,* June 22, 2001, A3; Lisa Takeuchi Cullen, "A Kinder, Softer Movie," *Time* 157 (July 2, 2001): 37; Ilene R. Prusher, "On the other side, 'Pearl Harbor' is a hard sell," *Christian Science Monitor,* July 13, 2001, at p. 1; Doug Struck and Shigehiko Togo, "Sanitized 'Pearl Harbor' Romances Japanese," *Washington Post,* July 15, 2001, A22; Mark Magnier, "Japan Moviegoers Giving 'Pearl Harbor' a Boost," *Los Angeles Times,* July 19, 2001, Part 3, p. 1.

8. Karen De Witt, "In Japan, Blacks as Outsiders," *New York Times,* December 10, 1995, Sec. 4, p. 4; Howard W. French, "Disdainful of Foreigners, the Japanese Blame Them for Crime," *New York Times,* September 30, 1999, A17.

9. See, e.g., Daniel I. Okimoto, *American in Disguise* (New York: Walker/Weatherhill, 1971); David Mura, *Turning Japanese: Memoirs of a Sansei* (New York: Anchor Books/Doubleday, 1991).

10. Arthur M. Schlesinger Jr., *The Disuniting of America: Reflections on a Multicultural Society,* 2d ed. (New York: W. W. Norton & Company, 1998), especially 13–19.

11. David Hackett Fischer, *Albion's Seed: Four British Folkways in America* (New York: Oxford University Press, 1989), 870.

12. Ian Haney López, *White by Law: The Legal Construction of Race* (New York: New York University Press, 1996), passim; Rogers M. Smith, *Civic Ideals: Conflicting Visions of Citizenship in U.S. History* (New Haven, Conn.: Yale University Press, 1997).

13. Philip P. Pan, "U.S. Naturalization Rate Drops; 35% of Nation's Foreign-Born Are Citizens, the Least This Century," *Washington Post,* October 15, 1999, at A1; U.S. Census Bureau, *Statistical Abstract of the United States: 2000* (120th ed.) (Washington, D.C.: U.S. Government Printing Office, 2000), Tables 48 and 49.

14. Noel Ignatiev, *How the Irish Became White* (New York: Routledge, 1995); Karen Brodkin, *How Jews Became White Folks and What That Says about Race in America* (New Brunswick, N.J.: Rutgers University Press, 1998); Matthew Frye Jacobson, *Whiteness of a Different Color: European Immigrants and the Alchemy of Race* (Cambridge, Mass.: Harvard University Press, 1998); Desmond King, *Making Americans: Immigration, Race, and the Origins of the Diverse Democracy* (Cambridge, Mass.: Harvard University Press, 2000).

15. Ibid.

16. U.S. Census Bureau, *Statistical Abstract of the United States: 2000,* Table 75. For a good overview of race, ethnicity, and religion in the United States, see Barry A. Kosmin and Seymour P. Lachman, *One Nation Under God: Religion in Contemporary American Society* (New York: Harmony Books, 1993), 114–156. See, too, Diana L. Eck, *A New Religious America: How a "Christian Country" Has Now Become the World's Most Religiously Diverse Nation* (New York: HarperSanFrancisco, 2001).

17. C. Eric Lincoln and Lawrence H. Mamiya, *The Black Church in the African American Experience* (Durham, N.C.: Duke University Press, 1990); Cheryl Townsend Gilkes, "Plenty Good Room: Adaptation in a Changing Black Church," *Annals of the American Academy of Political and Social Science 558* (July 1998): 101–121.

18. Robert C. Christopher, *Crashing the Gates: The De-WASPing of America's Power Elite* (New York: Simon and Schuster, 1989); Richard Brookhiser, *The Way of the WASP: How It Made America, and How It Can Save It, So to Speak* (New York: Free Press, 1991); William Grimes, "The Day of the WASP; Is It Time for an Epitaph to Ruling Elite?" *New York Times*, August 25, 1996, Sec. 4, p. 3.

19. U.S. Census Bureau, *Statistical Abstract of the United States: 2000,* Table 75.

20. Alan M. Dershowitz, *The Vanishing American Jew: In Search of Jewish Identity for the Next Century* (Boston: Little, Brown and Company, 1997); Craig Horowitz, "Without a Prayer?" *New York* 30 (July 14, 1997): 30–37, 101, 108.

21. U.S. Census Bureau, *Statistical Abstract of the United States: 2000,* Table 75.

22. On American Muslims, see, e.g., Eck, *A New Religious America,* 222–293; Jane I. Smith, *Islam in America* (New York: Columbia University Press, 1999). There is some dispute over the number of Muslims in America. Muslim organizations claim seven million adherents, while scholars and researchers who study the Muslim community think the number may be somewhere between 1.5 and 4.1 million. See Bill Broadway, "Number of U.S. Muslims Depends on Who's Counting," *Washington Post,* November 24, 2001, at A1. Considering the available evidence, the researchers Howard Fienberg and Iain Murray write, "While a precise figure remains elusive, '2 million Muslims, give or take a few hundred thousand' appears to be America's most accurate number - for now." Howard Fienberg and Iain Murray, "How many US Muslims? Our best estimate," *Christian Science Monitor,* November 29, 2001, 11.

23. Eck, *A New Religious America,* 80–221.

24. Herbert J. Gans, "Symbolic ethnicity: The future of ethnic groups and cultures in America," *Ethnic and Racial Studies* 2 (January 1979): 1–20.

25. Richard D. Alba, *Ethnic Identity: The Transformation of White America* (New Haven, Conn.: Yale University Press, 1990). See, too, Mary C. Waters, *Ethnic Options: Choosing Identities in America* (Berkeley: University of California Press, 1990).

26. In the 1990 census, 12,300,701 Americans listed Irish as their single ancestry. Most of these individuals were probably 100% Irish.

27. Dinitia Smith, "The Irish Are Ascendant Again," *New York Times*, October 3, 1996, C15, C20; Dan Barry, "From Poets to Pubs, Irish Imports Are in Demand," *New York Times*, March 17, 1997, at A1; Chris Jones, "The Makin' o' the Green; Sentimental or Literary, If It's Irish, It's Likely to Sell," *Chicago Tribune*, March 13, 1998, 5; Marilyn Halter, *Shopping for Identity: The Marketing of Ethnicity* (New York: Schocken Books, 2000), 119–124.

28. In 1990, the most recent year for which data are available, 56.6% of the residents of Pella, Iowa, had Dutch ancestry. Conversely, 41.8% of the people in Holland, Michigan, reported they had Dutch antecedents.

29. Michael Brenson, "Is 'Quality' an Idea Whose Time Has Gone?" *New York Times,* July 22, 1990, Sec. 2, at p. 1; Stephanie B. Goldberg, "The Law, a New Theory Holds, Has a White Voice," *New York Times,* July 17, 1992, A23; Steven A. Holmes, "A Rage for Merit, Whatever That Is," *New York Times,* July 30, 1995, Sec. 4, p. 6. See, too, Stephen L. Carter, "Academic Tenure and 'White Male' Standards: Some Lessons from the Patent Law," *Yale Law Journal* 100 (May 1991): 2065–2085; Barbara Flagg, " 'Was Blind, But Now I See': White Race Consciousness and the Requirement of Discriminatory Intent," *Michigan Law Review* 91 (March 1993): 953–1017; Barbara J. Flagg, "Fashioning a Title VII Remedy for Transparently White Subjective Decisionmaking," *Yale Law Journal* 104 (June 1995): 2009–2051.

30. Quentin Hardy, "School of Thought: The Unbearable Whiteness of Being; A Number of College Scholars Race to Caucasian Studies," *Wall Street Journal,* April 24, 1997, at A1; Margaret Talbot, "Getting Credit for Being White," *New York Times Magazine* (November 30, 1997): 116–119; John Yemma, " 'Whiteness studies' an attempt at healing," *Boston Globe,* December 21, 1997, at A1; V. Dion Haynes, "Sponsors Say Studying 'Whiteness' Can Loosen Racism's Grip on Society," *Chicago Tribune,* February 25, 1998, 4; Laurent Belsie, "Scholars unearth new field: white studies," *Christian Science Monitor,* August 14, 2001, at p. 2.

31. Barnaby Conrad III, *The Blonde: A Celebration of the Golden Era from Harlow to Monroe* (San Francisco: Chronicle Books, 1999); Natalia Ilyin, *Blonde Like Me: The Roots of the Blonde Myth in Our Culture* (New York: Touchstone/ Simon & Schuster, 2000).

32. On this topic, see Mia Tuan, *Forever Foreigners or Honorary Whites? The Asian Ethnic Experience Today* (New Brunswick, N.J.: Rutgers University Press, 1998).

33. Ted Anthony, "The English Conquest; Nearly a Quarter of the Human Population — Whether They Like It or Not — Are Using What Is Fast Becoming the World's First Global Language," *Chicago Tribune,* April 24, 2000, at p. 1; Ted Anthony, "The 'New Englishes'; Welcome or Resented, Our Language Is More Pervasive Than Ever, and the New Speakers, from Nigeria to India to Singapore, Are Reshaping It," *Chicago Tribune,* April 25, 2000, at p. 1. For a different viewpoint, see Barbara Wallraff, "What Global Language?" *Atlantic Monthly* 286 (November 2000): 52–56, 58–61, 64, 66.

34. Strobe Talbott, "The Birth of the Global Nation," *Time* 140 (July 20, 1992): 70–71; Pico Iyer, *The Global Soul: Jet Lag, Shopping Malls, and the Search for Home* (New York: Alfred A. Knopf, 2000).

35. Michelle Conlin, "Hey, What About Us?" *BusinessWeek* (December 27, 1999): 52–55; Aaron Bernstein, "Backlash," *BusinessWeek* (April 24, 2000): 38–42, 44; "Globalization: What Americans Are Worried About," *BusinessWeek* (April 24, 2000): 44.

36. Jacob M. Schlesinger and Christina Duff, "No Jingo Jangle: As Foreigners Again Gobble Up U.S. Firms, Where's the Backlash?" *Wall Street Journal,*

December 15, 1998, at A1; Gerald F. Seib and Carla Anne Robbins, "Kosovo Campaign Suggests U.S.'s Special Bond to Europe Survives Despite Demographic Shifts," *Wall Street Journal,* March 30, 1999, A18, A23.

37. Benjamin Franklin, *Writings* (New York: Library of America, 1987), 374.

38. Maldwyn Allen Jones, *American Immigration,* 2d ed. (Chicago: University of Chicago Press, 1992), 23–25, 29, 30, 39–40.

39. Frederick C. Luebke, *Bonds of Loyalty: German-Americans and World War I* (DeKalb: Northern Illinois University Press, 1974).

40. Peter Beinart, "Punditry: Mittel America," *New Republic Online,* August 13, 2001. www.thenewrepublic.com/punditry/beinart081301.html.

41. John Harmon McElroy, *American Beliefs: What Keeps a Big Country and a Diverse People United* (Chicago: Ivan R. Dee, 1999).

42. Milton M. Gordon, *Assimilation in American Life: The Role of Race, Religion, and National Origins* (New York: Oxford University Press, 1964); Nathan Glazer, "Is Assimilation Dead?" *Annals of the American Academy of Political and Social Science* 530 (November 1993): 122–136; Russell A. Kazal, "Revisiting Assimilation: The Rise, Fall, and Reappraisal of a Concept in American Ethnic History," *American Historical Review* 100 (April 1995): 437–471; Richard Alba and Victor Nee, "Rethinking Assimilation Theory for a New Era of Immigration," in Charles Hirschman, Philip Kasinitz, and Josh DeWind, eds., *The Handbook of International Migration: The American Experience* (New York: Russell Sage Foundation, 1999), 137–160.

43. Schlesinger, *The Disuniting of America,* 142.

44. William A. McGeveran Jr., ed., *The World Almanac and Book of Facts 2002* (New York: World Almanac Books, 2002), 595.

45. Donna R. Gabaccia, *We Are What We Eat: Ethnic Food and the Making of Americans* (Cambridge, Mass.: Harvard University Press, 1998). See, too, Richard Pillsbury, *No Foreign Food: The American Diet in Time and Place* (Boulder, Colo.: Westview Press, 1998).

46. Molly O'Neill, "New Mainstream: Hot Dogs, Apple Pie and Salsa," *New York Times,* March 11, 1992, at C1; Janet Day, "Salsa Reigns King over Ketchup," *Denver Post,* March 22, 1992, at I1; Robert Berner, "Ketchuping Up, Or a Classic Condiment Returns as Top Dog," *Wall Street Journal,* November 5, 1999, at A1.

47. John Fetto, "An All-American Melting Pot," *American Demographics* 23 (July 2001): 8–10.

48. These data are from the 1990 census. The 2000 census results on this topic are not yet available. U.S. Census Bureau, *Statistical Abstract of the United States: 2000,* Table 50.

49. In his 1903 classic, *The Souls of Black Folk,* W. E. B. Du Bois opined, "One ever feels his two-ness, — an American, a Negro; two souls, two thoughts, two unreconciled strivings; two warring ideals in one dark body, whose dogged strength alone keeps it from being torn asunder." W. E. B. DuBois, *The Souls of Black Folk* (1903; reprint, with an introduction by John Edgar Wideman, New York: Vintage Books/Library of America, 1990), 8–9. For essays that analyze DuBois's formulation, see Gerald Early, ed., *Lure and Loathing: Essays on Race, Identity, and the Ambivalence of Assimilation* (New York: Viking, 1993).

50. Dinesh D'Souza, *The End of Racism: Principles for a Multiracial Society* (New York: Free Press, 1995), 337–340, 360–381; Stephan Thernstrom and Abigail Thernstrom, *America in Black and White: One Nation, Indivisible* (New York: Simon & Schuster, 1997), 369–373; Gerald Early, "Dreaming of a Black Christmas," *Harper's Magazine* 294 (January 1997): 55–61; Marjorie Coeyman, "Black Pride Drives This Public School," *Christian Science Monitor*, October 6, 1998, B6–B7; "Kwanzaa Becomes $700 Million Business," *Ebony* 56 (December–2000): 42, 45.

51. G. Pascal Zachary, "Tangled Roots: For African-Americans in Ghana, the Grass Isn't Always Greener," *Wall Street Journal*, March 14, 2001, at A1.

52. Gary Marx, "In Somalia, U.S. soldiers find a bond of blood, color, heritage," *Chicago Tribune*, January 17, 1993, 8; Paul Taylor, "In S. Africa, U.S. Blacks Find a Promising Land," *Washington Post*, December 11, 1994, at A1; Charles C. Moskos and John Sibley Butler, *All That We Can Be: Black Leadership and Racial Integration the Army Way* (New York: Basic Books, 1996), 35–36; Jim Sleeper, *Liberal Racism* (New York: Viking, 1997), 96–117; Keith Richburg, *Out of America: A Black Man Confronts Africa* (New York: Basic Books, 1997); Philippe Wamba, *Kinship: A Family's Journey in Africa and America* (New York: Dutton, 1999); Lena Williams, *It's the Little Things: The Everyday Interactions that Get Under the Skin of Blacks and Whites* (New York: Harcourt, 2000), 48–49.

53. http://summit.asylee.com/about.cfm.

54. Michael Rogin, *Blackface, White Noise: Jewish Immigrants in the Hollywood Melting Pot* (Berkeley: University of California Press, 1996); Dale Cockrell, *Demons of Disorder: Early Blackface Minstrels and Their World* (New York: Cambridge University Press, 1997); Susan Gubar, *Racechanges: White Skin, Black Face in American Culture* (New York: Oxford University Press, 1997); W. T. Lhamon Jr., *Raising Cain: Blackface Performance from Jim Crow to Hip Hop* (Cambridge, Mass.: Harvard University Press, 1998).

55. Philip J. Deloria, *Playing Indian* (New Haven, Conn.: Yale University Press, 1998).

56. See, e.g., Norman Mailer, "The White Negro," in Robert Walser, ed., *Keeping Time: Readings in Jazz History* (New York: Oxford University Press, 1999), 242–246.

57. Lena Williams, "In Looks, a Sense of Racial Unity," *New York Times*, May 9, 1990, at C1; " 'Wiggers': White teens identify with black hip-hoppers," *Detroit News*, April 25, 1993, at 1A; Farai Chideya, *The Color of Our Future* (New York: William Morrow and Company, 1999), 86–112.

58. On the topic of African Americans and their hair, see Noliwe M. Rooks, *Hair Raising: Beauty, Culture, and African American Women* (New Brunswick, N.J.: Rutgers University Press, 1996); Ingrid Banks, *Hair Matters: Beauty, Power, and Black Women's Consciousness* (New York: New York University Press, 2000); Ayana D. Byrd and Lori L. Tharps, *Hair Story: Untangling the Roots of Black Hair in America* (New York: St. Martin's Press, 2001).

59. U.S. Census Bureau, *Statistical Abstract of the United States: 2000*, Table 51.

60. Ibid., Table 288.

61. For information about bilingual education, see Kenji Hakuta, *Mirror of Language: The Debate on Bilingualism* (New York: Basic Books, 1986); Rosalie Pedalino Porter, *Forked Tongue: The Politics of Bilingual Education* (New York: Basic Books, 1990); James Crawford, *Hold Your Tongue: Bilingualism and the Politics of "English Only"* (Reading, Mass.: Addison-Wesley Publishing Company, 1992), 75–89, 203–232; John J. Miller, *The Unmaking of Americans: How Multiculturalism Has Undermined the Assimilation Ethic* (New York: Free Press, 1998), 174–208; Christian J. Faltis and Paula M. Wolfe, eds., *So Much to Say: Adolescents, Bilingualism, and ESL in the Secondary School* (New York: Teachers College Press, 1999); David L. Leal and Frederick M. Hess, "The Politics of Bilingual Education Expenditures in Urban School Districts," *Social Science Quarterly* 81 (December 2000): 1064–1072.

62. J. N. Hook, *Family Names: How Our Surnames Came to America* (New York: Macmillan Publishing Company, 1982).

63. Brunner, ed., *TIME Almanac 2002*, 135. See, too, H. Amanda Robb and Andrew Chesler, *Encyclopedia of American Family Names* (New York: HarperCollins Publishers, 1995).

64. Stanley Lieberson and Kelly S. Mikelson, "Distinctive African American Names: An Experimental, Historical, and Linguistic Analysis of Innovation," *American Sociological Review* 60 (December 1995): 928–946.

65. Brunner, ed., *TIME Almanac 2002*, 135.

66. David Stout, "Whatever Happened to John?" *New York Times*, September 21, 1997, Sec. 1, p. 51; Maria Puente, "What's in a name? USA's changing face," *USA Today*, January 15, 1999, 8A.

67. U.S. Census Bureau, *Statistical Abstract of the United States: 2000*, Table 47.

68. William Booth, "One Nation, Indivisible: Is It History? Soon, No Single Group Will Comprise Majority," *Washington Post*, February 22, 1998, at A1; William Branigin, "Immigrants Question Idea of Assimilation," *Washington Post*, May 25, 1998, at A1; Amy Goldstein and Roberto Suro, "A Journey in Stages; Assimilation's Pull Is Still Strong, but Its Pace Varies," *Washington Post*, January 16, 2000, at A1.

69. I visited Tahlequah on September 5, 1999, and on October 30, 2000. Tahlequah erected the present-day bilingual street signs around 1965, according to Sally Ross, who was the city clerk at the time. Sally Ross, telephone conversation with author, November 22, 2000.

70. Carol Young, telephone conversation with author, January 18, 2001. Young, who is Pawnee and Kiowa, serves as the program coordinator of the Center for Tribal Studies and the co-chair of the Symposium on the American Indian at Northeastern State University. In addition, she is the driving force behind the Indian University Scholars Society, an honor society for Native American students at NSU. Young characterizes NSU as an "excellent" place for Indian students, and she spends much of her time recruiting them to the school.

71. Gary McClure, interview by author, Tahlequah, Oklahoma, October 30, 2000. McClure's wife is three-sixteenths Cherokee, and his two sons are enrolled members of the Cherokee Nation.

72. Vine Deloria Jr. and Clifford M. Lytle, _The Nations Within: The Past and Future of American Indian Sovereignty_ (New York: Pantheon Books, 1984), 2–15; Cesare Marino, "Reservations," in Mary B. Davis, ed., _Native America in the Twentieth Century: An Encyclopedia_ (New York: Garland Publishing, 1994), 554.

73. _Cherokee Nation v. Georgia,_ 30 U.S. 1 (1831).

74. _Worcester v. Georgia,_ 31 U.S. 515 (1832). For the quotation, see 31 U.S. 515 (1832), 561.

75. Janet A. McDonnell, _The Dispossession of the American Indian, 1887–1934_ (Bloomington: Indiana University Press, 1991). On the whites' largely successful efforts to take the Indians' land, see Paula Mitchell Marks, _In a Barren Land: American Indian Dispossession and Survival_ (New York: William Morrow and Company, 1998), 1–269.

76. Robert F. Berkhofer Jr., _The White Man's Indian: Images of the American Indian from Columbus to the Present_ (New York: Vintage Books, 1979), 113–194; Brian W. Dippie, _The Vanishing American: White Attitudes and U.S. Indian Policy_ (Lawrence: University Press of Kansas, 1982), 45–78, 95–196, 297–344; Frederick E. Hoxie, _A Final Promise: The Campaign to Assimilate the Indians, 1880–1920_ (Lincoln: University of Nebraska Press, 1984).

77. Deloria and Lytle, _The Nations Within,_ 215–243; Joane Nagel, _American Indian Ethnic Renewal: Red Power and the Resurgence of Identity and Culture_ (New York: Oxford University Press, 1996), passim.

78. Deloria and Lytle, _The Nations Within,_ 140–182; Marks, _In a Barren Land,_ 270–349.

79. For the most recent listing of tribes, see Department of the Interior, Bureau of Indian Affairs, "Indian Entities Recognized and Eligible to Receive Services from the United States Bureau of Indian Affairs," _Federal Register_ 65 (March 13, 2000): 13298–13303.

80. Peter Beinart, "Lost Tribes," _Lingua Franca_ 9 (May/June 1999): 32–41.

81. Gregory R. Campbell, "Indian Health Service," in Mary B. Davis, ed., _Native America in the Twentieth Century: An Encyclopedia_ (New York: Garland Publishing, 1994), 256–261; Stephen J. Kunitz, "The History and Politics of US Health Care Policy for American Indians and Alaskan Natives," _American Journal of Public Health_ 86 (October 1996): 1464–1473; Alyce Adams, "The Road Not Taken: How Tribes Choose between Tribal and Indian Health Service Management of Health Care Resources," _American Indian Culture and Research Journal_ 24:3 (2000): 21–38.

82. Duane Champagne, "Bureau of Indian Affairs (BIA)," in Mary B. Davis, ed., _Native America in the Twentieth Century: An Encyclopedia_ (New York: Garland Publishing, 1994), 80–84; Michael Satchell and David Bowermaster, "The worst federal agency," _U.S. News & World Report_ 117 (November 28, 1994): 61–64; William Claiborne, "At Indian Affairs, a Tough Act to Balance; Interior Official Challenges Convention to Seek Middle Ground for Tribes, Lawmakers," _Washington Post,_ November 17, 1998, A25; William Claiborne, " 'Brother, We Aren't with You'; Kevin Gover Enjoyed a Honeymoon with Tribes as Head of Indian Affairs. A Series of Bitter Disputes Has Ended It," _Washington Post,_ August 5, 1999, A3; William Claiborne, "Tribes and Tribulations: BIA Seeks to Lose

a Duty; Indians' Casino Rush Overwhelms Agency's Recognition Staff," *Washington Post,* June 2, 2000, A31; Ellen Nakashima, "At BIA, Seeking More for Tribes to Bet On; McCaleb Makes Pitch for Energy Development," *Washington Post,* July 24, 2001, A19; Tom Kenworthy, "Native Americans could win $10B over century-old dispute; David vs. Goliath battle over Indian trust fund may profit 500,000 people," *USA Today,* February 14, 2002, at 1A.

83. While researching this book, I went to 95 federal Indian reservations in 29 states: Iowa, Maine, Idaho, Texas, Kansas, Nevada, Oregon, Florida, Arizona, Montana, Alabama, Michigan, Colorado, Oklahoma, Nebraska, Louisiana, Minnesota, Wisconsin, Washington, California, Connecticut, Mississippi, New York, New Mexico, the Dakotas, the Carolinas, and Rhode Island. For the demographics of Indian Country, see Veronica E. Velarde Tiller, ed., *Tiller's Guide to Indian Country: Economic Profiles of American Indian Reservations* (Albuquerque, N.Mex.: BowArrow Publishing Company, 1996).

84. James Brooke, "Indian Country Finds a Capital in Denver," *New York Times,* February 22, 1999, A12.

85. "On Indian Reservations in the West, Violent Crime Soars," *New York Times,* August 16, 1998, Sec. 1, p. 28; William Claiborne, "As Law Forces Erode, Violent Crime Grows on Indian Lands," *Washington Post,* October 11, 1998, A3; Fox Butterfield, "Indians Are Crime Victims at Rate Above U.S. Average," *New York Times,* February 15, 1999, A12; Kevin Johnson, "Tribal police isolated in darkness, distance," *USA Today,* March 22, 2000, 19A, 20A.

86. The statistics about Indian gaming come from the National Indian Gaming Association at www.indiangaming.org/library/index.html. For helpful information about this topic, see Joseph G. Jorgensen, "Gaming and Recent American Indian Economic Development," *American Indian Culture and Research Journal* 22:3 (1998): 157–172; Jerry Useem, "The Big Gamble," *Fortune* 142 (October 2, 2000): 222–226, 228–230, 234–236, 238, 240, 242, 244; W. Dale Mason, *Indian Gaming: Tribal Sovereignty and American Politics* (Norman: University of Oklahoma Press, 2000); Jerome L. Levine, ed., *Indian Gaming Handbook, Part I,* 2001 Edition (Los Angeles: Holland & Knight, 2001); Jerome L. Levine, ed., *Indian Gaming Handbook, Part II,* 2001 Edition (Los Angeles: Holland & Knight, 2001).

87. Ibid.

88. Todd S. Purdum, "Ruling in California Crimps Indian Plans for a Casino Empire," *New York Times,* August 24, 1999, at A1; Andrew Pollack, "Las Vegas Glitz Is Set to Go West; Tribes in California Scramble to Expand Casinos After Vote," *New York Times,* March 10, 2000, at C1; David Plotz, "Jackpot: How Indians took over California politics," *New Republic* 222 (March 13, 2000): 26–29; William Booth, "Tribes Ride a Casino Dream; Fortunes, Apprehension Grow for California Indians," *Washington Post,* May 9, 2000, at A1.

89. William Claiborne, "Tribes' Big Step: From Casinos to Conglomerates," *Washington Post,* August 14, 1998, at A1; Kathy Khoury, "Big Business, Not Betting, as Boom for Many Tribes," *Christian Science Monitor,* September 22, 1998, at p. 1; Char Simons, "Enterprising tribes look beyond casinos," *Christian Science Monitor,* October 22, 2001, 20.

90. Marks, *In a Barren Land*, 316–377; Fergus M. Bordewich, *Killing the White Man's Indian: Reinventing Native Americans at the End of the Twentieth Century* (New York: Doubleday, 1996), 93–128, 313–315, 323–329; David E. Wilkins, *American Indian Sovereignty and the U.S. Supreme Court: The Masking of Justice* (Austin: University of Texas Press, 1997); Shepard Krech III, *The Ecological Indian: Myth and History* (New York: W. W. Norton & Company, 1999), 213–228.

91. Timothy Egan, "Senate Measures Would Deal Blow to Indian Rights," *New York Times*, August 27, 1997, at A1; Timothy Egan, "Now, a White Backlash Against Rich Indians," *New York Times*, September 7, 1997, Sec. 4, p. 3; Timothy Egan, "New Prosperity Brings New Conflict to Indian Country," *New York Times*, March 8, 1998, Sec. 1, at p. 1; Timothy Egan, "Backlash Growing as Indians Make a Stand for Sovereignty," *New York Times*, March 9, 1998, at A1; Brad Knickerbocker, "Tribal Nations Fight Challenges to Their Sovereignty," *Christian Science Monitor*, April 3, 1998, at p. 1; V. Dion Haynes, "In Twist of History, Native Americans Called Aggressors," *Chicago Tribune*, July 5, 1998, 5.

92. Ibid.

93. Ibid.

94. The Winter 1988 issue of *Human Organization* includes seven informative articles under the heading "Indian Language Renewal," while the entire Winter 1995 issue of *Bilingual Research Journal* — "Indigenous Language Education and Literacy" — is devoted to this topic. See, too, Gina Cantoni, ed., *Stabilizing Indigenous Languages* (Flagstaff: Northern Arizona University: Center for Excellence in Education, 1996); David H. DeJong, "Is Immersion the Key to Language Renewal?" *Journal of American Indian Education* 37 (Spring 1998): 31–46.

95. Marks, *In a Barren Land*, 377–380; Bordewich, *Killing the White Man's Indian*, 329–330, 336–339; Leslie Goffe, "Hitting the Genetic Jackpot," *Utne Reader* (May/June 1999): 76–78.

96. Wayne A. Cornelius, Philip L. Martin, and James F. Hollifield, eds., *Controlling Immigration: A Global Perspective* (Stanford, Calif.: Stanford University Press, 1994), especially the excellent chapters about France, Germany, Belgium, Britain, Italy, Spain, and Japan, respectively; Heinz Fassmann and Rainer Münz, eds., *European Migration in the Late Twentieth Century: Historical Patterns, Actual Trends, and Social Implications* (Laxenburg, Austria: International Institute for Applied Systems Analysis, 1994). See, too, Emma Daley, "New Wall for 'Fortress Europe,' " *Christian Science Monitor*, August 27, 1998, at p. 1; R. Jeffrey Smith, "Europe Bids Immigrants Unwelcome; Natives Resent Changes in 'Their Way of Life,' " *Washington Post*, July 23, 2000, at A1; Stephen Baker, Kerry Cappel, and Kate Carlisle, "Crime and Politics," *BusinessWeek* (March 18, 2002): 50–51.

97. Ibid.

98. Eighty-six percent of Canadians are of European descent (people from the British Isles outnumber Franco Canadians and other Europeans). Eleven percent of Canadians qualify as "visible minorities," a category the Canadian government defines to include the Chinese, South Asians, blacks, Arabs and West Asians, Filipinos, Southeast Asians, the Japanese, and Koreans. Three percent of Canadians

claim Chinese ancestry, making them the largest visible minority in Canada. Finally, three percent of Canadians are from an indigenous ethnic group. Data from the 1996 Canadian census are available at the Web site of Statistics Canada (www.statcan.ca).

99. Australia is 92% white and 7% Asian. McGeveran, ed., *The World Almanac and Book of Facts 2002,* 771.

100. U.S. Census Bureau, *Statistical Abstract of the United States: 2000,* Table 1353.

101. Michael S. Teitelbaum and Jay Winter, *A Question of Numbers: High Migration, Low Fertility, and the Politics of National Identity* (New York: Hill & Wang, 1998); Peter G. Peterson, *Gray Dawn: How the Coming Age Wave Will Transform America — and the World* (New York: Times Books/Random House, 1999), 66–84; Phillip J. Longman, "The World Turns Gray," *U.S. News & World Report* 126 (March 1, 1999): 30–35, 38–39; Peter Ford, "Can a graying Europe still support itself?" *Christian Science Monitor,* January 21, 2000, at p. 1; Anne Swardson, "Pensions Threaten European Economies; Governments Ill-Prepared for Crisis of Retiring Baby Boomers," *Washington Post,* April 26, 2000, at A1.

102. Philip L. Martin, "Germany: Reluctant Land of Immigration," in Wayne A. Cornelius, Philip L. Martin, and James F. Hollifield, eds., *Controlling Immigration: A Global Perspective* (Stanford, Calif.: Stanford University Press, 1994), 189–225; Hedwig Rudolph, "Dynamics of Immigration in a Nonimmigrant Country: Germany," in Heinz Fassmann and Rainer Münz, eds., *European Migration in the Late Twentieth Century: Historical Patterns, Actual Trends, and Social Implications* (Laxenburg, Austria: International Institute for Applied Systems Analysis, 1994), 113–126; William Drozdiak, "Germany Begins to Accept Changing Ethnic Makeup; Naturalization Process May Be Eased," *Washington Post,* April 28, 1997, at A1; William Drozdiak, "Immigrants to Become Citizens of Germany; New Legislation Sets Off Fierce Debate," *Washington Post,* November 28, 1998, A17; Deidre Berger, "Germany redefining Germans," *Christian Science Monitor,* January 11, 1999, at p. 1; Ayla Jean Yackley, "Turks, Fearing Loss of Heritage, Reject German Citizenship," *Chicago Tribune,* February 18, 2000, Sec. 1, p. 4; Jack Ewing et al., "Help Wanted," *BusinessWeek* (September 17, 2001): 52–53.

103. George Wehrfritz and Hideko Takayama, "The Japan That Can Say Yes," *Newsweek* 135 (June 5, 2000): 34–35.

Chapter 3: Latino America

1. This vignette draws upon my observations during my two visits to Hialeah. I went to Hialeah in May 2000 and February 2001.

2. The John F. Kennedy Library (Hialeah, Florida) Page. www.ci.hialeah.fl.us/library/about/

3. Latin Americans use the term America in reference to the entire Western Hemisphere. To Latin Americans, someone from Quito or Tegucigalpa is just as much an American, if not more so, than a Chicagoan or an Angeleno. Spanish speakers in the Western Hemisphere describe people from the United States as *norteamericanos,* or North Americans. Like most Americans, I use "United

States" and "America" interchangeably, even though many Latin Americans question this practice.

4. In fact, Miami-Dade's 650,601 Cubans account for 52.4% of the entire Cuban-American population. More than two-thirds (67.1%) of all Cuban Americans live in Florida.

5. Mireya Navarro, "Black and Cuban-American: Bias in 2 Worlds," *New York Times,* September 13, 1997, Sec. 1, p. 8; Mirta Ojito, "Best of Friends, Worlds Apart," in Correspondents of The New York Times, *How Race Is Lived in America: Pulling Together, Pulling Apart* (New York: Times Books/Henry Holt and Company, 2001), 23–39.

6. For an overview of the differences that separate the Cuban exiles in South Florida, see Mireya Navarro, "Miami's Exiles: Side by Side, Yet Worlds Apart," *New York Times,* February 11, 1999, at A1.

7. David Rieff, "From Exiles to Immigrants," *Foreign Affairs* 74 (July/August 1995): 76–89.

8. Alejandro Portes and Alex Stepick, *City on the Edge: The Transformation of Miami* (Berkeley: University of California Press, 1993).

9. Fouad Ajami, "TRB: Dire Straits," *New Republic* 222 (May 1, 2000): 6.

10. Rick Bragg, "Stand over Cuban Highlights a Virtual Secession of Miami," *New York Times,* April 1, 2000, at A1; April Witt, "Elian Impasse Widens Miami's Ethnic Divides; Cuban Americans Growing Frustrated," *Washington Post,* April 16, 2000, at A1.

11. I visited the Dominican Republic from May 25–27, 2000.

12. Sammy Sosa with Marcos Bretón, *Sosa: An Autobiography* (New York: Warner Books, 2000), 40.

13. William A. McGeveran Jr., ed., *The World Almanac and Book of Facts 2002* (New York: World Almanac Books, 2002), 790.

14. Harry Hoetink, "The Dominican Republic in the Nineteenth Century: Some Notes on Stratification, Immigration, and Race," in Magnus Mörner, ed., *Race and Class in Latin America* (New York: Columbia University Press, 1970), 96–121; Peter Winn, *Americas: The Changing Face of Latin America and the Caribbean* (New York: Pantheon Books, 1992), 277–280, 284–294; Silvio Torres-Saillant, "The Tribulations of Blackness: Stages in Dominican Racial Identity," *Latin American Perspectives* 25 (May 1998): 126–146; Ernesto Sagás, *Race and Politics in the Dominican Republic* (Gainesville: University Press of Florida, 2000).

15. Herbert S. Klein, *African Slavery in Latin America and the Caribbean* (New York: Oxford University Press, 1986).

16. Gail Edmondson and Elisabeth Malkin, "Spain's Surge," *Business Week* (May 22, 2000): 73–74, 76, 80; Mike Zellner and Raymond Colitt, "The Spanish Acquisition: The Final Adventure," *Latin Trade* 9 (April 2001): 40–45.

17. Mauricio Solaún and Sidney Kronus, *Discrimination Without Violence: Miscegenation and Racial Conflict in Latin America* (New York: John Wiley & Sons, 1973), 54–56.

18. Wynn, *Americas,* passim; Magnus Mörner, *Race Mixture in the History of Latin America* (Boston: Little, Brown and Company, 1967); Magnus Mörner, ed., *Race and Class in Latin America* (New York: Columbia University Press,

1970); Robert Brent Toplin, ed., *Slavery and Race Relations in Latin America* (Westport, Conn.: Greenwood Press, 1974); Jorge I. Domínguez, ed., *Race and Ethnicity in Latin America* (New York: Garland Publishing, 1994); Darién J. Davis, ed., *Slavery and Beyond: The African Impact on Latin America and the Caribbean* (Wilmington, Del.: SR Books, 1995); Claudio Esteva-Fabregat, *Mestizaje in Ibero-America,* trans. John Wheat (Tucson: University of Arizona Press, 1995); Thomas M. Stephens, *Dictionary of Latin American Racial and Ethnic Terminology,* 2d ed. (Gainesville: University Press of Florida, 1999); Alison Brysk, *From Tribal Village to Global Village: Indian Rights and International Relations in Latin America* (Stanford, Calif.: Stanford University Press, 2000).

19. Susan Ferriss, "Typical American still white to most in Mexico," *The Atlanta Constitution,* September 16, 1998, at A4; Marc Edelman, "Waiting for Fidel," *Dissent* 45 (Fall 1998): 13.

20. For a good overview of these issues, see Lester D. Langley, *America and the Americas: The United States in the Western Hemisphere* (Athens: University of Georgia Press, 1989); Michael J. Kryzanek, *U.S.-Latin American Relations,* 3d ed. (Westport, Conn.: Praeger, 1996).

21. McGeveran, ed., *The World Almanac and Book of Facts 2002,* 770, 775, 782, 784, 786, 787, 790, 791, 792, 800, 803, 829, 834, 837, 838, 839, 862, 863.

22. Ibid., 792.

23. CIA, *The World Factbook 2000 — Honduras,* available at www.cia.gov/cia/publications/factbook/geos/ho.html#People.

24. CIA, *The World Factbook 2000 — Guatemala,* available at www.cia/gov/cia/publications/factbook/geos/gt.html#People. See, too, Kay B. Warren, *Indigenous Movements and Their Critics: Pan-Maya Activism in Guatemala* (Princeton, N.J.: Princeton University Press, 1998); Greg Grandin, *The Blood of Guatemala: A History of Race and Nation* (Durham, N.C.: Duke University Press, 2000).

25. Hugh Thomas, *Cuba: The Pursuit of Freedom* (New York: Harper & Row, 1971), especially 168–189, 281–292, 429–432, 514–524, 601–602, 1100–1101, 1117–1126, 1432–1434, 1511–1529; Franklin W. Knight, "Slavery, Race, and Social Structure in Cuba During the Nineteenth Century," in Robert Brent Toplin, ed., *Slavery and Race Relations in Latin America* (Westport, Conn.: Greenwood Press, 1974), 204–227; Marianne Masferrer and Carmelo Mesa-Lago, "The Gradual Integration of the Black in Cuba: Under the Colony, the Republic, and the Revolution," in Robert Brent Toplin, ed., *Slavery and Race Relations in Latin America* (Westport, Conn.: Greenwood Press, 1974), 348–384; Aline Helg, *Our Rightful Share: The Afro-Cuban Struggle for Equality, 1886–1912* (Chapel Hill: University of North Carolina Press, 1995); Ada Ferrer, *Insurgent Cuba: Race, Nation, and Revolution, 1868–1898* (Chapel Hill: University of North Carolina Press, 1999).

26. Sanford J. Ungar, *Fresh Blood: The New American Immigrants* (New York: Simon & Schuster, 1995), 204–205.

27. CIA, *The World Factbook 2000 — Cuba,* available at www.cia/gov/cia/publications/factbook/geos/cu.html#People.

28. Ricardo Chavira, "Black Cubans continue to battle racism; Government panel studying problems," *Dallas Morning News,* September 17, 1998, at 1A; Eugene Robinson, "Cuba Begins to Answer Its Race Question," *Washington*

Post, November 12, 2000, at A1; Pedro Pérez Sarduy and Jean Stubbs, eds., *Afro-Cuban Voices: On Race and Identity in Contemporary Cuba* (Gainesville: University Press of Florida, 2000).

29. Ronald Fernandez, Serafín Méndez Méndez, and Gail Cueto, *Puerto Rico Past and Present: An Encyclopedia* (Westport, Conn.: Greenwood Press, 1998), 49–50.

30. Maxine W. Gordon, "Race Patterns and Prejudice in Puerto Rico," *American Sociological Review* 14 (April 1949): 294–301; Maxine W. Gordon, "Cultural Aspects of Puerto Rico's Race Problem," *American Sociological Review* 15 (June 1950): 382–392; E. Seda Bonilla, "Social Structure and Race Relations," *Social Forces* 40 (December 1961): 141–148; Melvin M. Tumin with Arnold S. Feldman, *Social Class and Social Change in Puerto Rico,* 2d ed. (Indianapolis: Bobbs-Merrill Company, 1971), 227–246; Thomas G. Mathews, "The Question of Color in Puerto Rico," in Robert Brent Toplin, ed., *Slavery and Race Relations in Latin America* (Westport, Conn.: Greenwood Press, 1974), 299–323; Jay Kinsbruner, *Not of Pure Blood: The Free People of Color and Racial Prejudice in Nineteenth-Century Puerto Rico* (Durham, N.C.: Duke University Press, 1996).

31. The Hispanic population of Puerto Rico is 96.3% Puerto Rican. Dominicans constitute 1.5% of the Latinos on the island. U.S. Census Bureau, *The Hispanic Population: 2000* (U.S. Census Bureau, May 2001), 5.

32. Fernandez, Méndez Méndez, and Cueto, *Puerto Rico Past and Present,* 105–107. For other recent sources, see Clara E. Rodríguez, *Puerto Ricans: Born in the U.S.A.* (Boston: Unwin Hyman, 1989), 49–84; Clara E. Rodríguez, "Challenging Racial Hegemony: Puerto Ricans in the United States," in Steven Gregory and Roger Sanjek, eds., *Race* (New Brunswick, N.J.: Rutgers University Press, 1994), 131–145; Ellis Cose, *Color-Blind: Seeing Beyond Race in a Race-Obsessed World* (New York: HarperCollins Publishers, 1997), 15–16, 198–206; Ivan Roman, "Puerto Ricans Confront Race Issue; Civil-Rights Activists Intend to Use New Census Figures to Expose Racism and Discrimination on the Island," *Orlando Sentinel,* March 31, 2001, at A1.

33. Rodríguez, *Puerto Ricans,* 49–84; Bonnie Urciuoli, *Exposing Prejudice: Puerto Rican Experiences of Language, Race, and Class* (Boulder, Colo.: Westview Press, 1996), passim.

34. Gonzalo Aguirre Beltrán, "The Integration of the Negro into the National Society of Mexico," in Magnus Mörner, ed., *Race and Class in Latin America* (New York: Columbia University Press, 1970), 11–27; Moisés González Navarro, "*Mestizaje* in Mexico During the National Period," in Magnus Mörner, ed., *Race and Class in Latin America* (New York: Columbia University Press, 1970), 145–155; Alan Knight, "Racism, Revolution, and *Indigenismo:* Mexico, 1910–1940," in Richard Graham, ed., *The Idea of Race in Latin America, 1870–1940* (Austin: University of Texas Press, 1990), 71–113; Richard Lee Marks, *Cortés: The Great Adventurer and the Fate of Aztec Mexico* (New York: Alfred A. Knopf, 1993); Hugh Thomas, *Conquest: Montezuma, Cortés, and the Fall of Old Mexico* (New York: Simon & Schuster, 1994); Boye Lafayette De Mente, *NTC's Dictionary of Mexican Cultural Code Words* (Lincolnwood, Ill.: NTC Publishing Group, 1996), xiv–xxxi, 75–77, 132–139, 160–162, 193–197; Enrique Krauze, *Mexico:*

Biography of Power: A History of Modern Mexico, 1810–1996, trans. Hank Heifetz (New York: HarperCollins Publishers, 1997), 51–59.

35. De Mente, *NTC's Dictionary of Mexican Cultural Code Words,* xiv–xxxi, 75–77, 132–139, 160–162, 193–197; Krauze, *Mexico,* 51–59.

36. Anthony DePalma, "Racism? Mexico's in Denial," *New York Times,* June 11, 1995, Sec. 4, p. 4; De Mente, *NTC's Dictionary of Mexican Cultural Code Words,* 75–77, 132–139, 160–162, 193–197; Tracey Eaton, "Mexican blacks want recognition; Many say their troubles ignored or overshadowed by Zapatistas," *Dallas Morning News,* March 4, 1996, at 1A; Tim L. Merrill and Ramón Miró, eds., *Mexico: A Country Study* (Washington, D.C.: U.S. Government Printing Office, 1997), 92, 95, 96–97.

37. Brysk, *From Tribal Village to Global Village,* 263–265; Kevin Sullivan, "A Civil Rights March, Mexico-Style; Rebels to Lead Caravan to Capital to Highlight Plight of Indians," *Washington Post,* February 25, 2001, A20; Ginger Thompson, "Mexican Rebels' Hopes Meet Hard Indian Reality," *New York Times,* March 3, 2001, A4; Ginger Thompson and Tim Weiner, "Zapatista Rebels Rally in Mexico City," *New York Times,* March 12, 2001, A6; Kevin Sullivan, "Rebels Arrive in Mexico City; Welcoming Crowd Shows Support for Indian Rights," *Washington Post,* March 12, 2001, A10; Ginger Thompson and Tim Weiner, "Zapatista Leaders Make Their Case to Mexico's Congress," *New York Times,* March 29, 2001, A4; Kevin Sullivan, "Measure on Mexican Indians' Rights Gets Mixed Reviews," *Washington Post,* April 30, 2001, A10; Dan Murphy, "Reforms falter for Mexican Indians," *Christian Science Monitor,* September 5, 2001, 6.

38. Kevin Burr, interview by author, Garden City, Kansas, October 31, 2000.

39. Donald D. Stull, Michael J. Broadway, and Ken C. Erickson, "The Price of a Good Steak: Beef Packing and Its Consequences for Garden City, Kansas," in Louise Lamphere, ed., *Structuring Diversity: Ethnographic Perspectives on the New Immigration* (Chicago: University of Chicago Press, 1992), 35–64; Deborah Sontag, "New Immigrants Test Nation's Heartland," *New York Times,* October 18, 1993, at A1; Rob Gurwitt, "Keeping the Heart in the Heartland," *Wilson Quarterly* 22 (Spring 1998): 28–36.

40. Mexican Americans and Mexican immigrants do not always get along very well in southwestern Kansas. *Newsweek* reports that there are periodic cultural clashes between the two groups in Garden City and Dodge City. Arian Campo-Flores, "Brown Against Brown," *Newsweek* 136 (September 18, 2000): 49, 51.

41. Burr, interview.

42. Ibid.

43. Ibid.

44. Nancie L. González, *The Spanish-Americans of New Mexico: A Heritage of Pride* (Albuquerque: University of New Mexico Press, 1967); Richard L. Nostrand, *The Hispano Homeland* (Norman: University of Oklahoma Press, 1992).

45. *Hernandez v. Texas,* 347 U.S. 475 (1954).

46. The literature on the ambiguous racial status of Mexicans in the United States focuses, appropriately, on Texas and California. See Tomás Al-

maguer, *Racial Fault Lines: The Historical Origins of White Supremacy in California* (Berkeley: University of California Press, 1994), 45–104; Camille Guerin-Gonzales, *Mexican Workers and American Dreams: Immigration, Repatriation, and California Farm Labor, 1900–1939* (New Brunswick, N.J.: Rutgers University Press, 1994), 51–75; Martha Menchaca, *The Mexican Outsiders: A Community History of Marginalization and Discrimination in California* (Austin: University of Texas Press, 1995); Neil Foley, *The White Scourge: Mexicans, Blacks, and Poor Whites in Texas Cotton Culture* (Berkeley: University of California Press, 1997).

47. Frederick G. Bohme, ed., *200 Years of U.S. Census Taking: Population and Housing Questions, 1790–1990* (Washington, D.C.: U.S. Government Printing Office, 1989), 60.

48. Ibid., 78.

49. Jack D. Forbes, "The Hispanic Spin: Party Politics and Governmental Manipulation of Ethnic Identity," *Latin American Perspectives* 19 (Fall 1992): 63–77; Lawrence Wright, "One Drop of Blood," *New Yorker* 70 (July 25, 1994): 50, 52, 53; Geoffrey Fox, *Hispanic Nation: Culture, Politics, and the Constructing of Identity* (Secaucus, N.J.: Birch Lane Press/Carol Publishing Group, 1996), 67–142; Clara E. Rodríguez, *Changing Race: Latinos, the Census, and the History of Ethnicity in the United States* (New York: New York University Press, 2000).

50. For background on the factors that lead Latinos to choose "Some Other Race" on the Census form in response to the race question, see Rodríguez, *Changing Race*, 129–152.

51. Rodríguez, *Changing Race*, 9. The racial data by Latino subgroup are from the 1990 census. As of March 2002, the 2000 census data on this topic were not yet available.

52. Melita Marie Garza, "Black Hispanics taking pride in their multifaceted heritage," *Chicago Tribune*, September 16, 1992, 4; Alisa Valdes, "Past Empowers Black Latinos; While Proud of Their African Roots, Many Face Prejudice from All Sides," *Boston Globe*, March 3, 1997, at B1; Delina D. Pryce, "Black Latina," *Hispanic* 12 (March 1999): 56; Veronica Chambers, "Secret Latina at Large," in Meri Nana-Ama Danquah, ed., *Becoming American: Personal Essays by First Generation Immigrant Women* (New York: Hyperion, 2000), 21–28.

53. Sometimes dark-skinned Hispanics resent the inclusion of Spanish Americans, whom they see as privileged whites, in the Latino category. But Spanish Americans do not always receive affirmative-action protections that benefit Latinos. (If one is of Spanish stock, by way of a multiracial country such as Cuba or Mexico, the person qualifies as a minority in America.) Prominent Spanish Americans of the past—this group includes the likes of Admiral David Farragut and the philosopher George Santayana—receive recognition as Hispanic heroes. Spanish actors such as Antonio Banderas and Penélope Cruz enjoy support from the Hispanic community as well as crossover success in Hollywood.

54. Only a small number of Americans (18,804) have ethnic ties to Uruguay. Argentine Americans are a much larger group, although their numbers — 100,864 — pale in comparison to those of the larger Hispanic subgroups.

55. The fact that Spanish is spoken in the United States by people largely of Mexican, Caribbean, and Central American ancestry blurs the boundaries in America between Spaniards and multiracial Latinos in the New World.

56. For overviews of Latino America, see, e.g., Fox, *Hispanic Nation;* Earl Shorris, *Latinos: A Biography of the People* (New York: W. W. Norton & Company, 1992); Ilan Stavans, *The Hispanic Condition: Reflections on Culture and Identity in America* (New York: HarperPerennial, 1996); Roberto Suro, *Strangers Among Us: How Latino Immigration Is Transforming America* (New York: Alfred A. Knopf, 1998); Juan Gonzalez, *Harvest of Empire: A History of Latinos in America* (New York: Viking, 2000); Arlene Dávila, *Latinos, Inc.: The Marketing and Making of a People* (Berkeley: University of California Press, 2001).

57. Rodolfo O. de la Garza et al., *Latino Voices: Mexican, Puerto Rican, and Cuban Perspectives on American Politics* (Boulder, Colo.: Westview Press, 1992), 63, 158; Suzanne Oboler, *Ethnic Labels, Latino Lives: Identity and the Politics of (Re)Presentation in the United States* (Minneapolis: University of Minnesota Press, 1995); Clyde Tucker and Brian Kojetin, "Testing racial and ethnic origin questions in the CPS supplement," *Monthly Labor Review* 119 (September 1996): 5; Leobardo F. Estrada, "Family Influences on Demographic Trends in Hispanic Ethnic Identification and Labeling," in Martha E. Bernal and George P. Knight, eds., *Ethnic Identity: Formation and Transmission Among Hispanics and Other Minorities* (Albany: State University of New York Press, 1993), 163–179.

58. de la Garza et al., *Latino Voices,* 69.

59. For data on how Hispanic subgroups view each other, see *The Washington Post/Kaiser Family Foundation*/Harvard University Survey Project, *National Survey on Latinos in America* (Menlo Park, Calif.: Henry J. Kaiser Family Foundation, May 2000), 70–73.

60. Laura Castañeda, "Media Explosion," *American Journalism Review* 23 (June 2001): 47.

61. Most panethnic Hispanic-American magazines are published in English, although *Latina,* a publication for Hispanic women, is a bilingual periodical.

62. Fox, *Hispanic Nation,* 40–66; Dávila, *Latinos, Inc.,* 153–180. See, too, Andrew Pollack, "The Fight for Hispanic Viewers; Univision's Success Story Attracts New Competition," *New York Times,* January 19, 1998, at C1; Kevin Baxter, "Univision Means Success in Any Language," *Los Angeles Times,* April 13, 1999, at p. 1; Rick Wartzman and Lisa Bannon, "Silent Treatment: A Media Mogul Who Steers Clear of Media? It Works for This One," *Wall Street Journal,* August 13, 1999, at A1; Martin Peers, "Is Sony Tuning Out Telemundo? Japanese Giant Strains to Revive Spanish Channel," *Wall Street Journal,* September 20, 1999, at B1; Ronald Grover, "Univision Peers into Cyberspace," *BusinessWeek* (January 17, 2000): 74, 76; Tim Dougherty, "Ratings Rebound," *Hispanic Business* 22 (July/August 2000): 80–82; Jayson Blair, "TV Advertising Drives Fight over Size of Spanish Audience," *New York Times,* July 17, 2000, at A1; Mimi Whitefield, "The Comeback Network," *Hispanic* 14 (July/August 2001): 26–28; Ronald Grover, "Media Giants Are Glued to Latino TV," *BusinessWeek* (September 24, 2001): 105–106; Kerry A. Dolan, "¡Viva la Televisión!" *Forbes* 168 (October 1, 2001): 70; Derek Reveron, "On with the Show," *Hispanic Business* 23 (December 2001): 60, 62.

63. Larry Rohter, "Aquí Se Habla English: A Talk-Show Twist," *New York Times,* July 26, 1992, Sec. 2, p. 23; Alisa Valdes, "Talk TV's Numero Uno; 100 Million Listen as Cristina Saralegui Tackles Latino Taboos," *Boston Globe,* February 10, 1998, at E1; Kevin Baxter, "In Any Language, It's More Than Idle Chat," *Los Angeles Times,* November 1, 1998, at p. 3; Mireya Navarro, "With Latin Flair (and Flare); Diverse Audience Presents a Balancing Act for Talk Show Host," *New York Times,* June 23, 1999, at E1; Arian Campo-Flores, "The Rudest of Them All," *Newsweek* 137 (April 30, 2001): 76.

64. Marie Arana, "Spanish-Language TV, a Channel to Latino Voters," *Washington Post,* August 17, 2000, C4; Dennis Farney, "Building Bloc: Both Candidates Woo Newsman with a Line to the Hispanic Vote," *Wall Street Journal,* October 3, 2000, at A1; Lydia Martin, "Making News," *Hispanic* 14 (January/February 2001): 62–64, 66.

65. Michael A. Fletcher, "The Blond, Blue-Eyed Face of Spanish TV; Activists Decry Shows as Sexist, Stereotypical — and Absent Darker Hues," *Washington Post,* August 3, 2000, at A1; Mireya Navarro, "Complaint to Spanish TV: Not Enough Americans; Few U.S. Plots for Growing U.S. Audience," *New York Times,* August 21, 2000, at B1.

66. Kevin Baxter, "United by Diversity," *Los Angeles Times,* April 15, 1999, F17.

67. Achy Obejas, "All Mexican, All the Time; Forget Latin Pop, Chicago's Spanish-Language FM Stations Battle It Out with Mexican Regional Music," *Chicago Tribune,* January 5, 2001, at Sec. 5, at p. 1.

68. Howard LaFranchi, "Will bilingual trend make US 'habla Español'?" *Christian Science Monitor,* June 30, 1999, at p. 1. The *Wall Street Journal* reports that some monolingual English-speaking Hispanics now feel pressure to learn Spanish, due to the Latino cultural renaissance of the late 1990s. See Evan Perez, "¿No Habla Español? Neither Do Latin Icons Estrada and Aguilera," *Wall Street Journal,* December 28, 2001, at A1.

69. Lizette Alvarez, "It's the Talk of Nueva York: The Hybrid Called Spanglish," *New York Times,* March 25, 1997, at A1.

70. Ilan Stavans, "The Sounds of Spanglish," in Ilan Stavans, ed., *The Essential Ilan Stavans* (New York: Routledge, 2000), 26–40. See, too, Alvarez, "It's the Talk of Nueva York"; Mike Clary, "Finding a 'Muy Friquiado' Way to Speak," *Los Angeles Times,* August 28, 1997, A5; David Adams, "Miami blends own brand of popular language: Cubonics," *St. Petersburg (Fla.) Times,* April 10, 1997, at 1B; Tracie Reddick, "Words in the mix," *Tampa Tribune,* October 31, 1997, at p. 1; Carmen Juri, "Understanding Spanglish; It's Really No Problema," *Seattle Times,* November 30, 1997, L4; Susy Schultz, "To speak or not to speak; Spanglish," *Chicago Sun-Times,* May 31, 1998, 7; Sam Dillon, "Click to Be Subsumed; On the Language of Cervantes, the Imprint of the Internet," *New York Times,* August 6, 2000, Sec. 4, p. 3; Allison Klein, "English, español mingle at border," *Baltimore Sun,* March 23, 2001, 2A.

71. Rebecca Gardyn, "Habla English?" *American Demographics* 23 (April 2001): 54–57.

72. For a general history of the island, see Arturo Morales Carrión, *Puerto Rico: A Political and Cultural History* (New York: W. W. Norton & Company, 1983).

73. Peter C. Stuart, *Isles of Empire: The United States and Its Overseas Possessions* (Lanham, Md.: University Press of America, 1999).

74. Fernandez, Méndez Méndez, and Cueto, *Puerto Rico Past and Present*, 185–188. The quotation appears on page 187.

75. U.S. Census Bureau, *Statistical Abstract of the United States: 2000* (120th ed.) (Washington, D.C.: U.S. Government Printing Office, 2000), Table 1339.

76. Cose, *Color-Blind*, 198.

77. José A. Cabranes, *Citizenship and the American Empire: Notes on the Legislative History of the United States Citizenship of Puerto Ricans* (New Haven, Conn.: Yale University Press, 1979).

78. Arlene M. Dávila, *Sponsored Identities: Cultural Politics in Puerto Rico* (Philadelphia: Temple University Press, 1997), 169–207.

79. Nancy Morris, *Puerto Rico: Culture, Politics, and Identity* (Westport, Conn.: Praeger, 1995), 69–169; Amílcar A. Barreto, *Language, Elites, and the State: Nationalism in Puerto Rico and Quebec* (Westport, Conn.: Praeger, 1998), 77–96.

80. David Jackson and Paul de la Garza, "Rep. Gutierrez Uncommon Target of a Too Common Slur; Capitol Security Aide Suspended for Insult," *Chicago Tribune*, April 18, 1996, at p. 1.

81. U.S. Census Bureau, *Statistical Abstract of the United States: 2000*, Table 45.

82. Francisco L. Rivera-Batiz and Carlos E. Santiago, *Island Paradox: Puerto Rico in the 1990s* (New York: Russell Sage Foundation, 1996), 65.

83. In Fiscal Year 1999, the federal government made $8,082,000,000 in direct payments to Puerto Ricans, with Social Security ($3,556,000,000), Medicare ($1,112,000,000), nutritional assistance ($1,088,000,000), and veterans benefits ($479 million) accounting for 77.1% of those payments. The total outlay was $8,851,000,000. Puerto Ricans paid $2,654,000,000 to the U.S. Treasury, mainly employee and employer contributions to Social Security, so the net balance was $6,197,000,000. U.S. Census Bureau, *Statistical Abstract of the United States: 2000*, Table 1341.

84. In 1998 Puerto Rico had $21,706,000,000 in imports; sixty-one percent, or $13,318,000,000, of these imports came from the mainland. Conversely, 91% of Puerto Rico's total exports that year ($28,109,000,000) went to the States. U.S. Census Bureau, *Statistical Abstract of the United States: 2000*, Table 1342.

85. Rivera-Batiz and Santiago, *Island Paradox*, 43–62; Mireya Navarro, "Puerto Rican Presence Wanes in New York," *New York Times*, February 28, 2000, at A1. For treatments of specific Puerto Rican communities, see Felix M. Padilla, *Puerto Rican Chicago* (Notre Dame, Ind.: University of Notre Dame Press, 1987), 56–98; Virginia E. Sánchez-Korrol, *From Colonia to Community: The History of Puerto Ricans in New York City*, 2d ed. (Berkeley: University of California Press, 1994), 11–50; Carmen Teresa Whalen, *From Puerto Rico to Philadelphia: Puerto Rican Workers and Postwar Economies* (Philadelphia: Temple University Press, 2001), passim.

86. Ibid.

87. A plurality of New York City's Puerto Ricans reside in the Bronx, where 24% of the population is Puerto Rican. Overall, there are 319,240 Puerto Ricans in the Bronx, compared to 213,025 in Brooklyn, 119,718 in Manhattan, 108,661 in Queens, and 28,528 in Staten Island.

88. Navarro, "Puerto Rican Presence Wanes in New York"; Susan Sachs, "Hispanic New York Shifted in 1990's," *New York Times,* May 22, 2001, B8.

89. Camden, New Jersey, is another heavily Puerto Rican city on the mainland. Nearly three out of ten, or 28.8%, of its 79,904 residents identify as Puerto Rican.

90. For some background on this issue, see Rodolfo O. de la Garza, "The Effects of Ethnicity on Political Culture," in Paul E. Peterson, ed., *Classifying by Race* (Princeton, N.J.: Princeton University Press, 1995), 333–353.

91. Rodríguez, *Changing Race,* 9. These data are from the 1990 census. The 2000 census data on this topic are not yet available.

92. In the November 1993 referendum, 48% of Puerto Ricans supported commonwealth, 46% voted for statehood, and 4% backed independence. The results were similar in the December 1998 referendum. Slightly more than one-half (50.3%) of Puerto Ricans chose "none of the above," while 46.5% voted for statehood, and 2.5% selected independence. Michael Barone and Richard E. Cohen with Charles E. Cook Jr., *The Almanac of American Politics 2002* (Washington, D.C.: National Journal, 2001), 1689.

93. Morris, *Puerto Rico,* 57–65.

94. Ibid.

95. Ivan Roman, "Woman Takes Reins in Puerto Rico," *Chicago Tribune,* January 3, 2001, Sec. 1, p. 3. For background on Governor Calderón, see Barone and Cohen, *The Almanac of American Politics 2002,* 1691–1693; "A New Governor Ushers in a New Era in Puerto Rico," *New York Times,* January 6, 2001, A8; Ana Radelat, "Sila María Calderón: The new face of Puerto Rican politics," *Hispanic* 14 (January/February 2001): 18.

96. Roman, "Woman Takes Reins in Puerto Rico."

97. For an overview of these issues, see Yossi Shain, "The Mexican-American Diaspora's Impact on Mexico," *Political Science Quarterly* 114 (Winter 1999–2000): 661–691. See, too, Paul Van Slambrouck, "Dual Allegiances Move Closer to Home," *Christian Science Monitor,* April 13, 1998, at p. 1; Sam Howe Verhovek, "Torn Between Nations, Mexican-Americans Can Have Both," *New York Times,* April 14, 1998, A12; Alejandro Carrillo, "Calling for Dual Nationality for Mexican-Americans," *Chicago Tribune,* May 22, 1998, Sec. 1, p. 27; William Branigin, "New Law in Mexico Allows Emigres to Call Two Nations Home," *Washington Post,* May 31, 1998, A3.

98. Ana Mendieta, "New bank ID rules help immigrants," *Chicago Sun-Times,* January 28, 2002, 11.

99. Many of the Mexican stores in the United States advertise their regional origins, to Durango, Sonora, Sinaloa, Guanajuato, or Michoacán states. As a result, you will see the Panadería Chihuahua or Michoacán Restaurant. There are many Latino neighborhoods where the residents trace their roots back to a single village or small town in Mexico.

100. Linda Robinson, "An opening to Cuba?" *U.S. News & World Report* 125 (September 28, 1998): 45–46; Serge F. Kovaleski, "Communist Cuba's Capitalist Contradictions," *Washington Post,* December 31, 1998, A29; Thomas W. Lippman, "U.S. Ready to Play Ball with Cuba; Clinton to Ease Trade Embargo, Using Orioles as Unofficial Envoys," *Washington Post,* January 5, 1999, at A1; Tim Golden, "U.S., Avoiding Castro, Relaxes Rules on Cuba," *New York Times,* July 7, 1999, at A1; Tim Padgett, "Cuba's New Look," *Time* 154 (December 6, 1999): 62–63; Laura Parker, "Dollars to Cuba," *USA Today,* December 6, 1999, at 1A.

101. Ginger Thompson, "Curious Americans Getting a Taste of Forbidden Island; U.S. Law Can't Hold Back Tide of Eager Tourists," *Chicago Tribune,* July 6, 1998, at Sec. 1, at p. 1; Mireya Navarro, "Cuba Draws the Curious, Despite the Law," *New York Times,* January 31, 1999, Sec. 5, p. 8; Joshua B. Rosenbaum, "Flouting Embargo, Adventure-Seeking Americans Head for Havana; Despite U.S. Ban on Tourism, There's More Than One Way for Vacationers to Visit Cuba," *Wall Street Journal,* December 27, 1999, at B1; Christopher Marquis, "Despite U.S. Restrictions Against Cuba, Door Opens Wider for Visits by Americans," *New York Times,* June 19, 2000, A10; Kevin Sullivan, "Americans Defy Cuba Embargo; Tens of Thousands Flock to Forbidden Island for the Beaches, Cigars and Rum," *Washington Post,* October 13, 2001, A23.

102. Dana Canedy, "On Land and Sea, Florida Plans for Turmoil After Castro's Death," *New York Times,* July 2, 2001, at A1.

103. de la Garza et al., *Latino Voices,* 25.

104. Jonathan Friedland, "¿Estás Preparado Para el Rock en Español?" *Wall Street Journal,* April 29, 1999, at B1; Peter Watrous, "For Latin Music, New Worlds to Conquer; English-Speaking Fans Discover a Spanish Voice," *New York Times,* May 24, 1999, at E1; Christopher John Farley, "Latin Music Pops," *Time* 153 (May 24, 1999): 74–79; Veronica Chambers and John Leland, "Lovin' La Vida Loca," *Newsweek* 133 (May 31, 1999): 72–74; Guy Garcia, "Another Latin Boom, but Different," *New York Times,* June 27, 1999, Sec. 2, p. 25; Diana A. Terry-Azíos, "Can the Explosion Last?" *Hispanic* 13 (March 2000): 22–24, 26; Carole Buia, "Best of both worlds," *Time* 158 (Fall 2001): 10–13.

105. Bruce Orwall, "Latin Translation: Colombian Pop Star Taps American Taste in Repackaged Imports," *Wall Street Journal,* February 13, 2001, at A1; Christopher John Farley, "The Making of a Rocker," *Time* 158 (Fall 2001): 14–16; Lydia Martin, "Shakira," *Hispanic* 14 (December 2001): 32–34, 36.

106. Brook Larmer, "Latino America," *Newsweek* 134 (July 12, 1999): 48–51; John Leland and Veronica Chambers, "Generation Ñ," *Newsweek* 134 (July 12, 1999): 52–58; Helene Stapinski, "Generación Latino," *American Demographics* 21 (July 1999): 62–68; Mireya Navarro, "Latinos Gain Visibility in Cultural Life of U.S.," *New York Times,* September 19, 1999, Sec. 1, p. 24.

Chapter 4: Unequal Life Chances?

1. I have been to Saint Paul numerous times since 1989; my most recent visit to the city was on August 15, 2001.

2. Bernard Stamler, "Talking the Tawk; New Yorkers Are Sounding More Like Everybody Else. Is It Curtains for the Accent People Love to Hate?" *New York Times,* September 20, 1998, Sec. 14, at p. 1; Mark Francis Cohen, "New York Postcard: Small Tawk," *New Republic* 219 (October 5, 1998): 11–12; Sara Hammel, "Do you speak Bostonian?" *U.S. News & World Report* 126 (January 25, 1999): 56–57. For a scholarly overview of the topic, see Walt Wolfram and Natalie Schilling-Estes, *American English: Dialects and Variation* (Malden, Mass.: Blackwell Publishers, 1998).

3. Ibid.

4. For the landmark study on issues related to language and discrimination, see Rosina Lippi-Green, *English with an Accent: Language, Ideology, and Discrimination in the United States* (London: Routledge, 1997).

5. As of October 1, 2001, the student population of the Saint Paul Public Schools was 31.9% white, 30.6% Asian, 25.3% black, 10.4% Latino, and 1.8% American Indian. Cindy Porter, telephone conversation with author, November 27, 2001.

6. More than one-quarter (26.7%) of the students in the Saint Paul Public Schools speak Hmong, while 7.6% claim Spanish as their native tongue. Over 1.2% of the students are native speakers of Somali, while 1.0% of them speak Vietnamese and another 1.0% is fluent in Khmer. In total, 41.2% of the Saint Paul Public School students come from homes where English is not spoken on a regular basis. Cindy Porter, telephone conversation with author, February 8, 2002.

7. Alberto Dávila, Alok K. Bohara, and Rogelio Saenz, "Accent Penalties and the Earnings of Mexican Americans," *Social Science Quarterly* 74 (December 1993): 902–916; Ross M. Stolzenberg and Marta Tienda, "English Proficiency, Education, and the Conditional Economic Assimilation of Hispanic and Asian Origin Men," *Social Science Research* 26 (March 1997): 25–51; Marie T. Mora, "Did the English Deficiency Earnings Penalty Change for Hispanic Men between 1979 and 1989?" *Social Science Quarterly* 79 (September 1998): 581–594; Alberto Dávila and Marie T. Mora, "The English-Skill Acquisition of Hispanic Americans during the 1980s," *Social Science Quarterly* 81 (March 2000): 261–275; Alberto Dávila and Marie T. Mora, "English Skills, Earnings, and the Occupational Sorting of Mexican Americans Along the U.S.-Mexico Border," *International Migration Review* 34 (Spring 2000): 133–157.

8. John Russell Rickford and Russell John Rickford, *Spoken Soul: The Story of Black English* (New York: John Wiley & Sons, 2000); Geneva Smitherman, *Black Talk: Words and Phrases from the Hood to the Amen Corner,* 2d ed. (Boston: Houghton Mifflin Company, 2000). For background on the controversy over Ebonics, see Theresa Perry and Lisa Delpit, eds., *The Real Ebonics Debate: Power, Language, and the Education of African-American Children* (Boston: Beacon Press, 1998); John Baugh, *Beyond Ebonics: Linguistic Pride and Racial Prejudice* (New York: Oxford University Press, 2000).

9. Lippi-Green, *English with an Accent,* passim; Mari J. Matsuda, "Voices of America: Accent, Antidiscrimination Law, and a Jurisprudence for the Last Reconstruction," *Yale Law Journal* 100 (March 1991): 1329–1407; Kelly

Hearn, "Pegged by an accent," *Christian Science Monitor,* December 18, 2000, 11, 16.

10. As Allison Uehling points out, "...protection against accent discrimination based on national origin does not apply to regional accents from around the United States typical of native speakers of English." See Allison Uehling, "Complaints About Communication Can Mask Accent Discrimination," *EEO Perspective* (March 2001). www.feds.com/eeo_lib/PERSPECTIVE/FEOR20010.

11. Lippi-Green, *English with an Accent,* 202–216; Cohen, "New York Postcard: Small Tawk"; Daniel Pearl, "Hush Mah Mouth! Some in South Try to Lose the Drawl," *Wall Street Journal,* December 13, 1991, at A1.

12. George Mair, *Oprah Winfrey: The Real Story* (Secaucus, N.J.: Birch Lane Press/Carol Publishing Group, 1994); Lynette Clemetson, "Oprah on Oprah," *Newsweek* 137 (January 8, 2001): 38–44, 46, 48; Peter Kafka and Peter Newcomb, eds., "The Forbes 400," *Forbes* 168 (October 8, 2001): 172, 174.

13. See, e.g., David Horowitz, *Hating Whitey and Other Progressive Causes* (Dallas: Spence Publishing Company, 1999), 58, 78, 181–182.

14. Jonathan Alter, "The Long Shadow of Slavery," *Newsweek* 130 (December 8, 1997): 58–63; Dinesh D'Souza, *The End of Racism: Principles for a Multiracial Society* (New York: Free Press, 1995), 67–114; Orlando Patterson, *Rituals of Blood: Consequences of Slavery in Two American Centuries* (Washington, D.C.: Civitas/Counterpoint, 1998).

15. *Plessy v. Ferguson,* 163 U.S. 537 (1896); *Brown v. Board of Education,* 347 U.S. 483 (1954).

16. C. Vann Woodward, *The Strange Career of Jim Crow* (New York: Oxford University Press, 1955); Stephan Thernstrom and Abigail Thernstrom, *America in Black and White: One Nation, Indivisible* (New York: Simon & Schuster, 1997), 25–52.

17. Neil Gotanda, "A Critique of 'Our Constitution is Color-Blind,'" *Stanford Law Review* 44 (November 1991): 1–68; Andrew Kull, *The Color-Blind Constitution* (Cambridge, Mass.: Harvard University Press, 1992).

18. Steven A. Holmes, "Quality of Life Is Up for Many Blacks, Data Say," *New York Times,* November 18, 1996, at A1; Henry Louis Gates, Jr., "The Two Nations Of Black America," *Brookings Review* 16 (Spring 1998): 4–7; Ellis Cose, "The Good News About Black America," *Newsweek* 133 (June 7, 1999): 28–32, 34–36, 38–40.

19. Ibid.

20. Bart Landry, *The New Black Middle Class* (Berkeley: University of California Press, 1987); Lawrence Otis Graham, *Our Kind of People: Inside America's Black Upper Class* (New York: HarperCollins, 1999).

21. Steven A. Holmes and Karen De Witt, "Black, Successful and Safe and Gone from Capital," *New York Times,* July 27, 1996, Sec. 1, at p. 1; Jonathan Kaufman, "Trading Places: Where Blacks Have More Than Whites, Racial Tension Erupts," *Wall Street Journal,* February 8, 2001, at A1.

22. D'Souza, *The End of Racism,* 254–258, 289–336; James Waller, *Face to Face: The Changing State of Racism Across America* (New York: Insight Books/Plenum Press, 1998).

23. Joe R. Feagin and Clairece Booher Feagin, *Discrimination American Style: Institutional Racism and Sexism* (Englewood Cliffs, N.J.: Prentice-Hall, 1978).

24. David O. Sears, Jim Sidanius, and Lawrence Bobo, eds., *Racialized Politics: The Debate about Racism in America* (Chicago: University of Chicago Press, 2000).

25. Leonard Steinhorn and Barbara Diggs-Brown, *By the Color of Our Skin: The Illusion of Integration and the Reality of Race* (New York: Dutton, 1999), 181–196.

26. D'Souza, *The End of Racism*, 387–429; Clarence Page, *Showing My Color: Impolite Essays on Race and Identity* (New York: HarperCollins Publishers, 1996), 70–99.

27. Gail Russell Chaddock, "Adverse impact?" *Christian Science Monitor*, November 30, 1999, 14–16.

28. Stephan Thernstrom and Abigail Thernstrom, *America in Black and White: One Nation, Indivisible* (New York: Simon & Schuster, 1997), 348–385. See, too, Ethan Bronner, "Colleges Look for Answers to Racial Gaps in Testing," *New York Times*, November 8, 1997, at A1; John Cloud, "Should SATs Matter?" *Time* 157 (March 12, 2001): 62–64, 66–67, 70; Mark Clayton, "In student test scores, a wider gap," *Christian Science Monitor*, August 29, 2001, at p. 1.

29. Paul Craig Roberts and Lawrence M. Stratton, *The New Color Line: How Quotas and Privilege Destroy Democracy* (Washington, D.C.: Regnery Publishing, 1995), especially 97–100. See, too, the six articles in the Symposium "Discrimination in Product, Credit and Labor Markets," in the Spring 1998 issue of the *Journal of Economic Perspectives*.

30. D'Souza, *The End of Racism*, 245–287.

31. Helen F. Ladd, "Evidence on Discrimination in Mortgage Lending," *Journal of Economic Perspectives* 12 (Spring 1998): 41–62; John Yinger, "Evidence on Discrimination in Consumer Markets," *Journal of Economic Perspectives* 12 (Spring 1998): 23–40. See, too, Allen R. Myerson, "Avis Finds Itself at the Center of Discrimination Complaints," *New York Times*, March 18, 1997, at D1; Alexandra Marks, "Cable Firms Unfair? The Picture Is Fuzzy," *Christian Science Monitor*, April 23, 1998, at p. 1; Timothy L. O'Brien, "For Banks, a Big Nudge to Do More," *New York Times*, July 5, 1998, Sec. 3, at p. 1.

32. David Rohde, "Forced to Open, Branches Profit and Refute Stereotype," *New York Times*, April 16, 1997, at B1; Roy S. Johnson, "Banking on Urban America," *Fortune* 137 (March 2, 1998): 128–130, 132; Roger O. Crockett, "They're Lining Up for Flicks in the 'Hood," *BusinessWeek* (June 8, 1998): 75–76; Michael A. Fletcher, "More Retailers Are Sold on Cities; They Say There's Money There After All," *Washington Post*, March 5, 1999, at E1; Paulette Thomas, "Selling Big Insurers on Inner-City Policies," *Wall Street Journal*, May 6, 1999, at B1; Kendra Parker, "Pent-Up Spending Energy," *American Demographics* 21 (November 1999): 40–42; Laurent Belsie, "Business flowing into inner city," *Christian Science Monitor*, July 6, 2000, at p. 1.

33. William Raspberry, "Of Two Minds About Race," *Washington Post*, April 27, 1998, A17; Brad Knickerbocker, "New face of racism in America," *Christian Science Monitor*, January 14, 2000, at p. 1; Lena Williams, *It's the*

Little Things: The Everyday Interactions that Get Under the Skin of Blacks and Whites (New York: Harcourt, 2000).

34. Jay MacLeod, *Ain't No Makin' It: Aspirations and Attainment in a Low-Income Neighborhood* (Boulder, Colo.: Westview Press, 1995), especially 11–24 and 135–151.

35. U.S. Census Bureau, *Statistical Abstract of the United States: 2000* (120th ed.) (Washington, D.C.: U.S. Government Printing Office, 2000), Tables 41, 42, 44, 45, 736, 737, 738, 741, 743, 744, 746, 750, 751, 753, 754, 755, 757, 758, 760, 761, and 762.

36. Ibid., Table 45.

37. Cheryl I. Harris, "Whiteness as Property," *Harvard Law Review* 106 (June 1993): 1707–1791. For other articles that explore similar issues, see Stephanie M. Wildman et al., *Privilege Revealed: How Invisible Preference Undermines America* (New York: New York University Press, 1996); Peggy McIntosh, "White Privilege: Unpacking the Invisible Knapsack," in Bart Schneider, ed., *Race: An Anthology in the First Person* (New York: Crown Trade Paperbacks, 1997), 120–126; George Lipsitz, *The Possessive Investment in Whiteness: How White People Profit from Identity Politics* (Philadelphia: Temple University Press, 1998).

38. Andrew Hacker, *Two Nations: Black and White, Separate, Hostile, Unequal*, 2d ed. (New York: Ballantine Books, 1995), 35–36.

39. U.S. Census Bureau, *Statistical Abstract of the United States: 2000*, Tables 737, 744, 753, 754; Charles Hirschman and Morrison G. Wong, "The Extraordinary Educational Attainment of Asian-Americans: A Search for Historical Evidence and Explanations," *Social Forces* 65 (September 1986): 1–27; Won Moo Hurh and Kwang Chung Kim, "The 'success' image of Asian Americans: its validity, and its practical and theoretical implications," *Ethnic and Racial Studies* 12 (October 1989): 512–538; Stacey J. Lee, *Unraveling the "Model Minority" Stereotype: Listening to Asian American Youth* (New York: Teachers College Press, 1996); Lucie Cheng and Philip Q. Yang, "Asians: The 'Model Minority' Deconstructed," in Roger Waldinger and Mehdi Bozorgmehr, eds., *Ethnic Los Angeles* (New York: Russell Sage Foundation, 1996), 305–344; Cliff Cheng, "Are Asian American Employees a Model Minority or Just a Minority?" *Journal of Applied Behavioral Science* 33 (September 1997): 277–290. There are six other articles about related topics in the September 1997 issue of the *Journal of Applied Behavioral Science*.

40. Ibid.

41. Robert B. Reich, *The Work of Nations: Preparing Ourselves for 21st-Century Capitalism* (New York: Alfred A. Knopf, 1991), 171–195, 219–240, 252–261, 268–300; Richard J. Herrnstein and Charles Murray, *The Bell Curve: Intelligence and Class Structure in American Life* (New York: Free Press, 1994), particularly 25–115, 509–511, 514–518, and 541–546; *The New York Times, The Downsizing of America* (New York: Times Books/Random House, 1996); William Julius Wilson, *When Work Disappears: The World of the New Urban Poor* (New York: Alfred A. Knopf, 1996), 3–146.

42. U.S. Census Bureau, *Statistical Abstract of the United States: 2000*, Tables 911, 912, 914; Donna L. Hoffman and Thomas P. Novak, "Bridging the Racial

Divide on the Internet," *Science* 280 (April 17, 1998): 390–391; Alan K. Ota, "Digital Haves and Have-Nots," *CQ Weekly* 57 (April 17, 1999): 866–868, 870; David E. Sanger, "Big Racial Disparity Persists in Internet Use," *New York Times*, July 9, 1999, A12; Michael J. Weiss, "Wired Nation," *American Demographics* 23 (March 2001): 53–60; Frederick M. Hess and David L. Leal, "A Shrinking 'Digital Divide'? The Provision of Classroom Computers across Urban School Systems," *Social Science Quarterly* 82 (December 2001): 765–778.

43. Coy Samons, telephone conversation with author, June 1, 2001; Coy Samons, interview by author, Allen, Kentucky, June 25, 2001.

44. Kathy J. Prater, "PHS principal to step down," *Floyd County (Ky.) Times*, February 2, 2001, A1, A2.

45. Dr. David Rudy, telephone conversation with author, May 8, 2001. Dr. Rudy is dean of the IRAPP; he served as the interim director of the East Kentucky Regional GEAR-UP Project.

46. One sees very few people of color in central Appalachia. Most of the people there trace their ancestry to Ireland, Germany, and the British Isles. I visited the area covered by the East Kentucky Regional GEAR-UP Project in July 1999 and June 2001.

47. Samons, telephone conversation; Samons, interview; Kevin Hall, interview by author, Pike County, Kentucky, June 25, 2001. I also interviewed Robert Osborne, the Pike County Schools coordinator for GEAR-UP, in Pike County, Kentucky, on June 25, 2001. These three gentlemen gave generously of their time. They introduced me to a number of key people affiliated with the East Kentucky Regional GEAR-UP Project. Mr. Samons, moreover, provided me with a wealth of information about GEAR-UP. Mr. Hall and Mr. Osborne took me to see firsthand the GEAR-UP summer programs at Millard High School in Millard, Kentucky, and Phelps High School in Phelps, Kentucky, on June 25, 2001.

48. Hall, interview; Samons, interview.

49. Richard Hofstadter, *Social Darwinism in American Thought* (1944; reprint, New York: George Braziller, 1959); Robert C. Bannister, *Social Darwinism: Science and Myth in Anglo-American Social Thought* (Philadelphia: Temple University Press, 1979); Carl N. Degler, *In Search of Human Nature: The Decline and Revival of Darwinism in American Social Thought* (New York: Oxford University Press, 1991).

50. Hugh Davis Graham, *The Civil Rights Era: Origins and Development of National Policy, 1960–1972* (New York: Oxford University Press, 1990); Robert C. Lieberman, "Race and the Organization of Welfare Policy," in Paul E. Peterson, ed., *Classifying by Race* (Princeton, N.J.: Princeton University Press, 1995), 156–187; Robert J. Samuelson, *The Good Life and Its Discontents: The American Dream in the Age of Entitlement, 1945–1995* (New York: Times Books/Random House, 1995).

51. See, e.g., Graham, *The Civil Rights Era*, passim; Thomas Byrne Edsall with Mary D. Edsall, *Chain Reaction: The Impact of Race, Rights, and Taxes on American Politics* (New York: W. W. Norton & Company, 1992), 4–5, 44–46, 94–95, 107–112, 165–166.

52. Graham, *The Civil Rights Era*, passim; Edsall and Edsall, *Chain Reaction*, passim.

53. Seymour Martin Lipset, "Equal Chances versus Equal Results," *Annals of the American Academy of Political and Social Science* 523 (September 1992): 63–74.

54. Gordon MacInnes, *Wrong for All the Right Reasons: How White Liberals Have Been Undone by Race* (New York: New York University Press, 1996); Jim Sleeper, *Liberal Racism* (New York: Viking, 1997); David Carroll Cochran, *The Color of Freedom: Race and Contemporary American Liberalism* (Albany: State University of New York Press, 1999).

55. Angela D. Dillard, *Guess Who's Coming to Dinner Now? Multicultural Conservatism in America* (New York: New York University Press, 2001).

56. MacLeod, *Ain't No Makin' It*, 247–250; William Julius Wilson, *The Declining Significance of Race: Blacks and Changing American Institutions*, 2d ed. (Chicago: University of Chicago Press, 1980); Richard D. Kahlenberg, *The Remedy: Class, Race, and Affirmative Action* (New York: New Republic Books/Basic Books, 1996).

57. Wilson, *When Work Disappears*, 149–206.

58. David Hage, David Fischer, and Robert F. Black, "America's other welfare state," *U.S. News & World Report* 118 (April 10, 1995): 34–37; Jill Quadagno, *The Color of Welfare: How Racism Undermined the War on Poverty* (New York: Oxford University Press, 1996); Martin Gilens, *Why Americans Hate Welfare: Race, Media, and the Politics of Antipoverty Policy* (Chicago: University of Chicago Press, 1999); Jason DeParle and Steven A. Holmes, "A War on Poverty Subtly Linked to Race," *New York Times*, December 26, 2000, at A1.

59. Public Law 104–193. See, too, R. Kent Weaver, *Ending Welfare as We Know It* (Washington, D.C.: Brookings Institution Press, 2000); Diana Zuckerman and Ariel Kalil, eds., "The Impact of Welfare Reform," *Journal of Social Issues* 56 (Winter 2000); Randy Albelda and Ann Withorn, eds., "Reforming Welfare, Redefining Poverty," *Annals of the American Academy of Political and Social Science* 577 (September 2001); Demetrios James Caraley, "Ending Welfare as We Know It: A Reform Still in Progress," *Political Science Quarterly* 116 (Winter 2001–02): 525–560.

60. U.S. Census Bureau, *Statistical Abstract of the United States: 2000*, Table 534.

61. Yochi J. Dreazen, "U.S. Racial Wealth Gap Remains Huge; Despite Booming Economy, Disparities Didn't Alter in the Course of the 1990s," *Wall Street Journal*, March 14, 2000, A2, A21. On the topic of the wealth gap, see Melvin L. Oliver and Thomas M. Shapiro, *Black Wealth/White Wealth: A New Perspective on Racial Inequality* (New York: Routledge, 1995); Dalton Conley, *Being Black, Living in the Red: Race, Wealth, and Social Policy in America* (Berkeley: University of California Press, 1999).

62. Jonathan Chait, "Painted Black: Robert Johnson, W.'s favorite race baiter," *New Republic* 225 (August 27 and September 3, 2001): 30–33; Brett Pulley, "The Cable Capitalist," *Forbes* 168 (October 8, 2001): 42–44, 46, 50, 54.

63. U.S. Census Bureau, *Statistical Abstract of the United States: 2000*, Table 533.

64. Ibid., Table 170.

65. Ibid., Table 629.

66. William A. McGeveran Jr., ed., *The World Almanac and Book of Facts 2002* (New York: World Almanac Books, 2002), 888.

67. U.S. Census Bureau, *Statistical Abstract of the United States: 2000*, Table 638.

68. Ibid., Table 438.

69. Ibid., Table 637.

70. MacLeod, *Ain't No Makin' It*, passim.

71. Patricia A. Turner, *I Heard It Through the Grapevine: Rumor in African-American Culture* (Berkeley: University of California Press, 1993); Robert C. Smith and Richard Seltzer, *Contemporary Controversies and the American Racial Divide* (Lanham, Md.: Rowman & Littlefield Publishers, 2000), 81–98.

72. Randall Kennedy, *Race, Crime, and the Law* (New York: Pantheon Books, 1997), 168–310.

73. William H. Grier and Price M. Cobbs, *Black Rage* (New York: Basic Books, 1968).

74. Paul Harris, *Black Rage Confronts the Law* (New York: New York University Press, 1997).

75. John H. McWhorter, *Losing the Race: Self-Sabotage in Black America* (New York: Perennial, 2001).

76. Michael A. Fletcher, "A Good-School, Bad-Grade Mystery; Educators Striving to Close Racial Gap in Affluent Ohio Suburb," *Washington Post,* October 23, 1998, at A1; Lynette Clemetson, "Trying to Close the Achievement Gap," *Newsweek* 133 (June 7, 1999): 36–37.

77. Claude M. Steele, "Thin Ice: 'Stereotype Threat' and Black College Students," *Atlantic Monthly* 284 (August 1999): 44–47, 50–54.

78. Audrey Edwards and Craig K. Polite, *Children of the Dream: The Psychology of Black Success* (New York: Doubleday, 1992); Jennifer L. Hochschild, "Middle-Class Blacks and the Ambiguities of Success," in Paul M. Sniderman, Philip E. Tetlock, and Edward G. Carmines, eds., *Prejudice, Politics, and the American Dilemma* (Stanford, Calif.: Stanford University Press, 1993), 148–172; Randall Robinson, *Defending the Spirit: A Black Life in America* (New York: Dutton, 1998), 265–274.

79. Ellis Cose, *The Rage of a Privileged Class* (New York: HarperCollins, 1993); Joe R. Feagin and Melvin P. Sikes, *Living with Racism: The Black Middle-Class Experience* (Boston: Beacon Press, 1994); Lawrence Otis Graham, *Member of the Club: Reflections on Life in a Racially Polarized World* (New York: Harper-Collins, 1995); Sam Fulwood III, *Waking from the Dream: My Life in the Black Middle Class* (New York: Anchor Books/Doubleday, 1996); Paul M. Barrett, *The Good Black: A True Story of Race in America* (New York: Dutton, 1999).

80. Hendrik Hertzberg, "TRB: Wounds of Race," *New Republic* 201 (July 10, 1989): 4.

81. Stephen L. Carter, *Reflections of an Affirmative Action Baby* (New York: Basic Books, 1991), 47–69.

82. David K. Shipler, *A Country of Strangers: Blacks and Whites in America* (New York: Alfred A. Knopf, 1997), 70–94.

83. The Dysart Unified School District includes El Mirage, a Hispanic-majority city; Surprise, an Anglo-majority town with a sizable Latino minority;

the multiethnic population of Luke Air Force Base; and a sliver of Youngtown, a mainly white community. It also encompasses a number of predominantly Anglo retirement communities — Sun Village, Happy Trails, Arizona Traditions, Sun City Grand, and the Sun City West expansion area. I learned a great deal about the communities in the Dysart Unified School District as a result of my interviews with the political leaders of Surprise and El Mirage. I interviewed Surprise Mayor Joan Shafer in Surprise, Arizona, on January 23, 2001, and I spoke to Surprise City Manager Bill Pupo by telephone on March 19, 2001. I interviewed El Mirage Mayor Roy Delgado and El Mirage Vice Mayor Norma Valdez in El Mirage, Arizona, on January 24, 2001.

84. Sue Anne Pressley, "School Fight in a Gray Area; Retirees in Phoenix Suburb Resist Taxation for Education," *Washington Post,* January 13, 1998, at A1.

85. Ibid.

86. Dr. Margo Olivares-Seck, interview by author, El Mirage, Arizona, January 23, 2001. The Superintendent graciously provided me with invaluable information about the Dysart Unified School District.

87. Olivares-Seck, interview.

88. Ibid.; David Madrid, "Dysart Bites Bullet, Seeks 8% Override," *Arizona Republic,* February 11, 2000; David Madrid, "Retiree Vote Uncertain in Override," *Arizona Republic,* April 14, 2000; David Madrid, "Dysart Banking on Retirees; Much at Stake in Override Vote," *Arizona Republic,* May 12, 2000; David Madrid, "Dysart Override Wins, 2–1; Voters Preserve Raises, Programs," *Arizona Republic,* May 19, 2000; David Madrid, "Raises Called Good Start for Dysart Staff; Teacher Pay Still Lags Peers'," *Arizona Republic,* June 10, 2000.

89. Dr. Margo Olivares-Seck, telephone conversation with author, December 20, 2001. In the 2001–2002 school year, 7,050 students attended the nine schools (six K-8 schools, one pre-K school, one alternative learning center, and one high school) in the Dysart Unified School District. The student population is presently 51.9% Hispanic, 38.5% Anglo, 6.8% black, 1.7% Asian, and 1.2% Native American. Dr. Margo Olivares-Seck, e-mail communication with author, December 10, 2001.

90. Dr. Olivares-Seck is a visible and accessible leader. She regularly shows up at the Dysart football games, for instance. Under her leadership, the test scores in the district have improved, the dropout rates have declined, and attendance is better as well. Olivares-Seck, telephone conversation.

91. U.S. Census Bureau, *Statistical Abstract of the United States: 2000,* Table 19.

92. McGeveran, ed., *The World Almanac and Book of Facts 2002,* 385.

93. Alison Stein Wellner, "The Forgotten Boomers," *American Demographics* 23 (February 2001): 46–51.

94. J. Madeleine Nash, "Fertile Minds," *Time* 149 (February 3, 1997): 48–56; Linda Feldmann, "Push to Tackle Social Woes in Their Infancy," *Christian Science Monitor,* February 6, 1997, at p. 1.

95. U.S. Census Bureau, *Statistical Abstract of the United States: 2000,* Table 635; Sue Kirchhoff, "Head Start Is Growing, But Is It Improving?" *CQ Weekly* 56 (June 27, 1998): 1743, 1745–1746; Robert E. O'Connor, "Race and Head

Start Participation: Political and Social Determinants of Enrollment Success in the States," *Social Science Quarterly* 79 (September 1998): 595–606.

96. Marjorie Coeyman, "Public Schools Open Doors to Four-Year-Olds," *Christian Science Monitor,* April 24, 1998, B4–B5; Jodie Morse, "Preschool for Everyone," *Time* 152 (November 9, 1998): 98.

97. Feldmann, "Push to Tackle Social Woes in Their Infancy."

98. Kenneth K. Wong, *Funding Public Schools: Politics and Policies* (Lawrence: University Press of Kansas, 1999); Douglas S. Reed, "Not in My Schoolyard: Localism and Public Opposition to Funding Schools Equally," *Social Science Quarterly* 82 (March 2001): 34–50.

99. Ibid.

100. Vincent J. Roscigno, "Race and the Reproduction of Educational Disadvantage," *Social Forces* 76 (March 1998): 1033–1061; Vincent J. Roscigno, "The Black-White Achievement Gap, Family-School Links, and the Importance of Place," *Sociological Inquiry* 69 (Spring 1999): 159–186; Vincent J. Roscigno, "Family/School Inequality and African-American/Hispanic Achievement," *Social Problems* 47 (May 2000): 266–290.

101. Marjorie Coeyman, "Schools question the benefits of tracking," *Christian Science Monitor,* September 21, 1999, 20. For a tendentious but informative summary of the debate over tracking, see Lissa J. Yogan, "School Tracking and Student Violence," *Annals of the American Academy of Political and Social Science* 567 (January 2000): 108–122.

102. U.S. Census Bureau, *Statistical Abstract of the United States: 2000,* Table 247.

103. The U.S. Department of Education provides a concise definition of this educational option: "Charter schools are public schools that come into existence through a contract with either a state agency or a local school board. The charter — or contract — establishes the framework within which the school operates and provides public support for the school for a specified period of time. The school's charter gives the school autonomy over its operation and frees the school from regulations that other public schools must follow. In exchange for the flexibility afforded by the charter, the schools are held accountable for achieving the goals set out in the charter including improving student performance." For information about charter schools, see Office of Educational Research and Improvement, U.S. Department of Education, *The State of Charter Schools 2000* (Washington, D.C.: U.S. Government Printing Office, January 2000). The quotation appears on page 1.

104. Mitchell L. Stevens, *Kingdom of Children: Culture and Controversy in the Homeschooling Movement* (Princeton, N.J.: Princeton University Press, 2001).

105. Terry M. Moe, *Schools, Vouchers, and the American Public* (Washington, D.C.: Brookings Institution Press, 2001).

106. U.S. Census Bureau, *Statistical Abstract of the United States: 2000,* Table 738.

107. Ibid., Tables 252 and 752.

108. Ibid., Table 764.

109. Ibid., Tables 249, 250, and 318.

110. Peter G. Peterson, *Will America Grow Up Before It Grows Old? How the Coming Social Security Crisis Threatens You, Your Family, and Your Country* (New York: Random House, 1996); Susan A. MacManus with Patricia A. Turner, *Young v. Old: Generational Combat in the 21st Century* (Boulder, Colo.: Westview Press, 1996). See, too, Mireya Navarro, "Florida Is Cutting-Edge Lab for Big Generational Shifts," *New York Times,* August 7, 1996, at A1; Mireya Navarro, "In Florida, the Young Are Gaining on the Old," *New York Times,* June 25, 1997, at A1.

111. Ibid.

112. Ibid.

113. Jonathan Cohn, "TRB: Profit motives," *New Republic* 219 (July 13, 1998): 6.

114. Richard Hogan and Carolyn C. Perrucci, "Producing and Reproducing Class and Status Differences: Racial and Gender Gaps in U.S. Employment and Retirement Income," *Social Problems* 45 (November 1998): 528–549.

115. Peterson, *Will America Grow Up Before It Grows Old?* 25, 128, 211; Marc Peyser, "Home of the Gray," *Newsweek* 133 (March 1, 1999): 51; Frederick R. Lynch, *Invisible Victims: White Males and the Crisis of Affirmative Action* (New York: Praeger, 1991), 177; Ronald J. Angel and Jacqueline L. Angel, *Who Will Care for Us? Aging and Long-Term Care in Multicultural America* (New York: New York University Press, 1997), 162–164; Kent L. Tedin, Richard E. Matland, and Gregory R. Weiher, "Age, Race, Self-Interest, and Financing Public Schools Through Referenda," *Journal of Politics* 63 (February 2001): 270–294.

116. Peyser, "Home of the Gray," 50–53; Peter G. Peterson, *Gray Dawn: How the Coming Age Wave Will Transform America — and the World* (New York: Times Books/Random House, 1999).

117. Lynch, *Invisible Victims,* 177.

118. Peter Applebome, "Rising Cost of College Imperils Nation, Report Says," *New York Times,* June 18, 1997, B8; Sue Kirchhoff, "Commission on College Costs Comes Back with a Warning," *Congressional Quarterly Weekly Report* 56 (January 24, 1998): 189; Tristan Mabry, "College Tuition Outpaces Inflation Again; Critics Call 3%-to-5% Boost Gouging, Defenders Cite Aid," *Wall Street Journal,* March 12, 1999, at A2; David R. Francis, "Seeing Past the Sticker Price," *Christian Science Monitor,* January 18, 2000, 17–18; Albert B. Crenshaw, "College Hopes Dim for the Poor; Financial Aid Has Fallen Steeply in Favor of Middle Class," *Washington Post,* February 25, 2001, H2.

119. www.gsfc.org/

120. www.firn.edu/doe/brfutures/

121. www.promisescholarships.org.

122. Angel and Angel, *Who Will Care for Us?* 165.

123. Peterson, *Will America Grow Up Before It Grows Old?* 22.

124. Mark A. Rothstein, ed., *Genetic Secrets: Protecting Privacy and Confidentiality in the Genetic Era* (New Haven, Conn.: Yale University Press, 1997). See, too, William F. Mulholland and Ami S. Jaeger, "Genetic Privacy and Discrimination: A Survey of State Legislation," *Jurimetrics Journal* 39 (Spring 1999): 317–326; Mark A. Hall, "Legal Rules and Industry Norms: The Impact of Laws Restricting Health Insurers' Use of Genetic Information," *Jurimetrics Journal*

40 (Fall 1999): 93–122; Mark A. Hall and Stephen S. Rich, "Laws Restricting Health Insurers' Use of Genetic Information: Impact on Genetic Discrimination," *American Journal of Human Genetics* 66 (January 2000): 293–307; Colin S. Diver and Jane Maslow Cohen, "Genophobia: What Is Wrong with Genetic Discrimination?" *University of Pennsylvania Law Review* 149 (May 2001): 1439–1482; Henry T. Greely, "Genotype Discrimination: The Complex Case for Some Legislative Protection," *University of Pennsylvania Law Review* 149 (May 2001): 1483–1505; Adriel Bettelheim, "Cures May Arise from Genome Mapping, but Congress Anticipates Headaches," *CQ Weekly* 59 (June 23, 2001): 1505–1506.

125. Ibid.

126. David Barton Smith, *Health Care Divided: Race and Healing a Nation* (Ann Arbor: University of Michigan Press, 1999).

127. Paul Cotton, "Is There Still Too Much Extrapolation from Data on Middle-aged White Men?" *JAMA: The Journal of the American Medical Association* 263 (February 23, 1990): 1049–1050; Paul Cotton, "Examples Abound of Gaps in Medical Knowledge Because of Groups Excluded from Scientific Study," *JAMA: The Journal of the American Medical Association* 263 (February 23, 1990): 1051, 1055.

128. Karen Wright, "The Body Bazaar," *Discover* 19 (October 1998): 114–118, 120; Rick Weiss, "A Look at . . . the Body Shop; At the Heart of an Uneasy Commerce," *Washington Post*, June 27, 1999, B3.

129. Roger Gosden, *Designing Babies: The Brave New World of Reproductive Technology* (New York: W. H. Freeman and Company, 1999); Rick Weiss, "Building a New Child; Embryo Screening Creates a Tool Against Disease — and Ethical Questions," *Washington Post*, June 30, 2001, at A1.

130. Philip Kitcher, *The Lives to Come: The Genetic Revolution and Human Possibilities* (New York: Simon & Schuster, 1996); Robert Wright, "Who Gets the Good Genes?" *Time* 153 (January 11, 1999): 67.

131. John Carey et al., "The Biotech Century," *BusinessWeek* (March 10, 1997): 78–90; Jeremy Rifkin, *The Biotech Century: Harnessing the Gene and Remaking the World* (New York: Jeremy P. Tarcher/Putnam, 1998); Walter Isaacson, "The Biotech Century," *Time* 153 (January 11, 1999): 42–43.

Chapter 5: The Geography of Race

1. I visited the grounds of the South Carolina Capitol on February 26, 2000, and on September 1, 2001.

2. David Firestone, "South Carolina Argues Future of a Rebel Flag," *New York Times*, November 13, 1999, A10; Sue Anne Pressley, "Remains of 22 Rebel Soldiers Reinterred in Charleston; Funeral Held as South Carolina Grapples with Confederate Flag Controversy," *Washington Post*, November 13, 1999, A2; David Firestone, "Bastion of Confederacy Finds Its Future May Hinge on Rejecting the Past," *New York Times*, December 5, 1999, Sec. 1, p. 29; David Firestone, "Battle Flag Is Lowered, but War Isn't Quite Over," *New York Times*, July 2, 2000, Sec. 1, p. 10.

3. Beth Reingold and Richard S. Wike, "Confederate Symbols, Southern Identity, and Racial Attitudes: The Case of the Georgia State Flag," *Social Science Quarterly* 79 (September 1998): 568–580; David Firestone, "Redesigned Georgia Flag Is Advanced by House," *New York Times,* January 25, 2001, A14; Dahleen Glanton, "Acting Quickly, Georgia Moves to Redesign Disputed State Flag," *Chicago Tribune,* January 25, 2001, Sec. 1, at p. 1; David Firestone, "The New South: Old Times There Are Not Forgotten," *New York Times,* January 28, 2001, Sec. 4, p. 4.

4. David Firestone, "Mississippi House Wants Voters to Decide Fate of Confederate Emblem on State Flag," *New York Times,* January 10, 2001, A12; Michael Schaffer, "The new battle of the states," *U.S. News & World Report* 130 (February 12, 2001): 28; Paul Duggan, "Mississippi Voters to Decide on Use of Confederate Emblem," *Washington Post,* March 25, 2001, A3; Kevin Sack, "Battle Lines Form Again on the Battle Flag," *New York Times,* April 4, 2001, A12; Dahleen Glanton, "In Mississippi, Flag Vote Shows Deep Divide; 'World Is Watching' State Referendum," *Chicago Tribune,* April 16, 2001, Sec. 1, at p. 1; David Firestone, "Mississippi Votes by Wide Margin to Keep State Flag That Includes Confederate Emblem," *New York Times,* April 18, 2001, A14; Paul Duggan, "In Miss., a Banner Day for a Rebel Yell," *Washington Post,* April 19, 2001, A2.

5. Tony Horwitz, *Confederates in the Attic: Dispatches from the Unfinished Civil War* (New York: Pantheon Books, 1998). See, too, Kevin Sack, "Symbol of the Old South Divides the New South," *New York Times,* January 21, 1996, Sec. 4, p. 5; Kevin Sack, "Symbols of Old South Feed a New Bitterness," *New York Times,* February 8, 1997, Sec. 1, at p. 1; Dahleen Glanton, "A Vivid Reminder; Across South, Rebel Flag Breeds Pride, Contempt," *Chicago Tribune,* August 7, 1999, at p. 1; "Rebels with a Cause," *Intelligence Report* (Summer 2000): 6–12; Patrik Jonsson, "Southern pride rising...rankling," *Christian Science Monitor,* January 26, 2001, at p. 1; "A New South at Last?" *Southern Political Report* (February 12, 2001): 1–4; Steve Lopez, "Ghosts of the South," *Time* 157 (April 30, 2001): 64–67, 69–70.

6. William Leach, *Country of Exiles: The Destruction of Place in American Life* (New York: Pantheon Books, 1999).

7. See, e.g., Tom Lewis, *Divided Highways: Building the Interstate Highways, Transforming American Life* (New York: Viking, 1997).

8. Borgna Brunner, ed., *TIME Almanac 2002* (Boston: Information Please, 2001), 139.

9. B. Drummond Ayres Jr., "Los Angeles, Long Fragmented, Faces Threat of Secession by the San Fernando Valley," *New York Times,* May 29, 1996, A12; William Booth, "They Are, Like, So Over L.A.; San Fernando Valley Considers Seceding to Form Nation's Sixth-Largest City," *Washington Post,* August 18, 1998, A3.

10. Sara Terry, "Integrated worship," *Christian Science Monitor,* September 12, 2001, at p. 11.

11. Mickey Kaus, *The End of Equality* (New York: New Republic Books/ Basic Books, 1992).

12. Malcolm Gladwell, "Symbol of Suburban Separatism; Until Teen's Death, Mall Had Refused Bus Stop for Inner-City Shoppers," *Washington Post,* February 6, 1996, at A1; Edward Barnes, "Can't Get There from Here," *Time* 147 (February 19, 1996): 33.

13. "Metropolitan Racial and Ethnic Change — Census 2000." This report was prepared by the scholars at the Lewis Mumford Center for Comparative Urban and Regional Research. The Mumford Center has a wealth of data on this topic on its Web site. See www.albany.edu/mumford/census/

14. Douglas S. Massey and Nancy A. Denton, *American Apartheid: Segregation and the Making of the Underclass* (Cambridge, Mass.: Harvard University Press, 1993); Michael Jones-Correa, "The Origins and Diffusion of Racial Restrictive Covenants," *Political Science Quarterly* 115 (Winter 2000–2001): 541–568.

15. Gary Orfield, Susan E. Eaton, and the Harvard Project on School Desegregation, *Dismantling Desegregation: The Quiet Reversal of Brown v. Board of Education* (New York: New Press, 1996); Gary Orfield, *Schools More Separate: Consequences of a Decade of Resegregation* (Cambridge, Mass.: Civil Rights Project/Harvard University, July 2001). www.law.harvard.edu/groups/civilrights/publications/resegregation01/schoolsseparate.pdf.

16. The strictest definitions of the South limit Dixie to the 11 states of the former Confederacy: Alabama, Arkansas, Florida, Georgia, Louisiana, Mississippi, Tennessee, Texas, Virginia, and the Carolinas.

17. In 2000, 35.6% of Americans lived in the South, 22.9% resided in the Midwest, 22.4% inhabited the West, and 19.0% dwelled in the Northeast. (The totals do not add to 100 because of rounding.)

18. U.S. Census Bureau, *Statistical Abstract of the United States: 2000* (120th ed.) (Washington, D.C.: U.S. Government Printing Office, 2000), Tables 26 and 50.

19. Patrick T. Reardon and Abdon M. Pallasch, "Poles Leading Immigrant Tide," *Chicago Tribune,* September 3, 1998, Sec. 1, at p. 1; Sanford J. Ungar, *Fresh Blood: The New American Immigrants* (New York: Simon & Schuster, 1995), 218–246.

20. For example, Milpitas, California, has a substantial Asian population (primarily Filipinos, Vietnamese, and Chinese, along with Asian Indians). Cicero, Illinois, is now one of America's most heavily Mexican cities outside of Texas and California. Delray Beach, Florida, continues to be the site of a well-known Haitian enclave. And Palisades Park, New Jersey, has a significant Korean shopping area. The town of 17,073 is 35.5% Korean.

21. For an excellent overview of the West's history, see Walter Nugent, *Into the West: The Story of Its People* (New York: Alfred A. Knopf, 1999).

22. Slightly more than four in ten Hawaiians, or 40.8% of the people in the Aloha State, are Asian (mainly Japanese, Filipino, and Chinese). Whites account for 22.9% of Hawaii's population, while multiracials constitute 18.1% of all Hawaiians, compared to 9.0% for Pacific Islanders and 7.2% for Hispanics.

23. U.S. Census Bureau, *Statistical Abstract of the United States: 2000,* Table 381; Michael Elliott, "The West at War," *Newsweek* 126 (July 17, 1995): 24–28; Erik Larson, "Unrest in the West," *Time* 146 (October 23, 1995): 52–66;

Terry McCarthy, "High Noon in the West," *Time* 158 (July 16, 2001): 18–21. This issue of *Time* contains a number of excellent articles about the West.

24. Earl Black and Merle Black, *Politics and Society in the South* (Cambridge, Mass.: Harvard University Press, 1987), 16–17; Sue Anne Pressley, "South Rises Again — with Yankees," *Washington Post*, December 27, 1998, at A1.

25. William H. Frey, "Black Movement to the South, and Regional Concentration of the Races," PSC Research Report No. 98-412 (Ann Arbor: Population Studies Center/University of Michigan, January 1998); William H. Frey, "Census 2000 Shows Large Black Return to the South, Reinforcing the Region's 'White-Black' Demographic Profile," PSC Research Report No. 01-473 (Ann Arbor: Population Studies Center/University of Michigan, May 2001).

26. Christina Nifong, "Hispanics and Asians Change the Face of American South," *Christian Science Monitor*, August 6, 1996, at p. 1; Haya El Nasser, "New face of the South; Recent Asian influx taking region by storm," *USA Today*, June 2, 1998, at 1A; Suzi Parker, "Hispanics reshape culture of the South," *Christian Science Monitor*, June 10, 1999, at p. 1; Sue Anne Pressley, "Hispanic Immigration Boom Rattles South; Rapid Influx to Some Areas Raises Tensions," *Washington Post*, March 6, 2000, A3.

27. I have visited Shullsburg and its environs multiple times, most recently on October 6, 2001.

28. Nearly 49% of Shullsburg residents told the Census Bureau in 1990 they had German forebears. Another 35% identified proudly with Ireland. And almost 30% had some sort of ancestral tie to England. Nearly 10% are at least part Swiss. In sum, most Shullsburgers are descended from Northern and Western Europeans.

29. *The New Ethnic Enclaves in America's Suburbs* (Albany, N.Y.: Lewis Mumford Center for Comparative Urban and Regional Research, July 9, 2001). http://mumford1.dyndns.org/cen2000/suburban/SuburbanReport/page1.html.

30. Angie Cannon, "A nation of new cities," *U.S. News & World Report* 130 (April 2, 2001): 16–18; Eric Schmitt, "To Fill Gaps, Cities Seek Wave of Immigrants," *New York Times*, May 30, 2001, at A1.

31. See, e.g., Kenneth J. Garcia, "The Big Uneasy," *San Francisco Chronicle*, June 16, 1996, at p. 1.Z.1.

32. I went to high school with a young African-American woman who said that her grandmother left a predominantly white community because she needed "a little color in her life."

33. Kevin Starr, *Americans and the California Dream, 1850–1915* (New York: Oxford University Press, 1973); Kevin Starr, *Inventing the Dream: California Through the Progressive Era* (New York: Oxford University Press, 1985); Kevin Starr, *Material Dreams: Southern California Through the 1920s* (New York: Oxford University Press, 1990); Kevin Starr, *Endangered Dreams: The Great Depression in California* (New York: Oxford University Press, 1996); Kevin Starr, *The Dream Endures: California Enters the 1940s* (New York: Oxford University Press, 1997).

34. Robert Reinhold, "They Came to California for the Good Life; Now They're Looking Elsewhere," *New York Times*, October 16, 1991, A16; Paul

Starobin, "Is the Dreamin' Over?" *National Journal* 24 (September 26, 1992): 2166–2169, 2171–2172.

35. Vincent J. Schodolski, "Boom Times Are Back in California; Economy and Population Surging," *Chicago Tribune*, January 29, 1997, Sec. 1, p. 4; Shelley Donald Coolidge, "California Dreaming Returns," *Christian Science Monitor*, January 30, 1998, at p. 1; John Cassidy, "The Comeback," *New Yorker* 74 (February 23 and March 2, 1998): 122–127.

36. Christopher Palmeri et al., "The Future of California," *BusinessWeek* (April 30, 2001): 110–114, 116; Robert Gavin, "Role Reversal for Western States; This Time, California Has It Easier in a Recession Than Its Neighbors," *Wall Street Journal*, March 6, 2002, B5.

37. Todd S. Purdum, "Non-Hispanic Whites a Minority, California Census Figures Show," *New York Times*, March 30, 2001, at A1; William Booth, "California's Ethnic Diversity Grows; State Has the Most Multiracial People," *Washington Post*, March 30, 2001, A3.

38. Dale Maharidge, *The Coming White Minority: California's Eruptions and America's Future* (New York: Times Books/Random House, 1996); Peter Schrag, *Paradise Lost: California's Experience, America's Future* (New York: New Press, 1998).

39. Booth, "California's Ethnic Diversity Grows."

40. Peter Skerry, *Mexican Americans: The Ambivalent Minority* (New York: Free Press, 1993).

41. Ungar, *Fresh Blood*, 116–119; Matthew Cooper, "So Long 'Dallas,' Hello High Tech," *Newsweek* 129 (April 21, 1997): 32; Maria Puente, "Bush counts on Hispanics' favor," *USA Today*, October 9, 1998, 19A; Robert D. Kaplan, *An Empire Wilderness: Travels into America's Future* (New York: Random House, 1998), 136.

42. Ungar, *Fresh Blood*, 130–135; Scott Baldauf, "US Checks Illegal Flow at Border," *Christian Science Monitor*, December 23, 1997, at p. 1; Douglas Holt, "Killings Spotlight Growing Danger for Border Patrol," *Chicago Tribune*, July 13, 1998, at Sec. 1, at p. 1; James Pinkerton, "Making a clean sweep," *Houston Chronicle*, October 10, 1999, at p. 1.

43. Anthony DePalma, "Drug Traffickers Smuggling Tons of Cash from U.S. Through Mexico," *New York Times*, January 25, 1996, A10; Sam Dillon, "Mexican Drug Gang's Reign of Blood," *New York Times*, February 4, 1996, Sec. 1, p. 10; Sam Dillon, "Canaries Sing in Mexico, but Uncle Juan Will Not," *New York Times*, February 9, 1996, A4.

44. Brownsville is 91.3% Hispanic; the vast majority of the city's residents are Mexicans and Mexican Americans. Nearly 74% of them are of Mexican descent. Slightly more than 17% of the city identifies as "other Latino."

45. Marjie Mugno Acheson et al., *Texas* (Houston: Lone Star Books, 1999), 518.

46. Allen R. Myerson, "North of the Border, Peso's Drop Is Hurting Stores," *New York Times*, January 17, 1995, at D1; Kris Axtman, "Border becomes a barrier for 'sister cities,' " *Christian Science Monitor*, November 2, 2001, at p. 1.

47. Scott Baldauf, "Politics is twice as complicated along border," *Christian Science Monitor*, June 14, 2000, 3.

48. Roberto Suro, "Rash of Brain Defects in Newborns Disturbs Border City in Texas," *New York Times,* May 31, 1992, Sec. 1, p. 18; David Grogan, "The Baby Killer," *People Weekly* 40 (September 27, 1993): 86–89; Mark Feldstein and Steve Singer, "The Border Babies," *Time* 149 (May 26, 1997): 72.

49. Andrew H. Malcolm, *The Canadians* (New York: Times Books, 1985), 185; Marion Botsford Fraser, *Walking the Line: Travels Along the Canadian/American Border* (San Francisco: Sierra Club Books, 1989); Howard Frank Mosher, *North Country: A Personal Journey Through the Borderland* (Boston: Houghton Mifflin Company, 1997).

50. Kaplan, *An Empire Wilderness,* 311.

51. To be sure, one sees Quebec's fleur-de-lis flying at establishments in South Florida, where hundreds of hotels, restaurants, and marinas fly the Canadian flag to welcome the cold-weather refugees every winter.

52. The Quebeckers' French cultural and linguistic identity emphatically separates them from both Americans and Canadian Anglophones, so the United States is more foreign to them than it is to native-born whites in English Canada. Since the cultural imperative to promote the French language remains overwhelmingly strong in Quebec, this province of 7.4 million people is in little danger of being subsumed by the English-speaking monolith south of it. Moreover, Quebec does not have a history of cultural and linguistic conflict with the United States, as it does with English Canada.

53. Raul A. Fernandez, *The Mexican-American Border Region: Issues and Trends* (Notre Dame, Ind.: University of Notre Dame Press, 1989); Leon C. Metz, *Border: The U.S.-Mexico Line* (El Paso, Tex.: Mangan Books, 1989); William Langewiesche, *Cutting for Sign* (New York: Pantheon Books, 1993); Oscar J. Martínez, *Border People: Life and Society in the U.S.-Mexico Borderlands* (Tucson: University of Arizona Press, 1994); Carlos G. Vélez-Ibáñez, *Border Visions: Mexican Cultures of the Southwest United States* (Tucson: University of Arizona Press, 1996); Rodolfo O. de la Garza and Jesús Velasco, eds., *Bridging the Border: Transforming Mexico-U.S. Relations* (Lanham, Md.: Rowman & Littlefield Publishers, 1997); Sebastian Rotella, *Twilight on the Line: Underworlds and Politics at the U.S.-Mexico Border* (New York: W. W. Norton & Company, 1998); Nancy Gibbs, "A Whole New World," *Time* 157 (June 11, 2001): 36–45. The June 11, 2001, issue of *Time* includes a number of informative articles about life in what the magazine refers to as "Amexica."

54. "A Country of 24 Million," *Time* 157 (June 11, 2001): 46–47.

55. Sam Howe Verhovek, "Pollution Puts People in Peril on the Border with Mexico," *New York Times,* July 4, 1998, A7.

56. For perspectives on this issue, see the Spring 2000 issue of *Natural Resources Journal* ("Articles from the La Paz Symposium on Transboundary Groundwater") and the Fall 2000 issue of *Natural Resources Journal* ("Water Issues in the U.S.-Mexico Borderlands").

57. Howard LaFranchi, "Where Mexico's voters are: here," *Christian Science Monitor,* June 19, 2000, at p. 1; Kevin Sullivan and Mary Jordan, "Mexican Campaign Trail Now Reaches U.S. Cities; 'No One Can Afford to Ignore Us,'" *Washington Post,* August 18, 2001, at A1.

58. Brunner, ed., *TIME Almanac 2002,* 716–717.

59. See Kaplan, *An Empire Wilderness*, 138–145, for similar observations. He describes the differences between the sister cities of Nogales, Sonora, and Nogales, Arizona.

60. Seymour Martin Lipset, *Continental Divide: The Values and Institutions of the United States and Canada* (New York: Routledge, 1990); J. L. Granatstein, *Yankee Go Home? Canadians and Anti-Americanism* (Toronto: Harper Collins Publishers, 1996). For recent polling data on this topic, see Chris Wood, "The Vanishing Border," *Maclean's* 112 (December 20, 1999): 20–23; Andrew Phillips, "Benign Neglect," *Maclean's* 112 (December 20, 1999): 24–25; Bruce Wallace, "What Makes a Canadian?" *Maclean's* 112 (December 20, 1999): 32–34, 36; Brenda Branswell, "A Southern Exposure," *Maclean's* 112 (December 20, 1999): 38–39; Ross Laver, "The Need to Take Risks," *Maclean's* 112 (December 20, 1999): 40–42; "Peering Inward and Outward," *Maclean's* 112 (December 20, 1999): 48–49.

61. Granatstein, *Yankee Go Home?* 246–277; Timothy C. Brown, "The Fourth Member of NAFTA: The U.S.-Mexico Border," *Annals of the American Academy of Political and Social Science* 550 (March 1997): 105–121; Gordon H. Hanson, "U.S.-Mexico Integration and Regional Economies: Evidence from Border-City Pairs," *Journal of Urban Economics* 50 (September 2001): 259–287.

62. Metz, *Border*, 398–403; Geri Smith and Elisabeth Malkin, "The Border," *BusinessWeek* (May 12, 1997): 64–70, 74; Sam Dillon, "A 20-Year G.M. Parts Migration to Mexico," *New York Times,* June 24, 1998, at D1; Geri Smith and Elisabeth Malkin, "Mexican Makeover," *BusinessWeek* (December 21, 1998): 50–52; Daniel B. Wood, "In Mexico, US industry finds uncertainty," *Christian Science Monitor,* November 1, 1999, 3; Daniel B. Wood, "Border factories hit hard by recession, winds of trade," *Christian Science Monitor,* January 23, 2002, at p. 2.

63. Charles J. Whalen, Paul Magnusson, and Geri Smith, "NAFTA's Scorecard: So Far, So Good," *BusinessWeek* (July 9, 2001): 54, 56.

64. Joel Millman, "Come on Down: What Southeast Was to U.S. Companies, Mexico Is Becoming," *Wall Street Journal,* October 29, 1999, at A1; Rafael Tamayo-Flores, "Mexico in the Context of the North American Integration: Major Regional Trends and Performance of Backward Regions," *Journal of Latin American Studies* 33 (May 2001): 377–407.

65. Peter Andreas, "The Escalation of U.S. Immigration Control in the Post-NAFTA Era," *Political Science Quarterly* 113 (Winter 1998–99): 591–615. See, too, Tim McGirk, "Border Clash," *Time* 155 (June 26, 2000): 24–27; Mireya Navarro, "On California's Urban Border, Praise for Immigration Curbs," *New York Times*, August 21, 2001, at A1.

66. Kris Axtman, "Illegal border crossings plunge amid security," *Christian Science Monitor,* November 9, 2001, 3; Daniel B. Wood, "At border, uptick in illegal crossings," *Christian Science Monitor,* January 24, 2002, at p. 1.

67. Donna Leinwand and Yasmin Anwar, "America's guard is down on porous frontier," *USA Today,* March 15, 2000, 21A, 22A; Mark Clayton and Gail Russell Chaddock, "Terrorists aided by a leaky US-Canada line," *Christian Science Monitor,* September 19, 2001, 3; Barbara Crossette, "Canada Pushes

Broad Antiterror Measure, Alarming Some Who Fear Erosion of Rights," *New York Times,* October 18, 2001, B4; Mary Beth Sheridan, "U.S. Moves to Tighten Security on Borders; In Wake of Terrorist Attacks, Congress and INS Are Changing Their Priorities," *Washington Post,* October 18, 2001, A8; Eric Pianin and Stephen Barr, "Lack of Funds for New Agents on U.S. Border Draws Criticism; Entry from Canada Remains Security Issue, Lawmakers Say," *Washington Post,* October 23, 2001, A21; Michael Grunwald, "Economic Crossroads on the Line; Security Fears Have U.S. and Canada Rethinking Life at 49th Parallel," *Washington Post,* December 26, 2001, at A1.

68. Kyle Johnson, " 'Drug Czar's' Plan to Shore Up Leaky Border Meets with Skepticism," *Christian Science Monitor,* August 27, 1998, 3; Kris Axtman, "Rising border traffic, more drugs," *Christian Science Monitor,* May 8, 2001, at p. 1.

69. Philip Shenon, "Teamsters May Stall Bush Goals for Mexican Trucks and Trade," *New York Times,* July 30, 2001, at A1; Tim Weiner, "Experts on Mexican Trucking Say Safety Issue Is Misleading," *New York Times,* August 2, 2001, at A1; Helen Dewar, "Senate Passes Mexican Truck Rules; Vote for Safety Requirements Threatens Bush Trade Policy," *Washington Post,* August 2, 2001, at A1; James C. Benton, "Debate over Mexican Trucks Hinges on Labor Issues as Well as Safety," *CQ Weekly* 59 (August 4, 2001): 1924–1925; Chris Kraul, "NAFTA May Deliver Blow to Mexican Truckers," *Los Angeles Times,* August 15, 2001, at A1; Lizette Alvarez, "Senate Votes to Let Mexican Trucks in U.S.," *New York Times,* December 5, 2001, A20.

70. Howard LaFranchi, "Flag Flap in El Paso Is Borderline Dispute," *Christian Science Monitor,* February 10, 1998, 3; Jose de Cordoba, "Oh, Say, Can You See That Very Big Flag Flying over Mexico?" *Wall Street Journal,* December 11, 1998, at A1; Howard LaFranchi, "¡Viva México! — with XXL flags," *Christian Science Monitor,* September 16, 1999, 6.

71. Granatstein, *Yankee Go Home?* 217–245; Anthony DePalma, "Tough Rules Protecting the Culture Make for Confusion and Surprises," *New York Times,* July 14, 1999, at E1; Joel Baglole, "Canada Loosens Up to Survive Flood of U.S. Media," *Wall Street Journal,* August 9, 2000, A18.

72. Anthony DePalma, "Canada Peeved and Puzzled by Big Neighbor to the South," *New York Times,* September 26, 1997, at A1; David Ivanovich, "To Canada, free trade isn't trouble-free; While volume up, southern partner seen as difficult," *Houston Chronicle,* November 7, 1997, at C1; Mark Heinzl, "Messy Canadian-U.S. Tomato Fight Alleges Dumping by State-of-the-Art Greenhouses North of the Border," *Wall Street Journal,* October 10, 2001, A13; Bernard Simon, "U.S.-Canada Tomato War Heats Up," *New York Times,* December 7, 2001, at W1; Mark Heinzl, "Quarrels Fray U.S.-Canada Ties; Washington Weighs Curbs on Wheat and Steel as Rancor Builds," *Wall Street Journal,* January 21, 2002, A9.

73. Anthony DePalma, "New Rules at U.S. Borders Provoke Criticism," *New York Times,* November 14, 1997, at A1; Ruth Walker, "Canadians shun US efforts to control border," *Christian Science Monitor,* February 8, 2000, 7; Anthony DePalma, "Slow Crawl at the Border," *New York Times,* October 21, 2001, Sec. 5, p. 12; Dean Paton, "Canada border loses easygoing ways — and

business," *Christian Science Monitor,* January 24, 2002, 3; Marci McDonald, "Checkpoint terror," *U.S. News & World Report* 132 (February 11, 2002): 52.

74. Jim Yardley, "Non-Hispanic Whites May Soon Be a Minority in Texas," *New York Times,* March 25, 2001, Sec. 1, p. 22.

75. Evan Osnos, "Sun Belt Is Magnet for Rust Belt Clout," *Chicago Tribune,* December 29, 2000, Sec. 1, at p. 1; John Dillin, "Most US growth comes in GOP Country," *Christian Science Monitor,* December 29, 2000, 2; Randal C. Archibold, "Census Costs States Seats in Congress," *New York Times,* December 29, 2000, at B1; Yochi J. Dreazen, "Census Shows Gains in South and West; Population Shifts Also Pare the Congressional Seats of Midwest, Northeast," *Wall Street Journal,* December 29, 2000, at A2; D'Vera Cohn and David S. Broder, "Nation Grows to 281 Million, Census Finds; Trends to Shift 12 House Seats to Republican-Leaning States," *Washington Post,* December 29, 2000, at A1.

76. U.S. Census Bureau, *Statistical Abstract of the United States: 2000,* Table 23.

77. Jonathan Friedland, "Mexicans Quietly Mull Tying Peso to Dollar," *Wall Street Journal,* September 28, 1998, A20, A25; Howard LaFranchi, "Mexicans start to sing, adios peso — hello $$$," *Christian Science Monitor,* January 12, 1999, at p. 1; Ruth Walker, "Time to trade-in Canada's loonie?" *Christian Science Monitor,* January 12, 1999, 6–7; Fred Langan, "For Canadians, what's worse than a weak loonie?" *Christian Science Monitor,* January 24, 2002, 7.

78. www.census.gov/epcd/www/naics.html.

79. http://naid.sppsr.ucla.edu/

80. On North American integration, see, e.g., Ronald Inglehart, Neil Nevitte, and Miguel Basañez, *The North American Trajectory: Cultural, Economic, and Political Ties among the United States, Canada, and Mexico* (New York: Aldine de Gruyter, 1996); Anthony DePalma, *Here: A Biography of the New American Continent* (New York: PublicAffairs, 2001).

Chapter 6: The Perils of Exclusion

1. Lena Williams, "For Nonwhite Dolls, a Growing Family," *New York Times,* November 1, 1990, at C1; Leah A. Samuel, "Demand Shows Diverse Dolls Are Nothing to Toy With," *Detroit News,* September 17, 1992, at E1; Sallie Han, "Push for Ethnically Diverse Dolls Not Just a Black and White Issue," *Los Angeles Daily News,* August 8, 1996, L19; Kristin Tillotson, "Hello, doll face; The demand for more "ethnic," or nonwhite, dolls reflects changes in demographics - and attitudes," *Minneapolis Star Tribune,* February 2, 2002, at 1E.

2. Maureen Tkacik, "Mattel Hopes Rapunzel's Flowing Tresses Take Barbie Sales Happily Ever After," *Wall Street Journal,* February 7, 2002, B7.

3. On the history of Barbie, see M. G. Lord, *Forever Barbie: The Unauthorized Biography of a Real Doll* (New York: Avon Books, 1995), passim; Ann duCille, *Skin Trade* (Cambridge, Mass.: Harvard University Press, 1996), 8–59; Marco Tosa, *Barbie: Four Decades of Fashion, Fantasy, and Fun,* trans. Linda M. Eklund (New York: Harry N. Abrams, 1998).

4. Mireya Navarro, "A New Barbie in Puerto Rico Divides Island and Mainland," *New York Times,* December 27, 1997, at A1.

5. Patricia Wen, "PC doll omits a minority; Barbie's presidential ambitions disenfranchise Asian-Americans," *Chicago Tribune*, June 12, 2000, Sec. 5, p. 5.

6. Kenneth B. Clark and Mamie P. Clark, "Racial Identification and Preference in Negro Children," in Eleanor M. Maccoby, Theodore M. Newcomb, and Eugene L. Hartley, eds., *Readings in Social Psychology*, 3d ed. (New York: Henry Holt and Company, 1958), 602–611; Ben Keppel, *The Work of Democracy: Ralph Bunche, Kenneth B. Clark, Lorraine Hansberry, and the Cultural Politics of Race* (Cambridge, Mass.: Harvard University Press, 1995), 97–131.

7. Judith D. R. Porter, *Black Child, White Child: The Development of Racial Attitudes* (Cambridge, Mass.: Harvard University Press, 1971), 62–86; Darlene Powell Hopson and Derek S. Hopson, *Different and Wonderful: Raising Black Children in a Race-Conscious Society* (New York: Prentice Hall Press, 1990), xix–xx, xxii, 127–128; Marguerite A. Wright, *I'm Chocolate, You're Vanilla: Raising Healthy Black and Biracial Children in a Race-Conscious World* (San Francisco: Jossey-Bass Publishers, 1998), 50–53.

8. Han, "Push for Ethnically Diverse Dolls Not Just a Black and White Issue."

9. Tillotson, "Hello, doll face."

10. "The History of Betty Crocker." www.GeneralMills.com/corporate/about/history/hist_betty.pdf.

11. Ibid.

12. Rebecca Quick, "Betty Crocker Plans to Mix Ethnic Looks for Her New Face; General Mills Wants to Blend Features of 75 Women to Make One Perfect Cook," *Wall Street Journal Europe*, September 12, 1995, at p. 1; Megan Rosenfeld, "Recipe for a New Betty Crocker; Take 75 Faces. Mix Liberally. Pour into Computer. Serve with Relish," *Washington Post*, September 12, 1995, at B1; Joseph A. Kirby, "Betty Crocker Gets Multicultural Makeover; Images of 75 Women Blended in Update of Icon," *Chicago Tribune*, March 20, 1996, 3; Elaine W. Shoben, "Getting the Skin Color 'Right,' " *Chicago Tribune*, March 28, 1996, 25; Steven V. Roberts, "Betty, meet Ashley, a '90s woman," *U.S. News & World Report* 120 (April 1, 1996): 10–11; Charles Paul Freund, "The New Face of Betty Crocker; Her Portrait as Drawn by Adam Smith's Invisible Hand," *Washington Post*, April 14, 1996, at H1.

13. Kirby, "Betty Crocker Gets Multicultural Makeover."

14. Marilyn Halter, *Shopping for Identity: The Marketing of Ethnicity* (New York: Schocken Books, 2000), 180.

15. www.bettycrocker.com.

16. Todd Wilkinson, "Attracting minorities to national parks," *Christian Science Monitor*, February 1, 1999, 3; Krista Reese, "At U.S. Parks, New Path to the Past; Sites and Exhibits Designed to Reach a Diverse Audience," *Washington Post*, March 23, 2001, at A1.

17. Jeffrey M. Humphreys, "Buying Power at the Beginning of a New Century: Projections for 2000 and 2001," *Georgia Business and Economic Conditions* 60 (July/August 2000). www.selig.uga.edu/forecast/GBEC/GBEC7800.PDF.

18. Halter, *Shopping for Identity*, passim; Arlene Dávila, *Latinos, Inc.: The Marketing and Making of a People* (Berkeley: University of California Press, 2001).

19. Scott Baldauf, "Surprise: More channels mean resegregation," *Christian Science Monitor,* August 6, 1999, at p. 1; Tamar Jacoby, "Adjust Your Sets: Meet the power behind segregated television. You," *New Republic* 222 (January 24, 2000): 21–25; Lisa de Moraes, "TV Networks Adding Some Color for Fall; New Minority Lead Roles Receive Little Applause," *Washington Post,* May 21, 2000, at A1; Thelma Adams, "The Networks Barely Hear the Latin Boom Outside," *New York Times,* October 29, 2000, Sec. 2, p. 35; Pamela Paul, "Soap Operas Battle the Suds," *American Demographics* 24 (January 2002): 26–30.

20. Diane Weathers, "And Along Came Tyson," *Essence* 27 (August 1996): 64–66, 126, 130–132; Marc Spiegler, "Marketing Street Culture: Bringing Hip-Hop Style to the Mainstream," *American Demographics* 18 (November 1996): 28–32, 34; Joshua Levine, "Badass sells," *Forbes* 159 (April 21, 1997): 142–144, 146–148; Christopher John Farley, "Hip-Hop Nation," *Time* 153 (February 8, 1999): 54–58, 60–64; Cathy Scott, "Rap goes from urban streets to Main Street," *Christian Science Monitor,* February 26, 1999, at p. 1; Charles Aaron, "Black Like Them," *Utne Reader* (March/April 1999): 68–73.

21. Ibid.

22. Richard Bernstein, *Dictatorship of Virtue: How the Battle over Multiculturalism Is Reshaping Our Schools, Our Country, and Our Lives* (New York: Vintage Books/Random House, 1995); Lawrence Levine, *The Opening of the American Mind* (Boston: Beacon Press, 1996); Sandra Stotsky, *Losing Our Language: How Multicultural Classroom Instruction Is Undermining Our Children's Ability to Read, Write, and Reason* (New York: Free Press, 1999).

23. Michael Eric Dyson, *I May Not Get There With You: The True Martin Luther King, Jr.* (New York: Free Press, 2000).

24. For a brief but excellent biography of Chavez, see Susan Ferriss and Ricardo Sandoval, *The Fight in the Fields: Cesar Chavez and the Farmworkers Movement* (New York: Harcourt Brace & Company, 1997).

25. Paul Van Slambrouck, "California bid for holiday honoring Cesar Chavez," *Christian Science Monitor,* April 10, 2000, 2–3; Rene Sanchez, "Honoring Chavez — and Hispanic Clout; Crusade for Holiday Signals Calif. Power Shift," *Washington Post,* April 24, 2000, A3; John Ritter, "Calif. seeks way to honor both Chavez, his work; Lawmakers want help for farm labor, along with holiday," *USA Today,* April 28, 2000, 2A.

26. Dinesh D'Souza, *The End of Racism: Principles for a Multicultural Society* (New York: Free Press, 1995), 201–243; Frederick R. Lynch, *The Diversity Machine: The Drive to Change the "White Male Workplace"* (New York: Free Press, 1997); Erin Kelly and Frank Dobbin, "How Affirmative Action Became Diversity Management: Employer Response to Antidiscrimination Law, 1961–1996," in John David Skrentny, ed., *Color Lines: Affirmative Action, Immigration, and Civil Rights Options for America* (Chicago: University of Chicago Press, 2001), 87–117.

27. Federal Glass Ceiling Commission, *Good for Business: Making Full Use of the Nation's Human Capital* (Washington, D.C.: Federal Glass Ceiling Commission, March 1995); John P. Fernandez, *Race, Gender, and Rhetoric: The True State of Race and Gender Relations in Corporate America* (New York: McGraw-Hill, 1999).

28. Jeremy Kahn, "Diversity Trumps the Downturn," *Fortune* 144 (July 9, 2001): 114–116; "America's 50 Best Companies for Minorities," *Fortune* 144 (July 9, 2001): 122–124, 126, 128.

29. Alison Stein Wellner, "Capitalist Dreams," *American Demographics* 24 (March 2002): 36–41.

30. Charlotte Steeh and Maria Krysan, "Poll Trends: Affirmative Action and the Public, 1970–1995," *Public Opinion Quarterly* 60 (Spring 1996): 128–158; David R. Williams et al., "Traditional and Contemporary Prejudice and Urban Whites' Support for Affirmative Action and Government Help," *Social Problems* 46 (November 1999): 503–527; Lawrence Bobo, "Race and Beliefs about Affirmative Action: Assessing the Effects of Interests, Group Threat, Ideology, and Racism," in David O. Sears, Jim Sidanius, and Lawrence Bobo, eds., *Racialized Politics: The Debate about Racism in America* (Chicago: University of Chicago Press, 2000), 137–164; Lawrence D. Bobo, "Race, Interests, and Beliefs about Affirmative Action: Unanswered Questions and New Directions," in John David Skrentny, ed., *Color Lines: Affirmative Action, Immigration, and Civil Rights Options for America* (Chicago: University of Chicago Press, 2001), 191–213.

31. Frederick R. Lynch, *Invisible Victims: White Males and the Crisis of Affirmative Action* (New York: Praeger, 1991); Michele Galen et al., "White, Male, and Worried," *BusinessWeek* (January 31, 1994): 50–55; Jonathan Kaufman, "Mood Swing: White Men Shake Off That Losing Feeling on Affirmative Action," *Wall Street Journal,* September 5, 1996, at A1.

32. Dana Y. Takagi, *The Retreat from Race: Asian American Admissions and Racial Politics* (New Brunswick, N.J.: Rutgers University Press, 1992); Myrtle P. Bell, David A. Harrison, and Mary E. McLaughlin, "Asian American Attitudes Toward Affirmative Action in Employment: Implications for the Model Minority Myth," *Journal of Applied Behavioral Science* 33 (September 1997): 356–377. See, too, Michael A. Fletcher, "For Asian Americans, a Barrier or a Boon? Washington State Debate over Affirmative Action Reveals Ambiguities on the Issue," *Washington Post,* June 20, 1998, A9; Paul Van Slambrouck, "Asian students struggle with high rate of success," *Christian Science Monitor,* March 18, 1999, at p. 1.

33. William G. Bowen and Derek Bok, *The Shape of the River: Long-Term Consequences of Considering Race in College and University Admissions* (Princeton, N.J.: Princeton University Press, 1998).

34. Adam Cohen, "When the Field Is Level," *Time* 154 (July 5, 1999): 30–34; Jodi Wilgoren, "New Law in Texas Preserves Racial Mix in States' Colleges," *New York Times,* November 24, 1999, at A1; Kenneth J. Cooper, "Colleges Testing New Diversity Initiatives; Success Is Uneven Without Traditional Affirmative Action," *Washington Post,* April 2, 2000, A4; Daniel Golden, "Fudge Factor: Some High Schools Finagle to Cram Kids into Top 10% of Class," *Wall Street Journal,* May 15, 2000, at A1; Rick Bragg, "Minority Enrollment Rises in Florida College System," *New York Times,* August 30, 2000, A18; Daniel Golden, "Admission: Possible; Hispanic Students Find a Way Around Affirmative-Action Ban," *Wall Street Journal,* June 26, 2001, at A1; Steven A. Holmes, "Leveling the Playing Field, but for Whom?" *New York Times,* July 1, 2001, Sec. 4, p. 6;

Adam Cohen, "Coloring the Campus," *Time* 158 (September 17, 2001): 48–49; Mark Sappenfield, "New scale to weigh college applicants," *Christian Science Monitor,* November 19, 2001, at p. 1.

35. I visited Storm Lake, Iowa, on April 30, 1999, and on September 15, 2000. This vignette draws upon my observations during those visits; my reading of the *Storm Lake Times,* the leading newspaper in the area, for the past three years; and my interviews with Michael Hanna, the principal of Storm Lake Senior High School, and Tina Donath of the *Storm Lake Times,* in Storm Lake, Iowa, on September 15, 2000. For background on Storm Lake, I relied upon the following sources: Roy Beck, *The Case Against Immigration* (New York: W. W. Norton & Company, 1996), 22–23, 100, 101, 105–107, 109–120; Steven A. Holmes, "In Iowa Town, Strains of Diversity; Local Jobs Attract Immigrants from Mexico and Southeast Asia," *New York Times,* February 17, 1996, Sec. 1, p. 6; Stephen J. Hedges, Dana Hawkins, and Penny Loeb, "The New Jungle," *U.S. News & World Report* 121 (September 23, 1996): 34–45; Marc Cooper, "The Heartland's Raw Deal," *Nation* 264 (February 3, 1997): 11–12, 14–17.

36. Ibid.

37. See, e.g., John S. Lapinski et al., "Poll Trends: Immigrants and Immigration," *Public Opinion Quarterly* 61 (Summer 1997): 356–383; Peter Burns and James G. Gimpel, "Economic Insecurity, Prejudicial Stereotypes, and Public Opinion on Immigration Policy," *Political Science Quarterly* 115 (Summer 2000): 201–225.

38. Daniel S. Hamermesh and Frank D. Bean, eds., *Help or Hindrance? The Economic Implications of Immigration for African Americans* (New York: Russell Sage Foundation, 1998); Frank D. Bean and Stephanie Bell-Rose, eds., *Immigration and Opportunity: Race, Ethnicity, and Employment in the United States* (New York: Russell Sage Foundation, 1999); George J. Borjas, *Heaven's Door: Immigration Policy and the American Economy* (Princeton, N.J.: Princeton University Press, 1999); Charles Hirschman, Philip Kasinitz, and Josh DeWind, eds., *The Handbook of International Migration: The American Experience* (New York: Russell Sage Foundation, 1999); Nelson Lim, "On the Back of Blacks? Immigrants and the Fortunes of African Americans," in Roger Waldinger, ed., *Strangers at the Gates: New Immigrants in Urban America* (Berkeley: University of California Press, 2001), 186–227.

39. Jeffrey Schmalz, "Miami's New Ethnic Conflict: Haitians vs. American Blacks," *New York Times,* February 19, 1989, Sec. 1, at p. 1; Marjorie Valbrun, "Caribbean Immigrants' Political Moves Stir Tensions," *Wall Street Journal,* June 30, 1998, A20; Alejandro Portes and Alex Stepick, *City on the Edge: The Transformation of Miami* (Berkeley: University of California Press, 1993), 55–56, 177–178, 185, 189–192.

40. Griff Witte, "Divisions Still Exist Among Area's Blacks," *Miami Herald,* February 4, 2001, 6BH.

41. Nancy Foner, ed., *Islands in the City: West Indian Migration to New York* (Berkeley: University of California Press, 2001).

42. James Davison Hunter, *Culture Wars: The Struggle to Define America* (New York: Basic Books, 1991); Philip Perlmutter, *Divided We Fall: A History of Ethnic, Religious, and Racial Prejudice in America* (Ames: Iowa State University

Press, 1992); David H. Bennett, *The Party of Fear: The American Far Right from Nativism to the Militia Movement,* 2d ed. (New York: Vintage Books/Random House, 1995).

43. Herbert McClosky and John Zaller, *The American Ethos: Public Attitudes toward Capitalism and Democracy* (Cambridge, Mass.: Harvard University Press, 1984); Everett Carll Ladd and Karlyn H. Bowman, "The Nation Says No to Class Warfare," *USA Today* 127 (May 1999): 24–26.

44. Robert M. Entman and Andrew Rojecki, *The Black Image in the White Mind: Media and Race in America* (Chicago: University of Chicago Press, 2000).

45. Lee Sigelman and Susan Welch, "The Contact Hypothesis Revisited: Black-White Interaction and Positive Racial Attitudes," *Social Forces* 71 (March 1993): 781–795; Christopher G. Ellison and Daniel A. Powers, "The Contact Hypothesis and Racial Attitudes among Black Americans," *Social Science Quarterly* 75 (June 1994): 385–400; Daniel A. Powers and Christopher G. Ellison, "Interracial Contact and Black Racial Attitudes: The Contact Hypothesis and Selectivity Bias," *Social Forces* 74 (September 1995): 205–226; Lee Sigelman et al., "Making Contact? Black-White Social Interaction in an Urban Setting," *American Journal of Sociology* 101 (March 1996): 1306–1332; Susan Welch and Lee Sigelman, "Getting to Know You? Latino-Anglo Social Contact," *Social Science Quarterly* 81 (March 2000): 67–83; Robert M. Stein, Stephanie Shirley Post, and Allison L. Rinden, "Reconciling Context and Contact Effects on Racial Attitudes," *Political Research Quarterly* 53 (June 2000): 285–303; F. Andrew Hanssen, "A Test of the Racial Contact Hypothesis from a Natural Experiment: Baseball's All-Star Voting as a Case," *Social Science Quarterly* 82 (March 2001): 51–66.

46. Richard Nadeau, Richard G. Niemi, and Jeffrey Levine, "Innumeracy about Minority Populations," *Public Opinion Quarterly* 57 (Fall 1993): 332–347; Lee Sigelman and Richard G. Niemi, "Innumeracy about Minority Populations: African Americans and Whites Compared," *Public Opinion Quarterly* 65 (Spring 2001): 86–94.

47. Lee Sigelman and Susan Welch, *Black Americans' Views of Racial Equality: The Dream Deferred,* 2d ed. (New York: Cambridge University Press, 1994); Howard Schuman et al., *Racial Attitudes in America: Trends and Interpretations,* 2d ed. (Cambridge, Mass.: Harvard University Press, 1997); Steven A. Tuch and Jack M. Martin, eds., *Racial Attitudes in the 1990s: Continuity and Change* (Westport, Conn.: Praeger, 1997). See, too, *The Washington Post*/Kaiser Family Foundation/Harvard University Survey Project, *The Four Americas: Government and Social Policy Through the Eyes of America's Multi-racial and Multi-ethnic Society* (Menlo Park, Calif.: Henry J. Kaiser Family Foundation, December 1995); *The Washington Post*/Kaiser Family Foundation/Harvard University Survey Project, *National Survey on Latinos in America* (Menlo Park, Calif.: Henry J. Kaiser Family Foundation, May 2000); *The Washington Post*/Kaiser Family Foundation/Harvard University Survey Project, *Race and Ethnicity in 2001: Attitudes, Perceptions and Experiences* (Menlo Park, Calif.: Henry J. Kaiser Family Foundation, August 2001).

48. "Active Hate Groups in the United States in the Year 2001," *Intelligence Report* (Spring 2002): 34–37.

49. Race (particularly antiblack violence) is the most common motivation for hate crimes, followed by religion (especially anti-Semitic acts); then sexual orientation (particularly attacks on gay males); and, finally, ethnicity/national origin (especially crimes against Hispanics). U.S. Census Bureau, *Statistical Abstract of the United States: 2000*, Table 338.

50. Arthur J. Magida, *Prophet of Rage: A Life of Louis Farrakhan and His Nation* (New York: Basic Books, 1996); Mattias Gardell, *In the Name of Elijah Muhammad: Louis Farrakhan and the Nation of Islam* (Durham, N.C.: Duke University Press, 1996); Robert Singh, *The Farrakhan Phenomenon: Race, Reaction, and the Paranoid Style in American Politics* (Washington, D.C.: Georgetown University Press, 1997).

51. Michael Kelly, "Playing with Fire," *New Yorker* 72 (July 15, 1996): 28–35; Joe Holley, "Who was burning the black churches?" *Columbia Journalism Review* 35 (September/October 1996): 26–33; Sarah A. Soule and Nella Van Dyke, "Black church arson in the United States, 1989–1996," *Ethnic and Racial Studies* 22 (July 1999): 724–742.

52. Pyong Gap Min, *Caught in the Middle: Korean Merchants in America's Multiethnic Cities* (Berkeley: University of California Press, 1996); Kwang Chung Kim, ed., *Koreans in the Hood: Conflict with African Americans* (Baltimore: Johns Hopkins University Press, 1999).

53. *The Washington Post*/Kaiser Family Foundation/Harvard University Survey Project, *The Four Americas: Government and Social Policy Through the Eyes of America's Multi-racial and Multi-ethnic Society* (Menlo Park, Calif.: Henry J. Kaiser Family Foundation, December 1995); *The Washington Post*/ Kaiser Family Foundation/Harvard University Survey Project, *National Survey on Latinos in America* (Menlo Park, Calif.: Henry J. Kaiser Family Foundation, May 2000); *The Washington Post*/Kaiser Family Foundation/Harvard University Survey Project, *Race and Ethnicity in 2001: Attitudes, Perceptions and Experiences* (Menlo Park, Calif.: Henry J. Kaiser Family Foundation, August 2001). For scholarly perspectives on these issues, see, e.g., James Jennings, ed., *Blacks, Latinos, and Asians in Urban America: Status and Prospects for Politics and Activism* (Westport, Conn.: Praeger, 1994); Wilbur C. Rich, ed., *The Politics of Minority Coalitions: Race, Ethnicity, and Shared Uncertainties* (Westport, Conn.: Praeger, 1996); Scott Cummings and Thomas Lambert, "Anti-Hispanic and Anti-Asian Sentiments among African Americans," *Social Science Quarterly* 78 (June 1997): 338–353; Paula D. McClain and Steven C. Tauber, "Black and Latino Socioeconomic and Political Competition: Has a Decade Made a Difference?" *American Politics Quarterly* 26 (April 1998): 237–252; Irwin L. Morris, "African American Voting on Proposition 187: Rethinking the Prevalence of Interminority Conflict," *Political Research Quarterly* 53 (March 2000): 77–98.

54. Harold M. Rose, "Blacks and Cubans in Metropolitan Miami's Changing Economy," *Urban Geography* 10 (September-October 1989): 464–486; Guillermo J. Grenier and Max J. Castro, "Triadic Politics: Ethnicity, Race, and Politics in Miami, 1959–1998," *Pacific Historical Review* 68 (May 1999): 273–292; Daryl Harris, "Generating Racial and Ethnic Conflict in Miami: Impact of American Foreign Policy and Domestic Racism," in James Jennings, ed., *Blacks,*

Latinos, and Asians in Urban America: Status and Prospects for Politics and Activism (Westport, Conn.: Praeger, 1994), 79–94.

55. Roberto Suro, *Strangers Among Us: How Latino Immigration Is Transforming America* (New York: Alfred A. Knopf, 1998), 243–258; James H. Johnson Jr., Walter C. Farrell Jr., and Chandra Guinn, "Immigration Reform and the Browning of America: Tensions, Conflicts, and Community Instability in Metropolitan Los Angeles," in Charles Hirschman, Philip Kasinitz, and Josh DeWind, eds., *The Handbook of International Migration: The American Experience* (New York: Russell Sage Foundation, 1999), 390–411. See, too, Kenneth B. Noble, "Blacks Say Life in Los Angeles Is Losing Allure," *New York Times,* January 8, 1995, Sec. 1, at p. 1; Joe Domanick, "The Browning of Black L.A.," *Los Angeles* 41 (May 1996): 74–79, 172; V. Dion Haynes, "Blacks Caught in L.A. Shift; Years of Political Gains Lost to Rising Hispanic Influence," *Chicago Tribune,* April 28, 1997, Sec. 1, at p. 1; Michael A. Fletcher, "In Rapidly Changing L.A., a Sense of Future Conflicts," *Washington Post,* April 7, 1998, at A1; Martin Kasindorf and Maria Puente, "Hispanics and blacks find their futures entangled," *USA Today,* September 10, 1999, 21A, 22A.

56. George E. Curry and Trevor W. Coleman, "Supreme Insult," *Emerge* 8 (November 1996): 38–40, 42–44, 46, 48.

57. Harriet Beecher Stowe, *Uncle Tom's Cabin* (1852; reprint, with an introduction by Raymond Weaver, New York: Modern Library, 1938). For a description of how Uncle Tom has been part of American popular culture over the years, see Linda Williams, *Playing the Race Card: Melodramas of Black and White from Uncle Tom to O. J. Simpson* (Princeton, N.J.: Princeton University Press, 2001), 45–135.

58. Robert B. Costello, ed., *Random House Webster's College Dictionary* (New York: Random House, 1991), 1450.

59. Joan Biskupic, "After a Quiet Spell, Justice Finds Voice; Conservative Thomas Emerges from the Shadow of Scalia," *Washington Post,* May 24, 1999, at A1.

60. Earl Shorris, *Latinos: A Biography of the People* (New York: W. W. Norton & Company, 1992), 169.

61. Sue Anne Pressley, "Use of Indian Mascots Brings Justice Dept. to N.C. Town," *Washington Post,* February 17, 1999, A3; Brooke A. Masters, "Team Names Go to Court; Redskins, Other Indian Logos Face Challenges," *Washington Post,* April 7, 1999, at B1; Douglas S. Looney, "If team names offend, must they change?" *Christian Science Monitor,* April 14, 2000, 19; James C. McKinley Jr., "Schools Urged to Stop Using Indian Names," *New York Times,* April 6, 2001, at B1; John J. Miller, "What's in a (Team) Name?" *National Review* 53 (April 16, 2001): 40–42; Manuel Perez-Rivas, "Mascot Skirmish Goes Local; Poolesville, Others Rethink Indian Team Names," *Washington Post,* April 24, 2001, at B1; Mary Otto, "Md. Activist Leads Effort to Reclaim Indian Names; Opponents Criticize Official's Tactics," *Washington Post,* September 3, 2001, at B1.

62. Carol Spindel, *Dancing at Halftime: Sports and the Controversy over American Indian Mascots* (New York: New York University Press, 2000).

63. Eric Schmitt, "Battle Rages over a 5-Letter Four-Letter Word," *New York Times,* September 4, 1996, A16; Mark Obmascik, "Indian request nets new name for squawfish," *Denver Post,* March 28, 1999, at A1; A. Jay Higgins, "Fighting Words; Maine moves to wipe ethnic slur off its map," *Boston Globe,* May 9, 1999, B6; Lisa Gutierrez, "The changing word on 'squaw'; Movement afoot to remove name from landmarks," *Kansas City (Mo.) Star,* April 15, 2000, at E1; Brian Ford, "Change for the better," *Tulsa World,* June 4, 2000, at p. 1; Matthew Barrows, " 'Squaw' Name Is Still All over the Map of the United States," *Cleveland Plain Dealer,* November 25, 2000, 16A; Archana Pyati and Kara Briggs, "Legislators Vote to Cut 'Squaw' from Place Names," *Portland (Ore.) Oregonian,* June 1, 2001, at A1.

64. See, e.g., Nina Eliasoph, " 'Everyday Racism' in a Culture of Political Avoidance: Civil Society, Speech, and Taboo," *Social Problems* 46 (November 1999): 479–502.

65. Michel Marriott, "Internet Unleashing a Dialogue on Race," *New York Times,* March 8, 1998, Sec. 1, at p. 1.

66. David Kamp, "The Color of Truth," *Vanity Fair* (August 1998): 124–131, 166–169; Michel Marriott, "Rock on a Roll," *Essence* 29 (November 1998): 116–118, 184, 186, 188; Christopher John Farley, "Seriously Funny," *Time* 154 (September 13, 1999): 66–70; Julia Reed, "The crack-up," *Vogue* 190 (September 2000): 628–631; Justin Driver, "The Mirth of a Nation: Black comedy's reactionary hipness," *New Republic* 224 (June 11, 2001): 29–33.

67. Nat Hentoff, *Free Speech for Me — But Not for Thee: How the American Left and Right Relentlessly Censor Each Other* (New York: Aaron Asher Books/ HarperCollins Publishers, 1992); Mari Matsuda et al., *Words That Wound: Critical Race Theory, Assaultive Speech, and the First Amendment* (Boulder, Colo.: Westview Press, 1993); Samuel Walker, *Hate Speech: The History of an American Controversy* (Lincoln: University of Nebraska Press, 1994), 127–158; Henry Louis Gates Jr. et al., *Speaking of Race, Speaking of Sex: Hate Speech, Civil Rights, and Civil Liberties* (New York: New York University Press, 1994); Edward J. Cleary, *Beyond the Burning Cross: A Landmark Case of Race, Censorship, and the First Amendment* (New York: Vintage Books/Random House, 1995); Laurence R. Marcus, *Fighting Words: The Politics of Hateful Speech* (Westport, Conn.: Praeger, 1996); Timothy C. Shiell, *Campus Hate Speech on Trial* (Lawrence: University Press of Kansas, 1998).

68. Howard Kurtz, *Hot Air: All Talk, All the Time* (New York: Times Books/ Random House, 1996), 228–308.

69. Hentoff, *Free Speech for Me — But Not for Thee,* 18–41; Randall Kennedy, *Nigger: The Strange Career of a Troublesome Word* (New York: Pantheon Books, 2002), 52, 137–141.

70. Mark Sappenfield, "New race-bias issue: the workplace climate," *Christian Science Monitor,* August 17, 1999, at p. 1; Aaron Bernstein, "Racism in the Workplace," *BusinessWeek* (July 30, 2001): 64–67.

71. For essays that explore the notion of "white trash," see Matt Wray and Annalee Newitz, eds., *White Trash: Race and Class in America* (New York: Routledge, 1997).

72. Joel Garreau, "Punch Lines That Hit the Mark; Jeff Foxworthy's Oddly Acceptable Redneck Roast," *Washington Post,* February 10, 1995, at B1; Kevin Sack, "2,000 Ways You Might Be a Redneck," *New York Times,* February 7, 1996, at C1; Greg Paeth, "King of the rednecks," *Cincinnati Post,* February 18, 1998, at 1B; Ed Will, "Foxworthy profits by staying in the red; Southern roots a boon for comic," *Denver Post,* October 22, 1998, E5.

73. Dahleen Glanton, "Celebrating the redneck within," *Chicago Tribune,* July 9, 2001, Sec. 1, p. 6. See, too, Bethany Bultman, *Redneck Heaven: Portrait of a Vanishing Culture* (New York: Bantam Books, 1996).

74. Kennedy, *Nigger,* passim. Randall Kennedy's book on the N-word is the definitive source on the topic.

75. Andrew Hacker, *Two Nations: Black and White, Separate, Hostile, Unequal,* 2d ed. (New York: Ballantine Books, 1995), 47.

76. Kennedy, *Nigger,* passim.

77. Ibid.

78. Michael A. Fletcher, "Hate Screens on the Web Raise Alarm; ADL Developing Way to Filter Out Sites," *Washington Post,* October 22, 1997, A16; Robert Marquand, "Hate Groups Market to the Mainstream," *Christian Science Monitor,* March 6, 1998, 4; Michael James, "Hate Online; Racists, neo-Nazis and gay bashers spread their message online," *Baltimore Sun,* October 26, 1998, at 1C; Achy Obejas, "Hate Rock," *Chicago Tribune,* March 16, 1999, at p. 1; Michel Marriott, "Rising Tide: Sites Born of Hate," *New York Times,* March 18, 1999, at G1; Connie Lauerman, "WWWIHate; Hatemongers of Every Kind Are Finding a Forum on the Internet," *Chicago Tribune,* May 7, 1999, at p. 1; Jared Sandberg, "Spinning a Web of Hate," *Newsweek* 134 (July 19, 1999): 28–29; Lisa Guernsey, "Mainstream Sites Serve as Portals to Hate," *New York Times,* November 30, 2000, at G1; "Active Hate Sites on the Internet in the Year 2001," *Intelligence Report* (Spring 2002): 38–43.

79. Viveca Novak, "Off the Bench?" *Time* 157 (February 26, 2001): 54–55; Charles Lane and Amy Goldstein, "At High Court, a Retirement Watch; Rehnquist, O'Connor Top List of Possibilities as Speculation on Replacement Grows," *Washington Post,* June 17, 2001, A4; Abraham McLaughlin, "Bush's judge picker could be picked," *Christian Science Monitor,* July 10, 2001, at p. 1; Lois Romano, "Positioned for a Call to Justice," *Washington Post,* July 10, 2001, at C1.

80. Paula D. McClain, "The Changing Dynamics of Urban Politics: Black and Hispanic Municipal Employment — Is There Competition?" *Journal of Politics* 55 (May 1993): 399–414; Robert Rosenblatt, "Blacks Dominate Postal Service, Latino Charges," *Los Angeles Times,* August 3, 1994, A3; Bill McAllister, "Postal Official: Too Many Blacks Hired; Lack of Hispanics in Big Cities Cited," *Washington Post,* August 3, 1994, at A1; Lori Rodriguez, "Black workers do fill a lot of jobs with city; But pointing that out has sparked a furor," *Houston Chronicle,* July 12, 1998, at A1; Hugh Davis Graham, "Affirmative Action for Immigrants? The Unintended Consequences of Reform," in John David Skrentny, ed., *Color Lines: Affirmative Action, Immigration, and Civil Rights Options for America* (Chicago: University of Chicago Press, 2001), 53–70.

81. Bernard Weinraub, " 'Beloved' Tests Racial Themes at Box Office; Will This Winfrey Film Appeal to White Audiences?" *New York Times,* October 13,

1998, at B1; Sharon Waxman, "Hollywood Tailors Its Movies to Sell in Foreign Markets; Studios Say 'Ethnic' Films Are Not Popular Overseas," *Washington Post,* October 26, 1998, at A1.

82. Cheo Hodari Coker, "Hollywood Blackout," *Premiere* 14 (October 2000): 29–30; George Alexander, "Fade to Black," *Black Enterprise* 31 (December 2000): 107–108, 110, 112, 114–115.

83. Michael Gross, *Model: The Ugly Business of Beautiful Women* (New York: William Morrow and Company, 1995), passim; Robin Givhan, "The White Stuff; On the Runway, Subtle Racism Puts Models of Color Out of Fashion," *Washington Post,* June 5, 1996, at C1; Veronica Webb, "Where Have All the Black Models Gone?" *Essence* 27 (September 1996): 108–110, 166, 168; Margo Jefferson, "Looking at What Black Looks Like," *New York Times,* June 11, 1997, C13; Anna Wintour, "Fashion's New Faces," *Vogue* (July 1997): 26; Allison Samuels, "Black Beauty's New Face," *Newsweek* 130 (November 24, 1997): 68; Bruce Horovitz, "Color them beautiful — and visible," *USA Today,* May 2, 2001, at 1B.

Chapter 7: Accommodating Diversity

1. Bob Quick and Ben Neary, "He always knew he'd win," *Santa Fe New Mexican,* March 4, 1998, A4.

2. Terry Pindell, *A Good Place to Live: America's Last Migration* (New York: Henry Holt and Company, 1995), 8–34.

3. Ibid.; James Brooke, "In Santa Fe, Residents Turn Cold Shoulder to Newcomers," *New York Times,* January 19, 1997, Sec. 1, p. 16; James Brooke, "Entrenched Hispanic Democrats Feel New Mexico's Sands Shifting," *New York Times,* July 15, 1997, at A1.

4. Mayor Larry Delgado, interview by author, Santa Fe, New Mexico, November 1, 2000.

5. Ibid.

6. Most of the information, including the quotations, in this paragraph comes from my interview with Mayor Delgado on November 1, 2000. As a rule, the *New Mexican* is an excellent source of information about Santa Fe politics and Mayor Delgado's administration. Two newspaper articles in particular were especially informative. See Ben Neary, "Delgado by a mile," *Santa Fe New Mexican,* March 4, 1998, A1, A4; Bob Quick and Ben Neary, "He always knew he'd win," *Santa Fe New Mexican,* March 4, 1998, A1, A4.

7. Delgado, interview.

8. Mayor Delgado took 42.8% of the vote in 2002. His strongest challenger, Councilor Patti Bushee, won 31.1%. Former City Manager Ike Pino, the brother of Debbie Jaramillo, took 18.3%, while Councilor Frank Montaño won only 7.9%. (The totals do not add to 100 because of rounding.) John T. Huddy, "Delgado Wins Another Term," *Albuquerque Journal,* March 6, 2002, at p. 1.

9. Steve Terrell, "Delgado's challenge: Forging new City Council into a team," *Santa Fe New Mexican,* March 6, 2002, at A1.

10. Delgado, interview.

11. www.gothamgazette.com/searchlight2001/dist20.html. I visited Flushing on April 25, 2001, so I am familiar with the demographics of this neighborhood.

12. To research this vignette, I relied on extensive secondary sources as well as the biographical data on John Liu's Web site: www.liunewyork.com. For commentary, see Somini Sengupta, "Bringing Asian Voice to the Council; Three Candidates in Flushing Want to Become the First," *New York Times*, March 30, 2000, at B1; Dennis Duggan, "Putting a New Face on the Body Politic," *Newsday*, July 22, 2001, G2; Bryan Virasami, "Pioneers: See How They Run; Flushing election may yield the city's first Asian-American official," *Newsday*, August 7, 2001, A23; Somini Sengupta, "In Flushing, a Chance to Make History," *New York Times*, September 7, 2001, B7; Bryan Virasami, " 'Breakthrough' Victory for Liu," *Newsday*, October 5, 2001, A12.

13. Ibid.

14. The four candidates in the September 2001 Democratic primary finished in the following order: John C. Liu (30.9%), Ethel Chen (28.6%), Terence Y. Park (20.8%), and Richard Jannaccio (19.7%). Similarly, four candidates were on the ballot in the November 2001 general election. Democrat Liu won with 55% of the vote, while Republican Ryan J. Walsh was a distant second with 33%. The Green Party's Paul D. Graziano took 7% of the vote. Independent candidate Martha Flores-Vazquez trailed with 5%. www.gothamgazette.com/searchlight2001/dist20.html.

15. Celia W. Dugger, "Queens Old-Timers Uneasy as Asian Influence Grows," *New York Times*, March 31, 1996, Sec. 1, at p. 1.

16. Vivian S. Toy, "Councilwoman Apologizes for Comments About Asians," *New York Times*, May 3, 1996, B3; Elizabeth Kolbert, "For Minorities, Divided Vote Dims Chances," *New York Times*, July 7, 1997, at B1; Jonathan P. Hicks, "Anti-Asian Remarks an Issue in Primary," *New York Times*, September 4, 1997, B4.

17. Jonathan P. Hicks, "New City Council a Portrait Composed by Term Limits," *New York Times*, November 11, 2001, Sec. 1A, p. 43.

18. Bryan Virasami, "Groundbreaking Win for Asian-Americans," *Newsday*, November 8, 2001, A56.

19. Maldwyn Allen Jones, *American Immigration*, 2d ed. (Chicago: University of Chicago Press, 1992), 200–211.

20. Michael Barone and Richard E. Cohen with Charles E. Cook Jr., *The Almanac of American Politics 2002* (Washington, D.C.: National Journal, 2001), 1348, 1350.

21. Thomas Byrne Edsall with Mary D. Edsall, *Chain Reaction: The Impact of Race, Rights, and Taxes on American Politics* (New York: W. W. Norton & Company, 1992).

22. Barone and Cohen, *The Almanac of American Politics 2002*, 28.

23. William B. Prendergast, *The Catholic Voter in American Politics: The Passing of the Democratic Monolith* (Washington, D.C.: Georgetown University Press, 1999).

24. Barone and Cohen, *The Almanac of American Politics 2002*, 28.

25. William H. Flanigan and Nancy H. Zingale, *Political Behavior of the American Electorate*, 8th ed. (Washington, D.C.: CQ Press, 1994); *The Washing-*

ton Post/Kaiser Family Foundation/Harvard University Survey Project, *National Survey on Latinos in America* (Menlo Park, Calif.: Henry J. Kaiser Family Foundation, May 2000).

26. Rodney E. Hero and Caroline J. Tolbert, "A Racial/Ethnic Diversity Interpretation of Politics and Policy in the States of the U.S.," *American Journal of Political Science* 40 (August 1996): 851–871.

27. Rhodes Cook, "Cities: Decidedly Democratic, Declining in Population," *Congressional Quarterly Weekly Report* 55 (July 12, 1997): 1645–1653; Rhodes Cook, "Suburbia: Land of Varied Faces and a Growing Political Force," *Congressional Quarterly Weekly Report* 55 (May 24, 1997): 1209–1217; Rhodes Cook, "America's Heartland: Neither One Mind nor One Heart," *Congressional Quarterly Weekly Report* 55 (September 20, 1997): 2243–2246, 2248–2249; Alison Mitchell, "Two Parties Seek to Exploit a Relentless Boom in the Suburbs," *New York Times,* May 4, 1999, A22; John Ritter, "Suburbs throw states to the right," *USA Today,* May 17, 2001, A3.

28. Flanigan and Zingale, *Political Behavior of the American Electorate,* 14–17.

29. Sidney Verba, Kay Lehman Schlozman, and Henry E. Brady, *Voice and Equality: Civic Voluntarism in American Politics* (Cambridge, Mass.: Harvard University Press, 1995), 37.

30. Virginia A. Chanley, Thomas J. Rudolph, and Wendy M. Rahn, "The Origins and Consequences of Public Trust in Government: A Time Series Analysis," *Public Opinion Quarterly* 64 (Fall 2000): 239–256; Clem Brooks and Simon Cheng, "Declining Government Confidence and Policy Preferences in the U.S.: Devolution, Regime Effects, or Symbolic Change?" *Social Forces* 79 (June 2001): 1343–1375; Greg M. Shaw and Stephanie L. Reinhart, "Poll Trends: Devolution and Confidence in Government," *Public Opinion Quarterly* 65 (Fall 2001): 369–388. It should be noted that there was a dramatic upsurge in the amount of confidence Americans had in the nation's institutions, particularly the federal government, in the aftermath of the September 11 terrorist attacks. Pamela Paul, "Faith in Institutions," *American Demographics* 24 (January 2002): 20–21.

31. et al., *Voice and Equality,* 228–266; Jan E. Leighley and Arnold Vedlitz, "Race, Ethnicity, and Political Participation: Competing Models and Contrasting Explanations," *Journal of Politics* 61 (November 1999): 1092–1114.

32. Wendy K. Tam Cho, "Naturalization, Socialization, Participation: Immigrants and (Non-) Voting," *Journal of Politics* 61 (November 1999): 1140–1155.

33. The turnout figures come from the state-level data in *The Almanac of American Politics 2002.*

34. For more information about this group, see Jack C. Doppelt and Ellen Shearer, *Nonvoters: America's No-Shows* (Thousand Oaks, Calif.: Sage Publications, 1999).

35. Michael A. Fletcher, "The Color of Campaign Finance; Report Contends Minorities' Political Clout Is Limited by System," *Washington Post,* September 23, 1998, A23; Jeffrey H. Birnbaum, *The Money Men: The Real Story of Fund-raising's Influence on Political Power in America* (New York: Crown Publishers, 2000).

36. *Buckley v. Valeo,* 424 U.S. 1 (1976).

37. Jennifer Steen, "Maybe You Can Buy an Election, But Not with Your Own Money," *Washington Post,* June 25, 2000, at B1.

38. Joel A. Thompson and Gary F. Moncrief, "The Implication of Term Limits for Women and Minorities: Some Evidence from the States," *Social Science Quarterly* 74 (June 1993): 300–309; W. Robert Reed and D. Eric Schansberg, "The House under Term Limits: What Would It Look Like?" *Social Science Quarterly* 76 (December 1995): 699–716; Stanley M. Caress, "The Influence of Term Limits on the Electoral Success of Women," *Women & Politics* 20:3 (1999): 45–63; Susan J. Carroll and Krista Jenkins, "Do Term Limits Help Women Get Elected?" *Social Science Quarterly* 82 (March 2001): 197–201. For journalistic commentary, see Hicks, "New City Council a Portrait Composed by Term Limits"; Richard Wolf, "States feel term limits' effects," *USA Today,* April 20, 1998, at 1A; Lois Romano, "With Term Limits, Political Rookies Abound; Incumbents Pack It In as Term Limits Hit Home," *Washington Post,* May 28, 1998, at A1; Michelle Boorstein, "Term Limits Shake up the Status Quo in Five State Capitols," *Los Angeles Times,* August 9, 1998, at A18; Amy Pyle, "Women to Play Largest Role Ever in Legislature," *Los Angeles Times,* November 23, 1998, at A3; Francis X. Clines, "Term Limits Bring Wholesale Change into Legislatures," *New York Times,* February 14, 2000, at A1; Antonio Olivo, "Term Limits a Mixed Blessing for Latinos," *Los Angeles Times,* July 2, 2000, at B1.

39. Ibid.

40. Tim Weiner and David E. Sanger, "Democrats Hoped to Raise $7 Million from Asians in U.S.," *New York Times,* December 28, 1996, Sec. 1, at p. 1; Paul Glastris, "Multicultural foreign policy in Washington," *U.S. News & World Report* 123 (July 21, 1997): 34.

41. James Sterngold, "For Asian-Americans, Political Power Can Lead to Harsh Scrutiny," *New York Times,* November 3, 1996, Sec. 1, at p. 36; David E. Kaplan and Julian E. Barnes, "Is the latest Red Peril actually a red herring?" *U.S. News & World Report* 123 (July 21, 1997): 29–30; Paul Van Slambrouck, "Asian Americans Forge Larger Political Role," *Christian Science Monitor,* February 24, 1998, at p. 1; L. Ling-chi Wang, "Race, Class, Citizenship, and Extraterritoriality: Asian Americans and the 1996 Campaign Finance Scandal," *Amerasia Journal* 24 (Spring 1998): 1–21.

42. Paul Van Slambrouck, "Native Americans wield new political clout," *Christian Science Monitor,* October 27, 1999, 3.

43. Barone and Cohen, *The Almanac of American Politics 2002,* 1598–1599; Brian Nutting and H. Amy Stern, eds., *Politics in America: 2002, The 107th Congress* (Washington, D.C.: CQ Press, 2001), 1062.

44. Ibid.

45. Hanna Rosin, "A 'Maturing' Christian Right; Diffuse Movement Turns More Mainstream, Less Loyal to GOP," *Washington Post,* April 7, 2000, A4.

46. Gary Washburn, "Pulaski Day Perfect for Politicians," *Chicago Tribune,* March 3, 1998, 3.

47. Oscar Corral, "Diaz Honors Diversity at Swearing-In," *Miami Herald,* November 18, 2001, at 1B.

48. Maria Puente, "Bush, Gore try bilingual approach to win voters; Some question whether 'Spanish strategy' works," *USA Today,* August 26, 1999, 4A.

49. Flynn McRoberts, "2 Texas candidates debate over Spanish-only debate," *Chicago Tribune*, March 1, 2002, Sec. 1, p. 5; Kris Axtman, "Qué es esto: ¿A Texas debate in Spanish?" *Christian Science Monitor*, March 1, 2002, at p. 1; Jim Yardley, "One Texas Candidate Cools on a Debate in Spanish," *New York Times*, March 1, 2002, A14; R. G. Ratcliffe and Jo Ann Zuniga, "Sanchez, Morales square off; Governor hopefuls spar over integrity," *Houston Chronicle*, March 2, 2002, at p. 1; Megan K. Stack, "Verbal Attacks Mark Texas Debate," *Los Angeles Times*, March 2, 2002, A16; Claudia Kolker, "Texas Candidates Debate in Spanish; Latinos Hold Key in Governor Race," *Boston Globe*, March 3, 2002, A13.

50. Louis Bolce, Gerald DeMaio, and Douglas Muzzio, "Blacks and the Republican Party: The 20 Percent Solution," *Political Science Quarterly* 107 (Spring 1992): 63–79; Louis Bolce, Gerald DeMaio, and Douglas Muzzio, "The 1992 Republican 'Tent': No Blacks Walked In," *Political Science Quarterly* 108 (Summer 1993): 255–270; R. W. Apple Jr., "G.O.P. Tries Hard to Win Black Votes, but Recent History Works Against It," *New York Times*, September 19, 1996, B11; Terry M. Neal, "In Outreach to Blacks, a GOP Credibility Gap; Bush's Inclusive Image Has Detractors," *Washington Post*, June 13, 2000, at A1.

51. Steven A. Holmes, "Minority Focus Raises Some Doubts," *New York Times*, August 14, 1996, A1.

52. Adam Nagourney with Janet Elder, "Poll of Delegates Shows Convention Solidly on Right," *New York Times*, July 31, 2000, at A1; Dahleen Glanton, "GOP Seeks Diverse Image; Critics Say It's Surface Only," *Chicago Tribune*, July 31, 2000, at p. 1; Faye M. Anderson, "The Republicans' Illusion of Inclusion," *New York Times*, August 1, 2000, A21; Dan Balz, "GOP Puts Focus on Diversity; Powell Calls on 'Party of Lincoln' to Act Like It," *Washington Post*, August 1, 2000, at A1; Brent Staples, "The Republican Party's Exercise in Minstrelsy," *New York Times*, August 2, 2000, A24; Martin Kasindorf, "On diversity, a split picture; TV image not representative of delegations," *USA Today*, August 2, 2000, 7A; Daniel LeDuc and R. H. Melton, "Delegations Reflect Gains in Grass-Roots Diversity," *Washington Post*, August 3, 2000, at A1.

53. Celia W. Dugger, "Immigrant Voters Reshape Politics," *New York Times*, March 10, 1996, Sec. 1, at p. 1; Steven A. Holmes, "Influx of Immigrants Is Changing Electorate," *New York Times*, October 30, 1996, A16.

54. Paul Glastris, "Immigration boomerang," *U.S. News & World Report* 122 (March 17, 1997): 24–26; Dan Carney, "Republicans Feeling the Heat as Policy Becomes Reality," *Congressional Quarterly Weekly Report* 55 (May 17, 1997): 1131–1136.

55. Neal, "In Outreach to Blacks, a GOP Credibility Gap"; Dana Milbank, "The Year of the Latino Voter? Only in Campaign Rhetoric," *Washington Post*, May 21, 2000, at B1; R. W. Apple Jr., "Courting of Voting Bloc Poses Question of Motive," *New York Times*, August 2, 2000, A16.

56. Glastris, "Multicultural foreign policy in Washington," 30–35; Yossi Shain, "Ethnic Diasporas and U.S. Foreign Policy," *Political Science Quarterly* 109 (Winter 1994–95): 811–841; Alexander DeConde, *Ethnicity, Race, and American Foreign Policy: A History* (Boston: Northeastern University Press, 1992).

57. Dan Morgan and Kevin Merida, "South Asia Rivals Had Money on South Dakota Senate Race; Ethnic Donors Play Powerful Role in U.S. Politics," *Washington Post,* March 24, 1997, at A1.

58. Glastris, "Multicultural foreign policy in Washington," 34.

59. Ibid.

60. Michael Dobbs, "Foreign Aid Shrinks, but Not for All; With Clout in Congress, Armenia's Share Grows," *Washington Post,* January 24, 2001, at A1.

61. Rodolfo O. de la Garza and Louis DeSipio, "Interests Not Passions: Mexican-American Attitudes toward Mexico, Immigration from Mexico, and Other Issues Shaping U.S.-Mexico Relations," *International Migration Review* 32 (Summer 1998): 401–422.

62. Glastris, "Multicultural foreign policy in Washington," 35; Steven Erlanger, "For 47 Years, a Lobby Group with Muscle Has Tirelessly Tended U.S.-Israeli Ties," *New York Times,* April 26, 1998, Sec. 1, p. 6; Ilene R. Prusher, "Sizing Up $3 billion in US aid," *Christian Science Monitor,* November 18, 1999, 6–7; U.S. Census Bureau, *Statistical Abstract of the United States: 2000* (120th ed.) (Washington, D.C.: U.S. Government Printing Office, 2000), Table 1318.

63. Ron Scherer, "Noshing it out on the New York campaign trail," *Christian Science Monitor,* April 19, 1999, at p. 1; Adam Nagourney, "White House and First Lady Are at Odds over Jerusalem," *New York Times,* July 9, 1999, at B1; Adam Nagourney, "First Lady Seeks Political Equilibrium with Jewish Voters," *New York Times,* August 3, 1999, B4; J. J. Goldberg, *Jewish Power: Inside the American Jewish Establishment* (Reading, Mass.: Addison-Wesley Publishing Company, 1996), 30.

64. María de los Angeles Torres, *In the Land of Mirrors: Cuban Exile Politics in the United States* (Ann Arbor: University of Michigan Press, 1999), passim; Miles A. Pomper, "Cuban-American Agenda Marked by New Diversity," *CQ Weekly* 57 (February 27, 1999): 467–470; Patrick J. Haney and Walt Vanderbush, "The Role of Ethnic Interest Groups in U.S. Foreign Policy: The Case of the Cuban American National Foundation," *International Studies Quarterly* 43 (June 1999): 341–361.

65. Walt Vanderbush and Patrick J. Haney, "Policy toward Cuba in the Clinton Administration," *Political Science Quarterly* 114 (Fall 1999): 387–408. See, too, Mireya Navarro, "Alliance of G.O.P. and Cuban-Americans Shows Rift," *New York Times,* October 22, 1996, A24; Douglas Waller, "Clinton's Cuban Road to Florida," *Time* 148 (October 28, 1996): 45–46; Steven Lee Myers, "Clinton Eases Law Punishing Allies for Trading in Cuba," *New York Times,* January 4, 1997, at A1.

66. Peter Wallsten, "Elián Case Forces a Fresh Look at Cuban-American Influence," *CQ Weekly* 58 (April 8, 2000): 827–829.

67. Karen DeYoung, "Anti-Castro Figure Named to State Dept.; Critics Vow to Block Bush Nominee, Citing Conflict of Interest, Iran-Contra Ties," *Washington Post,* April 15, 2001, A15; Karen DeYoung, "President Against Relaxing Cuban Economic Sanctions; Increase in U.S. Aid to Dissidents Supported," *Washington Post,* May 19, 2001, A5; Karen DeYoung, "Bush Continues a Clinton Policy on Cuba," *Washington Post,* July 17, 2001, A10; Karen DeYoung, "Pres-

ident Installs 2 Disputed Nominees; Action on State, Labor Dept. Picks Sidesteps Senate," *Washington Post,* January 12, 2002, at A1.

68. Representative Robert G. Clark Jr., interview by author, Jackson, Mississippi, June 5, 2001.

69. Ibid.

70. Today Robert Clark represents House District 47, a rural district of 21,046 in central Mississippi that encompasses parts of Holmes, Yazoo, and Attala counties. His district is 72% black and 26.2% white. I spent five hours traveling around Speaker Clark's district on June 5, 2001.

71. Clark, interview.

72. "Pioneer Black Mississippi Politician: Robert George Clark Jr.," *New York Times,* August 20, 1982, A18. Clark was the only African-American member of the Mississippi legislature during his first eight years in office. As a result, he served "almost as an unofficial governor to Mississippi blacks, who came to him from throughout the state with their problems," according to Jack Bass and Walter DeVries. See Jack Bass and Walter DeVries, *The Transformation of Southern Politics: Social Change and Political Consequence Since 1945* (New York: Basic Books, 1976), 209–210. The quotation appears on page 210.

73. Clark and his compatriots had quite a battle royal over this piece of legislation. The Education Reform Act of 1982 resulted in a compulsory school attendance law and reduced the student-teacher ratio by ten percent — and by 20 percent in the lower grades. Although Mississippi's schools continue to lag behind those in many states, Speaker Clark points out that things would be far worse if the Educational Reform Act of 1982 had not been enacted into law. Clark, interview.

74. Clark, interview.

75. Ibid.

76. Clark, interview; "Statement Made by Speaker Pro Tem Robert G. Clark"; David Firestone, "Mississippi House Wants Voters to Decide Fate of Confederate Emblem on State Flag," *New York Times,* January 10, 2001, A12; Paul Duggan, "Mississippi Voters to Decide on Use of Confederate Emblem," *Washington Post,* March 25, 2001, A3.

77. C. Vann Woodward, *Reunion and Reaction: The Compromise of 1877 and the End of Reconstruction* (Boston: Little, Brown and Company, 1951).

78. J. Morgan Kousser, *The Shaping of Southern Politics: Suffrage Restriction and the Establishment of the One-Party South, 1880–1910* (New Haven, Conn.: Yale University Press, 1974).

79. Bass and DeVries, *The Transformation of Southern Politics;* V. O. Key Jr., *Southern Politics in State and Nation* (New York: Alfred A. Knopf, 1949); Dewey W. Grantham, *The Life and Death of the Solid South: A Political History* (Lexington: University Press of Kentucky, 1988); Richard K. Scher, *Politics in the New South: Republicanism, Race, and Leadership in the Twentieth Century* (New York: Paragon House, 1992).

80. Edsall and Edsall, *Chain Reaction,* 37.

81. Earl Black and Merle Black, *Politics and Society in the South* (Cambridge, Mass.: Harvard University Press, 1987), 3–12, 175–194; Kenny J. Whitby and

Franklin D. Gilliam, Jr., "A Longitudinal Analysis of Competing Explanations for the Transformation of Southern Congressional Politics," *Journal of Politics* 53 (May 1991): 504–518; Richard Fleisher, "Explaining the Change in Roll-Call Voting Behavior of Southern Democrats," *Journal of Politics* 55 (May 1993): 327–341; Earl Black, "The Newest Southern Politics," *Journal of Politics* 60 (August 1998): 591–612.

82. Hastings Wyman, "Black Power in Dixie," *Southern Political Report* (May 21, 2001): 1.

83. Ibid.

84. Ibid.

85. Wyman, "Black Power in Dixie," 1–8.

86. In 1999, for instance, Democrat C. Jack Ellis was elected the first black mayor of Macon, Georgia. White flight has turned this central Georgia city into a black bastion. And James Perkins Jr. became the first African-American chief executive of Selma, Alabama, in 2000. He defeated Joe Smitherman, the former segregationist who had served as mayor for the past 36 years.

87. Nicol C. Rae, *Southern Democrats* (New York: Oxford University Press, 1994); James M. Glaser, *Race, Campaign Politics, and the Realignment in the South* (New Haven, Conn.: Yale University Press, 1996); Alexander P. Lamis, ed., *Southern Politics in the 1990s* (Baton Rouge: Louisiana State University Press, 1999); Terrel L. Rhodes, *Republicans in the South: Voting for the State House, Voting for the White House* (Westport, Conn.: Praeger, 2000).

88. *Southern Political Report*, November 20, 2000, 4–5.

89. Kevin Sack, "North Carolina Incumbent Finds Recipe for Success," *New York Times*, October 15, 1996, A22; Terry M. Neal, "Georgia's Centrist of Attention; Gov. Miller Called Model for Democrats," *Washington Post*, October 16, 1998, at A1; Kevin Sack, "3 G.O.P. Candidates for Governor Face Trouble," *New York Times*, October 22, 1998, A21; Peter Beinart, "The Carville Trick," *Time* 152 (November 16, 1998): 58; Jason Zengerle, "Man from Hope: Why Zell Miller screws the Democrats," *New Republic* 224 (February 12, 2001): 25–26.

90. Kevin Sack, "Democrats Buck 20-Year Trend, Faring Well in Once 'Solid' South," *New York Times*, November 4, 1998, at A1; Kevin Sack, "Black Turnout in the South Led to Surge by Democrats," *New York Times*, November 6, 1998, at A1.

91. John Harwood, "Dixie Coup: Democrats Rise Again, Give GOP Revolution Quite a Turn in South," *Wall Street Journal*, July 22, 1999, at A1.

92. The racial composition of Jacksonville, Florida's largest city, is 62.2% white, 28.7% black, 4.2% Latino, 2.7% Asian, and 1.6% multiracial.

93. Barone and Cohen, *The Almanac of American Politics 2002*, 360–425; Joan Carver and Tom Fiedler, "Florida: A Volatile National Microcosm," in Alexander P. Lamis, ed., *Southern Politics in the 1990s* (Baton Rouge: Louisiana State University Press, 1999), 343–376.

94. Barone and Cohen, *The Almanac of American Politics 2002*, 1436–1520; Bryan Curtis, "Lone Star: Can the Texas GOP survive W.'s departure?" *New Republic* 224 (February 12, 2001): 19–20; Richard Murray and Sam Attlesey,

"Texas: Republicans Gallop Ahead," in Alexander P. Lamis, ed., *Southern Politics in the 1990s* (Baton Rouge: Louisiana State University Press, 1999), 305–342.

95. For an overview of the prospects for minorities in Texas politics, see Patricia Kilday Hart, "Minority Report," *Texas Monthly* 29 (October 2001): 62, 64, 66.

96. Barry Yeoman, "Hispanic Diaspora," *Mother Jones* (July/August 2000): 34–41, 76–77; Arian Campo-Flores, "A Town's Two Faces," *Newsweek* 137 (June 4, 2001): 34–35.

97. Rick Badie, "Reed aims to recruit Hispanics for GOP; Latinos not focused on politics, leaders say," *Atlanta Constitution*, May 15, 2001, 1JJ.

98. Gail Russell Chaddock, "How Democrats plan to win Dixie," *Christian Science Monitor*, August 31, 2001, 2.

99. Niall A. Palmer, *The New Hampshire Primary and the American Electoral Process* (Westport, Conn.: Praeger, 1997); Hugh Winebrenner, *The Iowa Precinct Caucuses: The Making of a Media Event*, 2d ed. (Ames: Iowa State University Press, 1998); Randall E. Adkins and Andrew J. Dowdle, "Break Out the Mint Juleps? Is New Hampshire the 'Primary' Culprit Limiting Presidential Nomination Forecasts?" *American Politics Quarterly* 28 (April 2000): 251–269; Emmett H. Buell Jr., "The Changing Face of the New Hampshire Primary," in William G. Mayer, ed., *In Pursuit of the White House 2000: How We Choose Our Presidential Nominees* (New York: Chatham House Publishers/Seven Bridges Press, 2000), 87–144; Randall E. Adkins and Andrew J. Dowdle, "How Important Are Iowa and New Hampshire to Winning Post-Reform Presidential Nominations?" *Political Research Quarterly* 54 (June 2001): 431–444.

100. Ibid.

101. Frances E. Lee and Bruce I. Oppenheimer, *Sizing Up the Senate: The Unequal Consequences of Equal Representation* (Chicago: University of Chicago Press, 1999), 224.

102. As of March 2002, Nevada still had only two U.S. representatives. But the Silver State gained a House seat in reapportionment, so it will have three U.S. representatives next year.

103. Lee and Oppenheimer, *Sizing Up the Senate*, passim.

104. Matthew M. Hoffman, "The Illegitimate President: Minority Vote Dilution and the Electoral College," *Yale Law Journal* 105 (January 1996): 935–1021; Lawrence D. Longley and Neil R. Peirce, *The Electoral College Primer 2000* (New Haven, Conn.: Yale University Press, 1999), especially 154–161.

Chapter 8: Beyond Black and White

1. Herman J. Viola, *Ben Nighthorse Campbell: An American Warrior* (New York: Orion Books, 1993), 194–199.

2. Ibid., 199–203.

3. Ibid., 1–102.

4. Ibid., 103–141, 171–193.

5. Ibid., 204–309.

6. Ibid., xiii.

7. Michael Barone and Richard E. Cohen with Charles E. Cook Jr., *The Almanac of American Politics 2002* (Washington, D.C.: National Journal, 2001), 298–300; Brian Nutting and H. Amy Stern, eds., *CQ's Politics in America: 2002, The 107th Congress* (Washington, D.C.: CQ Press, 2001), 166–167.

8. ˙On points two and three, see Viola, *Ben Nighthorse Campbell,* 214–216, 230–231, 257–299.

9. The 2000 census found that Colorado was 74.5% white, 17.1% Hispanic, 3.7% black, 2.2% Asian, 1.7% mixed race, and 0.7% Indian.

10. David Duke, *My Awakening: A Path to Racial Understanding* (Mandeville, La.: Free Speech Press, 1999).

11. Thomas B. Edsall, "David Duke Says He'll Run for Rep. Livingston's Seat; Ex-Klansman Has Been Problem for GOP," *Washington Post,* December 21, 1998, A19; Michael Janofsky, "David Duke Heads North to Raise Money for House Race," *New York Times,* January 3, 1999, Sec. 1, p. 15; Tyler Bridges, "Southern Comfort: The coddling of David Duke," *New Republic* 220 (February 22, 1999): 13–14; Matt Labash, "David Duke, Louisiana's Long-Playing Nightmare," *Weekly Standard* 4 (April 26, 1999): 23–26; Kevin Sack, "Louisiana G.O.P. Facing David Duke, Again," *New York Times,* April 29, 1999, A18; Thomas B. Edsall, "Duke Is Fighting Forces of Change in Voting Today; Issues That Gained White Following Decade Ago Are Absent," *Washington Post,* May 1, 1999, A3; Kevin Sack, "David Duke Misses Louisiana Runoff but Has Strong Showing," *New York Times,* May 3, 1999, A22.

12. Ibid.

13. Douglas D. Rose, ed., *The Emergence of David Duke and the Politics of Race* (Chapel Hill: University of North Carolina Press, 1992); Tyler Bridges, *The Rise of David Duke* (Jackson: University Press of Mississippi, 1994); John C. Kuzenski, Charles S. Bullock III, and Ronald Keith Gaddie, eds., *David Duke and the Politics of Race in the South* (Nashville, Tenn.: Vanderbilt University Press, 1995); David Firestone, "A Dealing with David Duke Haunts Louisiana Governor," *New York Times,* June 22, 1999, A18.

14. Duke is the founder and president of the European-American Unity and Rights Organization. For more information about this hate group, see the organization's Web site at www.whitecivilrights.com.

15. "To Russia, with Books," *Intelligence Report* (Fall 2001): 16; Michael Perlstein, "Duke bilked backers, FBI says; Raid explained; no charges filed," *New Orleans Times-Picayune,* November 18, 2000, at p. 1 (national section); Michael Perlstein, "Duke says feds are trying to silence him," *New Orleans Times-Picayune,* December 12, 2000, at p. 1 (metro section); John Daniszewski, "Ex-Klansman David Duke Sets Sights on Russian Anti-Semites," *Los Angeles Times,* January 6, 2001, A2; Craig Timberg, "Va. Rescinds White History Declaration; Separatists Sought Salute," *Washington Post,* May 11, 2001, at B1; Darryl Fears, "Deep Distrust of Government Still Simmers; Many Americans Who Deplore Terrorist Acts of Sept. 11 Question or Criticize U.S. Actions," *Washington Post,* October 29, 2001, A2.

16. Nadine Cohodas, *Strom Thurmond and the Politics of Southern Change* (New York: Simon & Schuster, 1993), 20–26, 28–32, 38–39, 46–48, 63–67.

17. Kenneth O'Reilly, *Nixon's Piano: Presidents and Racial Politics from Washington to Clinton* (New York: Free Press, 1995), 96, 117–122, 128, 156, 158, 161.

18. Numan V. Bartley, *The Rise of Massive Resistance: Race and Politics in the South During the 1950's* (Baton Rouge: Louisiana State University Press, 1969).

19. Thomas Byrne Edsall with Mary D. Edsall, *Chain Reaction: The Impact of Race, Rights, and Taxes on American Politics* (New York: W. W. Norton & Company, 1992).

20. Edsall and Edsall, *Chain Reaction;* Edward G. Carmines and James A. Stimson, *Issue Evolution: Race and the Transformation of American Politics* (Princeton, N.J.: Princeton University Press, 1989); Robert Huckfeldt and Carol Weitzel Kohfeld, *Race and the Decline of Class in American Politics* (Urbana: University of Illinois Press, 1989).

21. Ibid.

22. Greenberg, *Middle Class Dreams,* 23–54; Edsall and Edsall, *Chain Reaction,* 163–164, 170–171, 181–185, 225–226, 230.

23. Jon F. Hale, "The Making of the New Democrats," *Political Science Quarterly* 110 (Summer 1995): 207–232.

24. Robin Toner, "Racial Politics: Back with a Vengeance," *New York Times,* November 24, 1991, Sec. 4, at p. 1.

25. David H. Bennett, *The Party of Fear: The American Far Right from Nativism to the Militia Movement,* 2d ed. (New York: Vintage Books/Random House, 1995), passim; Maldwyn Allen Jones, *American Immigration,* 2d ed. (Chicago: University of Chicago Press, 1992), 134–145.

26. For excellent analysis of the politics of race in America, see Edsall and Edsall, *Chain Reaction;* Kathleen Hall Jamieson, *Dirty Politics: Deception, Distraction, and Democracy* (New York: Oxford University Press, 1992), 15–120; Donald R. Kinder and Lynn M. Sanders, *Divided by Color: Racial Politics and Democratic Ideals* (Chicago: University of Chicago Press, 1996); Keith Reeves, *Voting Hopes or Fears? White Voters, Black Candidates, and Racial Politics in America* (New York: Oxford University Press, 1997); Tali Mendelberg, *The Race Card: Campaign Strategy, Implicit Messages, and the Norm of Equality* (Princeton, N.J.: Princeton University Press, 2001).

27. Timothy Bates and Darrell L. Williams, "Racial Politics: Does It Pay?" *Social Science Quarterly* 74 (September 1993): 507–522; Susan E. Howell and William P. McLean, "Performance and Race in Evaluating Minority Mayors," *Public Opinion Quarterly* 65 (Fall 2001): 321–343. See, too, Jim Sleeper, "The End of the Rainbow: America's changing urban politics," *New Republic* 209 (November 1, 1993): 20, 22–25; Jack E. White, "Bright City Lights," *Time* 142 (November 1, 1993): 30–32; Rogers Worthington, "Black Voters Look Beyond Race Politics," *Chicago Tribune,* November 7, 1993, 21; Kevin Sack, "Mayor Finds Old Issue Emerging in New Way," *New York Times,* July 15, 1996, at A7; Ben Wildavsky, "A painful plan to save Detroit's sorry schools," *U.S. News & World Report* 126 (March 15, 1999): 30; Vicki Lee Parker, "African-American Mayors Are Facing Squeeze Between Economics, Needs of Black Community," *Wall Street Journal,* October 12, 1999, A28.

28. Parker, "African-American Mayors Are Facing Squeeze Between Economics, Needs of Black Community"; Harry S. Jaffe and Tom Sherwood, *Dream City: Race, Power, and the Decline of Washington, D.C.* (New York: Simon & Schuster, 1994); Jonetta Rose Barras, *The Last of the Black Emperors: The Hollow Comeback of Marion Barry in the New Age of Black Leaders* (Baltimore: Bancroft Press, 1998); Michael H. Cottman, "Williams's Wary Approach to Race; Mayor Sees Better Services as One Way to Ease Tension," *Washington Post*, March 13, 1999, at A1.

29. Craig Timberg, "Barry Making His Return in a Much Different D.C.," *Washington Post*, March 8, 2002, at B1.

30. David T. Canon, *Race, Redistricting, and Representation: The Unintended Consequences of Black Majority Districts* (Chicago: University of Chicago Press, 1999), 34–51.

31. The Land of Lincoln elected the nation's first black female Senator, Carol Moseley-Braun, in 1992. Roland Burris, an African-American who was a statewide officeholder in Illinois for 16 years, sought the Democratic gubernatorial nomination in 1998 and 2002. Jesse White, the Illinois Secretary of State, is presently the state's highest-ranking black elected official.

32. Reeves, *Voting Hopes or Fears?*; Jack Citrin, Donald Philip Green, and David O. Sears, "White Reactions to Black Candidates: When Does Race Matter?" *Public Opinion Quarterly* 54 (Spring 1990): 74–96; Raphael J. Sonenshein, "Can Black Candidates Win Statewide Elections?" *Political Science Quarterly* 105 (Summer 1990): 219–241; Carol K. Siegelman et al., "Black Candidates, White Voters: Understanding Racial Bias in Political Perceptions," *American Journal of Political Science* 39 (February 1995): 243–265; Stephan Thernstrom and Abigail Thernstrom, *America in Black and White: One Nation, Indivisible* (New York: Simon & Schuster, 1997), 286–310; Baodong Lui, "The Positive Effect of Black Density on White Crossover Voting: Reconsidering Social Interaction Theory," *Social Science Quarterly* 82 (September 2001): 602–615.

33. Barone and Cohen, *The Almanac of American Politics 2002*, 468–469. See, too, Alex Salkever, "Governor's Race Shakes Hawaii's Liberal Base," *Christian Science Monitor*, May 21, 1998, 3; Michael Janofsky, "Shift in Politics and Economics Seen for Hawaii," *New York Times*, August 24, 1998, at A1.

34. Glen Grant and Dennis M. Ogawa, "Living Proof: Is Hawaii the Answer?" *Annals of the American Academy of Political and Social Science* 530 (November 1993): 137–154; Michael Haas, ed., *Multicultural Hawai'i: The Fabric of a Multiethnic Society* (New York: Garland Publishing, 1998).

35. Michael Haas, "Politics," in Michael Haas, ed., *Multicultural Hawai'i: The Fabric of a Multiethnic Society* (New York: Garland Publishing, 1998), 147–164.

36. Democrat Oren E. Long represented Hawaii in the U.S. Senate from 1959 to 1963.

37. Republican William Quinn served as governor from 1959 to 1963. He was succeeded by Democrat John A. Burns, who held the office from 1963 to 1973.

38. Jeff Kass, "For more diverse politics, go west," *Christian Science Monitor*, March 2, 1999, at p. 1.

39. Timothy Egan, "When to Campaign with Color," in Correspondents of The New York Times, *How Race Is Lived in America: Pulling Together, Pulling Apart* (New York: Times Books/Henry Holt and Company, 2001), 115–131.

40. The data about female legislators are from Nutting and Stern, eds., *CQ's Politics in America: 2002, The 107th Congress.*

41. Kathy Khoury, "Arizona voters create first all-female political lineup," *Christian Science Monitor,* December 23, 1998, 2–3; Martin Kasindorf, "Running Arizona; Five women hold the reins in the Grand Canyon State," *USA Today,* October 29, 1999, at 1A.

42. Kass, "For more diverse politics, go west."

43. For a useful overview of New Mexico politics, see Barone and Cohen, *The Almanac of American Politics 2002,* 1012–1031; F. Chris Garcia, "To Get Along or to Go Along? Pluralistic Accommodation versus Progress in New Mexico Politics and Government," in Richard W. Etulain, ed., *Contemporary New Mexico, 1940–1990* (Albuquerque: University of New Mexico Press, 1994), 25–56.

44. Himilce Novas, *The Hispanic 100: A Ranking of the Latino Men and Women Who Have Most Influenced American Thought and Culture* (Secaucus, N.J.: Citadel Press/Carol Publishing Group, 1995), 189–198.

45. Secretary of State Rebecca Vigil-Giron, interview by author, Santa Fe, New Mexico, November 3, 2000.

46. Ibid.

47. See, e.g., Tamala M. Edwards, "Young, G.O.P. and Black," *Time* 151 (May 25, 1998): 56.

48. Gary Franks, *Searching for the Promised Land: An African American's Optimistic Odyssey* (New York: ReganBooks, 1996).

49. Barone and Cohen, *The Almanac of American Politics 2002,* 1256–1258; Nutting and Stern, eds., *CQ's Politics in America: 2002, The 107th Congress,* 824–825.

50. Johanna McGeary, "Odd Man Out," *Time* 158 (September 10, 2001): 26.

51. Kevin Merida, "Would Powell Be a 'Black' Candidate? The Answer May Seem Obvious, but the Question Is More Complicated," *Washington Post,* September 17, 1995, C2; Steven Waldman et al., "Powell's Black Problem," *Newsweek* 126 (October 2, 1995): 42; David S. Broder, "Powell Faces Stiff Fight on Right Flank," *Washington Post,* October 29, 1995, at A1; Richard L. Berke, "Powell Record Is Criticized by Conservatives in G.O.P.," *New York Times,* November 3, 1995, A26; Paul Taylor and Dan Balz, "Conservatives Fire Away at Powell's Possible Bid; Leading Republican Figures Attack Retired General's Character and Military Background," *Washington Post,* November 3, 1995, A18; Henry Louis Gates, Jr., *Thirteen Ways of Looking at a Black Man* (New York: Random House, 1997), 72–102.

52. Elizabeth Kolbert, "A Little-Known Candidate with a Big Issue," *New York Times,* August 9, 1995, A16; Michael Abramowitz, "Keyes's National Effort Kindles Md. Memories," *Washington Post,* March 5, 1996, A6; James Dao, "Keyes Draws the Few, but Devoted," *New York Times,* September 1, 1999, A18; James N. Thurman, "Keyes stakes presidential bid on moral wake-up call," *Christian Science Monitor,* December 2, 1999, 3; Shailagh Murray, "GOP Candidate Keyes Mixes Hard-Right Stance with Appeal and Oratory, and Moves Up in

Polls," *Wall Street Journal*, January 21, 2000, A20; Michelle Cottle, "Campaign Journal: Crazy Like a Fox," *New Republic* 222 (January 24, 2000): 15–17; Larry Copeland, "Keyes is rarely written up, but won't be written off," *USA Today*, March 7, 2000, 10A.

53. Copeland, "Keyes is rarely written up, but won't be written off."

54. Jan Austin, ed., *Congressional Quarterly Almanac: 104th Congress, 2nd Session...1996*, Volume LII (Washington, D.C.: Congressional Quarterly, 1997), 11–5.

55. In calculating Keyes' showing in 2000, I relied on data from the Federal Election Commission. http://fecweb1.fec.gov/pages/2000presprim.htm#party.

56. Barone and Cohen, *The Almanac of American Politics 2002*, 1501–1503; Nutting and Stern, eds., *CQ's Politics in America: 2002, The 107th Congress*, 1000–1001.

57. Barone and Cohen, *The Almanac of American Politics 2002*, 411–414, 418–420; Nutting and Stern, eds., *CQ's Politics in America: 2002, The 107th Congress*, 242–243, 248–249.

58. Mireya Navarro, "The Latino Candidate: Yours, Mine or Ours?; Ferrer Faces Diverse Hispanic Electorate," *New York Times*, May 6, 2001, Sec. 1, p. 45.

59. Karl Ross, Jay Weaver, and Oscar Corral, "Cuban-American Vote Lifts Diaz to Miami Mayor's Post," *Miami Herald*, November 14, 2001, at 1A.

60. Ron Scherer, "Long Isolated, Haitians in the US May Enter Local, National Politics," *Christian Science Monitor*, September 22, 1994, at p. 2; Garry Pierre-Pierre, "Haitians Striving to Muster Political Clout," *New York Times*, March 16, 1998, at B1; Marjorie Valbrun, "Caribbean Immigrants' Political Moves Stir Tensions," *Wall Street Journal*, June 30, 1998, A20; Jonathan P. Hicks, "Bitter Primary Contest Hits Ethnic Nerve Among Blacks," *New York Times*, August 31, 2000, at A1; Michael Powell, "Primaries Reflect N.Y. Democrats' New Math," *Washington Post*, September 12, 2000, at A1; Eleanor Brown, "Brooklyn Dispatch: Black vs. Black," *New Republic* 223 (September 25, 2000): 18; Dana Candy, "Away from Haiti, Discovering the Politics of the Possible," *New York Times*, May 19, 2001, A8.

61. Ibid.

62. North Miami, Florida, a black-majority city of 59,880 with a sizable Haitian population, made history in 2001 when a Haitian American, Josaphat Celestin, defeated an African American, Arthur Sorey, to become mayor. Three of the five North Miami City Council members are Haitian American. For more about Celestin, see Candy, "Away from Haiti, Discovering the Politics of the Possible."

63. Navarro, "The Latino Candidate: Yours, Mine or Ours?"; Adam Nagourney, "Learning to Play Ethnic Politics in a Changing City," *New York Times*, May 11, 2001, at B1; Adam Nagourney, "Group Seeks Black-Latino Joint Effort for Mayor," *New York Times*, August 11, 2001, at B1; Dexter Filkins, "In Bid for Unity, Black and Hispanic Politicians Make Pledge to Back Ferrer," *New York Times*, August 18, 2001, B2; Dexter Filkins and Adam Nagourney, "Sharpton Endorses Ferrer in Mayoral Race," *New York Times*, August 28, 2001, at A1; Dexter Filkins and Adam Nagourney, "Courting Blacks and Latinos, Ferrer Is Walking Fine Line," *New York Times*, September 6, 2001, at A1; Michael

Powell, "Election Appeal to the 'Other' N.Y.; Latino-Black Coalition Fires Minority Challenge for Democrat's Mayoral Choice," *Washington Post*, September 9, 2001, A5; Adam Nagourney, "Ferrer's Choice: Appeal to Pride, or Embrace All," *New York Times*, September 27, 2001, at D1.

64. Ibid.

65. Adam Nagourney, "Green Beats Ferrer in Democratic Mayoral Runoff," *New York Times*, October 12, 2001, at A1; Jonathan P. Hicks, "Green's Campaign Angers Backers of Ferrer," *New York Times*, October 13, 2001, D3; Michael Cooper and Diane Cardwell, "Ferrer Doubts Green Victory After Miscount," *New York Times*, October 15, 2001, at F1; Adam Nagourney, "Heated Race Revisited, Amid Claims of Racism," *New York Times*, October 16, 2001, at D1; Michael Cooper, "Awaiting Tally, Democrats Try to Close Ranks," *New York Times*, October 16, 2001, D5; Dean E. Murphy and Michael Cooper, "Bloomberg Sees Race Overtones in Final Days of Green Effort," *New York Times*, October 17, 2001, at D1; Dean E. Murphy and Diane Cardwell, "Green Holds Quiet Meeting with Ferrer," *New York Times*, October 19, 2001, at D1; Adam Nagourney, "Ferrer Formally Concedes to Green in a Democratic Show of Unity," *New York Times*, October 20, 2001, at D1; Jack Newfield, "Can Mark Green Heal NYC?" *Nation* 273 (November 5, 2001): 20–22; Michael Tomasky, "The Untouchable," *New York* 34 (December 3, 2001): 34, 36.

66. Dean E. Murphy and Al Baker, "As Ferrer Embraces Green, Bloomberg Pours On the Salt," *New York Times*, October 21, 2001, Sec. 1A, p. 35; Adam Nagourney, "As Democrats Bicker, Bloomberg Era Begins," *New York Times*, November 8, 2001, at A1; Mirta Ojito, "City's Hispanics Shift, Moving Toward G.O.P.," *New York Times*, November 8, 2001, D5; Michael Cooper with Josh Barbanel, "Gains Among Hispanic, Black and Liberal Voters Helped Push Bloomberg to Victory," *New York Times*, November 10, 2001, D3; Jonathan Alter, "Betting on a Billionaire," *Newsweek* 138 (November 19, 2001): 44–52, 54; Ellis Cose, "A Warning Shot from Latin U.S.A.," *Newsweek* 138 (November 19, 2001): 55; Amanda Ripley, "Rudy's Unlikely Heir," *Time* 158 (November 19, 2001): 64–66; Fred Siegel, "Bloomberg's Bedfellows," *Weekly Standard* 7 (November 19, 2001): 12–13.

67. I have visited Representative Lipinski's district on a number of occasions. For background on Lipinski's career, see Barone and Cohen, *The Almanac of American Politics 2002*, 511–513; Nutting and Stern, eds., *CQ's Politics in America: 2002, The 107th Congress*, 312–313.

68. Barone and Cohen, *The Almanac of American Politics 2002*, 511–513; Nutting and Stern, eds., *CQ's Politics in America: 2002, The 107th Congress*, 312–313.

69. Ibid.; "Illinois," *Congressional Quarterly Weekly Report* 49 (December 21, 1991): 3702–3704; Bob Benenson, "Old Chicago Friends Now Foes, Lipinski and Russo Do Battle," *Congressional Quarterly Weekly Report* 50 (March 7, 1992): 566–569.

70. Thernstrom and Thernstrom, *America in Black and White*, 462–492; Wilma Rule and Joseph Zimmerman, eds., *United States Electoral Systems: Their Impact on Women and Minorities* (New York: Praeger, 1992); Bernard Grofman and Chandler Davidson, eds., *Controversies in Minority Voting: The Voting*

Rights Act in Perspective (Washington, D.C.: Brookings Institution, 1992); Chandler Davidson and Bernard Grofman, eds., *Quiet Revolution in the South: The Impact of the Voting Rights Act, 1965–1990* (Princeton, N.J.: Princeton University Press, 1994); Bernard Grofman, ed., *Race and Redistricting in the 1990s* (New York: Agathon Press, 1998).

71. Grofman, ed., *Race and Redistricting in the 1990s*, passim; James A. Barnes, "Minority Mapmaking," *National Journal* 22 (April 7, 1990): 837–839; Peter Bragdon, "Democrats' Ties to Minorities May Be Tested by New Lines," *Congressional Quarterly Weekly Report* 48 (June 2, 1990): 1739–1742; Michael Oreskes, "Seeking Seats, Republicans Find Ally in Rights Act," *New York Times,* August 20, 1990, A11; Richard L. Berke, "Redistricting Brings About Odd Alliance," *New York Times,* April 8, 1991, at A1; Richard L. Berke, "G.O.P. Tries a Gambit with Voting Rights," *New York Times,* April 14, 1991, Sec. 4, p. 5; James A. Barnes, "Minority Poker," *National Journal* 23 (May 4, 1991): 1034–1039; Jon Meacham, "Voting Wrongs," *Washington Monthly* 25 (March 1993): 28–32.

72. Ibid.; Richard L. Berke, "Strategy Divides Top Republicans; Redistricting and an Alliance with Minority Groups Stir Deep Disagreements," *New York Times,* May 9, 1991, A17; Beth Donovan, "New 'Majority Minority' Districts May Mean Lower Black Turnout," *Congressional Quarterly Weekly Report* 50 (March 7, 1992): 563–564; Kimball Brace et al., "Minority Turnout and the Creation of Majority-Minority Districts," *American Politics Quarterly* 23 (April 1995): 190–203.

73. Meacham, "Voting Wrongs"; Barnes, "Minority Poker"; Barnes, "Minority Mapmaking"; Berke, "Redistricting Brings About Odd Alliance"; Berke, "G.O.P. Tries a Gambit with Voting Rights"; Oreskes, "Seeking Seats, Republicans Find Ally in Rights Act"; Bragdon, "Democrats' Ties to Minorities May Be Tested by New Lines."

74. Barnes, "Minority Poker"; Chuck Alston, "Democrats Court Minorities to Counter GOP's Pitch," *Congressional Quarterly Weekly Report* 49 (May 4, 1991): 1103–1105.

75. For recent discussions of the effects of racial redistricting on the representation of black interests, see, e.g., Canon, *Race, Redistricting, and Representation;* Carol M. Swain, *Black Faces, Black Interests: The Representation of African Americans in Congress,* 2d ed. (Cambridge, Mass.: Harvard University Press, 1995), 193–243; David Lublin, *The Paradox of Representation: Racial Gerrymandering and Minority Interests in Congress* (Princeton, N.J.: Princeton University Press, 1997); Kenny J. Whitby, *The Color of Representation: Congressional Behavior and Black Interests* (Ann Arbor: University of Michigan Press, 1997); Christine Leveaux Sharpe and James C. Garand, "Race, Roll Calls, and Redistricting: The Impact of Race-Based Redistricting on Congressional Roll-Call," *Political Research Quarterly* 54 (March 2001): 31–51.

76. Canon, *Race, Redistricting, and Representation,* 147–200; Robert Singh, *The Congressional Black Caucus: Racial Politics in the U.S. Congress* (Thousand Oaks, Calif.: Sage Publications, 1998); Neil Pinney and George Serra, "The Congressional Black Caucus and Vote Cohesion: Placing the Caucus Within House Voting Patterns," *Political Research Quarterly* 52 (September 1999): 583–608.

77. Swain, *Black Faces, Black Interests,* 226–243; Lublin, *The Paradox of Representation,* 112–114; Kevin A. Hill, "Does the Creation of Majority Black Districts Aid Republicans? An Analysis of the 1992 Congressional Elections in Eight Southern States," *Journal of Politics* 57 (May 1995): 384–401; John R. Petrocik and Scott W. Desposato, "The Partisan Consequences of Majority-Minority Redistricting in the South, 1992 and 1994," *Journal of Politics* 60 (August 1998): 613–633.

78. Keith J. Bybee, *Mistaken Identity: The Supreme Court and the Politics of Minority Representation* (Princeton, N.J.: Princeton University Press, 1998), passim; J. Morgan Kousser, *Colorblind Injustice: Minority Voting Rights and the Undoing of the Second Reconstruction* (Chapel Hill: University of North Carolina Press, 1999).

79. Barone and Cohen, *The Almanac of American Politics 2002,* 378–381, 439–441, 443–446, 1165–1168, 1488–1490, 1518–1520; Nutting and Stern, eds., *CQ's Politics in America: 2002, The 107th Congress,* 215–216, 262–263, 266–267, 760–761, 990–991, 1014–1015. See, too, Kevin Sack, "Victory of 5 Redistricted Blacks Recasts Gerrymandering Dispute," *New York Times,* November 23, 1996, Sec. 1, at p. 1; Kevin Sack, "In the Rural White South, Seeds of a Biracial Politics," *New York Times,* December 30, 1998, at A1.

80. Lorraine Woellert, "Where Do You Draw the Line?" *Business Week* (January 15, 2001): 80–81; Robert Pear, "Race Takes Back Seat as States Prepare to Redistrict," *New York Times,* February 4, 2001, Sec. 1, p. 17; Laurent Belsie, "Redistricting forces black Democrats to pick sides," *Christian Science Monitor,* February 21, 2001, 2–3; Thomas B. Edsall, "Parties Play Voting Rights Role Reversal," *Washington Post,* February 25, 2001, A4; Eduardo Porter, "Hispanics Seek Increased Representation, and Republicans Are Very Eager to Help," *Wall Street Journal,* April 2, 2001, A24; Adam Clymer, "Shaping the New Math of Racial Redistricting," *New York Times,* July 15, 2001, Sec. 4, p. 16; Jason Zengerle, "Color Line: Whitening black districts," *New Republic* 225 (August 6, 2001): 12–14; Gregory L. Giroux, "New Twists in the Old Debate on Race and Representation," *CQ Weekly* 59 (August 11, 2001): 1966–1967, 1969, 1972–1973; David E. Rosenbaum, "As Redistricting Unfolds, Power Is Used to Get More of It," *New York Times,* August 13, 2001, A14; Jackie Calmes and Greg Hitt, "Virginia Redistricting Plan Tests Bush Pledge of More Diverse GOP," *Wall Street Journal,* August 30, 2001, A14.

81. Ibid.

82. Kevin Sack, "Democrats Face Facts of Redrawing Georgia," *New York Times,* August 22, 2001, A14; Thomas B. Edsall, "Georgia Democrats May Gain Up to 4 Seats in House," *Washington Post,* September 29, 2001, A24.

83. Thomas B. Edsall, "A Political Fight to Define the Future; Latinos at Odds over California's Two New Democratic Congressional Districts," *Washington Post,* October 31, 2001, A8.

84. See, e.g., Swain, *Black Faces, Black Interests,* 145–189.

85. Four white Democrats represent Hispanic-majority districts: Central California Democrat Cal Dooley, Los Angeles Democrat Howard Berman, San Diego Democrat Bob Filner, and Houston Democrat Gene Green. Philadelphia lawmaker Robert Brady, a Caucasian Democrat, represents a black-majority

district. An Anglo transplant from Upstate New York, Neil Abercrombie, represents Honolulu and environs in the U.S. House; his district is the most heavily Asian-American constituency in America. And Queens Democrat Joseph Crowley, Dallas Democrat Martin Frost, New York Democrat Eliot Engel, Southern California Republicans Steve Horn and Gary Miller, and Northern California Democrats Pete Stark and Zoe Lofgren represent majority-minority constituencies in which no ethno-racial group accounts for a majority of the residents. For background on these legislators, see Barone and Cohen, *The Almanac of American Politics 2002*, 192–194, 199–202, 209–212, 225–228, 257–260, 265–267, 287–289, 476–478, 1062–1064, 1089–1092, 1301–1303, 1503–1506, 1516–1518; Nutting and Stern, eds., *CQ's Politics in America: 2002, The 107th Congress*, 91–92, 96–97, 104–105, 116–117, 136–137, 142–143, 158–159, 288–289, 682–683, 702–703, 853–854, 1002–1003, 1012–1013.

86. Barone and Cohen, *The Almanac of American Politics 2002*, 1089–1092; Nutting and Stern, eds., *CQ's Politics in America: 2002, The 107th Congress*, 702–703.

87. Janelle Carter, "Latinos alter dynamics of 'black' House districts; Census shows possible peril for lawmakers," *USA Today*, August 20, 2001, 6A.

88. V. Dion Haynes, "Blacks Caught in L.A. Shift; Years of Political Gains Lost to Rising Hispanic Influence," *Chicago Tribune*, April 28, 1997, Sec. 1, at p. 1; Martin Kasindorf and Maria Puente, "Hispanics and blacks find their futures entangled," *USA Today*, September 10, 1999, 21A, 22A; Martin Kasindorf, "3 Calif. cities diverge on black-brown power clash," *USA Today*, September 10, 1999, 22A.

89. Thomas B. Edsall, "L.A. Politics Being Turned Inside Out; Council Redistricting Symbolizes Transfer of Power to Latinos," *Washington Post*, November 24, 2001, A4.

90. Adam Nagourney, "Bringing Diversity to the Politics of Distrust," *New York Times*, August 3, 1997, Sec. 4, p. 4; Alexandra Marks, "Politicians Shun Race-Baiting as Cities Grow More Diverse," *Christian Science Monitor*, September 12, 1997, 3; Terence Samuel, "Big Cities Shunning Racial Politics; Problem Solving Takes Precedence," *St. Louis Post-Dispatch*, September 21, 1997, at 1A; Sam Fulwood III, "Baltimore Voters Going Colorblind in Mayoral Race," *Los Angeles Times*, September 2, 1999, 5; Charles Cohen, "Racial politics subside in cities," *Christian Science Monitor*, November 2, 1999, at p. 1.

91. Barone and Cohen, *The Almanac of American Politics 2002*, 505–518; Dianne M. Pinderhughes, *Race and Ethnicity in Chicago Politics: A Reexamination of Pluralist Theory* (Urbana: University of Illinois Press, 1987); Gary Rivlin, *Fire on the Prairie: Chicago's Harold Washington and the Politics of Race* (New York: Henry Holt and Company, 1992); Dirk Johnson, "With Black Support, Daley Seems Sure of Re-election," *New York Times*, February 23, 1999, A14.

92. Alexandra Marks, "Unexpected twist in Philly mayoral race," *Christian Science Monitor*, October 14, 1999, 3; Fred Siegel, "Fair Philly: Why race matters less," *New Republic* 221 (November 1, 1999): 13–14.

93. Harry Bruinius, "The setting: a re-created Philadelphia," *Christian Science Monitor*, July 27, 2000, 2.

94. Mexicans constitute 29.5% of Dallas's population; moreover, they account for 82.9% of the city's Latinos. By contrast, Mexicans make up 27% of Houston's population — and 72.2% of its Hispanic community.

95. Carol Marie Cropper, "Racial Power Struggle in Dallas School System Takes New Turn," *New York Times,* October 12, 1997, Sec. 1, p. 21; Jim Yardley, "Houston School Chief to Test Hispanic Will," *New York Times,* February 9, 2001, A14.

96. Kris Axtman, "Houston mayoral race as face of future politics," *Christian Science Monitor,* November 29, 2001, at p. 1; Jim Yardley, "In Houston, a 'Nonpartisan' Race Is Anything But," *New York Times,* November 30, 2001, A24; Paul Duggan and Mike Allen, "Race in Houston Raises Hispanic Hopes; Bushes Boost Sanchez's Mayoral Bid as Latino Numbers Surge," *Washington Post,* November 30, 2001, at A1; Lianne Hart, "Brown Looks Set to Win Runoff, 3rd Term as Houston Mayor," *Los Angeles Times,* December 2, 2001, A45; Paul Duggan, "Houston's Democratic Mayor Pulls Ahead of GOP Challenger in Incomplete Vote Count," *Washington Post,* December 2, 2001, A2; John Williams, "Grass-roots effort put Brown over top; Sanchez's air attack fell short," *Houston Chronicle,* December 3, 2001, at A1; Jim Yardley, "Democrat in Houston Wins with Some National Help," *New York Times,* December 3, 2001, A12; Paul Duggan, "Houston Reelects Mayor in Close Race; Bush Family Backed Hispanic Challenger," *Washington Post,* December 3, 2001, A2.

Chapter 9: Conflict and Cooperation

1. Thomas H. O'Connor, *The Boston Irish: A Political History* (Boston: Back Bay Books, 1995), passim.

2. Ibid.; Michael Barone and Richard E. Cohen with Charles E. Cook Jr., *The Almanac of American Politics 2002* (Washington, D.C.: National Journal, 2001), 730, 732.

3. O'Connor, *The Boston Irish,* 285–288; Elizabeth Ross, "Ethnic Blocs Key in Boston Race," *Christian Science Monitor,* September 23, 1993, at p. 2; Elizabeth Ross, "Boston's Ethnic Power May Shift in Mayor Race," *Christian Science Monitor,* October 25, 1993, 8; "When Irish eyes are fading," *Economist* 329 (October 30, 1993): 27–28, 31; Elizabeth Ross, "Irish Hold on Mayoralty Ends in Boston," *Christian Science Monitor,* November 4, 1993, 6.

4. Ibid.

5. For the quotation attributed to Mayor Menino, see "When Irish eyes are fading," 31.

6. Ronald P. Formisano, *Boston Against Busing: Race, Class, and Ethnicity in the 1960s and 1970s* (Chapel Hill: University of North Carolina Press, 1991).

7. Stacy Teicher, "Closing a chapter on school desegregation," *Christian Science Monitor,* July 16, 1999, at p. 1.

8. In 1990, the most recent year for which data are available, 22.4% of Bostonians reported that they had Irish ancestry. Italian Americans were the second-largest white subgroup: More than one in ten Bostonians, or 10.5%, had Italian progenitors. Interestingly, only 6.7% traced some or all of their genealogy to England — after all, people of English ancestry founded Boston. German

Americans, not surprisingly, constituted the next largest white subgroup: They accounted for 5.9% of the people in Boston.

9. To learn more about the various ethnic groups that make up the city, I visited many of Boston's neighborhoods in late September 2000 and early October 2000.

10. O'Connor, *The Boston Irish*, 286, 289, 303.

11. Megan Tench, "Haitian Community Seeks Its Political Voice," *Boston Globe*, October 21, 2001, B3.

12. Bill Clinton and Al Gore, *Putting People First: How We Can All Change America* (New York: Times Books, 1992), 190.

13. Ibid.

14. For excellent background on Clinton's pre-presidential years, see David Maraniss, *First in His Class: A Biography of Bill Clinton* (New York: Simon & Schuster, 1995); Stanley B. Greenberg, *Middle Class Dreams: The Politics and Power of the New American Majority* (New York: Times Books/Random House, 1995), 181–214.

15. Maraniss, *First in His Class*, passim; Greenberg, *Middle Class Dreams*, 181–214.

16. Gwen Ifill, "Clinton Delivers a Mainstream Message with a Southern Accent," *New York Times*, December 27, 1991, A16; Richard D. Kahlenberg, *The Remedy: Class, Race, and Affirmative Action* (New York: New Republic Books/Basic Books, 1996), 190–198.

17. Greenberg, *Middle Class Dreams*, 181–214; Robin Toner, "To the Presidential Hopefuls, the Middle Class Is Royalty," *New York Times*, January 11, 1992, Sec. 1, at p. 1.

18. Steven A. Holmes, "Must Democrats Shift Signals on Blacks to Win the Presidency?" *New York Times*, November 10, 1991, Sec. 4, p. 3; Michel McQueen, "While Blacks Loom Large in Democratic Race, They Have No Natural Home Among the Rivals," *Wall Street Journal*, February 21, 1992, A16; Ronald Smothers, "Blacks Feel Like Wallflowers As No Candidates Woo Them," *New York Times*, March 2, 1992, at A1.

19. Jack W. Germond and Jules Witcover, *Mad as Hell: Revolt at the Ballot Box, 1992* (New York: Warner Books, 1993), 289–305; Gordon MacInnes, *Wrong for All the Right Reasons: How White Liberals Have Been Undone by Race* (New York: New York University Press, 1996), 13–21.

20. Gwen Ifill, "Clinton Waves at Blacks as He Rushes By," *New York Times*, September 20, 1992, Sec. 4, at p. 1; Thomas B. Edsall, "Black Leaders View Clinton Strategy with Mix of Pragmatism, Optimism," *Washington Post*, October 28, 1992, A16; Juan Williams, "The New Black Powers; Younger Leaders Lining Up with Clinton Have Clout But No Consensus," *Washington Post*, November 1, 1992, C2.

21. For Clinton's posturing on crime and welfare, see Clinton and Gore, *Putting People First*, 71–74, 164–168; Gwen Ifill, "Clinton, in Houston Speech, Assails Bush on Crime Issue," *New York Times*, July 24, 1992, A13; Gwen Ifill, "Clinton Presses Welfare Overhaul, Stressing Job Training and Work," *New York Times*, September 10, 1992, at A1.

22. Germond and Witcover, *Mad as Hell*, 423–424, 434, 513; Kenneth O'Reilly, *Nixon's Piano: Presidents and Racial Politics from Washington to Clinton* (New York: Free Press, 1995), 401–406.

23. Greenberg, *Middle Class Dreams*, 215–230.

24. For an overview of this period, see E. J. Dionne Jr., *They Only Look Dead: Why Progressives Will Dominate the Next Political Era* (New York: Simon & Schuster, 1996), 118–230.

25. Richard L. Berke, "Campaigns' Tenor Disappoints Black Voters," *New York Times*, October 30, 1994, Sec. 1, at p. 1; Isabel Wilkerson, "Many Blacks See Betrayal in This Year's Campaign; Losses by Democrats Are Called Bittersweet," *New York Times*, November 10, 1994, B4.

26. See, e.g., John Harwood, "Center Stage: Racially Tinged Issues Dominate the Debate as Campaigns Unfold," *Wall Street Journal*, July 24, 1995, at A1; Dan Balz, "Racial Issues Weigh Heavily on Minds of Nation's Voters," *Washington Post*, November 6, 1995, A10; Adam Nagourney, "On Volatile Social and Cultural Issues, Silence," *New York Times*, October 9, 1996, at A1.

27. Ann Devroy, "Clinton Orders Affirmative Action Review; At Stake: Principles and Political Base," *Washington Post*, February 24, 1995, at A1; Paul Richter, "Clinton Review of Affirmative Action May Signal a Shift," *Los Angeles Times*, February 25, 1995, at p. 1; Steven A. Holmes, "White House Signals an Easing on Affirmative Action," *New York Times*, February 25, 1995, Sec. 1, p. 9; Ann Devroy, "Clinton Study Backs Affirmative Action; Five-Month Review Supports Some Reforms," Washington Post, July 19, 1995, at A1; Todd S. Purdum, "President Shows Fervent Support for Goals of Affirmative Action," *New York Times*, July 20, 1995, at A1; John F. Harris, "Clinton Avows Support for Affirmative Action; 'Mend It, but Don't End It,' President Says in Speech," *Washington Post*, July 20, 1995, at A1. For the text of Clinton's speech about affirmative action on July 19, 1995, see *Public Papers of the Presidents of the United States: William J. Clinton 1995 - Book II — July 1 to December 31, 1995* (Washington, D.C.: U.S. Government Printing Office, 1996), 1106–1114.

28. Michael Tackett, "Jesse Jackson Weighs Ballot Options for '96," *Chicago Tribune*, June 30, 1995, Sec. 1, p. 11; Emily Church, "The Pull of a Party Castaway," *Congressional Quarterly Weekly Report* 53 (September 9, 1995): 2740; Roger Simon, "Primary Care: How Bill sandbagged Jesse," *New Republic* 216 (February 24, 1997): 15–18.

29. Evan Thomas et al., *Back from the Dead: How Clinton Survived the Republican Revolution* (New York: Atlantic Monthly Press, 1997), 31–44; Nicolaus Mills, *The Triumph of Meanness: America's War Against Its Better Self* (Boston: Houghton Mifflin, 1997), 180–205.

30. Dick Morris, *Behind the Oval Office: Winning the Presidency in the Nineties* (New York: Random House, 1997), 207–234.

31. Peter T. Kilborn and Sam Howe Verhovek, "Clinton's Welfare Shift Ends Tortuous Journey," *New York Times*, August 2, 1996, at A1.

32. David Johnston and Tim Weiner, "Seizing the Crime Issue, Clinton Blurs Party Lines," *New York Times*, August 1, 1996, at A1.

33. Ralph Nader received 651,771 popular votes in the 1996 presidential election, or 0.68% of all ballots cast. He was on the ballot in 22 states, and his

strongest showings came in states that Clinton won by a big margin — Oregon, Washington, Maine, New Mexico, California, Vermont — so his candidacy failed to help the Republicans in 1996.

34. For statistics on how the various demographic groups voted in 1996, see Marjorie Connelly, "Who Voted: A Portrait of American Politics, 1976–2000," *New York Times,* November 12, 2000, Sec. 4, p. 4.

35. Dennis Farney, "Minorities, Especially Blacks in the South, Put Democrats over the Top in Key Races," *Wall Street Journal,* November 5, 1998, A10; Terry M. Neal, "For Blacks, an Issue of Pressure vs. Prudence; African Americans Differ on What to Expect as Reward for Backing Democrats," *Washington Post,* November 23, 1998, A4.

36. Alison Mitchell, "Democrats Again Face Voter Doubts over Party's Values," *New York Times,* August 20, 1999, A18.

37. DeWayne Wickham, *Bill Clinton and Black America* (New York: Ballantine Books, 2002). See, too, Steven A. Holmes, "On Civil Rights, Clinton Steers Bumpy Course Between Right and Left," *New York Times,* October 20, 1996, Sec. 1, at p. 16; Michael K. Frisby, "Race Course: Clinton Stays Popular with Blacks in Spite of Fraying Safety Net," *Wall Street Journal,* June 13, 1997, at A1; Katharine Q. Seelye, "Blacks Stand by the President in His Time of Need," *New York Times,* February 16, 1998, A11; Richard L. Berke, "Once a Nemesis, Jackson Has Become the President's Spiritual Adviser," *New York Times,* March 6, 1998, A20; Jason Zengerle, "Family Therapy: Jesse plays the Chelsea card," *New Republic* 219 (September 14 and 21, 1998): 15–16, 18; Ceci Connolly and Robert E. Pierre, "Clinton's Strongest Constituency; To African Americans, President's Record Outweighs Personal Problems," *Washington Post,* September 17, 1998, at A1; Kevin Sack, "Blacks Stand by a President Who 'Has Been There for Us,'" *New York Times,* September 19, 1998, at A1; Ann Scales, "In the Loop," *Emerge* 10 (November 1998): 34–39.

38. Ibid.

39. Ronald Brownstein, "Clintonism," *U.S. News & World Report* 124 (January 26, 1998): 22–25, 28, 30–31; Robin Toner, "A Revival and a Party Transformed," *New York Times,* December 27, 2000, at A1.

40. Toner, "A Revival and a Party Transformed"; Jason DeParle and Steven A. Holmes, "A War on Poverty Subtly Linked to Race," *New York Times,* December 26, 2000, at A1.

41. Linda Chavez, *Out of the Barrio: Toward a New Politics of Hispanic Assimilation* (New York: Basic Books, 1991); Himilce Novas, *The Hispanic 100: A Ranking of the Latino Men and Women Who Have Most Influenced American Thought and Culture* (Secaucus, N.J.: Citadel Press/Carol Publishing Group, 1995), 101–104; Macarena Hernandez, "Conservative and Hispanic, Linda Chavez Carves Out Leadership Niche," *New York Times,* August 19, 1998, A28; "Linda Chavez," in Clifford Thompson, ed., *Current Biography Yearbook 1999* (New York: H. W. Wilson Company, 1999), 120–123; Steven A. Holmes, "Linda Chavez," *New York Times,* January 3, 2001, A12.

42. Steven Greenhouse, "Unions See Sign of Trouble in Bush's Choice for Labor," *New York Times,* January 4, 2001, A23; Mike Allen and Frank Swoboda, "Chavez Likely Will Face Intense Senate Hearings," *Washington Post,*

January 4, 2001, A12; Frank Swoboda and Thomas B. Edsall, "Unions Hope to Stop Chavez; Strategy Includes Pressuring Moderate Republicans," *Washington Post,* January 6, 2001, at A1; Steven Greenhouse, "Union Leaders Plan Fight Against Bush's Labor Selection," *New York Times,* January 7, 2001, Sec. 1, p. 15.

43. Steven A. Holmes, "Illegal Immigrant Lived in Labor Designee's Home," *New York Times,* January 8, 2001, at A1; Thomas B. Edsall and Manuel Roig-Franzia, "Chavez Is Under Fire over Illegal Immigrant; Guatemalan Lived in Designee's House," *Washington Post,* January 8, 2001, at A1; Steven Greenhouse and Raymond Bonner, "Bush Reaffirms His Confidence in Labor Choice," *New York Times,* January 9, 2001, at A1; Thomas B. Edsall and George Lardner Jr., "Bush Backs Chavez as Controversy Swells; Immigrant's Help Clouds Labor Choice," *Washington Post,* January 9, 2001, at A1; Manuel Roig-Franzia, "Mercado: Chavez Was 'Like a Friend'; Immigrant Says She Was Not an Employee," *Washington Post,* January 9, 2001, A4; Steven A. Holmes and Steven Greenhouse, "Bush Choice for Labor Post Withdraws and Cites Furor of Illegal Immigrant Issue," *New York Times,* January 10, 2001, at A1; David E. Sanger, "Lessons of a Swift Exit," *New York Times,* January 10, 2001, at A1; Dana Milbank and Thomas B. Edsall, "Chavez Pulls Out as Labor Nominee; Bush Pick Acknowledges She 'Wasn't Forthcoming' on Illegal Immigrant Issue," *Washington Post,* January 10, 2001, at A1.

44. Holmes, "Linda Chavez"; Novas, *The Hispanic 100,* 101–104; Thompson, ed., *Current Biography Yearbook 1999,* 120–123; Hernandez, "Conservative and Hispanic, Linda Chavez Carves Out Leadership Niche."

45. David E. Sanger, "In a Swift Action, Bush Names Choice for Labor Dept.," *New York Times,* January 12, 2001, at A1; Christopher Marquis, "A Washington Veteran for Labor, a Tested Negotiator for Trade; Elaine Lan Chao," *New York Times,* January 12, 2001, A17; Dana Milbank, "Bush Taps Chao for Labor Position; Nominee Praised by Union Leaders; Zoellick Named as Top Trade Negotiator," *Washington Post,* January 12, 2001, at A1; George Lardner Jr. and Frank Swoboda, "Chao Knows Her Way Around Labor; Union Leaders Welcome a Solid Conservative," *Washington Post,* January 12, 2001, A23; Steven Greenhouse, "Senate Panel Gives Warm Reception to New Labor Nominee," *New York Times,* January 25, 2001, A20; Frank Swoboda, "Chao Sails Through Hearing; Labor Nominee Notes Need to Adjust to New Economy," *Washington Post,* January 25, 2001, A6; Elizabeth Becker, "Family History Forges Labor Secretary's Convictions," *New York Times,* February 26, 2001, A10.

46. Joe Klein, "The Vision Thing," *New Yorker* 74 (October 19, 1998): 30–33; Howard Fineman, "The Bush Brothers," *Newsweek* 132 (November 2, 1998): 30–33; Rick Lyman with Mireya Navarro, "George W. and Jeb Bush Are Easily Elected Governors in Texas and Florida," *New York Times,* November 4, 1998, at B1. For background information about George W. Bush, Jeb Bush, and their family, see Bill Minutaglio, *First Son: George W. Bush and the Bush Family Dynasty* (New York: Times Books/Random House, 1999); Elizabeth Mitchell, *W: Revenge of the Bush Dynasty* (New York: Hyperion, 2000).

47. Maria Puente, "Bush counts on Hispanics' favor," *USA Today,* October 9, 1998, 19A; Eric Pooley, "The Bush Formula," *Time* 152 (November 16,

1998): 60–62; Kenneth T. Walsh, "Can he save the Republicans?" *U.S. News & World Report* 125 (November 16, 1998): 18–20, 23–26; A. Phillips Brooks, "Bush trying to cover bases on affirmative action policy; 'Affirmative access' talk appeals to both GOP and minority groups, but is criticized as being vague," *Austin American Statesman,* August 25, 1999, at A1; Terry M. Neal, "When Numbers Spell Words; Bush's Melding of Message, Audience Reflects Hispanic Demographics," *Washington Post,* September 15, 1999, A3; George Lardner Jr. and Edward Walsh, "George W. Bush: The Texas Record; Compassion Collides with the Bottom Line," *Washington Post,* October 24, 1999, at A1; Paul Duggan, "George W. Bush: The Texas Record; Youth Feel the Force of a Vow Kept; Juvenile Justice Overhaul Reflects Tougher Approach," *Washington Post,* November 9, 1999, at A1; Jim Yardley, "Hispanics Give Attentive Bush Mixed Reviews," *New York Times,* August 27, 2000, Sec. 1, at p. 1.

48. On George P. Bush, see, e.g., Frank Bruni, "A Young George Bush, P., on the Political Stage," *New York Times,* April 18, 2000, A22; Roxanne Roberts, "Another Bush, by George; Dubya's Nephew Adds a Little Something to the Name," *Washington Post,* July 18, 2000, at C1; Massie Ritsch, "The Bush with Muy Guapo Appeal," *Los Angeles Times,* July 27, 2000, at E1; Ellen Gamerman, "Young 'George P.' raises passion from party podium; Handsome Latino nephew excites GOP," *Baltimore Sun,* August 2, 2000, at 1A; Brian E. Crowley, "He's hot, he's Hispanic — and he's a Bush; Campaign finds nephew an asset," *Atlanta Constitution,* August 3, 2000, 15A.

49. "Jeb Bush," in Clifford Thompson, ed., *Current Biography Yearbook 1999* (New York: H. W. Wilson Company, 1999), 103–105. See, too, Mireya Navarro, "Chastened by Loss, Jeb Bush Looks Unbeatable in Florida," *New York Times,* May 12, 1998, at A1; Terry M. Neal, "In Fla. Race, Jeb Bush Finds 'Kinder, Gentler' Plays Well," *Washington Post,* May 30, 1998, at A1; S. C. Gwynne, "Kinder, Gentler — and in the Lead," *Time* 151 (June 8, 1998): 54–55; Mireya Navarro, "In Race for Governor, Democrat Is in Trouble," *New York Times,* October 23, 1998, A20; Dahleen Glanton, "In Florida Election, Jeb Bush Forging Solid Political Image," *Chicago Tribune,* November 1, 1998, Sec. 1, p. 3; Terry M. Neal, "Jeb Bush Has Many Promises to Keep; Diverse Voter Groups Gambled on Florida Republican's Shift to a Centrist Agenda," *Washington Post,* November 14, 1998, A2.

50. Rick Bragg, "Florida Will Award Vouchers for Pupils Whose Schools Fail," *New York Times,* April 28, 1999, at A1; Kenneth J. Cooper and Sue Anne Pressley, "Florida House Approves School Vouchers; Senate Votes Today," *Washington Post,* April 29, 1999, A2; Pamela Mercer, "Failure Holds New Fear for Florida Schools," *New York Times,* May 2, 1999, Sec. 1, p. 32; Steven A. Holmes, "Black Groups in Florida Split over School Voucher Plan," *New York Times,* May 30, 1999, Sec. 1, p. 17; Jodi Wilgoren, "Florida's Vouchers a Spur to 2 Schools Left Behind," *New York Times,* March 14, 2000, at A1; Jodi Wilgoren, "School Vouchers Are Ruled Unconstitutional in Florida," *New York Times,* March 15, 2000, A20; Sue Anne Pressley and Kenneth J. Cooper, "School Voucher Plan Struck Down; Florida to Appeal Judge's Ruling," *Washington Post,* March 15, 2000, at A1.

51. Rick Bragg, "Florida Governor Offers Plan for Diversity," *New York Times,* November 11, 1999, A18; Sue Anne Pressley, "Florida Plan Aims to End Race-Based Preferences," *Washington Post,* November 11, 1999, A15; Kenneth J. Cooper, "Fla. Minorities Plan: An Addition Challenge," *Washington Post,* December 22, 1999, A3; Peter T. Kilborn, "Jeb Bush Roils Florida on Affirmative Action," *New York Times,* February 4, 2000, at A1; Diane Roberts, "Tallahassee Dispatch: All Against One," *New Republic* 222 (February 21, 2000): 12, 14; Sue Anne Pressley, "Florida Protesters Vow to Fight End of Affirmative Action," *Washington Post,* March 8, 2000, A2; Matthew Rees, " 'One Florida' — Many Problems," *Weekly Standard* 5 (May 15, 2000): 27–29; Rick Bragg, "Minority Enrollment Rises in Florida College System," *New York Times,* August 30, 2000, A18.

52. Dana Canedy, "Changed Political Climate May Aid Jeb Bush," *New York Times,* September 28, 2001, A16.

53. See, e.g., Terry M. Neal, "When Numbers Spell Words; Bush's Melding of Message, Audience Reflects Hispanic Demographics," *Washington Post,* September 15, 1999, A3; Dana Milbank, "The Year of the Latino Voter? Only in Campaign Rhetoric," *Washington Post,* May 21, 2000, at B1; R. W. Apple Jr., "Courting of Voting Bloc Poses Question of Motive," *New York Times,* August 2, 2000, A16.

54. Bill Turque, *Inventing Al Gore: A Biography* (Boston: Houghton Mifflin Company, 2000); David Maraniss and Ellen Nakashima, *The Prince of Tennessee: The Rise of Al Gore* (New York: Simon & Schuster, 2000).

55. Barton Gellman, Dale Russakoff, and Mike Allen, "Where Did Bradley Go Wrong?; Many Believe Wounds Were Self-Inflicted," *Washington Post,* March 4, 2000, at A1; Eric Pooley with Karen Tumulty and Tamala M. Edwards, "How Al Came Back to Life," *Time* 155 (March 13, 2000): 41, 43–44, 46.

56. *Bush v. Gore,* 000 U.S. 00–949 (2000).

57. Connelly, "Who Voted: A Portrait of American Politics, 1976–2000."

58. Ibid.

59. For commentary on Bush's appointments, see David E. Sanger, "Democrat Chosen as Bush Completes Cabinet Selection," *New York Times,* January 3, 2001, at A1; Jim VandeHei, "Extending Diversity to Bush Subcabinet Will Be Tough Task," *Wall Street Journal,* February 6, 2001, A20; Jonathan Chait, "Color-Blind: Look who's for quotas," *New Republic* 224 (March 12, 2001): 16–17; Ellen Nakashima and Al Kamen, "Bush Picks as Diverse as Clinton's; Presidential Personnel Director Says Administration Is Not Relying on Quotas," *Washington Post,* March 30, 2001, A27; Dan Carney with Richard S. Dunham, " 'A Long Way from Tokenism,' " *BusinessWeek* (April 2, 2001): 74–76; Fred Barnes, "The Bush Quotas," *Weekly Standard* 6 (April 16/April 23, 2001): 18–19.

60. Jeanne Cummings, "Bush and Conservatives: Nomination Fight Speaks Volumes; Pickering Judicial Pick Pleases the Right, but Tardy Salvage Effort May Dismay Them," *Wall Street Journal,* March 7, 2002, A26; Michael Tackett, "Bush keeps GOP conservatives happy; Unlike his father, president follows Reagan's example," *Chicago Tribune,* March 10, 2002, Sec. 1, p. 8.

61. Ronald Brownstein, "Bush Walks Pragmatic Path That Clinton Made Familiar," *Los Angeles Times*, October 8, 1999, at A1; Howard Fineman, "Al and W's Balancing Act," *Newsweek* 134 (October 18, 1999): 22–26; Eric Pooley, "The Next Triangulator," *Time* 154 (October 18, 1999): 50–51; Terry M. Neal, "In South Carolina, Bush Steps Gingerly Around Racial Issues; Texan Tries to Woo Minorities Without Offending Conservatives," *Washington Post*, November 11, 1999, A14; Gustav Niebuhr, "Conservatives Warn Bush on Tilt to Abortion Rights," *New York Times*, April 15, 2000, A10; Richard L. Berke, "Grand Old Pragmatists," *New York Times*, April 22, 2000, at A1; Terry M. Neal, "GOP Right Accepts Bush's Move to Middle," *Washington Post*, May 27, 2000, at A1; Emily Pierce, "Bush's Center Strategy," *CQ Weekly* 58 (July 29, 2000): 21, 23–24; John Harwood and Jackie Calmes, "Texas Two-Step: Beyond Compassion, Bush Keeps Wooing Core Conservatives," *Wall Street Journal*, August 3, 2000, at A1; Thomas B. Edsall, "Bush Abandons 'Southern Strategy'; Campaign Avoids Use of Polarizing Issues Employed by GOP Since Nixon's Time," *Washington Post*, August 6, 2000, A19.

62. Neil A. Lewis, "Administration Backs Affirmative Action Plan," *New York Times*, August 11, 2001, A11; Edward Walsh, "Bush Backs Minority Program; High Court Brief Defends DOT Contracting Plan," *Washington Post*, August 11, 2001, at A1; Ellen Nakashima, "Bush Weighs Help for Minority Firms; New Rules Would Ease Bidding for U.S. Jobs Being Privatized," *Washington Post*, September 6, 2001, at A1.

63. Dana Calvo, "Bush to Break Language Barrier in Radio Address," *Los Angeles Times*, May 3, 2001, A15; Christopher Marquis, "Bush, and Democrats, Plan Speeches in Spanish," *New York Times*, May 5, 2001, A9; Arian Campo-Flores and Michael Isikoff, "On Vieques, No Hispanic Is an Island," *Newsweek* 137 (June 25, 2001): 32–33; Thomas B. Edsall, "Amnesty Proposal Is Huge Gamble for Bush; President Could Be Rewarded with Hispanic Vote but Risks Angering GOP's Conservative Wing," *Washington Post*, July 17, 2001, A2; Michael Duffy, "Out of the Shadows," *Time* 158 (July 30, 2001): 14–17; Howard Fineman and Arian Campo-Flores, "¿Cómo Se Dice 'Realignment'?" *Newsweek* 138 (August 6, 2001): 30; John O'Sullivan, "The Vex of Mex," *National Review* 53 (August 20, 2001): 20, 22, 24; Dana Milbank, "Attacks Shelve GOP Effort to Woo Hispanics," *Washington Post*, December 20, 2001, A4.

64. Mike Allen, "Bushes Join King Family on Holiday; Portrait of Civil Rights Leader Is Unveiled at White House Ceremony," *Washington Post*, January 22, 2002, A2; Francine Kiefer, "Surge in black approval a welcome sign for GOP," *Christian Science Monitor*, February 25, 2002, 2–3.

65. Janine DeFao, "Oakland Plan to Serve Non-English Speakers; Oakland Considers Hiring More Bilingual Employees," *San Francisco Chronicle*, April 4, 2001, A15; Benjamin Pimentel and Charles Burress, "Oakland orders city agencies to hire bilingual staff; Spanish, Chinese speakers sought," *San Francisco Chronicle*, April 25, 2001, at A1; Chip Johnson, "Melting pot law stirs up legal stew; Bilingual mandate may not be practical," *San Francisco Chronicle*, April 26, 2001, A17.

66. This vignette draws heavily upon my observations when I visited Oakland, California, on October 14, 2001.

67. Rick DelVecchio, "Blacks and Brown," *San Francisco Chronicle*, August 16, 1998, at p. 1.Z.1.

68. For biographies of the city's political leadership, see the City of Oakland's Web site at www.oaklandnet.com.

69. Marc Cooper, "Mayor Jerry Brown, Take II," *Nation* 274 (March 18, 2002): 22–24.

70. John Wildermuth, "Electorate still heavily white; Minorities making inroads slowly, poll shows," *San Francisco Chronicle*, January 10, 2002, A15.

71. For good overviews of how the initiative process has affected California's recent development, see Caroline J. Tolbert and Rodney E. Hero, "Dealing with Diversity: Racial/Ethnic Context and Social Policy Change," *Political Research Quarterly* 54 (September 2001): 571–604; Zoltan L. Hajnal, Elisabeth R. Gerber, and Hugh Louch, "Minorities and Direct Legislation: Evidence from California Ballot Proposition Elections," *Journal of Politics* 64 (February 2002): 154–177.

72. Barone and Cohen, *The Almanac of American Politics 2002*, 141–294.

73. Ibid.

74. William Booth, "In 'State' Visit, Zedillo Signals Mexico-California Thaw," *Washington Post*, May 19, 1999, A2. 75.

75. Paul Van Slambrouck, "A California governor who sees in shades of gray," *Christian Science Monitor*, May 21, 1999, 2, 4; Steve Lopez, "The Most Fearless Governor in America," *Time* 154 (October 11, 1999): 32–36; Paul Van Slambrouck, "California's brightest star is, well, gray," *Christian Science Monitor*, April 17, 2000, at p. 1; James Sterngold, "Power Crisis Abates, but It Hounds Gov. Davis," *New York Times*, October 5, 2001, A16; Mark Sappenfield, "Calif. governor tries to brighten his dimming star," *Christian Science Monitor*, November 15, 2001, at p. 1; David S. Broder and Dan Balz, "For Davis, Cruise to Reelection Turns Rocky; Polls Showing Slipping Support Among Democrats Lift GOP Hopes," *Washington Post*, March 1, 2002, A3.

76. Dale Maharidge, *The Coming White Minority: California's Eruptions and America's Future* (New York: Times Books/Random House, 1996), 141–175, 185–188, 255–267; Caroline J. Tolbert and Rodney E. Hero, "Race/Ethnicity and Direct Democracy: An Analysis of California's Illegal Immigration Initiative," *Journal of Politics* 58 (August 1996): 806–818; Irwin L. Morris, "African American Voting on Proposition 187: Rethinking the Prevalence of Interminority Conflict," *Political Research Quarterly* 53 (March 2000): 77–98; R. Michael Alvarez and Tara L. Butterfield, "The Resurgence of Nativism in California? The Case of Proposition 187 and Illegal Immigration," *Social Science Quarterly* 81 (March 2000): 167–179; Lina Y. Newton, "Why Some Latinos Supported Proposition 187: Testing Economic Threat and Cultural Identity Hypotheses," *Social Science Quarterly* 81 (March 2000): 180–193; M. V. Hood III and Irwin L. Morris, "Brother, Can You Spare a Dime? Racial/Ethnic Context and the Anglo Vote on Proposition 187," *Social Science Quarterly* 81 (March 2000): 194–206.

77. For the definitive treatment of Proposition 209, see Lydia Chávez, *The Color Bind: California's Battle to End Affirmative Action* (Berkeley: University of California Press, 1998).

78. William Booth, "A Plan to Write Off Bilingual Education; Californians to Vote on English-Immersion Proposal," *Washington Post*, February 28, 1998,

at A1; Don Terry, "Bilingual Education Facing Toughest Test," *New York Times,* March 10, 1998, at A1; Rene Sanchez and William Booth, "Calif. Rejection a Big Blow to Bilingualism; Decisive Vote Could Set Pace for Rest of Nation," *Washington Post,* June 4, 1998, A16; Frank Bruni, "The California Entrepreneur Who Beat Bilingual Teaching," *New York Times,* June 14, 1998, Sec. 1, at p. 1.

79. Marc Sandalow, "State GOP in Quandary over Minority Vote; Convention ends with few solutions," *San Francisco Chronicle,* September 29, 1997, at A1; Todd S. Purdum, "California G.O.P. Faces a Crisis as Hispanic Voters Turn Away," *New York Times,* December 9, 1997, at A1; Peter Beinart, "How the California G.O.P. Got a Spanish Lesson," *Time* 151 (May 18, 1998): 58; Rene Sanchez, "Both Parties Courting Latinos Vigorously; California GOP Tries Strategy of Inclusion," *Washington Post,* October 26, 1998, A12; Joel Kotkin, "GOP Wiped Out in Land of Reagan," *Wall Street Journal,* November 6, 1998, A14; Lou Cannon, "Reagan Country, Then and Now," *National Review* 51 (April 19, 1999): 46–49; Paul Van Slambrouck, "In the land of Reagan, a party in panic," *Christian Science Monitor,* June 25, 1999, 3; William Booth, "The Battle for California; With a New Script, the Action's in the Middle Series," *Washington Post,* June 27, 1999, at A1.

80. Ibid.

81. Greg Lucas, "Poll Shows Latinos' Dislike of Wilson Is Good for Davis," *San Francisco Chronicle,* October 29, 1998, at A1.

82. Barone and Cohen, *The Almanac of American Politics 2002,* 151.

83. Kotkin, "GOP Wiped Out in Land of Reagan."

84. Vincent J. Schodolski, "Bush Tries to Win over California Hispanics; Voting Patterns and Pete Wilson's Legacy Hobble His Candidacy," *Chicago Tribune,* April 11, 2000, Sec. 1, p. 9.

85. Paul Van Slambrouck, "California bid for holiday honoring Cesar Chavez," *Christian Science Monitor,* April 10, 2000, 2–3; Rene Sanchez, "Honoring Chavez — and Hispanic Clout; Crusade for Holiday Signals Calif. Power Shift," *Washington Post,* April 24, 2000, A3; John Ritter, "Calif. seeks way to honor both Chavez, his work; Lawmakers want help for farm labor, along with holiday," *USA Today,* April 28, 2000, 2A.

86. Carla Marinucci and John Wildermuth, "Governor's race spotlights GOP battle to close gender gap," *San Francisco Chronicle,* March 1, 2002, at A1; Martin Kasindorf, "Bush's man in danger in Calif.; Gubernatorial candidate slips in polls before GOP primary," *USA Today,* March 1, 2002, A3; John Harwood, "Riordan's Moderate Tack Alienates California Republicans; As Ex-Mayor Urges Party to Change, Voters Flock to Rival in Gubernatorial Primary," *Wall Street Journal,* March 1, 2002, A16; Mark Z. Barabak, "Governor Campaign Takes Sharp Right Turn," *Los Angeles Times,* March 3, 2002, at A1; James Sterngold, "Confounding Expectations, Political Neophyte Closes Gap in California Governor's Race," *New York Times,* March 3, 2002, Sec. 1, p. 26; V. Dion Haynes, "Ex-L.A. mayor on ropes; Lead in GOP race for governor of California vanishes," *Chicago Tribune,* March 4, 2002, Sec. 1, p. 5; Daniel B. Wood, "For Riordan, a shrinking California dream," *Christian Science Monitor,* March 4, 2002, at p. 1; Mark Z. Barabak, "Simon Trounces Riordan, Storms to GOP Nomination," *Los Angeles Times,* March 6, 2002, at A1.

87. For biographies of these legislators, go to the California Senate Web site (www.sen.ca.gov) and the California Assembly Web site (www.assembly.ca.gov).

88. The L.A. electorate in the mayoral contest on June 5, 2001, was 52% white, 22% Latino, 17% black, 6% Asian, and 3% Other. Hahn took 59% of the Anglo vote, 80% among blacks, 18% of the Latinos, and 65% of the Asians. Conversely, Villaraigosa's numbers were as follows: Anglos (41%), blacks (20%), Latinos (82%), Asians (35%). For excellent journalistic coverage of the election, see Todd S. Purdum, "Mayoral Race a Test for Los Angeles, and Hispanics," *New York Times*, March 21, 2001, A12; William Booth, "Los Angeles Confronts Its Future; Mayoral Race Reflects a Change in Priorities," *Washington Post*, April 9, 2001, at A1; Todd S. Purdum, "San Fernando Valley Crucial in Los Angeles Election," *New York Times*, May 28, 2001, A8; William Booth, "Visions, Styles Clash in L.A. Mayor's Race; As 2 Democrats Battle, City Readies for Big Shift," *Washington Post*, June 2, 2001, at A1; Todd S. Purdum, "New Electoral Math Changing the Script in Los Angeles Duel," *New York Times*, June 4, 2001, at A1; James Rainey and Greg Krikorian, "Hahn Won on His Appeal to Moderates, Conservatives," *Los Angeles Times*, June 7, 2001, at A1; Michael Finnegan and Erin Texeira, "For Blacks, New Clout in City Hall," *Los Angeles Times*, June 7, 2001, at A1; Todd S. Purdum, "Coalition Builder Wins Los Angeles Mayoral Race," *New York Times*, June 7, 2001, A14; Rene Sanchez, "In L.A., an Old Guard Victory; Hahn Wins Mayoral Race Despite Rising Latino Clout," *Washington Post*, June 7, 2001, at A1; Todd S. Purdum, "Los Angeles Race Bares Divisions," *New York Times*, June 10, 2001, Sec. 1, p. 20; Ellis Cose, "A Brownout in Los Angeles," *Newsweek* 137 (June 18, 2001): 32.

89. Ibid.

90. Delgadillo won the election based on his strong support from blacks (whom he carried 59%-41%) and Latinos (who backed him 79%-21%). Anglos, however, supported Mike Feuer by a 61%-39% margin. Similarly, Asians favored Feuer over Delgadillo (53%-47%). For coverage of this contest, see Jean Merl, "Delgadillo Beats Feuer in City Attorney Race," *Los Angeles Times*, June 6, 2001, A19; Jean Merl, "Latino, Black Votes Key for Delgadillo," *Los Angeles Times*, June 7, 2001, B12; Matea Gold, "An Upside Seen for Latinos, Despite Villaraigosa's Loss," *Los Angeles Times*, June 14, 2001, Part 2, at p. 1; Frank del Olmo, "Rocky: the Great Latino Hope," *Los Angeles Times*, June 17, 2001, M5; Jean Merl, "Life of Promise, Pressing New Issues," *Los Angeles Times*, July 1, 2001, Part 2, at p. 1; Gregory Rodriguez, "Rocky Delgadillo: Latino New Democrat," *Los Angeles Times*, August 5, 2001, M3.

91. Thomas B. Edsall, "Census a Clarion Call for Democrats, GOP; As Nation Changes, Parties Are Warned They Need New Tactics to Woo Voters," *Washington Post*, July 8, 2001, A5.

Epilogue: Reconcilable Differences?

1. Carl Quintanilla and Kevin Helliker, "What's a Hate Crime? South Dakota Cases Raise the Question," *Wall Street Journal*, August 27, 1999, at A1; Eric Davis, " '20/20' features Many Horses case," *Mobridge (S.Dak.) Tribune*, September 27, 2000, 3.

2. Ibid.

3. Fifty-nine percent of the residents of Mobridge identified as German in the 1990 census, the most recent year for which data are available. Thirteen percent of the townspeople were of Norwegian ancestry, while 8.9% had Irish roots, 7.8% chose United States or American as their ancestral identifier, and 6.4% had English progenitors.

4. I visited Mobridge, the Standing Rock Indian Reservation, and the Cheyenne River Indian Reservation on September 14, 2000. I benefited enormously from the insights into the local culture that I gained from Larry Atkinson during my three-hour interview with him on September 14, 2000. For some outside perspectives on the intersection of race, power, and economics in Mobridge, see Don Terry, "From '80 Crime, White-Sioux Tension Today," *New York Times,* February 20, 1996, at A1; Anita Parlow, "Revisiting a Murder Across Racial Divide; Indian Teen's Death in S. Dakota Was Subject of Long-Held Secret," *Washington Post,* May 3, 1996, at A1.

5. Northern South Dakota includes sizable swaths of virtually all-white counties interspersed with substantial concentrations of Native Americans in and around the reservations. Mobridge is part of Walworth County, which is predominantly white outside of the Bridge City. Moreover, Campbell County, north of Mobridge, is one of the whitest counties in America, as is Potter County, south of Mobridge. The Standing Rock Indian Reservation west and northwest of Mobridge consists of two counties: Corson County, South Dakota, and Sioux County, North Dakota. Corson County is 59.1% Indian and 37.1% white. Sioux County, though, is 83.2% Native American; only 14.3% of its residents identify as white. The Cheyenne River Indian Reservation encompasses Ziebach and Dewey counties; it is 72.9% Indian and 24.8% white. Since Mobridge occupies a central position in north-central South Dakota's cultural and economic life, many whites from homogeneous communities — and Native Americans from predominantly Indian areas — come to the town on a regular basis. Therefore, almost everyone in the Mobridge area is familiar with the issues discussed in this vignette.

6. Larry Atkinson, interview by author, Mobridge, South Dakota, September 14, 2000.

7. Ibid.

8. Ibid.

9. William A. Henry, "Beyond the Melting Pot," *Time* 135 (April 9, 1990): 28–31.

10. Dale Maharidge, *The Coming White Minority: California's Eruptions and America's Future* (New York: Times Books/Random House, 1996); Bob Greene, "New Minority Group Is on the Country's Horizon," *Chicago Tribune,* October 28, 1996, Sec. 3, at p. 1.

11. U.S. Census Bureau, *Statistical Abstract of the United States: 2000* (120th ed.) (Washington, D.C.: U.S. Government Printing Office, 2000), Table 16; Jennifer Cheeseman Day, *Population Projections of the United States by Age, Sex, Race and Hispanic Origin: 1995 to 2050,* U.S. Bureau of the Census, Current Population Reports, P25–1130 (Washington, D.C.: U.S. Government Printing Office, 1996).

12. Day, *Population Projections*, 23–29; Todd Gitlin, *The Twilight of Common Dreams: Why America Is Wracked by Culture Wars* (New York: Metropolitan Books/Henry Holt and Company, 1995), 107–117; John J. Miller, *The Unmaking of Americans: How Multiculturalism Has Undermined the Assimilation Ethic* (New York: Free Press, 1998), 142–144.

13. Anthony DePalma, "For Canadians, Is U.S. Gaze Friendly?" *New York Times*, September 28, 1996, Sec. 1, p. 4; Lansing Lamont, *Breakup: The Coming End of Canada and the Stakes for America* (New York: W. W. Norton & Company, 1994), 230–233; J. L. Granatstein, *Yankee Go Home? Canadians and Anti-Americanism* (Toronto: HarperCollins Publishers, 1996), 284.

14. Lawrence Wright, "One Drop of Blood," *New Yorker* 70 (July 25, 1994): 48–49; Linda Mathews, "More Than Identity Rides on a New Racial Category," *New York Times*, July 6, 1996, Sec. 1, at p. 7; Laurent Belsie, "Census nods to new views of ethnicity," *Christian Science Monitor*, July 28, 1999, 4; Ellis Cose, "Our New Look: The Colors of Race," *Newsweek* 134 (January 1, 2000): 30.

15. Laurent Belsie, "Scholars unearth new field: white studies," *Christian Science Monitor*, August 14, 2001, at p. 2.

16. See, e.g., Nancy Gibbs, "Baby, It's You! And You, And You . . . " *Time* 157 (February 19, 2001): 46–57.

17. Ray Kurzweil, *The Age of Spiritual Machines: When Computers Exceed Human Intelligence* (New York: Viking, 1999); Otis Port, "Artificial Intelligence," *BusinessWeek* (August 30, 1999): 117, 120.

18. Port, "Artificial Intelligence," 120.

19. Neil Howe and William Strauss, *Millennials Rising: The Next Great Generation* (New York: Vintage Books/Random House, 2000), 4.

20. Farai Chideya, *The Color of Our Future* (New York: William Morrow and Company, 1999). See, too, Howe and Strauss, *Millennials Rising*, 217–221; Christopher John Farley, "What Do Kids Really Think About Race?" in Borgna Brunner, ed., *The 1999 TIME Almanac* (Boston: Information Please, 1998), 360–362; Scott Shepard, "Gen-Millennium's View Of Color; Most Diverse Generation May Be One To Erase Race Line," *Wisconsin State Journal*, February 28, 1999, at 1B.

21. Howe and Strauss, *Millennials Rising*, 219.

22. Peter Grier and James N. Thurman, "Youths' shifting attitudes on race," *Christian Science Monitor*, August 18, 1999, at p. 1.

23. Boris I. Bittker, *The Case for Black Reparations* (New York: Random House, 1973); Richard F. America, ed., *The Wealth of Races: The Present Value of Benefits from Past Injustices* (New York: Greenwood Press, 1990); Randall Robinson, *The Debt: What America Owes to Blacks* (New York: Dutton, 2000); Adolph L. Reed Jr., "The Case Against Reparations," *Progressive* 64 (December 2000): 15–17; John McWhorter, "Against Reparations: Why African Americans can believe in America," *New Republic* 225 (July 23, 2001): 32–38.

24. Diane Cardwell, "Seeking Out a Just Way to Make Amends for Slavery; The Idea of Reparations for Blacks Is Gaining in Urgency, but a Knot of Questions Remain, Like: Which Blacks?" *New York Times*, August 12, 2000, B7; Michael Crowley, "On the Hill: Debt Relief," *New Republic* 223 (November 6, 2000): 18, 20, 22; Michael A. Fletcher, "Putting a Price on Slavery's Legacy; Call

for Reparations Builds as Blacks Tally History's Toll," *Washington Post*, December 26, 2000, at A1; Patrik Jonsson, "Movement to pay slavery reparations gains," *Christian Science Monitor*, January 12, 2001, 2–3; Tamar Lewin, "Calls for Slavery Restitution Getting Louder," *New York Times*, June 4, 2001, A15; Vern E. Smith, "Debating the Wages of Slavery," *Newsweek* 138 (August 27, 2001): 20–24.

25. Neil R. McMillen, *Dark Journey: Black Mississippians in the Age of Jim Crow* (Urbana: University of Illinois Press, 1989).

26. Stephan Thernstrom and Abigail Thernstrom, *America in Black and White: One Nation, Indivisible* (New York: Simon & Schuster, 1997), 44–45.

27. Only two counties in the northeastern corner of Mississippi are more than 90% white. Tishomingo County, Mississippi, is 94.3% white, while neighboring Itawamba County is 92.0% white.

28. Adam Nossiter, *Of Long Memory: Mississippi and the Murder of Medgar Evers* (Reading, Mass.: Addison-Wesley Publishing Company, 1994); Maryanne Vollers, *Ghosts of Mississippi: The Murder of Medgar Evers, the Trials of Byron de la Beckwith, and the Haunting of the New South* (Boston: Little, Brown and Company, 1995); Willie Morris, *The Ghosts of Medgar Evers: A Tale of Race, Murder, Mississippi, and Hollywood* (New York: Random House, 1998).

29. Adam Cohen, "Widow and the Wizard," *Time* 151 (May 18, 1998): 72–74; Paul Hendrickson, "From the Fires of Hate, an Ember of Hope; In 1966, the Klan Killed a Man. Now, Finally, His Family May See Justice Rise from the Ashes," *Washington Post*, July 22, 1998, at D1; Rick Bragg, "Jurors Convict Former Wizard in Klan Murder," *New York Times*, August 22, 1998, at A1.

30. Angie Cannon, "And justice for all, many years later," *U.S. News & World Report* 128 (March 13, 2000): 21–22; Vern E. Smith, "The Ghosts of Mississippi," *Newsweek* 135 (June 12, 2000): 39; Michael A. Fletcher, "Unsolved Killings, Unresolved Pain; Time and an Era's Prejudices Slow New Probes of South's Civil Rights Slayings," *Washington Post*, September 26, 2000, A3; Kim Cobb, "Chances dimming for trials in civil rights-era slayings; Survivors' efforts stymied by passage of time," *Houston Chronicle*, January 22, 2002, at A1.

31. Nadine Cohodas, *The Band Played Dixie: Race and the Liberal Conscience at Ole Miss* (New York: Free Press, 1997); Kevin Sack, "Old South's Symbols Stir a Campus," *New York Times*, March 11, 1997, A14.

32. Sue Anne Pressley, "Too Slowly for Many, Mississippi Faces a Hurtful Heritage," *Washington Post*, October 24, 1998, A3; Thomas B. Edsall, "With 'Resegregation,' Old Divisions Take New Form; Conservative Group Evokes South's Segregationist Past," *Washington Post*, April 9, 1999, A3.

33. Diane McWhorter, *Carry Me Home: Birmingham, Alabama: The Climactic Battle of the Civil Rights Revolution* (New York: Simon & Schuster, 2001).

34. David Firestone, "Old Southern Strategy Faces Test in Selma Vote," *New York Times*, September 10, 2000, Sec. 1, p. 18; Sue Anne Pressley, "Tight Race Evokes the Past; Longtime Selma, Ala., Mayor, a 'Reformed' Segregationist, in Runoff with Black Rival," *Washington Post*, September 10, 2000, A4; Sue Anne Pressley, "Selma Elects a Black Mayor," *Washington Post*, September 13, 2000, A27; Robin DeMonia, "Selma steps away from its troubled

past," *Christian Science Monitor,* October 2, 2000, at p. 1; Jeffrey Gettleman, "To Mayor, It's Selma's Statue of Limitations," *Los Angeles Times,* October 22, 2000, at A1; Tatsha Robertson, "For Mayor, Past Haunts 'New' Selma; First African-American to Lead City Hall Finds the Lines Are Blurred," *Boston Globe,* March 3, 2001, at A1.

35. Sue Anne Pressley, "Alabama Hamlet's Wounds from Racial Controversy Slow to Heal," *Washington Post,* April 7, 1996, A3; Eugene Robinson, "Black and White and Getting By; Between Hatred and Racial Harmony Is Lineville, Ala., Where Few Have It Easy," *Washington Post,* July 15, 1996, at A1; Roger Thurow, "Southern Cross: A Place Much Revered in Civil-Rights Lore Is Still Much Divided," *Wall Street Journal,* July 20, 1998, at A1; Roger Thurow, "Can Liver and Onions Lead People to Peace and Understanding?" *Wall Street Journal,* December 17, 1998, at A1; Vern E. Smith and Andrew Murr, "Up from Jim Crow," *Newsweek* 136 (September 18, 2000): 42–46.

36. Dahleen Glanton, "In Mississippi, Flag Vote Shows Deep Divide; 'World Is Watching' State Referendum," *Chicago Tribune,* April 16, 2001, at Sec. 1, at p. 1.

37. Kevin Sack, "After '63 Bombing, Hard Lives for Suspects," *New York Times,* May 20, 2000, at A1; Christopher John Farley, "The Ghosts of Alabama," *Time* 155 (May 29, 2000): 54–55; Kevin Sack, "A Bitter Alabama Cry: Slow Justice Is No Justice," *New York Times,* April 13, 2001, A12; Sue Anne Pressley, "Revisiting the South's Ugly Past; Ex-Klansman Finally Goes on Trial in Deadly '63 Birmingham Church Bombing," *Washington Post,* April 15, 2001, A5; Kevin Sack, "As Church Bombing Trial Begins in Birmingham, the City's Past Is Very Much Present," *New York Times,* April 25, 2001, A12; Kevin Sack, "Ex-Klansman Is Found Guilty in '63 Bombing," *New York Times,* May 2, 2001, at A1; Sue Anne Pressley and Dale Russakoff, "Guilty Verdict in '63 Bombing; Ex-Klansman Convicted of Murder of 4 Black Girls at Alabama Church," *Washington Post,* May 2, 2001, at A1.

38. For journalistic commentary about the panel's year-long history, see Alison Mitchell, "Defending Affirmative Action, Clinton Urges Debate on Race," *New York Times,* June 15, 1997, Sec. 1, at p. 1; Steven A. Holmes, "A Rose-Colored View of Race," *New York Times,* June 15, 1997, Sec. 4, p. 4; Kenneth T. Walsh, "Hand holding as policy," *U.S. News & World Report* 122 (June 23, 1997): 20–24; Gail Russell Chaddock, "Will 'Year of Dialogue' Matter?" *Christian Science Monitor,* June 12, 1998, at p. 1; Michael A. Fletcher, "Initiative on Race Ends Short of Its Soaring Goals," *Washington Post,* September 17, 1998, at A1; Steven A. Holmes, "Clinton Panel on Race Urges Variety of Modest Measures," *New York Times,* September 18, 1998, at A1; Charles Babington, "Like Commission, Clinton's Book on Race Languishes," *Washington Post,* June 20, 1999, A2.

39. Ibid.

40. The President's Initiative on Race, The Advisory Board's Report to the President, *One America in the 21st Century: Forging a New Future* (Washington, D.C.: U.S. Government Printing Office, 1998).

41. Cose, "Our New Look: The Colors of Race," 30; Roger Sanjek, "Intermarriage and the Future of Races in the United States," in Steven Gregory and

Roger Sanjek, eds., *Race* (New Brunswick, N.J.: Rutgers University Press, 1994), 116–122; Jack E. White, " 'I'm just who I am,' " *Time* 149 (May 5, 1997): 33–34; Roberto Suro, "Mixed Doubles," American *Demographics* 21 (November 1999): 56–62; Darryl Fears and Claudia Deane, "Biracial Couples Report Tolerance; Survey Finds Most Are Accepted by Families," *Washington Post*, July 5, 2001, at A1.

42. See, e.g., William H. Frey, "Immigrant and Domestic Migration Magnets, 1990–97," PSC Research Report No. 98-419 (Ann Arbor: Population Studies Center of the University of Michigan, July 1998); William H. Frey, "Immigration and Demographic Balkanization: Toward One America or Two?" in James W. Hughes and Joseph J. Seneca, eds., *America's Demographic Tapestry: Baseline for the New Millennium* (New Brunswick, N.J.: Rutgers University Press, 1999), 78–97; William H. Frey, "New Black Migration Patterns in the United States: Are They Affected by Recent Immigration?" in Frank D. Bean and Stephanie Bell-Rose, eds., *Immigration and Opportunity: Race, Ethnicity, and Employment in the United States* (New York: Russell Sage Foundation, 1999), 311–344. Frey's Web site — www.frey-demographer.org — is a valuable source of information on this topic, by the foremost expert in the field.

43. Ibid. The statistics regarding white flight from metropolitan areas come from a chart prepared by Frey for *American Demographics*. See David Whelan, "Trails South," *American Demographics* 23 (July 2001): 19.

44. Professor Robert D. Putnam and his collaborators on a multiyear research project did a series of polls after 9/11. As Putnam writes, "We were especially surprised and pleased to find evidence of enhanced trust across ethnic and other social divisions." Robert D. Putnam, "Bowling Together," *American Prospect* 13 (February 11, 2002). www.prospect.org/print/v13/3/putnam-r.html#chart.

45. Some observers have criticized what they thought were excessive displays of patriotism in the aftermath of 9/11. See Blaine Harden, "Flag Fever: the Paradox of Patriotism," *New York Times*, September 30, 2001, Sec. 4, at p. 1; Michael Elliott, "Don't Wear Out Old Glory," *Time* 159 (February 18, 2002): 84.

46. For information about the fund-raising efforts, see David France and David Noonan, "Blood Money," *Newsweek* 138 (December 17, 2001): 52–54, 56, 58–59; Steven Brill, "An Excess of Riches," *Newsweek* 139 (February 11, 2002): 40.

47. Eric Lichtblau, "Bias Against U.S. Arabs Taking Subtler Forms," *Los Angeles Times*, February 10, 2002, A20.

48. Dana Milbank and Emily Wax, "Bush Visits Mosque to Forestall Hate Crimes; President Condemns an Increase in Violence Aimed at Arab Americans," *Washington Post*, September 18, 2001, at A1; Blaine Harden, "Arab-Americans Are Finding New Tolerance Amid the Turmoil," *New York Times*, September 22, 2001, at B1.

49. These data are cited in a sidebar on page 26 of the July 10, 1995, issue of *Newsweek*.

Acknowledgments

Over the past seven years I have spoken to hundreds of Americans about race and ethnicity. Many of these conversations were informal, and a few were off-the-record. These discussions, of course, deepened my understanding of the many topics related to race and ethnicity.

The following people deserve special thanks for answering my questions: Professor Nabeel Abraham, Professor Brad Agnew, Larry Atkinson, Judy Bevins, Kevin Burr, Speaker Robert G. Clark Jr., Karen Conn, Mayor Larry Delgado, Mayor Roy Delgado, Tina Donath, Kevin Hall, Michael Hanna, Joy James, Victor Justice, Jim Kurtti, Jim Maniaci, Gary McClure, Dr. Margo Olivares-Seck, Robert Osborne, Cindy Porter, City Manager Bill Pupo, Roberto Ramirez, Sally Ross, Dr. David Rudy, Helen Samhan, Coy Samons, Mayor Joan Shafer, Vice Mayor Norma Valdez, Secretary Rebecca Vigil-Giron, Daisy West, and Carol Young.

On a related note, I would like to thank Art Cullen, the editor of the *Storm Lake Times,* for allowing me to use a vignette in *Visible Differences* that he had published in his newspaper — in a slightly different form.

Ronald Laitsch and Mary Lee Laitsch have done a wonderful job of representing my interests in the literary world. Whenever I have any questions about the publishing process, they are always willing to explain to me how things work. Even though they have a large number of clients, the Laitsches make me feel as if I can contact them whenever I think it is necessary to do so. Ron is also a lawyer, which gives him an advantage in the negotiating process, because of his ability to decipher the fine print in literary contracts. The Laitsches found a good home for this book, and I am grateful to them.

Frank Oveis, the senior editor at Continuum, was the person who made the decision to publish *Visible Differences*. Frank is the ideal editor: He is erudite, diligent, encouraging, and critical — in a constructive fashion — at the appropriate junctures. Frank read the manuscript multiple times and impressed me with his recall of its details. I especially appreciated the latitude Frank gave me to structure the book as I saw fit. My initial foray into the publishing world went quite well, in large part because of Frank's optimism, enthusiasm, and forbearance.

Visible Differences is dedicated to my father and mother, Mr. Eugene Pulera and Dr. Margaret Pulera, who taught me, through their words and deeds, to respect and appreciate the innate value of each human being. Their grace, tolerance, and inspiration inform every page of this book.

I thoroughly enjoyed writing *Visible Differences* due to the support and encouragement offered by my parents and my sister, Maria Pulera. They listened to my endless ruminations about race and ethnicity, faithfully clipped news articles for me, shared with me illuminating anecdotes from their personal experiences, and helped me in so many other ways. My parents provided me with the invaluable financial support that enabled me to travel to observe firsthand the demographics of many communities in the United States and elsewhere. They also proofread parts of the manuscript. I am extremely grateful to my family for their backing.

I lived at home with my parents in Wisconsin while working on this book, and it was a very congenial environment in which to write, do research, and conduct telephone interviews. Since 1996 my sister, Maria, has lived in California. Due to our frequent trips back and forth between Wisconsin and California — and our multiple telephone conversations each day — it was as if she had never left home.

All errors of fact or interpretation are mine alone.

Index